THE MAMMOTH BOOK OF
THE WORLD'S GREATEST
CHESS GAMES

Graham Burgess
John Nunn
John Emms

Foreword by Vishy Anand

CARROLL & GRAF PUBLISHERS
New York

Carroll & Graf Publishers
An imprint of Avalon Publishing Group, Inc.
245 W. 17th Street
New York
NY 10011
www.carrollandgraf.com

AVALON
publishing group incorporated

First published in the UK by Robinson Publishing Ltd 1998

This revised edition by Carroll & Graf 2004

Copyright © Graham Burgess, John Nunn and John Emms 1998, 2004

ISBN 0-7867-1411-5

Printed and bound in the EU

Contents

Foreword by Vishy Anand

In virtually every sport, there is a debate about who was the greatest of all time, and which was the best contest. Comparisons made over long periods of time are far from simple; comparing the tennis players of the past with those of today must take into account advances such as carbon-fibre rackets and scientifically designed training programs. A further difficulty is that for events pre-dating television, one often has to rely on written descriptions rather than video records. Chess is in a uniquely fortunate position in this respect; chess notation means that the great games of the past can be played over just as easily as those played last week.

This book aims to present the 112 greatest games of all time. Obviously not everyone will agree with the choice, but there is no doubt that these are all outstanding games. There are many old favourites, but also some less well-known encounters which will be new to most readers. Readers will meet not only the familiar names of world champions, but those of less familiar masters and grandmasters, correspondence players, etc.

At the moment, with a new millennium just begun, chess is looking to the future. The Internet is having an increasing impact for both disseminating chess information and providing a playing forum. The game will undoubtedly change in the years to come, but it will only be another evolutionary step in the long and rich heritage of chess. This book contains selected highlights from over 150 years of chess history; we can all learn from the experience of the past, and anyone who studies these games cannot fail to gain a greater understanding of chess.

As for the questions posed at the start of the foreword, was Mikhail Tal, who has more games in this book than any other player, really the most brilliant of all time? Were Botvinnik – Capablanca, AVRO tournament, Rotterdam 1938, Karpov – Kasparov, World Championship match (game 16), Moscow 1985, and Kasparov – Topalov, Wijk aan Zee 1999 really the greatest games in chess history? After playing over the 112 masterpieces in this book, you may form your own opinion; whether you agree or disagree, these games can hardly fail to give pleasure, instruction and entertainment.

Vishy Anand

Introduction

The aim of this book is simple: to present the 112 greatest chess games of all time, with annotations that enable chess enthusiasts to derive the maximum enjoyment and instruction from them.

The first problem we faced was the selection of the games: how could we choose just 112 from the treasure-house of chess history? Clearly the games should be great battles, featuring deep and inventive play. We decided that the prime consideration had to be the quality of the play, not just of the winner, but also of the loser. We rejected games where the loser offered little resistance, and those where the winner jeopardized victory by aiming for false brilliance. As one of the book's objectives is to help the reader gain a deeper understanding of all aspects of chess, we favoured games illustrating important concepts. The selection criteria were therefore as follows:

- Quality and brilliance of play by both contestants
- Instructive value
- Historical significance

Using these criteria, we selected a shortlist of 230 games; then each author voted on the games, rating each on a scale of 1 to 5, as follows:

5 one of the greatest 22 games ever played

4 in the top 56

3 in the top 112

2 the game is not in the top 112

1 the game is unsuitable for inclusion in the book

Thus the greatest possible score for a game was 15 votes. In the end just three games achieved this theoretical maximum.

This enabled us to select our 112 games, which were then allocated between the three annotators, 58 to Graham Burgess (who coordinated the whole project), 29 to John Nunn, and 25 to John Emms.

The annotator and the total number of votes for each game are indicated in the contents list.

Our primary aims in annotating each game were to provide an accurate set of notes, and to highlight the main instructive points. In some cases pre-existing notes, especially those by the players, proved a valuable source of ideas, but we repeatedly found major deficiencies in previous annotations. The most common problem was "annotation by result", i.e. the annotator praises everything the winner did, and criticizes all the loser's decisions. Few games between strong opponents are really so one-sided. Another common failing was the sheep-like tendency of annotators to copy earlier notes. Thus, if a game was poorly annotated in the tournament book, or in the winner's "best games" collection, then subsequent annotations were blighted. Of course, it would be unfair (and dangerous!) for us to be too critical of other annotators, especially considering that they were without computerized assistance, but in many cases there was clearly a definite lack of independent thought.

In this book we have aimed to present the truth about these games, warts and all. In some cases readers might feel that the games have lost some of their brilliance as a result, but we do not agree. On the contrary, it shows that many games which were hitherto regarded as rather one-sided were in fact massive struggles between almost evenly-matched players; only an 11th-hour slip at the height of the battle finally tipped the balance in the winner's favour. These new annotations often reveal new and instructive points in the games – so please don't skip a game just because you have seen it before. We were assisted in our work by a variety of computer software, most notably ChessBase, together with the Fritz and Junior analysis modules.

Each game starts with biographical information about the players (where a player has already been introduced, the reader is referred to the earlier material) and a summary of the game. The game and its detailed notes follow,

with a final review of the game's most instructive points. These games represent the pinnacle of human creativity on the chessboard (in one case, silicon 'creativity'!) and there is a great deal to be learnt from them. You may find it convenient to use two chessboards – one to keep track of the position in the main game, and another to play over the variations. Alternatively, and preferably, play over the moves using a suitable computer program (for example ChessBase). Keeping a program such as Fritz running in the background will reveal analytical points we had no space to include in the book.

We hope you enjoy reading this book as much as we enjoyed writing it. If there are any terms in this book that you don't understand, please refer to the extensive glossary in *The Mammoth Book of Chess*.

Graham Burgess
John Nunn
John Emms
January 2004

Symbols

+	check	!?	interesting move	
++	double check	?!	dubious move	
#	checkmate	?	bad move	
x	captures	??	blunder	
0-0	castles kingside	1-0	the game ends in a win for White	
0-0-0	castles queenside			
!!	brilliant move	½-½	the game ends in a draw	
!	good move	0-1	the game ends in a win for Black	

Game 1
Alexander McDonnell – Louis Charles de Labourdonnais
4th match, 16th game, London 1834
Sicilian Defence, Löwenthal Variation

The Players
Alexander McDonnell (1798–1835) was born in Belfast and established himself as the best player in England in the 1830s. Indeed, his superiority was such that he even played at odds when facing the best of the English players blindfold. Though his talent was undoubted, he had little experience facing opposition of his own level, and this showed when he faced Labourdonnais in their series of matches.

Louis Charles Mahé de Labourdonnais (1797–1840) was born on the French island of La Réunion, where his father had been governor. After settling in France, then the world's leading chess nation, he learned the game while in his late teens, and progressed rapidly; from 1820 up until his death he was regarded as the leading player. He was clearly a man who loved to play chess; even during his matches, he would play off-hand games for small stakes between the match games.

The Game
After some lacklustre opening play from McDonnell, Labourdonnais sets up a powerful mobile pawn centre, very much in the style of Philidor, the greatest French player prior to Labourdonnais. He plays extremely energetically to support and advance the pawns, and when McDonnell threatens to make inroads around and behind the pawns, he comes up with a fine exchange sacrifice. The tactics all work, and Black's pawns continue their advance towards the goal. The final position, once seen, is never forgotten: three passed pawns on the seventh rank overpowering a hapless queen and rook.

1	e4	c5
2	♘f3	♘c6
3	d4	cxd4
4	♘xd4	e5
5	♘xc6?!	

This somewhat cooperative exchange strengthens Black's control of the centre without giving White any compensating advantages. Moreover, it nullifies the main defect of Black's ambitious 4th move, i.e. the weakening of the d5-square. 5 ♘b5 has been the normal move ever since.

5	...	bxc6
6	♗c4	♘f6
7	♗g5	♗e7
8	♕e2?!	

By delaying development and exposing his queen to possible attack along the a6–f1 diagonal, White only encourages Black to advance in the centre. The fact that the queen exerts pressure on e5 is unlikely to be relevant before White has, at the least, got his king safely castled. He should instead try 8 ♘c3 or 8 ♗xf6 followed by 9 ♘c3.

8 ... d5

9 ♗xf6

9 exd5 cxd5 (9...♘xd5 is also possible, when Black has good piece-play) 10 ♗b5+ ♗d7 11 ♘c3 (after 11 ♗xd7+ ♘xd7 12 ♗xe7 ♕xe7 Black can comfortably maintain his pawn-centre) 11...d4 12 ♗xf6 ♗xf6 13 ♘d5 doesn't work for White after 13...♕a5+ 14 b4 (14 c3 ♗xb5 15 ♕xb5+ ♕xb5 16 ♘c7+ ♔d7 17 ♘xb5 ♖ab8 and b2 caves in) 14...♗xb5 15 bxa5 ♗xe2 16 ♘c7+? (after normal moves, White's shattered queenside pawns will give him a dreadful ending) 16...♔d7 17 ♘xa8 ♗a6 and the knight is trapped.

9 ... ♗xf6

10 ♗b3 0-0

11 0-0

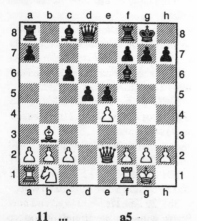

11 ... a5

Now Black threatens both 12...a4 and 12...♗a6. Thus Black manages to

use his a-pawn to cause White to make concessions in the centre.

12 exd5 cxd5

13 ♖d1 d4

14 c4?!

McDonnell decides to play actively, hoping that his own passed c-pawn will prove as strong as Black's d-pawn. However, this hope is unrealistic. Black's d-pawn is already well advanced, and ably supported by its neighbour, the e5-pawn. Moreover, Black's pieces are better mobilized and have more scope. If a modern grandmaster were to end up in this position as White, then he would not try to start a race, but rather develop the queen's knight, and aim to restrain and blockade the d-pawn, most likely chipping away at it with c3 at some point. However, this game was played almost a century before Nimzowitsch systematized the concept of "restrain, blockade, destroy" (though the third part would be hoping for too much in this instance), and, besides, in the early nineteenth century it was more standard for players to try to solve positional problems by lashing out aggressively. More prudent options include 14 c3 and 14 ♘d2.

14 ... ♕b6

15 ♗c2 ♗b7

Certainly not 15...♕xb2??, which loses the queen to 16 ♗xh7+.

16 ♘d2 ♖ae8!

Labourdonnais correctly perceives that his rooks belong on the e- and f-files, despite the fact that this leaves his rooks poorly placed to act on the queenside. The d-pawn is of course his main asset, but to create real threats Black will need to push his e-pawn, and this in turn may need the support of the f-pawn. If White could somehow set up a firm blockade on e4, then he would have good chances, so this square may be regarded as the focus of the battle.

16...♕xb2 strays off-course and dissipates Black's advantage after either 17 ♗xh7+ ♔xh7 18 ♖ab1 or 17 ♕d3 e4 (17...g6 18 ♖ab1 forces 18...e4 anyway) 18 ♘xe4 ♗xe4 19 ♕xe4 g6.

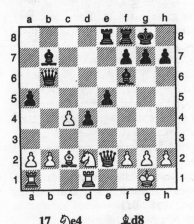

17 ♘e4   ♗d8

Black's threat of ...f5 forces White to act quickly if he is not to be overrun.

18 c5   ♕c6
19 f3   ♗e7

Preventing 20 ♘d6, which White's last move had made possible.

20 ♖ac1   f5

Black immediately begins the decisive advance. Note that he spends no time on prophylaxis against White's queenside play, confident that his pawn-storm will sweep everything from its path.

21 ♕c4+   ♔h8!

21...♕d5 would be annoyingly met by 22 ♕b5, threatening ♗b3.

21...♖f7? loses an exchange under far worse conditions than in the game:

22 ♗a4 ♕c8 23 ♗xe8 ♕xe8 24 ♘d6 ♗xd6 25 cxd6.

22 ♗a4   ♕h6

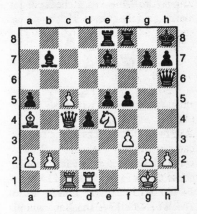

23 ♗xe8?!

23 ♘d6 is a better try, when Black must play extremely precisely to keep his advantage: 23...♖xd6 24 ♗xe8 ♗c7 25 c6 (25 ♕b3 e4 26 g3 should be met by 26...♗a6, with excellent play for Black, since 26...♖xe8 27 ♕xb7 ♕e3+ 28 ♔h1 ♕xf3+ 29 ♔g1 may yield no more than a draw) 25...e4 and now:

1) 26 cxb7? ♕xh2+ 27 ♔f1 exf3 28 gxf3 ♕h3+ 29 ♔e2 ♖xe8+ 30 ♔d3 ♕xf3+ 31 ♔c2 ♕xb7 is good for Black.

2) 26 h3?? ♕e3+ 27 ♔f1 (27 ♔h1 ♕f4) 27...♗h2 and Black wins.

3) 26 g3 ♕e3+ 27 ♔f1 ♕xf3+ 28 ♔g1 ♗xg3 (28...♗c8 is met by 29 ♗d7) and here:

3a) 29 hxg3 ♕xg3+ 30 ♔f1 (30 ♔h1 ♖f6) 30...d3 31 ♕c5 (31 cxb7 e3) 31...♖xe8 32 ♕g1 ♕f3+ 33 ♕f2 ♕xf2+ 34 ♔xf2 e3+ and ...♗a6 wins.

3b) 29 ♖f1 ♕e3+ 30 ♔g2 and now Black wins by sacrificing yet more material and using his swathe of pawns:

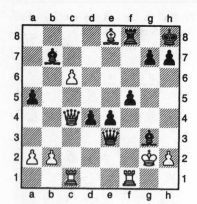

3b1) 30...♗e5 is not fast enough: 31 ♕c5 (not 31 cxb7? ♕h6) 31...♕d2+ 32 ♖f2 ♕g5+ 33 ♔h1 ♗d6 34 ♕xd6! (34 ♕c2 d3 allows Black to consolidate) 34...♕xc1+ 35 ♔g2 ♕g5+ 36 ♔h1! ♖xe8 (not 36...♕f6?? 37 ♕xf6 gxf6 38 cxb7 ♖xe8 39 ♖c2) 37 cxb7 gives Black no more than a draw.

3b2) 30...♕d2+! 31 ♔xg3 f4+ 32 ♔h3 f3 and mate cannot be prevented, e.g. 33 ♖g1 ♕h6+ 34 ♔g3 ♕f4+ 35 ♔f2 (35 ♔h3 ♖f6) 35...♕xh2+ 36 ♔f1 e3 followed by ...e2+; alternatively, 33 ♕c2 ♕h6+ 34 ♔g3 ♕g5+ 35 ♔f2 (35 ♔h3 ♖f4) 35...♕e3+ 36 ♔g3 f2+ 37 ♔g4 ♕f3+ 38 ♔h4 ♖f4+ 39 ♔g5 ♕g4#.

23 ...	fxe4
24 c6	exf3!
25 ♖c2	

25 cxb7? allows a forced mate: 25...♕e3+ 26 ♔h1 fxg2+ 27 ♔xg2 ♖f2+ 28 ♔g1 ♖e2+ 29 ♔h1 ♕f3+ 30 ♔g1 ♕g2#.

25 gxf3? ♕e3+ 26 ♔h1 ♕xf3+ 27 ♔g1 ♖f5 also forces mate in short order.

25 ...	♕e3+
26 ♔h1	♗c8
27 ♗d7	

White dare not let the c8-bishop out, e.g. 27 ♗f7 (trying to block off the rook instead) 27...♗g4 28 c7? (28 ♖f1 d3 29 ♖cf2 d2 is hopeless for White in any case) 28...fxg2+ 29 ♖xg2 ♗xd1 30 c8♕ ♕e1+ 31 ♖g1 ♗f3#.

27 ...	f2

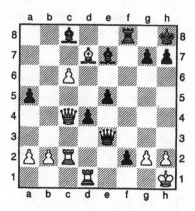

Black is threatening both 28...d3 and 28...♕e1+ 29 ♕f1 ♕xd1.

28 ♖f1	

Not 28 ♕f1? ♗a6.

28 ...	d3
29 ♖c3	♗xd7
30 cxd7	

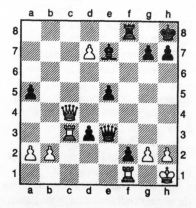

Not 30 ♖xd3? ♗e6 (30...♕e2 31
♖c3) 31 ♕c2 ♕c5.

   30 ...   **e4**

The threat is now ...♕e1, and there
isn't much White can do about it.

   31 ♕c8   **♗d8**

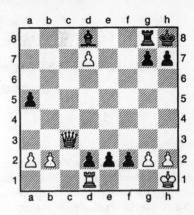

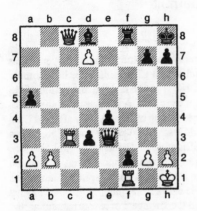

   32 ♕c4

32 ♕c6 ♕e1 is no different, and 32
♖cc1 is met by 32...♕f4.

   32 ...   **♕e1!**
   33 ♖c1   **d2**
   34 ♕c5   **♖g8**
   35 ♖d1   **e3**
   36 ♕c3

Now for a truly magical finish...

   36 ...   **♕xd1**
   37 ♖xd1   **e2**
             0-1

Lessons from this game:

1) A large mobile pawn centre is a
major strategic asset.

2) Don't be afraid to sacrifice to
press forward to your main strategic
goal (e.g. the advance of a pawn-centre, as in this game). An advantageous
position does not win itself against a
resourceful opponent, and at some
point it may become necessary to "get
your hands dirty" and analyse precise
tactical variations.

3) When pawns are far-advanced,
close to promotion, always be on the
lookout for tactical tricks involving
promotion. The final position of this
game should provide all the necessary
inspiration – make a mental note of it!

Game 2
The "Immortal Game"
Adolf Anderssen – Lionel Kieseritzky
London 1851
King's Gambit

The Players

Adolf Anderssen (1818–79) was undoubtedly one of the strongest players of his era and indeed he was crowned unofficial World Champion after handsomely winning the great London Tournament of 1851, which had the distinction of being the first international chess tournament ever held. A teacher of mathematics by profession, Anderssen began to take chess much more seriously after his London triumph. He kept his status as the world's strongest player until 1858, before losing convincingly in a match to the brilliant young American, Paul Morphy. Morphy's sudden retirement from the game, however, meant that Anderssen could once more take up the mantle as the leading player. Despite his numerous work commitments, he stayed active on the chess front, playing matches against many of his nearest rivals. In 1870 he won the strongest ever tournament at that time, in Baden-Baden, ahead of players such as Steinitz and Blackburne. Anderssen was certainly a chess player at heart. At London in 1851, he was asked why he had not gone to see the Great Exhibition. "I came to London to play chess" was his curt reply.

Lionel Kieseritzky (1806–53) was born in Tartu, in what is now Estonia, but settled in France in 1839. He became a frequent visitor to the Café de la Régence in Paris, where he gave chess lessons for five francs an hour, or played offhand games for the same fee. His main strength was his ability to win by giving great odds to weaker players. Kieseritzky was also an openings theoretician, who invented a line in the King's Gambit which is still considered a main variation today. However, despite his other achievements, he is still best remembered for the part he played in this game.

The Game

Dubbed the "Immortal Game" by the Austrian player Ernst Falkbeer, this is a game typical of the "romantic era" of chess, in which sacrifices were offered in plenty and most were duly accepted. Anderssen's love of combinations and his contempt for material are plain to see here. After some imaginative opening play, the game explodes into life when Anderssen plays a brilliant (and sound) piece sacrifice. Spurning more mundane winning lines, Anderssen raises the game onto another plane by a double rook offer, followed by a dazzling queen sacrifice, finishing with a checkmate using all three of his remaining minor pieces. In the final analysis it could be claimed that it's not all entirely sound, but this is merely a case of brilliance over precision.

1	e4	e5
2	f4	exf4
3	♗c4	♕h4+

It seems quite natural to force White to move his king, but the drawback of this check is that Black will be forced to waste time moving his queen again when it is attacked. Modern players prefer 3...♘f6 or 3...d5.

4	♔f1	b5?!

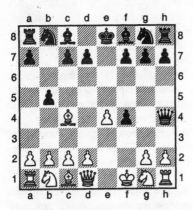

This counter-gambit was named after the American amateur player Thomas Jefferson Bryan, who was active in the chess circles around Paris and London in the middle of the nineteenth century. Kieseritzky also took a shine to it, especially after his pretty win over Schulten (see below). However, it has always been considered, to put it mildly, somewhat dubious. That said, it has been utilized by none other than Garry Kasparov, although the circumstances were hardly normal. After comfortably defeating Nigel Short for the PCA World Chess Championship in 1993, the audiences at the Savoy

Theatre in London were treated to some exhibition matches between the two players. Kasparov won the rapidplay games by the convincing margin of 4-0. Short, however, got some sweet revenge in the theme games, where the openings were chosen by the organizers. After two draws the proceedings were "spiced up" when Kasparov was forced to defend with the Bryan. Clearly disgusted with this choice, Kasparov could only last fifteen moves before resigning in a totally lost position, and storming off stage to vent his feelings to the powers-that-be. Still, Kasparov couldn't complain too much. *Batsford Chess Openings 2*, written by Garry Kasparov and Raymond Keene, only gives White a slight plus in this line!

5	♗xb5	♘f6
6	♘f3	

Kieseritzky's more pleasant experience with this line continued 6 ♘c3 ♘g4 7 ♘h3 ♘c6 8 ♘d5 ♘d4 9 ♘xc7+ ♔d8 10 ♘xa8 f3 11 d3 f6 12 ♗c4 d5 13 ♗xd5 ♗d6 14 ♕e1 fxg2+ 15 ♔xg2 ♕xh3+!! 16 ♔xh3 ♘e3+ 17 ♔h4 ♘f3+ 18 ♔h5 ♗g4# (0-1) Schulten-Kieseritzky, Paris 1844.

On this occasion the boot was firmly on the other foot!

6	...	♕h6
7	d3	

The more active 7 ♘c3 is probably better. Now 7...g5 8 d4 ♗b7 9 h4 ♖g8 10 ♔g1 gxh4 11 ♖xh4 ♕g6 12 ♕e2 ♘xe4 13 ♖xf4 f5 14 ♘h4 ♕g3 15 ♘xe4 1-0 was the start and the end of the infamous Short-Kasparov game.

7	...	♘h5

Protecting the f4-pawn and threatening ...♘g3+, but it has to be said that Black's play is a little one-dimensional. Once this idea is dealt with Black soon finds himself on the retreat.

8 ♘h4

As one would expect, the Immortal Game has been subjected to much analysis and debate from masters of the past and present. The sum of the analysis alone would probably be enough to fill up an entire book. One of the most recent annotators is the German GM Robert Hübner, who reviewed the game in his own critical way for *ChessBase Magazine*. From move seven to eleven inclusive, Hübner awarded seven question marks! Here, instead of 8 ♘h4, he recommends 8 ♖g1, intending g4. He follows this up with 8...♕b6 9 ♘c3 c6 10 ♗c4 ♕c5 11 ♕e2 ♗a6 12 ♗xa6 ♘xa6 13 d4 ♕a5 14 ♘e5 g6 15 ♘c4 ♕c7 16 e5, with a winning position for White. This all looks very correct, but then again Anderssen – Kieseritzky has always been noted for its brilliancy rather than its accuracy.

8 ...   ♕g5
9 ♘f5   c6

Here or on the next move Black should probably try to dislodge the f5-knight with ...g6. Hübner gives 9...g6 10 h4 ♕f6! 11 ♘c3 c6 12 ♗a4 ♘a6 13 d4 ♘g3+ 14 ♘xg3 fxg3+ 15 ♕f3 ♕xd4, which looks about equal.

10 g4   ♘f6
11 ♖g1!

An imaginative piece sacrifice. The idea is to gain masses of time driving the black queen around the board. This will give White an enormous lead in development.

11 ...   cxb5
12 h4!   ♕g6
13 h5

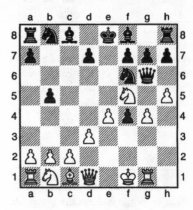

13 ...   ♕g5

Black is forced to bite the bullet. Returning the sacrificed piece with 13...♘xh5? doesn't relieve the pressure. Hübner then gives 14 gxh5 ♕f6 15 ♘c3 ♗b7 16 ♗xf4 g6 17 ♘xb5 with a winning position for White.

14 ♕f3   ♘g8

This abject retreat leaves Black's development in an almost comical state. In *The Development of Chess Style* Euwe suggested the counter-sacrifice 14...♘xg4, although it has to be said that 15 ♖xg4 ♕xh5 16 ♗xf4 doesn't look too appetising for Black either. Hübner continues with 16...d5 17 ♘c3 ♗xf5 18 exf5, when White is clearly better.

15 ♗xf4   ♕f6

Once more Black chooses the most aggressive option. Much more sober is the full retreat with 15...♕d8, although White's development advantage should still be decisive after 16 ♘c3. Instead Kieseritzky insists on plunging further into the fire.

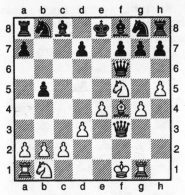

16	♘c3	♗c5
17	♘d5	

The game is already nearing its climax, as White initiates the grand concept of sacrificing both rooks. In the cold light of day 17 d4 should also be seriously considered. White wins after both the mundane 17...♗xd4 18 ♘d5 and the slightly more exciting 17...♗e7 18 ♗d6! ♗xd6 19 g5!.

17 ...   ♛xb2

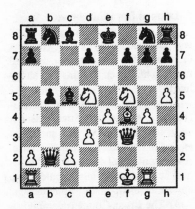

18 ♗d6!!(?)

And here is the immortal sacrifice. The two exclamation marks are for ingenuity, while the question mark is for the actual strength of the move. With 18 ♗d6 White says to Black "Take my rooks!". Given that Black can actually spoil the fun by choosing a resourceful option at move 19, it should be pointed out that objectively stronger moves do exist for White here. Hübner gives three possible wins:

1) 18 d4 ♛xa1+ (or 18...♗f8 19 ♘c7+ ♚d8 20 ♖e1) 19 ♚g2 ♛b2 20 dxc5 ♘a6 21 ♘d6+ ♚f8 22 ♗e5 ♛xc2+ 23 ♚h3 f6 24 ♘xf6 and the white attack breaks through.

2) 18 ♗e3 and now:

2a) 18...♛xa1+ 19 ♚g2 ♛b2 20 ♗xc5 ♛xc2+ 21 ♚h3 ♛xc5 22 ♖c1 d6 23 ♖xc5 ♗xf5 24 ♛xf5 dxc5 25 ♛c8#.

2b) 18...d6 19 ♗d4! ♗xd4 (White also wins if Black gives up his queen, e.g. 19...♛xd4 20 ♘xd4 ♗xd4 21 ♘c7+ ♚d8 22 c3) 20 ♘xd6+ ♚d8 21 ♘xf7+ ♚e8 22 ♘d6+ ♚d8 23 ♛f8+ ♚d7 24 ♛f7+ ♚xd6 25 ♛c7+ ♚e6 26 ♘f4+ ♚f6 27 g5#.

3) 18 ♖e1 and now:

3a) 18...♘a6 19 ♗d6 ♗b7 (or 19...♗xg1 20 e5 ♚d8 21 ♘xg7 ♗b7 22 ♛xf7 ♘e7 23 ♘e6+! dxe6 24 ♗c7+ ♚d7 25 ♛xe7+ ♚c8 26 ♛xe6#) 20 ♗xc5 ♘xc5 21 ♘d6+ ♚d8 22 ♘xf7+.

3b) 18...♗b7 19 d4 and once again White's attack is too strong.

So the assessment after 17...♛xb2 is that White has many ways to win. The one chosen leads to the most brilliant finish.

18	...	♛xa1+
19	♚e2	♗xg1?

By this stage I imagine Kieseritzky was too much in mid-flow not to capture the second rook. It would certainly have been less sporting to play the strong move 19...♛b2!, after which the outcome of the game remains far from certain.

20 e5!!

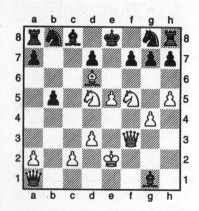

Blocking off the black queen and threatening 21 ♘xg7+ ♚d8 22 ♗c7#. Black has many defensive tries but none really do the trick:

1) 20...f6 21 ♘xg7+ ♚f7 22 ♘xf6 ♗b7 (or 22...♚xg7 23 ♘e8+ ♚h6 24 ♕f4#) 23 ♘d5+ ♚xg7 24 ♕f8#.

2) 20...♗b7 21 ♘xg7+ ♚d8 22 ♕xf7 ♘h6 23 ♘e6+ mates.

3) 20...♗a6 (the grimmest defence) 21 ♘c7+ ♚d8 22 ♘xa6 and now:

3a) 22...♕c3 (Falkbeer) 23 ♗c7+ ♕xc7 24 ♘xc7 ♚xc7 25 ♕xa8 ♘c6 26 ♘d6 ♘xe5 27 ♘e8+ ♚b6 28 ♕b8+ and 29 ♕xe5.

3b) 22...♗b6 (Chigorin) 23 ♕xa8 ♕c3 24 ♕xb8+ ♕c8 25 ♕xc8+ ♚xc8 26 ♗f8 h6 27 ♘d6+ ♚d8 28 ♘xf7+ ♚e8 29 ♘xh8 ♚xf8 30 ♚f3 and White rather mundanely wins the endgame.

3c) 22...♕xa2 23 ♗c7+ ♚e8 24 ♘b4 ♘c6 (what else?) 25 ♘xa2 ♗c5 26 ♕d5 ♗f8 27 ♕xb5 and White wins.

Kieseritzky's defence was in a sense far superior, as it ensured the game's immortality.

20 ...   ♘a6(!)

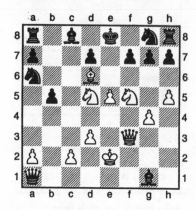

21 ♘xg7+   ♚d8
22 ♕f6+!!

The final glory in a game of many glories.

22 ...   ♘xf6
23 ♗e7# (1-0)

Lessons from this game:

1) It goes without saying that Black was punished in this game for his lack of respect for development. He had fun with his queen, but this was short-lived.

2) In the so-called romantic era of chess, defensive technique was not very well developed, and sacrifices tended to be readily accepted. Hence, Anderssen's 18 ♗d6 was a good practical bet, but such a move could prove unwise against a modern grandmaster.

3) The Bryan Counter-Gambit is a very dodgy opening. Just ask Garry Kasparov!

The "Evergreen Game"
Adolf Anderssen – Jean Dufresne
Berlin 1852
Evans Gambit

The Players

Adolf Anderssen (1818–79) was one of the greatest players of the nineteenth century. See Game 2 for more information.

Jean Dufresne (1829–93) was born in Berlin. When a hearing defect forced him to give up his career as a journalist, he devoted himself to chess and chess writing. Although not one of the leading players of his time, he was strong enough to score some successes against masters, and his writings proved influential: his *Kleines Lehrbuch des Schachspiels* was a popular beginners' guide, from which several generations of Germans learned their chess. Nowadays, outside Germany at least, he is mostly remembered as Anderssen's opponent in the Evergreen Game.

The Game

Like the "Immortal Game", this encounter did not take place under tournament conditions, but was a friendly game, just for the pleasure of playing chess. It has certainly given a great deal of pleasure to generations of enthusiasts ever since, and to this day articles appear now and then in chess magazines with some new nuance in the analysis of Anderssen's great combination.

The game starts with a sharp Evans Gambit – one of the most popular openings of the day. Dufresne chooses a somewhat offbeat sideline, losing a little time to frustrate the smooth development of White's position. Anderssen achieves a powerfully centralized position, and while Black tries to generate play on the flanks, White wrenches attention back to Black's king, stranded in the centre, with a stunning (though, it must be said, unnecessary) knight sacrifice. Dufresne, though, has considerable counterplay against the white king, making for a thrilling finale. When he misses his best chance to stay in the game, Anderssen pounces with a dazzling queen sacrifice to force an extremely attractive checkmate.

1	e4	e5
2	♘f3	♘c6
3	♗c4	♗c5
4	b4	♗xb4
5	c3	♗a5

5...♗e7 is the preference of many modern players, on the rare occasions when the Evans is played, but is by no means clearly better. One line runs 6 d4 ♘a5 7 ♘xe5 (7 ♗e2!? exd4 8

♛xd4 was Kasparov's choice in a game he won against Anand at the Tal memorial tournament, Riga 1995, but shouldn't lead to anything better than unclear play) 7...♘xc4 8 ♘xc4 d5 returning the pawn to bring about a relatively quiet position.

6 d4

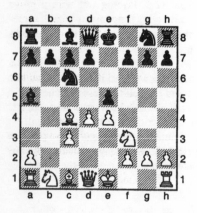

6 ...   exd4

6...d6 is the modern preference:

1) 7 ♕b3 ♕d7! is known as the Conservative Defence, and is a tough nut to crack – analysts have been trying for a long time, without denting it much. A recent try is 8 dxe5 ♗b6 9 ♘bd2 ♘a5 10 ♕c2 ♘xc4 11 ♘xc4 d5 12 ♗g5, with attacking chances.

2) After 7 0-0, 7...♗b6 has been the preferred move ever since its strength was realized by Emanuel Lasker. It is a tough defensive move, preparing to return the pawn to secure a good position, rather than riskily clinging to the material. The key idea is 8 dxe5 dxe5 9 ♕xd8+ (9 ♕b3 ♕f6 10 ♗g5 ♕g6 11 ♗d5 ♘a5 has been discovered by Murray Chandler to lead to satisfactory simplifications for Black) 9...♘xd8 10 ♘xe5 ♘f6 and in so far as winning

chances exist here, they are on Black's side.

7 0-0   d3?!

7...dxc3?!, known as the Compromised Defence, gives White a massive attack after 8 ♕b3 ♕f6 9 e5 ♕g6 10 ♘xc3 (10 ♗a3 is less convincing, and, interestingly, was played in a later game between the same players, but with colours reversed: 10...♘ge7 11 ♖e1 0-0 12 ♘xc3 ♗xc3 13 ♕xc3 d5 14 exd6 cxd6 15 ♗d3 ♕h6 16 ♖e4 ♗f5 17 ♖h4 ♕g6 18 ♖d1 ♗xd3 19 ♖xd3 ♘f5 20 ♖h3 ♖fe8 21 ♘h4 ♘xh4 22 ♖hg3 ♕f6 0-1 Dufresne – Anderssen, Berlin 1855).

7...♗b6 8 cxd4 d6 brings about the so-called "Normal Position" of the Evans, presumably because it can be reached via many natural move-orders. It offers White fair compensation and attacking chances, due to his fine centre and good development.

8 ♕b3!?

Naturally, White plays for the attack, immediately targeting the weak f7-pawn, rather than wasting time capturing the d3-pawn, but 8 ♖e1!?!? may well be a better way to pursue this aim, e.g. 8...♘f6 9 e5; 8...♘ge7 9 ♘g5!; 8...d6 9 ♕b3 ♕d7 (9...♕e7 10 e5 dxe5 11 ♗a3) 10 e5; or 8...♗b6 9 e5, when it is difficult for Black to develop and avoid coming under a heavy kingside attack.

8 ...   ♕f6

9 e5   ♕g6

Instead, 9...♘xe5?? 10 ♖e1 d6 11 ♕b5+ costs Black a piece.

In case you are thinking that Black's play looks very old-fashioned, considered that this position has been taken on, with success, as Black by Grandmaster Beliavsky (whom we meet in Games 78, 81 and 84), though his opponent did not play Anderssen's next move. Still, Beliavsky prepares his openings extremely thoroughly, so it is reasonable to assume that after 10 ♖e1 he has an improvement for Black that he considers viable.

10 ♖e1! ♘ge7

10...♗b6 intending 11...♘a5 may cause White more inconvenience.

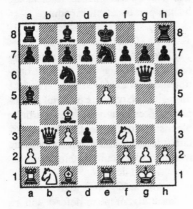

11 ♗a3 b5?!

This is the first truly "nineteenth-century" move of the game, and is reminiscent of Kieseritzky's 4...b5 in the Immortal Game. Rather than try to defend carefully, and to return the pawn, if necessary, in due course to deaden White's initiative, Black lashes out with a counter-sacrifice of a pawn. To a modern player, the logic is hard to see. Black's only consolation for White's lead in development is his extra pawn (the one of d3 cannot survive in the long term), and healthy, unweakened pawn-structure. These advantages are thrown away on a whim, Black hoping for some sort of counterattack on the b-file and a8–h1 diagonal. While it is true that Black does secure some

counter-threats, to start a tactical shoot-out from a strategically inferior position is a policy doomed to failure. However, such logic was foreign to ordinary masters in the 1850s – it was some decades yet before the writings of Steinitz (see Game 5) put the case for the methodical approach to chess. That said, lashing out with a move such as this is not always bad – sometimes specific tactics will justify outrageous, "illogical" moves.

11...a6 would prepare the b-pawn's advance, and give Black more realistic hope.

12 ♕xb5 ♖b8
13 ♕a4 ♗b6

13...0-0? would now lose a piece in view of 14 ♗xe7 overloading the c6-knight.

14 ♘bd2

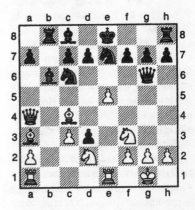

Anderssen brings his last minor piece into play and will now aim his pieces at Black's king, wherever it tries to hide.

14 ... ♗b7

Black has carried out the idea behind his ...b5 pawn sacrifice. 14...0-0 has been suggested, but if that is the best move, then why not just castle on move 11?

15 ♘e4

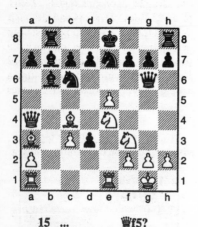

15 ...   ♕f5?

This lands Black in trouble, so it is worth looking at the alternatives:

1) 15...0-0 16 ♗xd3 threatens 17 ♘f6+, as in the game, and moreover 17 ♘eg5 is an idea after the queen moves, e.g. 16...♕h5 17 ♘eg5 h6?? 18 g4.

2) 15...♘d4 is an interesting and thematic attempt to use the pressure on the long diagonal to bring about some welcome exchanges. However, after 16 cxd4 ♗xe4 17 ♗xf7+! (a simple combination, with two decoys ready to set up a knight fork) 17...♕xf7 (17...♔xf7 18 ♖xe4 ♕xe4?? 19 ♘g5+) 18 ♖xe4 White will eventually emerge a pawn up, with Black's position still unconvincing.

3) 15...d2 16 ♘exd2 0-0 was Lasker's suggestion, but then material is level and White has all the chances. For instance a correspondence game with Tim Harding as White ended 17 ♘e4 ♖fe8 18 ♖ad1 ♖bd8?? (18...♘a5) 19 ♘eg5 1-0. Instead 17 ♗xe7 ♘xe7 18 ♕xd7 looks horribly materialistic,

but Black must be careful, for example:

3a) 18...♖bd8 19 ♕xe7 ♖xd2 (not 19...♗xf2+? 20 ♔xf2 ♖xd2+ 21 ♘xd2 ♕xg2+ 22 ♔e3) 20 e6! ♗xf2+ 21 ♔h1 ♗c5? 22 ♕xf7+! ♖xf7 23 exf7+ wins for White.

3b) 18...♘f5 19 e6 ♖bd8 20 exf7+ ♔h8 21 ♖e8 ♖dxe8 22 fxe8♕ ♕xe8 (22...♖xe8?? 23 ♗f7) 23 ♕xe8 ♖xe8 and Black must put his faith in the bishop-pair to save this ending.

16 ♗xd3   ♕h5
17 ♘f6+!?

17 ♘d6+!? is another interesting (pseudo-)sacrifice, but the best continuation is 17 ♘g3! ♕h6 18 ♗c1 ♕e6 19 ♗c4, winning material in simple fashion. This is rather an artistic blemish on the game, but we can certainly forgive Anderssen for wishing to win in spectacular fashion.

17 ...   gxf6
18 exf6   ♖g8

Black's attempt to defend will be based on threats to the white king.

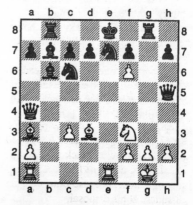

19 ♖ad1!

This move was criticized by Lasker, who suggested instead 19 ♗e4 ♕h3

20 g3 ⧄xg3+ 21 hxg3 ♕xg3+ 22 ♔h1 ♗xf2. Lasker now continued his analysis 23 ⧄e2, but this loses to 23...⧄d4!!. Instead 23 ♗xe7 might keep some advantage, e.g. 23...♕h3+ 24 ♘h2 ♕h4 25 ⧄e2 ⧄d4 26 ♗xb7 ⧄xe2 27 ♕xh4 ♗xh4, but the position is messy.

19 ...   ♕xf3?

After this White can prove a decisive advantage. Plenty of alternatives have been analysed in great depth at this point. The most interesting lines are:

1) 19...⧄xg2+? 20 ♔xg2 ⧄e5 also looks like quite a dangerous counter-attacking try, but White strikes first, in similar fashion to the game continuation: 21 ♕xd7+!! ⧄xd7 (21...♔xd7 22 ♗g6+) 22 ⧄xe7+ ♔d8 (22...♔f8 23 ⧄e5+) 23 ⧄xd7+! and now:

1a) 23...♔xd7 24 ♗f5++ ♔e8 (or 24...♔c6 25 ♗d7#) 25 ♗d7+ ♔d8 26 ♗e7#.

1b) 23...♔c8 24 ⧄d8+! ♔xd8 25 ♗f5+ ♔e8 26 ♗d7+ ♔d8 27 ♗e7#.

2) 19...⧄g4! is the best try, when it has been the subject of much debate whether White can win:

2a) 20 c4 has been recommended, but this artificial move appears inadequate: 20...⧄xg2+ (20...⧄f4? 21 ♗g6!) 21 ♔xg2 (21 ♔h1 ⧄xf2) 21...♕g4+ (not 21...⧄e5??, when 22 ♕xd7+ still works) 22 ♔f1 ♕xf3 looks most unconvincing for White:

2a1) 23 ⧄xe7+ ⧄xe7 24 ♕xd7+ ♔xd7 25 ♗f5++ (25 ♗e2+ ♔e6 26 ♗xf3 ♗xf3 leaves Black a piece up) 25...♔e8 26 ♗d7+ ♔f8 27 ♗xe7+ is no longer mate, because Black has the g8-square at his disposal.

2a2) 23 c5 ♕h3+ 24 ♔g1 (24 ♔e2 blocks the e-file, and allows 24...♗a5, with devastating threats for Black)

24...⧄e5 and it is Black who is attacking.

2b) The key line is 20 ⧄e4 ⧄xe4 (20...⧄xg2+ 21 ♔xg2 ♕g6+ 22 ♔f1 ♕xf6 23 ⧄de1) 21 ♕xe4 and although White's threats aren't too devastating here (to regain the piece, with an extra pawn or so, possibly starting with 22 ⧄e1), it is difficult for Black to find a decent move – indeed most moves worsen his position:

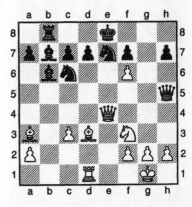

2b1) 21...♗a5 22 ♗xe7 ♗xc3 23 ♗a3+ ⧄e5 24 ⧄b1! d5 25 ♕a4+ wins.

2b2) 21...♕g6 22 ♕h4 (22 fxe7 ♕xe4 23 ♗xe4 ⧄xe7 is nothing special for White) 22...⧄f5 23 ♕f4 wins back the piece with a substantial advantage, e.g. 23...d6 24 ♗xf5 ♕h5 (24...♕xf6 25 ♗d7+ ♔e7 26 ⧄e1+) 25 ⧄e1+ ♔d8 26 ♗xd6 with a mating attack; 23...♕xf6 24 ♗xf5 and the d7-pawn falls with catastrophic effect; or 23...⧄cd4 24 cxd4 ♗xf3 25 ♕xf3 ⧄xd4 26 ⧄e1+ ♔d8 27 ♗e7+ ♔c8 (27...♔e8 28 ♗c5+ ♔d8 29 ♗xd4) 28 ♗a6+ and mate next move.

2b3) 21...d6 22 ⧄e1 ⧄e5 (22...♕a5 23 ♕xh7 is good for White, for example 23...♕xa3 24 ♗f5! cuts off the

king's escape and forces mate) 23
♗b5+! and after 23...♔f8 24 fxe7+
♔g7 (24...♔xe7 25 ♕xe5+) 25 ♕xb7
the e-pawn queens, while following
23...c6 24 ♗xd6 cxb5 25 ♕xe5 ♕xe5
26 ♖xe5 White will regain the sacrificed material with a lot of interest.

20   ♖xe7+!

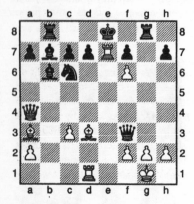

20   ...   ♘xe7?

Now Black is mated by force. Instead 20...♔f8? loses simply after 21
♖e3+, picking up Black's queen, but
20...♔d8 21 ♖xd7+! ♔c8 (21...♔e8?
22 ♖e7+ ♔d8 23 ♗e2+; 21...♔xd7? 22
♗f5++ ♔e8 23 ♗d7+ ♔d8 24 ♗xc6+
mates) 22 ♖d8+!! ♔xd8 (22...♖xd8?
23 gxf3 wins on material; 22...♘xd8?
23 ♕d7+!! ♔xd7 24 ♗f5++ forces
mate: 24...♔c6 25 ♗d7# or 24...♔e8
25 ♗d7#) needs careful analysis:

1) 23 ♗f5+ ♕xd1+ 24 ♕xd1+
♘d4 25 ♗h3! (25 g3 ♖g5 26 ♗h3 ♗f3
is less clear – Kasparov) 25...♗d5 26

♗e7+ ♔e8 27 cxd4 wins (Nunn). He
gives the sample line 27...♗a5 28 g3
c6 29 ♕c2 ♖g6 30 ♗g2! ♗xg2 31
♔xg2 ♖c8 32 ♕e4.

2) 23 ♗e2+ ♘d4 24 ♗xf3 ♗xf3 25
g3! ♖g5 (25...♗xd1 26 ♕xd1 "with a
boring but winning endgame" – Kasparov) 26 cxd4 ♗a5 27 ♗e7+ ♔c8 28
♕c2 ♗xd1 29 ♕xd1 is another line
cited by Nunn – Black is in trouble
since the f7-pawn cannot be held, and
then White's own far-advanced f-
pawn will be unstoppable.

21   ♕xd7+!!   ♔xd7
22   ♗f5++   ♔e8
22...♔c6 23 ♗d7#.
23   ♗d7+   ♔f8
23...♔d8 24 ♗xe7#.
24   ♗xe7# (1-0)

Lessons from this game:

1) Play in the centre has more effect than play on the wings – everyone
knows this of course, but it is all too
easily forgotten in the heat of battle.

2) Always analyse variations with
double checks extremely carefully –
however improbable they may look.

3) Before playing a spectacular
combination, check to see whether
there is a simpler, safer way to win
cleanly. Unless of course you want to
play a brilliancy that is still being
talked about a century and a half later,
in which case play the sacrifice and
keep your fingers crossed! (And don't
blame me if you follow that advice
and go on to lose.)

Johann Zukertort – Joseph Blackburne
London 1883
English Opening

The Players

Johann Zukertort (1842–88) was a Polish-born player, who for many years was considered second only to Wilhelm Steinitz in the chess world. In 1861 he enrolled in the faculty of medicine at Breslau University. Rather than attending lectures, however, Zukertort spent most of his waking hours playing chess, including many friendly games against Anderssen, and he was finally struck from the university register due to non-attendance. Zukertort gradually built up his reputation as a chess player, and this was enhanced when a match of off-hand games ended in a 5–2 victory over Anderssen in 1871. He arrived in London in 1872, and spent the rest of his life there as a professional player. Many successes in tournaments and match-play followed, including first place at the 1883 London Tournament, ahead of all the world's best, including Steinitz. His triumphs were rewarded with a battle against Steinitz in New Orleans in 1886, which has been recognized as the first official World Championship match. Steinitz won by the score of +10 =5 −5.

Joseph Blackburne (1841–1924) was for many years the leading English chess player, as well as being one of the world's best. Inspired by Paul Morphy's brief but explosive accomplishments in Europe, the eighteen-year-old from Manchester decided to learn the game. He proved to be an excellent student. After spending much of the 1860s developing his game, he made his breakthrough by winning the British Championship in 1868, and following this he became a full-time professional player. Blackburne's excellent results were helped by his brilliant combinative powers, his ability to create awesome kingside attacks, plus his knack of producing swindles from seemingly lost positions. The tournament book of Vienna 1873 called him "der schwarze Tod" (The Black Death), a nickname that has stuck ever since.

The Game

A deceptively quiet opening and a strategic middlegame give us no warning of the fireworks that eventually decide this battle. Blackburne starts off well, but then makes a minor slip, which Zukertort immediately exploits. The rest of the game is played to perfection by the Polish player, who builds up impressively on the kingside. When the position finally opens up, Blackburne appears to be fighting back strongly, but Zukertort's concept turns out to have hidden depth, and he wins by a spectacular combination. Look out in particular for White's sensational 28th move.

| 1 | c4 | e6 |
| 2 | e3 | |

Zukertort plays the early part of the game in a very innocuous way indeed, allowing Black to reach a comfortable position with no effort at all. Later on Richard Réti (see Game 22) was to develop a more potent, "hypermodern" method of development against 1...e6, involving a fianchetto of the king's bishop. At this particular moment, however, the theory of flank openings had not really developed at all.

2	...	♘f6
3	♘f3	b6
4	♗e2	♗b7
5	0-0	d5
6	d4	♗d6
7	♘c3	0-0
8	b3	♘bd7
9	♗b2	

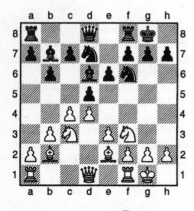

9 ...   ♕e7?!

After some effective opening play, Black now starts to drift. There are two basic pawn breaks for Black in this position, namely ...c7-c5 and ...e6-e5. Both advances will lead to pawn exchanges and thus an opening of the position. With 9...♕e7 Black connects his rooks and keeps his options open on which advance to make, but forgets one vital factor, the generalization that "in open positions bishops are better than knights". For this reason Black should take one move out to preserve his d6-bishop. Only after 9...a6! can Black safely continue with such moves as ...♕e7, ...♖ad8, ...dxc4 and ...e5 (or ...c5). Needless to say, Zukertort is quick to seize his chance.

10	♘b5!	♘e4
11	♘xd6	cxd6
12	♘d2	♘df6
13	f3	♘xd2
14	♕xd2	

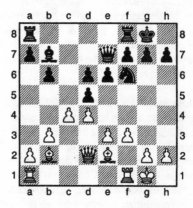

At the moment the position remains reasonably closed, but without being really blocked up. In effect it has the potential to become open and it is this situation which the bishops are waiting for. With his next move Blackburne allows just one open file, but in doing so he accepts a lifeless position. The advance 14...e5 is more enterprising, and ensures more counterplay, e.g.:

1) 15 cxd5 e4! (aiming to block the position: 15...♘xd5 16 e4 ♘f4 17

&c4! is clearly better for White) 16
&c4 &xd5 and Black has good control
over the central light squares, whereas
White's bishops haven't yet found
their scope.

2) 15 dxe5! dxe5 16 ℤfd1 (or 16
cxd5 ♘xd5 17 e4 ♘f4 and Black is
very active) 16...ℤfd8 17 ♕e1 and
White's bishop-pair is enough for a
small edge.

14	...	dxc4
15	&xc4	d5
16	&d3	ℤfc8
17	ℤae1!	

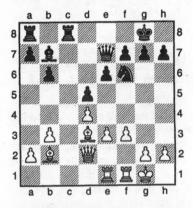

It is deep moves like this which often separate good players from great
players. Many players would have
been very tempted to oppose the only
open file with 17 ℤac1, but this would
have been an incorrect plan, leading
only to a mass exchange of the major
pieces on the c-file. It's true that White
could still advance in the centre later
on, but with fewer pieces on the board,
Black's defensive task would be
greatly eased. As we shall see later on,
the presence of white rooks is an important factor in the success of the attack.

This is not to say that giving up the
only open file is a business that should
be taken lightly. Here, however, White
correctly assesses that Black's occupation of the c-file is not so important,
especially as all the possible infiltra-
tion squares (i.e. c1-c5) are covered
more than adequately by White's
pieces and pawns.

As a further point it should be mentioned that this is definitely a case of
the "right rook". The other rook is ex-
cellently placed on f1, where it will
support the eventual advance of the f-
pawn.

17	...	ℤc7
18	e4	ℤac8
19	e5	♘e8
20	f4	g6
21	ℤe3	

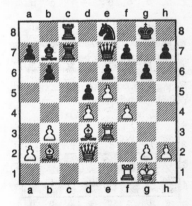

We now begin to see for sure that
Black's counterplay along the c-file is
proving to be more apparent than real.
Meanwhile, White's attack on the
kingside builds up at his leisure behind the impressive pawn-centre. The
next stage of the plan will involve
forcing the f4-f5 breakthrough with
moves such as g2-g4. Rather than

waiting to be squashed without a contest, with his next move Blackburne understandably tries to fight back. However, by doing so he stumbles into a long forced line, ending in a brilliant win for White.

21 ...   f5

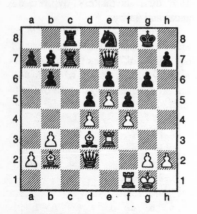

Despite the fact that this loses, it can hardly be criticized, especially as the alternatives are hardly enticing, e.g. 21...♘g7 22 g4 ♕h4 23 ♖g3 h5 24 f5! hxg4 25 fxg6 fxg6 26 ♗xg6 and White breaks through.

22 exf6   ♘xf6

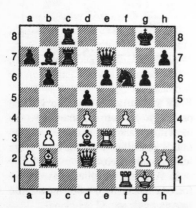

23 f5   ♘e4

23...gxf5 24 ♗xf5 is even worse, e.g. 24...♘e4 25 ♗xe4 dxe4 26 ♖g3+ ♚h8 27 d5+ e5 28 d6.

24 ♗xe4   dxe4
25 fxg6

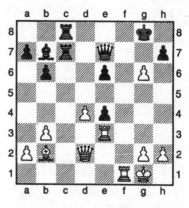

25 ...   ♖c2

Black bases all of his hopes on this move, which does seem to give him a lot more counterplay than he perhaps deserves. In any case, the alternative 25...hxg6 loses swiftly to 26 ♖g3, when Black's creaking kingside cannot stand up to the intense pressure, e.g.:

1) 26...♕e8 27 ♕h6 ♖h7 28 ♖xg6+ ♚h8 29 d5+ e5 30 ♗xe5+! ♕xe5 31 ♕f8+! ♖xf8 32 ♖xf8#.

2) 26...♚h7 27 d5 e5 (or 27...♗xd5 28 ♖h3+ ♚g8 29 ♖h8#) 28 d6 ♖d7 29 ♖h3+ ♚g8 30 dxe7 ♖xd2 31 ♗xe5 and ♖h8#.

3) 26...♕h7 27 ♖f6 ♖g7 28 ♖h3 wins the queen.

4) 26...♕g7 27 d5 e5 28 ♕g5 ♖e8 29 ♖f6 and again White wins.

26 gxh7+   ♚h8

The only move. Both 26...♚xh7 27 ♖h3+ ♚g8 28 ♕h6 and 26...♕xh7 27

♖g3+ ♔h8 28 d5+ e5 29 ♗xe5+ are winning for White.

27 d5+ e5

Suddenly it seems as if Black has dealt with the threats and White is left facing the loss of a piece. 28 d6 looks good, but Black can fight on after 28...♕g5!. Zukertort, however, has a dazzling queen sacrifice up his sleeve.

28 ♕b4!!

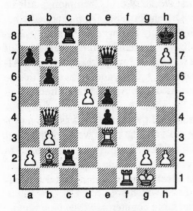

An extraordinary idea against which there is no defence. Accepting the offer with 28...♕xb4 leads to a forced mate in seven after 29 ♗xe5+ ♔h7 30 ♖h3+ ♔g6 (or 30...♔g8 31 ♖h8#) 31 ♖g3+ ♔h6 (other moves lead to quicker mates, e.g. 31...♔h7 32 ♖f7+ ♔h6 33 ♗f4+ ♔h5 34 ♖h7# or 31...♔h5 32 ♖f5+) 32 ♖f6+ ♔h5 33 ♖f5+ ♔h6 34 ♗f4+ ♔h7 35 ♖h5#. Other moves do no good either:

1) 28...♕e8 29 ♖f8+! ♕xf8 30 ♗xe5+ ♔h7 31 ♕xe4+ ♔h6 32 ♖h3+ ♔g5 33 ♖g3+ ♔h5 34 ♕g6+ ♔h4 35 ♖g4#.

2) 28...♖8c7 29 ♗xe5+ ♕xe5 30 ♕f8+ ♔xh7 31 ♖h3+ ♔g6 32 ♕h6#.

3) 28...♖e8 29 ♖f8+! ♕xf8 30 ♗xe5+ ♔xh7 31 ♕xe4+ ♔h6 32 ♖h3+

and White mates as in variation "1".

4) 28...♖2c7 defends against the flash moves, but after the prosaic 29 ♕xe4 Black can still resign.

28 ... ♖8c5

29 ♖f8+! ♔xh7

After 29...♕xf8 30 ♗xe5+ ♔xh7 31 ♕xe4+ ♔h6 32 ♖h3+ White mates in the usual way.

30 ♕xe4+ ♔g7

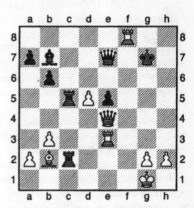

31 ♗xe5+ ♔xf8

32 ♗g7+ ♔g8

32...♔xg7 33 ♕e8# is mate.

33 ♕xe7 1-0

Lessons from this game:

1) Look out for sneaky knight moves. It's very easy to overlook annoying ones like Zukertort's 10 ♘b5, which secured the advantage of the two bishops.

2) Open files should be studied carefully. Sometimes they are the most important feature of the position. In this game, however, the open c-file was virtually irrelevant.

3) A queen sacrifice, based on a forced checkmate in seven moves, is a pleasing way to end the game!

Wilhelm Steinitz – Mikhail Chigorin
World Championship match (game 4),
Havana 1892
Ruy Lopez, Berlin Defence

The Players

Wilhelm Steinitz (1836–1900) was the first official World Champion, a title he received after defeating Zukertort in New Orleans in 1886. Despite actually being one year older than Paul Morphy, Steinitz really belonged to the next generation of chess players. By the time Steinitz was beginning to dedicate himself seriously to the game, in 1862, Morphy's chess career was already finished. After a few years living in Vienna, Steinitz came to England, and it was there that he developed his positional style, which contrasted with Anderssen's wholly combinative play.

Steinitz's importance was not just as a player of the game. He was also a profound thinker and teacher and became the most prolific chess writer of the nineteenth century. Unlike Philidor, who also advocated a positional approach to chess, Steinitz was able to persuade the world of its absolute importance. He was undoubtedly helped in this respect by his excellent results using his deep concepts of positional play.

Mikhail Chigorin (1850–1908) was one of the world's leading players towards the end of the nineteenth century. He twice challenged Steinitz for the world championship, in 1889 and 1892, but lost on both occasions, although the second match (+8 =5 –10) was close. Like many of his contemporaries, he was an exceptional tactician and he was also renowned for his imaginative approach to the opening, which is shown in his surprising invention against the Queen's Gambit (1 d4 d5 2 c4 ♘c6). At Vienna in 1903, where everyone was forced to play the King's Gambit Accepted, Chigorin won with ease, ahead of Pillsbury, Maróczy and Marshall. He also did much to develop chess activity in Russia, forming a chess club in St Petersburg and lecturing in many other cities.

The Game

After some peaceful opening play, Steinitz totally bewilders his distinguished opponent with some high-class manoeuvring. Not realizing the danger, Chigorin procrastinates over the right plan and is punished when Steinitz suddenly lashes out on the kingside with his h-pawn. Facing a sudden change in tempo, Chigorin is unable to cope and he finally falls prey to an irresistible attack on his king. Steinitz finishes with quite a flourish as an exquisite rook sacrifice rounds off some extremely subtle play.

1	e4	e5
2	♘f3	♘c6
3	♗b5	♘f6
4	d3	

This is the old way of playing against the Berlin. The modern method involves offering the e-pawn with 4 0-0. Although Black normally captures with 4...♘xe4, this is not done with the intention of keeping the extra pawn. After 5 d4 Black tends to enter the endgame arising after 5...♘d6 6 ♗xc6 dxc6 7 dxe5 ♘f5 8 ♕xd8+ ♔xd8, or to play the developing move 5...♗e7. The greedy 5...exd4 allows White to set up a powerful pin on the e-file with 6 ♖e1. Then 6...d5 7 ♘xd4 gives White an advantage, as both 8 ♘xc6 and 8 f3 are threatened.

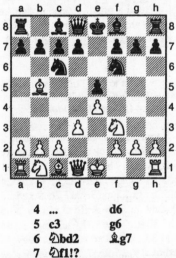

4	...	d6
5	c3	g6
6	♘bd2	♗g7
7	♘f1!?	

By delaying castling White is able to execute the classic Lopez knight manoeuvre. This knight can now emerge at either g3 or, on this occasion, e3 where it has a substantial influence over the centre. That said, Steinitz's

plan is a little bit too elaborate to give hope of a real advantage.

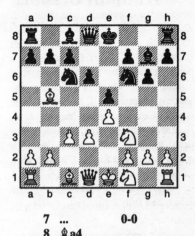

7	...	0-0
8	♗a4	

White withdraws the bishop in order to preserve it for later on. In game 2 of their match Steinitz had chosen instead 8 ♘e3 and Chigorin correctly countered in the centre immediately with 8...d5.

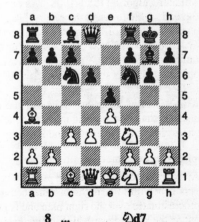

8	...	♘d7

The following manoeuvre with this knight proves rather time-consuming, without being especially constructive.

Perhaps Chigorin was lulled into a false sense of security by White's apparently slow opening play. Euwe recommended queenside expansion with 8...a6 9 ♘e3 b5 10 ♗b3 ♘a5 11 ♗c2 c5, which would virtually be taken for granted today. After 11...c5 Black's position possesses a certain amount of coordination, which is missing in the game continuation. Later on in their match Chigorin also improved on 8...♘d7 in another way, with an immediate lunge in the centre. The 14th game continued 8...d5!? 9 ♕e2 ♕d6 10 ♗c2 b6 11 ♘g3 ♗a6 12 0-0 dxe4 13 ♘xe4 ♘xe4 14 ♕xe4 ♗b7 and Black had fully equalized.

	9	♘e3	♘c5
	10	♗c2	♘e6
	11	h4!	

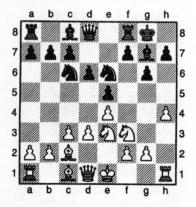

Probably the most important move of the entire game. Steinitz certainly enjoyed attacking in such a fashion. In some ways this offensive looks risky, because White has yet to complete his development, but his prophylactic measures in the centre have made it difficult for Black to obtain counterplay. This means that White can and

should create instant pressure on the black kingside. In particular the rook on h1 will enter the game under favourable circumstances.

Steinitz's idea of h2-h4 has not been lost on future generations. Just over a hundred years later the current World Champion used a very similar idea, with an equally favourable result.

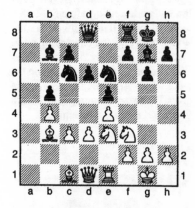

Kasparov – Short
*PCA World Championship
match (game 7), London 1993*

Here Kasparov had already castled, but the wing attack still carried a nasty sting. After 19 h4! ♗c8 20 h5! ♔h8 21 ♘d5 g5 22 ♘e3 ♘f4 23 g3 ♘xh5 24 ♘f5 ♗xf5 25 exf5 ♕d7 26 ♗xg5 h6 27 ♘h4 ♘f6 28 ♗xf6 ♗xf6 29 ♕h5 ♔h7 30 ♘g2 ♘e7 31 ♘e3 ♘g8 32 d4 exd4 33 cxd4 ♗xd4 34 ♘g4 ♔g7 35 ♘xh6! ♗f6 36 ♗xf7! Black was forced to resign.

(Back now to Steinitz – Chigorin.)

	11	...	♘e7

Finally Black hits on the correct plan, to aim for the ...d6-d5 advance.

Other moves are in danger of being either too slow or too panicky:

1) 11...h6 (too slow) 12 h5 g5 and now White should immediately occupy the outpost with 13 ♘f5 and follow up with 14 d4, securing a definite advantage.

2) 11...f5!? (too panicky) 12 exf5! (but not 12 h5 f4 13 ♘d5 g5 14 h6 ♗f6 15 ♗b3 ♔h8, when Black has not only survived, but has taken over the operation on the kingside) 12...gxf5 13 d4! exd4 14 ♘xf5 dxc3 15 ♘xg7 cxb2 16 ♗xb2 ♘xg7 17 ♘g5 and White has a very strong attack.

3) Perhaps Black's best alternative to 11...♘e7 is 11...h5, which makes it harder for White to expand on the kingside. Of course White can continue with 12 g4, but 12...hxg4 13 ♘xg4 ♘f4 14 ♘g5 d5 gives Black definite counterplay.

12	h5	d5

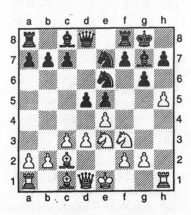

13 hxg6   fxg6?

This was an occasion where Black should have definitely adhered to the "capture towards the centre" principle. Perhaps Chigorin was seeking counterplay along the now half-open

f-file, but in reality all that Black has done is to weaken his king position. The threats down the h-file remain, while White will now also be able to find particular joy along the a2–g8 diagonal, which has suddenly become quite vulnerable.

After 13...hxg6 White should probably continue with 14 ♕e2, intending ♗d2 and 0-0-0. Notice that 14...♘f4 would not be too much of a worry. White could simply retreat with 15 ♕f1, before kicking the knight back with g2-g3.

14 exd5!

White normally doesn't release the tension in the centre like this without good reason, but here he is absolutely justified in his decision. The Lopez bishop will now find a nice home on the b3-square.

14	...	♘xd5
15	♘xd5	♕xd5
16	♗b3	♕c6
17	♕e2	

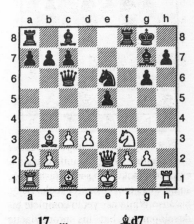

17 ...   ♗d7

Other moves have been suggested, but in all probability Black's position is beyond repair already. 17...♔h8 removes the black king from the pin, but after 18 &h6! the weaknesses in the black camp are becoming more and more apparent. In particular, the e5-pawn is basically a sitting duck. 17...a5, trying to chase the bishop off the diagonal with ...a4 is another try, although once more White can keep the advantage by either direct means with 18 ♘g5 ♕xg2 19 ♖xh7, or in a more positional way with 18 a4 ♕b6 19 ♕c2 and 20 ♗e3, as suggested by Neishtadt.

18 ♗e3

After obtaining positional domination, now is the right time to complete development. 18 ♘xe5? ♕xg2 would spoil all the earlier work.

    18 ...   ♔h8
    19 0-0-0   ♖ae8
    20 ♕f1!

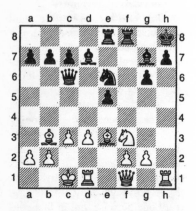

"More attacking than defensive" – Steinitz. This subtle queen retreat, which has many different purposes, is a move of star quality. Firstly White removes the queen from the e-file, thus eliminating many of Black's tactical tricks involving ...♘f4 and ...♘d4. There is also a much deeper aspect to

20 ♕f1, which becomes obvious very soon.

    20 ...   a5

Passive defence with 20...♖f5, intending ...♘f8, doesn't help Black. White should simply increase the pressure on the h-file with 21 ♖h4, when 21...♘f8 can be answered with 22 ♘g5!. Instead of 20...♖f5, we should consider two knight moves for Black.

1) 20...♘d4? 21 ♖xh7+! (another point of 20 ♕f1) 21...♔xh7 22 ♕h1+ ♗h6 23 ♕xh6#.

2) 20...♘f4 and now either 21 ♘g5 h6 22 ♘f7+ ♔h7 23 d4! ♕xg2 24 ♕xg2 ♘xg2 25 ♘xh6 (Ravinsky) or 21 d4! exd4 22 ♖xd4 looks very strong for White.

    21 d4!

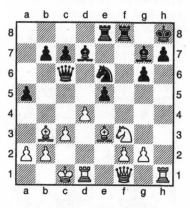

    21 ...   exd4
    22 ♘xd4   ♗xd4

Unfortunately Black must part with his defensive bishop, leaving him woefully weak on both the dark squares *and* the light squares! 22...♘xd4 allows White to mate after 23 ♖xh7+! ♔xh7 24 ♕h1+. Euwe also gives the depressing variations 22...♕a6 23 ♗c4 ♕a8 24 ♘f3 and 22...♕e4 23 ♗c2

♕g4 24 f3 ♕g3 25 ♘f5! gxf5 26 ♖xd7
as positionally winning for White.

23   ♖xd4!

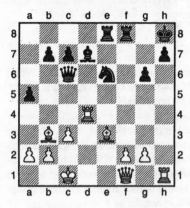

23   ...   ♘xd4?

Overlooking White's next brilliant
idea. Euwe gives 23...b5 24 ♕d3! as
winning for White, when 24...♘c5
runs into the usual rook sacrifice: 25
♖xh7+! ♚xh7 26 ♖h4+ ♚g7 27 ♕d4+
♕f6 28 ♗h6+ ♚h7 29 ♗xf8+ ♕xh4
30 ♕g7#. Black's final chance to prolong the agony lies in 23...♖e7, hoping
for 24 ♕d3? ♘c5, when White is
forced to give up one of his bishops for
that lowly knight. Instead White should
swing his rook across the fourth rank
to increase the pressure on h7.

24   ♖xh7+!

Revealing to his startled opponent
the real point of 20 ♕f1. The black
king will find itself checkmated in
mid-board.

24	...	♚xh7
25	♕h1+	♚g7
26	♗h6+	♚f6

| **27** | ♕h4+ | ♚e5 |
| **28** | ♕xd4+ | |

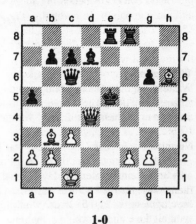

1-0

After 28...♚f5 White can choose
between 29 g4# and 29 ♕f4#.

Lessons from this game:

1) Don't dither with your plan!
Here Black wanders around aimlessly
for too long before deciding to carry
out the logical ...d5 advance, something which could have been achieved
as early as move eight. Be direct!

2) Look out for the unexpected.
Sometimes pedestrian developing
moves can be replaced by a sudden
idea which causes your opponent immediate problems. Steinitz's 11 h4 is
an example of such an effective idea.

3) A move which looks to have
merely one purpose, but in fact contains some heavily concealed threats,
often produces the desired result. Here
Steinitz's very deep 20 ♕f1 was too
much for Chigorin.

Game 6
Wilhelm Steinitz – Curt von Bardeleben
Hastings 1895
Giuoco Piano

The Players

Wilhelm Steinitz (1836–1900) was the first player to be recognized as World Champion, a title he held from 1886 to 1894, and one of the key figures in the development of chess. See Game 5 for more information.

Curt von Bardeleben (1861–1924) was born in Berlin. He studied law but never practised, finding the lure of the chessboard too strong to resist. He was undoubtedly an extremely talented player, capable of first-class results, but his temperament was unsuited to the hurly-burly of tough competitive play, with its inevitable setbacks. His standard of play would fall substantially after a disappointing loss, and he would sometimes withdraw from an event altogether.

The Game

For both players this was a turning point in the tournament. Steinitz had begun poorly, but starting with this game rallied to a respectable fifth place, whereas for von Bardeleben, who had the tremendous score of 7½/9 up to that point, it marked the start of a collapse. Steinitz plays a rather simple opening, common nowadays only at club level for its trappiness, but rare at top level because it brings matters to a premature crisis. However, von Bardeleben avoids the main lines, and lands in a position where structurally he is doing well, but his king is stranded in the centre. After a trade of inaccuracies, Steinitz plays an excellent pawn sacrifice to bring his knight into the attack. The finish is highly dramatic. It appears that Steinitz has over-reached, as Black finds a cunning defence based on White's back rank. However, this illusion is washed away by a staggering series of rook offers. This opens up a route for the white queen to come into the attack and bring about a beautiful mating finish.

1	e4	e5
2	♘f3	♘c6
3	♗c4	♗c5

This move characterizes the Giuoco Piano. The name means "Quiet Game", and seems rather inappropriate given the stormy events to come. However, when it received its name, the standard opening was the King's Gambit, and in comparison it is relatively "quiet".

4 c3

Instead 4 d3, or 5 d3 on the next move, would bring about the Giuoco Pianissimo. This is actually the modern preference, with White keeping open many plans, including queenside expansion with b4, play in the centre, and kingside activity, often involving the manoeuvre ♘bd2-f1-g3. Note that 4 d3 followed by ♘c3 is a deadly dull system that tends to be seen a lot in schools' chess.

4 ...   ♘f6

This healthy developing move forces White either to slow the pace with 5 d3 or else to open the centre before he is fully ready to do so.

5 d4   exd4
6 cxd4

White has set up an "ideal" pawn-centre, but he is unable to maintain it. Another logical attempt to achieve central dominance, 6 e5, is met by the thematic central thrust 6...d5!, assuring Black his full share of the play. Anyone who defends symmetrical king's pawn openings absolutely *must* know this idea.

6 ...   ♗b4+

This is the problem. If White had had time to castle before playing d4, then his pawns would have been able to steam-roller through in the centre, scattering Black's minor pieces in all directions before them.

7 ♘c3

Instead 7 ♗d2 ♗xd2+ 8 ♘bxd2 d5! breaks up White's pawn-centre, and gives Black a completely acceptable position.

7 ...   d5?!

Now, however, this move causes White rather less inconvenience. The key difference from the line in the previous note is that White retains his dark-squared bishop, and this greatly enhances his attacking prospects in the open position that now arises. Theory regards 7...♘xe4 as best, when White is struggling for equality in the notorious and thoroughly analysed complications after 8 0-0 ♗xc3 9 d5 ♗f6 10 ♖e1 ♘e7 11 ♖xe4 d6.

8 exd5   ♘xd5

9 0-0   ♗e6

It is too late for Black to grab the pawn:

1) 9...♘xc3 10 bxc3 ♗xc3? 11 ♕b3! ♗xa1 12 ♗xf7+ ♔f8 13 ♗a3+ ♘e7 14 ♗h5 g6 15 ♘g5 ♕e8 16 ♖e1 and White wins.

2) 9...♗xc3 10 bxc3 ♘xc3 11 ♕b3 gives White a huge attack without him having had to sacrifice.

10 ♗g5

Now White has the initiative in a position with level material.

10 ...   ♗e7

10...♕d7? 11 ♗xd5 ♗xd5 12 ♖e1+ ♗e7 13 ♘xd5 ♕xd5 14 ♗xe7 ♘xe7 gives White an extra tempo compared to the game.

11 ♗xd5   ♗xd5
12 ♘xd5

12 ♗xe7?! ♘xe7 13 ♖e1 is less effective, since after 13...0-0 14 ♖xe7 ♗xf3! 15 ♕e1 ♗c6 16 ♕e5 ♖e8 Black survives the pressure.

12 ...   ♕xd5
13 ♗xe7   ♘xe7
14 ♖e1

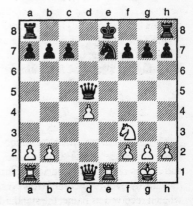

14 ...   f6
15 ♕e2

This move seems very natural and strong, but White had an excellent alternative in 15 ♕a4+!:

1) 15...c6? 16 ♕a3 gives Black no decent way to defend his knight, since 16...♕d7 allows 17 ♖xe7+ ♕xe7 18 ♖e1.

2) 15...♔f7 16 ♘e5+! fxe5 (declining the sacrifice by 16...♔g8 17 ♘g4 ♘g6 18 ♘e3 ♕f7 19 ♘f5 gives White a very strong position) 17 ♖xe5 ♕d6 (17...b5 18 ♕a3; 17...♕c6 18 ♕b3+ ♔f8 19 ♖ae1 ♖e8 20 ♖e6 ♕d7 21 ♖1e4 and the deadly threat of ♖f4+ decides the game in White's favour) 18 ♕c4+ ♔f8 19 ♖ae1 ♘g8 (19...♖e8 20 ♖1e3 g6 21 ♖e6 wins) 20 ♖d5 and then:

2a) 20...b5!? 21 ♕b3 ♕f6 22 ♕b4+ wins: 22...♔f7 23 ♕xb5 ♘e7 (23...♘h6 24 ♖d7+ ♔g6 25 ♖de7) 24 ♖xe7+ ♕xe7 25 ♖d7; or 22...♘e7 23 ♖xe7 ♕xe7 24 ♖f5+ ♔e8 25 ♕xb5+ ♕d7 26 ♖e5+ ♔d8 27 ♖d5.

2b) 20...♕c6 21 ♕b4+ ♔f7 22 ♖c5 ♕d6 23 ♕c4+ ♔f8 24 ♖xc7 ♘h6 25 ♖c8+ wins.

15 ...   ♕d7

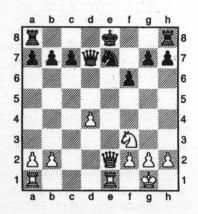

16 ♖ac1

Not the sharpest. White has a number of more forceful possibilities:

1) 16 d5 is Romanovsky's suggestion, but 16...♔f7 17 ♖ad1 (this is an improved version of the next note) 17...♖ad8 (17...♘xd5? 18 ♘g5+ fxg5 19 ♕f3+) 18 ♕e6+ ♔f8 might survive for Black.

2) 16 ♕e4!? c6 17 ♖e2 ♔f7 18 ♖ae1 keeps some pressure.

3) 16 ♖ad1! (Zaitsev) looks very strong. After 16...c6? 17 d5 White simply powers through, while 16...♔f7 17 ♕c4+ ♘d5? (bad, but otherwise how is Black to develop his pieces?) 18 ♘e5+ fxe5 19 dxe5 wins nicely.

16 ...   c6?!

Black underestimates the forthcoming square-vacating pawn sacrifice.

16...♔f7 has been regarded as a major improvement. White has a variety of attempts, but none that gives a serious advantage:

1) 17 ♕xe7+ ♕xe7 18 ♖xe7+ ♔xe7 19 ♖xc7+ ♔d6 20 ♖xg7 ♖hc8 followed by ...♖c7 is good for Black, whose king is very active (Réti).

2) 17 ♘e5+ fxe5 18 dxe5 is Colin Crouch's interesting suggestion in his book reanalysing the games from great Hastings tournament of 1895. However, it is hard to believe that White can have enough for the piece after 18...♕e6 19 ♖xc7 ♖hd8.

3) 17 ♘g5+ (Gufeld and Stetsko) 17...fxg5 18 ♕f3+ ♘f5 19 g4 will regain the material and provides some chance of White keeping an edge, but with his king also now exposed, it will be nothing serious, e.g. 19...c6 20 ♖e5 g6 21 gxf5, 19...♖ae8 20 ♖e5 or 19...♖hd8 20 ♖e5 ♔g8 21 ♖xf5.

17 d5!

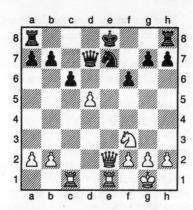

This excellent pawn sacrifice suddenly enlivens the struggle.

17 ...   cxd5
18 ᘯd4

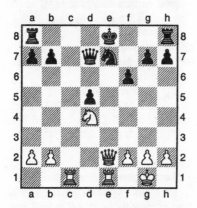

It is well worth a pawn to get such a wonderful square for the knight.

18 ...   ⬧f7
19 ᘯe6

White threatens 20 ᖴc7 ⬯d6 21 ⬯g4 g6 22 ⬯f4! ⬯xf4 23 ᘯxf4 followed by 24 ᘯxd5, winning the pinned knight on e7.

19 ...   ᖴhc8

Instead after 19...ᖴac8 20 ⬯g4 g6 21 ᘯg5+ ⬧e8 22 ᖴxc8+ White wins

on the spot, while 19...ᘯc6 20 ᘯc5 ⬯c8 21 ⬯h5+! is also devastating.

20 ⬯g4

Now the threat is to enter on g7.

20 ...   g6
21 ᘯg5+

The discovered attack on the black queen forces the reply.

21 ...   ⬧e8
22 ᖴxe7+!

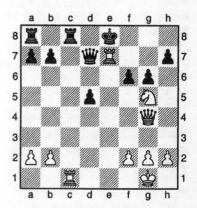

Starting one of the most famous sacrificial sequences in chess history. The rook cannot be taken, but Black has a cunning defensive idea.

22 ...   ⬧f8

Black suffers a disaster if he touches the rook: 22...⬯xe7 23 ᖴxc8+ ᖴxc8 24 ⬯xc8+ leaves White a piece up, while 22...⬧xe7 gives White a pleasant choice of winning lines:

1) 23 ⬯b4+ ⬧e8 (23...⬯d6 24 ⬯xb7+ ⬯d7 25 ᖴe1+ ⬧d6 26 ᘯf7+) 24 ᖴe1+ ⬧d8 25 ᘯe6+ safely wins the queen since White has two pieces covering e1.

2) 23 ᖴe1+ ⬧d6 24 ⬯b4+ ⬧c7 (24...ᖴc5 25 ᖴe6+) 25 ᘯe6+ ⬧b8 26 ⬯f4+ wins in view of 26...ᖴc7 27 ᘯxc7 ⬯xc7 28 ᖴe8#.

After Black's choice in the game, 22...♔f8, the black queen cannot be taken due to mate on the back rank. Meanwhile all four of White's pieces are under attack. Something dramatic is now needed.

23   ♖f7+!

23 ♖xc8+ ♖xc8 24 ♖f7+ ♔g8 25 ♖g7+ ♔h8 26 ♖xh7+ ♔g8 27 ♖g7+ ♔h8 is only a draw, since if White goes in for 28 ♕h4+? ♔xg7 29 ♕h7+ ♔f8 30 ♕h8+ ♔e7 31 ♕g7+ ♔d8 32 ♕f8+ ♔c7 the king escapes.

23   ...   ♔g8
24   ♖g7+!

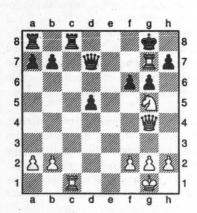

Aiming to decoy the black king so that the queen falls with check.

24   ...   ♔h8

24...♔f8 is no better: 25 ♘xh7+ ♔xg7 26 ♕xd7+.

25   ♖xh7+!   1-0

This "1-0" needs some explanation. von Bardeleben now saw the spectacular finish that awaited him, and elected to "resign" by simply leaving the tournament hall and not coming back. Obviously, this is rather poor sportsmanship.

After this devastating loss he even wanted to withdraw from the tournament. Ironically, this game is now virtually the only thing he is remembered for – perhaps the idea of gaining immortality as a loser is what upset him so much.

The key variation is 25...♔g8 26 ♖g7+ ♔h8 27 ♕h4+ ♔xg7 28 ♕h7+ ♔f8 29 ♕h8+ ♔e7 30 ♕g7+ ♔e8 (30...♔d8 allows White to save a couple of moves by 31 ♕f8+) 31 ♕g8+ ♔e7 32 ♕f7+ ♔d8 33 ♕f8+ ♕e8 34 ♘f7+ ♔d7 35 ♕d6#.

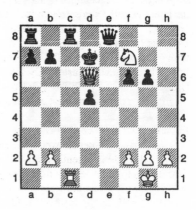

Lessons from this game:

1) If the opponent allows you to win a centre pawn, take it unless there is a very good reason not to.

2) It can be well worth sacrificing a pawn to gain a superb square for a piece, particularly if it is near the enemy king.

3) Try not to be too upset by a loss. Setbacks are inevitable, and it is most useful (though not necessarily very easy) to view each as a learning experience.

Harry Nelson Pillsbury – Emanuel Lasker
St Petersburg 1895/6
Queen's Gambit Declined, Semi-Tarrasch Defence

The Players

Harry Nelson Pillsbury (1872–1906) shot to fame when he won his first major tournament. No one had ever done this before and only Capablanca later achieved a success of a similar magnitude in his international debut. Although considered merely an outside bet for the first Hastings International in 1895, Pillsbury produced some magnificent chess, scoring fifteen wins, three draws and only three losses. He came first, ahead of Steinitz, Chigorin, Tarrasch and the reigning World Champion Lasker. This result catapulted Pillsbury to the top of the chess world, and his exceptional form continued in the first half of the St Petersburg Tournament, a round-robin tournament with Lasker, Steinitz and Chigorin (six games against each). After nine rounds Pillsbury was a clear leader with 6½ points. However, Pillsbury's play mysteriously collapsed in the second half, when he could muster only 1½ points, leaving him in third place behind Lasker and Steinitz. Pillsbury also caught syphilis at St Petersburg, which plagued him through the rest of his career and led to his premature death.

Emanuel Lasker (1868–1941) is one of the most famous chess players of all time. As a youngster Lasker showed incredible talent at both chess and mathematics and he fulfilled his potential in both fields. Lasker defeated Steinitz to become World Champion in 1894, a title he was to hold for twenty-seven years, which is still a record. Despite his victory over Steinitz, the chess world remained unimpressed, chiefly as the former World Champion was 32 years older than Lasker and his health was declining. Lasker, however, was still improving. In 1896 he proved his worth without doubt by winning four successive major events, including the St Petersburg tournament. Lasker continued to have excellent results, before beating Steinitz in a return match in 1896/7. During his chess career he still found time to pursue his mathematical studies, and in 1900 he was awarded his doctorate at Erlangen University. In chess Lasker was an exceptional tactician, but more than anything he was an immensely resourceful fighter. On countless occasions he was able to turn inferior positions to his advantage and his defensive qualities were without equal.

The Game

Lasker gets away with some provocative opening play to reach a very comfortable position with the black pieces. Undaunted, Pillsbury continues to plough ahead with a crude attack, but is rocked on his heels by a clever rook sacrifice from Lasker. Fighting hard, Pillsbury offloads some material to set up a defence, but at the vital moment, he misses the best line and allows Lasker to sacrifice again. This time there is no defence.

1	d4	d5
2	c4	e6
3	♘c3	♘f6
4	♘f3	c5
5	♗g5	

A popular move at the time, but this has now been replaced by the more direct 5 cxd5, when after 5...♘xd5 6 e4 ♘xc3 7 bxc3 cxd4 8 cxd4 ♗b4+ 9 ♗d2 ♗xd2+ 10 ♕xd2 0-0 Black has to play accurately against White's impressive-looking centre (see Game 58, Polugaevsky – Tal).

| 5 | ... | cxd4 |
| 6 | ♕xd4 | |

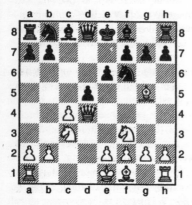

| 6 | ... | ♘c6 |

Lasker liked this move, although 6...♗e7 is probably more accurate, e.g. 7 cxd5 exd5 8 e4 ♘c6 9 ♗b5 0-0 10 ♗xc6 bxc6 with an equal position.

| 7 | ♕h4 | |

In the later game Pillsbury – Lasker, Cambridge Springs 1904, the American improved on his opening play with the subtle 7 ♗xf6!, and after 7...gxf6 8 ♕h4 dxc4 9 ♖d1 ♗d7 10 e3

♘e5 11 ♘xe5 fxe5 12 ♕xc4 ♕b6 13 ♗e2 ♕xb2 14 0-0 ♖c8 15 ♕d3 ♖c7 16 ♘e4 Black's weaknesses were obvious. Note that 7...♘xd4 8 ♗xd8 ♘c2+ 9 ♔d2 ♘xa1 10 ♗h4 favours White, who will pick up the trapped knight in the corner.

7	...	♗e7
8	0-0-0	♕a5
9	e3	♗d7
10	♔b1	h6
11	cxd5	exd5
12	♘d4	0-0

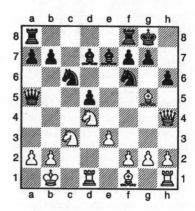

13 ♗xf6

It looks tempting to go "all-in" with 13 ♗xh6. Indeed, after 13...gxh6 14 ♕xh6 ♘g4 15 ♕f4 White has some menacing threats. However, Black doesn't have to capture the bishop immediately. Instead he can keep a cool head with 13...♘e4!, when 14 ♘xc6 ♘xc3+ 15 ♔c2 ♗xh4 16 ♘xa5 ♘xd1 wins for Black, as does 14 ♕f4 ♘xc3+ 15 bxc3 gxh6 16 ♕xh6 ♘xd4 17 ♖xd4 ♗f5+.

13   ...   ♗xf6

14 **♕h5**   **♘xd4**
15 **exd4**   **♗e6**
16 **f4**

The attempt to profit from the pin on the fifth rank with 16 ♘e4 fails after 16...♗xd4! 17 ♖xd4 ♕e1+ 18 ♕d1 ♕xd1+ 19 ♖xd1 dxe4 and Black has merely won a pawn. With 16 f4 White intends to launch an attack on the kingside. Meanwhile Black has his own ambitions on the other wing. Who will get in first?

16 ...   **♖ac8**
17 **f5**

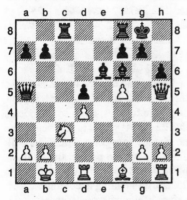

17 ...   **♖xc3!**

This move is the start of some real cut-and-thrust, where neither side is willing to go on the defensive. Of course 17...♗d7 is possible, but that's another, less exciting story.

18 **fxe6!**

Grabbing the rook leads to a catastrophe on the queenside for White. After 18 bxc3 ♕xc3 19 fxe6 ♖c8! White cannot defend against the many mating threats, e.g. 20 ♗e2 ♕b4+ 21 ♔a1 ♖c1+!! 22 ♖xc1 ♗xd4+ and mate next move. The desperate 20 ♕e2 ♗xd4 21 exf7+ ♔f8 22 ♕e8+ avoids mate, but

22...♖xe8 23 fxe8♕+ ♔xe8 is clearly hopeless for White.

18 ...   **♖a3!!**

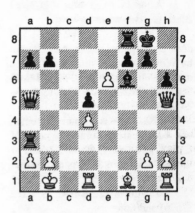

Moving the rook from one attacked square to another creates quite an impact. Lasker must have had this in mind when playing 16...♖ac8. White will have to capture the rook, as otherwise the decisive ...♖xa2 will follow. It's just a question of when to take the rook.

19 **exf7+?**

A mistake in a difficult position. It would have been more sensible to keep the e-file closed.

1) However, the apparently disruptive 19 e7? actually fails to do the trick after 19...♖e8 20 bxa3 ♕b6+ 21 ♔c2 (21 ♔a1 ♗xd4+ 22 ♖xd4 ♕xd4+ 23 ♔b1 ♖xe7 wins for Black, as White has no useful square to develop his bishop, e.g. 24 ♗b5 ♕e4+ 25 ♔a1 a6!) 21...♖c8+! 22 ♔d2 ♗xd4 and there is no defence:

1a) 23 ♗d3 ♕b2+ 24 ♗c2 ♕xc2+ 25 ♔e1 ♕f2#.

1b) 23 ♔e2 ♕e6+ 24 ♔f3 ♕e3+ 25 ♔g4 g6! 26 ♕xd5 h5+ 27 ♔h4 ♗f6+ 28 ♕g5 ♗xg5#.

Instead of 19 exf7+ or 19 e7, White can also make the most obvious move, that is grabbing the rook:

2) After 19 bxa3 ♕b6+ 20 ♔c2 Black has two ways forward:

2a) 20...♕c6+ 21 ♔b2 ♕b6+ is a draw by perpetual check. Any attempt by White to escape this is met by the most severe punishment, e.g. 21 ♔d3 ♗g5! 22 ♔e2 ♕xe6+ 23 ♔f3 ♕e3+ 24 ♔g4 f5#.

2b) 20...♖c8+ is a winning attempt, but it also carries some risk, e.g. 21 ♔d2 ♕xd4+ (21...♗xd4 22 ♕xf7+ ♔h8 23 ♔e2 and there is no obvious way to continue the attack) 22 ♔e1 (22 ♗d3 allows 22...♖c2+! 23 ♔xc2 ♕b2#) and now:

2b1) 22...♕c3+ 23 ♖d2 fxe6 and Black has definite compensation for the rook, but White is certainly still in the game.

2b2) 22...♕e3+ 23 ♗e2 (23 ♕e2? ♗c3+ 24 ♖d2 ♗xd2+ 25 ♔d1 ♖c1#) 23...♗c3+ 24 ♔f1 fxe6 25 ♗f3 also leads to immense complications.

| 19 | ... | ♖xf7 |
| 20 | bxa3 | ♕b6+ |

An excellent defensive resource. The white bishop can be captured with check, but at least the black queen is lured off the attack of the d-pawn. In any case king moves lead to a swift defeat:

1) 21 ♔a1 ♗xd4+ 22 ♖xd4 ♕xd4+ 23 ♔b1 ♕e4+ 24 ♔a1 (Black wins quickly after 24 ♔c1 ♖c7+ or 24 ♔b2 ♖f2+) 24...♕e1+ 25 ♔b2 ♖f2+ 26 ♔b3 ♕b1+ 27 ♔a4 (27 ♔c3 ♕b2+ 28 ♔d3 ♕d2# is mate) 27...♖f4+ 28 ♔a5 ♕b6#.

2) 21 ♔c2 ♖c7+ 22 ♔d2 ♕xd4+ 23 ♗d3 (23 ♔e2 also leads to mate after 23...♖e7+ 24 ♔f3 ♕e3+ 25 ♔g4 ♖e4+ 26 ♔f5 ♖f4+ 27 ♔g6 ♕e8#) 23...♖c2+! 24 ♔xc2 ♕b2#.

| 21 | ... | ♕xb5+ |
| 22 | ♔a1 | ♖c7? |

There is no rest for White. Now the threat is 23...♖c1+! 24 ♖xc1 ♗xd4+ and mate follows. Even so, it appears that 22...♕c4! would have given White no chance to erect a defensive wall. The only way to protect the vital d4-pawn would be with 23 ♕g4, but then 23...♖e7, intending to continue ...♖e4, leaves White with no defence.

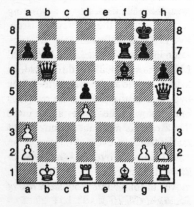

21 ♗b5

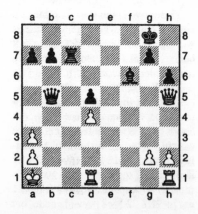

23 罝d2 罝c4

Another vital moment has arisen. Black threatens both 24...奧xd4+ and 24...罝xd4, with the added idea of doubling the major pieces on the c-file. White has to decide between active and passive defence, and it is by no means an easy choice.

24 罝hd1

Or:

1) 24 罝b1 豐c6 25 豐d1 loses to 25...罝xd4 26 罝xd4 豐c3+ 27 罝b2 奧xd4, when White is trapped in a lethal pin.

2) 24 豐g4 also doesn't work after 24...豐c6, e.g. 25 ⭐b2 豐b6+ 26 ⭐a1 罝xd4 27 豐c8+ ⭐f7 28 豐d7+ ⭐g6 29 豐e8+ ⭐h7 or 25 ⭐b1 奧g5 26 罝dd1 豐b6+ 27 ⭐a1 奧e3!.

3) However, the active 24 罝e1! looks like a good move. Suddenly White has threats of his own, including 罝e8+ and the simplifying 豐e8+. Indeed, there seems to be no decisive continuation for Black, e.g.:

3a) 24...奧xd4+? allows a decisive counterattack after 25 罝xd4! 罝xd4 26 罝e8+ ⭐h7 27 豐f5+ g6 28 豐f7#.

3b) 24...罝xd4 is no better. White wins with 25 罝e8+ ⭐h7 26 豐f5+ g6 27 豐xf6, threatening mate on h8.

3c) Black could also try the quiet 24...⭐f8, preventing 豐e8 and 罝e8 ideas, but this is too slow to have any real chance of working. It should be remembered, after all, that Black is the exchange down. White can simply play 25 罝f2, pinning the bishop and creating the opportunity of a counter-sacrifice of the exchange on f6. For example 25...罝xd4? 26 罝xf6+! gxf6 27 豐xh6+ ⭐f7 28 豐h7+ ⭐f8 29 豐e7+ ⭐g8 30 豐d8+ ⭐g7 31 罝e7+ and now it's Black's king on the run.

3d) 24...豐c6 is probably the best choice. This does allow White to exchange queens with 25 豐e8+, but after 25...⭐h7! (forcing White to exchange improves Black's pawn structure) 26 豐xc6 bxc6 27 ⭐b1 奧xd4 28 罝c2 奧c3 Black still has good compensation for the exchange.

24 ... 罝c3?

This prepares an imaginative sacrifice on a3. Nevertheless, it was objectively better to carry out the intended doubling on the c-file. After 24...豐c6! Black threatens the deadly 25...罝c1+ and forces White to relinquish his material advantage with interest:

1) 25 ⭐b2 豐b6+ 26 ⭐a1 罝xd4 27 罝xd4 奧xd4+ 28 罝xd4 豐xd4+ 29 ⭐b1 豐g1+ and the g2-pawn drops with check.

2) 25 ⭐b1 is a better try, planning to meet 25...豐b6+? with 26 罝b2. However, Black has the very strong reply 25...奧g5!. Now, moving the d2-rook allows 26...罝c1+, so White must give up the exchange. However, after 26 豐e2 奧xd2 27 豐xd2 豐d6! Black immediately wins another pawn. Together with White's shaky king position, this promises Black a winning advantage.

25 豐f5?

Finally White commits a fatal error. 25 罝e1! is a particularly difficult move to see, as the rook had deliberately bypassed this option on the previous move. Nevertheless, the fact that the black rook is no longer attacking d4 makes 罝e1 an even stronger option now than on move 24. This type of move is described as a "hesitation move" in John Nunn's book *Secrets of Practical Chess*.

Let's examine the variations:

1) 25...♕c4 26 ♔b2! ♖xa3 (or
26...♗xd4 27 ♖e8+ ♔h7 28 ♕f5+ g6
29 ♕f7+ ♗g7 30 ♕g8#) 27 ♖e8+ ♔h7
28 ♕f5+ g6 29 ♖e7+!! ♗xe7 30 ♕f7+
♔h8 31 ♕e8+ ♔g7 32 ♕xe7+ ♔g8 33
♕xa3 and White wins.

2) 25...♖xa3 26 ♖e8+ ♔h7 27
♕f5+ g6 28 ♕e6! h5 29 ♖e7+! ♗xe7
30 ♕xe7+ ♔h6 31 ♕xa3 and again
White prevails.

3) Just as on the previous move,
25...♕c6 is Black's best try. After 26
♕e8+ ♔h7 27 ♕xc6 bxc6 28 ♔b1
♖xa3 29 ♖e6 ♖c3 30 ♖c2 ♖d3 31
♖cxc6 ♖d2 32 ♖c2 ♖d1+ 33 ♔b2
♗xd4+ 34 ♔b3 White has an edge, although a draw is the most likely outcome.

    25 ...   **♕c4**
    26 ♔b2

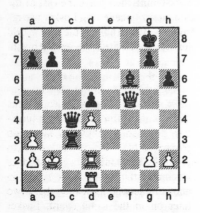

White seems to have everything
covered, but Black's next move, the
third rook offer in the game, shatters
this illusion.

    26 ...   **♖xa3!!**
    27 ♕e6+   **♔h7!**

Black also wins after 27...♔h8 28
♕e8+ ♔h7 29 ♔xa3 ♕c3+ 30 ♔a4
a6!, but 27...♔h7 is certainly cleaner.

    28 ♔xa3

Declining the sacrifice doesn't help,
for example 28 ♔b1 ♗xd4 29 ♖xd4
♕xa2+ 30 ♔c1 ♖c3#, or 28 ♔a1
♗xd4+ 29 ♔b1 ♕b4+ 30 ♔c1 ♖c3+
31 ♖c2 ♖xc2+ 32 ♔xc2 ♕c3+ 33 ♔b1
♕b2#.

    28 ...   **♕c3+**

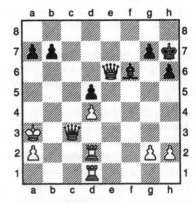

              0-1

After 29 ♔a4 b5+! 30 ♔xb5 ♕c4+
31 ♔a5 ♗d8+ 32 ♕b6 Black has the
pleasant choice between 32...axb6#
and 32...♗xb6#.

Lessons from this game:

1) Study your own games! Despite
being on the wrong end of a brilliancy
here, Pillsbury didn't just erase the
game from his memory. He looked
long and hard for an improvement and
was ready to unleash 7 ♗xf6! next
time around.

2) Often attack is the best form of
defence. Instead of passive resistance,
the more active 24 ♖e1 or 25 ♖e1
would have saved White.

3) Sacrificing two rooks, followed
by driving the king up the board to
checkmate, is a pleasing way to win!

Wilhelm Steinitz – Emanuel Lasker

St Petersburg 1895/6
Queen's Gambit Declined

The Players

We have already met both Steinitz and Lasker in earlier games (see Game 5 for more information on Steinitz and Game 7 for more about Lasker). By the time of this particular meeting between the two giants of the chess world, Steinitz had already lost the title of World Champion to Lasker, who was now proving his worth by a convincing demonstration at this tournament, which he won by a big margin ahead of Steinitz, Pillsbury and Chigorin. In his six games against Steinitz in the St Petersburg event, Lasker scored three wins, two draws and one loss, which is shown here.

The Game

Steinitz introduces a new concept in a well-worn opening, which presents Lasker with some early difficulties. Lasker reacts badly to the new circumstances and leaves the opening with clear disadvantage. Steinitz then plays the rest of the game in an accurate and imaginative fashion, never once letting Lasker use his renowned fighting abilities. Faced with problem after problem, the new World Champion finally breaks and Steinitz's relentless attack reaps the reward his ingenious play deserves.

1	d4	d5
2	c4	e6
3	♘c3	♘f6
4	♗f4	

4 ...   ♗e7

These days 4 ♗f4 is very uncommon, since it has been shown that the active 4...c5 offers Black a problem-free position. If White is intent on playing ♗f4 lines, he tends first to play 4 ♘f3 and only after 4...♗e7 does he commit the bishop to f4. In fact, in another encounter between these two later on in the same event, Lasker showed that he had learned from this encounter. The third Steinitz – Lasker game went 4...c5 5 e3 ♘c6 6 ♘f3 a6 7 dxc5 ♗xc5 8 cxd5 ♘xd5 9 ♘xd5 exd5 10 ♗d3 ♗b4+ 11 ♔e2 with equality.

5 e3   0-0
6 c5!?

This move, which introduces an extremely adventurous scheme by

White, was quite a surprise at the time. A bind is established on the queenside and Black has to play actively or else run the risk of being squashed and suffocated to death.

6 ...   ♘e4?

Predictably, Lasker seeks activity, but this proves to be the wrong way to find counterplay. In particular Black's central pawn-structure becomes compromised, and the e4-pawn becomes a liability. What are Black's other options in this position? *Handbuch* gives 6...b6 7 b4 a5 8 a3 as better for White, but more recent games have shown this to be the way forward. One very important theoretical battle was Lerner – Geller, USSR Championship, Riga 1985, which continued 8...axb4 9 axb4 ♖xa1 10 ♕xa1 ♘c6 11 ♕a4 bxc5!! 12 ♕xc6 cxd4 with a dangerous initiative for the sacrificed piece.

7   ♘xe4   dxe4
8   ♕c2   f5
9   ♗c4   ♘c6

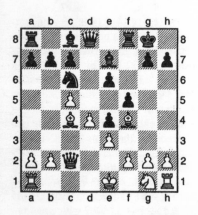

10   a3

This quiet move is a useful prophylactic device, preventing ...♘c6-b4-d5 ideas from Black, and also making a

retreat-square on a2 available for the light-squared bishop, which is destined to do good work on the enticing a2–g8 diagonal.

10   ...   ♗f6

Black can actually trap the f4-bishop here with 10...g5 11 ♗g3 f4, but following 12 ♕xe4 fxg3 13 hxg3 ♖f7 14 d5! White has more than enough compensation for the piece.

11   0-0-0

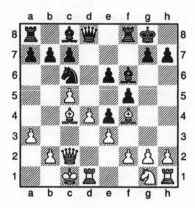

An excellent decision. Black's counterplay revolves around the advance ...e5. Putting the rook on d1 further dissuades Black from this lunge. With 11 0-0-0 Steinitz changes direction, preparing the move f3, which will pose Black some problems in the centre. White can also hope to initiate a kingside attack.

11   ...   ♔h8

This move breaks the pin of the e6-pawn, making it easier for Black to realize his goal of ...e5. In fact, Black already has to be careful in this position. 11...b6? runs into 12 d5!, which leads to a complete disaster. 11...♘e7, intending ...♘d5, has been suggested as an alternative defence. Then White can still keep the initiative in the centre and on the kingside with 12 g4!, e.g. 12...g5 13 ♗g3 ♔h8 14 h4! and the attack is gathering momentum by the move.

12 f3   ♕e7!

Not surprisingly Lasker begins to fight hard in what can only be described as a miserable position. The obliging 12...exf3 13 ♘xf3 leaves Black with absolutely no prospects, while White could slowly prepare to open lines on the kingside with the eventual g2-g4.

13 ♗g3!

Very clever play from White. What could be more natural than grabbing a pawn with 13 fxe4? Well, this was exactly what the World Champion was hoping for. Following 13...e5! 14 dxe5 ♘xe5 Black suddenly takes over the initiative. Note that 15 exf5 ♗xf5! makes matters worse for White, as after 16 ♕xf5 ♘xc4 Black's swift counterattack has reached menacing proportions.

13 ...   f4!?

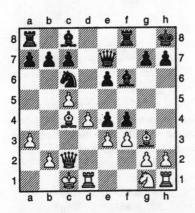

Once more a typical move from Lasker, who won many games from suspicious positions just by complicating matters. Unfortunately on this particular day he met Steinitz in an irrepressible mood.

14 ♕xe4!!

This brilliant piece sacrifice kills Black's attempt at snatching the initiative. Lasker was once more hoping that White would grab the offered pawn. After 14 ♗xf4 e5 15 dxe5 ♘xe5 both 16 ♗xe5 ♗xe5 17 f4 ♗f6 18 ♗d5 ♗f5 19 ♗xb7 ♖ab8 and 16 ♕xe4 ♗f5! 17 ♕xf5 ♘xc4 leave Black firmly on the offensive. After 14 ♕xe4 White gains only two pawns for the piece. On the other hand, Black is reduced to a grim defensive job, which would not have suited Lasker at all.

14 ...   fxg3
15 hxg3   g6

By relinquishing a third pawn Lasker hopes to use the semi-open g-file for defence. If instead 15...g5 White tightens his grip over the e5-square with 16 f4!, after which it is extremely difficult to see what Black can do to prevent White's steamroller of an attack. 16...gxf4 17 gxf4 ♗d7 18 g4 looks totally grim, so Black should try to block the game up with 16...g4. Nevertheless, following 17 ♘e2 the analysis is overwhelmingly in White's favour, e.g.:

1) 17...♖f7 18 ♕c2 b6 19 e4 ♗g7 20 e5 h6 21 ♕g6 ♕e8 (or 21...bxc5 22 d5 ♘d8 23 dxe6 ♘xe6 24 f5 ♕g5+ 25 ♕xg5 ♘xg5 26 f6 ♗f8 27 ♘f4 ♔g8 28 e6!) 22 ♗d3 is a variation given by none other than Garry Kasparov, who annotated the game for *ChessBase Magazine*. Following 22...♕g8 White wins neatly with 23 ♖xh6+ ♗xh6 24 ♕xh6+ ♖h7 25 ♗xh7 ♕xh7 26 ♕f8+ ♕g8 27 ♖h1#.

2) 17...♗d7 18 ♖h6! ♖f7 19 ♖dh1
♖g8 20 ♕d3 and the threat of e5 is decisive, e.g. 20...♘a5 21 ♗a2 ♖gg7 22
e4 ♕e8 23 b4! ♗b5 24 ♕c2 ♗a4 25
♕b2 ♘c6 26 e5 ♗d8 27 b5 ♘b8 28
♘c3, winning the bishop on a4.

16 ♕xg6   ♗d7

Black can snatch one of the three
pawns back with 16...♖g8 17 ♕e4
♖xg3, but this only allows White to
bring the knight into the attack with
tempo after 18 ♘e2 ♖g7 19 ♘f4. It is
clear that Black cannot afford such
greed.

17 f4

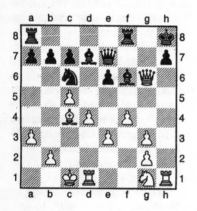

17 ...   ♖f7?

Lasker finally cracks under the
strain of having to defend a miserable
position for a long time. 17...♖g8! offers more hope, although it has to be
said that White retains a significant
initiative after 18 ♕e4, e.g. 18...♖xg3
19 ♘e2 ♖g7 20 ♖h6 followed by
♖dh1. It is also worth mentioning that
after 17...♖g8 White can play 18
♖xh7+, which leads to a draw by perpetual check following 18...♔xh7 19
♕xf6+ ♕g7 20 ♕h4+. Black can avoid
the draw with 19...♖g7, although this

is risky in view of White's attack after
20 ♘f3.

After 17...♖f7? the game is over as
a contest. Black's defences become
uncoordinated and White's attack is
allowed to power through.

18 g4   ♖g7

After 18...♖g8 White simply replies 19 ♕h5!, followed by g5.

After the text-move, 19 ♕h5 allows
Black to defend with ...♗e8-g6, but
White has an alternative square.

19 ♕h6!   ♖xg4
20 ♗d3   ♖g7

Or 20...♖h4 21 ♖xh4 ♗xh4 22 ♘f3
♗f2 23 ♖h1 ♗xe3+ 24 ♔b1 and h7
collapses.

21 ♘f3   ♕f7

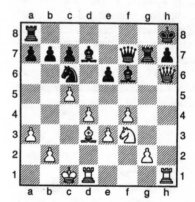

22 g4!

The rest of the game must have been
very pleasurable for Steinitz. White's
attack virtually plays itself. A collapse
on h7 is simply unavoidable.

22	**...**	**♖ag8**
23	**g5**	**♗d8**
24	**♖h2!**	**♖g6**
25	**♕h5!**	**♖6g7**
26	**♖dh1!**	**♕xh5**
27	**♖xh5**	**♖f8**

28 ♖xh7+   ♖xh7

The loss of the d7-bishop cannot be avoided by 28...♔g8, as White replies 29 ♖xg7+ ♔xg7 30 ♖h7+ and 31 ♖xd7. Black could already resign.

29 ♖xh7+   ♔g8
30 ♖xd7   ♖f7
31 ♗c4!

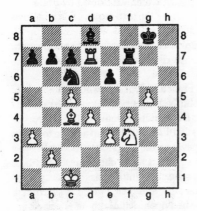

1-0

After 31...♖xd7 32 ♗xe6+ ♖f7 33 g6 White will be four pawns up.

Lessons from this game:

1) Always be careful to study carefully the consequences before allowing your pawn-structure to change. Lasker hoped that he would gain enough activity to counterbalance his compromised structure after 6...♘e4, but was proved wrong by Steinitz's imaginative play.

2) If your opponent shocks you in the opening (as in this case with 6 c5), don't panic into moving quickly. Take a deep breath and try to weigh up the novel idea in objective fashion. In most cases you'll find that the new move is not any better than its predecessors and that its main strength is indeed its surprise value.

3) It is often worth giving up material to kill off any chances of counterplay. This is shown with great effect by Steinitz's 13 ♗g3! and 14 ♕xe4!. With absolutely no attacking chances to relieve the purely defensive task at hand, even great fighters such as Lasker are going to make mistakes.

Game 9
Harry Nelson Pillsbury – Emanuel Lasker
Nuremberg 1896
French Defence

The Players

This game features the same players as Game 7, which was won by Lasker.

The Game

Pillsbury creates one of the classic examples of the sacrificial breakthrough, whereby a seemingly impregnable position is ripped apart by a series of sacrifices.

Starting from a slightly unusual line of the French Defence, in which he has loosened his queenside in return for greater mobility, Pillsbury conceives a grandiose plan to attack the black king, which Lasker has decided to leave in the centre, defended by a strong barricade of pawns. Firstly Pillsbury gives up a pawn to divert a black piece to the queenside, and then a pawn on the kingside to loosen Black's position and bring a knight to an active square. Lasker then misses his best chance to retain a viable position and plunge the game into a mass of murky complications. Pillsbury pounces. First an exchange, and then a piece is sacrificed, and all the lines to the black king are smashed open. Although he is a rook up, Lasker has no defence. In desperation, he gives up his queen, but the resulting endgame is hopeless.

1	**e4**	**e6**
2	**d4**	**d5**
3	**♘c3**	**♘f6**
4	**e5**	**♘fd7**
5	**f4**	**c5**
6	**dxc5**	

An unusual idea, but far from bad. Instead White normally develops so as to support the d4-pawn.

6	**...**	**♘c6**
7	**a3**	**♘xc5**

7...♗xc5 would be more standard, but less ambitious.

8 b4!?

This move loosens White's queenside but severely reduces the activity of Black's knights – probably a good trade-off for White.

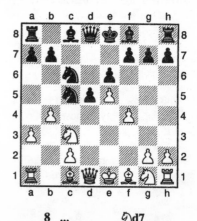

8	**...**	**♘d7**

8...d4?! looks like it should be better, but there is a tactical problem pointed out by John Nunn: 9 ♘ce2 d3

(9...♘e4 10 ♘f3) 10 ♘g3 ♕d4 11 c3!
♕xc3+ 12 ♗d2 wins a piece for inadequate compensation, e.g. 12...♕c4 13
♖c1 ♕d5 14 bxc5 ♗xc5.

9	♗d3	a5
10	b5	♘cb8
11	♘f3	♘c5
12	♗e3	♘bd7
13	0-0	

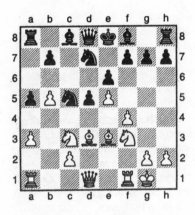

13 ...   g6

Not with the idea of fianchettoing
the bishop, but to delay White's intended f4-f5 advance. Lasker has decided that his king will be safest in the
centre, and aims to make it as difficult
as possible for White to break through
to it. Note that if White has to support
f5 with g4, his own king will also become considerably exposed after a
later f5 gxf5, gxf5.

14 ♘e2

White has the greater freedom of
movement, but must play energetically
to justify the weakening of his queenside.

14	...	♗e7
15	♕e1	♘b6
16	♘fd4	♗d7
17	♕f2	

This cunning move lends support to
possible f-file play and threatens to
win a pawn by 18 ♘xe6.

17 ...   ♘ba4

17...♕c7 followed by ...♘ca4 and
...♘c4 is a more secure way for Black
to play on the queenside.

18 ♖ab1

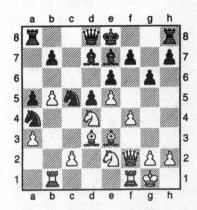

Both preventing ...♘b2 and supporting the b-pawn.

18 ...   h5

Lasker further discourages White's
plan of g4 and f5, by making the preparatory advance that much harder.
However, it eats another tempo, and
Pillsbury manages to engineer a tactical f5 breakthrough without any support from the g-pawn.

18...♘xd3 19 cxd3 ♗xa3? is not a
good pawn-grab in view of 20 ♖a1
♕e7 21 ♘c2, winning a piece.

18...0-0!? was still possible (e.g. 19
g4 f5), though a switch of plans.

19 b6!?

White makes inroads into the
queenside. If Black reacts passively,
White will be able to make good use of
the b5-square, but if Black makes the
critical reply and wins the a3-pawn,

several pieces will be diverted from the defence of the king. Undoubtedly Pillsbury's great combination was already coming together in his mind at this stage – one would not give Lasker an extra passed a-pawn on a whim!

19   ...   ♘xd3

19...♘xb6? is wholly bad due to the familiar theme 20 ♘xe6!.

20   cxd3   ♗xa3

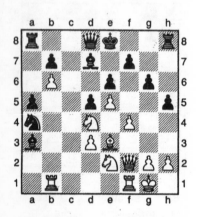

21   f5!

Disrupting Black's kingside structure and freeing f4 for the knight. "Pillsbury possessed an unparalleled technique when it came to unleashing the explosive powers of his pieces." – Euwe.

21   ...   gxf5

21...exf5? 22 ♘f4 gives White a massive attack without the need for sacrifices.

22   ♘f4

One of White's ideas is now to bring the queen to g7 via g3, but Black's next move is an, albeit understandable, over-reaction to this.

22   ...   h4?

The critical position for the combination, and therefore for the evaluation of the two sides' strategies, arises after 22...♗b4! 23 ♕g3 (23 ♕f3?! h4 24 ♘xf5? exf5 25 ♘xd5 ♗c6 exploits the queen's position on f3 to force exchanges) 23...♔f8 24 ♘xd5! (24 ♘xf5 exf5 25 ♘xd5 is unconvincing) and now if Black wishes to take the knight on d5 he must first nudge the white queen to a worse square:

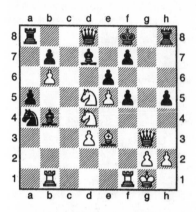

1) 24...exd5! 25 ♘xf5 (25 e6 is tempting, but messy and unnecessary) 25...♗xf5 (the knight generates too many threats from f5 to be tolerated) 26 ♖xf5 ♕e7 (26...♕d7 27 ♖bf1 ♔e8 28 ♕g7 ♖f8 29 e6 ♕xe6 30 ♖e5) 27 ♖bf1 ♔e8 (27...♕e6 28 ♖xf7+ comes to the same thing; 27...♖h7 28 ♕g6) 28 ♖xf7 ♕xf7 29 ♖xf7 ♔xf7 30 ♕f3+ ♔e6 (no better are 30...♔g7 31 ♕f6+ ♔g8 32 e6 ♖h7 33 ♗d4, 30...♔g8 31 ♕xd5+ ♔f8 32 e6 ♖h7 33 ♗d4 and 30...♔e7 31 ♕f6+) 31 ♕f6+ ♔d7 32 ♕f7+ ♔c6 33 ♕e6+ ♔b5 34 ♕xd5+ with two possible defences:

1a) 34...♘c5 35 ♗xc5 ♗xc5+ 36 d4 ♖hc8 37 dxc5 ♖xc5 38 ♕xb7 ♖a6 (38...♖d8 39 e6!, e.g. 39...♖d2 40 ♕d7+! ♖xd7 41 exd7 ♖d5 42 b7) 39 e6 ♖xb6 40 ♕d7+ and 41 e7 wins.

1b) 34...♗c5 35 ♗xc5 ♘xb6 (or 35...♘xc5 36 d4, etc.) 36 ♕d6 should win for White.

2) 24...h4! 25 ♕f4 and here:

2a) 25...♘c3 is the solid approach. 26 ♘xc3 (sacrificial ideas look unconvincing here, e.g. 26 ♘c7 ♘xb1 27 ♖xb1 or 26 ♘f6 ♘xb1) 26...♖xc3 27 ♖fc1 (not 27 ♘xf5? exf5 28 ♗c5+ ♔e8) and White enjoys some queen-side pressure, but the game is not at all clear.

2b) 25...exd5 adopts a "show-me" attitude. 26 ♖xb4! axb4 27 ♘xf5 with another choice for Black:

2b1) 27...♗xf5? 28 ♕xf5 ♕e7 (28...♕e8 is answered by 29 ♕g6 followed by e6) 29 ♗g5 ♕e8 30 e6 ♘c5 (30...♘c3 31 ♕g6 ♘e2+ 32 ♔h1 ♘g3+ 33 hxg3 hxg3+ 34 ♔g1 would work if the black queen could reach a suitable square on the a7–g1 diagonal, but unfortunately it is on the wrong square) 31 e7+! (31 ♕f6 ♖h7; 31 exf7? ♕e6) 31...♔g8 32 ♗f6 ♖h6 and now 33 ♕g5+! ♖g6 34 ♕xh4 ♖xf6 35 ♕xf6 is the simplest way for White to win.

2b2) 27...♖h7 28 ♕xb4+ and paradoxically, the black king is safest in the centre:

2b21) 28...♔g8? 29 ♕g4+ ♔h8 (29...♔f8? 30 ♗h6+ mates) 30 e6! decisively opens the long diagonal to h8: 30...♗xe6 31 ♗d4+ f6 32 ♕g6.

2b22) 28...♕e8 29 ♘d6+ ♔f8 30 ♘f5+ gives White a draw – it seems risky to try for more (e.g. 30 ♘xf7+ ♕e7).

To summarize this analysis: Black should have played 22...♗b4, when after 23 ♕g3 ♔f8 24 ♘xd5! h4! 25 ♕f4, he should choose between 25...♘c3, with a complex battle in prospect, and 25...exd5 26 ♖xb4! axb4 27 ♘xf5

♖h7, which appears to be a forced draw.

23 ♖a1

23 ♘xf5 exf5 24 ♘xd5 is a less convincing sacrificial attempt, since Black has more pieces ready to defend his king.

23 ... ♗e7

23...♕e7 loses to 24 ♘xf5!.

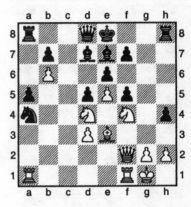

24 ♖xa4! ♗xa4

At the cost of "just" an exchange, White has removed the irritating black knight and drawn a defensive bishop off-side.

25 ♘dxe6! fxe6

26 ♘xe6

"The great virtuoso of the break-through presents his *chef d'oeuvre*. Black, a clear rook ahead, must now lose, play as he will. To have foreseen all this is a brilliant piece of work by Pillsbury. There are few combinations on record to be compared to it." – Euwe. Of course, it is not clear to what extent Pillsbury played by intuition, and how far he had seen in the lines following 22...♗b4, but there is no doubting Euwe's conclusion.

26 ... ♗d7

Lasker is convinced that White's play is sound and, true to his nature, seeks the best practical chances of saving the game. However, this is practically equivalent to resignation, since the "practical chances" are little more than a way to prolong the agony. The critical continuation was 26...♕c8 27 ♕xf5! (threatening, amongst other things, 28 ♗g5!) 27...♕c6 (27...♖g8 28 ♕f7+ ♔d7 29 ♘c5+ ♔c6 30 ♕xe7 and the black pieces are too poorly placed to put up a decent defence to the mating threats) 28 ♗g5! ♕xb6+ 29 d4 ♕b4 (29...♔d7 30 ♘c5++ ♔c7 31 ♗xe7 with a winning attack) 30 ♕f7+ ♔d7 31 ♗xe7 ♕xe7 32 ♘c5+ ♔d8 33 ♘xb7+ ♔d7 34 e6+, winning the black queen.

27	♘xd8	♖xd8
28	♗c5	

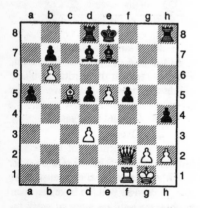

White is clearly winning; his queen is too powerful and Black's army too poorly coordinated. The rest of the game is a nice example on the theme "using a queen actively to harass loose pieces".

28	...	♖c8
29	♗xe7	♔xe7

30	♕e3	♖c6
31	♕g5+	♔f7
32	♖c1	♖xc1+
33	♕xc1	♖c8
34	♕e1	h3

34...a4 35 ♕xh4 a3 36 ♕h7+ ♔e8 (36...♔e6 37 ♕g7!) 37 ♕g6+ ♔f8 38 ♕d6+ ♔e8 39 ♕xa3 eliminates the passed a-pawn and with it Black's last hope.

35	gxh3	♖g8+
36	♔f2	a4
37	♕b4	♖g6
38	♔f3	a3
39	♕xa3	♖xb6
40	♕c5	♖e6
41	♕c7	♔e7
42	♔f4	b6
43	h4	♖c6
44	♕b8	♗e8
45	♔xf5	♖h6
46	♕c7+	♔f8
47	♕d8	b5
48	e6	♖h7
49	♔e5	b4
50	♕d6+	1-0

Lessons from this game:

1) Great ingenuity is needed to break through a defensive wall – it may be necessary to loosen the opponent's position by play on both wings, and to sacrifice material to divert crucial defensive pieces.

2) When facing a massive sacrificial attack, keep calm and try to find ways to interfere with the smooth operation of the attacking pieces – this may mean striking at the reinforcements, rather than the advanced units.

3) A queen on an open board can overpower a large number of uncoordinated pieces, especially if one of them is a king.

Game 10
Emanuel Lasker – William Napier
Cambridge Springs 1904
Sicilian Defence, Dragon Variation

The Players

Emanuel Lasker (1868–1941) was one of the all-time greats and held the World Championship for a record 27 years (see Game 7 for more information).

William Napier (1881–1952) was born in England, but his family emigrated to the United States when he was five years old. His international chess career was very short but he was a successful competitor during the period 1900–5, one of his achievements being to win the British Championship in 1904. Had he continued playing chess, he might have risen to the top, but he retired from international chess, became a US citizen in 1908 and embarked on a successful business career. Napier had an attractive combinative style and although he left relatively few games, many of them are worth studying.

The Game

Lasker was famous for his fighting spirit and ability to induce mistakes by his opponents; both qualities are evident in this game. Lasker plays over-aggressively in the opening, and should have been punished for neglecting his development. Instead of refuting Lasker's opening positionally, Napier goes in for tactics which rapidly become a whirlwind of complications spreading over the whole board. Both players handle the tactics brilliantly and at the critical moment Lasker, not content with a slight endgame advantage, goes for broke. For a fleeting instant Napier has the chance to score the success of his career by beating the World Champion, but instead he adopts a tempting but unsound continuation. Lasker springs his trap and liquidates to a winning ending.

1	e4	c5
2	♘c3	♘c6
3	♘f3	g6
4	d4	cxd4
5	♘xd4	♗g7
6	♗e3	d6
7	h3	♘f6
8	g4	

Launching an attack before completing your development is always a risky business, but Lasker's idea is to drive away the black knight from f6 by g4-g5. This will make it much harder for Black to develop counterplay by ...d5, his traditional response when confronted by a kingside attack in the Dragon. Although this push of the g-pawn is a valid idea in certain Sicilian variations, here the fact that White has had to spend a further tempo on the preparatory h3 casts doubt on the idea.

The normal continuation today is 8 ♗c4.

8	...	0-0

The simplest reply; the threat of g5 is not so strong that Black need take any special measures against it.

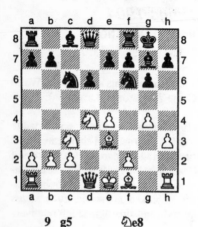

9 g5   ♘e8

Black could even have continued 9...♘h5, for example 10 ♘xc6 (10 ♗e2 ♘f4) 10...bxc6 11 ♗e2 ♖b8 and his counterplay against b2 and c3 is more important than the threat to the knight on h5.

10 h4?!

This is going too far. White continues with his plan of attacking on the kingside, but every pawn move is a non-developing move, and he simply cannot afford to leave his king in the centre for so long. 10 ♕d2 followed by 11 0-0-0 would have been safer and better.

10 ...   ♘c7

Now Black is threatening to open the position up by 11...d5, when White's lack of development will become serious.

11 f4

In order to meet 11...d5 by 12 e5, keeping the position closed, but it is yet another pawn move.

11 ...   e5!

Napier hits on the correct answer to White's plan. A central counterattack is usually the best response to a flank attack, and this applies particularly when the opposing king is still in the centre.

12 ♘de2

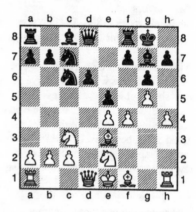

12 ...   d5?

This move is the trigger for the exciting complications which follow, but it is a mistake since these should ultimately give White the edge. The simple 12...♗g4 would have been very strong, for example 13 ♕d2 (13 ♖g1 ♕d7 14 ♕d2 exf4 and 15...♘e5 is also good for Black) 13...exf4 14 ♗xf4 ♘e5 15 0-0-0 ♘e6 16 ♗g3 ♘c4 17 ♕d3 ♖c8 and Black has a very strong attack (18...♘xb2 is the immediate threat) for which White has not the slightest compensation.

13 exd5

Forced, as 13 ♘xd5 exf4 14 ♗xf4 (14 ♘xc7 ♕xc7 15 ♗xf4 ♕b6 and 14 ♗c5 ♖e8 are also very good for Black) 14...♘xd5 15 exd5 ♘d4 16 ♘xd4 ♕xd5 17 ♖h2 ♗xd4 gives Black a massive attack.

13 ...   ♘d4

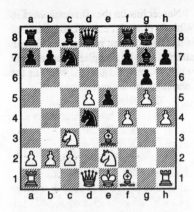

14 ⌦xd4

White must retain his dark-squared bishop since 14 ♗xd4 exd4 15 ⌦xd4 is virtually winning for Black after 15...⌦xd5 16 ⌦de2 (or 16 ⌦xd5 ♕xd5 17 ⌦f3 ♕c6 18 ♗e2 ♗xb2 19 ♖b1 ♗c3+) 16...⌦e3 17 ♕xd8 ♖xd8 18 ♖c1 ♗f5.

14 ...   ⌦xd5!

The point of Black's play.

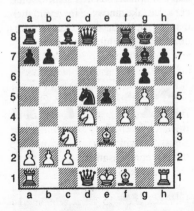

15 ⌦f5!

Lasker responds in style. After 15 ⌦xd5 exd4 (15...♕xd5 loses a piece after 16 ♕f3) 16 ♗g2 dxe3 17 0-0 ♗e6 18 ♖e1 ♗xd5 (18...e2 19 ♖xe2

♗g4 20 ⌦e7+ and 21 ♕xd8 is unclear) 19 ♕xd5 ♕c7 White's weak pawns and exposed king give Black the advantage.

15 ...   ⌦xc3
16 ♕xd8

Enabling the knight to check on e7.

16 ...   ♖xd8
17 ⌦e7+

Better than 17 ⌦xg7 ⌦d5 18 0-0-0 (18 ♗d2?! exf4 19 0-0-0 ♗g4 20 ♗g2 ♗xd1 21 ♖xd1 ⌦e3 is very good for Black) 18...♗g4! (18...⌦xg7 19 c4 ♗e6 20 cxd5 ♖ac8+ 21 ♔b1 ♗xd5 22 ♖xd5 ♖xd5 23 ♗g2 ♖d3 24 ♖e1 favours White) 19 ♖xd5 ♖xd5 20 ♗g2 ♖d7 21 fxe5 ♗xg7 22 c3 when White faces an uphill struggle to draw.

17 ...   ♔h8

Not 17...♔f8 18 ♗c5 ⌦e4 19 ♗a3 ⌦d6 20 ⌦xc8 ♖axc8 21 0-0-0 ♔e7 22 ♗h3 ♖c6 23 ♖he1 and White wins.

18 h5!

Just when the complications are at a maximum, Lasker suddenly revives his kingside attack, even in the absence of queens. The alternative 18 ⌦xc8 (18 bxc3 exf4 19 ♗d4 ♖e8 wins a pawn) 18...exf4 (after 18...⌦d5? 19 0-0-0 ♖axc8 20 ♗xa7 ⌦xf4 the two bishops give White the edge) 19 ♗xf4 (19 ♗d2 ♖e8+ 20 ♔f2 ⌦e4+ and Black wins) 19...♖axc8 20 ♗d3 ♖e8+ 21 ♔f2 ⌦d5 22 ♗c1 ⌦b4 would have given Black a clear advantage.

18 ...   ♖e8!

White gains a clear advantage after 18...⌦d5 19 ⌦xd5 ♖xd5 20 h6 ♗f8 21 ♗c4 or 18...gxh5 19 f5 ⌦e4 20 f6 ♗f8 21 ♖xh5 ⌦g3 22 ♖h4 ⌦xf1 23 ♔xf1 ♗xe7 24 fxe7 ♖e8 25 ♗c5.

19 ♗c5

There is nothing better than simply defending the knight as 19 hxg6 ♖xe7

20 &c5 &d5 21 &xe7 &xe7 is slightly
better for Black, while 19 h6 &f8 20
bxc3 &xe7 21 &c5 exf4+ 22 &xe7
&xe7 23 &g1 &e6 gives Black excellent compensation for the exchange.

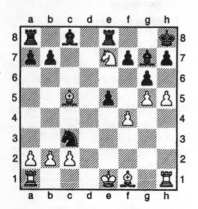

19 ...   gxh5

A key moment. Black decides to
prevent hxg6 directly, but 19...exf4
was also tempting, pinning the knight.
In fact the move played appears more
accurate, since 19...exf4 leads to a significant advantage for White:

1) 20 bxc3 &xe7+! (better than
20...&xc3+ 21 &f2 &xa1, when 22
&c4! leads to equality after 22...&c3
23 &xf7 &xe7 24 hxg6 &xf7 25 gxf7
&e6! 26 f8&+ &xf8 27 &xf8 &d4+
28 &e1 f3 or 22...b6 23 &xf7 &b7 24
&xa1 bxc5 25 &xe8 &xe8 26 &e1) 21
&xe7 &xc3+ 22 &f2 &xa1 23 &c4
(23 hxg6 fxg6 24 &d3 &d4+ 25 &f3
&g7 is good for Black) 23...&d4+ 24
&f3 &f5 with a slight plus for Black.

2) 20 hxg6! fxg6 21 &c4 b5
(21...&f5 22 bxc3 &xc3+ 23 &f2 &e4
24 &d5 &xd5 25 &xd5 and 21...&d7
22 bxc3 &xc3+ 23 &f2 &xa1 24
&xa1 &g7 25 &h1 are very good for
White) 22 &f7 &b7 23 &h2 &d5 24

&xe8 &xe8 25 0-0-0 &xe7 26 &d7
(26 &xe7 &xb2+ 27 &xb2 &xe7 offers Black more chances) 26...&c6 27
&xe7 &xe7 28 &xe7 f3 with an advantage for White, although winning this
endgame would be far from easy.

20 &c4?

White could have secured an edge
by 20 bxc3 &f8 (20...b6? 21 &d6
wins) 21 &b5 and now:

1) 21...&xe7 22 &xe8 &xc5 23
&xf7 exf4 24 &xh5! (24 &xh5 &f5
25 &f3 &e8+ 26 &f1 &e3 is unclear)
24...&g7 25 g6! (25 &d5 &g4 is safe
for Black) 25...hxg6 26 &xg6 and
White is clearly better.

2) 21...&xe7! 22 &xe7 &xe7 23
&xh5 &g4 (not 23...exf4? 24 &d3) 24
&h4 &f5. Although White has some
extra material, there would be few
winning chances in view of his scattered pawns.

Lasker evidently felt that this simple line would be insufficient to win
and so bravely went in for a more
complex alternative. However, there
was a serious flaw in his idea which
could have cost him the game.

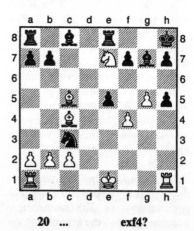

20 ...   exf4?

This costs Black the first half-point. 20...♗e6? is even worse, because 21 ♗xe6 fxe6 22 bxc3 ♗f8 23 ♗d6 exf4 (23...♗xe7 24 ♗xe5+ ♔g8 25 ♖xh5 should win for White) 24 ♗e5+ ♗g7 25 ♗f6 ♖xe7 26 ♗xe7 ♗xc3+ 27 ♔e2 ♗xa1 28 ♖xa1 leaves Black with insufficient compensation for the piece. 20...♗f8 is better; after 21 ♗xf7 ♗xe7 (21...♖xe7 22 ♗xe7 ♗xe7 23 bxc3 exf4 24 ♖xh5 ♔g7 25 ♗d5 favours White) 22 ♗xe8 ♗xc5 23 bxc3 ♗f5 24 ♗xh5 exf4 we have transposed to an unclear variation mentioned in line "1" of the previous note.

Best of all is 20...♘e4! 21 ♗xf7 ♗g4! (21...♖f8 also favours Black, but is less clear) 22 ♗xe8 ♖xe8 23 ♗a3 ♘g3 (23...exf4 24 0-0 ♘xg5 is also very good for Black) 24 ♖h2 exf4 and Black has overwhelming compensation for the exchange – he has one pawn already, White's king is trapped in the centre and his knight is hopelessly pinned. While this line may not appear very complex, the sheer number of alternatives at each move makes Black's task far from easy. Moreover, one of the themes of the game is Black's desire to maintain his knight at c3 in order to prevent White from castling queenside. It would not have been easy to overcome the psychological block about moving it away, even though the bishop on g4 proves an effective substitute. It is also worth mentioning that I have seen this game annotated many times without any mention of 20...♘e4!.

21 ♗xf7   ♘e4?

This tempting but unsound idea costs Black the second half-point. The correct line was 21...♖f8 (another move concerning which the annotators have been oddly silent) 22 ♗xh5 (22 ♘g6+ hxg6 23 ♗xf8 ♗xf8 24 bxc3 ♗f5 is good for Black) 22...♘e4 23 ♘g6+ ♔g8 (23...hxg6 24 ♗xg6+ ♔g8 25 ♗xf8 ♗xb2 26 ♗xe4 ♗xa1 27 ♗d6 gives White an advantage) and White can either force a draw by 24 ♘e7+ or head for an unclear position with 24 ♘xf8 ♗xb2 25 ♖d1 ♗c3+ 26 ♔f1 ♘xc5.

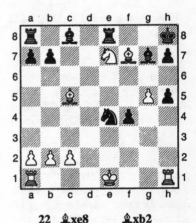

22	♗xe8	♗xb2
23	♖b1	♗c3+
24	♔f1	♗g4

24...♘xc5 loses after 25 ♗xh5 ♘e4 26 ♔g2 ♘g3 27 ♗g6 ♘xh1 28 ♖xh1.

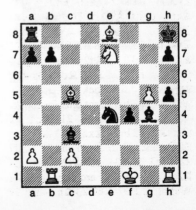

The point of Napier's idea: two of White's minor pieces are attacked and both White's rooks are vulnerable to a knight fork. Lasker finds a brilliant defence, returning the sacrificed material to liquidate favourably.

25 ♗xh5!   **♗xh5**

Or 25...♘g3+ 26 ♔g2 ♗xh5 27 ♖b3 ♘xh1 28 ♖xc3 ♔g7 29 ♔xh1 and White wins.

26 ♖xh5   **♘g3+**

White wins after 26...♘d2+ 27 ♔f2 ♘xb1 28 g6 ♔g7 29 ♖xh7+ ♔f6 30 g7.

27 ♔g2   **♘xh5**

28 ♖xb7   **a5**

Attempting to counterattack by 28...♖d8 29 ♖xa7 ♖d2+ 30 ♔f3 ♖xc2 rebounds after 31 ♘f5 ♔g8 32 ♘h6+ ♔h8 33 ♖a8+ ♔g7 34 ♖g8#.

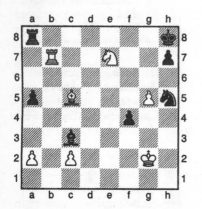

The wild complications have led, oddly, to material equality. However, all the white pieces are more active than their enemy counterparts – the contrast between the knights is particularly extreme. Lasker now exploits one vulnerable black piece after another to win a pawn, while maintaining his pressure.

29 ♖b3!   **♗g7**

Leaving g7 free for the knight is no better: 29...♗a1 30 ♖h3 ♘g7 31 ♖h6 ♘e8 32 ♔f3 ♔g7 33 ♔xf4 is winning for White.

30 ♖h3   **♘g3**

31 ♔f3   **♖a6?!**

31...♖e8 would have put up more resistance, but 32 ♗d6 ♘f1 33 ♔xf4 will win in the long run.

32 ♔xf4   **♘e2+**

Or 32...♘f1 33 ♖h1 ♘d2 34 ♖d1 and wins.

33 ♔f5   **♘c3**

34 a3   **♘a4**

35 ♗e3   **1-0**

Since there is no defence to the threat of 36 g6 winning another pawn.

Lessons from this game:

1) It is risky to start an attack before you have brought your pieces into play and safeguarded your king by castling.

2) The correct response to a flank attack is usually a counterattack in the centre.

3) In wild complications, piece activity is often more important than a material head-count.

4) If your opponent has sacrificed material for an attack, it may be possible to stifle his attack by returning the extra material.

Game 11

Georg Rotlewi – Akiba Rubinstein

Lodz 1907/8

Queen's Gambit Declined

The Players

Akiba Rubinstein (1882–1961) was one of the world's best players in the period 1907–22. Born in the small Polish town of Stawiski, he learned chess at the age of 16 – unusually late for one who goes on to become a great player. A few years later he moved to Lodz and his chess developed rapidly. By 1907 he was already recognized as one of the leading masters and in the following five years he won a whole string of major international events. Rubinstein challenged Lasker for the World Championship and a match was arranged, but a poor performance by Rubinstein at St Petersburg 1914 followed by the outbreak of the First World War dashed his hopes of a title match. After the war years Rubinstein's career continued successfully and in 1922 he agreed terms with Capablanca, who had taken the title away from Lasker the previous year. However, he was unable to raise the necessary finance and his hopes of becoming World Champion faded for ever. Rubinstein effectively retired from chess in 1932, with his mental health in poor shape. Destitution and the Second World War cast a further shadow over his declining years and he became one of the many great masters who suffered poverty and deprivation in later life.

Georg Rotlewi (1889–1920) was a Polish player who achieved considerable success in his short career. His best result was probably fourth place in the enormously strong tournament at Karlsbad 1911 with a score of 16/26 (including only two draws!). Shortly after this he contracted a serious illness and never played again.

The Game

Rubinstein was primarily a positional player whose endgame play was of unparalleled subtlety, but when he was provoked he could be a fierce attacker. Rotlewi plays the opening too naïvely, and soon relinquishes the initiative. In symmetrical positions, the advantage of a single tempo can have a disproportionate influence on the play. Here Rubinstein exploits White's inaccuracies with great energy, first inducing Rotlewi to weaken his kingside and then crashing through with one of the most stunning combinations ever played.

1	d4	d5
2	♘f3	e6
3	e3	c5
4	c4	♘c6

5 ♘c3   ♘f6

In such positions both sides tend to play a kind of waiting game. White should certainly be considering the plan of dxc5, followed by queenside expansion with a3 and b4. However, he would prefer to wait until Black plays ...♗e7 or ...♗d6, since then the exchange on c5 will gain a tempo. Black, of course, is in exactly the same situation. These days the most popular move is 6 a3, making progress while waiting for the f8-bishop to move. Black often replies 6...a6, and the war of nerves continues.

6 dxc5

Although in this game the result is a transposition, such an early exchange on c5 rather plays into Black's hands.

6 ...   ♗xc5
7 a3   a6

Black is in no mood to try exploiting White's sixth move. 7...0-0 8 b4 ♗d6 is more natural, when Black retains the option of playing ...a5 without losing a tempo.

8 b4   ♗d6
9 ♗b2   0-0

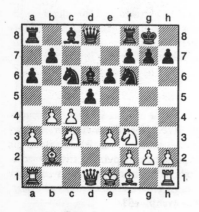

10 ♕d2?!

A poor choice. White cannot take three times on d5 because Black would win the queen by ...♗xb4+, and this move intends to step up the pressure

against d5 by ♖d1. However, the scheme backfires and White's queen ends up in an exposed position on d2. The correct way to introduce the ♖d1 plan is by 10 ♕c2, while the most popular line today is 10 cxd5 exd5 11 ♗e2, with a typical isolated d-pawn position.

10 ...   ♕e7!

Rubinstein crosses White's plan by simply offering the d-pawn. If White doesn't take it, then Black can play ...♖d8 and the d-pawn will be secure.

11 ♗d3?

Fatal inconsistency. The only merit to having the queen on d2 is the threat to d5, so it is quite wrong to play ♕d2 but then refuse the pawn – White ends up with the worst of both worlds. Most annotators have dismissed 11 cxd5 exd5 12 ♘xd5 ♘xd5 13 ♕xd5 out of hand on the basis that 13...♗e6 or 13...♖d8 gives Black a dangerous attack. That may be, but accurate play is necessary for Black to prove that he has enough for the pawn, and even then it is doubtful whether he can do more than force a draw. Black may try:

1) 13...♘xb4 14 axb4 ♗xb4+ is unsound after 15 ♔e2.

2) 13...♖d8 14 ♕b3 ♗e6 15 ♕c3 f6 16 ♗c4 and Black does not have enough for the pawn.

3) 13...♗e6! 14 ♕d3 (not 14 ♕g5? ♗xb4+, nor 14 ♕d1? ♘xb4! 15 axb4 ♗xb4+ 16 ♘d2 ♖fd8 17 ♗d4 ♖xd4 18 exd4 ♗b3+ 19 ♕e2 ♗xd2+ 20 ♔xd2 ♕b4+ and Black wins) 14...♖ac8! (14...♘xb4 15 axb4 ♗xb4+ 16 ♗c3 is unsound, while 14...♖fd8 15 ♕c3 is again bad for Black) 15 ♗e2 (15 ♘d4 ♘xd4 16 ♕xd4 f6 threatens 17...♗e5 while 15 ♖d1 ♖fd8 16 ♕b1 ♘xb4 17 axb4 ♗xb4+ 18 ♘d2 ♗b3 19 ♗d3

&xd1 20 &xd1 ♛h4 is very good for
Black) 15...♖fd8! (15...&xb4+ 16 axb4
♘xb4 17 ♛b1 ♘c2+ 18 &f1 ♘xa1 19
♛xa1 favours White) 16 ♛b1 &d5 17
0-0 &e4 18 ♛a2 (not 18 ♛e1 ♘xb4!)
and now Black has nothing better than
18...&d5 with a draw.

11 ... dxc4

Of course. White now loses one
tempo because he has moved his f1-
bishop twice and one tempo because
his queen is misplaced. Thus not only
has "Black" become "White", but he
has been presented with an extra move
into the bargain!

12 &xc4 b5
13 &d3 ♖d8

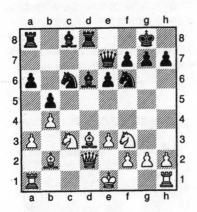

14 ♛e2

White decides that his queen is too
vulnerable to stay on the d-file. Indeed, after 14 0-0 &xh2+ (14...♘e5
15 ♘xe5 &xe5 16 ♖fd1 &b7 is similar to the game and also favours Black)
15 ♘xh2 ♘e5 16 &xh7+ ♘xh7 17
♛c2 ♘c4 Black has a clear advantage.

14 ... &b7
15 0-0 ♘e5

A key move. Black breaks the symmetry to his own advantage.

16 ♘xe5 &xe5
17 f4

White cannot proceed with his normal development, since both 17 ♖fd1
♛c7 and 17 ♖ac1 &xh2+ cost material. Therefore he is reduced to drastic
measures to drive the bishop off the
a1–h8 diagonal.

17 ... &c7

The bishop retreats, but White has
weakened his kingside.

18 e4

This move prepares to meet ...e5 by
f5. If White continues 18 ♖fd1, then
18...e5 19 ♖ac1 exf4 20 exf4 &b6+ 21
&h1 ♛e3 22 f5 ♛f4 is very good for
Black.

18 ... ♖ac8

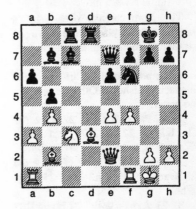

The diagram shows a very favourable situation for Black. Both his
rooks are occupying active positions,
while White's have yet to enter the
game.

19 e5?

White's aim is to force exchanges
by playing a piece to e4, but this further weakening allows Black a forced
win. White should have tried 19 ♖ac1
or 19 ♖ad1, although in either case

19...e5 20 f5 &b6+ 21 &h1 &d4 gives Black a large positional advantage.

19 ...   &b6+

20 &h1   ♘g4!

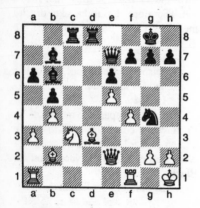

The storm breaks over White's kingside. Every black piece is in a position to participate in the attack.

21 &e4

Attempting to block off one of the menacing bishops. Other moves are no better:

1) 21 ♕xg4? ♖xd3 22 ♘e2 (22 ♖ac1 ♖d2) 22...♖c2 23 &c1 h5 24 ♕xh5 &xg2+ 25 &xg2 ♕b7+ wins.

2) 21 ♘e4 ♖xd3! 22 ♕xd3 &xe4 23 ♕xe4 ♕h4 24 h3 ♕g3 25 hxg4 ♕h4#.

3) 21 &xh7+ &xh7 22 ♕xg4 ♖d2 wins.

4) 21 h3 ♕h4 22 ♕xg4 ♕xg4 23 hxg4 ♖xd3 wins material because of the threat of mate by 24...♖h3#.

21 ...   ♕h4

The brilliance of Rubinstein's final combination is only slightly marred by the fact that he could have won relatively simply by 21...♘xh2! 22 ♖fc1 (22 &xh7+ &xh7 23 ♕h5+ &g8 24 &xh2 ♖d2 and 22 &xb7 ♘xf1 both

win for Black while 22 ♖fd1 ♕h4 23 g3 ♕xg3 is similar to 22 ♖fc1) 22...♕h4 (22...♘f1 23 ♕g4 h5! 24 ♕h3 ♖xc3 25 ♖xc3 &xe4 26 ♖xf1 ♖d2 also wins) 23 g3 ♕xg3 24 ♕xh2 (24 &xb7 ♘g4) 24...&xe4+ (not 24...♕f3+ 25 &xf3 &xf3+ 26 ♕g2 &xg2+ 27 &xg2 ♖d2+ 28 &h1 ♖xb2 29 ♘a4!) 25 ♘xe4 ♕f3+ 26 ♕g2 ♖xc1+ 27 ♖xc1 ♕h5+ 28 ♕h2 ♖d1+ 29 ♖xd1 ♕xd1+ 30 &g2 ♕c2+ 31 &h3 ♕xe4 and White can resign.

22 g3

Or 22 h3 ♖xc3 23 &xc3 (23 &xb7 ♖xh3+ 24 gxh3 ♕xh3+ 25 ♕h2 ♕xh2# and 23 ♕xg4 ♖xh3+ 24 ♕xh3 ♕xh3+ 25 gxh3 &xe4+ 26 &h2 ♖d2+ 27 &g3 ♖g2+ 28 &h4 &d8+ 29 &h5 &g6# both result in mate) 23...&xe4 24 ♕xg4 (24 ♕xe4 ♕g3 mates) 24...♕xg4 25 hxg4 ♖d3 26 &h2 ♖xc3 with a decisive material advantage.

22 ...   ♖xc3!!

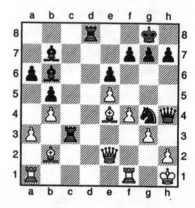

This queen sacrifice provides a stunning finish.

23 gxh4

There is nothing better than to accept, for example 23 &xb7 (23 &xc3 &xe4+ 24 ♕xe4 ♕xh2#) 23...♖xg3

24 ♖f3 (24 ♗f3 ♘xh2 25 ♕xh2 ♖h3 and 24 ♖ad1 ♖xd1 25 ♖xd1 ♖h3 are also dead lost) 24...♖xf3 25 ♗xf3 ♘f2+ 26 ♔g1 (26 ♔g2 ♕h3+ 27 ♔g1 ♘e4+ 28 ♔h1 ♘g3#) 26...♘e4+ 27 ♔f1 ♘d2+ 28 ♔g2 ♘xf3 29 ♕xf3 (29 ♔xf3 ♕h5+) 29...♖d2+ wins.

23 ... ♖d2!

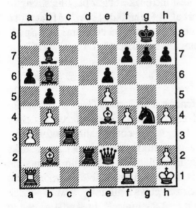

The amazing activity of Black's pieces proves too much for White's numerically superior forces.

24 ♕xd2

The lines 24 ♕xg4 ♗xe4+ 25 ♖f3 ♖xf3, 24 ♖xc3 ♗xe4+ 25 ♕xe4 ♖xh2# and 24 ♗xb7 ♖xe2 25 ♗g2 ♖h3 also lead to mate in a few moves.

24 ... ♗xe4+
25 ♕g2 ♖h3!

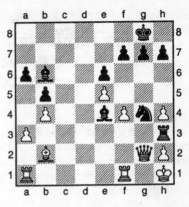

0-1

The final position deserves a diagram. White cannot avoid a rapid mate, for example 26 ♖f2 ♖xh2+ 27 ♔g1 ♗xf2+ 28 ♔f1 ♗d3# or 26 ♖f3 ♗xf3 27 ♕xf3 ♖xh2#.

Lessons from this game:

1) The advantage of moving first is a valuable but fragile asset – take good care of it!

2) In symmetrical positions a single tempo can play a decisive role. The first player to undertake aggressive action can force his opponent into a permanently passive role.

3) Two bishops attacking the enemy king along adjacent diagonals make a dangerous team.

Game 12
Akiba Rubinstein – Emanuel Lasker
St Petersburg 1909
Queen's Gambit Declined

The Players

In 1909 both Rubinstein and Lasker were near the peak of their playing strength. Indeed, they tore the rest of the field apart at St Petersburg, sharing first place with 14½ points, a massive 3½ points ahead of third-placed Duras and Spielmann. For more information on the two players, see Game 7 (Lasker) and Game 11 (Rubinstein).

The Game

Once more Lasker employs an inferior defence to the Queen's Gambit, but unlike his game against Pillsbury (Game 7) he doesn't get a chance to correct his error this time. Rubinstein fails to find the most punishing continuation, but what he plays is certainly enough to secure a small plus. In typical fashion Lasker seeks complications, sacrificing a pawn to gain the initiative. Rubinstein accepts the pawn, perhaps unwisely, but for him this is the only questionable decision of the game. Faced with a defensive task, Rubinstein plays brilliantly, first to squash Lasker's counterplay and then to go onto the attack himself. Lasker is forced to enter a terrible endgame, which is the equivalent of resignation against someone of Rubinstein's legendary technique.

1	d4	d5
2	♘f3	♘f6
3	c4	e6
4	♗g5	c5?!

This lunge in the centre was quite popular at the time, but is probably a bit premature here. Black normally winds up with an isolated d-pawn that can be quite difficult to defend. The unpinning move 4...♗e7 is more normal.

5	cxd5	exd5
6	♘c3	cxd4
7	♘xd4	♘c6?

This is most certainly a mistake. Black should unpin immediately with 7...♗e7, when White can decide between 8 e3, or fianchettoing the bishop with 8 g3 and 9 ♗g2. In either case White is slightly better.

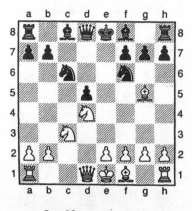

8 e3?

Returning the compliment. After 8 ♗xf6! Black is forced to play the very ugly 8...gxf6, as 8...♕xf6 9 ♘db5 presents Black with some very difficult problems. Following 9...♗b4 10 ♘c7+ ♔f8 11 ♘xd5! White is a pawn up with an excellent position.

8 ...   ♗e7
9 ♗b5   ♗d7!

Lasker begins his legendary technique of defending a difficult position. Here he offers a pawn in an attempt to seize the initiative.

10 ♗xf6!?

Rubinstein decides to grab the material, although there is something to be said for playing the more sober 10 0-0, when Black's difficulties surrounding the d-pawn will not go away.

10 ...   ♗xf6
11 ♘xd5   ♗xd4
12 exd4   ♕g5!

The double threat against d5 and g2 forces White to part with his bishop, leaving Black with some development advantage to compensate for the sacrificed pawn. Note that 13 ♘c7+? ♔d8 14 ♘xa8 ♕xb5 leaves Black with a very strong attack.

13 ♗xc6   ♗xc6

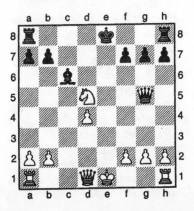

14 ♘e3

Again 14 ♘c7+ ♔d7 favours Black, as 15 ♘xa8 runs into 15...♖e8+!.

14 ...   0-0-0

Lasker criticized this over-ambitious move after the game. It does seem the logical continuation to Black's previous play, but it becomes apparent that White has some hidden defensive resources. It is better simply to regain the pawn with 14...♗xg2, e.g.:

1) 15 ♘xg2 ♕xg2 16 ♕e2+ ♔d8! 17 0-0-0 ♖e8 is fine for Black, according to Lasker. The d4-pawn actually acts as a shield for the black king, while all of his major pieces will soon become very active.

2) 15 ♖g1! was preferred by Rubinstein, and this does seem to be a bigger test for Black. After the forced line 15...♕a5+ 16 ♕d2 ♕xd2+ 17 ♔xd2 ♗e4, Rubinstein liked 18 ♖g4 ♗g6 19 f4, intending f5. However, Black still retains counterchances after 19...♖d8 20 f5 ♗h5 21 ♖xg7 ♖xd4+ 22 ♔c3 ♖h4. It must also be noted that the immediate 18 ♖xg7? is a mistake. Black can incarcerate the white rook with 18...♗g6!, and force White to give up the exchange with ...♔f8.

15 0-0   ♖he8
16 ♖c1!

An extremely subtle defence. At first sight this does not seem an adequate response to the threat of 16...♖xe3, but White's idea is very deep.

16 ...   ♖xe3

The only alternative is to side-step the pin with 16...♔b8, but White can then activate his rook with 17 ♖c5!. After 17...♕f4 18 d5 ♖xe3 19 ♕c1! White keeps the advantage in a similar way to the actual game. Certainly Lasker didn't like the look of Black's position after 19...♖e4 20 dxc6 bxc6 21 ♕c3. Both Black's king and pawns are very weak. Indeed, following 17 ♖c5 perhaps Black's best option is to seek sanctuary in the endgame with 17...♕xc5 18 dxc5 ♖xd1 19 ♖xd1. Although White has an extra pawn, the fact that he has a bishop against a knight promises Black some drawing chances.

17   ♖xc6+   bxc6

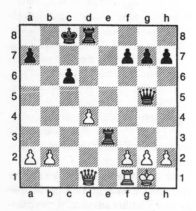

18   ♕c1!!

The whole point of Rubinstein's previous play, beginning with 16 ♖c1. The rook is pinned to the queen and cannot be saved. Naturally Lasker had been hoping for 18 fxe3? ♕xe3+ 19 ♔h1 ♕xd4, when Black is even slightly better.

18   ...   ♖xd4

Lasker thought that better defensive chances were offered by 18...♖e5!? 19 ♕xc6+ (but not 19 f4 ♖c5! 20 dxc5 ♕d5) 19...♔b8 20 dxe5 ♕xe5, although after 21 ♖c1 one would expect that White's extra pawn and Black's weaker king would soon become decisive factors.

19   fxe3   ♖d7

20   ♕xc6+   ♔d8
21   ♖f4!

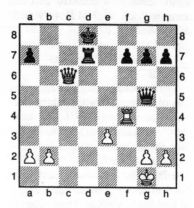

Rubinstein plays the rest of the game in a faultless manner. By placing his rook on the fourth rank White threatens to decide the issue immediately by smoking the black king out into the open. The first threat is 22 ♕a8+ ♔e7 23 ♖e4+ ♔d6 24 ♕f8+ and Black is mated after 24...♔c6 25 ♖c4+ ♔b6 26 ♕b8+ ♖b7 27 ♕d6+ ♔a5 28 b4+ ♔a4 29 ♕a6+ ♕a5 30 ♕xa5#. Lasker finds the right defence, but is immediately faced with another problem.

21   ...   f5

Preventing White from using the e4-square. Other lines don't work, e.g.:

1) 21...♕a5 22 ♕a8+ ♔e7 23 ♖e4+ ♔f6 24 ♕c6+ ♔g5 25 h4+ and 26 ♕xd7.

2) 21...♖d1+ 22 ♔f2 ♖d2+ 23 ♔e1! and the natural 23...♕xg2 loses to 24 ♖d4+!, when 24...♖xd4 allows 25 ♕xg2, while 24...♔e7 25 ♕d6+ ♔e8 26 ♕d8# is mate.

22   ♕c5   ♕e7

Lasker is forced into a lost ending. Once more 22...♖d1+ loses after 23

♔f2 ♖d2+ 24 ♔e1 ♕xg2 25 ♕a5+
and 26 ♕xd2, while 22...g6 23 ♕f8+
again leads to a decisive checking
spree with 23...♔c7 24 ♖c4+ ♔b6 25
♕b4+ ♔a6 26 ♖c6#.

23	♕xe7+	♔xe7
24	♖xf5	♖d1+
25	♔f2!	

Classic technique. White gives up
one of his extra pawns to activate his
king. In contrast 25 ♖f1 ♖d2 offers
Black more chances to draw. After 26
♖b1 Black doesn't attempt to retrieve
a pawn with 26...♖e2, as 27 ♔f1!
♖xe3? 28 ♖e1 leads to a won king and
pawn endgame. Instead Black continues with 26...♔e6, when, despite the
two-pawn advantage, it is very difficult for White to make progress.

25	...	♖d2+
26	♔f3	♖xb2
27	♖a5	♖b7

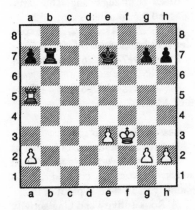

28 ♖a6!

Another excellent move. The a6-
square is the ideal place for the white
rook. Now the black rook remains tied
to the a7-pawn, while the black king
cannot move onto the third rank. Black
can now only sit and wait while White

gradually pushes his king and pawns
up the board.

28	...	♔f8
29	e4	♖c7
30	h4	♔f7
31	g4	♔f8
32	♔f4	♔e7
33	h5!	

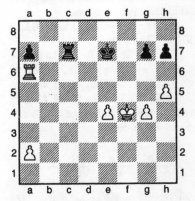

The white pawns slowly move up
the board. Lasker now decided to prevent any further advance, but in doing
so created a specific weakness on g6.

33 ... h6

Nevertheless, passive defence also
loses, although some accurate play is
required by White. After 33...♔f7 34
♔f5 ♔e7 35 g5 ♔f7 36 e5 ♔e7 37 g6
h6 Black is on the verge of defeat. The
most obvious method for White is to
target the g7-pawn. This can be done
by manoeuvring the rook to g8 or f7,
but this is not as simple as it first
seems, e.g.:

1) 38 ♖e6+ and now:

1a) 38...♔d7 39 ♖f6! ♔e8 (White
wins after 39...gxf6 40 g7 ♖c8 41
exf6) 40 ♖f7 ♖xf7+ 41 gxf7+ ♔xf7
42 e6+ ♔e7 43 ♔e5 with a won king
and pawn endgame.

1b) 38...♔f8! 39 ♖d6 ♔e7 40 ♖a6 leaves Black in some trouble, as the natural waiting move 40...♖b7 allows 41 ♖e6+ ♔f8 42 ♖c6!, followed by ♖c8 and ♖g8. However, Black is still alive after 40...♔e8!.

2) 38 ♖a3! is perhaps the most convincing move. The main ideas are ♖b3-b8 and ♔e4, followed by ♖f3 and ♖f7. Black has no defence, e.g.:

2a) 38...♔d7 39 ♖d3+ ♔e7 40 ♖b3 ♖d7 41 ♖b8 wins.

2b) 38...♖b7 39 ♖c3 ♔d7 40 e6+ ♔e7 41 a4! ♔d6 42 ♖d3+ ♔e7 43 ♔e5 ♖c7 44 ♖d5 a6 45 a5 ♔e8 46 ♖d7! ♖xd7 47 exd7+ ♔xd7 48 ♔d5 and we see the advantage of White's far-advanced pawns.

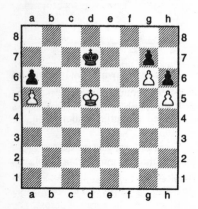

All pawn races are easily won, while after 48...♔e7 49 ♔c6 ♔e6 50 ♔b6 ♔d6 51 ♔xa6 ♔c6 52 ♔a7 ♔c7 53 a6 ♔c8 54 ♔b6, the white king races to the kingside.

	34	♔f5	♔f7
	35	e5	♖b7
	36	♖d6	♔e7
	37	♖a6	♔f7

38   ♖d6

Repeating the position is merely a tease for Lasker. Rubinstein is merely marking time before the final finesse.

38	...	♔f8
39	♖c6	♔f7
40	a3!	**1-0**

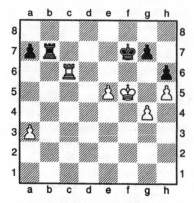

Black is in zugzwang. The variations tell the complete story.

1) 40...♖e7 41 e6+ ♔g8 42 ♔g6 ♖e8 43 e7, followed by ♖d6-d8.

2) 40...♔e7 41 ♔g6 ♔d7 42 ♖d6+ ♔c8 43 e6.

3) 40...♔f8 41 ♔g6 ♖d7 42 ♖c8+ ♔e7 43 ♔xg7.

Lessons from this game:

1) Brilliant defence can be just as powerful and imaginative as brilliant attack. Rubinstein's concept, culminating with 18 ♕c1, is proof of this.

2) Rook activity and king activity are powerful tools in the endgame. Witness Rubinstein's 25 ♔f2! and 28 ♖a6!.

3) Rubinstein was the absolute master of rook and pawn endgames.

Game 13
Ossip Bernstein – José Capablanca
Exhibition game, Moscow 1914
Queen's Gambit Declined

The Players

Ossip Bernstein (1882–1962) was born in the Ukraine into a rich family. He was able to devote a great deal of time to chess while studying law at Heidelberg University. His best years as a player were between 1905 and 1914, when he performed prominently in many major tournaments, sharing first place with Rubinstein at Ostend 1907. After losing his fortune in the revolution of 1917 he moved to Paris, where he became an outstanding financial lawyer. In 1932, after a long time away from the game, Bernstein took up chess once more. He was awarded the grandmaster title in 1950 and two years later he also gained the title of International Arbiter. In his later years he still played actively, representing France at the Amsterdam Olympiad in 1954. Also in that year there was a flash of his previous skill when he was awarded the brilliancy prize for a victory over Najdorf in Montevideo.

José Raúl Capablanca (1888–1942) is one of the legends in chess history. Born in Cuba, he learned chess at the age of four and gave due notice of his talent when, barely a teenager, he defeated Corzo, who won the national championship in the same year, in an informal match. Capablanca was educated in America, and spent much of his free time playing masters at the Manhattan Chess Club. Even in his younger days it was obvious to everyone that Capablanca was a natural-born chess player. Positionally and in the endgame he had no equal, but as his countless wins against other tacticians show, he was also at home in highly complex positions. At one stage of his career Capablanca lost only one tournament game in ten years, which gave him an aura of invincibility. It came as absolutely no surprise when, in Havana during 1921, he finally met with Lasker and took the world title, without losing a single game.

The Game

Capablanca possessed a distinctive style, which was both classical and direct; this game is a perfect illustration. After playing a sound opening he accepts the so-called hanging pawns, which can either be viewed as a strength or a weakness. The Cuban follows up by stunning the chess world with a new and somewhat controversial concept. Bernstein tries in vain to search for a refutation, but is slowly pushed backwards as Capablanca's activity increases. Annoyed by Capablanca's passed pawn, Bernstein thinks he has spotted a way to eliminate it. Capablanca, however has seen one move further. This one crushing move is enough for victory.

1	d4	d5
2	c4	e6
3	♘c3	♘f6
4	♘f3	♗e7
5	♗g5	0-0
6	e3	♘bd7
7	♖c1	b6
8	cxd5	exd5
9	♕a4	

This early queen move was favoured by Czech Grandmaster Oldřich Duras, and is a playable alternative to both 9 ♗d3 and 9 ♗b5. White's intention is to exchange the light-squared bishops by ♗a6, thus weakening some of the light squares on the queenside and eliminating one of Black's important defenders of the hanging pawns that are about to arise.

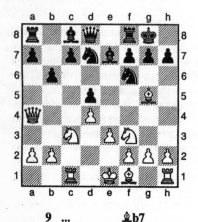

9	...	♗b7

At the time Capablanca thought this was a better move than the immediate 9...c5!?, after which White can win a pawn by 10 ♕c6. However, later on it became apparent that Black receives plenty of play for the pawn after 10...♖b8 11 ♘xd5 ♘xd5 12 ♕xd5 ♗b7 13 ♗xe7 ♕xe7. The game Levitina – Chiburdanidze, Women's World

Championship match (game 13), Volgograd 1984 continued 14 ♕g5 ♕xg5 15 ♘xg5 cxd4 16 exd4 ♖fe8+ 17 ♔d1 ♖ed8! 18 ♘f3 ♗xf3+ 19 gxf3 ♘e5 20 ♖c3 ♖xd4+ and Black had regained the pawn with an excellent position.

10	♗a6	♗xa6
11	♕xa6	c5
12	♗xf6?!	

This move is one of the reasons for White's later problems in the game. True, it does eliminate one defender, but it is still rather committal. There's an old principle in chess which is certainly very applicable in the opening stages: "Always make an obvious move before one you are not sure about!" Here White knows he must castle kingside at some point, so why not do it now? Indeed the natural 12 0-0 probably ensures an edge for White. If Black then tries to simplify with 12...♕c8 he finds that his centre soon comes under a severe attack. Gheorghiu – M. Brunner, Mendrisio 1989 continued 13 ♕xc8 ♖axc8 14 dxc5 bxc5 15 ♖fd1 ♘b6 16 ♗xf6 ♗xf6 17 ♘xd5 ♘xd5 18 ♖xd5 ♗xb2 19 ♖cxc5 and White had simply won a pawn.

12	...	♘xf6
13	dxc5	bxc5

Forming the set of "hanging pawns" on c5 and d5. These pawns are so named because they cannot be defended by pawns on adjacent files (Black has neither a b-pawn nor an e-pawn). As a consequence of exchanges they more often than not also stand on half-open files (White has no c- and d-pawns). A big argument centres around the strengths and weaknesses of this pair. Their strength lays in the number of important squares they control in the centre, plus their ability to attack by advancing. Their weakness becomes apparent when they are forced to be defended by pieces, thus diminishing the relative activity of these pieces. It's normally true that these pawns also become weaker as more pieces are exchanged.

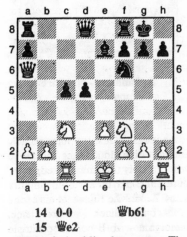

14 0-0   ♛b6!
15 ♛e2

White feels obliged to retreat. The alternative 15 ♛xb6 axb6 improves Black's pawn-structure, as well as giving him a useful half-open a-file on which to operate.

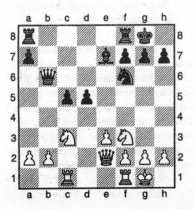

15 ...   c4!

Perhaps the most significant move of the game. At the time this was played it would have been clearly condemned, but for the fact that Capablanca made it work quite beautifully. A dogmatic advocate of the classical school of chess would have immediately pointed to the weakness it creates on d4, which can now be occupied by any white piece, plus the absolute elimination of any ...d4 ideas, which in effect further weakens the d5-pawn. It's true that these static considerations do favour White, but that doesn't take into account all of the new dynamic possibilities available to Black. Perhaps it is most effective to hear Capablanca's own view on the subject:

"White's plan from the start was to work against the weakness of Black's hanging c- and d-pawns, which must be defended by pieces. The general strategy for such positions is for White's rooks to occupy the c- and d-files attacking Black's hanging pawns, while Black's rooks defend these pawns from the rear. Again the awkward position of Black's bishop at e7 rendered it useless, except for the purpose of defending the pawn on c5. It is against such strategy on the part of White that the text-move (15...c4) is directed. By it the defensive bishop becomes an attacking piece, since the long diagonal is open to him; and what is more important, White's b-pawn is fixed and weakened and becomes a source of worry for White, who has to defend it also with pieces, and thus cannot use those pieces to attack the black hanging pawns. The fact that the text-move opens d4 for one of White's knights is of small consequence, since if White posts a knight there his attack on Black's d5-pawn is blocked for the moment, and thus Black has time to assume the offensive."

This powerful argument changed people's concept of this type of position, and influenced future generations of grandmasters. Take the following example, played almost fifty years later.

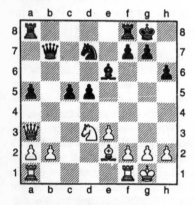

M. Bertok – R. Fischer
Interzonal tournament,
Stockholm 1962

In this position the future World Champion followed Capablanca's lead with 17...c4! and following 18 ♘f4 ♖fb8 19 ♖ab1?! ♗f5 20 ♖bd1 ♘f6 21 ♖d2 g5! he had achieved a very favourable position. Bertok now felt obliged to sacrifice a piece with 22 ♘xd5? ♘xd5 23 ♗xc4 ♗e6, but after 24 ♖fd1 ♘xe3! 25 ♕xe3 ♗xc4 26 h4 ♖e8 27 ♕g3 ♕e7 28 b3 ♗e6 29 f4 g4 30 h5 ♕c5+ 31 ♖f2 ♗f5 he resigned. However, even if White had played the superior continuation 22 ♘h5 ♘e4 23 ♖c2 ♕b4! Black would have had excellent winning chances.

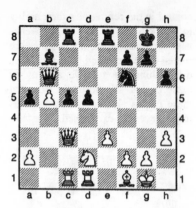

J. Timman – N. Short
Candidates match (game 1),
El Escorial 1993

Another leap of thirty years and this time it's England's Nigel Short who benefits from the Cuban's teachings. Here Short played 21...c4!, and after 22 a4 ♖e6 23 ♖c2 ♖ce8 24 ♘f3 ♘e4 25 ♕a1 ♖f6 Black was doing fine. Timman now followed the principle of possessing the d4-square, but this proved to be a decisive mistake. After 26 ♖d4? ♖xf3! 27 gxf3 ♕g6+ 28 ♗g2 ♘g5 29 ♖c1 ♘xf3+ 30 ♔f1 ♘h2+ 31 ♔g1 ♘f3+ 32 ♔f1 ♘xd4 33 ♕xd4 ♕f5 Black was a pawn up and went on to win very comfortably.

(*Back now to the game Bernstein – Capablanca.*)

Capablanca concludes that after 15...c4, White should already be looking for equality. He gives the simplifying continuation 16 e4 as White's best move, and after 16...dxe4 17 ♘xe4 ♘xe4 18 ♕xe4 ♗f6 the position does seem to be heading for a draw.

    16 ♖fd1?   **♖fd8**
    17 ♘d4

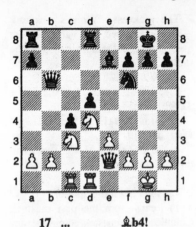

17 ... &b4!

The fruits of Black's revolutionary 15th move are beginning to show. The dark-squared bishop, hitherto so quiet on e7, now takes up an active role, putting pressure on the c3-knight, and thus dissuading White from breaking with b2-b3. Evidently Bernstein was not dissuaded enough.

18 b3

18 Wc2 prevents Black from creating a passed pawn, but Black can still increase the pressure against the b-pawn with Harry Golombek's suggestion of 18...Eab8.

18 ... Eac8
19 bxc4

Giving Black a crucial passed pawn, but it's already becoming hard to suggest an alternative for White. Certainly 19 Da4 Wa5 doesn't improve matters, as after a timely ...c3, the knight would have no way back from a4.

19 ... dxc4
20 Ec2 &xc3
21 Exc3 Dd5
22 Ec2

22 Exc4? Dc3 wins the exchange.

22 ... c3
23 Edc1 Ec5

24 Db3 Ec6
25 Dd4 Ec7

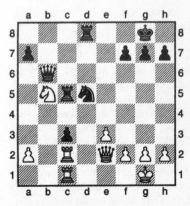

26 Db5?

Falling into a sneaky trap, which finishes the game abruptly. White should have remained passive with 26 We1, although after 26...Edc8 27 De2 Ec4! Black's c-pawn remains a thorn in White's flesh. It cannot be extracted by 28 Dxc3? Exc3 29 Exc3 Exc3 30 Exc3 Dxc3 31 Wxc3, as Black mates on the back rank after 31...Wb1+.

26 ... Ec5

27 Dxc3??

It still wasn't too late to crawl back with 27 ♘d4.

27	...	♘xc3
28	♖xc3	♖xc3
29	♖xc3	

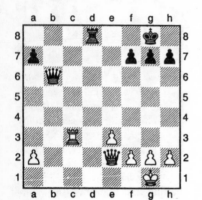

Bernstein must have been expecting 29...♕b1+ 30 ♕f1 ♕xa2. Capablanca's next move is a thunderbolt.

29	...	♕b2!!

0-1

The weakness of White's back rank is cruelly exposed. The variations are quite simple, but rather striking all the same:

1) 30 ♕xb2 ♖d1#.

2) 30 ♕e1 ♕xc3 31 ♕xc3 ♖d1+ 32 ♕e1 ♖xe1#.

3) 30 ♕c2 ♕a1+ 31 ♕c1 ♖d1+ 32 ♕xd1 ♕xd1#.

4) 30 ♖c2 ♕b1+ 31 ♕f1 ♕xc2 and the queen is also lost.

Lessons from this game:

1) Learn from the past masters. Countless grandmasters admit that they are influenced by the top players from yesteryear. As we have seen, both Bobby Fischer and Nigel Short were direct beneficiaries of Capa's brave new idea.

2) Always be aware of back-rank mates. They can often give rise to some surprising tactics (e.g. 29...♕b2 in this game).

3) Capablanca was a genius!

Aron Nimzowitsch – Siegbert Tarrasch
Preliminary event, St Petersburg 1914
Queen's Gambit Declined

The Players

Aron Nimzowitsch (1886–1935) was one of the strongest players in the world during the 1920s and was also influential as a thinker and writer. He was born in Riga and rose to prominence before the First World War. The war interrupted his career for six years but when Nimzowitsch was able to resume international competition he rapidly advanced into the world elite. After a succession of tournament victories, his challenge for the World Championship was accepted by Capablanca in 1926. However, Nimzowitsch was unable to raise the necessary money and when the world title passed to Alekhine in 1927, the new champion preferred to play a title match against Bogoljubow (some have said that this was because Alekhine regarded Nimzowitsch as the more dangerous opponent). After 1931 he could not maintain his level of play and was no longer a realistic title contender. Nimzowitsch fell ill in 1934 and died from pneumonia some months later.

Nimzowitsch was, along with Réti, one of the most prominent members of the so-called Hypermodern school of chess, which introduced many new ideas into the game, especially in the area of opening play (see the introduction to Game 22, Réti – Bogoljubow, for more details). Nimzowitsch's influence on opening theory was especially profound and a number of opening lines bear his name. The two most important are the Nimzo-Indian Defence (1 d4 ♘f6 2 c4 e6 3 ♘c3 ♗b4), and the French Defence line 1 e4 e6 2 d4 d5 3 ♘c3 ♗b4, which is called the Nimzowitsch Variation in most non-English speaking countries. Both are still in everyday use. Nimzowitsch wrote three important books of which two, *My System* (1925) and *Chess Praxis* (1929) are regarded as classics of chess literature and are still in print.

Siegbert Tarrasch (1862–1934), another all-time great, was one of the best players in the world for two decades. Born in Breslau, he spent most of his life in Nuremberg where he was a practising doctor of medicine. Tarrasch had an unusually long chess career. He gained the German master title in 1883 and in the period 1888–94 won a number of strong tournaments. In 1903 he challenged Lasker for the world title and terms were agreed, but the match collapsed after Tarrasch asked for a postponement. Further tournament successes followed, but it was not until 1908 that he finally played a World Championship match against Lasker. However, by now Tarrasch was perhaps slightly past his prime, and he lost decisively (+3 =5 −8). Tarrasch continued to play for another two decades and represented Germany in the 1927 London Olympiad. Like Nimzowitsch, Tarrasch had a considerable influence on opening play and his name is attached to the Tarrasch Defence to the Queen's Gambit (1 d4 d5 2 c4 e6 3 ♘c3 c5) and the Tarrasch Variation of the French Defence (1 e4 e6 2 d4 d5 3 ♘d2).

Tarrasch was a great chess teacher and had the knack of reducing complex ideas to simple, easily-remembered rules. Unfortunately, he carried this too far and believed that chess could ultimately be reduced to a set of formulae. The Hypermodern school were particularly antagonistic to his dogmatic views; indeed, Tarrasch and Nimzowitsch had a famous feud which made clashes between them real needle contests. The lifetime score between these two players favoured Nimzowitsch (+5 =5 −2) but the score is distorted by three Nimzowitsch wins during the 1920s when Tarrasch was already more than sixty years old. While all their encounters are interesting, the honour of the greatest brilliancy belongs to Tarrasch.

The Game

Nimzowitsch's opening play is fairly insipid, but Tarrasch makes no real attempt to refute it and soon a near-symmetrical position is reached. We have already seen (Game 11, Rotlewi – Rubinstein) how important tempi are in such positions and in this game Nimzowitsch squanders time with an odd knight manoeuvre. Tarrasch gradually increases his central control and finally the stage is set for a double bishop sacrifice. In desperate trouble, Nimzowitsch tries to find counter-play against Tarrasch's king, but suffers the indignity of having his own king chased all the way up the board.

| 1 | d4 | d5 |
| 2 | ♘f3 | c5 |

The characteristic move of the Tarrasch Defence. In this opening Black often ends up with an isolated d-pawn, but Tarrasch believed that the active piece-play Black obtains fully compensates for the weakness of the pawn.

| 3 | c4 | e6 |
| 4 | e3 | |

These days the most critical line is considered to be 4 cxd5 exd5 5 g3, since from g2 the bishop is ideally posted to exert pressure on Black's d5-pawn.

| 4 | ... | ♘f6 |
| 5 | ♗d3 | |

An insipid move. We explained in Game 11 (Rotlewi – Rubinstein) that there is often a battle for tempo in such

symmetrical Queen's Gambit positions. White normally delays moving his f1-bishop, because if Black then exchanges on c4 White will have to move his bishop twice; similarly, Black will try to delay moving his f8-bishop. The most natural move is 5 ♘c3.

| 5 | ... | ♘c6 |

The harmlessness of White's last move may be demonstrated by the fact that after 5...dxc4 6 ♗xc4 we would arrive at a standard position of the Queen's Gambit Accepted (1 d4 d5 2 c4 dxc4 3 ♘f3 ♘f6 4 e3 c5 5 ♗xc4), but with Black having an extra tempo.

| 6 | 0-0 | ♗d6 |

Neither side really seems to care about opening finesses, which seems odd given their dispute away from the board about how the opening should be handled. This was Black's last chance to take on c4, whereas after the text-move a more or less symmetrical position is reached.

7 b3   0-0

Black should not try to hunt down White's bishop before completing his development, since 7...♘b4 8 cxd5 ♘xd5 9 ♕xd3 exd5 10 dxc5 ♗xc5 11 ♕b5+ ♘d7 12 ♘c3 is very good for White.

8 ♗b2   b6

Once again Black is content to maintain the symmetry. After 8...cxd4 9 exd4 ♘b4 10 ♘c3 ♘xd3 11 ♕xd3 Black equalized comfortably in Janowsky – Marshall, match (game 3), New York 1916.

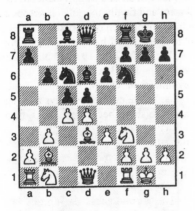

9 ♘bd2

In queen's pawn openings the players often face the decision as to whether to develop the queen's knight at d2 or c3 (d7 or c6 for Black). It is wrong to play ♘c3 when the c-pawn is still at c2, as the move c2-c4 is blocked, but if the pawn has already advanced to c4 then the decision is more difficult. However, in the majority of cases the knight is better at c3

than at d2, for the obvious reason that the enemy pawn on d5 severely restricts a knight developed at d2. Only if there is some special motivation should one bring the knight out to d2. Nimzowitsch's move is not a major error because, as we shall see, there is one plan which requires the knight to be on d2. However, having played the knight to this less active square, automatic moves will not do – White must justify his decision.

After 9 ♘c3 White would have had the slight advantage typical of a quiet symmetrical position.

9 ...   ♗b7
10 ♖c1   ♕e7
11 cxd5?!

This does not fit in with 9 ♘bd2. The only reason for playing the knight to d2 rather than c3 is to avoid blocking the b2-bishop, and White could have utilized this factor by 11 ♘e5. Then the attempt to liquidate with 11...cxd4 12 exd4 ♗a3 13 cxd5 ♘xe5 14 ♗xa3 ♕xa3 15 dxe5 ♘xd5 would give White a very dangerous attack after 16 ♖c4, for example the greedy 16...♕xa2 would run into 17 ♗xh7+! ♔xh7 18 ♕h5+ ♔g8 19 ♘e4! f6 (19...♖fd8 20 ♘g5 ♖d7 21 ♖h4 ♔f8 22 ♕h8+ ♔e7 23 ♕xg7 ♖f8 24 ♘xe6 wins) 20 ♘d6 ♖ad8 21 ♘xb7 ♖d7 22 ♘d6 with a clear advantage for White. Black should be content to meet 11 ♘e5 by 11...♖fd8, with a roughly level position.

11 ...   exd5
12 ♘h4?!

An extravagant manoeuvre which, by threatening to occupy f5, more or less forces Black to reply ...g6; White's hope is that the b2-bishop will be well placed to exploit the weakening of the a1–h8 diagonal. The downside is that the knight manoeuvre costs a tempo, and this allows Black to step up the pressure in the centre.

It is interesting to note how the actively-placed knight on c6 prevents many natural moves by White, for example 12 ♖c2 ♘b4 or 12 ♕e2 ♘b4 13 ♗b1 ♗a6; in contrast the d2-knight isn't doing very much. Perhaps 12 dxc5 bxc5 13 ♗xf6 ♕xf6 14 e4 is best, completely changing the nature of the position, although Black retains an edge after 14...♘b4 15 ♗b1 ♖fe8.

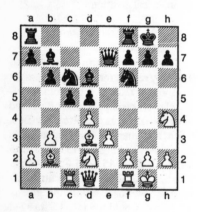

12	...	g6
13	♘hf3	♖ad8
14	dxc5	bxc5

White's main problem is that he has no square for his queen, which is now uncomfortably placed opposite Black's rook (15 ♕e2 is met by 15...♘b4).

15 ♗b5

Relatively best. Now White can play ♕e2, since the reply ...♘b4 does not come with gain of tempo.

| 15 | ... | ♘e4 |
| 16 | ♗xc6? | |

White should not have made this exchange voluntarily, as Black obtains two dangerous bishops, both pointing at White's kingside. We saw in Game 11 (Rotlewi – Rubinstein) that such bishops form a dangerous pair. Apparently White wanted to play ♕c2, but saw that the immediate 16 ♕c2 allows 16...♘b4 17 ♕b1 ♘xd2 18 ♘xd2 d4 with a strong attack; hence this preliminary exchange. However, White should have played 16 ♕e2, keeping the queen nearer the threatened kingside; in this case Black would have some advantage but no immediate breakthrough.

| 16 | ... | ♗xc6 |
| 17 | ♕c2 | |

17 ♘xe4 dxe4 18 ♘d2 is little better since after 18...♗b5 19 ♖e1 ♗d3 the invulnerable bishop is a thorn in White's flesh.

| 17 | ... | ♘xd2 |
| 18 | ♘xd2 | |

Or 18 ♕xd2 d4 19 exd4 ♗xf3 20 gxf3 ♕h4 and Black wins.

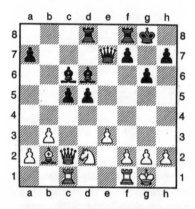

The critical position. White's kingside is devoid of defensive pieces and Black's bishops occupy menacing positions. However, the immediate attacking attempt 18...♕h4 is repulsed by 19 ♘f3. The key to many kingside attacks is to include all the available pieces in the attack; every extra attacking unit increases the chances of success.

18 ...   d4!

This preliminary pawn offer allows the c6-bishop to join in the fun.

19 exd4

White may as well take, as 19 ♘c4 loses to 19...♗xh2+! 20 ♔xh2 ♕h4+ 21 ♔g1 ♗xg2 22 ♔xg2 ♕g4+ 23 ♔h1 ♕f3+ 24 ♔g1 ♖d5 25 ♖fd1 ♖h5 followed by mate.

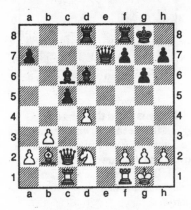

19 ...   ♗xh2+!

The first part of the classic double bishop sacrifice. It was made famous by the game Em. Lasker – Bauer, Amsterdam 1889 and has demolished many a kingside in the years since. Nimzowitsch was of course aware of the idea, but there was little he could do to prevent it.

20 ♔xh2   ♕h4+
21 ♔g1   ♗xg2
22 f3

The only chance, as 22 ♔xg2 ♕g4+ 23 ♔h1 ♖d5 24 ♕xc5 ♕h5+ 25 ♔g1 ♕g5+ 26 ♔h1 ♖xc5 and 22 f4 ♕g3

are hopeless. Now 22...♕g3 fails to 23 ♘e4.

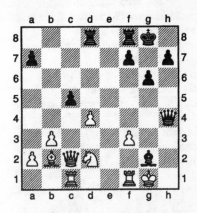

22 ...   ♖fe8!

The last black piece joins the attack. Tarrasch threatens the instantly decisive 23...♖e2.

23 ♘e4

The alternative is 23 ♖fe1, but then Black wins by 23...♖xe1+ 24 ♖xe1 ♕xe1+ 25 ♔xg2 ♕e2+ 26 ♔g3 (26 ♔g1 ♖d5) 26...♖d5 27 f4 ♖h5 28 ♕c1 ♕h2+ 29 ♔f3 ♖h3+ 30 ♔e4 ♕g2+ 31 ♔e5 ♕c6 with unavoidable mate.

23 ...   ♕h1+
24 ♔f2   ♗xf1

Effectively the end of the game, because 25 ♖xf1 loses the queen to 25...♕h2+.

25 d5

Nimzowitsch struggles on, hoping to generate some counterplay along the long diagonal (remember his knight manoeuvre at move 12!).

25 ...   f5

Black could have won more easily by 25...♕g2+ 26 ♔e3 (26 ♔e1 ♕xf3) 26...f5 when the best White can hope for is to reach an ending an exchange and two pawns down. However, the text-move is also sufficient for an easy victory.

    26 ♕c3

26 ♘f6+ ♔f7 27 ♘xe8 ♖xe8 leads to a quick mate.

    26 ...   ♕g2+

    27 ♔e3

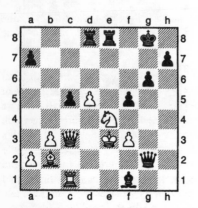

Now White threatens mate himself, but Black strikes first.

    27 ...   ♖xe4+

    28 fxe4   f4+

Black could have mated more quickly by 28...♕g3+ 29 ♔d2 ♕f2+ 30 ♔d1 ♕e2#. Perhaps Tarrasch overlooked it, but in view of the personal animosity between the two players it is also possible that he preferred the humiliating game continuation out of sadism.

    29 ♔xf4   ♖f8+

    30 ♔e5

If 30 ♔e3, then 30...♕f2#.

    30 ...   ♕h2+

    31 ♔e6   ♖e8+

    32 ♔d7   ♗b5# (0-1)

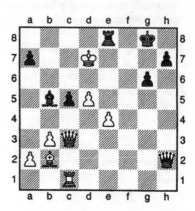

Lessons from this game:

1) In queen's pawn openings, c4 followed by ♘c3 is usually more active than c4 followed by ♘bd2.

2) Bring every piece you can into your attack – invite everyone to the party!

3) The double bishop sacrifice is a standard technique for demolishing the opposing kingside. It usually requires at least a queen and a rook for support.

José Capablanca – Frank Marshall
New York 1918
Ruy Lopez (Spanish), Marshall Attack

The Players

José Raúl Capablanca (1888–1942) was one of the greatest players of all time and held the World Championship from 1921 to 1927. For more details see Game 13.

Frank Marshall (1877–1944) was one the world's leading players in the first quarter of the twentieth century. Born in New York, he learned chess at the age of 10 and soon decided to become a professional player – then a relatively rare breed. By 1904, when he won a tournament ahead of the World Champion Lasker, he was certainly one of the ten leading players in the world. Marshall's aggressive tactical style was well suited to tournament play but it was noticeable that he scored very poorly against the absolutely top players, such as Lasker and Capablanca. Perhaps because of this, he was not regarded as a possible world championship contender. Marshall continued to play successfully until the late 1920s, but even when advancing years started to take their toll he played regularly and enthusiastically. In the entertaining book *Frank J. Marshall's Best Games of Chess* (1942) he wrote "I started when I was ten years old and I am still going strong. In all that time I don't believe a day has gone by that I have not played at least one game of chess – and I still enjoy it as much as ever." The words of a man who loved chess.

Marshall was not a great opening theoretician, but two of his gambit lines are still mainstream openings today. One is the Marshall Gambit in the Semi-Slav (1 d4 d5 2 c4 e6 3 ♘c3 c6 4 e4 dxe4 5 ♘xe4 ♗b4+ 6 ♗d2 ♕xd4) and the other is the famous Marshall Attack, for which see the game below.

The Game

The story behind this game makes it one of the most famous in chess history. Marshall had prepared a surprising new attacking line on the black side of the Ruy Lopez (in fact there had been a few isolated games with it before, but it is not clear whether Marshall knew of these earlier examples). Capablanca, against whom Marshall had a dreadful score, was the ideal opponent on whom to spring the surprise (as an aside, the oft-repeated story that Marshall saved up his idea for eight years seems a distinct exaggeration). Capablanca accepted the sacrifice, but had to weather a vicious attack against an opponent who had prepared the whole line at home. Almost miraculously, Capablanca found his way through the complications and won the game. Despite this inauspicious start, the Marshall Attack is today regarded as one of Black's main defences against the Ruy Lopez.

1	e4	e5
2	♘f3	♘c6
3	♗b5	a6
4	♗a4	♘f6
5	0-0	♗e7
6	♖e1	b5
7	♗b3	0-0
8	c3	d5

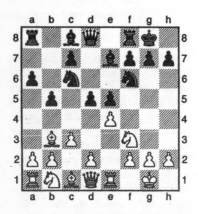

This move introduces the Marshall Attack. Black offers his e-pawn in order to gain time and develop an attack against the white king. I suspect that most players, when faced with a new and dangerous move, would look for a safe route out of trouble, but Capablanca's intuition told him that White's position could be defended and he decided to confront Marshall's idea head-on.

9	exd5	♘xd5
10	♘xe5	♘xe5
11	♖xe5	♘f6

Partly as a result of this game, 11...♘f6 is now regarded as unsound. Later on, Marshall himself introduced the move 11...c6, which is the foundation of the modern method of handling the Marshall Attack.

12   ♖e1

White's move-order is slightly unusual, but it transposes to the more natural sequence 12 d4 ♗d6 13 ♖e1 (today 13 ♖e2 is regarded as equally strong) 13...♘g4 14 h3 ♕h4 15 ♕f3.

12	...	♗d6
13	h3	♘g4!

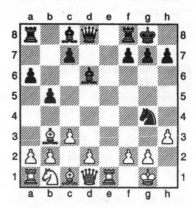

Black's attack gathers momentum. Thanks to Black's gambit, White has no minor pieces defending his kingside; moreover, his entire queenside is still at home. Black's attack certainly looks very dangerous, and White only survives because his queen and light-squared bishop prove very effective.

14   ♕f3!

The piece sacrifice cannot be accepted: 14 hxg4 ♕h4 15 ♕f3 ♗h2+ (not 15...♗xg4 16 g3 ♕h5 17 ♕h1 ♖ae8 18 ♖e3 and White defends) 16 ♔f1 ♗xg4 17 ♕e4 (or 17 ♖e4 ♗f4) 17...♗f4 18 g3 ♕h2 and White will lose his queen under unfavourable conditions. Curiously, in *My Chess Career* (1920), Capablanca gave the alternative 15...♕h2+ 16 ♔f1 ♗xg4 17 ♕xg4 ♕h1+ 18 ♔e2 ♖ae8+ as the winning line for Black, overlooking 19 ♗e6!, which wins for White instead. It is surprisingly common for even very strong players to assess a position accurately, but then give a concrete variation that contains a serious flaw. The reason, of course, is that a player of Capablanca's strength will "know" that taking the knight cannot be good and his mind isn't really on the job when it comes to providing a "proof" for lesser mortals.

14 ...   ♕h4

Black presses on with his attack, ignoring both his knight and the attacked rook on a8.

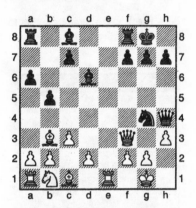

15 d4!

This move provides a clear illustration that development counts for more than material in such tactical situations; White's first priority is to bring his queenside pieces into play. The alternatives are bad:

1) 15 ♖e8 ♗b7 16 ♖xf8+ ♖xf8 17 ♕xg4 ♖e8 18 ♔f1 ♕e7 19 ♕d1 ♕e5 20 g3 ♕e4 with a winning attack.

2) 15 ♖e4 h5 16 d4 ♗b7 17 ♖xg4 hxg4 18 ♕xb7 ♖ae8 19 ♗e3 ♖xe3 also wins for Black.

3) 15 hxg4 ♗h2+! 16 ♔f1 ♗xg4 17 ♕e4 ♗f4! 18 g3 ♕h2 19 ♖e3 (19

♗xf7+ ♔xf7 20 ♕d5+ ♔g6 21 ♖e6+ ♗xe6 22 ♕xe6+ ♔h5 wins for Black – White has only succeeded in exchanging off his few developed pieces) 19...♖ae8 20 ♕d5 ♗xg3! 21 ♖xg3 (21 ♕xf7+ ♔h8!) 21...♗e2+ 22 ♔e1 ♗f3+ and mates.

15 ...   ♘xf2!

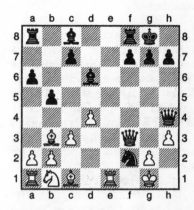

Black now threatens 16...♘xh3+.

Again White cannot take the knight: 16 ♕xf2 ♗h2+ (but not 16...♗g3?? 17 ♕xf7+) 17 ♔f1 ♗g3 18 ♕e2 (now 18 ♕xf7+ ♖xf7+ is check) 18...♗xh3 19 gxh3 ♖ae8 20 ♗e3 ♗xe1 21 ♕xe1 ♕xh3+ 22 ♔f2 ♕h2+ 23 ♔f1 ♕xb2 and wins.

16 ♖e2!

A strong move, but decades of analysis have shown that the most convincing refutation of Black's play is 16 ♗d2! (not 16 ♖e8? ♘xh3+ 17 gxh3 ♗b7 18 ♖xf8+ ♖xf8 with an enormous attack for Black) 16...♗b7 (16...♘g4 17 ♖e8) 17 ♕xb7 ♘d3 18 ♖e2 ♕g3 (18...♖ae8 19 ♕f3 ♖xe2 20 ♕xe2 ♕g3 21 ♕f3!) 19 ♔f1! ♘f4 (19...♕h2 20 g4! ♕xh3+ 21 ♕g2 ♕h4 22 ♗e3 wins) 20 ♖f2! ♕d3+ (20...♕h2 21 ♗xf4 ♗xf4 22 g3 ♕xh3+ 23 ♕g2

♕xg3 24 ♗xf7+ ♔h8 25 ♕xg3 ♗xg3 26 ♖f3 keeps the extra piece) 21 ♔g1 ♘e2+ 22 ♖xe2 ♕xe2 23 ♕f3 ♕xf3 24 gxf3 and White consolidates his extra material.

One can hardly criticize Capablanca's move since after it White retains a clear advantage, no matter how Black continues.

16 ...   ♗g4

The only chance, since 16...♘g4 (16...♘xh3+ 17 gxh3 ♗xh3 18 ♖e4 and 16...♗xh3 17 gxh3 ♘xh3+ 18 ♔f1 are also hopeless for Black) 17 g3 ♕xh3 (17...♗b7 18 ♕xf7+ ♖xf7 19 gxh4 ♗f3 20 ♖c2 ♘f6 21 ♗xf7+ ♔xf7 22 ♖f2 wins) 18 ♕xa8 ♗xg3 19 ♕g2 ♗h2+ 20 ♔f1 leaves Black with totally inadequate compensation for the rook.

17 hxg4

Not 17 ♕xf2 ♗g3 18 hxg4 (18 ♕f1? ♗xe2 19 ♕xe2 ♖ae8 is even lost for White) 18...♕h2+ 19 ♔f1 ♗xf2 20 ♔xf2 ♕h4+ with an unclear position.

17 ...   ♗h2+

After 17...♘xg4, 18 ♗f4 defends.

18 ♔f1

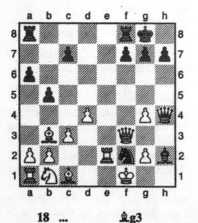

18 ...   ♗g3

The best chance, since 18...♘h1 19 ♗e3 ♘g3+ 20 ♔e1 ♘xe2+ 21 ♔xe2 ♖ae8 22 ♘d2 ♗d6 23 ♖f1 ♕e7 24 ♔d3 and 18...♘xg4 19 ♕h3 ♕f6+ 20 ♔e1 h5 21 ♕xh5 ♗g3+ 22 ♔d2 are relatively simple wins for White.

19 ♖xf2

Capablanca also thought 19 ♔e1 playable, but 19...♘h3+ 20 ♔d1 ♘g1 21 ♕e4 ♘xe2 22 ♕xe2 ♖ae8 23 ♕f3 ♕h1+ 24 ♔c2 ♕e1 25 ♗d2 ♖e2 gives Black more counterplay than in the game.

19 ...   ♕h1+

20 ♔e2

Now Black has to decide whether to take the rook or the bishop.

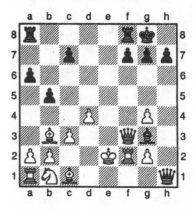

20 ...   ♗xf2

After the game this move was criticized, and 20...♕xc1 was suggested as an improvement. In that case White may try:

1) 21 ♕xg3 ♕xb2+ 22 ♔d3 (22 ♘d2 ♕xa1 23 ♖xf7 ♔h8 favours White but is not completely clear) 22...♕xa1 23 ♔c2 was Golombek's suggestion, but 23...♖ae8 24 ♕xc7 ♖e1 25 ♘d2 ♔h8! 26 ♗xf7 b4 gives Black dangerous counterplay.

2) 21 ♖f1! ♖ae8+ (21...♕xb2+ 22 ♘d2 ♖ae8+ 23 ♔d3 is an easy win) 22 ♔d3 ♖e3+ (the only chance) 23 ♕xe3 ♕xf1+ 24 ♔c2 ♗d6 (or 24...♗f4 25 ♘d2 ♕xa1 26 ♕xf4 with a decisive material advantage) 25 ♗d5, and now White frees himself by ♗f3 followed by ♕e2.

Thus 20...♕xc1 was no better than Marshall's move.

21	♗d2	♗h4
22	♕h3	♖ae8+
23	♔d3	♕f1+
24	♔c2	

These moves were all forced. White has two pieces for a rook, an advantage sufficient to win provided that he can develop his queenside pieces.

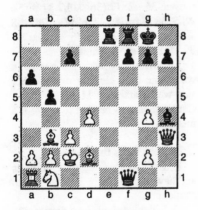

24   ...   ♗f2

Perhaps 24...♗e1 was a better practical chance, as it gives White the opportunity to go wrong by 25 ♘a3 ♖e2 26 ♖d1 ♕f2 27 ♘b1 c5 28 dxc5 ♗xd2 29 ♖xd2 ♖d8, when Black even wins. However, after the correct 25 ♕f3 ♕e2 26 ♕xe2 ♖xe2 27 ♔d3 ♖fe8 28 ♗d5 ♗f2 29 ♗f3, followed by a4, White liberates his rook along the a-file.

25   ♕f3   ♕g1

After 25...♕e2, Capablanca gave the line 26 ♘a3 ♖xd2+ 27 ♔xd2 ♕xa1 28 ♕xf2 ♕xb2+ 29 ♘c2 c5 30 ♗d5, but if Black continues 30...b4 the position appears quite unclear. However, 26 a4! ♕e1 27 axb5 ♖xd2+ 28 ♘xd2 ♕xa1 29 ♕xf2 axb5 30 ♘f3 is much more convincing, as White will soon exert intolerable pressure on f7.

26   ♗d5!

This move is one of those inconspicuous but important moves which make all the difference between a smooth technical victory and allowing the opponent messy counterplay. After 26 a4? ♗e3! 27 ♗xe3 ♖xe3 28 ♘d2 ♕xa1 29 ♕xe3 bxa4 30 ♗d5 a3 we have the mess, whereas after the text-move, which threatens 27 ♕d1, Black's counterplay is far more limited.

26   ...   c5

Black must react quickly, or else White frees himself with ♕d1 followed by ♘a3. Note that 26...♗e3 fails to 27 ♗xe3 ♖xe3 28 ♘d2.

27	dxc5	♗xc5
28	b4	

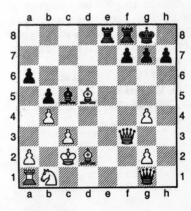

28   ...   ♗d6

28...♗e3 is still refuted by 29 ♗xe3 ♖xe3 30 ♘d2 ♕xa1 31 ♕xe3.

29 a4

White finally brings his a1-rook into play. If Black allows axb5 followed by ♖a6, then White will have no trouble exploiting his material advantage, so Marshall makes a desperate attempt to mix things up.

29 ...   a5

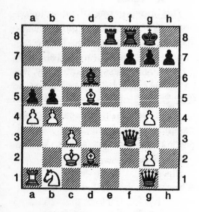

30	**axb5**	**axb4**
31	**♖a6**	**bxc3**
32	**♘xc3**	**♗b4**

White's king has been stripped of its defensive pawn-cover, but Black's pieces are in no position to make use of this. Indeed, there is little he can do to stop the b-pawn.

33 b6   ♗xc3

Or 33...♖e7 34 b7 ♖c7 35 ♖a8 ♕b6 36 ♖xf8+ ♔xf8 37 ♕f5 and wins.

34	**♗xc3**	**h6**
35	**b7**	**♖e3**
36	**♗xf7+**	**1-0**

White can force mate in four more moves: 36...♖xf7 (36...♔h7 37 ♕f5+ ♔h8 38 ♖xh6#) 37 b8♕+ ♔h7 38 ♖xh6+ ♔xh6 (38...gxh6 39 ♕xf7#) 39 ♕h8+ ♔g6 40 ♕h5#.

An amazingly accurate game, in which the only clear error by either side was Marshall's 11...♘f6 – but a Capablanca was needed to prove it a mistake.

Lessons from this game:

1) Believe in your own abilities and have the confidence to face up to challenges.

2) When defending, developing your pieces is usually more important than grabbing material.

3) Capablanca really was a genius!

Game 16
Edwin Adams – Carlos Torre
New Orleans 1920
Philidor Defence

The Players
Edwin Adams (1885–1944) was born in New Orleans. He is best known as having been Torre's trainer, and for this game and its sensational combination.

Carlos Torre Repetto (1905–78) was born in Merida, Yucatan, and is the strongest player ever to have come from Mexico. There are certain parallels between his career and that of Paul Morphy: having proved himself against the best of the North American players, he travelled to Europe and achieved some remarkable successes, most notably his fifth place in the Moscow tournament of 1925, including a brilliant win over Emanuel Lasker. However, in 1926, following severe misfortunes in both his professional and personal life, he suffered a nervous breakdown and never played tournament chess again. He was finally awarded the grandmaster title in 1977, on the basis of his results in the mid-1920s. In his games he used the opening system 1 d4 ♘f6 2 ♘f3 e6 (or 2...g6) 3 ♗g5 to great effect, and as a result this popular opening is nowadays known as the Torre Attack.

The Game
What starts as a normal training game – a young talent against his teacher – takes on immortal status when the teacher finds a spectacular combination. From a fairly quiet opening, Torre fails to resolve the problem of his weak back rank, and it is this that Adams exploits with a series of astonishing queen offers. Torre refuses the offer for as long as he can, but eventually he runs out of options – the queen must be taken and the back rank collapses. A highly appealing feature is that White's back rank is also weak, but this does not provide quite enough counterplay for Black to survive.
There have been questions asked about whether Torre and Adams really played this game, or whether it is a composition. I imagine there will always be doubts about any such brilliant game that was played neither under tournament conditions nor with any eye-witnesses. It would take us too far afield to go into details here, but the evidence for this game being fabricated strikes me as purely circumstantial, and presents no compelling reason to assert that the game was definitely not played. So let's just enjoy the game. If it was composed, then let's enjoy the composition!

1	e4	e5	3	d4	exd4
2	♘f3	d6	4	♕xd4	

This treatment of the Philidor Defence was favoured by Morphy in his time. White centralizes his queen and the f3-knight continues to support a possible e5 push. The drawback is that White will need to surrender the bishop-pair to maintain his queen in the centre.

4	...	♘c6
5	♗b5	♗d7
6	♗xc6	♗xc6
7	♘c3	

7 ♗g5 was Morphy's choice, but is rendered harmless by the precise reply 7...♗e7! 8 ♕xg7 ♗f6, the key point being 9 ♕xh8 ♗xh8 10 ♗xd8 ♗xb2!.

The text-move should not give White much advantage either, but the move has scored well in practice. White has more space and his game is very easy to play.

7	...	♘f6
8	0-0	♗e7
9	♘d5	♗xd5

Torre sees no way to put his bishop-pair to use and gives up one of the clergymen to eliminate White's powerful knight.

10	exd5	0-0
11	♗g5	c6
12	c4	cxd5

The liquidation 12...♘xd5 13 cxd5 ♗xg5 14 ♘xg5 ♕xg5 15 dxc6 bxc6 16 ♕xd6 gives White the more pleasant pawn-structure.

13	cxd5	♖e8

13...h6, partly with hindsight, could be suggested.

14	♖fe1	a5

This is certainly not the most useful move imaginable, and this fact has been seized upon by those who seek to cast doubt on this game's credibility. However, the move is not without

point: one idea is to play ...♖a6 and then either ...♖b6 or ...♕b6, while another is simply to secure c5 as a square for the knight later on. Torre may also have been thinking of the more ambitious plan of ...a4 and ...♖a5, threatening the d5-pawn. It is quite common even for strong players to try slightly unrealistic ideas in a misguided attempt to generate winning chances as Black. The results, as here, tend to be somewhat unfortunate.

Again one might suggest 14...h6, possibly then meeting 15 ♗h4 with 15...♕b6 creating counterplay against the d5-pawn.

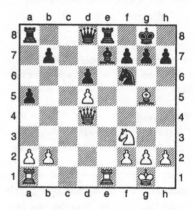

15	♖e2	

Doubling rooks on the e-file is an effective answer to Black's idea. Black now fails to sense the danger and simply develops his a8-rook.

15	...	♖c8?

Instead 15...♘d7 16 ♖ae1 f6 followed by ...♘e5 is not too bad for Black. Nor was it too late to remove the main danger by 15...h6.

Now everything is set for the great combination.

16	♖ae1	

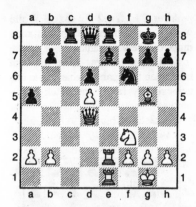

White threatens 17 ♗xf6, when in reply 17...gxf6, horribly exposing the black king, would be compulsory.

16 ...   ♕d7

16...h6 17 ♗xf6 gxf6 18 ♕g4+ ♔h7 gives White a choice of devastating continuations, for instance the simple 19 ♘h4 or 19 ♕h5 ♔g7 20 ♘d4 ♗f8 21 ♘f5+ ♔h8 22 ♘xh6 ♖xe2 23 ♘f5+ ♔g8 24 ♕xe2, but not 19 ♖xe7? ♕xe7! since after 20 ♖xe7?? ♖c1+ it is White who is mated on the back rank.

17 ♗xf6   ♗xf6

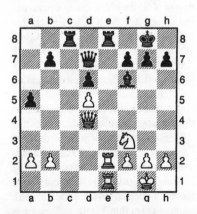

We are now treated to one of the most spectacular sequences in chess

history – six consecutive queen offers. Black can never take the queen due to mate on e8.

18 ♕g4!!   ♕b5

The e8-rook is attacked twice, so Black must keep it defended twice. Note that the whole combination is only possible because the e1-rook is defended by the knight on f3. If the minor pieces were magically to vanish from the board, White's combination would not work due to 18...♖xe2, when 19 ♕xd7? would allow 19...♖xe1#.

19 ♕c4!!

Some writers have claimed that 19 ♕a4?? is bad because of 19...♕xe2. This is true, but I'll leave it for the reader to find a simpler answer to White's blunder!

The text-move puts the queen *en prise* again, but this time to two black pieces. However, since they are both needed to cover e8, the queen is again invulnerable.

19 ...   ♕d7
20 ♕c7!!

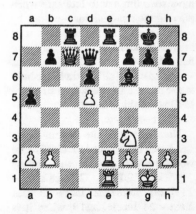

The same theme, but White has now penetrated into the midst of Black's forces. As Nunn puts it, "It is especially attractive that the queen slides cheekily along the black rook's line of attack."

20 ... ♕b5

20...♕d8 would be answered by 21 ♕xc8!.

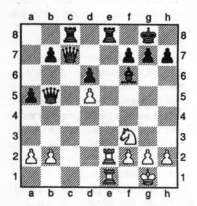

It appears that Black is coping quite well with the multiple queen offers – perhaps all White has done is to find a very striking way to force a repetition of moves? Note that White need only have seen this far to feel safe when playing the combination – a draw by repetition is his "safety net" if it proves impossible to find anything better. However, Black's defence is very fragile, and all it takes is one little tap at its base for the whole structure to come crashing down.

21 a4!!

Note that if White continued instead with the obvious 21 ♕xb7??, he would be very rudely awakened by 21...♕xe2! 22 ♖xe2 (22 ♕xc8 ♕xe1+ 23 ♘xe1 ♖xc8) 22...♖c1+ 23 ♘e1 ♖xe1+ 24 ♖xe1 ♖xe1#, when it is *Black* who wins, by exploiting *White's* weak back rank!

21 ... ♕xa4

After 21...♕xe2 22 ♖xe2 White wins since neither black rook may move off the back rank.

Still, after the text-move it is not immediately apparent what White has achieved by luring the black queen onto a4.

22 ♖e4!!

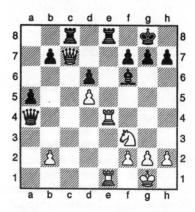

This is the point. White is able to introduce another idea into the position – the rook can control, with gain of tempo, one of the squares on the a4–e8 diagonal. If the black queen can be run out of squares on that line, then this will sever the black king's lifeline. White's main threats are now 23 ♕xc8 ♖xc8 24 ♖xa4 and 23 b3 ♕b5 24 ♕xb7, so Black has no time to breathe.

22 ... ♕b5

No choice. Black must respond to the threats, while the white queen is still invulnerable because of disaster on e8, and 22...♕xe4 23 ♖xe4 again overloads both black rooks.

Now the position is identical to that which occurred after Black's 20th move, except that White's a-pawn has vanished and his rook has been shifted from e2 to e4. In the earlier position,

21 ♕xb7 was a blunder because of 21...♕xe2. Aha!

    23 ♕xb7!!   1-0

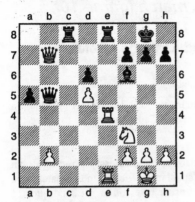

The white queen covers the squares b5, c6 and d7 and, now that the a4-square is also covered and there is no killing counter-sacrifice on e2, this completes the domination of the black queen. It has finally been run out of squares and now it is either mate or loss of a "full" queen. John Nunn wrote that he was particularly impressed by this combination as a young player: "This combination had a profound effect on me. It suddenly seemed that chess was worth all the blunders and lost games, if only one could produce such a beautiful and profound combination."

Lessons from this game:

1) Spare a thought for your back rank. If it is possible to open up some "luft", an escape-hatch for your king, without a serious loss of time or weakening of your king's defences, it is well worth considering.

2) If your opponent's position is only hanging together by a slender thread, use all your ingenuity to find a way to cut this thread.

3) If you want everyone to believe that you really did play a fantastic combination, be sure to play it in a tournament game!

Game 17

Emanuel Lasker – José Capablanca
*World Championship match (game 10),
Havana 1921*
Queen's Gambit Declined, Orthodox Defence

The Players
We have already seen both players in action in this book. For further information
on Lasker, see Game 7, and to find out more about Capablanca, refer to Game 13.

The Game
Here we see Capablanca in tremendous form, remorselessly grinding down
Lasker in a game that effectively sealed Capablanca's victory in the match. In a
fairly normal Queen's Gambit position, Lasker takes on an isolated queen's
pawn. However, he fails to play dynamically enough to make use of his active
pieces, and Capablanca is able to execute some elegant exchanging manoeuvres.
To the untrained eye it looks as if the game is heading for a draw, but Capablanca
secures an edge, which he turns into a serious endgame advantage. He increases
the pressure in all sectors of the board, and eventually, having started off with just
one moderately weak pawn, Lasker is left with nothing but weaknesses. Robbed
of all counterplay, bound and gagged, he can do little but await the execution.
What makes this game so remarkable is that Capablanca was able to render one
of the most resourceful players of all time so completely helpless.

1	d4	d5
2	c4	e6
3	♘c3	♘f6
4	♗g5	♗e7
5	e3	0-0
6	♘f3	♘bd7
7	♕c2!?	

7 ♖c1 leads to quieter play, and is
the traditional main line.

7 ...   **c5**

This is the most logical reply to the
queen move.

8 ♖d1

8 0-0-0 is the most popular move
nowadays, following its successful
use by Kasparov.

8 ...   **♕a5**

9 ♗d3

9 cxd5 is the main alternative.

9 ...   **h6**

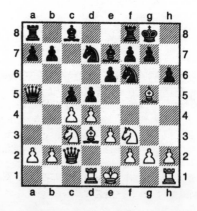

10 ♗h4   cxd4

Another possibility is 10...dxc4 11 ♗xc4 ♘b6 12 ♗e2 ♗d7 13 ♗xf6 (13 0-0 ♖ac8) 13...gxf6.

11 exd4

11 ♘xd4 is met by 11...♘e5.

11 ...   dxc4

12 ♗xc4   ♘b6

13 ♗b3   ♗d7

14 0-0

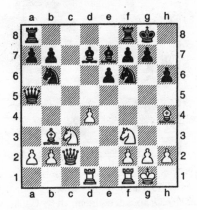

White has the freer game, but also the long-term liability of an isolated queen's pawn. White's plan has to be to attack, since if Black can exchange a few pairs of pieces without making positional concessions, he will obtain a very pleasant game.

14 ...   ♖ac8

Oddly enough, in a later encounter Ståhlberg – Capablanca, Moscow 1935, Capablanca deviated here with 14...♗c6, but got a difficult position after 15 ♘e5 ♗d5 16 ♘xd5 ♘bxd5 17 ♕e2 ♖ad8 18 f4.

15 ♘e5

15 ♕e2 has been claimed as a better try. This is probably true, but not for the reasons hitherto cited. After 15...♘bd5 we have:

1) 16 ♘e5?! allows Black the excellent temporary exchange sacrifice 16...♖xc3! (the line generally given is 16...♗c6 17 ♘g6!? with an edge for White, e.g. 17...fxg6 18 ♕xe6+ ♔h7 19 ♗xf6 ♗xf6 20 ♘xd5 ♗xd5 21 ♕xd5) 17 bxc3 (17 ♘xd7?! ♘xd7 18 ♗xe7 ♖xb3 19 ♗xf8 ♕xa2; 17 ♗xf6? ♗b5) 17...♘xc3, and then:

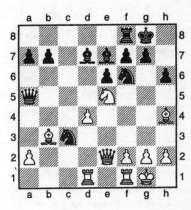

1a) 18 ♕d2 ♘fe4 is obviously good for Black.

1b) 18 ♕e1 ♗b4! (18...♗b5 19 ♘c4 ♕b4 20 ♖c1 ♗xc4 21 ♗xc4 ♕xc4 22 ♕xc3 ♕xc3 23 ♖xc3 ♘e4 24 ♗xe7) 19 ♗xf6 (19 ♘xd7 ♘xd7; 19 ♘c4 ♕h5!) 19...♗b5 20 ♗xg7 (20 ♘d3 gxf6 21 ♘xb4 ♕xb4) 20...♘e2+ 21 ♕xe2 ♗xe2 should be winning for Black.

1c) 18 ♕f3 ♗b5 19 ♕xb7 ♗xf1 20 ♘c6 ♕b5 works well for Black, as 21 ♘xe7+ ♔h8 22 ♕xb5 ♗xb5 makes it hard for White to retrieve the knight from e7.

2) White does better to play 16 ♘xd5 ♘xd5 17 ♗xd5 ♖xh4 18 ♗xb7, though after 18...♖c7 (not 18...♗b5? 19 ♕e1!) 19 ♗a6 ♗f6, White's extra pawn is unlikely to be of much use in

view of Black's bishop-pair and play against d4.

15 ...   **♗b5**

Capablanca begins a fine exchanging manoeuvre.

16 ♖fe1

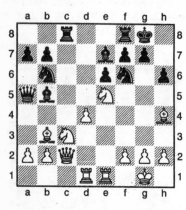

16 ...   **♘bd5!**

Capablanca tended to make awkward defensive tasks look effortless. Here is what happened when a lesser mortal tried a more ambitious move: 16...♗c4 17 ♗xc4 ♘xc4 18 ♗xf6 ♗xf6 19 ♘d7 ♖fd8 20 ♘xf6+ gxf6 21 ♖d3 with a decisive attack for White, Euwe – Landau, Noordwijk 1938.

17 ♗xd5?

With this move White throws away his position's dynamic potential. This was the moment to play for an attack: 17 ♗xf6 ♗xf6 (17...♘xf6? 18 ♘g6! intending ♖xe6 gives White a strong attack) 18 ♗xd5 exd5 19 ♘g4!? (19 ♕f5 ♗c6 20 ♘g4 ♗g5 21 f4 g6 defends) 19...♗g5 20 f4 ♗xf4 21 ♕f5 ♗g5 22 ♕xd5 a6 23 a4 ♖cd8 24 ♕xb7 ♗xa4 25 b4 ♕f5 26 ♘xh6+ ♗xh6 27 ♘xa4 ♕c2 28 ♘c5 ♗e3+ 29 ♔h1 ♗xd4 30 ♕xa6 ♗xc5 with a draw, according to analysis by Breyer. It is

worth continuing this line: 31 ♖c1 ♖fe8 32 ♖f1 ♕e2 33 ♕xe2 ♖xe2 34 bxc5 ♖dd2 35 ♖g1 ♖c2 36 c6 ♖xg2! and the mate threat forces White to allow a perpetual or to lose his c-pawn.

17 ...   **♘xd5**
18 ♗xe7   **♘xe7**
19 ♕b3

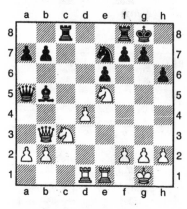

19 ...   **♗c6**

19...♗a6 was condemned by Capablanca on the basis of 20 ♘d7 "followed by ♘c5", but there are two problems with this:

1) 20...♗c4 21 ♕c2 (21 ♕xb7 ♖c7) 21...♖fd8 22 ♘c5 ♖c7, with an advantage for Black, is indicated by Nunn.

2) After 20...♖fd8 21 ♘c5 b6 22 ♘xa6 (22 ♘xe6 ♗c4 23 ♕xc4 ♖xc4 24 ♘xd8 ♕b4 doesn't give White enough) 22...♕xa6 White still cannot remove his liability by 23 d5 since after 23...♖xd5 24 ♘xd5 exd5 25 ♖xd5 ♖xd5 26 ♕xd5 Black has the back-rank trick 26...♕e2!, securing an excellent ending.

20 ♘xc6   **bxc6**
21 ♖e5

21 ♘a4 ♖fd8 22 ♖e5 ♖d5 23 f4 (aiming to play ♘c3, forcing ...♖xe5,

when dxe5 would liquidate White's weakness) 23...♕d8 keeps the pressure on.

21 ...   ♕b6

22 ♕c2   ♖fd8
23 ♘e2

"Probably White's first mistake. He wants to take a good defensive position, but he should instead have counterattacked with ♘a4 and ♖c5." – Capablanca. Of course, the fact that White is on the defensive suggests that he has already made some inaccuracies. The immediate 23 ♖c5? fails to 23...♖xd4!, while 23 ♘a4 ♕b8 24 ♖c5 ♖d6, followed by tripling on the d-file, is comfortable for Black.

23 ...   ♖d5
24 ♖xd5

24 ♖e3 ♘f5 25 ♖b3 ♕d8 26 ♖b4 ♕d7 27 ♖c4 e5! wins the d-pawn, as 28 ♕c3 exd4 29 ♘xd4? ♖d8 picks off a piece.

24 ...   cxd5

Now Black has a clear structural advantage: there is no weakness in Black's position to counterbalance the isolated (and now firmly "blockaded") d4-pawn. "The apparently weak black a-pawn is not actually weak because White has no way to attack it." – Capablanca. Here we see that Capablanca understood one of the axioms of modern chess ("a weakness is not a weakness unless it can be attacked") long before it became a generally accepted piece of chess wisdom.

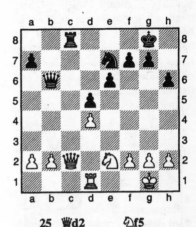

25 ♕d2   ♘f5
26 b3

A rather passive move, preventing ...♖c4. While it also frees the white queen from the burden of defending b2, there isn't a great deal the queen can actually do.

26 ...   h5!

Cementing the knight on f5 by hindering any ideas of g2-g4 and "also to make a demonstration on the kingside, preparatory to further operations on the other side." – Capablanca. This is an instructive remark. Capablanca does not rush to attack on the wing where he expects to make progress in the long term, but instead seeks to make gains on the other side. This is useful in two ways. Firstly, if Black goes straight for queenside play, White may seek counterplay on the kingside, which could prove dangerous if Black has not taken suitable precautions. Secondly, the queenside attack may well not turn out to be decisive in itself. In that event, it might be enough for Black to tie White up on the queenside, and swing his forces over for a kingside attack. This scenario is particularly applicable when, as here, there are major pieces still on the board. The chessboard is not two halves loosely glued together, but rather an organic whole, where events on one side can have implications over the entire battlefield.

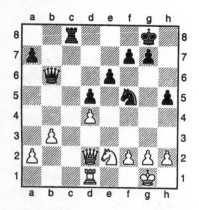

27   h3

Preparing g4, but as just discussed, the new weaknesses created may help Black to play on the kingside later on.

27 ♘g3 does not solve White's problems either: 27...♘xg3 28 hxg3 ♖c6 29 ♕f4 ♖c2 30 ♖d2 ♖c1+ 31 ♔h2 ♕c6 (31...♕b5 is also strong, when in view of the threat of 32...♕f1, White has nothing better than 32 ♖d3 ♕xd3 33 ♕xc1 ♕xd4, with a pawn-down queen ending) 32 g4 hxg4 33 ♕xg4 ♖c3 34 ♕g5 f6 35 ♕f4 ♖e1! 36 f3 g5! 37 ♕b8+ (37 ♕xf6 ♕c7+ 38 f4

♕h7+ mates) 37...♔g7 38 ♕xa7+ ♔g6 wins the rook, because 39 ♖f2 allows the "Monopoly board" mate with 39...♖c8 followed by ...♕h8+ and ...♕h4 or ...♕h1#.

27   ...   h4

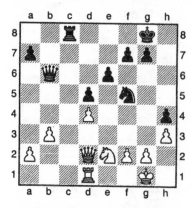

Capablanca perceives that White will eventually need to play g4, and so ensures that this move will cause further weaknesses. Note that Black's h4-pawn can in no way be regarded as a weakness since it is firmly guarded by the knight which is entrenched on f5. The only way to dislodge this knight is by g4, when an *en passant* capture will liquidate any potential weakness in Black's structure.

28   ♕d3   ♖c6
29   ♔f1   g6
30   ♕b1

30 ♕d2 ♕c7 threatens to penetrate on c2.

30   ...   ♕b4!
31   ♔g1   a5!
32   ♕b2   a4

Far from being a liability, Black's a-pawn is a device for breaking up White's queenside pawns. It is striking how White starts off with one major weakness, but because it ties up his all his pieces to defend it, the disease spreads throughout the whole of his position, and what were healthy pawns on both sides of the board are transformed into weaknesses just as severe as that on d4.

33 ♕d2

The best way to put up resistance, since 33 ♖b1 a3 34 ♕a1 ♖c2 is just horrible.

33 ... ♕xd2

34 ♖xd2 axb3

35 axb3

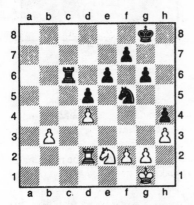

35 ... ♖b6

A delicate touch typical of Capablanca. The rook is heading for the a-file, but on its way stops off on b6 to force the white rook to take a passive role on d3. 35...♖a6 36 ♖b2 would give White more counterplay.

36 ♖d3

36 ♖b2 ♖b4 now wins a pawn.

36 ... ♖a6

Now that the white rook is just staring at two weak pawns.

37 g4

White needs to activate his king. Instead 37 ♖d2 drops a pawn to 37...♖a1+

38 ♔h2 ♖b1, while 37 ♘c3 ♖a1+ 38 ♔h2 ♖c1 allows White to hold things together for the time being with 39 ♘b5, but after 39...♖c2 40 ♔g1 he can undertake little while Black brings up his king.

37 ... hxg3

38 fxg3

38 ♘xg3 ♖a1+ 39 ♔g2 ♘d6 40 ♔f3 ♖b1 41 ♔e3 ♖b2 again leaves White tied up and helpless.

38 ... ♖a2

39 ♘c3 ♖c2

Threatening 40...♘xd4, so White must move his knight.

40 ♘d1

40 ♘a4 was no better according to Capablanca.

40 ... ♘e7

The knight has done a fantastic job on f5, but now sees greener pastures on the queenside. Moreover, White's b-pawn, though weak, is also a passed pawn, requiring constant surveillance.

41 ♘e3 ♖c1+

42 ♔f2 ♘c6

43 ♘d1

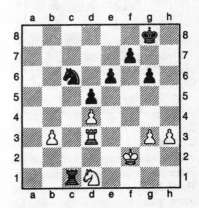

Lasker sets a little trap, of the type he was famous for.

43 ...   ♖b1!

43...♘b4? 44 ♖d2 ♖b1 45 ♘b2 ♖xb2?! (45...♘c6 keeps the pieces on, but meanwhile White has improved his position considerably) 46 ♖xb2 ♘d3+ 47 ♔e2 ♘xb2 48 ♔d2 traps the knight, leading to a drawn king and pawn ending.

44 ♔e2

The b-pawn was indefensible in any case. By surrendering it now Lasker hopes for some activity in return. Since this comes to nothing, he might have done better with 44 ♔e1 ♘a5 45 ♔d2 ♖xb3 (45...♘xb3+?? 46 ♔c2) 46 ♖xb3 ♘xb3+ 47 ♔c3, and though knight and pawn endings with a clear extra pawn are generally winning, there is scope for tricks and there is plenty of work still to be done.

44 ...   ♖xb3

45 ♔e3

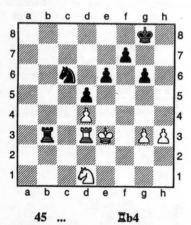

45 ...   ♖b4

It is often tempting to follow the principle "when material ahead, exchange pieces", but there is no need to do so indiscriminately. Here Black's rook is far more active than White's so he refuses the exchange.

46	♘c3	♘e7
47	♘e2	♘f5+
48	♔f2	g5
49	g4	♘d6

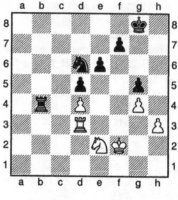

50	♘g1	♘e4+
51	♔f1	♖b1+
52	♔g2	♖b2+
53	♔f1	♖f2+
54	♔e1	♖a2

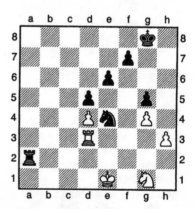

"All these moves have a meaning. The student should study them carefully." – a typical comment from Capablanca. The "meaning" he refers to is to activate the black pieces to the maximum extent relative to their white counterparts before advancing the king for the *coup de grâce*.

55	♔f1	♔g7
56	♖e3	♔g6
57	♖d3	f6
58	♖e3	♔f7
59	♖d3	♔e7
60	♖e3	♔d6
61	♖d3	♖f2+
62	♔e1	♖g2
63	♔f1	♖a2
64	♖e3	e5
65	♖d3	

Or:

1) 65 ♘e2 ♘d2+ 66 ♔f2 e4 67 ♖c3 ♘f3 68 ♔e3 ♘e1 69 ♔f2 ♘g2 leaves White helpless, for example 70 ♔xg2 (70 ♔f1 ♘f4) 70...♖xe2+ 71 ♔f1 ♖d2.

2) 65 ♘f3 ♘d2+ and Black wins following the exchange of knights.

65	...	exd4
66	♖xd4	

66 ♘e2 ♔c5 67 ♘xd4 is no improvement since 67...♔c4 68 ♖d1 ♘c3 wins the knight.

66	...	♔c5
67	♖d1	d4
68	♖c1+	♔d5
	0-1	

"The black pawn will advance and White will have to give up his knight for it. This is the finest win of the match and probably took away from Dr Lasker his last real hope of winning or drawing the match." – Capablanca.

Lessons from this game:

1) If you have an isolated queen's pawn, it is necessary to play energetically and aggressively. Otherwise the pawn is liable to become a static weakness that could easily cost you the game.

2) "A weakness is not a weakness unless it can be attacked."

3) When the opponent's position is paralysed on one wing, see if you can take advantage of this by making additional gains in other parts of the board before undertaking decisive action.

4) In a winning ending don't give the opponent any more counterplay than you have to – and ideally stamp out his activity altogether. Then bring your king up and promote a pawn.

Geza Maróczy – Savielly Tartakower
Teplitz-Schönau 1922
Dutch Defence

The Players

The Hungarian Geza Maróczy (1870–1951) was one of the world's strongest players at the start of the twentieth century. His second place at Nuremberg 1896 signalled his arrival on the world stage, and over the decade 1899–1908 he achieved consistently good results in numerous tournaments. In 1906 he signed an agreement with Lasker to play a world-title match, but owing to a combination of circumstances the match never took place. Although Maróczy achieved some further successes after the title bid collapsed, he started to play less often and more erratically. After the First World War he lived in various countries before returning to Hungary, which he represented in the Olympiads of 1927, 1930 and 1933. Maróczy effectively retired in 1936, although he did participate in one tournament in 1947.

Maróczy had a positional style, and was especially famed for his handling of the endgame. Some of his queen and pawn endings are regarded as classics and are still quoted today as model examples. His name is attached to one important opening system – the Maróczy Bind (pawns on c4 and e4 against the Sicilian).

Savielly Tartakower (1887–1956) was born in Rostov-on-Don, but he left Russia in 1899 and settled in Vienna. He had already become a leading player before the First World War, winning matches against Spielmann and Réti, but it was in the 1920s that his career reached its peak. In 1924 Tartakower moved to Paris and in the subsequent six years won a number of tournaments. While he was undoubtedly one of the top ten players during this period, he was not generally regarded as a potential challenger for the world title. During the 1930s his results slowly tailed off, although he remained a strong and active player until 1950.

Tartakower's playing style is hard to define. He would often experiment in the openings, and he seemed to love paradoxical ideas. His best games are absolutely first-class, but sometimes his love of the eccentric cost him valuable points. Tartakower's writings are highly regarded, although little has been translated into English. His two-volume *My Best Games of Chess* is an excellent games collection, containing not only very fine analysis but also some humour.

The Game

Tartakower adopts the Dutch Defence, an opening quite popular today but which was regarded as offbeat at the time this game was played. In the Dutch, one of Black's main plans is to launch a kingside attack, but to begin with Maróczy does not seem to realize the potential danger. A few casual moves by White allow

Black to make a brilliant rook sacrifice. What makes this sacrifice special is that it is largely positional – Black obtains a few pawns, but his main compensation lies in his unshakeable grip on the position. Maróczy struggles, but the net tightens ever so slowly. Finally, the pressure becomes too much and White's position collapses.

1	d4	e6
2	c4	f5

This is the characteristic move of the Dutch Defence, a combative opening which often leads to double-edged play. One of Black's main ideas is to control e4, and use this square as a jumping-off point for a kingside attack.

3 ♘c3

These days almost all the main lines against the Dutch involve playing an early g3 and ♗g2. The fianchettoed bishop not only exerts pressure on the key squares e4 and d5, but also provides a secure defence against Black's projected kingside attack.

3	...	♘f6
4	a3	

The best moment for playing g3 has already passed. If now 4 g3, then Black has the additional option of playing 4...♗b4, exchanging off the knight which controls e4. The move played rules out ...♗b4, but I think few present-day players would consider this threat so strong as to spend a tempo preventing it.

4	...	♗e7
5	e3	0-0
6	♗d3	

White adopts straightforward, classical development aimed at fighting for the e4-square. If he can eventually play e3-e4 then his play will be justified, but Black should be able to prevent this.

6	...	d5

The simplest antidote to White's plan – Black solidifies his grip on e4.

7 ♘f3

7 ♘ge2 c6 8 f3 intends e4, but after 8...♗d6 White cannot achieve his aim, for example 9 c5 ♗c7 10 e4 fxe4 11 fxe4 ♘g4 and Black wins.

7 ... c6

Black must consolidate his centre before occupying the e4-square. If 7...♘e4, then 8 cxd5 exd5 9 ♕b3 and Black must make the concession of taking on c3 to avoid losing material.

8	0-0	♘e4
9	♕c2	

Although White's pieces are aimed at e4, Black's knight is solidly entrenched. The only way to displace the knight is to arrange f2-f3, but after 9 ♘e5 ♘d7 10 ♘xd7 ♗xd7 11 f3 ♘xc3 12 bxc3 White has no advantage as his queenside pawns are weak.

9 ... ♗d6

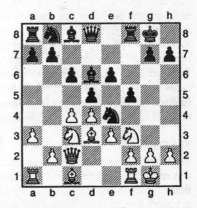

Black's pieces start to line up against White's kingside. Although a serious threat is still some way off, it is not easy for White to counter Black's slow-motion build-up because the c1-bishop is blocked in and White's pieces cannot easily be fed across to the kingside.

10   b3   ♘d7
11   ♗b2

White would like to exchange off his inactive dark-squared bishop, but after 11 a4 ♕e7 Black has prevented ♗a3.

11   ...   ♖f6

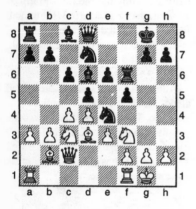

12   ♖fe1?!

White's plan is to play g3 and ♗f1-g2 after all, which bears out the point made in the note to White's third move. However, this plan involves a considerable loss of time, and it would have been better to play 12 ♘e2, which not only switches this knight to the kingside, but also prepares ♘e5 to block off the dangerous d6-bishop.

12   ...   ♖h6

Threatening 13...♗xh2+ 14 ♘xh2 ♕h4.

13   g3   ♕f6

13...♘df6, heading for g4, is another promising plan as 14 ♘e5 ♗xe5 15 dxe5 ♘g4 is very good for Black.

14   ♗f1

White must already take care: 14 ♘d2? ♘xf2! 15 ♔xf2 ♖xh2+ 16 ♔g1 (16 ♔f3 ♕g5 mates next move, while 16 ♔f1 ♕h6 wins for Black) 16...♕g5 with decisive threats.

14   ...   g5
15   ♖ad1?

White simply cannot afford a wasted tempo in view of the gathering storm on the kingside, and this rather pointless move is the final provocation. 15 ♗g2 was compulsory, when the sacrifice 15...g4 16 ♘d2 ♘xf2 17 ♔xf2 ♖xh2 fails to 18 ♘f1. Instead Black should play 15...♕g6, heading for h5; he still has a dangerous attack although White might hold on by continuing ♘d2-f1.

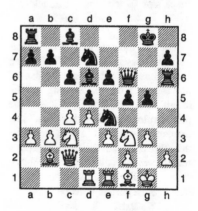

15   ...   g4
16   ♘xe4

After 16 ♘d2 ♘xf2! (16...♖xh2 17 ♔xh2 ♕h4+ 18 ♔g1 ♗xg3 19 fxg3 ♕xg3+ is only a draw) 17 ♔xf2 ♖xh2+ 18 ♔g1 (18 ♗g2 ♗xg3+ 19 ♔g1 f4! is strong as 20 exf4? ♕xd4+ mates)

18...♗xg3 19 ♖e2 ♖xe2 20 ♗xe2 (20 ♘xe2 ♕h4 21 ♘xg3 ♕xg3+ 22 ♔g2 ♕xe3+ 23 ♔h1 ♕h6+ 24 ♔g1 f4 is very good for Black) 20...♕h4 21 ♘f1 ♗f2+ 22 ♔g2 ♘f6 Black is clearly better – he has three pawns for the piece and a continuing attack.

16 ... fxe4

17 ♘d2

17 ♘h4 loses to 17...♖xh4 18 gxh4 ♕xh4.

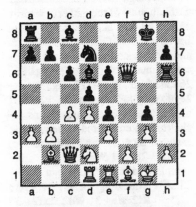

17 ... ♖xh2!!

Black could have continued the attack slowly, for example by 17...♘f8 18 ♗g2 ♗d7 19 ♘f1 ♖g6, intending ...h5 and then ...♘h7-g5-f3, but Tartakower's judgement is excellent. The sacrifice presents White with enormous practical problems, and analysis shows that Black retains the advantage even against perfect defence.

18 ♔xh2 ♕xf2+

19 ♔h1

Or 19 ♗g2 ♕xg3+ (the slower 19...♘f6 is also very strong, but a forced win cannot be bad) 20 ♔g1 ♕h2+ 21 ♔f2 (21 ♔f1 ♘f6 leaves White absolutely helpless, e.g. 22 ♖e2 ♘h5 23 ♖f2 ♗g3 24 ♘b1 ♗d7 25

♖dd2 ♗h4 and wins) 21...♗g3+ 22 ♔f1 b6 23 ♘xe4 (the only chance) 23...♗b7! 24 ♖d2 dxe4 25 ♕xe4 ♖f8+ 26 ♔e2 ♗xe1 27 ♔xe1 ♕g1+ 28 ♔e2 ♖f2+ 29 ♔d3 ♕b1+ 30 ♔c3 ♕e1 31 ♕xe6+ (31 ♔b4 c5+) 31...♔h8 32 ♕e8+ (had Black played 23...♗a6? instead of 23...♗b7 earlier in this sequence, White would gain the advantage here by 32 ♔b4!) 32...♘f8 33 ♕e5+ ♔g8 34 ♕g5+ ♘g6 35 ♕d8+ ♔g7 36 ♕c7+ ♔h6 37 ♕h2+ ♔g5 and wins.

19 ... ♘f6

Not 19...♕xg3 20 ♘b1, when the white queen can switch to the kingside. The knight must be kept pinned for as long as possible.

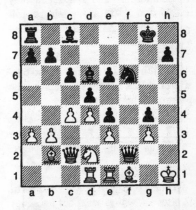

20 ♖e2

Thus White unpins the knight, but on e2 the rook obstructs the queen's path along the second rank. The alternative was 20 ♖c1 (20 ♗g2 loses straight away, to 20...♘h5), but after 20...♘h5 21 ♘xe4 ♕xc2 22 ♘f6+ (22 ♖xc2 dxe4 23 c5 ♗c7 24 ♔g1 ♘xg3 25 ♗c4 ♗d7 26 ♖f2 ♖f8 27 ♖xf8+ ♔xf8 is even worse) 22...♘xf6 23 ♖xc2 ♗xg3 24 ♖ee2 h5 Black has a clear advantage. The two connected passed pawns offer very good compensation for the exchange, especially as Black retains a grip on the position.

20 ...   ♕xg3

21 ♘b1

A natural move allowing the queen to join the defence. The alternative was 21 ♕c3 (defending e3 to prepare ♖g2; the immediate 21 ♖g2 ♕h3+ 22 ♔g1 ♕xe3+ is bad) 21...♘h5 22 ♖g2 ♕h4+ 23 ♔g1 ♘g3 24 ♖h2 g5 25 ♖f2 ♘f5 with a position of a type we will meet several times. Black still has only three pawns for the rook, but White's position is hopeless. The knight on f5 is very well-placed, attacking e3 and preparing for ...♘h4-f3+. White has no counterplay and Black can play ...♗d7 and ...♖f8 at his leisure, followed by pushing the h-pawn or ...♘h4 as appropriate.

21 ...   ♘h5

21...♕h4+ 22 ♖h2 ♕g5 is also possible, but Black prefers to improve the position of his knight.

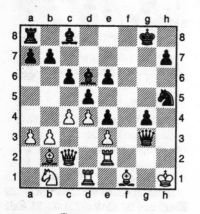

22 ♕d2

After 22 ♗c1 ♗d7 23 ♖g2 ♕h4+ 24 ♔g1 ♘g3 25 ♖h2 ♕g5, followed

by ...♘f5, Black again sets up his typical winning position.

22 ...   ♗d7

Activating the rook. It is amazing how leisurely Black can afford to be when building up his attack; the reason is that the closed pawn structure affords White no prospects of active play.

23 ♖f2

After 23 ♕e1 ♕f3+ (23...♖f8 24 ♘d2) 24 ♖g2 (24 ♔g1 ♘g3 25 ♖g2 ♘xf1 26 ♕xf1 ♕xe3+ 27 ♕f2 ♕h3 28 c5 ♖f8 29 ♕e2 ♗g3 is very good for Black, e.g. 30 ♖f1 ♖f5! 31 ♖xf5 exf5 and the four connected passed pawns are too much) 24...♕h3+ 25 ♔g1 ♖f8 26 ♘d2 ♗g3 27 ♕e2 (27 ♖xg3 ♕xg3+ 28 ♕xg3 ♘xg3 29 ♗c3 ♘f5 30 ♖e1 h5 favours Black; the three pawns, including two connected passed pawns, are worth more than an inactive bishop) 27...♖f3 28 ♖c1 White is reduced to complete passivity. Black can win by 28...♘g7 (heading for f5) 29 ♘xf3 exf3 30 ♖f2 ♕h4 31 ♕d2 ♗xf2+ 32 ♕xf2 g3 33 ♕c2 f2+ 34 ♔g2 e5 and the activation of the light-squared bishop finishes White.

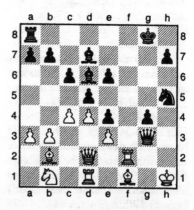

23 ...   ♛h4+
24 ♔g1?!

White's best chance is to return some material immediately by 24 ♖h2 ♗xh2 25 ♕xh2. Black can retain the advantage by either 25...♘g3+ 26 ♔g2 ♕xh2+ 27 ♔xh2 ♘f5 28 ♖e1 h5 or 25...♕g5 26 ♗e2 ♘g7 27 ♖g1 h5, followed by 28...♘f5, but White is still fighting.

24 ...   ♗g3?!

After 24...♘g3! 25 ♖h2 ♕g5 26 ♖f2 ♘f5 White's position is hopeless. He has no counterplay at all and Black can continue with 27...♘h4 followed by ...♘f3+, or even the gradual advance of the h-pawn.

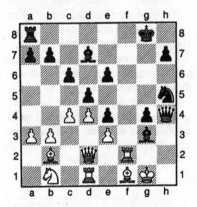

25 ♗c3?!

White gives up the exchange in an unfavourable way. 25 ♖g2 ♖f8 26 ♕e2 ♖f3 is also bad, for example 27 ♗c3 ♗d6 28 ♗e1 g3 29 ♘d2 ♕g4 30 ♖c1 ♘g7 31 ♕d1 ♘f5 32 ♗e2 ♘h4 33 ♘xf3 exf3 34 ♗xf3 ♘xf3+ 35 ♔f1 h5 and the h-pawn decides. Therefore the best chance is 25 ♖h2! ♗xh2+ 26 ♕xh2 ♕g5, with play similar to that after 24 ♖h2 – Black remains clearly better but White is not dead.

25 ...   ♗xf2+

In this position the elimination of Black's dark-squared bishop doesn't help White much.

26 ♕xf2   g3
27 ♕g2   ♖f8

Black's threat is 28...♖f2 29 ♕h1 ♖h2.

28 ♗e1

There is no defence:

1) 28 ♕h1 ♕g5 29 ♖e1 ♖f2 30 ♗g2 ♘g7, followed by ...♘f5-h4, and Black wins.

2) 28 ♖d2 ♖f3 29 ♖e2 ♕g5 30 ♗e1 h6 (30...♖xe3 31 ♗d2 is bad as the black queen is unguarded; after the text-move, however, 31...♖xe3 is a threat) 31 ♗d2 (or 31 ♕h1 e5 32 dxe5 ♗g4 33 ♗h3 ♖f2 34 ♗xf2 gxf2+ 35 ♔xf2 ♕f5+ 36 ♔g1 ♗xh3 with a winning position for Black) 31...♘f6 32 ♘c3 ♘g4 33 ♘d1 ♘h2 34 ♖e1 ♖f8 and White cannot prevent 35...♘f3+.

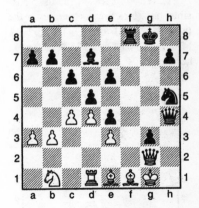

28 ...   ♖xf1+

Black must avoid 28...♕h2+ 29 ♕xh2 gxh2+ 30 ♔xh2 ♖xf1 31 ♘d2 ♖f8 32 ♗h4 and the win is no longer simple, but 28...e5! is even more clear-cut than the text – after 29 ♖d2

♕g5 30 ♖e2 ♗g4 White's position collapses immediately.

29 ♔xf1   e5

30 ♔g1

Black also wins after 30 ♗xg3 ♘xg3+ 31 ♔f2 ♗g4 32 ♖e1 ♘f5+ 33 ♔f1 ♔h8 or 30 ♔e2 ♗g4+ 31 ♔d2 ♕h2 32 ♕xh2 gxh2.

30 ...   ♗g4

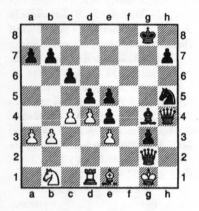

31 ♗xg3

31 ♖d2 ♗f3 32 ♗xg3 ♘xg3 33 ♕h2 ♕g5 34 ♔f2 ♘f5 35 ♕g1 ♗g4 is hopeless.

31 ...   ♘xg3

32 ♖e1   ♘f5

33 ♕f2

After 33 ♔f1 ♔h8 Black wins the white queen.

33 ...   ♕g5

34 dxe5

Or 34 ♔f1 exd4 35 exd4 ♗h3+ 36 ♔e2 ♕g4+ 37 ♔d2 e3+ 38 ♖xe3 ♕xd4+ 39 ♔e2 ♗g4+ with a total catastrophe.

34 ...   ♗f3+

35 ♔f1   ♘g3+

0-1

Since 36 ♔g1 ♘h1+ leads to a quick mate.

Lessons from this game:

1) If your opponent is building up an attack, it is essential to take defensive measures in good time.

2) Sacrifices are not necessarily short-term investments; sometimes they only pay off after 15 or 20 moves.

3) If the defender has no active plan, then the attacker can afford to take his time and bring all his reserves into play.

Game 19

Friedrich Sämisch – Aron Nimzowitsch

Copenhagen 1923
Queen's Indian Defence

The Players

Friedrich Sämisch (1896–1975) was a German bookbinder before devoting himself to chess full-time. His most notable successes as a player were his match victory over Richard Réti and his third place at the strong Baden-Baden event in 1925, behind Alekhine and Rubinstein. In his later years Sämisch proved himself to be an excellent lightning chess player, yet paradoxically he was also terrible in time-trouble. He lost more games on time than any of his contemporaries. In fact, in one tournament he lost all thirteen games on time!

By 1923 Aron Nimzowitsch (see Game 14) had left Latvia and had moved to Copenhagen, where he spent the rest of his life. Nimzowitsch was also beginning to play the best chess of his career and the 1920s were full of tournament successes for him. In this particular event Nimzowitsch remained unbeaten, scoring six wins and four draws.

The Game

Nimzowitsch has a slight disadvantage from the opening, but Sämisch releases the tension too early, allowing his opponent to equalize. Then, as Sämisch's play becomes planless, Nimzowitsch embarks on a space-gaining operation on the kingside. At the critical moment, he offers a very deep piece sacrifice. His return is not immediately obvious, but slowly Sämisch realizes that despite having more pieces, he is fast running out of moves...

Emanuel Lasker hailed this as the "Immortal Zugzwang Game".

1	d4	♘f6
2	c4	e6
3	♘f3	

Avoiding Nimzowitsch's favourite defence, the Nimzo-Indian (see Game 25). Nevertheless, after 3 ♘f3 Black is still able to adopt the strategy of controlling the centre with pieces rather than pawns.

3	...	b6

3...b6 introduces the Queen's Indian Defence, which was another favourite of the Hypermodern school.

The black bishop is fianchettoed on b7, from where it will exert useful pressure on the important e4-square. The Queen's Indian reached the height of its popularity in the 1980s, when it became extremely commonplace in grandmaster tournaments, if only because White was tending to avoid the Nimzo-Indian. It has a reputation for extreme solidity, with some games ending in colourless draws. This fact has put off some of today's more dynamic players, and likewise, it has never enjoyed the same popularity at club level. However, the Queen's Indian remains a very well respected opening.

4 g3   ♗b7

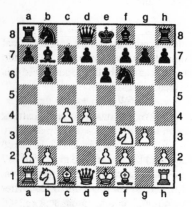

5 ♗g2   ♗e7
6 ♘c3   0-0
7 0-0   d5

Black reverts to the classical method of placing his pawns in the centre. The main line now runs 7...♘e4!, which fits in better with the concept of piece control.

8 ♘e5   c6

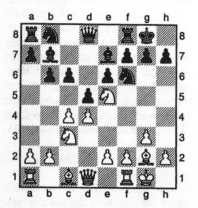

9 cxd5?!

This move lets Black get away with his slightly unusual seventh move. It seems rather unnatural to release the tension in the centre at such an early stage, especially as the c4-pawn is protected by the knight on e5. Instead of 9 cxd5, the move 9 e4! is generally regarded as the best method of increasing the pressure. Either capture is a concession, but otherwise Black's lack of space leaves him with some problems completing his development:

1) 9...dxc4 10 ♘xc4 leaves White with an impressive centre with two pawns abreast. Black can attempt to disrupt White's harmony by 10...♗a6, as after 11 b3 Black wins a pawn with 11...b5!? 12 ♘e3 b4 13 ♘e2 ♗xe2 14 ♕xe2 ♕xd4. However, after 15 ♗b2 White's two bishops and possibility of a kingside attack promise a good deal of compensation for the pawn.

2) After 9...dxe4 10 ♘xe4 ♘xe4 11 ♗xe4 White again enjoys an advantage as Black has problems developing his queenside. Note that 11...f6 can be met by the surprising 12 ♘g6!, when capturing the knight is fatal. After 12...hxg6 13 ♗xg6 ♗b4 14 ♕h5 and Black has to give up a rook to avoid an immediate checkmate.

3) 9...♘bd7? falls into another trap: 10 ♘xc6! ♗xc6 11 exd5 exd5 12 cxd5 ♗b7 13 d6 ♗xg2 14 dxe7 ♕xe7 15 ♔xg2 left White a pawn up in Kavalek – Raičević, Amsterdam IBM 1975.

9 ...   cxd5
10 ♗f4   a6

Despite his shattering loss in this game, Sämisch chose to repeat the variation in a game played two years later. Sämisch – Haida, Marienbad 1925

continued instead 10...♘bd7 11 ♖c1
♖c8 12 ♕b3 ♘xe5 13 ♗xe5 ♕d7 14
a3 ♗a6 15 ♖fe1 ♗c4 with an equal
position.

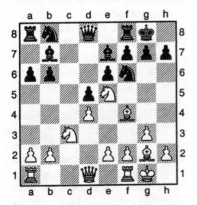

With 10...a6 Black starts an ambitious plan of expanding on the queenside. In particular, after ...b5, Black
hopes to secure the c4-square, which
could prove to be a excellent outpost
for the b8-knight.

11 ♖c1

The main reason why White suffers
so badly in this game is his failure to
find a suitable plan of action, or to put
it less kindly, any plan at all! To be
fair, even without the pressure of a
tournament situation, it is difficult to
suggest a really constructive idea. The
only pawn break White has is e2-e4.
Unfortunately this advance requires
some preparation and even then it
hardly improves White's position. Playing e4 will automatically lead to a
mass exchange of pawns and pieces,
saddling White with an isolated d-
pawn in a simplified position. The
weakness of the isolated pawn becomes more prominent as pieces are
exchanged. Here is a sample variation:

11 ♖e1 b5 12 a3 ♘bd7 13 e4 dxe4 14
♘xe4 ♘xe4 15 ♗xe4 ♗xe4 16 ♖xe4
♖c8 17 ♘xd7 ♕xd7 18 ♗e5 ♖fd8,
and the d4-pawn has become a real liability, especially as Black can always
play a timely ...f6.

11 ...   b5
12 ♕b3   ♘c6

This presents White with a tactical
opportunity, which probably should
have been taken. Black can avoid this
with 12...♘bd7.

13 ♘xc6

13 ♘xd5!?, uncovering an attack
on the c6-knight, is another possibility
for White. After 13...♘xd5 14 ♘xc6
♗xc6 15 ♖xc6 ♘xf4 16 gxf4 ♕xd4 17
e3, White's pieces are more active.
13...♘xd4 is stronger for Black. After
14 ♘xe7+ ♕xe7 15 ♕e3 ♗xg2 16
♔xg2 ♕b7+ 17 f3 ♘f5 18 ♕f2 we
reach a roughly level position.

13 ...   ♗xc6
14 h3?

The first move that can really be
criticized, and by now it has become
obvious that White is drifting, completely without a plan. There can be no
other explanation for this move. In fact
here White does seem to have a reasonable continuation, which includes
relocating his knight, which is quite
ineffective on c3, to a much stronger
post. One possible line would be 14
♗g5! ♕d7 (or 14...♘d7 15 ♗xe7 ♕xe7
16 e3 ♖fc8 17 ♘e2 ♘b6 18 ♘f4 ♘c4
19 ♕c2 ♗b7 20 ♕e2 and the knight
heads to c5 via d3) 15 e3 h6 16 ♗xf6
♗xf6! 17 ♘e2, followed by ♘f4-d3-
c5.

14 ...   ♕d7
15 ♔h2

Another move from the same stock
as 14 h3. Again 15 ♗g5 is the right

idea. Now Sämisch doesn't get another chance.

15 ...   ♘h5

Nimzowitsch decides to expand on the kingside with ...f5, which will give him more space. The only minus side of this operation is that the e5-square will become an possible outpost for a white piece. In this particular position, however, White's army is in no position to exploit such a weakness. Nimzowitsch also mentions an alternative method for Black, starting with 15...♛b7 and intending ...♘d7-b6-c4.

16 ♗d2   f5

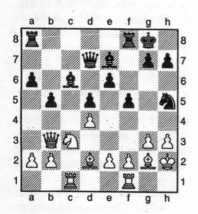

Black now has a major clamp on the position, with more space on both the kingside and queenside. Of course White would love to shift his knight one square to the right. On d3 it would patrol the important squares c5, e5 and f4, whereas on c3 it looks rather redundant. Notice also that the move h3 has proved to be worse than merely a waste of time. Black's attack on the kingside is all the more powerful, as White has already weakened himself on this side.

17 ♕d1

Preparing the sneaky e2-e4, which would uncover an attack on the h5-knight. Nimzowitsch, however, saw a brilliant concept, and so actually encouraged Sämisch to go through with the "cheap trick".

17	...	b4
18	♘b1	♗b5
19	♖g1	♗d6!
20	e4	

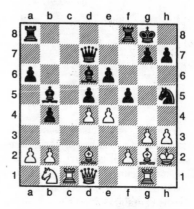

20 ...   fxe4!

Virtually forced, as 20...♘f6 allows the fork 21 e5, while 20...g6 loses a pawn to 21 exd5. Even so, this piece sacrifice all fits in with Black's grand scheme.

21 ♕xh5   ♖xf2

For the investment of the knight Black has obtained an assortment of goodies, including two pawns, occupation of the seventh rank, and the incarceration of the white queenside. Even so, it's a bit difficult at this stage to believe that White can't do anything. But the fact is that he is totally lost!

22	♕g5	♖af8
23	♔h1	♖8f5
24	♕e3	♗d3

Threatening to trap the queen with ...⬛e2, although in fact this could have been achieved immediately with 24...⬛e2 25 ♛b3 ♝a4 26 ♝xe4. Then again, that line would have deprived the chess world of quite a beautiful finish.

25 ⬛ce1   h6!!

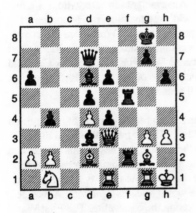

0-1

Perhaps it's Nimzowitsch's entire concept rather than this single, quiet but deadly move which deserves the two exclamation marks. 25...h6 simply underlines the helplessness of White's plight. White is in fact in zugzwang here, i.e. every possible move only leads to a deterioration of his position. In fact White would like to pass, but

the rules state that players must move alternately! Let's just go through a few legal white moves:

1) 26 ♝c1 loses a piece after 26...♝xb1.

2) 26 ⬛c1 loses White's queen to 26...⬛e2.

3) 26 ♚h2 allows 26...⬛5f3, winning the queen.

4) 26 g4 allows 26...⬛5f3 27 ♝xf3 ⬛h2#.

The queen, the g2-bishop, the g1-rook and the d2-bishop all cannot move without losing material. This leaves White with just a few spare pawn moves before self-destruction sets in. After 26 a3 a5! 27 axb4 axb4 28 b3 ♚h8! 29 h4 ♚g8 White must finally lose material.

Lessons from this game:

1) When you have control of the centre, it is usually a good policy to maintain or increase the tension, rather than release it (as Sämisch did with 9 cxd5).

2) "A bad plan is better than no plan at all."

3) Zugzwang is normally seen more in the endgame rather than the middlegame, but when it does arise in a complex position, it is an extremely powerful weapon.

Ernst Grünfeld – Alexander Alekhine
Karlsbad 1923
Queen's Gambit Declined, Orthodox Defence

The Players

Ernst Grünfeld (1893–1962) was a strong Austrian grandmaster who, for a few years in the 1920s, was probably in the world's top ten players. He continued to play in the 1930s, but with less success, and the Second World War effectively ended his career, although he did play in a couple of small events in Vienna just after the war. Today he is chiefly remembered for having invented the Grünfeld Defence (1 d4 ♘f6 2 c4 g6 3 ♘c3 d5) which is one of those workhorse openings played day in, day out by grandmasters all round the world.

Alexander Alekhine (1892–1946) was one of the greatest players of all time and held the World Championship from 1927 to 1935 and from 1937 until his death in 1946. Born into the Russian aristocracy, he was taught chess by his mother and soon displayed a remarkable talent for the game. After some successes in relatively minor tournaments, he was invited to play in the famous 1914 St Petersburg tournament, which included all the world's leading players. Alekhine's third place indicated that he had arrived among the chess elite. The First World War and the Revolution interrupted Alekhine's career, but after he left Russia in 1920 he started a run of impressive tournament successes, which led to a challenge for the World Championship in 1927. Few expected the almost unbeatable Capablanca to lose, but Alekhine's preparation was better and, aided by his ferocious will-power, Alekhine gained the title after a marathon battle of 34 games. Unlike many world champions, actually gaining the title did not undermine his determination and over the next few years Alekhine dominated the chess world. He successfully defended his title twice against Bogoljubow, but Alekhine seemed reluctant to face his most dangerous challengers and never allowed Capablanca a return match. A fondness for alcohol cost Alekhine the title in 1935 when he faced the Dutchman Euwe. The gentlemanly Euwe offered Alekhine a return match and, after giving up the bottle, Alekhine regained his title in 1937. Alekhine's results just before the Second World War were definitely less impressive than formerly, and had a projected match with Botvinnik taken place he might well have lost the title. The war intervened, and during the war years Alekhine played in a number of (not very strong) tournaments in German-occupied territory. After the war, negotiations for a match with Botvinnik resumed and terms were agreed, but Alekhine died of a heart attack before the match could take place.

Alekhine had a preference for attacking play and tactics, but he could handle all types of position well. The games produced while he was at his peak are models of attacking play; he had the rare ability to confront his opponents with all sorts of problems without risking his own position.

The Game

After some subtle opening play, Alekhine manages not only to nullify White's advantage of the first move but even to gain a slight positional advantage. Many players would have tried to increase this advantage by slow positional manoeuvring, but Alekhine's methods are far more direct. A series of threats keeps Grünfeld off-balance, until finally Alekhine strikes with a deadly combination.

1	d4	♘f6
2	c4	e6
3	♘f3	d5
4	♘c3	♗e7
5	♗g5	♘bd7
6	e3	0-0
7	♖c1	c6

Although the Queen's Gambit Declined remains a popular opening, these days attention has shifted to other variations. White often plays the Exchange Variation (cxd5 at some stage), while Black tends to prefer the Tartakower Variation (5...0-0 6 e3 h6 7 ♗h4 b6).

8 ♕c2

8 ♗d3 is another important line. The text-move delays developing the f1-bishop, hoping to win the battle for tempo (see Games 11 and 14, Rotlewi – Rubinstein and Nimzowitsch – Tarrasch respectively, for similar situations) – Black may play ...dxc4 and White doesn't want to move his bishop twice.

| 8 | ... | a6 |
| 9 | a3 | |

This line was played several times in the 1920s but is now considered harmless. 9 cxd5 exd5 10 ♗d3 is almost the only continuation played today. Both 9 a3 and 9 cxd5 are motivated by the above-mentioned battle for tempo; 9 a3 is a slightly useful move which just waits for ...dxc4, while 9 cxd5 rules out the possibility of ...dxc4 before developing the bishop.

9 ... **h6**

Inserting ...h6 is useful for Black if he intends ...dxc4 followed by a queenside pawn advance, because White will sooner or later line up against h7 and Black benefits from having removed the vulnerable pawn from the line of fire. On the other hand, if Black intends ...dxc4 followed by ...♘d5, then he should not insert ...h6, because it gives White the chance to avoid a bishop exchange by ♗g3.

10 ♗h4

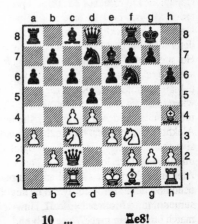

10 ... **♖e8!**

The battle for tempo continues. This is a useful move since after ♗xc4 followed by ♗a2 and ♗b1, the white queen's possible arrival on h7 will not be mate. In Grünfeld – Maróczy, Vienna 1922 Black did not take this precaution and fell into an poor position after 10...dxc4 11 ♗xc4 b5 (if 11...♘d5, then 12 ♗g3) 12 ♗a2 ♗b7 13 ♗b1 ♖e8 14 ♘e5 ♘f8 15 0-0.

11 ♗d3

White's concedes the battle for tempo. Alekhine himself suggested 11 h3, but one gains the impression that the moves White is playing to delay touching his f1-bishop are becoming steadily more pointless. 11 ♗g3 is another idea, but after 11...dxc4 12 ♗xc4 b5 13 ♗a2 c5 14 dxc5 ♘xc5 15 ♖d1 ♕b6 16 b4 ♘cd7 17 ♗b1 ♘f8 the position is roughly equal.

11	...		dxc4
12	♗xc4		b5
13	♗a2		c5

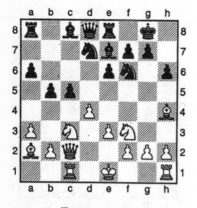

14 ♖d1?!

White is aiming to set up a mating attack by ♗b1 followed by the elimination of the d7-knight by ♖xd7. However, if this fails then White will end up with the wrong rook on d1. The alternatives are:

1) 14 0-0 cxd4 (Alekhine also suggested 14...♕b6) 15 exd4 ♗b7 16 ♘e5 (16 ♖fd1 ♕b6 17 ♘e5 was played in Grünfeld – Teichmann, Karlsbad 1923 and now 17...♘xe5 18 dxe5 ♕c6 19 f3 ♕c5+ 20 ♔h1 ♕xe5 would have won a pawn) 16...♘f8 (16...♘b6 is also possible) 17 ♖fd1 ♖c8 18 ♕e2 ♕b6 19 f3 ♖ed8 with equality, Réti – Teichmann, Karlsbad 1923.

2) 14 dxc5 ♘xc5 15 ♗b1 (15 0-0 ♕d3) 15...♗b7 16 0-0 (Alekhine gave the line 16 ♗xf6 ♗xf6 17 ♕h7+ ♔f8 18 ♘xb5 axb5 19 ♖xc5 ♗xb2 and Black is better) 16...♖c8 17 ♖fd1 ♘cd7 (not 17...♕b6? 18 ♗xf6 ♗xf6 19 ♕h7+ ♔f8 20 b4! and White is winning) 18 ♗xf6 ♗xf6 19 ♕h7+ ♔f8 20 ♘d4 ♗e7 and the position is roughly level, Heinonen – Vuorinen, correspondence game 1987.

Line "2" demonstrates the value of 10...♖e8! – Black can often afford to allow the queen to reach h7.

14	...		cxd4
15	♘xd4		

15 exd4 ♗b7 leads to an inferior type of isolated d-pawn position in which White has lost time.

15	...		♕b6

16 ♗b1   ♗b7!

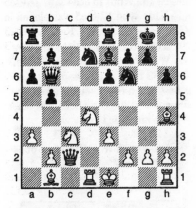

This is the critical moment. Can White make use of his pressure against Black's kingside?

17 0-0

White admits that his plan has led to nothing. Perhaps he had intended 17 ♘dxb5, when 17...axb5 18 ♖xd7 g5 (the only move) 19 ♖xe7 ♖xe7 20 ♗g3 gives White good play for the sacrificed exchange, e.g. 20...♗xg2 21 ♗e5! ♗xh1 22 ♗xf6 ♔f8 23 ♕h7 ♔e8 24 ♗g6! with a very strong attack. However, Alekhine had prepared the surprising refutation 17...♕c6! 18 ♘d4 ♕xg2 and it is White's kingside that is broken up.

17 ...   ♖ac8

The pawn structure is almost symmetrical, but Black has the advantage. Thanks to White's ♖c1-d1, Black is ahead in development and White will have to waste more time finding a comfortable spot for his queen.

18 ♕d2?!

A further inaccuracy. The obvious square for the queen is e2 and it may be that Grünfeld rejected 18 ♕e2 because of 18...♗xa3, but after 19 ♘cxb5

♗b4 20 ♘a3 White has good chances of equalizing.

18 ...   ♘e5

The knight is heading for c4 when, thanks to White's previous move, Black will gain another tempo.

19 ♗xf6

White is aiming to exchange as many pieces as possible; by eliminating this knight he clears the way for a later ♗e4.

19 ...   ♗xf6

20 ♕c2

20 ♗e4 is not possible straight away because 20...♖xc3 21 ♗xb7 ♖d3 wins material. White must put his queen on e2 before ♗e4 is viable, but first of all he forces a weakening of Black's kingside.

20 ...   g6

Now there is no need for Black to allow ♕h7+.

21 ♕e2   ♘c4

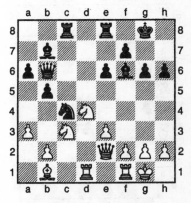

22 ♗e4   ♗g7

The point of forcing ...g6 is that 22...♘xa3 now fails to 23 ♕f3 ♗xe4 24 ♘xe4 ♗xd4 25 ♖xd4 and White wins material.

23 ♗xb7   ♕xb7

24 **♖c1**

White has defended against the immediate threats, but Black has a long-term advantage; his bishop is more active than either of White's knights and his pieces combine to exert unpleasant pressure on White's queenside pawns. However, Black should not rush to win a pawn, e.g. 24...♖ed8 25 ♖fd1 ♛b6 26 ♘e4 (not 26 ♘f3? ♘xb2) 26...♗xd4 (26...f5 27 ♘c3) 27 exd4 ♖xd4 28 b3 ♖xd1+ 29 ♖xd1 ♘xa3 30 ♛b2! gives White a dangerous counterattack.

Alekhine now increases his advantage in typically dynamic style.

24 ...　　　　e5
25 ♘b3　　　e4

Threatening 26...♘xa3. White can meet this threat but the advance of the e-pawn has secured another advantage for Black – a new outpost for his knight at d3.

26 ♘d4　　　♖ed8
27 ♖fd1　　　♘e5

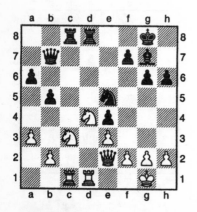

28 ♘a2?!

Moving the knight offside is the final error. 28 ♖c2 is also bad in view of 28...♘d3 29 ♘xe4 ♛xe4 30 ♖xc8 ♖xc8 31 ♖xd3 ♖c1+ 32 ♖d1 ♛b1 33 ♖f1 ♖xf1+ 34 ♛xf1 ♛xb2 with a winning ending for Black. The correct plan was to eliminate the cramping e4-pawn by 28 f3 exf3 29 gxf3. Then 29...♖xd4 30 exd4 ♘xf3+ looks strong, but White can hang on by 31 ♔h1 ♗xd4 32 ♛g2, so the simple 29...♘c4 is best, when Black retains a large positional advantage, especially because White's kingside is now weak.

28 ...　　　　♘d3

Cutting off the rook's defence of d4.

29 ♖xc8　　　♛xc8

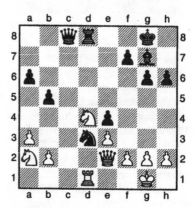

30 f3?!

White allows a beautiful finish. 30 ♘c3 f5 31 f3 would have been a much tougher defence; after 31...♗xd4 32 exd4 ♛c4 33 d5 ♛c5+ 34 ♔f1 ♘f4 35 ♛d2 (35 ♛f2 e3 36 ♛g3 g5 wins, while 35 ♛e1 ♘xd5 36 ♘xd5 ♖xd5 37 ♖xd5 ♛xd5 38 fxe4 fxe4 leaves Black a good pawn up) 35...e3 White can try:

1) 36 ♛e1 ♖e8 37 b4 ♛d6 38 g3 (if 38 ♘e2, then 38...♘xe2 followed by 39...♛xh2) 38...e2+ 39 ♘xe2 ♖xe2 40 ♛c3 ♖xh2 41 gxf4 ♖h1+ 42 ♔e2 ♖xd1 43 ♔xd1 ♛xd5+ and the extra pawn should be enough for a win.

2) 36 ♕d4 e2+! 37 ♘xe2 ♖xd5! 38 ♕xc5 ♖xd1+ 39 ♔f2 ♘d3+ is the beautiful point of Black's play.

30 ...   ♖xd4!

A crushing blow. White cannot take the rook as 31 exd4 ♗xd4+ 32 ♔f1 ♘f4 33 ♕xe4 (or 33 ♕d2 ♕c4+ 34 ♔e1 e3) 33...♕c4+ 34 ♔e1 ♘xg2+ 35 ♔d2 ♗e3+ wins White's queen.

31 fxe4

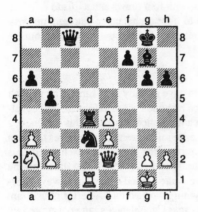

White hopes to regain the piece by means of the double attack on d3 and d4, but there is a horrible surprise waiting for him.

31 ...   ♘f4!

32 exf4   ♕c4!

A wonderful finish to the game; White must lose a piece.

33 ♕xc4   ♖xd1+

34 ♔f1   ♗d4+

0-1

Lessons from this game:

1) Even if no material sacrifice is involved, playing for an attack usually involves a positional commitment which may prove a handicap if the attack fails.

2) Advantages do not increase of their own accord; purposeful play is necessary to increase an advantage.

3) A knight firmly entrenched in the middle of the opposing position is often a decisive advantage.

Game 21
José Capablanca – Savielly Tartakower
New York 1924
Dutch Defence

The Players

Capablanca (see Game 13 for more information) was now in the middle of his reign as World Champion, and at the height of his powers. However, he had started badly at the New York tournament, with four draws and a loss to Réti. He desperately needed to win some games to have a chance of catching up with Lasker. Tartakower (see Game 18) by contrast was having an excellent tournament, undefeated and sharing the lead.

The Game

Tartakower employs the Dutch, which we have already seen him using to such devastating effect in Game 18. Capablanca responds with straightforward development, rather than getting embroiled in a theoretical dispute in his opponent's territory. Capablanca gets the better of a tense middlegame, and evolves the plan of a positional attack down the h-file. Although the queens are exchanged, this plan is effective in the endgame too. Tartakower tries to counterattack on the queenside, and indeed he appears to have made a good deal of headway. However, Capablanca turns out to have everything worked out. A series of brilliant moves, sacrificing two pawns with check, sees Capablanca's king penetrate into the heart of Tartakower's kingside, to add its support to a passed pawn. The small but superbly coordinated army of king, rook and pawn generates deadly threats against the black king, and this leaves Black paralysed. Capablanca can then regain his pawns with interest. It is an extremely instructive ending.

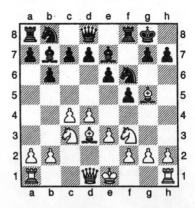

1	d4	e6
2	♘f3	f5
3	c4	♘f6
4	♗g5	♗e7
5	♘c3	0-0
6	e3	b6
7	♗d3	♗b7

Black's set-up is quite reasonable, but he still has the unsolved problem of finding a constructive role for his queen's knight. He is not helped in this by his slightly inflexible pawn structure – moving either the d- or e-pawn will leave light-square weaknesses.

8 0-0 ♕e8

Black seeks play on the kingside, with, if permitted, ...♕h5 followed by ...♘g4.

9 ♕e2! ♘e4

Black seeks simplifications. 9...♕h5 10 e4 would thwart Black's intentions and give White a pleasant advantage.

10 ♗xe7 ♘xc3
11 bxc3 ♕xe7
12 a4!?

White intends to loosen Black's queenside structure, and in the process to liquidate his own potentially vulnerable queenside pawns. Note that this move also prevents the annoying possibility ...♕a3.

12 ... ♗xf3

This is surely an overreaction to White's plan. 12...d6 seems sensible, preparing ...♘d7 and/or ...e5. This makes use of the fact that his exchanging manoeuvre lent his f5-pawn the f8-rook's support.

Instead 12...♘c6 is met by 13 ♖fb1 followed by c5.

13 ♕xf3

"Now it happens – as usual in mobile pawn formations – that the bishop is superior to the knight. The rest of the game is a very fine example of the utilization of such an advantage." – Alekhine.

13 ... ♘c6
14 ♖fb1 ♖ae8

Alekhine suggested two alternatives to this move: 14...g5 and 14...♘a5, e.g. 15 c5 bxc5 16 ♖b5 c4.

15 ♕h3

Side-stepping ...e5 ideas and preparing to stifle Black's potential play in the centre and on the kingside by playing f4.

15 ... ♖f6

15...g5 would give better chances of a real fight developing.

16 f4 ♘a5
17 ♕f3 d6

17...c5 allows White to choose between playing on the kingside (18 g4) or the queenside (18 ♖b5).

18 ♖e1

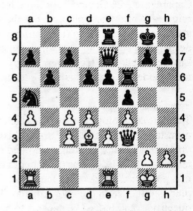

18 ... ♕d7?!

The critical line is 18...e5! 19 e4 and now:

1) 19...exf4? 20 exf5 (20 e5 should also be good) 20...♕xe1+ 21 ♖xe1 ♖xe1+ 22 ♔f2 ♖e3 23 ♕d5+ ♔f8 24 ♕a8+ (but not 24 ♗e4?? c6) 24...♔e7 (24...♔f7 25 ♗e4) 25 ♕g8 favours White, since 25...♖xd3? (25...♖f7 26 ♗e2) 26 ♕xg7+ ♖f7 27 f6+ ♔e6 28 d5+ is a disaster for Black.

2) 19...♘b3! (much better) 20 ♖ad1 exd4 and then:

2a) 21 ♗c2?! ♘c5 22 e5 d3 and now White must avoid 23 exf6?? (23 ♗xd3 ♘xd3 24 ♕xd3 must be played, though this is unimpressive for White) 23...♕xe1+ 24 ♖xe1 ♖xe1+ 25 ♔f2 dxc2 and Black wins.

2b) 21 e5 dxe5 22 fxe5 (22 ♖xe5 ♖e6 23 ♗c2 ♘a5 24 cxd4 ♘xc4 25

♗xf5 ♘xe5 26 ♗xe6+ ♕xe6 27 dxe5 is less convincing) 22...♖e6 23 ♗c2 ♘a5 24 cxd4 g6 25 c5 bxc5 26 ♕c3 ♘c6 27 ♗b3 ♘xd4 28 ♗xe6+ ♘xe6 29 ♕c4 is a tricky ending to assess, but White's chances on the queenside look quite good.

	19	e4	fxe4
	20	♕xe4	g6
	21	g3	

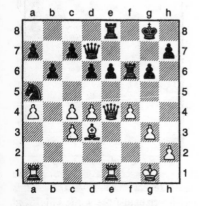

White telegraphs his intention of breaking up Black's kingside by h4-h5, but there is little Black can do about it.

| | 21 | ... | ♔f8 |
| | 22 | ♔g2 | ♖f7 |

22...♕c6 23 ♕xc6 ♘xc6 is one way to take queens off. It does not involve the positional concessions that we see in the game, but loses some time. White would still continue with 24 h4 (rather than 24 c5 ♘a5 25 cxd6 cxd6 26 ♖e3 ♖c8, which is unconvincing for White).

| | 23 | h4 | d5 |

Tartakower sees no sensible way to defend his kingside other than to exchange queens. However, this involves some concessions. 23...♘xc4 24 ♗xc4

d5 25 ♗xd5 ♕xd5 26 a5! is an echo of what happens in the game – White makes progress by threatening to penetrate with a rook via the a-file.

	24	cxd5	exd5
	25	♕xe8+	♕xe8
	26	♖xe8+	♔xe8
	27	h5	

Since White's attacking ideas were based on making positional gains, they are just as applicable in the ending too. There is no sensible way for Black to stop the white rook entering on the h-file.

| | 27 | ... | ♖f6 |

27...gxh5 28 ♖h1 ♔f8 29 ♖xh5 wins a pawn.

| | 28 | hxg6 | hxg6 |

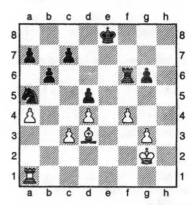

How would you assess this ending? It may seem that the c3-pawn is a serious weakness, but it turns out that the g6-pawn is just as easily attacked. Moreover, it is far easier for White to create a passed pawn on the kingside than it is for Black on the queenside. Thus White should play very actively, rather than trying to defend his queenside.

| | 29 | ♖h1 | ♔f8 |

30 Rh7	Rc6
31 g4	♘c4
32 g5	

"Threatening Rh6 followed by f5, and against it there is nothing to be done." (Alekhine)

32 ...	♘e3+
33 ♔f3	♘f5

"Or 33...♘d1 34 Rh6 ♔f7 35 f5 Rxc3 36 fxg6+ ♔g8 37 ♔e2 ♘b2 38 ♗f5 with an easy win." (Alekhine)

34 ♗xf5	

Capablanca sees a rook ending as the simplest way to win. His rook is very active, he has a passed pawn, and he has foreseen a superb way to introduce his king into the thick of battle.

34 ...	gxf5

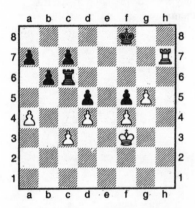

Glancing at this position superficially, we see that White is about to lose a pawn. A deeper look shows that White has made enormous progress.

35 ♔g3!	

"Decisive! White sacrifices material in order to obtain the classical position with king on f6, pawn on g6 and rook on h7, whereupon the pawns tumble like ripe apples." (Alekhine)

35 ...	Rxc3+

36 ♔h4	Rf3
37 g6!	

A memorable move, making way for the king.

37 ...	Rxf4+
38 ♔g5	Re4
39 ♔f6!	

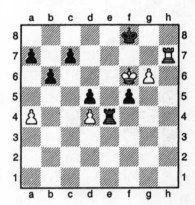

Again highly instructive. White does not take the f5-pawn; instead this pawn will shield the white king from checks. It does not matter at this point that Black has a mobile passed pawn, as White's threats are so immediate.

39 ...	♔g8
40 Rg7+	♔h8
41 Rxc7	Re8

White was threatening mate, so the rook must go passive.

42 ♔xf5	

Now that Black is wholly passive, White kills off any counterplay by eliminating this pawn.

42 ...	Re4
43 ♔f6	Rf4+
44 ♔e5	Rg4
45 g7+	♔g8

45...Rxg7 46 Rxg7 ♔xg7 47 ♔xd5 ♔f6 48 ♔c6 is a trivially won king and pawn ending.

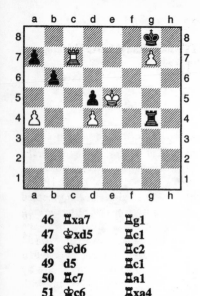

46	♖xa7	♖g1
47	♔xd5	♖c1
48	♔d6	♖c2
49	d5	♖c1
50	♖c7	♖a1
51	♔c6	♖xa4

52 d6   1-0

This ending provides a superb example of a number of important endgame themes: passed pawns, rook activity, king activity and an admirable avoidance of materialism when the initiative is at stake.

Lessons from this game:

1) Don't be intimidated because your opponent knows a lot about an opening. If you play sensible moves you should get a reasonable position.

2) A positionally justified plan of attack can be just as effective in an ending as in the middlegame.

3) Initiative, piece activity and mating attacks are a part of endgame play too – be prepared to sacrifice for them.

Richard Réti – Efim Bogoljubow
New York 1924
Réti Opening

The Players

Richard Réti (1889–1929) was born in what was then Hungary but he later adopted Czechoslovakian nationality. Réti was one of the leading figures in the so-called "Hypermodern" school of chess, which revolutionized chess thinking in the period after the First World War. The new ideas introduced by the Hypermoderns had a particular impact on opening play. It had always been accepted that opening play had three main objectives: to develop the pieces, bring the king into safety and control the centre. This last had been taken to mean occupying the centre with pawns, and the ideal central formation was thought to be pawns on d4 and e4 with White, or d5 and e5 with Black. The Hypermodern school held that central control was possible without the physical occupation of the centre by pawns; instead, the pieces would exert control from a distance. In keeping with this theory, Réti favoured openings involving the fianchetto of the bishops (i.e. b3 + ♗b2 and g3 + ♗g2 with White, and the analogous development with Black). From b2 and g2 the bishops would exert an influence on all four central squares (d4, e4, d5 and e5). If Black tried to occupy the centre with his own pawns, the idea was that the persistent pressure exerted by the bishops would cause the enemy centre to collapse, opening the way for White's own pawns to advance in the centre without resistance. These new theories proved controversial, and would never have gained any credence had they not been backed up by practical successes.

Although Réti was one of the world's leading players in the early 1920s, he was never in a position to challenge for the world championship and his early death deprived the chess world of one of its most profound thinkers. He left behind two classics of chess literature (*Modern Ideas in Chess* and the unfinished *Masters of the Chess Board*) and a collection of games bearing the hallmarks of a great chess artist.

The ideas of the Hypermoderns were gradually assimilated into chess thinking; one of their theories which has gained universal acceptance is that a pawn-centre which is insufficiently supported by pieces is not strong, but weak. Many opening systems have been developed with the specific purpose of luring the opponent into a premature central advance; this over-extension is then punished by a vicious counterattack.

Efim Bogoljubow (1889–1952) was born the same year as Réti, in the Ukraine, but became a German citizen in 1927. Although his career was far longer than Réti's, his greatest achievements were also in the 1920s. His best result was victory in the Moscow 1925 tournament, where he took first prize by a massive 1½ point margin over a field that included all the leading players of the time with the exception of Alekhine. This and other successes led him to challenge Alekhine for the world championship in 1929, but he lost decisively (+5 =9 −11). A second world-title match against Alekhine in 1934 again ended in defeat (+3 =15 −8). Although Bogoljubow continued to compete with some success during the late 1930s, his results gradually declined, although he won the German Championship as late as 1949.

The Game

The current game, which won the first brilliancy prize at the extremely strong New York 1924 tournament, is one of the most elegant examples of Hypermodern opening play. White's opening appears modest, but its latent power is revealed when Réti opens the position up and his bishops suddenly develop tremendous power. Bogoljubow tries to free himself tactically, but is demolished by a refined combination.

	1	♘f3	♘f6
	2	c4	e6
	3	g3	

White already commits himself to the fianchetto development of his bishop on g2.

3 ...   d5

There is nothing especially wrong with Black's play, but he has to take care not to allow his c8-bishop to become permanently blocked in. In some of Réti's other games from New York 1924, his opponents preferred to develop this bishop to f5 before playing ...e6, thus avoiding the problems that Bogoljubow faces later in this game.

	4	♗g2	♗d6
	5	0-0	0-0
	6	b3	

White's other bishop will also be fianchettoed. This is a particularly natural reaction when, as here, Black has set up his central pawns on light squares. This leaves the central dark squares d4 and e5 slightly weak and the bishop on b2 is well placed to exploit this.

6 ...   ♖e8

To modern eyes, Black's opening play appears rather naïve. He is arranging his pieces so as to be able to force through the advance ...e6-e5, and thereby obtain the ideal classical d5-e5 pawn centre, but he is never able to achieve this. The result is that his pieces end up misplaced.

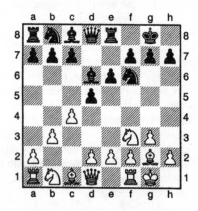

7 ♗b2   ♘bd7

As an example of the Hypermodern theory in action, the line 7...e5 8 cxd5 e4 9 ᐸe1 ᐸxd5 10 d3 exd3 11 ᐸxd3 c6 12 e4 shows how, once Black's pawn centre has been demolished, White can himself gain the ascendancy in the centre.

8 d4

In an earlier round of the same tournament, Réti (against Yates) had played 8 d3, but after 8...c6 9 ᐸbd2 e5 10 cxd5 cxd5 11 ♖c1 ᐸf8 Black was able to develop the c8-bishop and so solve his main problem. 8 d4 is much stronger since, by covering the e5-square, White makes it virtually impossible for Black to advance his e-pawn. Unlike some of the Hypermoderns, who stuck to their principles dogmatically, Réti was not averse to pushing a central pawn if he could see a concrete benefit in doing so.

8 ... c6

The main reason for Black's loss is that he fails to realize the danger posed by Réti's subtle play and takes no counter-action until it is too late. Here 8...dxc4 9 bxc4 c5 would have at least challenged White's central control.

9 ᐸbd2 ᐸe4

With this Black definitely gives up his plan to contest e5, but 9...e5 10 cxd5 cxd5 11 dxe5 ᐸxe5 12 ᐸxe5 ♗xe5 13 ♗xe5 ♖xe5 14 ᐸc4 ♖e8 15 ᐸe3 ♗e6 16 ♕d4 ♕d7 17 ♖fd1 would have given White a large positional advantage in view of Black's weak isolated d-pawn.

Perhaps 9...b6 was relatively best, in order to develop the problem c8-bishop at b7.

10 ᐸxe4 dxe4
11 ᐸe5 f5

The only move, since 11...ᐸf6 12 ♕c2 would soon lead to the loss of the e4-pawn.

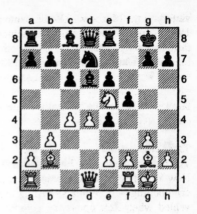

12 f3

An instructive moment. White has a definite advantage, since both his own bishops are actively placed, while Black's c8-bishop is still buried on its original square. Nevertheless, given time Black will eventually solve this problem, perhaps by exchanging the e5-knight and then playing ...b6, ...♗b7 and ...c5. Therefore, White cannot afford to waste time; quick action is necessary to exploit his advantage. Réti decides to open the game up before Black has a chance to coordinate his forces.

12 ... exf3
13 ♗xf3

Far more dynamic than 13 exf3, since White intends to play e4, opening the position up even further.

13 ... ♕c7?

Black wants to force White to exchange knights himself, but the tempo that Black spends on this move turns out to be largely wasted. The best defence was 13...ᐸxe5 14 dxe5 ♗c5+ 15 ♔g2 ♗d7 (Black should not swap queens, because then the c8-bishop would never move). In this way Black can at least bring his queenside pieces into play by ...♕e7 and ...♖ad8, even though his light-squared bishop remains poorly placed.

14 ♘xd7   ♗xd7
15 e4

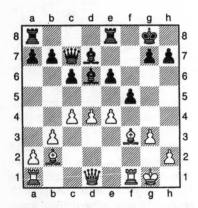

The triumph of Réti's Hypermodern strategy: it is not Black but White who forms the ideal two-abreast pawn centre. White's pawn advance is even more effective for being delayed until his pieces are able to support the pawns.

15 ...   e5

At last Bogoljubow decides to make a fight of it, but in the resulting complications White always has a head-start because his bishops are far more effectively placed. The alternatives are no better:

1) 15...c5 16 e5 ♗f8 17 d5 and the white pawns dominate the centre.

2) 15...fxe4 16 ♗xe4 (threatening 17 ♕h5) 16...g6 17 ♕d3 with a very strong kingside attack.

3) 15...♗f8 16 ♕d3 ♖ad8 avoids an immediate catastrophe, but after either 17 e5 or 17 ♖ad1 White has more active pieces and greater central control.

16 c5   ♗f8

After 16...♗e7 17 b4 Black would also be in difficulties, as any exchange in the centre would only serve to bring a white piece to a more active position.

17 ♕c2!

An excellent move, avoiding the tempting 17 exf5 ♗xf5 18 ♗xc6 ♕xc6 19 ♖xf5, which wins a pawn, but allows Black's pieces to develop great activity. After 19...♖ad8 (not 19...g6 20 ♖f3 exd4, however, as 21 ♖xf8+! ♖xf8 22 ♕xd4 gives White a winning attack) 20 b4 exd4 21 ♗xd4 ♕e6 22 ♖f4 (22 ♕g4 g6 23 ♖f4 ♕xg4 24 ♖xg4 h5 loses a piece) 22...g6 there is no satisfactory way to meet the threat of 23...♗h6. When one has a positional advantage, it is important not to cash it in too soon; winning a pawn may not help if the opposing pieces suddenly spring to life.

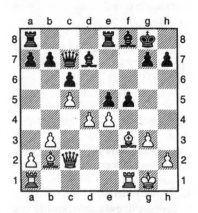

The text-move both attacks the f5-pawn directly, and, by defending c5, threatens dxe5.

17 ...   exd4

There is no choice, as after 17...f4 18 gxf4 exf4 19 e5, followed by ♗e4, the f4-pawn will not survive for long, while 17...fxe4 18 &xe4 attacks e5 and h7.

18 exf5   &ad8

After 18...&e5 19 &xd4 (Black can defend after 19 &c4+ &h8 20 f6 &xc5 21 fxg7+ &xg7 22 &xd4 &xd4+ 23 &xd4 &b6) 19...&xf5 20 &xe5 (20 &c3 &e6 21 &xc6 &xc6 22 &xf5 gains a pawn, but the resulting position would be tricky to win) 20...&xe5 21 &c4+ &e6 22 &e4 White wins the exchange for a pawn. Although this material advantage does not always guarantee a win, here the open files favour the rooks so I would expect White to win in the long run.

19 &h5!

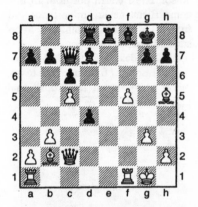

The last phase of the struggle begins. The question is no longer one of central control, but of a direct assault. All White's pieces, except for the a1-rook, are well placed to attack the enemy king, and the advanced pawn on f5 fulfils a critical role in some lines.

Flexibility is important in chess. If one has an advantage, it is worth keeping an eye open for a means of transforming this advantage into one of a different type. In this game Réti, after

strategically outplaying his opponent, did not stubbornly persist in trying to decide the game by purely positional means; instead, he took the opportunity to convert his advantage into a flowing attack.

19 ...   &e5

After 19...&e7 20 &xd4 &xf5 21 &xf5 &xd4 22 &xf8+ &xf8 23 &xh7 Black's exposed king would be defenceless.

20 &xd4   &xf5?

Black decides to regain his pawn, but this allows a beautiful finish. The last chance was 20...&d5 21 &c4 &h8, although after 22 &g4! (22 f6 &h3 is less clear) White retains his extra pawn. One possible continuation runs 22...b6 23 cxb6 axb6 24 &ad1 b5 25 &c3 c5 26 &xg7+! &xg7 27 f6 and White should win.

21 &xf5   &xf5
22 &xf5   &xd4

Material equality has been restored, and in view of the opposite-coloured bishops Black would only have to survive the next few moves for a draw to be more or less certain.

23 &f1

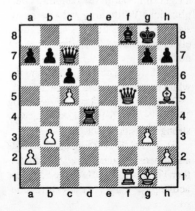

However, Réti has calculated the finish to perfection: there is no defence to the threats along the f-file.

23 ...   Ξd8

The other variation is an echo of the finish that occurs in the game: after 23...♕e7 24 ♗f7+ ♔h8 25 ♗d5! White uses his bishop to prevent the rook participating in the defence, and there is no way to defend Black's trapped bishop (25...♕f6 loses to 26 ♕c8).

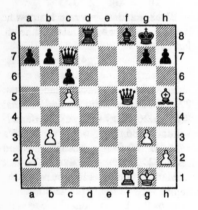

24 ♗f7+   ♔h8
25 ♗e8!   1-0

A worthy finish by the great chess artist. By using the bishop to block the enemy rook, White sets up a *double* attack on the f8-bishop, and to this there is no defence, e.g. 25...♗e7 26 ♕f8+ or 25...Ξxe8 26 ♕xf8+.

Lessons from this game:

1) Central control is an important objective of opening play, but this does not necessarily mean the occupation of the centre by pawns; control can be exerted by pieces from a distance.

2) A single badly-placed piece can poison one's entire position. In this game Black never really recovered from his handicap of an inactive light-squared bishop.

3) Stay flexible. Be ready to transform advantages from one type to another, or to switch from positional play to attack.

Game 23
Richard Réti – Alexander Alekhine
Baden-Baden 1925
Alekhine Reversed

The Players

Richard Réti (1889–1929) was one of the world's leading players in the early 1920s, an opening theoretician and a profound thinker on the game. For more details see Game 22.

Alexander Alekhine (1892–1946) was one of the greatest players in history; he held the World Championship from 1927 to 1935 and from 1937 until his death. For more details see Game 20.

The Game

Alekhine was famed for his attacking powers and they are never more evident than in this game. A slightly lax opening by Black allows White some positional pressure. Rather than defend passively, Alekhine, typically, chooses to counter-attack. At the critical moment he hurls a rook into White's position. Faced with a thicket of enormously complex variations, Réti chooses the wrong move and falls victim to a tactical storm which continues right into the endgame. The fact that the new annotations below tell a different story to the generally accepted version in no way detracts from Alekhine's genius.

1	g3	e5
2	♘f3	

A very unusual move. Réti's idea is to reach an Alekhine Defence (1 e4 ♘f6) with colours reversed and with the extra tempo g3. The problem is that Black is able to choose a variation in which the extra tempo is no asset. Réti had many good ideas in the opening, but this isn't one of them.

2	...	e4
3	♘d4	d5

Alekhine correctly pointed out that after 3...c5 4 ♘b3 c4 5 ♘d4 ♗c5 6 c3 ♘c6 a line of the Alekhine Defence is reached in which the extra tempo g3 is quite useless (it gets a bit confusing when an opening is named after one of

the players!). In this case White would be fighting for equality.

4	d3	exd3

A very timid reaction. 4...♘f6 would be a more natural response, maintaining the pawn at e4 for the moment.

5	♕xd3	♘f6
6	♗g2	♗b4+

Alekhine himself criticized this move. It is true that it enables Black to castle quickly, but White's development is accelerated.

7	♗d2	♗xd2+
8	♘xd2	0-0

A leading present-day openings manual offers the move 8...♘bd7, even though 9 ♕e3+ ♕e7 10 ♕xe7+ ♔xe7 11 0-0-0 is good for White.

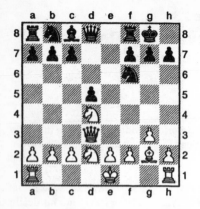

9 c4

A good move. Réti gives Black no time to consolidate and at once eliminates his central pawn, at the same time increasing the scope of his bishop. After a slightly inaccurate opening, both sides start to play very well.

9 ...   ♘a6

The best defence, as after 9...c5 10 ♘4b3 dxc4 11 ♕xc4 Black would just lose a pawn.

10 cxd5   ♘b4

11 ♕c4   ♘bxd5

12 ♘2b3

Securing the knight on d4. 12 0-0 is less accurate, because 12...♘b6 leaves the queen without a really good square. After the text-move, 12...♘b6 13 ♕c2 would favour White.

12 ...   c6

Aiming to retain Black's main asset, the strongly posted knight on d5. Of course, White can drive the knight away by playing e4, but this would block the action of his bishop on the long diagonal. Réti soon decides to undermine Black's queenside pawn chain by b4-b5, thereby also destabilizing the d5-knight. This is a strong but rather slow plan, and Alekhine is

forced to search for counterplay on the opposite side of the board.

13 0-0   ♖e8

14 ♖fd1   ♗g4

Aiming for counterplay against e2.

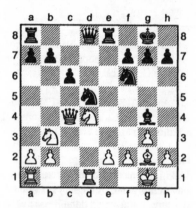

15 ♖d2

Relatively best, since after 15 h3 ♗h5 Black will gain control of e4 by ...♗g6. 15 ♘c5 ♕e7 is even worse, as 16 ♖d2? fails to 16...♘e3.

15 ...   ♕c8

A typical manoeuvre: Black aims for the exchange of light-squared bishops by ...♗h3. 15...♕e7 16 ♕c5 would favour White, as without queens White would be free to pursue his queenside attack.

16 ♘c5

Clearing the way for the b-pawn's advance.

16 ...   ♗h3

17 ♗f3

White cannot grab a pawn: 17 ♗xh3 ♕xh3 18 ♘xb7 ♘g4 19 ♘f3 ♘de3 20 fxe3 ♘xe3 21 ♕xf7+ ♔h8 22 ♘h4 ♖f8 would cost him his queen.

17 ...   ♗g4

18 ♗g2   ♗h3

19 ♗f3   ♗g4

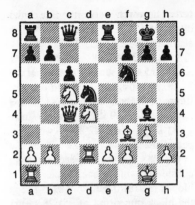

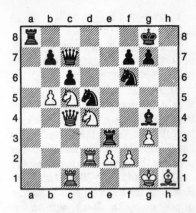

White does not wish to retreat to the less active square h1, but Alekhine persists in opposing bishops. Of course Réti could have drawn by repeating moves, which would have been no disgrace against Alekhine, but he decides to play on. While this decision was objectively correct, he might have been regretting it after the game!

20 ♗h1   h5

Black aims to soften up White's kingside by ...h4 and ...hxg3. This not only opens the h-file, but also weakens the pawn on g3.

21 b4

Playing e4 doesn't give White any advantage, e.g. 21 e4 ♘b6 22 ♕c3 ♕c7 23 b4 ♘bd7 and Black eliminates the powerful c5-knight.

21	...	**a6**
22	**♖c1**	**h4**
23	**a4**	**hxg3**
24	**hxg3**	**♕c7**
25	**b5!**	

This move has often been criticized, but it appears stronger than 25 e4 ♘b6 26 ♕b3 ♘bd7 when Black has comfortable equality.

25	...	**axb5**
26	**axb5**	**♖e3!**

Just as White's queenside attack arrives, this spectacular rook sacrifice energizes Black's counterplay.

27 ♘f3?

This is the critical moment of the game. White has several plausible moves to meet the threat of 27...♖xg3+ and it is certainly not easy to decide which is the most appropriate. Alekhine's own annotations claimed that Black has the advantage against any reply; other annotators have generally followed his lead. As we shall see, this is not correct. Réti had two lines leading to a clear draw, and a third which would have given him a slight advantage (although the result should still be a draw).

In my opinion, this does not detract from Alekhine's achievement. When playing at his best, Alekhine had a special ability to provoke complications without taking excessive risks. Even had Réti found the best line, the game would almost certainly have ended in a draw. In fact Réti, as so often with Alekhine's opponents, lost his way and made a fatal error. Here are the alternatives in (roughly) ascending order of merit:

1) 27 fxe3?? ♕xg3+ 28 ♗g2 ♘xe3 mates.

2) 27 bxc6? ♖xg3+ 28 ♗g2 (28 fxg3 ♕xg3+ 29 ♗g2 ♘e3 mates) 28...♘e3! 29 fxe3 ♗h3 and wins.

3) 27 ♗g2?! ♖xg3 28 e3 (28 e4 ♖xg2+ 29 ♔xg2 ♘f4+ with a very strong attack, e.g. 30 ♔h1 ♕e5 31 bxc6 ♕h5+ 32 ♔g1 ♗f3 and wins) 28...♘xe3 29 fxe3 ♕e5 and Black has very good compensation for the piece.

4) 27 ♗xd5 cxd5 28 ♕b4 and now Black can force a draw by 28...♖xg3+ or play on by 28...♖ee8, with an unclear position.

5) 27 ♗f3 ♗xf3 28 exf3 cxb5 29 ♘xb5 ♕a5 30 ♖xd5 ♖e1+ 31 ♖xe1 ♕xe1+ 32 ♔g2 ♘xd5 (not 32...♖a1? 33 ♖d8+ ♔h7 34 ♕h4+ ♔g6 35 f4 and White wins) 33 ♕xd5 ♖a1 34 ♕d8+ ♔h7 35 ♕h4+ ♔g8 with perpetual check.

6) 27 ♔h2! ♖aa3! and now:

6a) 28 ♘db3 ♖e5 (28...♕e5 29 fxe3 ♕h5+ 30 ♔g1 ♕h3 31 ♗xd5 ♕xg3+ 32 ♔h1 ♕h3+ is a draw) and Black's pieces are very active.

6b) 28 ♘cb3 ♕e5 with a further branch:

6b1) 29 fxe3 ♕h5+ 30 ♔g1 ♕h3 31 ♗xd5 ♘xd5! (better than forcing an immediate draw) 32 ♘f3 ♕xg3+ 33 ♔h1 ♗xf3+ (33...♘xe3 34 ♖d8+ ♔h7 35 ♘g5+ ♔h6 36 ♘xf7+ ♔g6 37 ♘h8+ ♔h6 is a draw) 34 exf3 ♕xf3+ 35 ♔h2 ♕xe3! and White is in difficulties, e.g. 36 ♖d3 ♕f2+ 37 ♔h1 ♖a2 38 ♖d2 ♖xd2 39 ♘xd2 ♕xd2, 36 ♖e2 ♕h6+ 37 ♔g1 ♖xb3 or 36 ♖xd5 cxd5 37 ♕c8+ ♔h7 38 ♕c2+ g6 with an advantage for Black in every case.

6b2) 29 bxc6 bxc6 30 fxe3 ♕h5+ 31 ♔g1 ♕h3 (Alekhine stopped his analysis here, implying that Black is

better; however, it seems to be a draw) 32 ♗xd5 (32 ♗f3 ♕xg3+ 33 ♔h1 is also a draw) 32...♘xd5 33 ♘f3 ♕xg3+ (33...♘xe3? 34 ♖d8+ wins) 34 ♔h1 ♗xf3+ 35 exf3 ♕xf3+ 36 ♔h2 ♕xe3 37 ♕xc6 (possible thanks to the preliminary exchange on c6) 37...♖xb3 38 ♕c8+ ♔h7 39 ♕f5+ ♔h6 40 ♖c6+ g6 41 ♖xg6+ fxg6 42 ♕f8+ with perpetual check.

6c) 28 ♘d3! (nobody seems to have considered this move, which again blocks the third rank but also keeps the black queen out of e5) 28...♘h5 (28...♖xg3 29 fxg3 ♘h5 30 ♖g1 ♘e3 31 ♕c1 ♖c3 32 ♕e1 wins for White, while 28...♘e4 29 ♗xe4 ♖xe4 30 ♕xd5 cxd5 31 ♖xc7 ♖xd4 32 ♖xb7 ♗xe2 33 ♖xe2 ♖axd3 34 ♖e8+ ♔h7 35 ♖ee7 gives White a very favourable ending) and now:

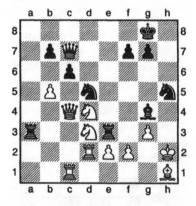

6c1) 29 ♗xd5 ♖xg3! (29...♘xg3 30 ♗xf7+ ♔f8 31 ♘f4 ♘f1+ 32 ♔g1 refutes the attack) 30 ♗xf7+ (not 30 fxg3 ♕xg3+ 31 ♔h1 ♕h3+ 32 ♔g1 cxd5 33 ♕c2 ♘f4 and Black wins) 30...♔h8 (30...♔f8 31 ♕c5+ ♔xf7 32 ♘e5+ and 33 fxg3 wins for White) 31 fxg3 (31 f4? ♕d8 and Black wins)

31...♕xg3+ 32 ♔h1 with perpetual check.

6c2) 29 ♕xd5! ♘xg3 (29...♖xg3 loses to 30 ♕e5) 30 ♔g1 ♘xe2+ (there is nothing better as 30...♕a5 31 bxc6 ♕xd2 32 cxb7 ♖e8 33 ♖b1! ♖xd3 34 b8♕ ♕d1+ 35 ♖xd1 ♖xd1+ 36 ♔g2 ♖xb8 37 ♔xg3 ♗xe2 38 ♕e5 ♖d8 39 ♘f5 wins for White) 31 ♘xe2 ♖xe2 32 ♕c5 and White is slightly better as he has a piece for two pawns. However, after 32...♖xd2 33 ♕xa3 ♕d8 34 ♘e1 cxb5 35 ♗xb7, for example, White has only one pawn left and so his winning chances are near zero.

After Réti's choice Black decides the game with a series of hammer blows. White's moves are virtually forced until the end of the game.

27 ...   cxb5

28 ♕xb5

28 ♕d4 is strongly met by 28...♖e4.

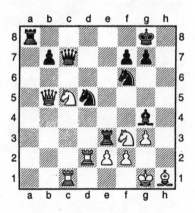

28 ...   ♘c3!

29 ♕xb7

After 29 ♕c4 b5 the queen cannot continue to defend e2.

29 ...   ♕xb7

A much stronger continuation than 29...♘xe2+ 30 ♖xe2 ♕xb7 31 ♖xe3,

when the resulting position offers few winning prospects.

30 ♘xb7   ♘xe2+

31 ♔h2

Or 31 ♔f1 ♘xg3+ 32 fxg3 ♗xf3 33 ♗xf3 ♖xf3+ 34 ♔g2 ♖aa3 (34...♖xg3+ 35 ♔xg3 ♘e4+ is also effective) 35 ♖d8+ ♔h7 36 ♖h1+ ♔g6 37 ♖h3 ♖fb3 with a decisive attack.

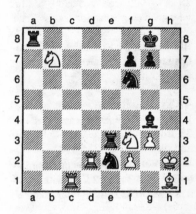

There are several pieces hanging in this remarkable position, but the winning move does not involve taking any of them!

31 ...   ♘e4!

31...♖xf3 32 ♖xe2 ♖xg3 33 fxg3 ♗xe2 should be a draw.

32 ♖c4

The best defence is 32 ♖d8+ (32 fxe3 ♘xd2 loses at once) 32...♖xd8 33 fxe3, when Black's only clear-cut win is by means of the beautiful continuation 33...♖d5! 34 ♖c4 (White must skewer Black's minor pieces, otherwise 34...♗h5+ wins out of hand) 34...♘2xg3 (34...♖h5+ 35 ♘h4) 35 ♗g2 ♘f1+!! 36 ♔g1 (after 36 ♗xf1 ♗xf3 White cannot meet the threat of 37...♗h5+) 36...♖d1 37 ♗xf1 ♗xf3 with the deadly threat of 38...♘d2.

Curiously, Alekhine made no mention of 32 ♖d8+.

| 32 | ... | ♘xf2 |
| 33 | ♗g2 | |

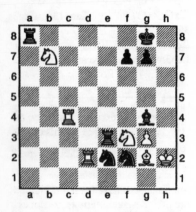

33 ...   ♗e6

Black could have won more simply by 33...♘e4 34 ♖dc2 ♖a6, with the lethal threat of 35...♖h6+, but Alekhine's

move is also decisive. The remaining moves are forced.

34	♖cc2	♘g4+
35	♔h3	♘e5+
36	♔h2	♖xf3
37	♖xe2	♘g4+
38	♔h3	♘e3+
39	♔h2	♘xc2
40	♗xf3	♘d4

0-1

White loses a piece after 41 ♖f2 ♘xf3+ 42 ♖xf3 ♗d5.

Lessons from this game:

1) A fianchettoed bishop combined with a pawn advance on the opposite wing is a standard technique for exerting strategic pressure.

2) Active counterplay is better than passive defence.

3) In order to play a game such as this it helps if you can calculate at least ten moves ahead!

Game 24
Akiba Rubinstein – Alexander Alekhine
Semmering 1926
Queen's Indian Defence

The Players

Akiba Rubinstein (1882–1961) was one of the world's best players in the period 1907–22 and one of the best endgame players of all time. For more details see Game 12.

Alexander Alekhine (1892–1946) was one of the greatest players in history; he held the World Championship from 1927 to 1935 and from 1937 until his death. For more details see Game 20.

The Game

Just as in Game 23 (Réti – Alekhine), most commentators have been intimidated by Alekhine's own annotations, but it turns out that these annotations are not especially accurate. The opening line chosen by Rubinstein is not thought to cause Black any real problems; indeed Alekhine's vigorous response seems to lead to clear equality. Alekhine misses a chance to gain an advantage, but then Rubinstein goes wrong in turn. The result is a dazzling display of tactics by Alekhine.

1	d4	♘f6
2	c4	e6
3	♘f3	b6
4	g3	♗b7
5	♗g2	♗b4+

Today this line of the Queen's Indian is rarely played, the currently popular lines being 5...♗e7 and the earlier alternative 4...♗a6.

6 ♘bd2

A harmless move which justifies the check on b4. As mentioned in the notes to Game 14 (Nimzowitsch – Tarrasch), in queen's pawn openings it is almost always better to develop the b1-knight on c3 rather than d2. Here Black is willing to spend a tempo to tempt the knight to the inferior d2-square. White should not have fallen in with this plan – 6 ♗d2 is better and

is the reason that this line is unpopular today.

6	...	0-0
7	0-0	d5

Alekhine suggests 7...♖e8, so that the bishop can retreat to f8 after White's a3, but the move played is natural and strong.

8	a3	♗e7
9	b4	c5

As usual, Alekhine adopts the most active continuation. Given that this appears entirely satisfactory for Black, there is little reason to analyse another move.

10	bxc5	bxc5
11	dxc5	

Attempting to exert pressure along the b-file leads to nothing: 11 ♖b1 ♕c8 12 ♕b3 ♗a6 13 ♘e5 ♘c6 and

Black has at least equalized since his a6-bishop is very well-placed. Instead Rubinstein contents himself with simple development but Black has already solved all his opening problems.

11   ...   ♗xc5

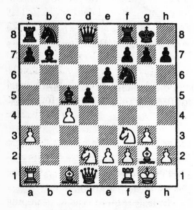

12   ♗b2   ♘bd7

Here there is a specific reason for developing the knight on d7 rather than c6. After 12...♘c6, White could gain the initiative by 13 cxd5 ♘xd5 (13...exd5 14 ♘b3 gives White a favourable isolated d-pawn position) 14 ♕c2 ♗e7 15 e4. The text-move avoids blocking the b7-bishop, so that 13 cxd5 can be met by 13...♗xd5, retaining control over e4.

13   ♘e5?

Rubinstein aims for exchanges, but the result is to leave his dark-squared bishop in an exposed position. He should have played the quiet 13 ♕c2, with equality.

13   ...   ♘xe5
14   ♗xe5   ♘g4
15   ♗c3

This is forced since 15 ♗b2 ♕b6 forks b2 and f2 – the weakness of f2 is a recurrent theme in this game.

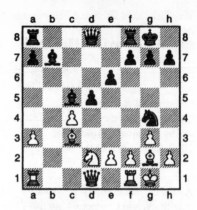

15   ...   ♖b8?

Alekhine misses the chance to gain the advantage by 15...♕b6, and now:

1) 16 ♕e1 d4 17 ♗a5 and Black stands better after either 17...♕xa5 18 ♗xb7 ♖ab8 19 ♗g2 ♖b2 20 ♘e4 ♕c7 or 17...♕a6 18 ♗xb7 ♕xb7 19 ♖b1 ♕c6 – in both cases White has no compensation for his weak c-pawn and Black's central pawn majority.

2) 16 e3 (Alekhine gave this as the correct reply to 15...♕b6, but Black has a strong continuation) 16...♘xf2! with two lines:

2a) 17 ♔xf2 ♗xe3+ 18 ♔e2 (after 18 ♔e1 d4 19 ♗a5 ♕xa5 20 ♗xb7 ♖ab8 21 ♖b1 ♕xa3 Black has three pawns and a continuing attack for the piece) 18...♗h6 19 ♕c2 ♕e3+ 20 ♔d1 d4 21 ♗xb7 dxc3 22 ♗xa8 ♖d8! 23 ♗d5 exd5 and Black wins after 24 c5 cxd2 25 c6 ♖e8 or 24 ♖f3 ♕g1+ 25 ♖f1 ♕d4.

2b) 17 ♖xf2 ♗xe3 18 ♕e2 dxc4 19 ♗xb7 (19 ♘xc4? ♗xf2+ 20 ♕xf2 ♕xf2+ 21 ♔xf2 ♗xg2 22 ♔xg2 ♖fc8 wins for Black, while 19 ♖b1 ♗xf2+ 20 ♕xf2 ♕xf2+ 21 ♔xf2 ♗xg2 22 ♔xg2 ♖ab8 gives Black a clear endgame advantage) 19...♗xf2+ 20 ♕xf2

♛xb7 21 ♘xc4 ♖fd8 and Black is distinctly better. A rook and two pawns are normally worth more than a bishop and a knight, especially when, as here, there are plenty of open files for the rooks and there is no secure central outpost for the knight.

The text-move covers the b7-bishop and so threatens 16...d4.

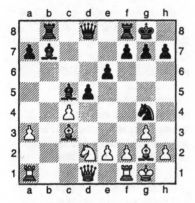

16 ♖b1?

Rubinstein misses his chance. The safest continuation was 16 cxd5! ♗xd5 17 ♘e4 (not 17 e4 ♘xf2 18 ♖xf2 ♗xf2+ 19 ♔xf2 ♛b6+ 20 ♔f1 ♗b7 21 ♗f3 ♖fd8 with a dangerous initiative for Black) 17...♗xe4 18 ♛xd8 (18 ♗xe4 ♛xd1 19 ♖axd1 ♗xa3 might also be drawn, but White would have to work hard to save his half-point) 18...♖fxd8 19 ♗xe4 and Black cannot exploit the slightly loose white pieces, for example 19...♖b3 20 ♗a5 ♖d4 21 ♖fc1 ♗f8 22 ♗d3 and everything is safe.

Contrary to Alekhine's opinion, White could also have played 16 h3 ♘xf2 (not 16...♗xf2+ 17 ♖xf2 ♘e3 18 ♛a4 ♘xg2 19 ♖xg2 d4 20 ♗a5) 17 ♖xf2 and now:

1) 17...♛g5 18 ♘f3! (Alekhine only considered 18 ♘f1) 18...♗xf2+ (18...♛xg3 19 ♗d4 ♗xd4 20 ♛xd4 is very good for White) 19 ♔xf2 with a slight advantage for White.

2) 17...♛c7 (best) 18 ♛e1! (18 ♗b4 ♗xf2+ 19 ♔xf2 ♖fc8 favours Black, for example 20 cxd5? a5 or 20 ♖c1 a5 21 ♗c3 dxc4 22 ♗xb7?! ♛c5+ 23 ♔f1 ♖xb7 24 ♘xc4 ♛xc4 25 ♗d2 ♛xc1 26 ♗xc1 ♖b1 and Black wins) 18...♗xf2+ (18...♛xg3 19 ♗b4 ♗xf2+ 20 ♛xf2 is unclear) 19 ♛xf2 dxc4 may be very slightly better for Black. Comparing this position with line "2b" in the note to Black's 15th move, the only major difference is that here White has an extra e-pawn. This emphasizes what a chance Alekhine missed with 15...♖b8?.

The move played is an error tipping the balance in Black's favour.

16 ... d4

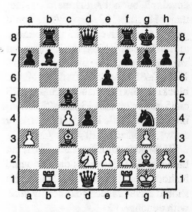

17 ♖xb7?

After this further mistake White falls victim to a typically vicious Alekhine combination. 17 ♗xb7? dxc3 18 ♘e4 ♘xf2! 19 ♘xf2 ♛xd1 20 ♖fxd1 c2 also loses, so the only chance was

17 ♗b4!. After 17...♗xg2 18 ♔xg2 ♕c7 Black has some advantage due to the weak c4-pawn, but White would have avoided an immediate disaster.

| 17 | ... | ♖xb7 |
| 18 | ♗xb7 | |

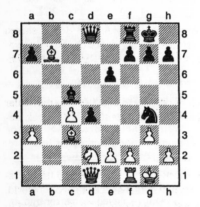

At this point many players would have automatically played the obvious 18...dxc3, but not Alekhine!

18 ...   ♘xf2!

This is a clear-cut win but, contrary to Alekhine's opinion, 18...dxc3 would also have won. The analysis runs 19 ♘e4 ♘e3! (not 19...♘xf2 20 ♘xf2 ♗xf2+ 21 ♔xf2 ♕b6+ 22 c5 ♕xb7 23 ♕c2 ♕b2 24 ♖c1 ♕xa3 25 ♕xc3 ♕xc3 26 ♖xc3 ♖c8 with a likely draw) 20 ♕xd8 (20 ♕b3 ♘xf1 21 ♔xf1 ♕b6 is hopeless) 20...♖xd8 21 fxe3 (21 ♖c1 c2 loses at once, while 21 ♘xc5 ♘xf1 22 ♔xf1 c2 23 ♘b3 f5! 24 c5 ♖d1+ 25 ♔g2 ♖b1 only lasts slightly longer) 21...♗xe3+ 22 ♔g2 c2 23 ♘c3 ♖b8! (simpler than 23...c1♕ 24 ♖xc1 ♗xc1 25 c5) 24 ♗e4 c1♕ 25 ♖xc1 ♗xc1 with an easy win for Black.

19 ♔xf2

Somewhat surprisingly, White cannot avoid a complete disaster:

1) 19 ♖xf2 dxc3 is fatal.

2) 19 ♗a5 ♘xd1 20 ♗xd8 d3+ 21 ♔h1 (21 e3 ♘xe3) 21...dxe2 22 ♖e1 ♖xd8 23 ♖xe2 ♗xa3 with two extra pawns.

3) 19 ♕a1 dxc3 20 ♘b3 ♗e3! 21 ♔g2 ♕b6 with crushing loss of material.

| 19 | ... | dxc3+ |
| 20 | e3 | |

Black wins easily after 20 ♔e1 cxd2+ 21 ♕xd2 ♕b6 22 ♗e4 (22 ♗f3 ♖d8 wins at once) 22...♗xa3 23 ♔d1 (23 ♗xh7+ ♔h8 24 ♕c2 f5 costs a piece) 23...♖d8 24 ♗d3 e5.

20 ...   cxd2

Not only does Black have an extra passed pawn on the seventh rank, but White's king is exposed and his pawns are hopelessly weak and scattered.

21	♔e2	♕b8
22	♗f3	♖d8
23	♕b1	♕d6
24	a4	f5
25	♖d1	♗b4
26	♕c2	♕c5
27	♔f2	a5
28	♗e2	g5
29	♗d3	f4

0-1

30 ♗xh7+ ♔h8 31 ♕e4 ♕xe3+ 32 ♔g2 ♖d4 33 ♕xe3 fxe3 wins a piece.

Lessons from this game:

1) Timid opening play by White often gives Black the opportunity to seize the initiative himself.

2) Even very strong players sometimes fall victim to the weakness of f2 (f7 for Black).

3) Your next move may seem forced, but it is worth taking a few seconds to see if there might be an alternative.

Game 25
Paul Johner – Aron Nimzowitsch
Dresden 1926
Nimzo-Indian Defence

The Players
Paul Johner (1887–1938) was a Swiss player and musician, who won or shared the Swiss Championship six times. His best success was his victory in a quadrangular tournament in Berlin 1924, where he came ahead of Rubinstein, Teichmann and Mieses.

We have already met Aron Nimzowitsch in Games 14 and 19. This particular game was played one year after the publication of his first major chess book, entitled *Die Blockade*. Enough said!

The Game
This is probably one of Nimzowitsch's most creative achievements at the chessboard. As early as move 12 he implements a plan that shocks the chess world. The incredible thing is that it seems to work! Certainly Johner has no answer to the unique problems facing him. He looks on as a virtual spectator as his pawns are blocked and then his position dismantled bit by bit. A game of pure joy!

1	d4	♘f6
2	c4	e6
3	♘c3	♗b4

Nimzowitsch's own defence, which is generally known as the Nimzo-Indian (the name "Nimzowitsch Defence" is reserved for 1 e4 ♘c6, even though this is a far less important opening). In the nineteenth century virtually all the top players would have played 3...d5 here (if they hadn't already played ...d5 on move one), controlling the centre in a classical way by occupying it with pawns. However, Nimzowitsch discovered another way to play for Black, which seems very normal now, but at the time was quite revolutionary. His concept was to control the centre with pieces rather than pawns, a kind of long-distance

command, which has the advantage of retaining much flexibility. This theory was one of the key ideas of the Hypermodern school of chess, led by Richard Réti and Nimzowitsch himself.

4	e3	0-0
5	♗d3	c5
6	♘f3	♘c6
7	0-0	♗xc3
8	bxc3	d6
9	♘d2!	

Nimzowitsch praises this move, which plans to meet a subsequent ...♘a5 with ♘b3. In the event of an exchange on b3 White would recapture with the a-pawn, thus improving his pawn structure on the queenside.

9	...	b6

Following on from the last note, Black now feels ready for the advance

10...e5, planning to meet 11 d5 ♘a5 12 ♘b3 with 12...♘b7. Nowadays, retreating the knight to e7 is more usual, with the immediate 9...e5 10 d5 ♘e7.

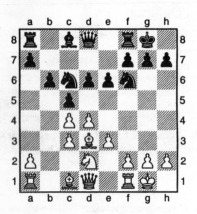

10 ♘b3?

Preventing ...♘a5, but this move allows Black to take the initiative in the centre. In his book *My System* Nimzowitsch prefers 10 f4!, which he would have met by 10...e5 11 fxe5 dxe5 12 d5 ♘a5 13 ♘b3 ♘b7 14 e4 ♘e8, intending to blockade the protected passed pawn with ...♘ed6. Knights are particularly effective at blocking enemy pawns, as their jumping properties mean that they can still influence other parts of the game. In particular, from d6 the knight exerts pressure on White's weak c4-pawn, which can be further attacked by ...♗a6. For White's part, he has a semi-open f-file and the possibility of the thrust a4-a5. Nimzowitsch assesses the chances as even. After 10 ♘b3, however, Black can strive for the advantage.

10 ...   e5
11 f4

After 11 d5 Nimzowitsch intended 11...e4!, when 12 ♗e2 ♘e5 favours

Black. Nimzowitsch also likes Black after 12 dxc6 exd3, but is 13 ♕xd3 ♕c7 14 e4 ♕xc6 15 f3 ♗a6 16 ♗f4 really so bad for White?

11 ...   e4!
12 ♗e2

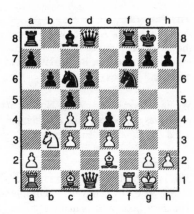

12 ...   ♕d7!!

This move, together with the subsequent queen manoeuvre, astounded the chess world at the time it was played, but its concept has been an inspiration to many grandmasters since. Nimzowitsch's main idea was first to restrain, then blockade and finally destroy. Here Black starts the restraining part of the plan. The only possible action for White in this position is on the kingside. He would like to expand there with g4, so Black basically takes steps to prevent this. The fact that the queen blocks the bishop for the moment is quite irrelevant. The whole picture will be seen in a few moves' time.

In *My System* Nimzowitsch writes "Black sees in White's kingside pawns (f-, g- and h-pawns) a qualitative majority. The text move involves a complicated method of restraint. A simpler one could have been achieved with

12...♘e8! 13 g4 f5 14 dxc5 dxc5 15 ♕d5+ ♕xd5 16 cxd5 ♘e7 17 ♖d1 ♘d6 and Black has a better game." However, a different note by Nimzowitsch, in B. Nielsen's book, *Nimzowitsch, Denmark's Chess Teacher*, explains his dislike for the simpler method. Nimzowitsch states that the sequence 14 d5 (instead of 14 dxc5) 14...♘e7 15 g5 leads to a petrification of the position. So although objectively there's nothing wrong with 12...♘e8, it allows White the chance to reach a totally blocked and virtually drawn position. The same accusation could in no way be levelled at 12...♕d7.

13 h3?!

This move is bypassed by Nimzowitsch, but has been universally criticized elsewhere, as it weakens the g3-square, and this can prove to be important in some variations. Here are a few suggested improvements for White:

1) Szabo mentions 13 f5!?, saying "It is interesting to note that, even for this important matter, the opinion of the great Danish master is nowhere to be found. We must assume that he considered 13 f5 not worthy of a mention because of 13...♘e7 14 g4 h5." This line should probably be expanded a little further. Black certainly doesn't get his desired blockade after 15 g5 (15 h3 hxg4 16 hxg4 ♘h7! and ...♘g5) 15...♘h7 16 f6, but White also pays a certain price for this achievement, i.e. a lack of pawn-cover for his own king. Following 16...♘f5 17 fxg7 ♘xg7 18 ♗xh5 (or 18 h4 ♕h3 19 ♕e1 ♘f5) 18...♘xg5 19 ♔h1 ♕h3 Black's pieces are very active.

2) 13 ♗d2!? is a suggestion of Larsen's. The idea is to activate this problem bishop via e1 to h4. After 13...♘e7 14 ♗e1 Larsen gives three lines:

2a) 14...♘g4 15 ♕d2 f5 "and it is not easy to storm the white position".

2b) 14...♘f5? is now effectively met by 15 ♗f2, followed by g4, kicking the knight away.

2c) Larsen also mentions the idea 14...♗a6!?, intending to meet 15 ♗h4 (? – Larsen) with 15...♘f5 16 ♗f2 cxd4. However, it seems that White can in fact play 16 ♗xf6, because after 16...♘xe3 17 ♕c1 ♘xf1 18 ♗h4, the knight on f1 is trapped. 18...♘xh2 19 ♔xh2 leads to a very unclear position, where it's difficult to say whether the rook and pawns are stronger than the two minor pieces.

13 ... ♘e7

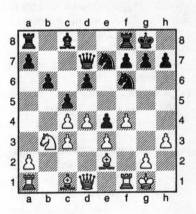

14 ♕e1?

Discounting the small glimmer of a chance at move eighteen, this was White's last chance to make a fight of it in the positional battle.

1) After 14 ♗d2 Nimzowitsch likes the idea 14...♘f5, intending 15...♘g3 exchanging off the e2-bishop, which protects the weak c4-pawn. He gives

the variation 15 ♕e1 g6 16 g4 ♘g7 17 ♕h4 ♘fe8 18 a4 (preventing ...♕a4) 18...f5 19 g5 ♘c7 20 d5 (Nimzowitsch doesn't mention 20 a5!?, which looks like a good move) 20...♗a6 (a preventative measure directed against 21 a5, for now the reply could be 21...b5) 21 ♔f2 ♕f7 22 ♖fd1 (22 ♕h6? ♘xd5! 23 cxd5 ♗xe2 24 ♔xe2 ♕xd5 25 ♘c1 ♘h5! with permanent imprisonment of the white queen; Black wins by promoting his queenside pawns) 22...♔h8, with a small advantage to Black, who plans ...♘h5, ...♔g7 and finally ...h6. Instead of 14...♘f5, Larsen prefers 14...h5, sacrificing the h-pawn to win the c-pawn. After 15 ♗xh5 ♘xh5 16 ♕xh5 ♕a4! (but not 16...♗a6 17 f5!) 17 f5 f6 Black has an edge, especially as 18 ♖f4? fails to 18...♗xf5! 19 ♖xf5 g6. After 14...h5 White can also try 15 ♗e1, but Black remains better with 15...♘f5 16 ♗f2 g6, e.g. 17 g4 hxg4 18 hxg4 ♘g7 19 g5 ♘g4.

2) 14 ♔h2 protects the g3-square in readiness for ...♘f5, but Black can prepare the blockade with 14...g6. Then 15 g4 can be answered by 15...h5 16 ♖g1 ♔g7!, preparing ...♖h8.

3) The direct 14 g4!? is another suggestion from Szabo, and it certainly needs to be taken seriously. After 14...h5 15 g5 Black can take a draw with 15...♕xh3 16 gxf6 ♕g3+ 17 ♔h1 ♕h3+ or try 15...♘e8 16 ♗xh5 ♕xh3. However, White can then play 17 ♖f2!, planning to annoy the queen with ♖h2. Perhaps the slower 14...g6 is stronger, intending ...♔g7, ...♖h8 and only then ...h5!.

14   ...   h5!

This important restraining move is an essential part of Black's plan.

15 ♗d2

The weakness of g3 is shown in the Nimzowitsch's variation 15 ♕h4 ♘f5 16 ♕g5 ♘h7 17 ♕xh5 ♘g3, winning the exchange.

15   ...   ♕f5!
16 ♔h2   ♕h7!

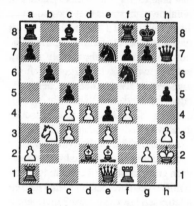

Nimzowitsch's restraining manoeuvre ...♕d8-d7-f5-h7 has finally been completed. With the black queen now sitting on the same file as the white king, White can hardly contemplate the advance g2-g4. This leaves White with absolutely nothing to do on the kingside, as well as the queenside. Black has time to coordinate his forces for the "blockade and destroy" part of the plan!

17 a4   ♘f5

It is more accurate to play the immediate 17...a5!. Nimzowitsch was under the impression that after the text-move 18 a5 could be answered by 18...♘g4+, when 19 hxg4 hxg4+ 20 ♔g1 g3 wins, but as Larsen points out, the variation 19 ♗xg4 hxg4 20 axb6 gxh3 21 gxh3 is not clear at all, and certainly more than White deserves. Again Black can draw with 21...♘xd4 22 cxd4 ♕xh3+ 23 ♔g1 ♕g4+ 24 ♔f2

♕f3+ 25 ♔g1 ♕g4+, but after 21...♘h4 22 ♕g3 it is not easy to suggest a way forward for Black.

18 g3 a5!

Finally preventing any a4-a5 ideas that White might entertain. You could say that ...a5 leaves the b6-pawn as a weakness, but it has been shown in many games that the pawn on b6 is easier to defend (and more difficult to attack) than the one on a4. The most striking example of the difference in these weaknesses is shown in the famous fifth game of the Spassky – Fischer World Championship match in Reykjavik in 1972. Here Fischer used a variation of the Nimzo-Indian that had been popularized by the German grandmaster Robert Hübner: 1 d4 ♘f6 2 c4 e6 3 ♘c3 ♗b4 4 ♘f3 c5 5 e3 ♘c6 6 ♗d3 ♗xc3+ 7 bxc3 d6 (a modern refinement over Nimzowitsch's play: Black delays castling) 8 e4 e5 9 d5 ♘e7 10 ♘h4 h6 11 f4 ♘g6 12 ♘xg6 fxg6 13 fxe5 dxe5 14 ♗e3 b6 15 0-0 0-0 16 a4? a5! 17 ♖b1 ♗d7 18 ♖b2 ♖b8 19 ♖bf2 ♕e7 20 ♗c2 g5 21 ♗d2 ♕e8 22 ♗e1 ♕g6 23 ♕d3 ♘h5 24 ♖xf8+ ♖xf8 25 ♖xf8+ ♔xf8 26 ♗d1 ♘f4 27 ♕c2? ♗xa4! and Spassky resigned due to 28 ♕xa4 ♕xe4, hitting g2 and e1.

19 ♖g1 ♘h6
20 ♗f1 ♗d7
21 ♗c1 ♖ac8

The main assault will start on the kingside in a few moves' time. Black is so confident of its success that he doesn't mind the rest of the board being blocked up. Indeed here he positively encourages White to block with d4-d5, by creating some concealed threats against the c4-pawn.

22 d5 ♔h8

23 ♘d2 ♖g8

Only now, after much preparation, does Black show signs of commencing the attack. Of course White is now totally lost.

24 ♗g2 g5

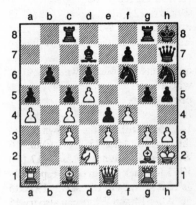

25 ♘f1 ♖g7
26 ♖a2 ♘f5
27 ♗h1 ♖cg8
28 ♕d1 gxf4!
29 exf4 ♗c8
30 ♕b3 ♗a6
31 ♖e2

After 31 ♗d2 Nimzowitsch gives the pretty line 31...♕g6! 32 ♗e1 ♘g4+ 33 hxg4 hxg4+ 34 ♔g2 ♗xc4! 35 ♕xc4 e3 and to prevent the mate on h3 White is forced to give up the queen with 36 ♘xe3 ♘xe3+ 37 ♔f2 ♘xc4.

31 ... ♘h4!

Black's positional masterpiece has been completed, and he now completely dominates the board. The rest is of the game is simply tactics. Tactics tend to flow freely from a position of strength, and this game is no exception. For example, if White now plays 32 ♘d2 Black wins in a pleasing fashion by 32...♗c8! 33 ♘xe4 (or 33 ♕d1

♗xh3! 34 ♔xh3 ♕f5+ 35 ♔h2 ♘g4+
36 ♔h3 ♘f2+ 37 ♔h2 ♕h3#) 33...♕f5!
34 ♘f2 ♕xh3+! 35 ♘xh3 ♘g4#. White
can spoil the fun a little with 34 g4, but
34...hxg4 35 ♘xd6 ♕d7 is still hopeless for White.

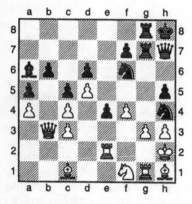

32	♖e3	♗c8
33	♕c2	♗xh3!
34	♗xe4	

Again 34 ♔xh3 allows mate after
34...♕f5+ 35 ♔h2 ♘g4+ 36 ♔h3
♘f2+ 37 ♔h2 ♕h3#.

| 34 | ... | ♗f5 |

Nimzowitsch: "Best, for ...h4 can
no longer be withstood. After the fall of
White's h-pawn the defence is hopeless."

| 35 | ♗xf5 | ♘xf5 |

36	♖e2	h4
37	♖gg2	hxg3+
38	♔g1	♕h3
39	♘e3	♘h4
40	♔f1	♖e8!

0-1

Black intends 41...♘xg2 42 ♖xg2
♕h1+ 43 ♔e2 ♕xg2+. 41 ♔e1 doesn't
help after 41...♘f3+ 42 ♔d1 ♕h1+,
with mate in three.

Lessons from this game:

1) The Nimzo-Indian is one of the
soundest defences to 1 d4.

2) The art of restraint is a very important concept. In *My System* Nimzowitsch asks himself the question "Was
...♕d8-d7-f5-h7 an attacking manoeuvre?", before answering in his own
way "Yes and no(!). No, since its whole
idea was to restrain White's kingside
pawns. Yes, since every restraining action is the logical prelude to an attack,
and since every immobile complex
tends to be a weakness and therefore
must sooner or later become an object
of attack." Who can argue with this
logic?

3) Positional domination is often
the precursor to a decisive tactical
flourish. In this game Black only begins the tactics around move thirty. Ten
moves later White is forced to resign.

Game 26
José Capablanca – Rudolf Spielmann
New York 1927
Queen's Gambit Declined, Westphalia Defence

The Players

José Raúl Capablanca (1888–1942) was one of the greatest players of all time and held the World Championship from 1921 to 1927. For more details see Game 13.

Rudolf Spielmann (1883–1942) was an Austrian professional player who spent most of his adult life in Germany before fleeing from the Nazis to Sweden. He was a leading player for an unusually long time, without ever reaching the absolute top ranks of world chess. A very active player, by the time he registered his first major success (2nd place at San Sebastian 1912), Spielmann had already competed in about 25 tournaments! After the First World War his career resumed, but far more than most masters he was prone to the occasional catastrophic failure. His style tended towards sacrificial attacks, and these were often based on intuition. When his intuition was working, he could produce brilliant games, but when it wasn't functioning the result was often a disaster. In the late 1920s, Spielmann's play became somewhat less erratic, and during the period 1926–9 he was one of the world's top ten players. His best results were first place at Semmering 1926 and joint second at Karlsbad 1929. Spielmann continued to play with slightly less success during the 1930s, before the outbreak of the Second World War effectively ended his career.

The Game

Capablanca had the unusual ability to dispose of very strong opponents without any great effort. At first glance, there is little special about this game; the decisive combination, while attractive, is not really very deep. The simplicity is deceptive; a closer look shows that the combination resulted from very accurate play in the early middlegame.

1	d4	d5
2	♘f3	e6
3	c4	♘d7

An unusual move-order which soon transposes into a known, if rather uncommon, line of the Queen's Gambit Declined. This variation was played several times at the 1927 New York tournament (a six-player event in which the players met each other four times).

4	♘c3	♘gf6
5	♗g5	♗b4
6	cxd5	

White should not give up his important dark-squared bishop by 6 ♗xf6. It is true that Black cannot reply 6...♘xf6 because of the fork 7 ♕a4+, but 6...♕xf6 7 e3 c5 gives him good counterplay.

6 ...   exd5

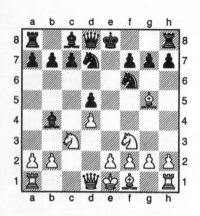

7 ♕a4

A move which is rarely played today. The current main line runs 7 e3 c5 8 ♗d3 c4 (8...0-0 9 0-0 ♗xc3 10 bxc3 c4 11 ♗c2 ♕a5 12 ♘e5 ♕xc3 13 ♘xd7 ♘xd7 favoured White in Alekhine – Vidmar, New York 1927) 9 ♗f5 ♕a5 10 ♕c2 0-0 11 0-0 ♖e8 with a slight advantage for White.

The other Capablanca – Spielmann game at New York 1927, which was played in the first cycle, continued 7 ♕b3 c5 8 a3 ♗xc3+ 9 ♕xc3 c4 10 ♕e3+ ♕e7 11 ♕xe7+ ♔xe7 with equality. This time Capablanca improves.

7 ...   ♗xc3+?!

Spielmann immediately goes awry. He does not want to waste time defending the bishop, but the long-term weakening of the dark squares turns out to be serious. The best reply was 7...c5! 8 dxc5 (after 8 e3 0-0 9 ♗d3 b6 10 0-0 ♗b7 Black completes his development) 8...♗xc3+ (now that White's pawns have been broken up, this exchange is justified) 9 bxc3 0-0

10 ♕d4 ♕c7 (10...♕a5 11 ♕b4!) 11 ♗xf6 ♘xf6 and Black will eventually regain the pawn on c5, with a roughly equal position.

8 bxc3   0-0
9 e3   c5

9...♕e8 sets the trap 10 ♗d3? ♘e5, but after 10 ♕c2 ♕e6 11 ♗d3 ♘e4 12 ♗f4 White retains a slight advantage because of his active bishops, e.g. 12...c5 13 c4! and the position starts to open up.

10 ♗d3

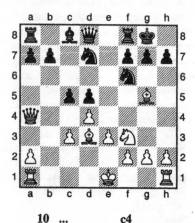

10 ...   c4

The start of an ambitious plan to expand on the queenside while restraining White in the centre. Unfortunately for Black, this plan is time-consuming and his development is simply not good enough to justify such optimistic play. However, accurate play is required to demonstrate this.

10...♕e8 would be met by 11 ♗xf6 ♘xf6 12 ♕xe8 ♖xe8 13 dxc5 ♘d7 14 ♗b5 and it isn't clear how Black will regain his pawn.

11 ♗c2   ♕e7

Alekhine suggested the interesting plan 11...♖e8 12 0-0 ♖e6, in order to harass White's queen. However, after 13 &f5 &a6 14 &b5! (14 &c2 &f8! is fine for Black) 14...&a5 (14...&b6? 15 &xd5) 15 &b1 White retains the advantage (now 15...&f8? fails to 16 &xf6 &xf6 17 &xc8 &xc8 18 &xb7).

12 0-0 a6

This position occurred in the game Farago – Sifrer, Ljubljana 1992, when Black continued 12...h6 13 &h4 &e6 14 &d2 &b6 15 &a5 &e4 16 &xe4 dxe4 17 f3 &d5. Now White should have played 18 &b4 exf3 19 &xf3 &g4 20 &f2 and Black cannot prevent e4 by White, as 20...f5? fails to 21 &af1. The theme of forcing through e3-e4 is typical of this type of position and also arises in Capablanca – Spielmann.

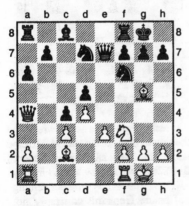

13 &fe1 &e6

Black intends to play ...b5 to activate his queenside pawns, followed by ...&b7 to prevent White's e4. However, the immediate 13...b5 14 &a5 &b7 is bad after 15 &c7 threatening both 16 &xb7 and 16 &xf6. Black must prevent the threatened 14 e4, so unpinning the f6-knight is the only choice.

14 &d2

Renewing the threat of e4.

14 ... b5
15 &a5!

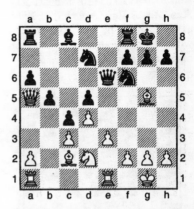

An excellent move. The queen on a5 appears to be doing little to support White's central play, but Capablanca intends to combine the threat of e4 with queenside play by a4. It is the combination of these two threats on different parts of the board that overstretches Black's defences.

15 ... &e4?!

Spielmann switches plans and instead of controlling e4 from afar, he decides to simply block it. However, it turns out that his position cannot stand another non-developing move. He should have stuck to his original idea with 15...&b7. It is true that White can eventually force through e4 by 16 f3 (16 a4 &c6 is ineffective) 16...&fe8 17 h3 (Black gains counterplay after either 17 e4 dxe4 18 fxe4 &g4 19 &xf6 &xf6 or 17 a4 &c6 18 e4 dxe4 19 fxe4 &g4 – in the latter line 20 &xf6 &xf6 21 d5 fails to 21...&xd5! 22 exd5 &xd5 23 g3 &e2), but Black would avoid an immediate disaster.

16 &xe4 dxe4

17 a4   ♕d5

The alternative 17...♖b8 18 ♖eb1 ♕d5 costs Black a pawn after 19 ♗f4 ♖b6 20 axb5 ♖xb5 (20...axb5 21 ♗a4 ♗a6 22 ♗c7 ♖g6 23 ♗xb5) 21 ♖xb5 axb5 22 ♖b1. The text-move aims to win a tempo by attacking the bishop on g5, thus gaining time for ...♗b7.

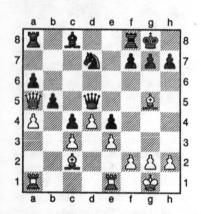

18 axb5!

This piece sacrifice is the refutation. Neither 18 ♗f4 ♗b7 19 ♖eb1 ♗c6 nor 18 ♗e7 ♖e8 19 axb5 ♗b7 20 ♗b4 axb5 21 ♕c7 ♕c6 gives White more than a slight advantage.

18 ...   ♕xg5

18...♗b7 19 bxa6 defends the g5-bishop and wins two pawns.

19 ♗xe4

In return for the piece White obtains three pawns, including a monster passed a-pawn.

19 ...   ♖b8

After 19...♖a7 White reveals the main point of his combination: 20 b6! ♕xa5 21 bxa7 ♕xa1 22 ♖xa1 ♘b6 23 ♖b1 and wins.

20 bxa6

There is no stopping White's a-pawn, so Black tries to drum up some counterplay against White's kingside, but the bishop on the long diagonal proves an effective defender.

20 ...   ♖b5
21 ♕c7   ♘b6
22 a7   ♗h3

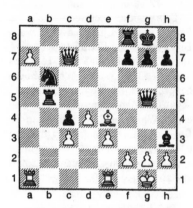

23 ♖eb1   ♖xb1+

Or 23...♖c8 24 ♕xb6 ♖xb6 25 ♖xb6 with an easy win.

24 ♖xb1   f5

24...♘d5 25 ♕a5 is decisive.

25 ♗f3   f4
26 exf4   1-0

Black's position is a total wreck and the finish might be 26...♖xf4 27 ♖xb6 ♖xf3 (27...♖f8 28 ♕xc4+ ♔h8 29 ♖b8) 28 a8♕+ ♖f8 29 ♕xc4+ mating.

Lessons from this game:

1) The power of the two bishops increases as the position opens up. If you have two bishops against a bishop and knight (or two knights) then look for pawn thrusts to open lines.

2) Changing your plan mid-stream is usually a bad idea.

3) An advanced passed pawn which cannot be blockaded usually costs the opponent a piece.

Game 27
Alexander Alekhine – Geza Maróczy
Bled 1931
Queen's Gambit Declined

The Players
We have already come across Alexander Alekhine in Games 20, 23 and 24. After wresting the world title from Capablanca in 1927, Alekhine was now busy cementing his position as the number one player in the world, while actively seeking to avoid a return match with the Cuban. To prove his supremacy Alekhine won some very strong tournaments, including San Remo (1930), Bled (1931) and London (1932). Alekhine refused to play in any tournament where Capablanca was competing, and the two did not meet again until 1936 in Nottingham, when Capablanca won.

We were introduced to Geza Maróczy in Game 18. Amongst his other duties in the 1930s, he was the controller for the two World Championship clashes between Alekhine and Euwe.

The Game
After a reasonably normal opening, Alekhine raises the tension in the position by accepting a pawn weakness in return for attacking chances against the black king. Meeting resolute defence, Alekhine presses on without fear, sacrificing his central pawn and throwing everything into the attack. One minor slip by Maróczy is enough for Alekhine's attack to come crashing through. It was shown after the game that Black could have defended his position, but finding such defences is always easier in the cold light of day than in the heat of battle. Alekhine's use of the entire board is particularly impressive.

1	d4	d5
2	♘f3	♘f6
3	c4	e6
4	♗g5	♘bd7
5	e3	h6
6	♗h4	♗e7
7	♘c3	0-0
8	♖c1	c6
9	♗d3	a6

At first sight this little pawn move on the queenside looks quite insignificant. What, for example, is Black going to do about developing the c8-bishop, which is currently hemmed in by its own pawns? In fact Black does have a cunning plan, which involves expanding with pawns on the queenside. The idea is simply to capture on c4 with ...dxc4. After ♗xc4 Black will follow up with ...b5, attacking the bishop, and then prepare a timely ...c6-c5 break. This will put pressure on the white centre and prepare to develop the so-called "problem bishop" on b7, where it can influence the game on the a8–h1 diagonal.

Nevertheless, when playing with the black pieces in a later game, Alekhine himself preferred a more direct move-order with 9...dxc4 10 ♗xc4 b5 11 ♗d3 and only now 11...a6. In Euwe – Alekhine, World Championship match (game 28), Amsterdam 1935, the defending champion benefited immediately from this sequence when the Dutch challenger went astray with 12 e4?. This slip allowed Alekhine to pounce with 12...♘xe4!. Now 13 ♗xe7 ♘xc3 14 ♖xc3 ♕xe7 15 ♖xc6 ♗b7 16 ♖c7 ♗xf3 17 ♕xf3 ♕b4+ 18 ♔f1 ♕xb2 and 14 ♗xd8 ♘xd1 15 ♔xd1 ♖xd8 16 ♖xc6 ♗b7 17 ♖c7 ♗xf3+ 18 gxf3 ♘f6 are both very good for Black. Euwe tried 13 ♗xe4, but after 13...♗xh4 14 ♗xc6 ♖a7 15 0-0 ♘b6 16 ♘e4 ♗e7 17 ♘e5 ♖c7 18 ♕d3 ♘c4 19 ♘xc4 ♖xc6 the weakness of the d4-pawn was beginning to tell, and White had to work hard for the draw.

The right way forward for White after 11...a6 is to attack the queenside with 12 a4!. This move directly opposes Black's plan of ...c6-c5. Fischer – Spassky, World Championship match (game 12), Reykjavik 1972 saw White keeping an edge after 12...bxa4 13 ♘xa4 ♕a5+ 14 ♘d2 ♗b4 15 ♘c3 c5 16 ♘b3 ♕d8 17 0-0 cxd4 18 ♘xd4 ♗b7 19 ♗e4!.

10	0-0	dxc4
11	♗xc4	c5
12	a4!	

Alekhine liked this move, which prevents Black's intended expansion with ...b5 and prepares for the imminent Isolated Queen's Pawn (IQP), one of the most common types of position seen in master chess. The safer way to play would be with 12 ♕e2 or 12 ♗d3.

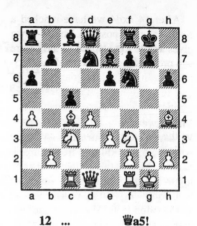

12	...	♕a5!

Maróczy's play in this game is also quite energetic, mixing defence and counterattack in just the right proportions. Of course, he does go wrong later on, but this is only after being subjected to a storming attack from Alekhine.

13	♕e2	cxd4
14	exd4	

Accepting the isolated pawn is the most aggressive course and one which is typical of Alekhine's style. In any case Alekhine dismissed the alternative 14 ♘xd4 with 14...♘e5 15 ♗b3 ♘g6 16 ♗g3 e5, and Black is fine.

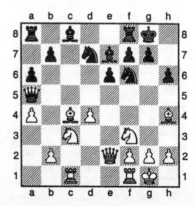

After 14 exd4 we have reached a finely balanced position. The d4-pawn gives White extra space in the centre and protects the important e5- and c5-squares. In particular it makes it virtually impossible for Black to free his position by the ...e6-e5 advance. White can often build up menacing pressure on the kingside and in the centre and will very often launch a direct attack against the black king, using his more active pieces. On the other hand, although rather passive, Black's position is extremely solid. He has no weaknesses, and he can hope to further free his position with timely exchanges. He can huddle in defence, safe in the knowledge that winning chances will arise later on. In the late middlegame and endgame the structural weakness which White possesses will become more and more prominent, and it is here where Black will hope to make his move. It's enough to say that many grandmasters like to play with the isolated pawn, but just as many are prepared to defend against it. It is purely a matter of taste.

14 ...   ♘b6

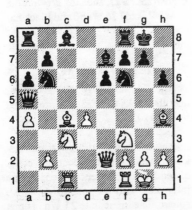

15 ♗d3!

"In for a penny, in for a pound." Once White has committed himself to a kingside attack, it's no good worrying about the little a-pawn. In fact Black can already grab it with 15...♘xa4, but Alekhine pointed out that White's initiative would be substantial after 16 ♘e4. Instead Maróczy continues to defend with a cool head.

15 ...   ♗d7
16 ♘e5   ♖fd8!

We can see the hidden dangers for Black more clearly if he does decide to go pawn-grabbing on the queenside. If 16...♗xa4 the tactics on the kingside start with 17 ♘g6!. 17...♖fe8 18 ♘xe7+ ♖xe7 19 ♗xf6 gxf6 20 ♘e4 gives White a very strong attack, not dissimilar to the game, while the capture 17...fxg6 loses to 18 ♕xe6+ ♔f7 19 ♘xa4 ♘xa4 20 ♗xg6 ♖f8 21 ♖c8!, whereupon Black is lost in all variations:

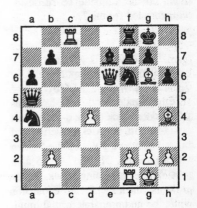

1) 21...♖xc8 22 ♗xf7+ ♔f8 23 ♗g6 ♕d5 24 ♕xc8+.
2) 21...♕d5 22 ♗xf7+.
3) 21...♗d8 22 ♗xf7+ ♖xf7 23 b4! ♕b6 24 ♕xb6 ♘xb6 25 ♖xd8+.

Maróczy's choice is far more sensible and another case of good practical defence. Black prepares the clever retreat ...♗e8, targeting the d4-pawn, which is a much bigger fish than a4. When the pawn on d4 goes, so does much of White's control over the important central squares.

17 f4!?

A sure sign of Alekhine's dynamic mood on this particular day. In his notes to the game he actually questioned the logic of this committal move and suggests that the simple 17 ♕f3 should be taken into consideration. Now 17...♘xa4 18 ♘e4! once more promises White a strong attack, while 17...♗xa4 18 ♕xb7 also favours White. Black's best option is 17...♗c6 18 ♘xc6 bxc6 19 ♖fd1, which Alekhine assessed as slightly better for White.

After 17 f4 White is prepared to give up the d4-pawn and allow Black serious counterplay on the d-file. Will the attack on the kingside be sufficient compensation for this?

17	...	♗e8
18	♘g4	♖xd4
19	♗xf6	♗xf6
20	♘xf6+	gxf6
21	♘e4	♖ad8?!

Perhaps understandably, Black goes for a counterattack on the d-file against the d3-bishop, but Alekhine criticized this move, which gives up the f-pawn without a fight. 21...♘d7 22 f5 also gives White a menacing attack, but after the stubborn 21...f5! 22 ♘f6+ ♔f8 White has no immediate way through on the kingside. Alekhine considered the calm 23 b3, but gave no follow-up for White. This in itself can be taken as a sign that Black has sufficient resources after 21...f5.

After 21...♖ad8 Black is still in the game, but the pendulum has swung significantly in White's favour. It does, however, require some quite brilliant play by Alekhine to prove this.

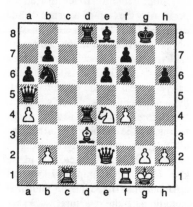

| 22 | ♘xf6+ | ♔f8 |
| 23 | ♘h7+! | |

Knight moves to the edge of the board are quite paradoxical, and hence difficult to visualize. It's very possible that Maróczy underestimated the strength of this idea, which forces the black king into the centre of the board, where it is more vulnerable to attack. If now 23...♔g7, then 24 ♕g4+ ♔h8 25 ♕h4! ♖xd3 26 ♕xh6 and Black has no good defence to White's mating threats.

| 23 | ... | ♔e7 |
| 24 | f5 | ♖8d6 |

After 24...♖xd3? White can disconnect the rooks with 25 f6+!, followed by 26 ♕xd3+.

25 b4!

Another powerful blow from Alekhine, which either deflects the black queen from the defence of e5, or else interferes with its path to an active square. The immediate 25 ♕h5 is met by 25...♕d2, when Black can create some threats of his own.

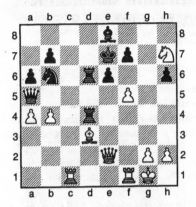

25 ...   ♕xb4

After 25...♖xb4, 26 ♕h5 gains in strength, as Black no longer has the reply 26...♕d2. Now 26...♖xd3 27 f6+ wins the black queen, so Alekhine gave the line 26...e5 27 f6+ ♔d8 28 ♕xh6 ♖xd3 29 ♕f8 ♖d7 30 ♖c5! ♕xa4 31 ♖xe5, which should be winning for White, e.g. 31...♖d5 32 ♕e7+ ♔c8 33 ♕xe8+ ♕xe8 34 ♖xe8+ ♖d8 35 ♖xd8+ ♔xd8 36 ♘g5 ♔e8 37 ♖e1+ ♔f8 38 ♖e7.

Instead of 29...♖d7 Black could also try to defend with 29...♘c8, but 30 ♘g5! gives White a winning attack, e.g. 30...♖f4 31 ♘xf7+ ♔d7 32 ♕g7! ♖xf1+ (or 32...♕b6+ 33 ♔h1 ♖xf1+ 34 ♖xf1 ♗xf7 35 ♕xf7+ ♔d8 36 ♕g8+ ♔c7 37 f7 ♕f2 38 f8♕!) 33 ♔xf1! and the white f-pawn proves decisive.

26 ♕e5

Threatening a pretty checkmate with 27 ♕f6+ ♔d7 28 ♘f8#.

26 ...   ♘d7

27 ♕h8!   ♖xd3?

Maróczy finally cracks under the strain of having to defend a difficult position for a long time. Alekhine gave an alternative win after 27...♕b6 with the further deflection 28 a5!. Then 28...♕a7 loses as in the game to 29 f6+ ♔d8 30 ♕xe8+!, while 28...♕xa5 29 ♖c8 is also the end.

However, in *The Chess Sacrifice*, Vuković points out that 27...♖c6! is a much more stubborn defence. Further analysis by Nunn concludes that after 28 ♖xc6 bxc6 29 fxe6 fxe6 30 ♘f6 ♗f7 31 ♘xd7 ♖xd7 32 ♗g6 ♕c5+ 33 ♔h1 ♕f2 34 ♕a1 ♕xf1+ 35 ♕xf1 ♗xg6 White has some advantage, but whether this would be enough to win is quite another matter. Black can also try 30...♘xf6 31 ♕xf6+ ♔d7 but his more exposed king gives White some winning chances after, for instance, 32 ♕xh6 (32...♖xd3? 33 ♕h7+).

28 f6+   1-0

28...♔d8 allows a fitting finale after 29 ♕xe8+! ♔xe8 30 ♖c8#, while 28...♘xf6 29 ♕xf6+ ♔d7 30 ♘f8# is also mate.

Lessons from this game:

1) Remember "edge moves". Alekhine won this game with a lethal cocktail of moves near to the side of the board, e.g. 23 ♘h7+, 25 b4 and 27 ♕h8. This type of move is often quite difficult to visualize.

2) Pawns are good defenders! 21...f5 would have not only kept the extra material, but also this extra pawn could have been used as a barricade.

3) Kasparov was right when he said "Alekhine's attacks came suddenly, like destructive thunderstorms that erupted from a clear sky."

Vsevolod Rauzer – Mikhail Botvinnik

USSR Championship, Leningrad 1933

Sicilian Defence, Dragon Variation

The Players

Vsevolod Rauzer (1908–41) is mainly remembered for a number of aggressive opening systems that he developed for White. We shall see the Richter-Rauzer Attack in Games 36, 39 and 97, while the Yugoslav Attack (see Game 67) ought really to be named after him too, as indeed it is in Russian. He was one of the leading group of Soviet players in the period 1927–37, though he never won the Soviet Championship. Thereafter a serious illness brought his playing career to a premature end. His life also ended prematurely: he died in Leningrad in 1941.

Mikhail Botvinnik (1911–95) was one of the greatest players of all time, and a key figure in the development of chess in the Soviet Union. He was born in Kuokkala, near St Petersburg. He learned to play chess at the age of 12 and made remarkably fast progress, qualifying for the USSR Championship when he was 16, overstating his age in order to be allowed to play. As a young man he was very determined and hard-working, and these qualities were a trademark throughout his long career. He was astute, level-headed and realistic. His approach was to prove effective not only on the chessboard but also in the ever-changing politics of the USSR: for one prominent individual to remain in favour for a prolonged period was no mean feat. Two subsequent victories in the Soviet Championship made it clear that he was the great hope for Soviet chess, and in international events in the mid-1930s he established himself as a legitimate challenger for the world title; he was clearly in the same class as Alekhine and Capablanca. However, the Second World War intervened, and frustrated his hopes of a title match. He was fortunate to escape from Leningrad before the siege began in 1941. He spent the war years in the Urals, to where his wife, a ballet dancer in the Kirov, had been evacuated. Botvinnik was not an obsessive chess player; he also pursued a successful career as an engineer. However, when this career was threatening his study time for chess, he wrote to Molotov to arrange a cut in his working hours!

After the war, and following Alekhine's death in 1946, FIDE assumed control of organizing the world championship. In 1948 Botvinnik emerged as convincing winner of the match-tournament to determine a new champion, and thus became a Hero of the Soviet Union. He held on to the world title until 1963, except for two occasions when he lost the title for one year, to Smyslov (1957–8) and Tal (1960–1). On each occasion he made good use of the champion's right to a return match. On the whole his title defences were none too convincing, but during the 1950s he did not play very frequently, and each time he was almost emerging from semi-retirement to face a younger, more strongly motivated opponent. The fact that he kept his title through these challenges was a remarkable demonstration of his strength of character and the effectiveness of his methods.

After losing the title for the last time, to Petrosian in 1963, he began to play more frequently in tournaments, with considerable success and occasional brilliance, as we shall see in Game 57, Botvinnik – Portisch. He finally retired from competitive play in 1970, to concentrate on his work with chess-playing computers. However, it must have been a bitter disappointment to him that the artificial-intelligence approach, which he advocated, fell by the wayside as brute-force machines made steady progress towards top-grandmaster level.

The Game

Botvinnik plays an uncompromising opening, to which Rauzer replies in a somewhat hesitant manner. Botvinnik is able to use tactical means to smash open the centre. For several moves Rauzer follows the right path, but just when he has a chance to emerge from the complications with a reasonable game, he gives Botvinnik the opportunity to raise his initiative to a more intense level. With an unexpected and unusual manoeuvre, he launches a surprisingly powerful attack with his queen, knight and a far-advanced passed pawn. With suitable back-up from the Dragon bishop and two centralized rooks, the attack quickly proves decisive.

1	e4	c5
2	♘f3	♘c6

2...d6 3 d4 cxd4 4 ♘xd4 ♘f6 5 ♘c3 g6 is the standard Dragon. Now 6 ♗e2 (6 ♗e3 ♗g7 7 f3 is the Yugoslav Attack) 6...♗g7 7 ♗e3 ♘c6 transposes to the game.

3	d4	cxd4
4	♘xd4	♘f6
5	♘c3	d6

This system is known, for want of a better name, as the Classical Sicilian.

6	♗e2	

By this time, Rauzer had not yet developed the line (now the most popular in this position) that was to bear his name, 6 ♗g5 e6 7 ♕d2, the Richter-Rauzer Attack. Thus Botvinnik is able to use this move-order to reach a Dragon Sicilian while avoiding some of White's sharper attacking ideas – though it is amusing to note that the sharpest of these, the Yugoslav Attack,

the main line in modern practice, was also yet to be invented by this same Rauzer!

6	...	g6

Although one generally associates Botvinnik with very solid opening play, in his earlier years he used the Dragon Sicilian to good effect. 6...e5 was later devised by Boleslavsky, after whom it is named, and is considered extremely solid. As a result, 6 ♗e2 is quite rare in modern practice.

7	♗e3	♗g7
8	♘b3	♗e6
9	f4	0-0
10	0-0	

10 g4 was tried by Alekhine against Botvinnik at the Nottingham tournament of 1936. Botvinnik replied in excellent fashion, and secured a comfortable draw after 10...d5! 11 f5 ♗c8 12 exd5 ♘b4 13 d6 ♕xd6 14 ♗c5 ♕f4! 15 ♖f1 ♕xh2 16 ♗xb4 ♕g3+ 17

♖f2 ♕g1+ 18 ♖f1. Botvinnik's play is to this day still considered the correct handling of 10 g4.

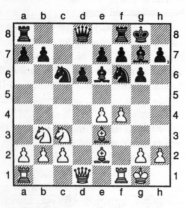

```
10 ...              ♘a5
11 ♘xa5
```

11 f5 ♗c4 gives Black satisfactory play, by using thematic Dragon devices: 12 ♘xa5 (not 12 e5?! ♗xe2 13 ♕xe2 dxe5 14 ♖ad1 ♕c7 15 ♘b5 ♕c4!) 12...♗xe2 13 ♕xe2 ♕xa5 and now:

1) 14 g4 ♖ac8! 15 g5 (15 ♗d4 ♕b4 16 ♖ad1 ♕c4!) 15...♖xc3 (this exchange sacrifice, undermining White's protection of his e4-pawn, is one of the main themes in the Dragon Sicilian) 16 gxf6 ♖xe3 17 ♕xe3 ♗xf6 18 c3 ♖c8 gives Black excellent compensation for the exchange.

2) 14 ♗d4 ♘d7 15 ♗xg7 ♔xg7 16 ♘d5 ♘f6! is equal, since after 17 ♘xf6 exf6 Black's pawns may appear ugly, but White's backward e-pawn is just as weak as anything in the black structure.

```
11 ...              ♕xa5
12 ♗f3
```

12 ♕d2 was cited as an improvement by Botvinnik, but Black's game

is obviously satisfactory even in this case.

```
12 ...              ♗c4
13 ♖e1              ♖fd8
14 ♕d2
```

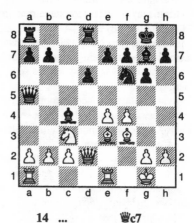

```
14 ...              ♕c7
```

The undefended queen on a5 is a tactical liability (the move ♘d5, unveiling an attack from the white queen, is a typical theme), so it relocates to a square where it puts pressure on the c-file and potentially the b8–h2 diagonal.

15 ♖ac1?!

This move is far too slow. Perhaps Rauzer had in mind some scheme involving b3 and ♘d5. Whatever it was, Botvinnik gives him no chance to play it by immediately seizing the initiative. White ought to have taken his opponent's lead, and improved the position of his queen (i.e. 15 ♕f2).

```
15 ...              e5!
```

This move ensures that the centre will be blasted open to the maximum degree. Both the d8-rook and the g7-bishop (and to some extent the black queen) have sensitive targets at the end of their lines, so any opening of the position will enhance the effectiveness of at least one of them.

16 b3?!

White can be forgiven for missing his opponent's stunning reply, but alarm bells ought to have been ringing – his pieces are set up for some sort of combinative blow.

16 fxe5 dxe5 17 ♕f2 is the best way to bail out – by opening only the d-file, White manages to avoid serious trouble.

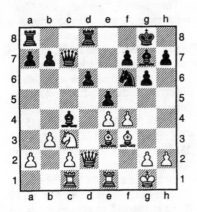

16 ... d5!!

It is always nice to be able to play a move like this – there are four pieces trying to stop this advance, yet Black can play it. Moreover, the move creates such serious threats that Black need not move his attacked bishop for now. Grandmaster Jonathan Mestel once expressed a general principle: the more pieces there are trying to stop a pawn-break, the more effective it will be if carried out successfully. Here we have a case in point.

17 exd5!

Rauzer's heart must have sunk as he analysed the various possible sequences of captures here, and he realized that

he had completely lost control of the game. However, he made the right decision at this point, as other moves are worse:

1) 17 bxc4? dxe4.

2) 17 ♘xd5 ♗xd5 18 exd5 e4 19 ♗e2 ♘xd5 is dreadful for White.

3) 17 fxe5 ♘xe4! (17...dxe4? 18 ♕f2 exf3 19 exf6 ♗xf6 20 ♘e4 and suddenly Black's loose pieces tell against him) 18 ♗xe4 dxe4 19 ♕f2 ♗xe5 (after 19...♕xe5 20 ♘xe4 White has escaped the worst) 20 ♘xe4 f5 leaves White in difficulties.

17 ... e4!

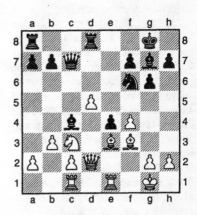

18 bxc4

This move may not be too bad, but a clearer solution to White's problems is to take the pawn with his knight:

1) 18 ♗xe4 ♘xe4 19 ♘xe4 ♗xd5 20 ♕d3 (20 ♘g3 ♗c3) 20...♕c6 (or 20...f5!?) 21 ♗f2 f5 (21...♖e8 has been claimed to be very good for Black, but 22 ♘d6!? is an interesting reply) 22 ♘g5 ♗xg2 favours Black in view of his better structure and long-term lack of safety for the white king.

2) 18 ♘xe4! ♘xd5 19 ♔h1 (certainly not 19 bxc4? ♘xe3 20 ♕xe3??

♗d4) 19...♘xe3 20 ♕xe3 ♗d4 and now:

2a) 21 ♕d2 and now Black must choose carefully:

2a1) 21...♗b2?! 22 ♕b4 ♗xc1 (22...♗d5 23 ♖cd1!?) 23 ♘f6+ (23 ♕c3!? is also awkward) 23...♔h8 24 ♕c3 ♗d2 25 ♕b2 (25 ♕a1 ♗e6 26 ♘d5+ ♗c3 27 ♘xc7 ♗xa1 28 ♘xa8 ♗c3 is at least OK for Black) 25...♗e6! 26 ♘d5+ ♗c3 is meant to be good for Black, but 27 ♘xc3 still looks worrying for the black king – after 27...♔g8 28 ♘e4 ♕xf4 29 ♘f6+ ♔f8 30 ♘d5! ♖xd5 31 ♕h8+ ♔e7 32 ♕xa8 the winning chances are with White.

2a2) 21...♗e6 and here, rather than 22 c4 ♗e5 23 ♕c2 ♗xf4, which is good for Black (Botvinnik), 22 ♖cd1 ♗e5 23 ♕b4!? keeps White in the game.

2b) 21 ♘f6+!? ♗xf6 (21...♔h8 22 ♘e8!; 21...♔f8? 22 ♕e4 ♗e6 23 ♘xh7+ ♔g8 24 ♘g5 ♗d5 25 ♕xd4 ♗xf3 26 ♕f2 gives White two extra pawns and attacking chances) 22 bxc4 ♕xc4 23 ♗xb7 ♖ab8 24 ♗f3 ♕xa2 and Black's a-pawn shouldn't be enough to give him real winning chances.

18 ...   exf3

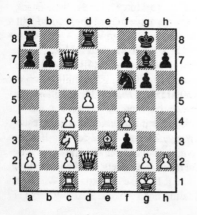

19 c5

Black's energetic play has reduced White's pawn structure to rubble. However, there is a large amount of this rubble, some of it in rather threatening places, and there is a limit to the speed at which Black can clear it – great precision is still required.

19 ...   ♕a5

Now 20...♘xd5 represents a major threat.

20 ♖ed1?!

This natural, "useful" move does not answer the specific requirements of the position, which turn out to be to keep the queens on and seek a tactical means to maintain at least part of the pawn-centre he has been temporarily granted – in other words to build something out of the "rubble".

1) 20 d6? fails to 20...♘g4! 21 ♘e4 ♕xd2 22 ♗xd2 (22 ♘xd2? ♘xe3 23 ♖xe3 ♗d4) 22...f2+! 23 ♘xf2 ♗d4.

2) 20 ♖cd1 would also be met by 20...♘g4 since after 21 ♘e4 ♕xd2 22 ♖xd2 f5 the ...♗c3 idea exploits the line-up of the white rooks along the e1–a5 diagonal.

3) 20 ♕d3! is the critical move:

3a) 20...♘g4?! (presumably Botvinnik would have played this if Rauzer had chosen 20 ♕d3) 21 ♘e4 f5 22 ♘g5 f2+ 23 ♗xf2 ♘xf2 24 ♔xf2 ♕xc5+ 25 ♔g3! ♖xd5 (25...♕xd5?? 26 ♖e8+) 26 ♕b3 and the pin causes problems.

3b) Botvinnik found the best reply, 20...b6!, breaking up White's centre pawns (e.g. 21 gxf3 bxc5 or 21 cxb6 axb6), in analysis nearly thirty years after the game!

20 ...   ♘g4!
21 ♗d4

Again, White could be forgiven for missing that this move allows Black to launch a winning attack using his queen and knight. The best chance was 21 ♘e4 ♕xd2 22 ♗xd2 ♗d4+ 23 ♔h1 fxg2+ 24 ♔xg2 ♖xd5, though the ending is grim in view of White's many weaknesses.

21 ...   f2+

22 ♔f1

22 ♔h1 ♖xd5! 23 ♘xd5 f1♕+! wins the queen: 24 ♖xf1 ♕xd2.

22 ...   ♕a6+

23 ♕e2

There was nothing better: 23 ♘e2 ♖xd5 24 c3 ♖e8!; 23 ♕d3 ♗xd4 24 ♕xa6 ♘xh2+ 25 ♔e2 f1♕+! 26 ♖xf1 bxa6 is winning for Black.

23 ...   ♗xd4

24 ♖xd4

If White plays 24 ♕xa6?, then Black wins a piece by 24...♘e3+ 25 ♔e2 (25 ♔xf2? ♘xd1++) 25...f1♕+! (yet again the white rook is diverted by this heroic pawn's final act) 26 ♖xf1 bxa6.

24 ...   ♕f6!

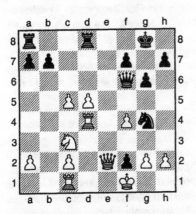

Completing a memorable queen manoeuvre. Consider how unlikely this scenario looked after White's 20th move.

25 ♖cd1

Black's attack also proceeds briskly after other moves:

1) 25 ♕d2 is met by 25...♕h4! (rather than 25...♖e8 26 ♘e4 ♖xe4 27 ♖xe4 ♕h4 28 h3).

2) 25 ♕d3 ♖e8! (25...♕h4 26 ♕g3) 26 g3 (26 ♘e4? ♘xh2+ 27 ♔xf2 ♕xf4+; 26 ♖e4? ♖xe4 27 ♘xe4 ♕xf4) 26...♖e3 27 ♘e4 ♕f5 28 ♕c4 ♕h5! 29 h4 ♘h2+ 30 ♔g2 (30 ♔xf2 ♕f3+ 31 ♔g1 ♖e2) 30...♕f3+ 31 ♔xh2 ♖e1 32 ♕f1 ♖xc1! winning.

25 ...   ♕h4

26 ♕d3   ♖e8

27 ♖e4   f5

28 ♖e6   ♘xh2+

29 ♔e2   ♕xf4

0-1

Botvinnik's comment was "This was my first game to become widely known. It is probably my best effort from those years."

Lessons from this game:

1) If White does not seize the initiative from the opening, then Black will – and in an Open Sicilian he will do so very quickly.

2) A pawn-break in the centre is a powerful weapon – always analyse such moves to see if they might work, even if there seem to be enough pieces preventing them.

3) The introduction of a queen into an attack often has a devastating effect; the defender should be very careful to avoid an unwelcome royal visit.

Game 29
Mikhail Botvinnik – José Capablanca
AVRO tournament, Rotterdam 1938
Nimzo-Indian Defence

The Players

Mikhail Botvinnik (1911–95) was World Champion 1948–57, 1958–60 and 1961–3. By 1938 he had already achieved considerable success at top level, but had yet to establish himself as the challenger to Alekhine – a challenger the AVRO tournament was designed to select. For an account of Botvinnik's career, see Game 28.

José Raúl Capablanca was still an extremely formidable opponent in 1938; just two years earlier he had shared first prize with Botvinnik in the Nottingham tournament, ahead of Euwe, Alekhine, Lasker, et al. However, the format of the AVRO tournament – each round in a different city – certainly did not favour the older players, especially those with ailing health – Capablanca was suffering from *angina pectoris*. It was the only tournament in his entire career in which he lost more games than he won.

The Game

This is a strategic battle on the grand scale, culminating with a scintillating sacrificial combination. Capablanca chooses an ambitious plan of infiltrating on the queenside at the cost of giving White more prospects in the centre. Hitherto this had been considered a reasonable plan with this type of structure; as a result of this game it came to be seen as rather dubious. Botvinnik relentlessly pushes on in the centre, bravely sacrificing a pawn on the queenside to fuel his initiative. Capablanca defends well, and just when he seems to be consolidating, Botvinnik finds a fantastic combination, and there is no saving the black position. The notes presented here ask, for the first time, what would have happened if Capablanca had not allowed the combination. The answer is an endgame variation as beautiful as the combination itself.

1	d4	♘f6
2	c4	e6
3	♘c3	♗b4
4	e3	d5
5	a3	♗xc3+
6	bxc3	c5
7	cxd5	exd5
8	♗d3	0-0
9	♘e2	b6

10	0-0	♗a6

Capablanca methodically prepares to exchange off his bishop before it becomes "bad", and before its counterpart creates dangerous threats on the kingside. The drawback is that after White's reply, Black's knight is poorly placed on a6.

11	♗xa6	♘xa6

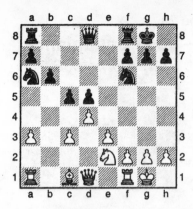

12 &b2?!

12 &d3! was Botvinnik's later preference, giving Black less leeway in how to reply. White would still be happy to see 12...c4, while 12...&c8 limits Black's scope for counterplay on the c-file. 12 f3 is another possibility.

12 ...   &d7

13 a4

13 &d3 &a4 could prove annoying for White, who has no pieces that can conveniently oust the queen from a4.

13 ...   &fe8?!

13...cxd4! 14 cxd4 &fc8 gives Black more counterplay, and is undoubtedly the correct way to play. However, at the time the power of White's central strategy was underestimated, and Capablanca was probably trying to extract the maximum winning chances from the position.

14 &d3   c4?!

"This is a really serious positional error. Black evidently assumed that White would be unable to advance the e-pawn later, and Black's superiority would tell on the queenside... However, Black's superiority on the queenside happens in this case to be of no

great consequence, and the breakthrough e3-e4 proves inevitable. Black should have contented himself with the modest defence 14...&b7." – Botvinnik. Instead 14...&c7 15 dxc5 bxc5 16 c4 gives White a definite positional plus.

15 &c2

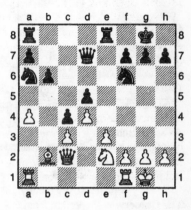

15 ...   &b8

Black is planning ...&c6-a5-b3, either tying White up on the queenside or forcing him to surrender the a-pawn. Against sluggish play from White, this would indeed be a highly effective plan. 15...&h5 followed by ...f5 was a reasonable way to try to frustrate White's central advance. Then White would have had to consider the alternative plan of undermining the f5-pawn by h3 and g4. This would take careful preparation, and give Black more hope of real counterplay.

16 &ae1   &c6

Capablanca's positional sense must have been telling him that his queenside play was sufficient to counterbalance White's central push. However, his knight spends a great deal of time coming round to b3, and although the a4-pawn does drop, by then White is creating some real threats.

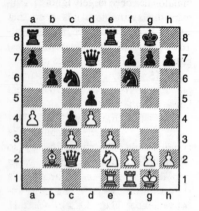

17 ᐀g3

Now Black's ...᐀h5 idea is ruled out.

17 ...   ᐀a5

17...᐀e4 is instructively met by 18 ᐀h1!, preserving the knight from exchange and preparing f3, followed by the h1-knight's return to the action and a continued central advance; for example 18...f5 19 f3 ᐀f6 20 ᐀g3 is clearly better for White. The more pieces remain on the board, the more potent White's advance will be. Firstly there will then be more targets for the advancing pawns; secondly White will have greater prospects of launching an attack on the black king.

18 f3!   ᐀b3
19 e4   ᐁxa4
20 e5   ᐀d7

Now 21...᐀bc5 is threatened. White can obviously afford neither an exchange of queens nor a black knight landing on the square d3. The immediate 20...᐀c5? fails to 21 ᐀e2, leaving both black knights attacked.

21 ᐁf2!

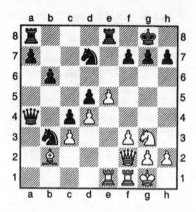

Neatly side-stepping the threat. From here the queen supports the f-pawn's advance.

21 ...   g6
22 f4   f5
23 exf6

Naturally White must keep the game open to make his local superiority of force on the kingside tell.

23 ...   ᐀xf6
24 f5

It is now very difficult for Black to defend. He tries to do so by exchanging off the rooks on the e-file.

24 ...   ᐀xe1
25 ᐀xe1   ᐀e8

Instead, a defence on the f-file is more easily broken down: 25...᐀f8 26 ᐁf4! and then:

1) 26...ᐁa2 27 fxg6! ᐁxb2 28 g7 ⬦xg7 (28...᐀f7 29 ᐁb8+ ⬦xg7 30 ᐀f5+ ⬦g6 31 ᐁg3+ mates) 29 ᐀f5+ ⬦h8 30 ᐁd6 (not 30 ᐁh6?? ᐁf2+!) 30...᐀f7 31 ᐁxf6+! and White forces mate.

2) 26...ᐁd7 27 ᐀e6 ᐀a5 (27...᐀e4 28 ᐁe5 ᐀xg3 29 ᐀e7 wins the black queen, and with it the game, as in the resulting position the white queen will pick off Black's pawns very quickly)

28 ♗a3 ♖f7 29 ♕g5! and White has a large advantage.

26 ♖e6!   ♖xe6

Or:

1) 26...♘e4? 27 ♘xe4 dxe4 28 fxg6! wins, e.g. 28...♕d7 29 gxh7+ ♔xh7 30 ♕f5+.

2) 26...♔f7? 27 ♖xf6+! ♔xf6 28 fxg6+ ♔xg6 (28...♔e7 29 ♕f7+ ♔d8 30 g7) 29 ♕f5+ ♔g7 30 ♘h5+ ♔h6 (30...♔g8 31 ♕g5+ ♔f7 32 ♕f6+ ♔g8 33 ♕g7#) 31 h4 ♖g8 32 g4 ♕c6 33 ♗a3! forces mate.

3) 26...♘g4? 27 ♕e2 doesn't help Black at all.

27 fxe6   ♔g7
28 ♕f4   ♕e8

Not 28...♕a2? 29 ♘f5+! gxf5 30 ♕g5+ ♔f8 31 ♕xf6+ and mate in two more moves.

29 ♕e5

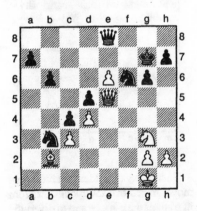

Considering how much danger he appeared to be in a few moves ago, it looks as if Capablanca has defended his position rather well. However, his next move, although very natural, allows a surprising combination that has become extremely famous.

29 ...   ♕e7?

It is strange that the question of what happens if Black avoids the combination has been largely ignored. Perhaps the assumption has been that Black can do little active, and if he allows ♗a3, then the e-pawn will be too strong and White will make progress easily. However, things are not so simple, as a well-timed ...♘a5-c6 offers hope of counterplay.

1) First of all, it is worth mentioning that 29...♘a5? is premature; the knight should only retreat from b3 (so allowing ♗c1) when the white e-pawn is more vulnerable, and so the knight's arrival on c6 causes White more inconvenience. Thus 30 ♗c1 ♘c6 31 ♗h6+ ♔xh6 32 ♕xf6 (threatening mate in two with 33 ♘f5+) 32...♘e7 (32...♕d8 33 ♕xd8 ♘xd8 34 e7) 33 h4 (threatening mate in two by the quiet move 34 ♘h5!) 33...♕d8 34 ♘f5+ wins the queen.

2) 29...h6 is the critical move:

2a) 30 ♕c7+ ♔g8 and the e-pawn needs protection.

2b) 30 ♗a3 ♕d8 31 ♘e2 ♘a5 32 e7 ♕d7 33 ♘f4 ♘c6 34 ♕e6 ♕xe6 35 ♘xe6+ ♔g8 (35...♔f7? 36 ♘d8+; 35...♔h8? 36 ♘c7) 36 ♘d8 and now Black should play either 36...♘a5 or 36...♘b8, with a good game.

2c) 30 ♘e2!?, rerouting the knight, doesn't give a clear win either after 30...♘a5 31 ♘f4 (31 ♕c7+ ♔g8 32 ♘f4 is met by 32...g5 33 ♕e5 ♘g4) 31...♘c6 32 ♕c7+ ♘e7 33 ♗a3 (33 ♕xa7 g5 34 ♘e2 ♔g6 35 ♕xb6 ♘c6 and the e6-pawn falls) 33...g5 and here:

2c1) 34 ♘e2 ♘fg8 intending ...♕c6 or ...♔f6.

2c2) 34 ♗xe7 gxf4 35 ♕xa7 ♔g6 36 ♗xf6 ♔xf6 37 ♕xb6 ♕xe6 38

♕xe6+ ♔xe6 39 ♔f2 ♔f5 40 ♔f3 ♔g5 with a drawn king and pawn ending.

2c3) 34 ♕xa7 gxf4 35 ♕xe7+ ♕xe7 36 ♗xe7 leads to a complicated ending which seems OK for Black.

2d) 30 h4!? (Nunn) is a logical attempt, aiming to play h5 to gain control of the f5-square:

2d1) 30...b5? (30...a5? 31 h5 is a similar story) 31 h5 a5 32 ♗a3 (32 hxg6 should be good too) 32...b4 33 cxb4 and White should win.

2d2) 30...♕e7? 31 h5 ♘a5 32 hxg6 and Black is too slow with his counterplay.

2d3) 30...h5 (this leaves g5 too weak) 31 ♗a3 ♘a5 (31...♕d8 32 ♕g5!) 32 ♕c7+ ♔g8 33 ♗e7 ♘g4 34 ♕d7 ♕xd7 35 exd7 wins a piece, leaving White with a won ending.

2d4) 30...♘a5 is the best try.

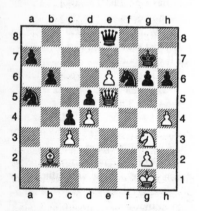

Now White has several tempting ideas, but it is surprisingly hard to prove a clear-cut win. However, there is a way: 31 ♗c1! ♕e7 (31...♘c6? 32 ♗xh6+ ♔xh6 33 ♕xf6 ♔h7 34 h5) 32 ♗g5! ♘c6 (32...hxg5 33 hxg5 ♘c6 34 gxf6+ ♕xf6 35 ♕xd5 ♘d8 36 ♕d7+ ♔f8 37 d5 ♕g5 38 ♘f1 and White

wins) 33 ♗xf6+ ♕xf6 34 ♕xd5 ♕xh4 (Black's only chance) 35 ♕d7+ ♘e7 36 d5 ♔f6 37 d6 ♕xg3 38 ♕xe7+ ♔e5 (it looks as if White cannot prevent a perpetual, but...) 39 ♕g7+! ♔xd6 (39...♔xe6 40 ♕e7+ and 41 d7 or 39...♔f5 40 ♕f7+ ♔g5 41 d7 ♕e1+ 42 ♕f1 ♕d2 43 e7 wins) 40 ♕d7+ ♔c5 41 ♕d4+ ♔b5 42 ♕e4 (the key point is to arrive at this square, which prevents perpetual check) 42...♕b8 (42...♕d6 43 e7 ♕d1+ 44 ♔h2 ♕h5+ 45 ♔g3 escapes from the checks easily) 43 e7 ♕e8 44 ♕d5+ and 45 ♕d8 wins.

We return now to the position after Capablanca's actual move, 29...♕e7.

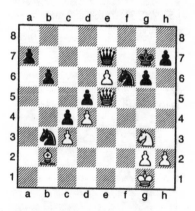

30 ♗a3!!

There are two ideas behind this move: to remove the blockader from in front of the e-pawn and to divert the queen from defending the f6-knight. Black's main defensive idea is to give perpetual check, but Botvinnik has everything worked out.

30 ...   ♕xa3

30...♕e8 is no good, as Black has lost two tempi compared to lines of the last note . 31 ♕c7+ ♔g8 32 ♗e7

♘g4 and now White's e-pawn proves its worth: 33 ♕d7 ♕a8 34 ♗d6 and White wins.

31 ♘h5+!

This temporary knight sacrifice is the second link in the chain.

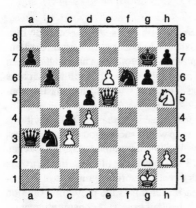

31 ... gxh5

31...♔h6 32 ♘xf6 ♕c1+ 33 ♔f2 ♕d2+ 34 ♔g3 ♕xc3+ 35 ♔h4 ♕xd4+ fails to the killer blow 36 ♘g4+.

32 ♕g5+ ♔f8
33 ♕xf6+ ♔g8
34 e7!

A poetic finish to White's strategy of central advance: a centre pawn will inevitably promote. Black's attempts to give perpetual are doomed as the white king can safely walk up the board.

Instead 34 ♕f7+ ♔h8 35 e7? ♕c1+ 36 ♔f2 ♕d2+ 37 ♔g3 ♕g5+ (37...♕xc3+? 38 ♔h4 ♕xd4+ 39 ♔xh5 ♕e5+ 40 ♔g4 ♕e4+ 41 ♔h3 ♕e3+ 42 g3 ♕h6+ 43 ♔g2 ♕d2+ 44 ♕f2 and White wins) 38 ♔f3 ♘d2+ 39 ♔e2 ♕xg2+ (it is important to remove this pawn) 40 ♔d1 ♕g1+ 41 ♔c2 (41 ♔xd2 ♕xh2+ 42 ♔c1 ♕g1+ 43 ♔b2 ♕h2+!) 41...♕b1+ 42 ♔xd2 ♕d3+ 43 ♔e1 ♕e3+ 44 ♔f1 ♕c1+ 45

♔f2 ♕d2+ 46 ♔g3 ♕g5+ 47 ♔f3 ♕g4+ 48 ♔f2 ♕h4+ 49 ♔f1 ♕h3+ is perpetual check.

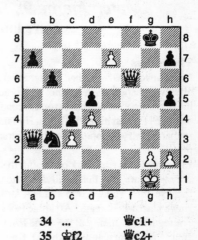

34 ... ♕c1+
35 ♔f2 ♕c2+
36 ♔g3 ♕d3+
37 ♔h4 ♕e4+
38 ♔xh5 ♕e2+

38...♕g6+ 39 ♕xg6+ hxg6+ 40 ♔xg6 and the king stops his counterpart from approaching the pawn.

39 ♔h4 ♕e4+
40 g4 ♕e1+
41 ♔h5 1-0

Lessons from this game:

1) An attack based on the gradual advance of a central pawn majority may take a long time to develop, but generates tremendous force.

2) Believe in yourself and your ideas – as Botvinnik did when he let his a-pawn go in order to concentrate on his attack.

3) When there is a far-advanced passed pawn near the enemy king, be on the lookout for tactical methods, utilizing threats to the king, to free a path for the pawn.

Max Euwe – Paul Keres

Match (game 9), Rotterdam 1939/40

Queen's Indian Defence

The Players

Max Euwe (1901–81) had a long involvement with chess which covered virtually every aspect of the game, but paradoxically he was an amateur throughout
his playing career and chess took second place to his profession as a mathematics
teacher. He lived his entire life in Holland and single-handedly popularized chess
in that country, a popularity which persists today and which forms a lasting memorial.

Euwe made his first mark on the international scene in the early 1920s, but it was
only ten years later that he advanced to the top with a succession of good tournament results. These led to a match for the World Championship in 1935, when
Euwe narrowly defeated Alekhine (+9 =13 −8) to gain the ultimate title. Euwe is
not regarded as being at the same level as the other world champions of the period (Capablanca and Alekhine). One reason for this is the prevailing opinion
that Alekhine only lost the 1935 match as a result of excessive consumption of alcohol coupled with a failure to take Euwe seriously. The other reason is that
Euwe only held the title for two years, since Alekhine (now off the bottle) regained the World Championship in 1937 with the one-sided score +10 =11 −4. It
is worth remarking that Alekhine and Capablanca made it as hard as possible for
potential challengers to actually get a title match, whereas Euwe immediately offered Alekhine the chance to regain his title. Euwe's chess was curtailed during
the Second World War, but when international activity started again (fittingly, in
Holland) Euwe registered one of the best tournament results of his career, second
place behind Botvinnik at Groningen 1946. However, Euwe's playing career
then went into decline although he still played actively right up to his death.

Euwe was involved with chess on many other fronts. He was a prolific and successful author, with *The Middle Game* (1965, with H. Kramer) being perhaps the
most notable of a generally high-quality output. He became President of the International Chess Federation (FIDE) in 1970, a post he held for eight years. This
was a potentially difficult period for FIDE and although some of his decisions
were criticized at the time, in retrospect his presidency may be assessed as a success. Euwe was also interested in the development of chess-playing computers,
so there was hardly one area of chess activity in which Euwe did not have an influence.

Paul Keres (1916–75) was one of the strongest players never to become World
Champion. He lived in Estonia throughout his life and in that country he is regarded as something of a national hero.

In his youth, Keres could not find suitable opponents and so played hundreds of games by correspondence. Evidently this was good practice for over-the-board play, as he won the Estonian Championship in 1934/5. Keres's advance to the world top was astonishingly quick. He burst onto the international scene at the 1935 Warsaw Olympiad, and only two years later he tied for first (with Fine) at Margate 1937, beating Alekhine in their individual game. Later in 1937 he won a very strong event at Semmering, and this was sufficient to gain him an invitation to AVRO 1938, an event which was intended to select a challenger to meet Alekhine for the World Championship. Keres finished joint first with Fine, but Keres had the superior tie-break and so gained the right to challenge Alekhine. Unfortunately, war broke out and hopes of a title match faded. Estonia was assimilated into the USSR in 1940, and Keres competed in some Soviet events. However, it was not long before Estonia was occupied by Germany, and Keres took part in a number of events in German-occupied territories. When the war ended, Estonia was back in Soviet hands. The historical details of this period are both unclear and controversial, but in any case Keres returned to Estonia and resumed playing in Soviet tournaments. In the World Championship Tournament of 1948, Keres finished joint third and this was the only time Keres was able to challenge for the ultimate title.

Keres had an exceptionally long career at the top and was within the top eight for an incredible quarter of a century. In 1971, when numerical rankings were introduced, Keres was still in the top ten. His tournament successes are so numerous that we can hardly mention them all here, but he was a Candidate seven times, and won the Soviet Championship three times. In 1975, shortly before his death, he convincingly won a strong tournament in Tallinn, his home town. On the way back from a tournament in Vancouver (which he won with 8½/10) he suffered a heart attack and died on 5th June 1975.

The Game

This game is an excellent illustration of Keres's dynamic style. Euwe makes a slip in the early middlegame, allowing Keres to gain the initiative. The next phase of the game is quite complex and neither player handles it perfectly. Keres then seizes the chance to make a positional queen sacrifice, obtaining only a rook and a piece for the queen but developing amazing activity for his pieces. Euwe can do little but wriggle, and Keres finishes with an attractive mating combination.

1	d4	♘f6
2	c4	e6
3	♘f3	b6
4	g3	♗b7
5	♗g2	♗e7
6	0-0	0-0
7	♘c3	♘e4

8 ♕c2

This system often leads to a quick draw, but not in this game! These days, if White is playing for a win then he usually chooses 8 ♗d2.

8	...	♘xc3
9	♕xc3	d6

A slightly unusual line. Today the alternatives 9...♗e4, 9...f5 and 9...c5 are all regarded as equalizing. 9...♗e4 is the preferred choice of players aiming for a draw.

10 ♕c2   f5

Control of e4 is critical in the Queen's Indian Defence, so Black must prevent White from establishing a large and solid pawn centre by e2-e4. Black must also take care to avoid a favourable d4-d5 by White; for example 10...♘c6?! 11 d5 exd5 12 cxd5 ♘b4 13 ♕b3 ♘xd5 14 ♘d4 c6 15 ♘xc6 ♗xc6 16 ♗xd5 favours White due to Black's weak d-pawn.

11 ♘e1

White hopes to exchange bishops, and then transfer his knight to f4 to exploit the weakening of e6 created by Black's ...d6. However, this plan is hard to realize and 11 d5 e5 12 e4 is a more combative line, with an edge for White.

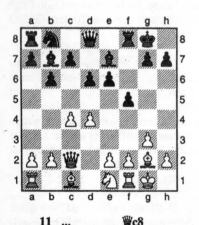

11 ...   ♕c8

Keres recommended 11...♗xg2 12 ♘xg2 e5 (12...c6 13 e4 ♘a6 14 exf5 exf5 15 ♕a4 ♕c8 16 ♖e1 gave White some advantage in Alekhine – Keres,

Buenos Aires Olympiad 1939, while 12...♕d7 13 e4 fxe4 14 ♕xe4 d5 15 ♕g4 ♗d6 16 cxd5 exd5 17 ♕xd7 ♘xd7 18 ♗f4 also gives White an edge) as Black's best, in order the keep the knight out of f4, although White still has a faint edge after 13 dxe5 dxe5 14 ♖d1.

12 e4

Not 12 d5 ♘d7 13 dxe6 ♘c5 and Black regains the pawn under favourable circumstances.

12 ...   ♘d7

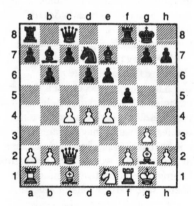

13 d5?

After this Black liquidates favourably in the centre. The critical line was 13 exf5 exf5 (13...♗xg2 14 ♘xg2 exf5 15 d5 and e6 is weak) and now:

1) 14 d5 c6! and Black frees himself. It is true that he will probably end up with an isolated d-pawn, but White's development is so poor he cannot exploit it.

2) 14 ♕e2 ♗xg2 15 ♘xg2 ♗f6 16 ♗e3 ♕b7 17 ♘f4 ♖ae8 18 ♕c2 ♖e4 with equality, Vidmar – Szabo, Budapest 1940.

3) 14 ♗h3 is White's best chance for an advantage. Then 14...g6 (after

14...♗e4 15 ♕d1 Black must take care
otherwise his bishop will be trapped
by d5 followed by f3) 15 ♗h6 ♖e8 is
best, when White is just slightly better.

13 ...   fxe4

14 ♕xe4

Black gains the advantage after either 14 dxe6 ♘c5 or 14 ♗xe4 ♘f6 15
♗g5 h6 16 ♗xf6 ♗xf6 17 dxe6 ♗xe4
18 ♕xe4 ♖e8.

14 ...   ♘c5

15 ♕e2

Not 15 ♕c2 exd5, which is very
awkward for White, e.g. 16 cxd5 ♗a6,
16 b4 ♘a6 or 16 ♗xd5+ ♗xd5 17
cxd5 ♕f5.

15 ...   ♗f6

Unpinning the e6-pawn.

16 ♗h3

This looks dangerous, but if the pin
along the h3–c8 diagonal leads to
nothing, White might well regret having abandoned the long diagonal to the
control of the bishop on b7. In fact, it
is already hard for White to equalize
completely: after 16 dxe6 ♗xg2 17
♘xg2 ♕xe6 Black is slightly more
comfortable because of his better development.

16 ...   ♖e8!

With the tactical threat 17...exd5.

17 ♗e3

The threat is 18 ♗xc5 followed by
19 ♗xe6+, but Black can meet this
threat. 17 dxe6 ♘xe6 18 ♕g4 is also
ineffective after 18...♘d4!, with the
idea 19 ♕xc8? ♘e2#.

17 ...   ♕d8

18 ♗xc5

White executes his threat, but it
meets with a surprising reply. 18 dxe6
♘xe6 would have been just slightly
better for Black.

18 ...   exd5!

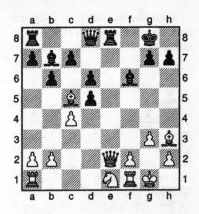

19 ♗e6+?

Now White loses a pawn. 19 ♗e3
was the best chance, but after 19...d4
20 ♗g2 ♗xg2 21 ♘xg2 dxe3 22 ♘xe3
♗d4 23 ♖ae1 ♗xe3 24 fxe3 ♖e5
Black obtains a small but persistent
advantage due to White's isolated e-
pawn.

19 ...   ♔h8

20 ♖d1

White also ends up a pawn down after 20 cxd5 ♗xd5 or 20 ♗a3 ♕e7 21
cxd5 ♗xd5.

20 ...   dxc5

20...bxc5 was also very good, for
example 21 ♘g2 dxc4 or 21 cxd5
♗xd5 22 ♖xd5 ♕e7.

21 ♘g2

White clears e1 for his rook and attempts to activate his knight. After 21
cxd5 Black has several good alternatives, for example 21...♘d4, 21...♗xd5
22 ♖xd5 ♕e7 or 21...♗xb2 22 ♕xb2
♖xe6.

21 ...   d4?

The activity of Black's bishops is
more important than consolidating the
extra pawn. Therefore the correct line
was 21...♗d4!; after 22 ♘f4 dxc4 23
♕h5 ♕f6 24 ♗f7 ♖e5 25 ♘g6+ ♕xg6

26 ♗xg6 ♖xh5 27 ♗xh5 ♗xb2 Black has a huge pawn-mass in return for the exchange.

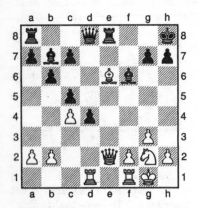

22 f4?

The correct plan – White must try to support his well-placed e6-bishop by f5 and ♘f4 – but incorrectly executed. After 22 ♖fe1! ♗c8 (or else f4-f5, followed by ♘f4) 23 ♕g4 ♗xe6 24 ♖xe6 ♖xe6 25 ♕xe6 ♕e8 26 ♕xe8+ ♖xe8 27 ♔f1 Black has an extra pawn, but his bishop is severely restricted by his own pawns, so it is doubtful whether he could win.

After this rather scrappy phase, the rest of the game is pure magic.

22 ...   d3!

Keres pinpoints the flaw in Euwe's last move. First of all he sacrifices a pawn to clear the d4-square for his dark-squared bishop...

23 ♖xd3   ♕xd3!

...then he offers his queen to eliminate the well-placed bishop on e6. 23...♗d4+ 24 ♔h1 ♕f6 is far less clear after 25 f5 ♗xb2 26 ♖d7, when White has counterplay.

24 ♕xd3   ♗d4+
25 ♖f2

After 25 ♔h1 ♖xe6 White is in a fatal pin and there is little to be done against the threat of ...♖ae8 followed by ...♖e2, e.g. 26 f5 ♖e3 27 ♕d2 ♖ae8 28 f6 ♖e2 29 fxg7+ ♔xg7 30 ♕g5+ ♔h8 and wins. White therefore offers the exchange, but Black need not take it.

25 ...   ♖xe6
26 ♔f1   ♖ae8

Much stronger than 26...♗xf2 27 ♔xf2 ♖ae8 28 ♘h4, when the pressure is somewhat relieved.

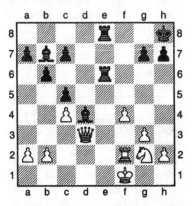

Black has only a rook and a piece for the queen, but just look at his piece activity! His bishops, operating on adjacent diagonals (see also Games 11 and 14, Rotlewi – Rubinstein and Nimzowitsch – Tarrasch respectively), tear into White's king position, while his rooks threaten to penetrate decisively along the e-file.

27 f5

A desperate attempt to free himself by clearing f4 for the knight. The most resilient defence is 27 ♖d2, but Black wins all the same by 27...♗e4 28 ♕b3 (28 ♕a3 ♗f5 is very similar) 28...♗f5! (transferring the bishop to h3 is the key idea) 29 ♕d1 (or 29 ♕f3 ♗h3 30 ♕d1 ♖e4 and then ...g5) 29...♗h3 30 ♖c2 (White is totally paralysed and can only await Black's intentions) 30...g5! 31 b3 gxf4 32 gxf4 ♖e4 33 ♕c1 ♖g8 34 ♖f2 ♖g4 followed by 35...♗xg2+ 36 ♖xg2 ♖gxf4+.

27 ...   ♖e5

28 f6

In order to deflect the g7-pawn and so prevent a later ...g5. White also loses after 28 ♖d2 ♗e4 29 ♕b3 ♖xf5+ 30 ♘f4 g5 or 28 ♖f4 ♖e2.

28 ...   gxf6

Certainly not 28...♗xf2 29 ♔xf2 ♖e2+? 30 ♕xe2 ♖xe2+ 31 ♔xe2 since 31...♗xg2 32 f7 actually loses for Black.

a b c d e f g h

29 ♖d2

29 ♖xf6 fails to 29...♗xg2+ 30 ♔xg2 ♖e2+.

29 ...   ♗c8!

Now that the pawn is on f6, the continuation 29...♗e4 30 ♕b3 ♖f5+ 31 ♘f4 is not so clear. However, the transfer of the bishop to the c8–h3 diagonal creates new threats.

30 ♘f4

Or 30 ♕f3 ♗h3 31 ♖xd4 (31 ♕xf6+ ♔g8) 31...cxd4 32 g4 ♖e1+ 33 ♔f2 ♖1e2+ and Black wins.

30 ...   ♖e3

There is more than one solution to the problem, for example 30...♖e1+ 31 ♔g2 ♖8e3 32 ♕c2 ♗g4 33 h4 ♗f3+ 34 ♔h3 ♖h1+ 35 ♖h2 ♗e4 36 ♕d2 ♗f5+ 37 ♔g2 ♖b1 is also decisive. However, the method chosen is the most elegant.

31 ♕b1

White must prevent 31...♖e1+.

31 ...   ♖f3+

32 ♔g2

32 ...   ♖xf4!

Introducing an attractive mating finish.

33 gxf4   ♖g8+

34 ♔f3

Or 34 ♔h1 (34 ♔f1 ♖g1+ wins) 34...♗b7+ and Black mates on the following move.

34 ...   ♗g4+

0-1

Since 35 ♔e4 (35 ♔g3 ♗f5+) 35...♖e8+ leads to mate after 36 ♔d5 ♗f3+ or 36 ♔d3 ♗f5#.

Lessons from this game:

1) If the position is equal, then playing too hard for the advantage is risky.

2) Piece activity is often more important than a small amount of material (such as a pawn or the exchange for a pawn).

3) Be flexible. Just because a bishop is active on one diagonal doesn't mean that another diagonal might not be even better.

Efim Geller – Max Euwe
Candidates tournament, Zurich 1953
Nimzo-Indian Defence

The Players

Efim Geller was born in 1925 in Odessa (Ukraine). He has had a long and successful career, and during most of the 1950s and 1960s was among the world's elite, qualifying for the Candidates stage of the World Championship no fewer than six times, coming particularly close to qualifying for a title match in 1962. He played in the Soviet Championship a record 23 times. His style of play has always been aggressive, and particularly in his early career he would often stake everything on one big attack (in this book we see one example where this went horribly wrong, and another where it worked perfectly). His opening knowledge has always been well respected, and in the 1970s was chosen as a second by Spassky and Karpov. He has continued to produce important games into the 1990s.

Max Euwe (1901–81) was World Champion 1935–7. By 1953 he was no longer one of the main challengers for the world title, but played with great energy in this Candidates tournament, and certainly deserved a higher placing than 14th (out of 15) – of his five wins in the tournament, two were brilliant enough to have made it into this collection! For more details on Euwe's career, see Game 30.

The Game

Geller tries an aggressive line against Euwe's Nimzo-Indian. Euwe chooses a subtle move-order with slightly delayed castling. Geller does not seem perturbed and continues to channel his pieces towards the black king. Visually, at least, his attack reaches quite frightening proportions, but then Euwe makes a surprising rook sacrifice to draw the white queen even further into his position, and to grant his other rook access to the key square c2. This opens the floodgates for Black's counterattack. Geller has one problematic chance to stay in the game, but misses it and is quickly overwhelmed.

1	d4	♘f6	5 a3	♗xc3+
2	c4	e6	6 bxc3	b6
3	♘c3	♗b4		
4	e3			

4 a3 ♗xc3+ 5 bxc3 c5 6 e3 comes to the same thing.

4 ... c5

6...0-0 7 ♗d3 b6 8 ♘e2 ♗b7 9 0-0 would allow White to save a tempo by ♘g3, e4 and f4 (rather than f3-f4, as in the game), unless Black were to play ...d5, but White would welcome the liquidation of the weak c4-pawn and the opening of the position which that would bring about.

7 ♗d3   ♗b7

A slightly unusual move-order from Black. The bishop would usually aim to go to a6 to put pressure on the c4-pawn, but here it stops off at b7 to hinder White's attempts to play a quick e4. Note that this idea only makes sense if Black delays castling – see the note to Black's 6th move.

8 f3   ♘c6
9 ♘e2   0-0
10 0-0   ♘a5
11 e4

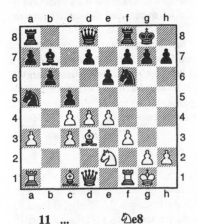

11 ...   ♘e8

This retreat looks odd at first sight, but has for a long time been a standard part of Black's armoury in the Nimzo-Indian. Black wishes to avoid the unpleasant pin ♗g5. In most positions, such a pin would be only an inconvenience, but with the black dark-squared bishop gone, and Black's other minor pieces making for the c4-pawn, the pin would be a real menace, creating instant and severe defensive problems. The manoeuvre ...♘e8, introduced by

Capablanca, is not merely a passive move; the knight can come to d6 to intensify the pressure on c4, and makes way for a possible advance of Black's f-pawn, attacking White's imposing centre.

12 ♘g3

The knight heads for an attacking post on the kingside and takes control of the f5-square. As Bronstein commented, "defending the c4-pawn is pointless; it was already doomed by White's 5th move". In effect then, the Sämisch Nimzo-Indian is a gambit by White: the c4-pawn is undead rather than alive, and White must act with all the urgency that gambit play entails.

12 f4 f5 illustrates an idea mentioned in the previous note.

12 ...   cxd4
13 cxd4   ♖c8
14 f4   ♘xc4
15 f5

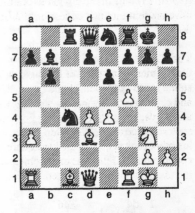

Here we see another key aspect of Black's plan for defending his kingside coming into play. White is now threatening to push his pawn on to f6. If he allows that, then Black will find his king position blasted wide open. In

particular, if Black plays ...♘xf6, then the deadly ♗g5 pin would appear. The fact that it has cost White a pawn is far less significant that the open f-file, intensifying the pressure.

15 ...   f6

That said, I wonder if in this specific instance Black wasn't being a little stereotyped in his thinking – "everyone knows you can't allow f6 in this type of position". However, 15...b5 doesn't look at all bad, since Black can generate very quick pressure on the white centre, e.g. 16 f6 ♘xf6 and now:

1) 17 e5 ♘d5 18 ♕h5 (18 ♗xh7+ ♔xh7 19 ♕h5+ ♔g8 20 ♘e4 f6) 18...g6.

2) 17 ♗g5 ♕b6 18 ♗xf6 (18 ♗xc4 ♖xc4 19 ♗xf6 gxf6 20 ♔h1 ♕xd4 21 ♕g4+ ♔h8) 18...gxf6.

In all cases Black seems to be doing well.

16 ♖f4

White brings in his big guns for an all-or-nothing attack. 16 a4 e5 17 ♗xc4+ ♖xc4 18 dxe5 fxe5 19 ♕b3 was tried in Polugaevsky – Averbakh, USSR Championship, Leningrad 1956, with White enjoying a fair initiative in return for the pawn.

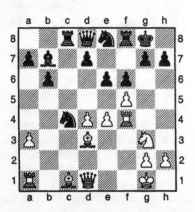

16 ...   b5!

As Bronstein observes, Euwe played more than 70 games against Alekhine, so was well accustomed to facing massive attacks. He does not panic and go into passive defence, nor does he embark on a hasty counterattack, but rather prepares to activate his forces, ready for whatever is to come. His masterplan, as we shall see, is to draw White's major pieces so far into his own camp that they will be uselessly placed when Black finally launches his counterattack. The initial tactical point of 16...b5 is to prepare 17...♕b6, when the pin of, and pressure against, the d4-pawn slows down White's transfer of queen and rook to the h-file. This is what has become known as "active prophylaxis" or "prophylactic thinking". Black perceives White's plan, and finds a way to frustrate it that at the same time furthers his own plans.

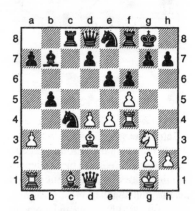

17 ♖h4

Or:

1) 17 ♗xc4 ♖xc4 18 ♖h4 ♕c7 19 ♗e3 ♖c2 is given as unclear by Botvinnik in the *Encyclopedia of Chess Openings*.

2) 17 ♕h5 is well met by 17...♕b6 18 ♘e2 ♘e5!.

17	...	♕b6
18	e5	♘xe5
19	fxe6	♘xd3
20	♕xd3	

20 exd7 can be met by 20...♕c6 or 20...♖xc1 21 ♖xc1 ♘xc1.

20	...	♕xe6
21	♕xh7+	♔f7
22	♗h6	

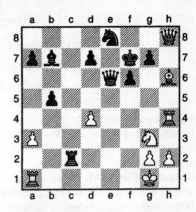

24 ♖c1?

White had to play 24 d5 ♗xd5 (24...♕b6+ 25 ♔h1 ♕f2 26 ♖g1 ♗xd5 27 ♖e4!) 25 ♖d1! (25 ♖d4? ♖xg2+ 26 ♔f1 ♖xh2) 25...♖xg2+ 26 ♔f1 gxh6 27 ♕xh6 (and not 27 ♖xh6? ♖xg3; nor 27 ♖xd5?! ♕xd5 28 ♖e4 ♘g7 29 ♔xg2 f5), though Black still has the better practical chances.

24	...	♖xg2+
25	♔f1	♕b3
26	♔e1	♕f3

0-1

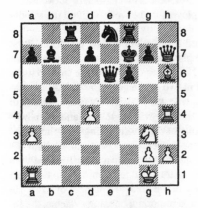

22 ... **♖h8!?**

22...♖c4 is, according to Bronstein, more accurate, preparing the ...♖h8 idea.

22...♕d5 23 ♖e4 (certainly not 23 ♘e4?? ♕xd4+) 23...♖c6 intending ...♖e6 looks good. At the very least Black's threats on the long diagonal keep several of White's pieces tied up, and therefore unable to participate in his flagging attack.

23 ♕xh8 ♖c2

The point – Black launches a whirlwind counterattack against the white king.

Lessons from this game:

1) Accepting a complex of weakened pawns can be equivalent to offering a gambit, with all the risk and commitment that a gambit entails.

2) Pieces that have advanced far into enemy territory may turn out to be useless in defending their own king.

3) When the opponent suddenly turns defence into counterattack, don't panic. Calmly reassess the position and look for your best hope of salvaging something from the position.

Max Euwe – Miguel Najdorf
Candidates tournament, Zurich 1953
Benoni Defence

The Players

Max Euwe (1901–81) was World Champion 1935–7. For more information, see Game 30.

Miguel Najdorf (1910–97) was one of the most colourful characters of twentieth-century chess. He was one of the top ten players in the world around the middle of the century and inspired an upsurge in chess activity in Argentina.

He was born in Warsaw, originally named Moishe Mieczslaw Najdorf. When war broke out in 1939, he was one of the players who chose not to try to return home from the Buenos Aires Olympiad. He subsequently became an Argentine citizen and changed his name. He played in two of the great Candidates tournaments of the 1950s, performing well, though he was never really in the running to qualify for a world championship match. His play was aggressive and often brilliant, but also impulsive – and this was one of the shortcomings that held him back when facing world-class opposition. He remained passionate about his chess well into his eighties, promoting events in Argentina and performing with gusto in tournaments as late as 1996, when he travelled to Groningen to take part in an event celebrating the 50th anniversary of the great tournament of 1946. He gave his name to one of the most popular and important opening systems, the Sicilian Najdorf (1 e4 c5 2 ♘f3 d6 3 d4 cxd4 4 ♘xd4 ♘f6 5 ♘c3 a6). Although he was not the first to play 5...a6, he introduced what are now viewed as the main strategic ideas behind it (a quick ...e5 and rapid, aggressive queenside development). The Najdorf has been a favourite of World Champions Fischer and Kasparov, and its popularity is currently as great as ever.

The Game

Najdorf plays the opening in provocative style. Rather than acquiesce to the type of game for which Najdorf is clearly aiming, Euwe cuts across his plans with a daring and heavily committal sequence of moves. The entire fate of the game rides on whether he can keep his grip on certain key squares, and when this grip is challenged, Euwe is ready to sacrifice material to achieve his strategic goals. Black goes a rook up, but is unable to solve the main problem of his position – the fact that his position is cut in two, with the queenside pieces unable to come quickly enough to the aid of their king. White's attack crashes through, and although Najdorf manages to return the material to avoid immediate disaster and to get his pieces into play, White's superiority is by now unchallenged and he wins efficiently.

1	d4	♘f6
2	c4	g6
3	g3	♗g7

Other moves:

1) 3...c6 intending ...d5 is a sound but dull way to play for sterile equality.

2) 3...d5 is the Fianchetto Grünfeld. Compared to the standard Grünfeld (which we see in Game 53), White benefits from the fact that his knight is not yet on c3, but the time already spent on g3 makes it somewhat less efficient for him to build a centre with e2-e4.

4	♗g2	0-0
5	♘c3	c5

5...d6 would be a more standard King's Indian move, keeping open Black's options of a strategy based on either ...e5, ...c5, or piece play against White's pawn-centre. With his actual move, Black seems to be aiming for a Benoni set-up.

6 d5

White indicates that he wants a complex battle. If he wished to play for an edge in a quiet position, then 6 ♘f3 was possible, when after 6...cxd4 (6...d6 7 0-0 ♘c6 is more aggressive) 7 ♘xd4 White has a spatial plus and it is not easy for Black to generate active counterplay.

6 ...   e5

Black's idea with this move was probably to reach the line 6...d6 7 ♘f3 e5 while denying White the possibility of 8 dxe6 ♗xe6 9 ♘g5. This position has been the subject of considerable debate, but it is currently the view that 9...♗xc4 10 ♗xb7 ♘bd7 11 ♗xa8 ♕xa8 12 0-0 d5 gives Black excellent compensation. Back in 1953, the verdict on the exchange sacrifice was less

clear. Note that these ideas do not always work – after 5 ♘f3 (instead of 5 ♘c3) 5...d6 6 0-0 c5 7 d5 e5?! 8 dxe6 ♗xe6 9 ♘g5 ♗xc4 10 ♗xb7 ♘bd7, 11 ♘a3! is good for White, as the bishop has no decent square, and 11...♖b8 12 ♘xc4 ♖xb7 13 ♘xd6 is obviously bad for Black.

7 ♗g5!?

White devises a plan to "take advantage" of Black's unusual move-order. Whether it is any better than 7 ♘f3 d6 8 0-0, when White can play solidly for a positional edge, is open to question. However, from a practical angle, Euwe doubtless wanted to deny Najdorf the type of game he was aiming for – instead of settling into the slow grind of a King's Indian/Benoni structure, Black will now have to solve some very concrete short-term problems.

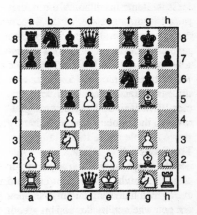

7 ...   h6

True to his style, Najdorf seeks an immediate solution to the problem, forcing the bishop to declare its intentions. The alternative is 7...d6:

1) 8 ♘e4 ♗f5 is no problem for Black, e.g. 9 ♕d2? ♗xe4 10 ♗xf6 (10

♗xe4 ♘xe4) 10...♗xg2!? 11 ♗xd8 ♖xd8.

2) 8 ♕d2 stops ...h6 and may be followed up by the advance of White's h-pawn.

8 ♗xf6　　　♕xf6
9 d6!?

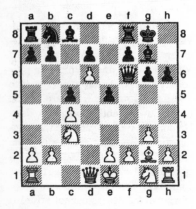

This, then, is the plan. White intends to justify the surrender of the important dark-squared bishop by clogging up the development of Black's queenside, and using the d5-square as a base for his own operations. However, there are major risks associated with this plan. If White is unable to keep the initiative, then the pawn will hardly prove tenable on d6 in the long term. Moreover, while Black's queenside development may be frustrated for now, the knight has access to c6, and the light-square long diagonal is open for potential use by the bishop – both of which were unthinkable prior to White's 9th move. On top of that, White is neglecting his kingside development, and leaving his king in the centre. If White lets up the pace for an instant, these factors will immediately tell against him. "White's problem is

to hold the pawn and at the same time strive to attack Black's kingside while it is deprived of the needed support of the queenside pieces. Euwe copes with this problem brilliantly." – Bronstein.

9 ...　　　♘c6
10 e3

Necessary to prevent ...♘d4.

10 ...　　　b6
11 ♗d5

Activating the bishop while using a simple tactical device (11...♕xd6?? 12 ♗xf7+) to keep the d6-pawn defended.

11 ...　　　♔h8

Now the d6-pawn is threatened in earnest, so White's hand is forced. 11...♗a6 intending ...♖ab8 and ...b5 was an alternative suggested by Najdorf, though this does not solve the fundamental problem of his position being divided in two.

12 ♘e4　　　♕d8

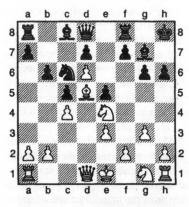

It appears that Black has already solved his problems: ...f5 will follow, forcing the knight to retreat from e4, and Black will engulf the d6-pawn and win easily. If it were not for the small matter of Black's king, that would be the case. However...

13 h4!   f5
14 ♘g5

It becomes apparent that it will be several moves before Black will really threaten to capture the knight, and so White has bought himself some time to generate his attack.

14 ...   ♗b7
15 g4!

It is not yet clear where the g1-knight should go, as there are no routes open towards the black king. Nor is it obvious how the position of the major pieces can best be improved, so White aims to open some lines.

15 ♘f7+? ♖xf7 16 ♗xf7 would of course be a horrible betrayal of White's aims so far in the game. White's target is to attack the king, not to make a dodgy exchange grab. Play might continue 16...♘b4 17 f3 ♕f6 18 ♗d5 ♗xd5 19 cxd5 e4, when White's position is a total wreck.

15 ...   e4

With this move, Black seeks to move the bishop to free a square for his king, and so threaten ...hxg5. White must find a way to oppose this plan. Deciding how to do so is easier because of the main drawback of 15...e4 – it gives White the f4-square. Other moves:

1) 15...♘a5 16 ♗xb7 ♘xb7 17 ♕d5 threatens ♕xb7 and ♘f7+ (White doesn't mind winning the exchange if it doesn't entail positional suicide, of course). 17...♕c8 can be met by 18 h5! making immediate use of the h-file now that the black queen has taken its eye off the g5-knight.

2) 15...♕f6!? 16 ♘f7+ (16 gxf5 ♕xf5 17 ♖h2 is possible too) 16...♖xf7 (forced; 16...♔h7?? 17 g5 wins the

black queen) 17 g5 ♕xd6 18 ♗xf7 gives Black some compensation for the exchange, but maybe not enough, e.g. 18...♘d4 19 ♖h3 ♖f8 20 ♗d5.

16 ♘e2   ♗xb2

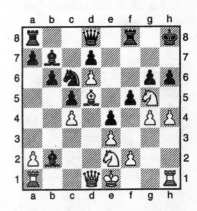

17 ♘f4

Euwe decides he cannot afford to spend time saving his queen's rook – which in any case is unlikely to be able to participate in the attack in the near future – and goes straight for the king.

17 ...   ♕f6

Instead:

1) 17...hxg5 18 ♘xg6+ ♔g7 19 ♘xf8 ♕xf8 20 hxg5 gives White dangerous attacking chances.

2) 17...♗xa1 18 gxf5 (18 ♕xa1+? ♕f6 19 ♘xg6+ ♔g7 is wholly inadequate for White) 18...♗c3+ 19 ♔f1 is similar to the game continuation:

2a) 19...hxg5?? allows a forced mate: 20 hxg5+ ♔g7 21 ♕h5!? (21 ♘h5+ also mates just as quickly) 21...gxh5 22 ♘xh5+ ♔h8 23 ♘f6+ ♔g7 24 ♖h7#.

2b) 19...♕f6 transposes to the game.

2c) 19...♖xf5 is the only way to give this move-order independent significance, but then White continues by 20 ♘xg6+ ♔g7 21 ♘xe4 ♖xd5 (21...♔xg6? 22 ♕g4+; 21...♗f6 22 ♕g4 ♖xd5 23 ♘e5+ wins; 21...♔h7 22 ♕g4 ♖xd5 23 cxd5) 22 ♕xd5 ♘a5 23 ♕f5 ♗xe4 24 ♕xe4 with a winning attack.

18 gxf5!?

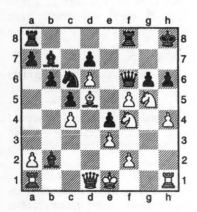

18 ...   ♗xa1

18...gxf5 19 ♖b1 ♗e5 20 ♕h5 gives White powerful threats without him having to sacrifice a rook:

1) 20...♗xd6 21 ♘g6+ ♔g7 22 ♘xf8 ♖xf8 23 ♘f7 and then:

1a) 23...♘d8 24 ♘xd6 ♗xd5 (or 24...♕xd6? 25 ♖g1+ ♔h7 26 ♗xb7 ♘xb7 27 ♖d1 and ♖xd7+) 25 ♖d1 ♕c3+ 26 ♔f1 ♗xc4+ 27 ♔g2 ♗e6 28 ♖hg1 ♔h7 29 ♔h1 ♕f6 30 ♖g2 and ♖dg1 with a winning attack.

1b) 23...♖xf7? 24 ♖g1+ ♔f8 25 ♗xf7 ♕xf7 26 ♕xh6+ (the loose bishop on d6 causes Black's downfall) 26...♔e7 27 ♖g7 wins.

1c) 23...♗e7 24 ♖g1+ ♔h7 25 ♖d1 (instead 25 ♘g5+ ♔h8 26 ♘f7+ is a draw) keeps Black tied up.

2) 20...♗xf4 21 exf4 is a reason-able way for Black to continue. The

following line is a sample of White's attacking ideas: 21...♘d8 22 ♖d1 ♗xd5 23 ♖xd5 ♘b7 24 ♖xf5 ♕a1+ 25 ♔e2 ♕xa2+ 26 ♔f1 ♕xc4+ 27 ♔g2 ♔g7 28 ♖e5 ♘xd6 29 ♖e7+ ♔f7 30 ♘xf7 ♘xf7 31 ♖c1 ♕a2 32 ♖c2 ♕b3 33 ♖c3 ♕a2 34 ♖g3+ ♔f8 35 ♖xd7 ♕e6 36 ♖c7 intending ♖g6 with a winning attack.

19 ♘xg6+   ♔g7

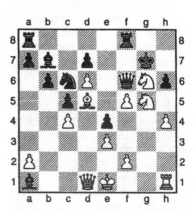

20 ♘xe4

Bronstein criticized this move as unnecessary (though in no concrete lines did he show that it allowed Black a good defence), recommending in-stead 20 ♘f4:

1) 20...♗c3+ 21 ♔f1 ♕xf5 22 ♖g1 hxg5 23 ♕h5 ♖f6 (23...♗f6 24 hxg5) 24 ♖xg5+ ♕xg5 25 ♕xg5+ ♔h8 26 ♘g6+ ♔h7 27 ♗xe4 wins.

2) 20...♕c3+ 21 ♔f1 leaves Black without any defence (this was Bron-stein's point), e.g. 21...hxg5 (21...♖xf5 22 ♕g4; 21...♕e5 22 ♖g1; 21...♗a6 22 ♘xe4 ♗xc4+ 23 ♔g1) 22 hxg5 ♖xf5 23 ♖h7+! wins.

20 ...   ♗c3+

20...♕xf5 should be met by 21 ♘f4, as in the game. Instead the apparently

strong 21 ♕xa1+? is well met by
21...♘d4! (21...♔xg6? 22 ♖g1+) 22
♗xb7 (22 ♖g1? ♗xd5 23 ♘e7+ ♔h7
24 ♘xf5 ♘c2+ 25 ♔d2 ♘xa1 26 cxd5
♖xf5) and now, instead of 22...♕f3? 23
♕xd4+ (23 0-0 is also good) 23...cxd4
24 ♖g1 ♔h7 25 ♘xf8+ ♖xf8 26 ♘g5+
hxg5 27 ♗xf3 ♖xf3 with a winning
rook ending for White, thanks in no
small part to the pawn on d6, after
22...♔xg6! 23 exd4 ♖ae8 it is suddenly White who is in some trouble.

21 ♔f1   ♕xf5

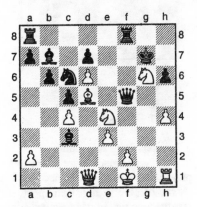

Now the g6-knight is loose and
White must be careful about Black's
pressure on f2.

22 ♘f4

White rescues his knight and blocks
the f-file. The principal threat is 23
♘g3 followed by 24 ♕g4+.

The alternative 22 ♖g1 ♕h3+ 23
♖g2 ♕h1+ 24 ♖g1 ♕h3+ is a draw.

22 ...   ♔h8!

The alternatives all clearly fail:
22...♗e5 23 ♘g3 ♕h7 24 ♕g4+ ♔h8
25 ♘g6+; 22...♕e5 23 ♖g1+ ♔h7 24
♘g5+!; 22...♗f6 23 ♘g3 ♕h7 24
♕g4+.

23 ♘xc3   ♖ae8

23...♘d8 24 ♖g1 (24 ♗xb7 ♘xb7
25 ♘cd5 just gives Black extra defensive options) 24...♔h7 25 ♕a1 ♗xd5
26 ♘cxd5 ♘e6 27 ♖g6 (27 f3 ♕f7)
27...♕e4 28 ♔g1 is good for White:
28...♘d4 (28...♖xf4 29 ♘xf4 ♖f8 30
♖g2 leaves White material ahead with
Black still tied up) 29 exd4 ♖xf4 30
♘xf4 ♕xf4 31 ♕b1 ♖g8 32 ♖xg8+
♔xg8 33 ♕g6+ and White's main
trump in this ending turns out to be the
far-advanced d6-pawn!

24 ♘ce2

White wishes to bring this knight
more fully into the kingside attack.

24 ♖g1 was a natural alternative, as
the knight is still capable of doing good
work from c3, for example 24...♖f6
(24...♔h7 25 ♕f3) 25 ♕f3 with ideas
of ♘e4 or ♕g3.

24 ...   ♖g8

24...♗a6 is a more constructive defensive move, freeing the knight from
its pin, so that ...♘e5 is a possible resource.

25 h5   ♖g5

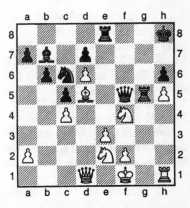

26 ♘g3   ♖xg3

Black will need to give back the exchange in any case, and at least this

way he inflicts some structural damage. However, with material now level, White's positional dominance quickly decides the game.

Note that 26...♕g4 self-traps the queen after 27 ♗f3.

27   fxg3   ♖xe3
28   ♔f2

28 ♖h2 is also good, intending ♖f2, unpinning the knight and so effectively bringing two pieces into the attack.

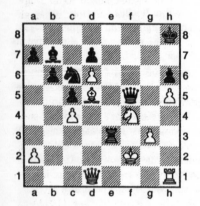

28   ...   ♖e8

28...♖c3 is no better: 29 ♖e1 (29 ♕a1? ♕c2+ 30 ♘e2 ♘d4) 29...♕c2+ (29...♖c2+ 30 ♔g1) 30 ♕xc2 ♖xc2+ 31 ♔g1 ♖xa2 32 ♖e7! and Black's position collapses.

29   ♖e1   ♖xe1
30   ♕xe1

Now there is no saving the black king, as the white pieces can just walk in – there are no defences left.

30   ...   ♔g7

31	♕e8	♕c2+
32	♔g1	♕d1+
33	♔h2	♕c2+
34	♘g2	♕f5

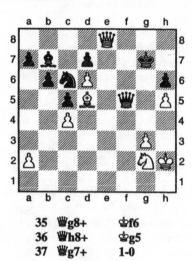

35	♕g8+	♔f6
36	♕h8+	♔g5
37	♕g7+	1-0

Lessons from this game:

1) There is much more to opening play than developing your pieces! The choice of plan in the opening often sets the tone for the whole game.

2) Having embarked on a heavily committal course, there may be no way back. If the only way to achieve your strategic aims is by sacrificing material, then this is the path you must take.

3) Splitting the opponent's position in two with a pawn wedge is a powerful idea, especially if your pieces can be brought into an attack on the enemy king.

Game 33

Yuri Averbakh – Alexander Kotov

Candidates tournament, Zurich 1953

Old Indian Defence

The Players

Yuri Averbakh (born 1922) is a Soviet grandmaster who became a world-renowned expert on the endgame. He played 15 times in the Soviet Championship, winning it in 1954, but in the 1960s he started to play less and turned to writing and chess administration. The first edition of his famous endgame encyclopaedia was published in three volumes from 1956–62, with some updated volumes appearing more recently. It is still regarded as a standard reference work, although in the 1990s the use of computer databases has had a major impact on this area of chess theory.

Alexander Kotov (1913–81) was probably one of the world's top ten players in the period 1948–54. Although he was successful in local events as a teenager, it was not until 1939 that Kotov made a breakthrough – second place (behind Botvinnik) in the USSR Championship. After the war Kotov had a number of successes, but far and away his greatest achievement was first place in the 1952 Saltsjöbaden Interzonal, a massive three points clear of a world-class field. Thus Kotov qualified for the Candidates tournament of the following year, in which this game was played. However, Kotov failed to live up to the promise of his Interzonal result, and finished joint eighth. In later years Kotov became a successful author and is best known for *Think Like a Grandmaster* (1971), a ground-breaking work describing thought-processes at the board. Despite his writing, Kotov still took part in occasional tournaments and I (JN) gained the first part of my grandmaster title with a last-round draw against him in 1977.

The Game

Kotov adopts a solid but slightly passive opening, and the central pawn-structure soon becomes blocked. There follows a period of slow manoeuvring, with both sides jockeying for position. White holds a slight advantage throughout this phase, but then the balance of the game is disturbed as Averbakh tries to clear up the situation on the kingside. This gives Kotov the chance he needs to make a brilliant queen sacrifice. The white king is hunted for almost twenty moves before finally succumbing to Black's attack.

1	d4	♘f6
2	c4	d6
3	♘f3	♘bd7
4	♘c3	e5

5	e4	♗e7

This development is more passive than ...g6 and ...♗g7, which would lead to a King's Indian Defence.

6	**♗e2**	**0-0**
7	**0-0**	**c6**
8	**♕c2**	

8 ♖e1 followed by 9 ♗f1 is a popular alternative.

| 8 | ... | **♖e8** |
| 9 | **♖d1** | **♗f8** |

A typical manoeuvre. The rook's line of action is cleared to exert latent pressure against the white pawn on e4. The intention is to induce White to resolve the central tension by playing d5. In general, it is in White's interests to avoid this for as long as possible, since a fluid central structure makes it hard for Black to decide where to put his pieces.

Curiously, Black often re-deploys his dark-squared bishop by means of ...g6 and ...♗g7, which might make a cynic ask "Why not play the King's Indian and save two tempi?". Good question, actually.

| 10 | **♖b1** | |

10 b4!? would have been an interesting attempt to anticipate Black's next move.

| 10 | ... | **a5** |

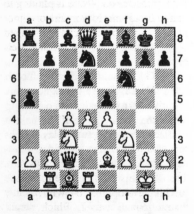

11 d5

This lets Black off rather lightly. White could have kept more options open with 11 b3 but even the move played is sufficient to give White a slight advantage.

Note that 11 a3 is bad, since after 11...exd4 12 ♘xd4 a4 White's queenside pawns become blockaded.

11	...	**♘c5**
12	**♗e3**	**♕c7**
13	**h3**	**♗d7**
14	**♖bc1**	

White would like to expand on the queenside by b3, a3 and b4 but the immediate 14 b3 cxd5 15 cxd5 (15 exd5 is positionally bad) loses to 15...♘cxe4, so first of all White defends his queen.

| 14 | ... | **g6** |
| 15 | **♘d2** | |

Further preparation. 15 b3 ♘h5 would have given Black reasonable counterplay, so White takes the precaution of preventing ...♘h5.

| 15 | ... | **♖ab8** |

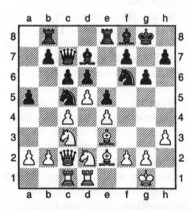

16 ♘b3

Black's last move prepared to meet 16 b3 by 16...cxd5 17 cxd5 b5, and again Black has some counterplay. Therefore White now changes his plan and decides to eliminate the active knight on c5.

  16   **...**   **♘xb3**
  17 **♕xb3**   **c5**

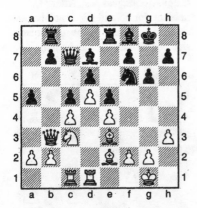

Black blocks the queenside. It will now take White several moves to prepare b4 (for example, by ♕c2, a3 and ♖b1), during which time Black will try to generate counterplay on the kingside.

  18 **♔h2**

A rather odd move. It seems more logical to prepare b4 by 18 ♕c2 ♔h8 19 a3 ♘g8 20 ♕d2 (preventing ...♗h6). If Black reacts passively, White will play b4, while 20...f5 is met by 21 exf5 gxf5 22 f4 and in both cases White retains his slight advantage.

  18   **...**   **♔h8**
  19 **♕c2**   **♘g8**
  20 **♗g4**   **♘h6**

20...♗h6 would be a more solid line, exchanging off his "bad" bishop, but then Black would be left defending a slightly worse position with no prospects of active play. Kotov prefers to keep his bishop.

  21 **♗xd7**   **♕xd7**
  22 **♕d2**   **♘g8**

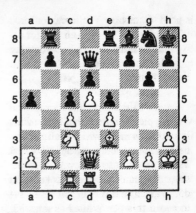

  23 **g4**

Evidently Averbakh was preparing this plan when he played ♔h2, but it seems unnecessarily double-edged. White can always meet ...f5 by f3, when it will take Black a long time to create any real threats on the kingside. Therefore White should simply aim for b4 and avoid creating any weaknesses on the other side of the board; then White would have a clear advantage.

The strategy of playing g4 is familiar in certain King's Indian positions, but in those cases White is playing to cramp Black. Here two pairs of minor pieces have already been exchanged so a cramping strategy is much less effective.

  23   **...**   **f5**
  24 **f3**   **♗e7**
  25 **♖g1**   **♖f8**
  26 **♖cf1**   **♖f7**

Black does not want to play ...f4, as this would block the kingside and reduce Black's counterplay there to zero. Then White would be free to pursue his preparations for b4 without any distraction. However, Black steadfastly refuses to push his f-pawn and it is hard to see how White can enforce it. Therefore, if White is aiming for active play he must undertake something himself on the kingside.

27 gxf5   gxf5
28 ♖g2?

Some annotators have criticized White's earlier moves, but in my view it is only this move which really upsets the balance of the position. Now that White has exchanged pawns on f5 the kingside cannot become blocked, and so ...f4 is a threat. Therefore 28 f4! was correct, when White has some advantage because Black's king is awkwardly placed in the corner. One line runs 28...♗f6 29 exf5 ♕xf5 30 ♘b5 ♖d8 31 ♕xa5! ♕c2+ 32 ♔g2 ♕xc4 33 ♕xd8! ♗xd8 34 ♘xd6 ♕xd5 35 ♖d1 ♕xg2+ 36 ♔xg2 ♖g7+ 37 ♔f3 with a very favourable ending for White, as his pieces are all more active than their enemy counterparts.

28 ...   f4!

Kotov pounces on Averbakh's mistake.

29 ♗f2   ♖f6

Suddenly Black has the deadly threat of 30...♖h6.

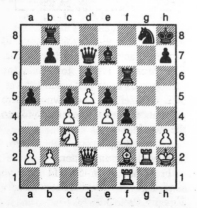

30 ♘e2?

The obvious move aiming to solidify the kingside by playing ♘g1. However, 30 ♕e1 ♖h6 31 h4, unpleasant though it looks, was best. After 31...♘f6 (heading for h5 and g3) Black has the advantage but the game is far from over.

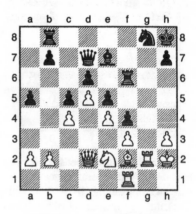

30 ...   ♕xh3+!!

This brilliant sacrifice introduces one of the most exciting king-hunts of the twentieth century. In a sense Black is risking little, because he always has perpetual check in reserve, but it is still an impressive idea.

31 ♔xh3   ♖h6+
32 ♔g4   ♘f6+
33 ♔f5

The king is obviously in great danger, but it is not easy to finish it off because Black doesn't have much light-square control.

33 ...   ♘d7

This wins, but White's next move allows him to struggle on for some time. Black could have won more quickly with the incredible 33...♘g4!, threatening 34...♖f8+ 35 ♔xg4 ♖g8+ 36 ♔f5 ♖f6# while at the same time blocking the ♖g5 defence which occurs in the game. The only way for White to avoid immediate mate is by 34 ♘xf4, but after 34...♖g8! (34...♖f8+ 35 ♔xg4 ♖g8+ is unclear after 36 ♘g6+ ♖gxg6+ 37 ♔f5 ♖h5+ 38 ♖g5 ♗xg5 39 ♔g4, when Black has no way to win) 35 ♘h5 ♖hg6 36 ♕g5 ♗xg5 37 ♔xg4 ♗f4+ 38 ♔h3 ♖xg2 39 ♘xf4 exf4 Black's extra material guarantees an easy win.

34 ♖g5

The only other way to meet the threat of 34...♖f8+ 35 ♔g4 ♖g8+ 36 ♔f5 ♖f6# is by 34 ♖g7, but then Black wins with 34...♖f8+ 35 ♔g4 ♗xg7 36 ♖g1 ♖g8 37 ♔f5+ ♔f7 38 ♖xg8 ♖h5+ 39 ♔g4 ♘f6#.

34 ...	♖f8+
35 ♔g4	♘f6+
36 ♔f5	♘g8+
37 ♔g4	

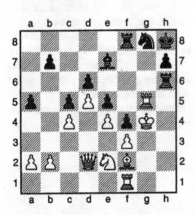

| **37 ...** | ♘f6+ |

Kotov repeats moves to reach the time-control, but as a result makes the win slightly more complicated. The simplest line was 37...♗xg5 and now:

1) 38 ♖g1 ♘f6+ 39 ♔f5 ♘g4+ 40 ♔xg4 (40 ♔xg5 ♖g8+ 41 ♔f5 ♖f6#)

40...♗d8 41 ♘xf4 ♖g8+ 42 ♘g6+ ♖gxg6+ 43 ♔f5 ♖h5+ wins.

2) 38 ♔xg5 ♖f7 39 ♗h4 ♖g7+ 40 ♔f5 ♖hg6 41 ♗g5 ♘h6+ mates.

3) 38 ♕e1 ♘f6+ 39 ♔f5 ♘g4+ 40 ♔xg4 ♖g8 41 ♔f5 ♗d8 42 ♗h4 ♗xh4 43 ♕xh4 ♖xh4 also wins.

38 ♔f5   ♘xd5+

Necessary in order to avoid a threefold repetition of the position, but the capture of White's d5-pawn actually makes the win more complex.

39 ♔g4	♘f6+
40 ♔f5	♘g8+
41 ♔g4	♘f6+
42 ♔f5	♘g8+
43 ♔g4	♗xg5!

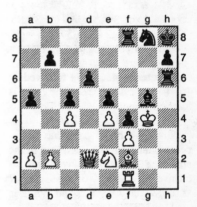

With the time-control at move 40 passed, Black finds the winning line. The threat is simply to retreat the bishop to e7 or d8 and resume the attack with ...♘f6+. The pawn structure prevents the white pieces coming to the aid of the king.

44 ♔xg5

There is nothing better:

1) 44 ♕d1 ♗e7 45 ♘xf4 ♘f6+ 46 ♔g5 ♘g4+ 47 ♔xg4 ♖g8+ 48 ♘g6+ ♖gxg6+ 49 ♔f5 ♖h5#.

2) 44 ♗e3 fxe3 45 ♕d3 (45 ♕d1
♗f4 46 ♘xf4 ♖xf4+ 47 ♔g3 ♖ff6 48
f4 e2 49 ♕xe2 ♖fg6+ 50 ♔f3 ♖h3+
wins) 45...♘f6+ 46 ♔f5 ♘d5+ 47
♔xg5 (47 ♔g4 ♘f4) 47...♖g6+ 48
♔h4 ♖fg8 with a quick mate.

44 ...   ♖f7

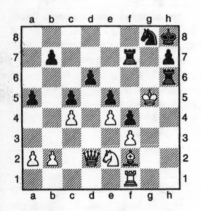

Threatening 45...♖g7+ followed by
46...♖f6# or 46...♘e7#. The reply is
forced.

45 ♗h4   ♖g6+

Now that the d5-pawn has disappeared, the winning line given in the
note to Black's 37th move is inconclusive: 45...♖g7+ 46 ♔f5 ♖hg6 47
♕xd6! ♖xd6 48 ♔xe5 and White is

still alive. However, Black finds an effective alternative.

46 ♔h5   ♖fg7
47 ♗g5

After 47 ♕xd6 ♖xd6 48 ♗g5 ♖dg6
White loses his bishop.

47 ...   ♖xg5+
48 ♔h4   ♘f6

White is given no peace. The new
threat of 49...♖h5# forces him to jettison more material.

49 ♘g3   ♖xg3
50 ♕xd6   ♖3g6

Having digested another snack,
Black renews his mating threat.

51 ♕f8+   ♖g8

0-1

Lessons from this game:

1) Blocking the pawn structure alters the whole course of the game and
so deserves careful thought.

2) Keep your eye open for surprise
tactics. Such opportunities often only
last for one move so you are unlikely
to get a second chance.

3) If the pawn-structure prevents
defensive pieces coming to the aid of
their king, the attacker may have a local superiority of material even if he
has made heavy sacrifices.

Game 34
Paul Keres – Vasily Smyslov
Candidates tournament, Zurich 1953
English Opening

The Players
Paul Keres (1916–75) was one of the strongest players never to become World
Champion. For more information see Game 30.

Vasily Smyslov was born in Moscow in 1921. He has enjoyed an extremely long
career, and is a very well respected figure in the chess world. He first came to
prominence in the 1940s, and made a good showing at the 1948 World Championship match-tournament. By the 1950s he was ready to challenge Botvinnik's
hold on the world title, and it seems a little unfair that he was only World Champion for one year: 1957–8. He convincingly won two Candidates tournaments
and played three matches with Botvinnik. One match, in 1954, was drawn, while
Smyslov won in 1957 and Botvinnik in 1958, with an overall score of +18 =34
−17 in Smyslov's favour. In the 1960s and 1970s Smyslov remained a leading
player, but did not challenge for the world title again. However, in a quite remarkable run of success, he again managed to reach the Candidates final in 1983, and
it was only Garry Kasparov who prevented him from reaching a fourth world
championship match. To this day, despite advancing years and failing eyesight,
he still plays with great enthusiasm, in particular in the annual Women vs Veterans events.
Throughout his playing career he has stressed the concept of harmony in chess
(and not only in chess – away from the board he was a professional opera singer).
When he was young he was particularly influenced by the writings of both
Nimzowitsch and Tarrasch – perhaps his style was the product of harmonizing
these two opposing theories. His chess has always been undogmatic: he excels in
simplified positions and the ending, but when the position demands it, he has no
qualms about launching fierce attacks.

The Game
Keres described the game as follows: "Should I have succeeded in winning this
then I would have been at the head of the tournament with every chance of
emerging with final victory, but a draw too would not have extinguished my
hopes, and therefore I should not have played in too risky a style in this game.
However, I once again repeated a mistake I had made so often before and staked
everything on one card. I offered my opponent an extremely complicated piece
sacrifice, acceptance of which would have submitted Smyslov's king to a fierce
attack. But, after long reflection, Smyslov discovered an excellent defence and
once I had sacrificed the chance of securing equality in favour of an ill-considered

plan, the consequences were soon apparent. I suffered an ignominious defeat and in so doing I had not only thrown away all chances of first place but was once again back in fourth place."

This is a grandiose game of attack and counterattack at the highest level, and a dire warning against "playing for a win" rather than playing good, correct chess.

1	c4	♘f6
2	♘c3	e6
3	♘f3	c5
4	e3	♗e7
5	b3	0-0
6	♗b2	b6
7	d4	cxd4
8	exd4	d5
9	♗d3	♘c6
10	0-0	♗b7

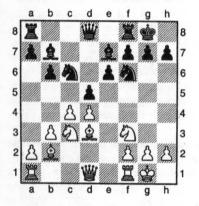

In a fairly tame opening, both players have developed systematically. However, it is worth noting that the "tameness" can prove deceptive; Keres often launched vicious attacks from quiet positions of this very type. It is now time for him to decide on a plan of attack. The main strategic question involves the bishop on b2: White hopes that the pressure along the a1–h8 diagonal will bear fruit, while Black will be happy if he can keep the bishop just staring at an immobilized

pawn on d4. With this in mind, it is no surprise that neither player is keen to resolve the c4-d5 pawn tension.

11 ♖c1

11 ♕e2?! ♘b4 12 ♗b1?! dxc4 13 bxc4 ♗xf3 14 ♕xf3 ♕xd4 is a reasonably safe pawn-grab, since White cannot then snare a piece by 15 a3 ♘a6 16 ♕b7 because of 16...♗d6 17 ♕xa6 ♗xh2+ 18 ♔xh2 ♕h4+ 19 ♔g1 ♘g4, with a standard mating attack for Black.

11	...	♖c8
12	♖e1	♘b4
13	♗f1	♘e4
14	a3	

14 ♘xe4 dxe4 15 ♘e5 may well be preferable, but is nothing special for White.

14	...	♘xc3
15	♖xc3	

Not 15 ♗xc3? in view of 15...♘a2.

| 15 | ... | ♘c6 |

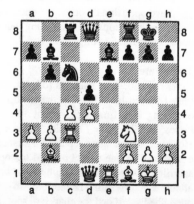

White now embarks upon the highly ambitious plan of transferring both rooks to the kingside for an all-out attack. It would be surprising if Black's position could really be taken by storm in this way, but resourceful defence will be needed.

16 ♘e5?!   ♘xe5
17 ♖xe5   ♗f6
18 ♖h5

The consistent follow-up, threatening 19 ♖xh7 ♔xh7 20 ♕h5+ ♔g8 21 ♖h3. If White were instead to retreat, Black would have a very comfortable position, e.g. 18 ♖e1 dxc4 19 ♖xc4 ♕d5 with play against the isolated queen's pawn.

18 ...   g6

18...dxc4 is possible, when 19 ♖xh7 can be met by 19...g6, which can be compared to the game continuation, and not 19...♔xh7? 20 ♕h5+ ♔g8 21 ♖h3 ♗h4 22 ♖xh4 with a strong attack.

19 ♖ch3!?

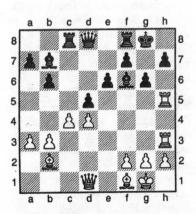

This "quiet" rook sacrifice brings about the crisis-point of the game. Clearly, neither player could work out by analysis whether the rook could be safely taken or not, and both relied on their intuition. Smyslov said of this position "I thought for a long time and very much wanted to take the rook, the more so because I could not see how White could win". However, he found a safer alternative, which emphasized his positional advantages, and challenged Keres to try to find a way to mate on the kingside with both his rooks intact.

19 ...   dxc4!?

19...gxh5 20 ♕xh5 ♖e8 21 a4! is the surprising point behind the sacrifice; by coming to a3, the hitherto dormant bishop will cut off the king's escape-route via f8:

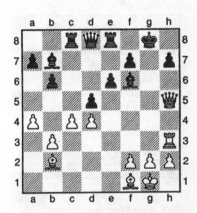

1) 21...dxc4 allows White's threat: 22 ♕xh7+ ♔f8 23 ♗a3+ ♖e7 24 ♖g3 wins the black queen after 24...♔e8 25 ♖g8+.

2) 21...♕e7 (hoping to reopen the escape-route, but too slow) 22 ♕h6 (22 ♕xh7+?! ♔f8 23 ♖g3 ♕b4) forces 22...♗h4, when White regains most of the sacrificed material while keeping his attack.

3) 21...♕d6 22 c5! with a further branch:

3a) 22...bxc5 23 ♕xh7+! (23 ♕h6 ♗xd4! has the simple idea of giving up the queen for the rook, leaving Black with two rooks versus the white queen) 23...♔f8 24 ♕h6+ ♗g7 25 ♕xg7+ ♔xg7 26 dxc5+ amounts to an excellent exchange sacrifice by White.

3b) 22...♕d8 23 c6 ♖xc6 24 ♗a3 ♖d6 25 ♕h6 (threatening 26 ♖g3+ ♔h8 27 ♗d3; 25 ♗b5!? is also possible) 25...e5 (25...♗xd4 is met by 26 ♗d3 ♗g7 27 ♖g3) 26 ♕xh7+ ♔f8 27 ♕h6+ ♔e7 28 ♖f3! (not 28 dxe5? ♗xe5 29 ♖e3 ♔d7) 28...♗h8 (28...♔d7 29 ♗xd6 ♖e6 30 ♗xe5 ♗xe5 31 ♖xf7+ ♖e7 32 ♖f8 wins a lot of material) 29 ♗xd6+ ♕xd6 30 ♖xf7+ and the black queen drops off.

3c) 22...♕f4! 23 ♕xh7+ (23 ♖f3? ♕h4) 23...♔f8 has generally been considered difficult for Black, and on the basis of this Smyslov's decision to decline the sacrifice to have been objectively correct. However, White has no clear way through here, e.g.:

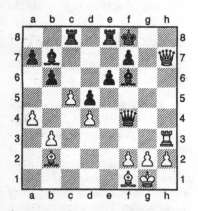

3c1) 24 ♗a3 bxc5 25 ♗xc5+ ♖xc5! (after 25...♖e7 26 ♖g3 ♔e8 27 ♗b5+ White's initiative continues) 26 dxc5 looks inadequate for White.

3c2) 24 c6 ♖xc6 25 ♗a3+ ♖e7 26 ♖g3 ♔e8 also looks unconvincing for White.

3c3) 24 cxb6 ♕d6 (to stop the ♗a3+ idea, but maybe more trouble than it's worth; Black may do better to try to weather the storm after either 24...axb6 25 ♗a3+ ♖e7 26 ♖g3 ♔e8 or 24...a6!? 25 ♗a3+ ♖e7 26 ♖g3 ♔e8) 25 ♖f3 ♔e7 (25...♗g7 26 ♖g3 ♗f6 27 ♕h6+ ♔e7 28 ♖f3 transposes) 26 ♕h6 e5! (better than 26...♗h8 27 ♕h4+ f6 28 ♕h7+ ♔d8 29 ♕xb7) 27 ♗a3 ♕xa3 28 ♕xf6+ ♔d7 29 ♗b5+ ♗c6 30 ♗xc6+ ♖xc6 31 ♖xf7+ ♕e7 32 ♕xd5+ ♕d6 and White's initiative grinds to a halt – even though he has plenty of pawns, they are not sufficiently far advanced to compensate for the rook.

20 ♖xh7?

Keres rushes headlong into an attack which is doomed to fail. Perhaps under different circumstances, with less at stake, he would have calmly reassessed the situation, and found the alternative plan, which would have enabled him to save the game: 20 ♕g4! (20 bxc4? gxh5 21 ♕xh5 now gives White nothing for the rook in view of 21...♗e4) and now:

1) 20...c3 21 ♗xc3 ♖xc3 22 ♖xc3 ♕xd4 23 ♕xd4 ♗xd4 24 ♖c7 gxh5 25 ♖xb7 leads to a drawish ending, though White will have to be a little careful. This line was given by Bronstein.

2) 20...cxb3 invites White to demonstrate his attacking ideas: 21 ♖xh7 ♖c2 22 ♗d3 (22 ♖3h6 ♗g7 23 ♗d3 ♕f6) 22...♕c7 (22...♖xb2? 23 ♗xg6! ♗g5 24 ♕h5) 23 ♖3h6 ♖c1+ (23...♗g7 24 ♕h4) 24 ♗xc1 ♕xc1+ 25 ♗f1 and now:

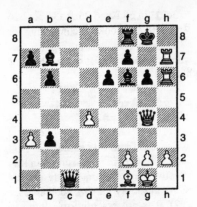

2a) 25...♗a6?? 26 ♖xg6+ mates.

2b) 25...♕c2? (defending g6, but giving White precious time to coordinate his attacking forces) 26 ♕h3 and then:

2b1) 26...b2?? 27 ♖h8+ ♗xh8 28 ♖xh8+ ♔g7 29 ♕h7+ ♔f6 30 ♖xf8 ♕c7 (30...b1♕ 31 ♕xf7+ ♔g5 32 ♕f4+ ♔h5 33 ♖h8#) 31 f4! b1♕ 32 ♕h4+ ♔f5 (32...♔g7 33 ♕h8#) 33 ♖xf7+! ♔e4 (33...♕xf7 34 ♕g5+ ♔e4 35 ♕e5#) 34 ♖xc7 and White is a rook up.

2b2) 26...♖c8 27 ♖h8+ ♗xh8 28 ♖xh8+ ♔g7 29 ♖h7+ and Black has only a choice of ways to lose:

2b21) 29...♔f8 30 ♕h6+ ♔e8 (or 30...♔e7 31 ♕g5+ ♔e8 32 ♕f6 ♕f5 33 ♗b5+ ♗c6 34 ♗xc6+ ♖xc6 35 ♖h8+ ♔d7 36 ♕d8#) 31 ♕f4 ♕f5 (31...♕c7 32 ♗b5+ ♔f8 33 ♕f6) 32 ♕d6 ♕f6 33 ♗b5+ wins.

2b22) 29...♔f6 30 f4! (threatening ♕h4+; 30 ♕h4+ g5 31 ♖h6+ ♔e7 32 ♕xg5+ ♔d7 33 ♕g7 ♖e8) 30...♔e7 31 ♕h4+ ♔d6 (31...♔e8 32 ♕f6) 32 ♖xf7 with a decisive attack.

2c) 25...♗g7 26 ♕h4 ♗a6 (Black should not try to avoid the perpetual check by 26...♗xh6 27 ♖xh6 ♕xh6?

28 ♕xh6 b2 29 ♗d3 ♖c8 30 f3) 27 ♖h8+ (27 h3? is no winning attempt, as is demonstrated most simply by 27...♗xh6 28 ♖xh6 ♕xh6! 29 ♕xh6 b2, winning) 27...♗xh8 28 ♖xh8+ ♔g7 29 ♖h7+ ♔g8 30 ♖h8+ with a draw.

20 ... c3!

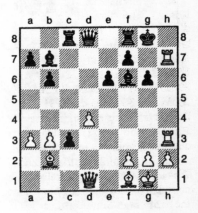

The fact that so much of White's army is tied up in a do-or-die kingside attack means that he is unable to hold together his collapsing centre and queenside.

21 ♕c1

There was nothing better. 21 ♗xc3 ♖xc3 overloads the h3-rook, while 21 ♗c1 ♕xd4 rules out any hope of White bringing his queen into the attack. At least the text-move sets a little trap.

21 ... ♕xd4!

21...cxb2?? 22 ♕h6 (22 ♖h8+ ♗xh8 23 ♕h6 also mates, and demonstrates another typical mating theme against the fianchettoed position) 22...b1♕ (22...♕xd4 23 ♖h8+ ♗xh8 24 ♕h7#) 23 ♖h8+ ♗xh8 24 ♕xh8#.

22 ♕h6

By now the reader should have no trouble seeing White's threat!

22	...	**♖fd8!**
23	**♗c1**	

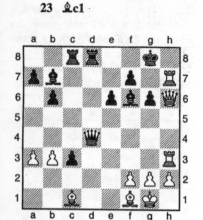

White is "only" a pawn down, but what a pawn! Moreover, Black's counterattack will be irresistible.

23	...	**♗g7**
24	**♕g5**	**♕f6**
25	**♕g4**	

Naturally, an exchange of queens would leave White with no hope at all.

25	...	**c2**
26	**♗e2**	**♖d4!**

Smyslov provokes the f-pawn forward to make way for some threats of his own.

27	**f4**	**♖d1+**
28	**♗xd1**	**♕d4+**
	0-1	

Lessons from this game:

1) "Playing to win" is often a less effective way of getting the desired result than simply playing good chess.

2) It is not essential to capture a sacrificed piece. Always have a look to see if there is a good alternative to accepting – or a good *zwischenzug* that can be played before taking the material.

3) Even two rooks may not constitute an effective attacking force if they lack sufficient back-up from the other pieces. Central control, as always, is a major factor in supporting (or refuting) an attack.

Game 35
Mikhail Botvinnik – Vasily Smyslov
World Championship match (game 14), Moscow 1954
King's Indian Defence, Fianchetto Variation

The Players

Mikhail Botvinnik (1911–95) was World Champion 1948–57, 1958–60 and 1961–3. For an account of Botvinnik's career, see Game 28.

Vasily Smyslov (born 1921) was World Champion 1957–8. For more information see Game 34.

The Game

Smyslov surprises Botvinnik with an opening that did not form a part of his regular repertoire. Botvinnik plays the very line that Smyslov was expecting, and for which he had prepared a surprise. A highly complicated position soon arises. After some intricate tactics, Smyslov makes an excellent queen sacrifice, and with a well-coordinated army of minor pieces buzzing around his king, Botvinnik quickly succumbs.

1	d4	♘f6
2	c4	g6
3	g3	♗g7
4	♗g2	0-0
5	♘c3	d6

Smyslov was by no means a regular King's Indian player, but in this game he has something specific in mind in the line he could expect Botvinnik to play.

It is an interesting fact that most of Botvinnik's opponents in world championship matches resorted to the King's Indian, especially when they were trailing and desperately needed a win to keep their chances alive.

6	♘f3	♘bd7
7	0-0	e5
8	e4	c6
9	♗e3?!	

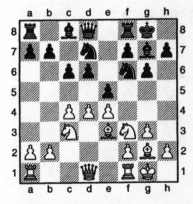

At that time it was still not clear whether White should first prepare this move by 9 h3, which is the standard move here. Botvinnik was of the view that it was unnecessary, but the powerful rejoinder that Smyslov had prepared for this game was sufficient for White to abandon 9 ♗e3 for many decades. It was virtually unseen in competitive play until the 1990s. It has recently enjoyed a very modest revival – it now appears that it leads to interesting play, but in which White can hardly hope for any advantage.

9 ...   ♘g4
10 ♗g5   ♛b6!

10...f6 had been played a few times by Bronstein, but 11 ♗c1 f5 12 ♗g5 gives White some advantage – Black has exposed his kingside a little too much.

11 h3   exd4!

11...♘gf6 is too passive, e.g. 12 ♛d2 exd4 13 ♘xd4 ♘c5 (13...♘e5!?) 14 ♖ad1 ♖e8 15 ♖fe1 ♘fd7 16 ♗e3 leaves White a little better.

12 ♘a4   ♛a6
13 hxg4   b5

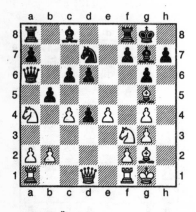

14 ♘xd4

This is a major decision-point for White:

1) 14 cxb5 cxb5 15 ♘xd4 bxa4 16 e5 ♗b7 (16...♖b8!?) 17 ♗xb7 ♛xb7 18 exd6 ♛xb2 is somewhat better for Black.

2) 14 ♗e7 ♖e8 15 ♗xd6 bxa4 16 e5!? (16 ♘xd4 ♘e5 is good for Black, e.g. 17 ♗xe5 ♗xe5 18 f4 ♗xg4; 16 c5 ♖xe4 17 ♖e1 ♖xe1+ 18 ♛xe1 ♘f8 is fine for Black because 19 ♛e8 ♛b7 threatens ...♗xg4) 16...c5!? (16...♛xc4 is possible too) 17 b4 (or 17 ♘xd4 ♗b7 18 ♘b5 ♗xg2 19 ♔xg2 ♗xe5) 17...cxb4 18 ♛xd4 (18 ♘xd4 and 18 ♖b1!? are other ideas) 18...♗b7 19 ♖ae1 ♖ac8 20 c5 ♛b5 gave Black the advantage in Yusupov – Kasparov, Linares 1992, because White's c- and e-pawns have lost their mobility and are now rather weak.

3) 14 c5!? and now:

3a) 14...dxc5 15 ♘xc5 (15 ♗e7?! bxa4 is the same exchange sacrifice as after 14...bxa4 15 ♗e7) 15...♘xc5 16 ♗e7 ♘e6 17 ♗xf8 ♔xf8 may not give Black quite enough compensation, as his position is a little loose.

3b) 14...bxa4 15 cxd6 (15 ♗e7?! dxc5 is a good exchange sacrifice – a standard King's Indian theme) 15...c5 16 ♗e7 ♖e8 17 e5 led to an unclear, messy game in Fominykh – Chuprov, Omsk 1996.

14 ...   bxa4

15 ♘xc6

15 b3 ♘e5 (15...♕b6?! 16 ♘xc6!) 16 ♗e7 (16 f3 d5! blows open the centre to Black's advantage) 16...♗xg4 17 f3 ♖fe8 18 ♗xd6 ♖ad8 works nicely for Black.

15	...	**♕xc6**
16	e5	**♕xc4**
17	♗xa8	**♘xe5**

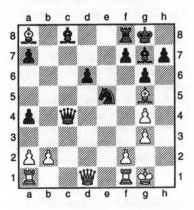

Black has achieved excellent compensation for the exchange.

18 ♖c1

Or:

1) 18 ♗g2 ♗e6 19 ♕xd6 ♕xg4 20 ♗f4 ♘f3+ 21 ♗xf3 ♕xf3 22 ♕d1 ♕b7 is somewhat better for Black.

2) 18 ♗e7?! ♗xg4! with the two possibilities:

2a) 19 ♕d5 ♖e8! 20 ♗h4 (20 f4 ♘f3+) 20...♘f3+ 21 ♔g2 ♘xh4+ 22 gxh4 ♗e2 23 ♕xc4 ♖xc4 24 ♖fc1 d5 and Black regains the exchange with a couple of extra pawns.

2b) 19 ♗d5 ♕c7 20 f3 ♗xf3 21 ♗xf3 ♕xe7 is really bad for White, who is material down with a position riddled with weaknesses.

3) 18 ♕xd6 ♗e6 19 ♗g2 ♕xg4 and now:

3a) 20 ♗f4 ♘f3+ 21 ♗xf3 ♕xf3 22 ♕d1 ♕b7 gives Black potent threats: both mating ideas against the white king and the plan of removing White's queenside pawns.

3b) 20 ♗e7 ♖e8 threatens both 21...♘f3+ and 21...♘c4.

3c) 20 ♗h6!? seeks a tactical solution to White's problems, but 20...♗xh6 (20...♘f3+? 21 ♗xf3 ♕xf3 22 ♗xg7 ♗h3?? is of course no good now that White gets his mate in first: 23 ♕xf8#; 20...♘c4 21 ♕f4 ♕xf4 22 ♗xf4 ♘xb2 is another fairly good option) 21 ♕xe5 ♗g7 22 ♕a5 ♗xb2 gives Black all the chances.

18 ... ♕b4!?

18...♗xg4 is an interesting alternative, e.g. 19 f3 (19 ♖xc4?! ♗xd1) 19...♕b5 20 fxg4 (20 ♕d5 ♕b6+ 21 ♔h1 ♗e6) 20...♖xa8 21 ♕xd6 ♘xg4 is difficult for White to survive.

18...♕b5 looks quite good too: 19 ♕xd6 (19 ♗e7 ♗xg4 20 ♕d5 ♕d7 leaves Black with a useful initiative) 19...♗xg4 20 ♗g2 ♕xb2 21 f3 ♗e6 22 ♖f2 ♕b6 23 ♕xb6 axb6 with a very difficult ending for White.

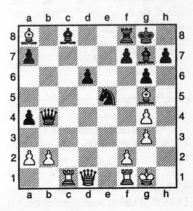

19 a3!

Botvinnik finds the best defensive chance. Instead 19 ♗g2 ♗a6 20 ♖e1 ♘d3 21 ♖e4 ♕b5 22 ♗e7 ♘xc1 23 ♗xf8 ♘e2+ 24 ♖xe2 ♕xe2 25 ♕xe2 ♗xe2 26 ♗xd6 ♗xb2 is not a tenable ending.

19 ...   ♕xb2
20 ♕xa4

20 ♗e4 is also reasonable, with the simple idea of keeping the bishop active so that a later ...♗xg4 can be met by f3.

20 ...   ♗b7!

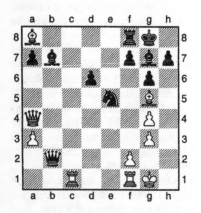

Smyslov perceives the great importance of the f3-square, and is prepared even to sacrifice his queen to gain use of it for his minor pieces. The game has reached its most critical point.

21 ♖b1?

21 ♗xb7 ♕xb7 22 ♖c3 gives White excellent drawing chances, for example 22...h6 (22...♘f3+ 23 ♖xf3 ♕xf3 24 ♗e7 eliminates the d-pawn) 23 ♗f4 ♘f3+ 24 ♖xf3 ♕xf3 25 ♗xd6 ♖d8 and Black is only a little more active.

21 ...   ♘f3+
22 ♔h1

22 ♔g2 (allowing a double check is never very natural, but there's no way

for Black to exploit it here) 22...♗xa8 23 ♖xb2 ♘xg5+ 24 f3 ♗xb2 seems to give White more hope of survival, as his king is a little less likely to find itself in a mating net than in the game continuation.

22 ...   ♗xa8!

Definitely the best continuation. Other moves:

1) 22...♕xb1? 23 ♖xb1 ♗xa8 24 ♗e7 ♘d2+ 25 ♔g1 ♘xb1 26 ♗xf8 ♗xf8 27 ♕b4 traps the knight, winning.

2) 22...♘d2+?! 23 ♗xb7 ♘xb1 is also quite good for Black, though not as strong or elegant as the move in the game. Several sources have then given 24 ♗c6?!, oddly, as good for White, but then 24...♘a3 is playable, since 25 ♗c1 (presumably the idea) runs into 25...♕e2.

23 ♖xb2   ♘xg5+
24 ♔h2   ♘f3+
25 ♔h3   ♗xb2

Here Black's three pieces are far stronger than the white queen, so Black has a decisive advantage.

26 ♕xa7   ♗e4!

Black intends to end the game with a direct attack on the beleaguered white king. With Black's pieces well coordinated and supporting one another so efficiently, it is very difficult for White to put up any meaningful resistance. When, as here, there is looseness in their position, three pieces can easily prove weaker than a queen; when there is no looseness, the queen can only thrash around. White's rook might be able to help the queen to drum up trouble, but it has trouble even finding a route into play; all its natural entry routes are covered.

27 a4

White's only hope of counterplay is with his a-pawn, but it is very slow: its queening square is covered twice, its path is blocked by the queen, and it can get no back-up from the rook.

27   ...   ♔g7
28   ♖d1

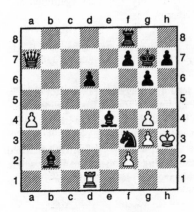

28   ...   ♗e5

28...♘g5+ 29 ♔h2 (29 ♔h4? ♗g2! 30 ♔xg5 ♗f6+ 31 ♔f4 ♖e8 32 ♕e3 h6! 33 ♕xe8 ♗g5#) 29...h5 30 gxh5 ♖h8 is another way to pursue the attack, but Smyslov prefers to increase the harmony of his position.

29   ♕e7   ♖c8!
30   a5

30 ♖xd6 ♖c1 wins on the spot.

30   ...   ♖c2
31   ♔g2   ♘d4+

31...♘g5+ 32 ♔f1 ♗xg3 33 ♕a7 is less clear (and not 33 ♕xg5? ♖xf2+ 34 ♔g1 ♖h2 35 ♔f1 ♗f3; nor 33 fxg3? ♗g2+ and 34...♘f3#).

32   ♔f1

32 ♔h3 ♖xf2 33 ♖xd4 ♗g2+ 34 ♔h2 (34 ♔h4 ♗f1!) 34...♗xd4 35 ♕xd6 ♗e4+! (35...♖d2?? 36 ♕b4) 36 ♔h3 ♖d2 leads to mate or win of the queen:

1) 37 g5 ♗f5+ 38 g4 ♖d3+ 39 ♔g2 (39 ♔h2 ♗g1+) 39...♗e4+ 40 ♔f1 ♗f3.

2) 37 ♕f4 ♖e2 38 ♕c1 ♗g2+ 39 ♔h2 ♗f1+ 40 ♔h1 ♖f2 intending ...♗e2-f3, etc.

3) 37 ♕b4 ♖d1 38 g5 ♗f3 finally closes in to give mate.

32   ...   ♗f3
33   ♖b1

33 ♖e1 ♗xg3 34 ♕e3 ♗xf2 35 ♕xf2 ♖xf2+ 36 ♔xf2 ♔f6 37 ♔e3 ♔e5 (37...♘c2+?? 38 ♔xf3 ♘xe1+ 39 ♔g3 denies the knight any useful checks, and thus the a-pawn cannot be stopped; incidentally this illustrates a useful point to bear in mind in knight and pawn endings: if a king is two squares diagonally away from a knight, it is most unlikely that the knight will be able to gain a tempo with a check) 38 ♔d3+ ♔d5 39 a6 ♘c6 is an easy enough win for Black.

33   ...   ♘c6
0-1

White has no counterplay and 34...♗d4 will win in short order.

Lessons from this game:

1) Players with a predictable opening repertoire are easy to prepare for. Here Smyslov was able to choose an opening that was somewhat unusual for him because he could narrow his preparation down to a few lines.

2) In the King's Indian it is often worth Black's while to sacrifice a pawn or an exchange to blast open the dark squares.

3) Three well-coordinated minor pieces that have plenty of squares where they are securely defended generally prove stronger than a queen that has few targets to attack.

Game 36

Paul Keres – Laszlo Szabo

USSR – Hungary Match-Tournament,
Budapest 1955

Sicilian Defence, Richter-Rauzer Attack

The Players

Paul Keres (1916–75) was one of the strongest players never to become World Champion. For more details see Game 30.

Laszlo Szabo (born 1917) was one of the leading Hungarian players for over 20 years. In 1935 he won the Hungarian Championship for the first of nine times, but it was not until after the Second World War that Szabo made an impact on the international scene. Although he was a successful tournament player, Szabo did not achieve comparable results in World Championship cycles. He qualified three times for the Candidates, his best result being at Amsterdam 1956, where he finished in joint third place. Despite advancing years, he has continued to compete into the 1990s.

The Game

A slip by Szabo in the opening is punished in brutal style by Keres, the whole game being over in just 23 moves. Keres wastes no time in mounting his assault; incredibly, 22½ of Keres's 23 moves are towards the enemy king (the '½' is 8 0-0-0)! The final breakthrough provides an elegant finish to a model game.

1	e4	c5
2	♘f3	d6
3	d4	cxd4
4	♘xd4	♘f6
5	♘c3	♘c6
6	♗g5	e6
7	♕d2	♗e7
8	0-0-0	0-0
9	f4	a6?

In a sharp opening such as the Sicilian, it is often not enough to play "natural" moves. Of course, ...a6 is a fundamental part of many Sicilian systems but each position must be considered individually, and in this specific situation it is a mistake. The standard lines are 9...♘xd4 10 ♕xd4 ♕a5 and 9...h6 10 ♗h4 e5, both of which lead to complex play.

10 e5!

At the time, Szabo's 9...a6 was a new move; many players would react to an innovation cautiously, but not Keres. He immediately spots the flaw in Black's idea and exploits it vigorously. The central breakthrough initiated by the text-move creates dark-squared weakness in Black's position, which are only rendered more serious by the inevitable exchange of dark-squared bishops.

10 ... dxe5

11 ♘xc6   bxc6
12 fxe5

More dynamic than 12 ♕xd8 ♖xd8 13 ♖xd8+ ♗xd8 14 fxe5, when Black saves the piece by 14...h6 and avoids any serious difficulties.

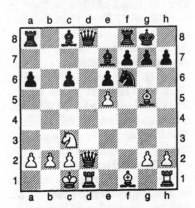

12 ...   ♘d7

There are two alternatives:

1) 12...♕xd2+ 13 ♖xd2 ♘d5 14 ♗xe7 ♘xe7 15 ♗d3 is a miserable ending for Black. White has a fine outpost for his knight at d6, whereas Black has no correspondingly good square for his knight. If it moves to d5, then it can be driven away by c2-c4.

2) 12...♘d5 13 ♗xe7 (13 ♘e4 is also promising) 13...♕xe7 14 ♘e4 and again Black suffers due to the weak d6-square.

13 h4

13 ♗xe7 ♕xe7 14 ♕e3 would have guaranteed White some positional advantage, but Keres prefers to play for a direct attack. Now ...♗xg5 by Black will open the h-file, while otherwise Black's queen is tied to d8.

13 ...   ♖b8

Black intends to free himself with 14...♕b6, threatening mate on b2.

14 ♕e3

Countering Black's threat.

14 ...   ♖e8

This is a cumbersome method of freeing the black queen, but the alternative 14...h6 would have invited 15 ♗xh6! gxh6 16 ♕xh6 and now:

1) 16...♕c7 17 ♗d3 f5 18 g4! ♘xe5 19 gxf5 ♘xd3+ 20 ♖xd3 ♗f6 21 ♖g1+ ♗g7 22 f6 and wins.

2) 16...♕b6 17 ♗d3 f5 18 ♖h3 ♕xb2+ 19 ♔d2 ♘xe5 20 ♖g3+ ♔f7 21 ♕h5+ ♔f6 22 ♘e4+ fxe4 23 ♖f1+ ♘f3+ 24 ♖fxf3+ exf3 25 ♕g5+ ♔f7 26 ♕g6#.

3) 16...♖b4 17 g4! (avoiding the trap 17 ♗d3 ♖xh4! 18 ♖xh4 ♗g5+) 17...♖e8 18 ♗d3 ♘f8 19 ♖df1 with the threat of 20 ♖xf7 ♔xf7 21 ♖f1+ ♗f6 (21...♔g8 22 ♖xf8+) 22 ♖xf6+ ♔e7 23 ♕g7#. If Black defends by 19...♕d7, then 20 ♖xf7 ♔xf7 21 ♗h7! ♖f4 22 ♕xf4+ ♔g7 23 ♗d3 gives White three pawns and a very strong attack for the piece.

15 ♖h3

White utilizes the time to bring his other rook into an attacking position.

15 ...   ♕a5

If Black exchanges queens then White has a clear endgame advantage, for example 15...♕b6 16 ♖xb6 ♗xg5+ 17 ♕e3 ♗xe3+ 18 ♖xe3 or 15...♗xg5 16 hxg5 ♕b6 17 ♕xb6 ♖xb6 18 ♖e1 ♖d8 19 ♗d3 g6 20 ♘e4. Thus Black decides to keep the queens on, and hopes to tie White to the defence of the vulnerable e5-pawn.

16   ♗xe7   ♖xe7
17   ♖g3

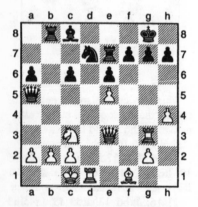

For the moment White need not worry about his e-pawn, as 17...♘xe5 runs into 18 ♕xe5 with a back-rank mate.

17   ...   ♖e8

By covering the back rank, Black renews his threat to the e-pawn and hopes to induce the defensive ♖e1. The alternatives are little better:

1) 17...♕b4 18 ♕g5 g6 (White wins material after 18...♕xb2+ 19 ♔d2) 19 b3, with h5 to come.

2) 17...♔f8 18 ♖e1 ♕b4 19 b3 and Black's threats have dried up, while White is ready for ♕g5 and h5, etc.

3) 17...g6 and now:

3a) 18 h5 may be favourable for White but it is unnecessarily murky:

18...♕xe5 19 ♕xe5 ♘xe5 20 ♖d8+ ♔g7 21 ♘e4 (threatening 22 ♘d6 and 22 ♗xa6) 21...♖b4 22 c4 (22 h6+ ♔xh6 23 ♘f6 ♖f4 24 ♘g8+ ♔g7 25 ♘xe7 ♖xf1+ 26 ♖d1 ♖xd1+ 27 ♔xd1 ♗d7 is also unclear) 22...f5! 23 a3 ♖bb7 24 ♘d6 ♖bd7 25 h6+ ♔xh6 26 ♘xc8 ♖xd8 27 ♘xe7 f4 28 ♖b3 ♖d7 29 ♘c8 is not clear. Black has two pawns for the piece, and the knight on c8 is seriously out of play.

3b) 18 ♖e1! (simple and strong) 18...♕b4 19 b3 ♕xh4 (or else White's attack proceeds with h5) 20 ♖h3 ♕b4 (20...♕g4 21 ♘e4 h5 22 ♘f6+ ♘xf6 23 exf6 wins) 21 ♘e4 with a crushing attack.

18   ♖xd7!

A somewhat surprising sacrifice because it does not give rise to any immediately deadly threats. However, by eliminating the danger to the important e5-pawn, White frees his pieces to attack the real target – Black's king. Soon White will have at least three pieces attacking the enemy kingside, where Black doesn't have a single defensive piece. Szabo's only chance is to stir up some confusion by penetrating with his queen, but it turns out that the queen by itself cannot accomplish much.

18   ...   ♗xd7
19   ♗d3

The threat is simply 20 ♕g5 g6 21 h5, followed by a lethal sacrifice on g6.

19   ...   h6

There is no defence:

1) 19...♕b6 20 ♕h6 ♖g1+ 21 ♔d2 ♕f2+ 22 ♘e2 g6 23 h5 ♖e7 24 hxg6 fxg6 25 ♗xg6 ♕xg3 (or 25...♔h8 26 ♖f3) 26 ♘xg3 hxg6 27 ♘e4 and White wins.

2) 19...♕b4 20 ♕g5 ♕xb2+ 21 ♔d2 g6 22 h5 ♖ed8 23 ♕f6! (threatening 24 h6; not, however, 23 hxg6 fxg6! 24 ♗xg6 ♗e8+ 25 ♗d3+ ♗g6 and Black wriggles out) 23...♕b4 (23...♗e8 24 h6 ♔f8 25 ♖xg6 ♖xd3+ 26 ♔xd3 wins) 24 hxg6 fxg6 25 ♖xg6+ hxg6 26 ♕xg6+ ♔f8 27 ♕h6+ mates.

3) 19...g6 20 h5 and the attack proceeds as in the above lines.

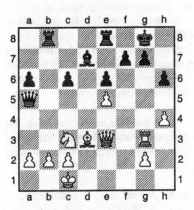

20 ♕f4

White must avoid 20 ♕xh6? ♕xe5 but, as Keres himself points out, White could also have won by 20 ♕e4 ♔f8 (20...g6 21 ♖xg6+ fxg6 22 ♕xg6+ ♔f8 23 ♕xh6+ mates) 21 ♖xg7 ♕b6 (21...♔xg7 22 ♕h7+ ♔f8 23 ♕xh6+ ♔e7 24 ♕f6+ ♔f8 25 ♗g6 also forces mate) 22 ♖xf7+ ♔xf7 23 ♕h7+ ♔f8 24 ♕xh6+ and again Black's king perishes.

The text-move is equally effective, since Black has no answer to the twin threats of 21 ♕f6 and 21 ♖xg7+.

20 ...   ♔f8

Meeting the first threat but not the second. 20...♕b4 21 ♕xh6 ♕xb2+ 22 ♔d2 and 20...♕b6 21 ♕xh6 also lose straight away, so the best defence is

20...♕c5. However, a few accurate moves suffice to end the game: 21 ♘e4 (not 21 ♕f6? ♕e3+) 21...♕g1+ 22 ♔d2 ♔f8 23 ♘d6 ♖e7 24 ♕g4 ♕f2+ (or 24...g6 25 ♕f4) 25 ♗e2 g6 26 ♖f3, followed by ♕xg6, and Black's position crumbles.

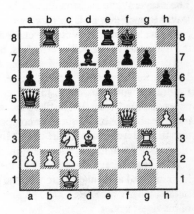

21 ♖xg7!

The second white rook also sacrifices itself to further White's attack. This time the calculation is simple.

21 ...   ♔xg7
22 ♕f6+   ♔f8

Or 22...♔g8 23 ♕xh6 f5 24 exf6 and Black can only prevent mate by giving away almost all his pieces.

23 ♗g6   1-0

Now mate is inevitable.

Lessons from this game:

1) A new move in the opening is not necessarily a good move.

2) Rooks are not normally developed via the third rank, but it can be a way to switch them quickly into attacking positions.

3) The elimination of defensive pieces is often the key to a successful attack.

David Bronstein – Paul Keres
Interzonal tournament, Gothenburg 1955
Nimzo-Indian Defence

The Players

David Bronstein is a player to whom results have always been of secondary importance; he considers himself a chess artist, to whom originality and beauty are the real goals in chess. Nevertheless, he did achieve some outstanding results, and came within a whisker of winning the world championship. He was born in 1924 in the Kiev region in the Ukraine, and progressed rapidly in the late 1940s. He drew a world championship match with Botvinnik in 1951, but thereafter never qualified again. His results have ever since been highly erratic, as more and more he abandoned the quest for competitive success. He was one of the key figures in the development of the King's Indian Defence, and the dynamic handling of positions with formal but unexploitable "weaknesses" – some of the most important new strategic concepts since the Hypermodern theories in the 1920s. He has remained a popular figure with the public, as shown by the great success of his autobiographical work *The Sorcerer's Apprentice*, in which he presents many of his finest games.

Paul Keres (1916–75) was one of the strongest players never to become World Champion. For more details see Game 30.

The Game

Bronstein seizes the initiative with a surprising and unusual sequence of moves in the opening. He sacrifices a whole piece to open up Black's kingside. There is no mate, but rather awkward, prolonged defensive difficulties for Black. At the critical moment Keres misses his chance to get a decent game; he plays a passive move, and there is no way back after this. Further passive defence is forced, and Bronstein starts to claw back the sacrificed material bit by bit, until he has rook and three pawns for two minor pieces. He then wraps up the game efficiently.

1	d4	♘f6
2	c4	e6
3	♘c3	♗b4
4	e3	c5
5	♗d3	b6
6	♘ge2	♗b7
7	0-0	cxd4
8	exd4	0-0

In this fairly normal-looking Nimzo-Indian position, Bronstein conceives a daring attacking plan, based on Black's slow queenside development and the possible exposure of the b4-bishop. There is a certain logic to this, as otherwise Black would have succeeded in retaining maximum flexibility with his d-pawn and queen's knight without paying any price.

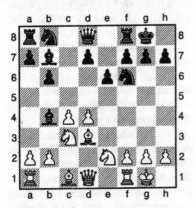

9 d5!   h6!?

Keres sees fit to challenge White's idea head-on. His move prevents ♗g5 and threatens to take on d5 – he wouldn't mind having an isolated d-pawn if it were an extra pawn!

Instead 9...exd5 10 cxd5 ♘xd5 11 ♘xd5 ♗xd5 12 ♗xh7+ ♔xh7 13 ♕xd5 gives White a large positional advantage as Black's isolated d-pawn is very weak, while 9...♘a6 is a relatively "safe" move, which leaves Black a little worse.

10 ♗c2   ♘a6

11 ♘b5!?

An imaginative idea. Bronstein wants to force the pace, and obliges Black to follow him down a complex path, which sees both White's pawn-centre and Black's kingside defences decimated.

Instead 11 a3 ♗d6 (11...♗xc3 12 ♘xc3 ♖c8 13 dxe6 dxe6 14 b3 ♕xd1 15 ♖xd1 ♖fd8 is a line cited by Pachman – White has an edge in view of his bishop-pair) looks a little odd, but may be OK, e.g. 12 ♘b5 ♗e5 (either

keeping the bishop active or provoking a weakening advance) 13 f4 (13 d6 ♘e4 and again it is not so easy for White, e.g. 14 f3 ♕h4) 13...♗b8 14 d6 ♘c5 and White has problems maintaining his pawn on d6 – Black's firm control of e4 is useful.

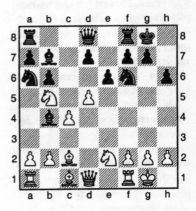

11 ...   exd5

White was threatening to win the bishop by 12 a3, so there wasn't much real choice. 11...♖e8 gives the bishop a square on f8, but after 12 a3 ♗f8 White maintains a substantial spatial plus without difficulty.

12 a3   ♗e7

13 ♘g3!   dxc4

13...♖e8 14 ♕f3 ♘c5 15 ♘f5 gives White a very menacing attack without, as yet, any need to sacrifice.

14 ♗xh6!

White embarks on a sacrificial attack, the soundness of which is not 100% clear. However, it was undoubtedly the right course at this point – Bronstein's 11th move had already committed him. Black faces an arduous defensive task.

14 ...   gxh6
15 ♕d2   ♘h7?

This rather passive move allows White to build his attack methodically. Other moves:

1) 15...♖e8? (worse still) 16 ♕xh6 ♗f8 17 ♕g5+ ♔h8 18 ♘d6! with the variations:

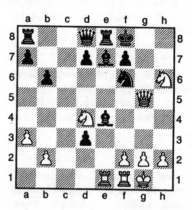

1a) 18...♗xd6 19 ♕h6+ ♔g8 20 ♘h5 ♘xh5 (20...♗xh2+ 21 ♔h1 alters nothing, of course) 21 ♗h7+ ♔h8 22 ♗g6+ ♔g8 23 ♕h7+ ♔f8 24 ♕xf7#.

1b) 18...♗d5 19 ♘xe8! ♘xe8 (or 19...♕xe8 20 ♕xf6+ ♗g7 21 ♕f5 and White will be a rook up) 20 ♕h5+ ♔g7 21 ♕h7+ ♔f6 22 ♕f5+ ♔g7 (22...♔e7 23 ♕e5+ ♗e6 24 ♘f5#) 23

♘h5+ ♔h6 24 ♕h7+ ♔g5 25 f4+ ♔g4 26 ♕f5+ ♔h4 27 g3#.

1c) 18...♕e7 19 ♘gf5 ♘h7 (White can meet 19...♕e6 by 20 ♖ae1) 20 ♕h5 ♕f6 21 ♘xf7+ (21 ♘e7!? ♕g7 22 ♘xf7+ ♕xf7 23 ♕xf7 ♖xe7 isn't very clear – Black has three pieces for the queen, and is reasonably well mobilized) 21...♔g8 22 ♘5h6+ ♗xh6 23 ♘xh6+ ♔f8 (23...♔g7? 24 ♘g4) 24 ♗xh7 should be enough to win.

2) 15...♘c5! is a better, more active defence. 16 ♖ae1 (Bronstein's intention, preventing ...♗e4; after 16 ♕xh6 ♗e4 it is not clear how White might proceed) 16...♘d3 17 ♗xd3 (17 ♕xh6 can be met by 17...♘h7 or 17...♘e8 18 ♖e5 f5) 17...cxd3 18 ♘f5 ♗e4 19 ♘bd4 ♖e8 20 ♘xh6+ ♔f8 21 ♕g5 and now:

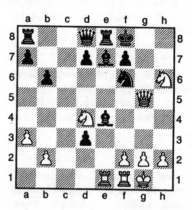

2a) 21...♗c5 is an interesting try, but I believe it can be refuted: 22 ♖xe4! ♖xe4 23 ♘df5 ♔e8 24 ♕g7 ♕c7 25 b4! (to run the bishop out of squares; other moves are less effective) and now:

2a1) 25...♗f8?? 26 ♕xf7+.

2a2) 25...♗d6?? 26 ♕xf7+ ♔d8 27 ♕xf6+.

2a3) 25...♗xf2+ 26 ♔h1 d5 27 ♕xf6 ♖d8 28 ♘g7+ ♔f8 29 ♘hf5! wins – the threat is 30 ♘e6+, and 29...♗d4 30 ♘xd4 ♖d6 31 ♘ge6+ ♖dxe6 32 ♘xe6+ ♖xe6 33 ♕xe6 leaves White a rook up.

2a4) 25...♗e7 26 ♕xf7+ ♔d8 27 ♘xe7 ♖xe7 (27...♘e8 28 ♕d5) 28 ♕xf6 d5 (28...♕e5 29 ♘f7+; 28...d6 29 ♘f5) 29 ♕g5! intending to regain the exchange while neutralizing Black's d-pawns.

2b) 21...♗g6 22 ♖xe7 (22 ♖e6? is flashy and bad – the rook cannot be touched due to 22...dxe6?? 23 ♕xg6 fxg6 24 ♘xe6#, but 22...♘e4 23 ♕e5 ♗f6 would be embarrassing for White) 22...♖xe7 (22...♔xe7? 23 ♘hf5+ forces mate: 23...♗xf5 24 ♘xf5+ ♔e6 25 ♖e1+ ♔d5 26 ♘e7++ ♔c4 27 ♖c1+ ♔b3 28 ♕b5+ ♔a2 29 ♕c4+ ♔xb2 30 ♕c3+ ♔a2 31 ♖a1#) 23 ♕xf6 ♖e4 24 ♕h8+ ♔e7 25 ♘hf5+ ♗xf5 26 ♘xf5+ ♔e6 and here:

2b1) 27 ♘g7+ ♔e7 (moving up the board is very risky: 27...♔d6 28 ♕h7; 27...♔d5 28 ♕h5+) 28 ♘f5+ repeats.

2b2) 27 ♕h3 with very dangerous attacking chances for what is now quite a small material investment.

In conclusion, 15...♘c5 was certainly the best defensive try, but White has enough resources to carry on playing for a win, with a draw in hand in most lines.

16 ♕xh6   f5

As is so often the case, the consequence of one passive move is that further passive play is forced. In the lines following 15...♘c5, we saw that Black was able to play constructive moves in defence, whereas now he must play this weakening pawn move to prevent mate or catastrophic material loss.

Meanwhile each of White's moves is purposeful, and makes progress towards the goal.

17 ♘xf5   ♖xf5

17...♖f7? 18 ♕g6+ ♔f8 19 ♘bd6 ♗xd6 20 ♕xd6+ ♔g8 21 ♘h6+ is devastating.

17...♗f6 18 ♖ae1 ♖f7 (18...♘g5 19 f4) 19 ♕g6+ ♔f8 20 ♘bd6 wins for White.

18 ♗xf5   ♘f8

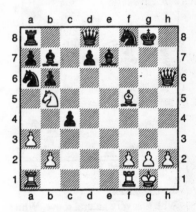

Black is still marginally up on material, but White's pieces are far better placed. He will now aim to swing a rook round to g4.

19 ♖ad1	**♗g5**
20 ♕h5	**♕f6**
21 ♘d6	**♗c6**
22 ♕g4	**♔h8**
23 ♗e4!	

Bronstein decides that the most efficient way to break his opponent's resistance is to eliminate his best-placed piece – the c6-bishop. Rounding up pawns can wait until later.

23 ...   ♗h6

White was threatening to play 24 ♗xc6 dxc6 25 ♘e4, so there was little choice.

23...♗f4 is an attempt to hang on to the c4-pawn, but it leaves the king more exposed, e.g. 24 ♗xc6 (24 ♖d5 is flashy, but after 24...♗xd5 25 ♗xd5 ♘e6 26 ♕h5+ ♔g8 27 ♘e4 ♕xb2, the c-pawn might prove troublesome) 24...dxc6 25 ♘f5 ♕g5 26 ♕h3+ ♔g8 27 ♖fe1 with a big attack.

24 ♗xc6   dxc6

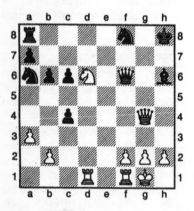

25 ♕xc4

With this very natural move, White establishes a material plus. 25 ♘f5 is also possible, playing directly for an attack, e.g. 25...♖e8 26 ♕h3 ♖e6 27 ♖d4.

25	...	♘c5
26	b4	♘ce6
27	♕xc6	♖b8
28	♘e4	♕g6
29	♖d6	♗g7
30	f4!	♕g4
31	h3	♕e2
32	♘g3	♕e3+
33	♔h2	♘d4

33...♘xf4 is met by 34 ♕c7! (threatening both 35 ♕xb8 and 35 ♕xg7+ ♔xg7 36 ♘f5+, and far better than 34

♖h6+ ♘h7 35 ♕d6 ♗e5 36 ♕e7 ♕xg3+ 37 ♔xg3 ♘g6+ 38 ♕xe5+ ♘xe5 39 ♖e1) 34...♗e5 35 ♕xb8.

| 34 | ♕d5 | ♖e8 |
| 35 | ♘h5 | |

35 ♕h5+! followed by 36 ♖xd4 ♗xd4 37 ♘f5 fatally overloads the black queen.

| 35 | ... | ♘e2 |
| 36 | ♘xg7 | ♕g3+ |

36...♔xg7? 37 ♕g5+ ♔f7 38 ♖f6+ ♔e7 39 ♕g7+ is annihilation.

| 37 | ♔h1 | ♘xf4 |

37...♔xg7 was the only way to stay vaguely in the game, though there is no real hope for Black.

38 ♕f3

This is a typical "safety" move in time-trouble in a clearly winning position. There is no objective reason to avoid 38 ♘xe8.

| 38 | ... | ♘e2 |
| 39 | ♖h6+ | |

39 ♕h5+ would actually mate more quickly, but the text-move is devastating enough.

1-0

Lessons from this game:

1) If the opponent seems to have taken a few liberties in the opening (in this game he had retained more flexibility than is normal) identify any concrete drawbacks in his scheme, and let this guide your choice of plan.

2) When under attack, always try to find the most active, constructive defensive moves.

3) To consolidate an advantage, subduing enemy counterplay is more important than grabbing extra material.

Donald Byrne – Robert Fischer

Rosenwald, New York 1956

Grünfeld Defence, Russian System

The Players

Donald Byrne (1930–76) was the brother of the prominent American grandmaster Robert Byrne. Donald Byrne's own successes include first place in the US Open Championship in 1953. He also represented the USA in three Olympiads (1962, 1964 and 1968).

Robert James Fischer (born 1943) is probably the most famous chess player of all time, and in many people's view he is also the strongest. He has certainly done more to popularize chess than any other player before or since. His celebrated 1972 World Championship Match with Boris Spassky in Reykjavik was headline news in most countries.

At the age of six Fischer got hold of a chess set and was immediately absorbed in the game. "All I want to do, ever, is to play chess." At the age of fourteen he caused the first of many sensations by winning the US Championship, which he continued to capture year after year. He initially found things less straightforward on the international circuit, but he still looked like a good bet to break the Soviet domination of the World Championship single-handedly, which was his burning ambition. Too inexperienced in his first two attempts in 1959 and 1962, Fischer looked set when he was comfortably leading the Sousse Interzonal in 1967. However, a dispute with the organizers, an extremely common occurrence in Fischer's career, led to him withdrawing from the event. He was forced to wait three more years for another chance, but this time there were no mistakes. He destroyed the rest of the field at the 1970 Palma Interzonal. The rest is history. Unbelievable 6–0 wins over top grandmasters Mark Taimanov and Bent Larsen were followed by another convincing victory over Petrosian and finally success in Reykjavik over Spassky. Victories from each of these last three matches earn a place in this collection (Games 61, 62 and 64).

The Game

Described in *Chess Review* by Hans Kmoch as "the game of the century", Fischer indeed plays with remarkable imagination and calculation for one so young. After a standard opening Byrne allows himself the minor extravagance of moving his bishop twice. This seems insignificant, but Fischer sees a small chance and latches onto it. The result is some brilliant sacrificial play. Byrne makes a gallant attempt to confuse the issue, but Fischer is more than ready with a dazzling 17th move, which offers his queen. After this the game is over as a contest. Byrne takes the queen but Fischer takes everything else, including White's king.

1	♘f3	♘f6
2	c4	g6
3	♘c3	♗g7
4	d4	0-0
5	♗f4	d5
6	♕b3	dxc4
7	♕xc4	c6
8	e4	♘bd7

More recently Black has played 8...b5 9 ♕b3 ♕a5, with the idea of ...b4. Miles – Kasparov, Match (game 2), Basle 1986 continued 10 ♗d3 ♗e6 11 ♕d1 ♖d8 12 0-0 ♗g4 13 e5 ♘d5 14 ♘xd5 cxd5 15 ♖c1 ♕b6 16 ♖c5 ♘d7 17 ♖xb5 ♗xf3 18 ♕a4! ♗xg2!? 19 ♖xb6 ♘xb6 20 ♕a6 ♗xf1 21 ♔xf1 e6 with an unclear position.

| 9 | ♖d1 | ♘b6 |
| 10 | ♕c5 | ♗g4 |

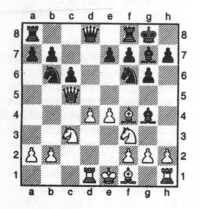

11 ♗g5?

With this move White violates the opening principle "Do not move a piece twice in the opening!". Nevertheless, it must be said that Byrne was a little unfortunate to be punished so brutally for this "crime". Playing with the black pieces, a serious mistake in the opening can often prove to be fatal. The comfort of the white pieces and

that extra tempo, however, means that one can usually remain relatively unscathed after just one bad move. This is certainly not the case here, although it takes some exceptionally imaginative play by Fischer to prove so. If the white knight were removed from c3, then Black would be able to unleash the powerful fork ...♘xe4. This logic provides the basis for Fischer's startling reply, which Byrne must certainly have overlooked.

Instead of Byrne's inferior move, White should be content with the simple developing move 11 ♗e2, e.g. 11...♘fd7 12 ♕a3 ♗xf3 13 ♗xf3 e5 14 dxe5 ♕e8 15 ♗e2 ♘xe5 16 0-0 and White had a slight edge in Flear – Morris, Dublin 1991.

11 ...   ♘a4!!
12 ♕a3

Accepting the offer with 12 ♘xa4 ♘xe4 quickly leads to a disaster for White, e.g.:

1) 13 ♕xe7 ♕a5+! 14 b4 ♕xa4 15 ♕xe4 ♖fe8 16 ♗e7 ♗xf3 17 gxf3 ♗f8 and the pin on the e-file is decisive.

2) 13 ♗xe7 ♘xc5 14 ♗xd8 ♘xa4 15 ♗g5 ♗xf3 16 gxf3 ♘xb2 and not only is Black a pawn up, but White's pawns are also a complete mess.

3) 13 ♕c1 ♕a5+ 14 ♘c3 ♗xf3 15 gxf3 ♘xg5 and Black regains the sacrificed piece, once more with a winning position.

4) After 13 ♕b4 both 13...♘xg5 14 ♘xg5 ♗xd1 15 ♔xd1 ♗xd4 16 ♔e1 ♕d5 and 13...a5!? 14 ♕xb7 ♘xg5 15 ♗e2 (after 15 ♘xg5 ♗xd1 16 ♔xd1 ♕xd4+ Black wins the knight on a4) 15...♘xf3+ 16 gxf3 ♖b8 look very good for Black.

With 12 ♕a3, Byrne hoped that the pressure on e7 would dissuade Black from grabbing the e-pawn. Nevertheless, Fischer was not going to be denied.

| 12 | ... | ♘xc3 |
| 13 | bxc3 | ♘xe4! |

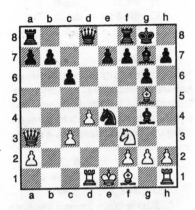

This capture is a logical follow-up to Black's previous play. True, White can now win an exchange, but Fischer had accurately calculated that the problems White encounters down the open e-file more than makes up for this. Indeed, Byrne was eventually forced to agree, and decline the material on offer.

| 14 | ♗xe7 | ♛b6 |
| 15 | ♗c4 | |

Grabbing the rook allows the black pieces to flood into the game with a gain of time. After 15 ♗xf8 ♗xf8 16 ♛b3 ♘xc3! (the tactics simply flow for Black; it also has to be said that the simple 16...♛xb3 17 axb3 ♖e8 18 ♗e2 ♘xc3 19 ♖d2 ♗b4 also looks very strong) 17 ♛xb6 (17 ♛xc3 ♗b4 pins and wins the queen) 17...axb6 18 ♖a1 ♗xf3 19 gxf3 ♗a3 20 ♔d2 ♗b2 21 ♖e1 ♘d5 Black starts to pick off White's woefully weak pawns.

| 15 | ... | ♘xc3! |

16 ♗c5

Black recovers the bishop after 16 ♛xc3 ♖fe8 17 ♛e3 ♛c7, while 16 ♗xf8 is still no good after 16...♗xf8 17 ♛xc3 ♗b4.

| 16 | ... | ♖fe8+ |
| 17 | ♔f1 | |

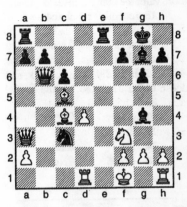

| 17 | ... | ♗e6!! |

This clever retort, a bishop retreat which is very difficult to detect, must have come as a complete shock to Byrne, who was probably hoping for 17...♘b5? 18 ♗xf7+! ♔xf7 19 ♛b3+ ♗e6 20 ♘g5+, when the tables would suddenly be turned in White's favour.

18 ♗xb6

There is no way out for White. The most engaging line is 18 ♗xe6, when Black can carry out a version of Philidor's (smothered) Mate by 18...♛b5+ 19 ♔g1 ♘e2+ 20 ♔f1 ♘g3++ 21 ♔g1 ♛f1+! 22 ♖xf1 ♘e2#.

Other moves fail to put up any sort of resistance, e.g. 18 ♛xc3 ♛xc5! 19 dxc5 ♗xc3 20 ♗xe6 ♖xe6 and Black's extra pawn is just one of his pluses, or 18 ♗d3 ♘b5 19 ♛a4 ♛c7. In this last variation it's not particularly surprising that an attempt to regain the pawn with 20 ♗xb5 cxb5 21 ♕xb5 runs into disaster following 21...b6 22 ♗a3 ♗c4+.

After 18 ♗xb6 Black can go on a (discovered) checking spree, picking up assorted material along the way. This bag of goodies proves to be far more valuable than the invested queen.

18	...	♗xc4+
19	♔g1	♘e2+
20	♔f1	♘xd4+
21	♔g1	

21 ♖d3 is hardly likely to work, and doesn't after 21...axb6 22 ♕c3 ♘xf3.

21	...	♘e2+
22	♔f1	♘c3+
23	♔g1	axb6
24	♕b4	♖a4
25	♕xb6	♘xd1

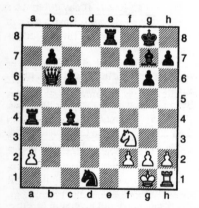

The dust has settled and Black has managed to amass a total of one rook, two bishops and one pawn for the queen. Furthermore, White now has to waste more time releasing his h1-rook and Black can take this opportunity to pluck another couple of pawns. In fact White could quite easily resign here, but it's always difficult to do so when one has the extra queen.

26	h3	♖xa2
27	♔h2	♘xf2
28	♖e1	♖xe1
29	♕d8+	♗f8
30	♘xe1	♗d5
31	♘f3	♘e4
32	♕b8	b5
33	h4	h5
34	♘e5	♔g7
35	♔g1	

Black now starts the final onslaught against the white king. It's very entertaining how all of Black's pieces play a part in driving the white monarch along the back rank and into a mating net.

35	...	♗c5+
36	♔f1	♘g3+
37	♔e1	♗b4+

37...♗b3 actually forces mate more quickly, but it's a very secure feeling to check all of the way to checkmate.

38	♔d1	♗b3+
39	♔c1	♘e2+
40	♔b1	♘c3+
41	♔c1	♖c2# (0-1)

Lessons from this game:

1) Opening principles exist for a reason. Here Byrne flouted them with 11 ♗g5 and paid the full penalty. The really great players know when to break, and when not to break the rules, but lesser mortals should beware.

2) Material sacrifices are always more likely to work if your opponent's king is stuck in the middle and a central file is open. In this case it's possible that a move such as Fischer's 13...♘xe4 can be played on intuition rather than calculation.

3) Even at the age of thirteen, Fischer was someone to be reckoned with!

Game 39
Mikhail Tal – Aleksandrs Koblencs
Training game, Riga 1957
Sicilian Defence, Richter-Rauzer Attack

The Players

Mikhail Tal (1936–92) had perhaps the most remarkable and unique talent of all chess players. Although others could sometimes match his results, no one, before or since, has ever matched the way he achieved them. Tal was a born attacking genius. He would launch attacks that looked to others like sheer recklessness, but painstaking analysis would later show that Tal's intuition and feel for the initiative had been right – perhaps there would be ways to survive, but all attempts at simple refutations of Tal's sacrifices would crumble upon detailed examination. Over the board, his opponents found the problems he posed them quite impossible to deal with. He quite literally changed the way chess was played; not by his writings or theories, but quite simply by checkmating everyone. In an interview given in 1979, when asked whether his style had become more positional, Tal replied, "I'd be glad to get to heaven, but my sins won't allow it! Today the squares d5, f5 and e6 (my visiting cards, so to speak) are so well covered! Have a poke in there – there are four defenders!" Like Morphy a century earlier, Tal showed the world that the general level of defensive play was inadequate.

Tal was born in Riga, the capital of Latvia, which for most of his life was a part of the Soviet Union. The original Latvian form of his name was Mihails Tals. He learned to play at an early age, but was no prodigy; it was not until he was into his teens that he began to study the game seriously, working in close association with Koblencs. He then made rapid progress. Tal was also extremely bright and quick-witted away from the board, going to university at the age of 15. He won the Latvian Championship in 1953 and had an impressive debut in the USSR Championship in 1956. Then in the period 1957–60 something incredible happened. Tal became completely unstoppable. Consecutive victories in the USSR Championship in 1957 and 1958 were followed by first place in the Portorož interzonal in 1958, two and a half points ahead of the field, an extremely convincing victory in the 1959 Candidates tournament (including a 4–0 whitewash of the young Fischer) and a 12½–8½ crush of Botvinnik to become the youngest world champion up to that time. Few would have thought at that point that he would soon become the youngest ex-World Champion ever, but it was then that his worst enemy – his health – intervened, as it was to do repeatedly throughout his career. Even as a youngster it was clear to his doctors that Tal was not destined to enjoy a long, healthy life. In particular he was in and out of hospital with kidney problems. He did not help matters by smoking and drinking to excess, but much of this was to dull the pain from which, especially in his later years, he was rarely free. He suffered a bout of kidney problems shortly before his title defence in

1961, and lost badly in the match. He never again challenged for the world title. For the next thirty years he was among the world's top players, and during the periods when his health would permit he achieved world-beating results. In 1979, for instance, he rose to second place in the world rankings, close on the heels of Anatoly Karpov.

His talent was deeply respected by his grandmaster colleagues. Botvinnik famously commented, "If Tal would learn to program himself properly then it would become impossible to play against him." Petrosian stated that Tal was the only living chess genius that he knew. Grandmaster Sosonko reports that at the 1985 Taxco Interzonal, one prominent grandmaster said "None of us can hold a candle to Misha."

Tal loved chess. Right up to the end of his life, when he was severely weakened by his final illness, he would play blitz chess as much as he could – and still to a very high standard. In his younger days he would even "escape" from hospital to visit the local chess club. The joy of playing, of sacrificing, of executing a beautiful combination – this was everything to Tal.

Tal was a prolific chess journalist; he edited the Latvian chess magazine *Sahs* from 1960 to 1970, making it one of the world's most important chess magazines. He also left behind for posterity one of the greatest books of all time, *The Life and Games of Mikhail Tal*.

We have selected for this book more games by Tal than by any other player. We could easily have included a dozen more.

Aleksandrs Koblencs (1916–93) was born in Riga and became one of the leading Latvian players and trainers. In 1949 he started working with the young Mikhail Tal, and helped to shape his then rather uncoordinated talent into the play that was to take the chess world by storm over the next decade. He was Tal's trainer from 1955 to 1979. His many writings included the entertaining book *Study Chess with Tal*, with training exercises based around Tal's finest games.

The Game

The game that follows is a rather bizarre and highly complex masterpiece. Tal plays an aggressive opening involving a rapid kingside pawn advance. After a rather odd episode in moves 19–22, when both players miss chances to be clearly better, Koblencs tries to emulate Game 31, Geller – Euwe, by sucking White's pieces deep into his kingside. It appears both players were held under the spell of that game, since in neither player's notes is the idea of Black trying to win the white queen, trapped in the corner, even mentioned – it is assumed that Black will play for the counterattack. After a prolonged period of chaos, with several pieces on both sides left *en prise* but unable to be taken, Tal crashes through. The mechanism for his final attack is quite unique. The only fly in the ointment is that there were other ways to win, and that Black in fact had an astonishing drawing resource close to the end. Of course, mistakes are inevitable in such a complex struggle, and they in no way detract from both players' achievement.

1	e4	c5
2	♘f3	♘c6
3	d4	cxd4
4	♘xd4	♘f6
5	♘c3	d6
6	♗g5	e6
7	♕d2	

This move was developed by Rauzer (see Game 28) in the 1930s. His idea of castling queenside proved so effective that his name was added to that of Richter (who advocated 6 ♗g5, but with the altogether more crude and less effective idea of playing 7 ♘xc6 bxc6 8 e5), and the opening became known as the Richter-Rauzer Attack. It can lead to many types of play: intricate battles in the centre, long forcing sequences with early simplifications, or – as here – the standard Sicilian opposite-wing attacks.

7	...	♗e7
8	0-0-0	0-0
9	♘b3	

This is known as the Podebrady Variation, after the town where it was first played. White avoids an exchange of knights, and increases the pressure on the d6-pawn. However, White must always be wary of actually grabbing this pawn if the positional price is too high.

9	...	♕b6
10	f3	a6
11	g4	♖d8
12	♗e3	♕c7
13	h4	b5
14	g5	♘d7

This was at the time a topical position. Tal now plays the most vigorous move at his disposal.

15 g6!?

Tal actually played this position on three occasions: firstly in this training game, and later in two tournament games. 15 h5 is possible too, but since Black can choose to ignore the pawn when it arrives on g6, the move h4-h5 can turn out to be a loss of time.

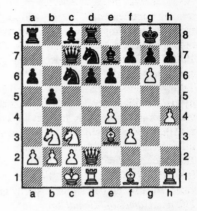

15 ... hxg6!

Tal commented "This looks risky, but appears to be best". His other opponents both chose different moves here:

1) 15...fxg6 16 h5 gxh5 17 ♖xh5 ♘f6 (17...b4? 18 ♘d5 exd5 19 ♕xd5+ ♔h8 20 ♖xh7+ ♔xh7 21 ♕h5+ ♔g8 22 ♗c4+ mates) 18 ♖g5 gave White a strong attack in Tal – Mohrlock, Varna Olympiad 1962.

2) 15...♘c5 16 gxf7+ ♔xf7 17 ♗h3 ♘a4 18 f4 ♘b4 19 f5 e5 20 ♘xa4! ♘xa2+ 21 ♔b1 bxa4 22 ♘a5! ♖b8 23 ♕d5+ ♔f8 24 ♔xa2 ♕xc2 (24...♖b5 25 ♕c6 ♕xa5 26 f6! wins) 25 ♖d2 ♖xb2+ 26 ♔a1 ♕c3 27 ♕d3 1-0 Tal – Stoltz, Telegraph game 1959.

16	h5	gxh5
17	♖xh5	♘f6
18	♖h1	

Often when retreating a rook on an open h-file against the enemy king such as this, it would go to the second rank, to allow the other rook to come behind it. Here, though, more immediate threats can be generated by putting the queen in front of the rook, and having her majesty lead the attack.

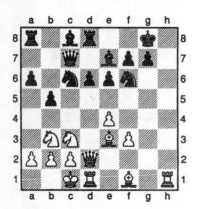

18 ...   d5

Black reacts to prevent ♕h2 and, in accordance with the standard procedure when attacked on the wing, to open the centre. However, 18...♘e5 should, in view of the next note, be regarded as a better defence.

19 e5?!

White sacrifices another pawn to keep the initiative. However, 19 ♗f4! ♗d6 20 ♗xd6 ♕xd6 21 f4 is Timman's suggestion, when White has ideas of e5 and ♕h2. His attacking chances here look better than those in the game, and he has sacrificed less too.

19 ...   ♘xe5

After 19...♕xe5?? 20 ♗f4 ♕f5 21 ♗d3 White wins material.

20 ♗f4

20 ♕h2 is tempting, but after 20...♔f8 21 ♕h8+ ♘g8 22 ♖h7 ♗f6, the fact that the queen has no escape from h8 proves fatal: 23 ♗c5+ ♕xc5! 24 ♘xc5 ♘g6 and Black regains the

queen, keeping a two-pawn advantage. We should bear this theme in mind, since it crops up again later on.

20 ...   ♗d6
21 ♕h2

White furthers his attack, seeing that the obvious 21...♘d3+?? would actually fail disastrously to 22 ♔b1!.

21 ...   ♔f8

21...♘g6 22 ♗xd6 ♕xd6 looks like quite a reasonable alternative.

22 ♕h8+   ♘g8?!

Koblencs recounts that his motivation behind this move came from the strong impression that the game Geller – Euwe, Candidates tournament, Zurich 1953 (Game 31) had made on him. Although famous examples of strategic ideas enrich our understanding of chess, a strong player must be able to assess when a model can be followed, and not copy an idea on a whim, because of a superficial similarity. Compare Tal's queen in twelve moves' time to that of Geller at the end of his game with Euwe! 22...♔e7 is the safe and sensible move, when White must drop back his queen, 23 ♕h3 (23 ♕h4 ♘xf3 is worse, while 23 ♕xg7? ♖g8 24 ♕h6 ♘d3+ is now a real problem), and it is debatable whether the attack is really worth the pawns.

23 ♖h7   f5
24 ♗h6   ♖d7

White has been methodically bringing all his pieces to bear on the g7-pawn. However, Black now threatens 25...gxh6 and 25...♘g6. Consider how you might continue, and compare it with Tal's actual continuation.

25 ♗xb5!

Tal wastes no time at all preparing to bring the rook to g1. As long as it survives on b5, the bishop attacks the d7-rook and in some lines its potential guard on the e8-square is important. This move also takes care of the threatened 25...gxh6.

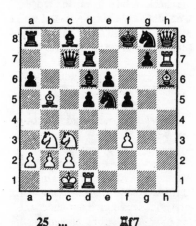

25 ... 𝕏f7

25...♘g6! is a natural move that has gone unmentioned by previous annotators, although it is only by a miracle that White isn't losing on the spot. The critical line runs 26 ♘d4! (26 ♗xd7? is answered by 26...♗f4+ and not 26...♘xh8? 27 ♗xg7+ ♔e7 28 ♗xe6!) 26...𝕏e7 (26...♘xh8 27 ♘xe6+) 27 ♗xg7+ 𝕏xg7 28 ♗d7!! ♕xd7 29 ♘xe6+ ♕xe6 30 ♕xg7+ ♔e8 31 ♘xd5, e.g.:

1) 31...♗d7 and then:

1a) 32 ♘f6+ ♘xf6 33 ♕xg6+ ♔d8 34 𝕏h8+ ♔c7 35 𝕏xa8 appears to work nicely, but Black has the horrible counterblow 35...♕e3+! 36 ♔b1 (36 𝕏d2?? ♕e1+ 37 𝕏d1 ♗f4+ 38 ♔b1 ♕xd1#) 36...♕xf3 forking the white rooks, when White will be grovelling for an unlikely draw.

1b) 32 ♕xg8+ ♕xg8 33 ♘f6+ ♔d8 (33...♔f8 34 ♘xd7+ ♔e8 35 ♘f6+ ♔f8 36 ♘xg8) 34 ♘xg8 ♔c7 35 ♘f6 is very good for White.

2) 31...a5! (countering the threat of 32 ♘c7+ ♗xc7 33 ♕xc7 by making room for 33...♗a6) leaves White with no particularly convincing continuation.

26 𝕏g1 𝕏a7

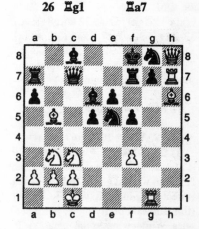

The parallel with Geller – Euwe is clear. The white queen on h8 and h7-rook are quite useless when it comes to defending their own king. Therefore everything depends on how effective they are at attacking his opposite number. Since there is no immediate breakthrough, and most of White's pieces are effectively positioned, it is time to look around and see if any reserves can be brought up – is any piece not pulling its weight?

27 ♘d4!

White has a spectacular alternative in 27 ♗xa6!, with the aim of diverting a piece from guarding g7 or e6. Then:

1) 27...𝕏xa6? 28 𝕏gxg7 is terminal.

2) 27...♗xa6 28 ♘d4 ♘d3+ (if 28...♗c8 then 29 ♘db5, or 28...♔e7 29 ♕xg8) 29 cxd3 ♗f4+ 30 ♔b1 ♗xd3+ 31 ♔a1 ♕e5 32 𝕏hxg7 𝕏xg7 33 ♗xg7+ 𝕏xg7 34 ♘xe6+ and wins.

3) 27...♘xf3 28 ♘b5 (28 ♖gxg7 ♖xg7 29 ♗xg7+ ♕xg7 30 ♖xg7 ♖xg7 and White's back rank saves Black from immediate catastrophe) 28...♗f4+ (28...♘xg1 29 ♘xc7 ♖axc7 30 ♗xc8) 29 ♔b1 ♗xh6 (29...♕e5 30 ♗xf4 ♕xf4 31 ♖gh1! ♖xa6 32 ♕xg8+! ♗e7 33 ♖xg7) 30 ♘xc7 ♖xa6 (30...♘xg1 31 ♗xc8 ♖axc7 32 ♗xe6; 30...♖axc7 31 ♗xc8 ♖xc8 32 ♖g6 planning ♖hxh6) 31 ♖g3 should win.

27 ...   ♘g4

To reduce the pressure on g7. Others:

1) 27...♕b6? 28 ♖gxg7 mates.

2) 27...♘c4 28 ♘xf5! ♗f4+ 29 ♔b1 exf5 30 ♘xd5 ♕e5 31 ♗xc4 ♗xh6 32 ♖xh6 wins, e.g. 32...♕d4 33 ♖gh1 (threatening mate in two) 33...♖fd7?! (this allows a pretty mate, but otherwise White wins as he pleases) 34 ♕xg8+! (34 ♘b6?? ♕d1+) 34...♔xg8 35 ♘e7++ ♔f8 36 ♘g6+ ♔e8 37 ♖h8#.

3) 27...♗c5 is met by 28 ♗e8 and now:

3a) 28...♔xe8 29 ♖gxg7 ♖xg7 30 ♖xg7 ♘f7 31 ♖xg8+ ♔e7 (31...♔d7 32 ♖g7) 32 ♘xf5+ wins.

3b) 28...♖xd4 29 ♗xf7 ♘d3+ (or 29...♕xf7 30 ♗xg7+) 30 cxd3 ♕xf7 31 ♗xg7+ ♗xg7 32 ♖hxg7 ♕xg7 33 ♖xg7 ♖xg7 and this particular queen vs bits position is a straightforward win for White.

28 fxg4   ♗e5

Or:

1) 28...gxh6 29 gxf5 ♗f4+ (White wins after 29...♗g3 30 ♖xf7+) 30 ♔d1 ♗g5 (30...♗g3 31 ♖xf7+) 31 ♖xh6 wins, e.g. 31...♕f4 32 ♖xg5 ♕xg5 33 ♖g6.

2) 28...♗f4+ 29 ♗xf4 ♕xf4+ 30 ♔b1 ♕xd4 31 ♖gh1 ♖fb7 32 ♗e8!

(threatening 33 ♕xg8+ again; 32 g5? e5 33 g6 ♗e6) 32...♖xb2+ 33 ♔c1 (33 ♔xb2? ♖b7+ 34 ♔c1) 33...♕f4+ 34 ♔xb2 ♕b4+ 35 ♔c1 ♕f4+ 36 ♔d1 and the checks soon run out: 36...♕d4+ 37 ♔e2 ♕c4+ (37...♕xg4+ 38 ♔e1 ♕g3+ 39 ♔d1 ♕f3+ 40 ♘e2) 38 ♔f2 ♕f4+ (38...♕d4+ 39 ♔f1) 39 ♔e1.

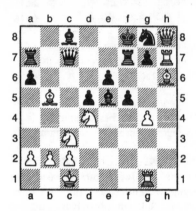

29 ♘c6!?

29 ♗e8! ♔xe8 30 ♘xe6 (30 ♕xg8+ ♖f8 31 ♘xe6 ♖xg8 32 ♘xc7+ ♖xc7 is less clear) 30...♗xe6 31 ♕xg8+ ♔e7 (31...♖f8? 32 ♕xe6+ ♕e7 33 gxf5!; 31...♔d7? 32 gxf5!) 32 gxf5 ♗xc3 (32...♗xf5? 33 ♘xd5+; 32...♖xf5 33 ♖gxg7+ ♗xg7 34 ♖xg7+ ♖f7 35 ♕xf7+! ♗xf7 36 ♘xd5+ simplifies into a winning ending) 33 ♗g5+ ♗f6 (33...♔d6 34 ♗f4+) 34 ♗xf6+ ♔xf6 (34...gxf6 35 ♖e1) 35 fxe6 is hopeless for Black.

29 ...   ♗xc3
30 ♗e3!?

The threat of ♗c5+ is sufficient to force Black's reply.

30 ...   d4

This move has the drawback of cutting off Black's bishop from the defence of g7.

31 Rgh1!

Threatening 32 Wxg8+ Kxg8 33 Rh8#.

31 ... Rd7

31...Rf6? 32 Bg5 Rb7 (32...axb5 33 Bxf6 Wf4+ 34 Kb1) 33 Bxf6 Wf4+ 34 Kb1 gxf6 35 Rxb7 Bxb7 36 Ne7! not only puts several pieces *en prise*, but also wins.

32 Bg5

32 gxf5 opens up some more lines towards the black king, and is worth investigating in view of the note to Black's 33rd move below. The main threat is fxe6, renewing the threat to force mate by the queen sacrifice Wxg8+. 32...Rd5 is a valiant defensive effort, but seems inadequate: 33 fxe6 Bxe6 34 Rf1+ Rf5 (34...Bf5 35 Bc4) 35 Rxf5+ Bxf5 36 Bc4 Bxh7 37 Wxh7 Wxc6 38 Wxg8+ Ke7 39 Bg5+ Kd6 40 Wf8+ Kc7 41 Wd8+ Kb7 42 Bd5 wins the queen.

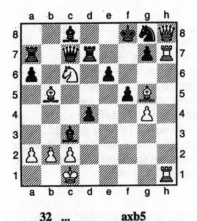

32 ... axb5

Finally the bishop that was sacrificed on move 25 is captured! 32...d3?

33 bxc3 axb5 34 Rh6!! transposes to the game.

33 Rh6!?

This move introduces the idea Rf6+, meeting ...gxf6 with Bh6+, but this threat isn't as strong as Koblencs assumed.

33 ... d3?

Black should play 33...Wxc6! 34 Rf6+ (34 bxc3? We4 35 Rf6+ Ke7!) 34...gxf6 35 Bh6+ Rg7 36 Bxg7+ Ke7 37 Bxf6++ Kd6 38 Be5+ Kd5 39 Rxa7 Bxb2+ with a perpetual. I find it quite shocking – almost beyond belief – that Black can have this saving resource. However, it does appear to be true!

34 bxc3 d2+
35 Kd1 Wxc6

In despair, Black allows White's main idea. But there was now no saving line.

36 Rf6+ Rf7

36...gxf6 37 Bh6+ Rg7 38 Bxg7+ Ke7 39 Bxf6++ Kd6 (39...Kf8 40 Bg7+ Ke7 41 Bh6+) 40 Be5+ Kd5 41 Bb8 wins.

37 Wxg7+ 1-0

Lessons from this game:

1) Study the classics, but don't let the ideas from them cloud your thinking in completely different positions.

2) Don't be intimidated by extremely messy positions. The play still tends to be based on simple tactical ideas – just a large quantity of them.

3) Never give up hope. Even when defending against the most massive of attacks, there may well be a saving resource.

Lev Polugaevsky – Rashid Nezhmetdinov
RSFSR Championship, Sochi 1958
Old Indian Defence

The Players

Lev Polugaevsky (1934–95) was born in Mogilev, in what is now Belarus. He was one of the world's top grandmasters from the late 1960s to the early 1980s. During this period he was a world championship candidate three times, reaching the semi-finals in 1977, losing to Korchnoi, who went on to challenge Karpov in 1978. He competed in the USSR Championship on twenty occasions, sharing first place three times running at the end of the 1960s. In 1981 his classic book *Grandmaster Preparation* was published, a brilliant source of inspiration for all those hoping to become top players. As well as many of his best games, and insights into his methods, the book contains a large chapter on the birth and development of his famous double-edged invention in the Sicilian Najdorf (1 e4 c5 2 ♘f3 d6 3 d4 cxd4 4 ♘xd4 ♘f6 5 ♘c3 a6 6 ♗g5 e6 7 f4 b5!?), the Polugaevsky Variation. Polugaevsky really cared about his work, and spoke out against the tendency for lazy authors to throw books together quickly and without much thought or effort. His great strengths as a player were his strategic understanding and deep opening preparation, while his Achilles' Heel was his tactical vision, which let him down in some crucial games.

Rashid Nezhmetdinov (1912–74) was born in Aktiubinsk, Kazakhstan, but spent most of his life in Kazan, the capital of the Tartar Republic. In his youth he showed a remarkable talent for both chess and draughts and when he was 18 he was champion of Kazan at both. Nezhmetdinov won the championship of the Russian Republic five times and also competed often in the Soviet Championship. Nezhmetdinov is best known for his open attacking play and the spectacular combinations that featured regularly in his games. Mikhail Tal paid tribute to him in the classic book *Learn from the Grandmasters*. Tal, who annotated one of his three losses to Nezhmetdinov in the book, said of the recently deceased player "Players die, tournaments are forgotten, but the works of great artists are left behind them to live on for ever in memory of their creators."

The Game

Polugaevsky plays ambitiously in the opening, erecting a powerful centre, but losing time by having to move his queen twice. Nezhmetdinov spots a small chink in the armour, seizes his chance and refuses to give up the initiative for the rest of the game. In an intricate position one minor slip by Polugaevsky is enough to set off some major fireworks, involving a fantastic queen sacrifice, culminating in a king-hunt leading to checkmate. This game has everything!

1	d4	♘f6
2	c4	d6
3	e4	e5
4	♘c3	exd4
5	♕xd4	♘c6
6	♕d2	g6
7	b3	♗g7
8	♗b2	0-0
9	♗d3	♘g4!

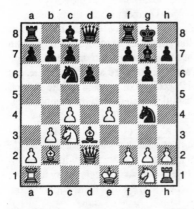

White's two pawns on e4 and c4 create a strong bind in the centre, and typical moves from Black will allow White to catch up in development and gain a comfortable advantage. Black must seek activity as soon as possible and 9...♘g4 is the perfect way to do this. Now Black has ideas of ...♕h4, ...♘ge5 and the pawn break ...f5.

10 ♘ge2

Already White has to be a little careful how he develops his pieces. 10 ♘f3 looks the most natural move, but then Black can play 10...♘ge5! 11 ♗e2 (or 11 ♘xe5 dxe5, when Black has a pleasant outpost on d4 for his knight) 11...♘xf3+ 12 ♗xf3 ♘d4 13 ♗d1 f5 14 exf5 ♗xf5 and Black has a powerful initiative. This was converted into a victory very convincingly in

Alatortsev – Boleslavsky, USSR Championship, Moscow 1950: 15 ♘e2 ♘xe2 16 ♗xe2 ♗xb2 17 ♕xb2 ♕g5! 18 g3 ♖ae8 19 0-0 ♗h3 20 f4 ♗xf1! 21 fxg5 ♖xe2 22 ♕c3 ♗g2 23 ♕d3 ♗f3 24 ♖f1 ♖g2+ 25 ♔h1 ♗c6! 26 ♖xf8+ ♔xf8 27 ♕f1+ ♖f2+ 0-1.

10 ... ♕h4

11 ♘g3

Efim Geller mentions 11 g3 as a possible improvement for White. It should be mentioned that then the tempting 11...♘ce5 12 gxh4 ♘f3+ is good for Black after 13 ♔f1 ♘xd2+ 14 ♔g2 f5!, but not so good if White chooses the superior 13 ♔d1! ♘xf2+ 14 ♔c2 ♘xd2 15 ♔xd2 ♘xh1 16 ♖xh1, when the two pieces outweigh the rook.

11 ... ♘ge5

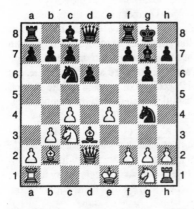

12 0-0

Delaying castling also gives Black plenty of play. Geller gives the lines:

1) 12 ♗c2 ♘d4! 13 ♗d1 c5 14 ♘d5 ♗h6 15 f4 ♗xf4 16 ♘xf4 ♕xf4 and Black has won a pawn.

2) 12 ♗e2 ♗h6 13 ♕d1 f5 14 exf5 gxf5 15 ♘d5 f4 and White's king is still stuck in the centre.

12   ...   f5

This move is very natural, and gives Black a powerful attack, but why didn't Nezhmetdinov play the obvious switchback 12...♘g4 here? After 13 h3 ♘xf2 14 ♕xf2 (both 14 ♔xf2 ♗d4+ 15 ♔f3 ♘e5+ and 14 ♖xf2 ♕xg3 are very strong for Black) 14...♗d4 White is forced to give up his queen for two minor pieces. However, following 15 ♕xd4 ♘xd4 16 ♘d5 White has some compensation, e.g.:

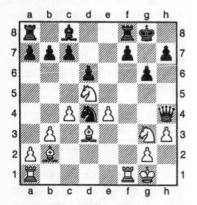

1) 16...♘e6? 17 ♗f6 and the double threat of ♗xh4 and ♘e7# wins.

2) 16...♕xg3 17 ♘e7+ ♔g7 18 ♗xd4+ f6 19 ♖f3 ♕g5 20 ♘d5 c5 21 ♗b2 and White will increase the pressure on f6 with ♖af1.

3) 16...c5 (probably the best move) 17 ♘e2 ♘xe2+ 18 ♗xe2 f5 19 ♖f4 ♕h6 20 ♖af1 and now Black can play 20...♗e6 as after 21 ♘c7 he has the resource 21...g5!.

Despite the fact that Black gains material after 12...♘g4, one can understand Nezhmetdinov's reluctance to hand over the initiative to White. After 12...f5 at least it's Black who has all the fun.

13   f3

Now 13 f4? will certainly be met by 13...♘g4!, when 14 h3 ♗d4+ 15 ♔h1 ♕xg3 16 hxg4 ♕h4# is mate. The next few moves witness Black's attack building up very swiftly.

13	**...**	**♗h6**
14	**♕d1**	**f4**
15	**♘ge2**	**g5**
16	**♘d5**	**g4**
17	**g3!**	

The only way to fight back. After the greedy 17 ♘xc7 g3! 18 h3 it is no surprise that Black crashes through with the standard sacrifice 18...♗xh3 19 gxh3 ♕xh3, when White has no useful way to defend his position.

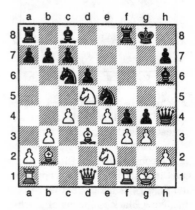

17   ...   fxg3!?

Good enough to keep an initiative, but 17...♕h3! is objectively better. Geller gives 18 ♘exf4 ♗xf4 19 ♘xf4 ♖xf4 20 gxf4 g3 21 hxg3 ♕xg3+ leading to a perpetual check, but after 22 ♔h1 Black can play on with 22...♕h4+ 23 ♔g1 ♗h3! 24 ♕e1 (or 24 ♖f2 ♕g3+ 25 ♔h1 ♕xf2 26 ♕g1+ ♗g2+! 27 ♕xg2+ ♕xg2+ 28 ♔xg2 ♘xd3) 24...♕xe1 25 ♖fxe1 ♘xd3 with a clear advantage in the endgame.

18 hxg3   ♕h3
19 f4

An important moment. It would be easy for Black to continue with abandon by playing 19...♘f3+ 20 ♔f2 ♕h2+ but after 21 ♔e3! the white king is surprisingly safe in the middle of the board, while suddenly Black has to deal with nasty threats including ♖h1 and ♘xc7. Instead Nezhmetdinov elevates the attack onto another level.

19 ...   ♗e6!

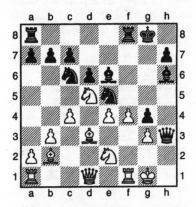

An imaginative idea. Black concentrates on coordinating his forces for a final assault on the white king, not afraid of giving up his c-pawn in the process. Now 20 fxe5 allows Black to remove a vital defender with 20...♗xd5, as 21 exd5 loses to 21...♗e3+.

20 ♗c2?

Under immense pressure, Polugaevsky slips up, although at this stage it is far from clear why this plausible move should lose. Three other alternatives come into consideration.

1) Against the prophylactic 20 ♗c1 Geller gives 20...♘d4, but after 21 ♘xd4 I don't see anything better than

21...♕xg3+ 22 ♔h1 with a draw by perpetual check. An attempt to do better with 22...♗xd5 leads nowhere after 23 fxe5 ♕h3+ 24 ♔g1 g3 25 ♖xf8+ ♖xf8 26 ♘f3 g2 27 ♗e2 ♗xe4 28 ♗xh6. Instead of 20...♘d4, perhaps now is the time for 20...♘f3+ 21 ♔f2 ♕h2+. After 22 ♔e3 Black returns to the long diagonal with 22...♗g7, not fearing 23 ♖h1 ♕g2 24 e5 due to 24...♗f5 and the opening of the centre favours Black, whose king remains the safer of the two.

2) 20 ♗b1 avoids the later tricks involving ...♘b4, but cuts off White's protection on the back rank. Black retains a big initiative after 20...♗xd5:

2a) 21 ♕xd5+ ♖f7 22 ♗c3 ♖e8 23 ♗c2 ♘f3+ 24 ♔f2 ♘e7 and White is in trouble, e.g. 25 ♕e6 ♕h2+ 26 ♔e3 ♘f5+! 27 exf5 ♖xe6+ 28 fxe6 ♖e7 29 ♗f5 ♕h5.

2b) 21 cxd5 ♘e7 22 ♔f2 (22 ♗xe5 dxe5 23 ♖f2 is stronger, but Black can still complicate matters by means of 23...♗xf4! 24 gxf4 exf4, when the two advanced pawns are very threatening) 22...♖xf4+!! (Geller) 23 gxf4 ♘7g6 and despite the extra rook, Geller concludes that White cannot meet Black's numerous threats. The main idea is just to push the g-pawn with 24...g3+ 25 ♔e1 g2 26 ♖g1 ♘xf4 27 ♗xe5 dxe5 28 ♘xf4 ♗xf4 29 ♕d3 ♕h2. White has one move to defend against this threat, but this isn't enough, e.g. 24 ♕c1 g3+ 25 ♔e1 g2 26 ♖g1 ♘xf4 27 ♘xf4 ♕g3+ 28 ♔e2 ♕f3+ 29 ♔e1 ♗xf4 and 24 ♕d4 g3+ 25 ♘xg3 ♘xf4 26 ♖g1 ♗g7 27 ♕d1 ♘g4+ 28 ♔e1 ♗xb2, both of which win for Black.

3) The active 20 ♘xc7 is difficult to refute, even though Black has two possible sacrifices on f4:

3a) 20...♖xf4!? 21 ♘xf4! ♕xg3+ 22 ♔h1 ♗xf4 23 ♖xf4 ♘xd3 24 ♘xe6 is unclear. Black always has a perpetual, but it is not clear that there is anything more. Note, however, that 21 gxf4? g3 22 ♘xg3 ♕xg3+ 23 ♔h1 ♕h3+ 24 ♔g1 ♗g4! 25 ♕c2 ♖f8! gives Black a winning attack.

3b) 20...♗xf4 has been the published "refutation" of 20 ♘xc7. Now both 21 ♘xf4 ♕xg3+ 22 ♘g2 ♖xf1+ 23 ♗xf1 ♘f3+ and 21 gxf4 g3 win for Black. This leaves 21 ♖xf4 ♖xf4, when 22 ♘xe6 ♖f3 is given by Geller, but what about the greedy 22 ♘xa8 instead? 22...♖f3 23 ♗c2 ♘xc4!? 24 bxc4 ♖xg3+ 25 ♘xg3 ♕xg3+ is another perpetual. Black can try 22...♖f8 23 ♘c7 ♘f3+ 24 ♔f2 ♘fd4+!? (24...♘fe5+ 25 ♔g1 draws) when 25 ♔g1 runs into 25...♘xe2+ 26 ♕xe2 ♕xg3+ 27 ♕g2 ♕e3+ 28 ♔h1 ♖f3, but 25 ♔e3 ♖f3+ 26 ♔d2 ♕h6+ 27 ♔c3 is a complete mess.

20	...	♖f7
21	♔f2	♕h2+
22	♔e3	

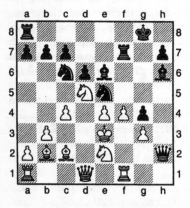

| 22 | .... | ♗xd5 |
| 23 | cxd5 | |

After 23 exd5 ♖e8 White can hardly hope to survive the open e-file, so White's last hope lies with 23 ♕xd5. Still, it's hard to visualize the thunderbolt coming in two moves' time.

| 23 | ... | ♘b4 |
| 24 | ♖h1 | ♖xf4!! |

A fabulous move, which is the start of a long combination, forcing the white king to trudge up the board to its death. White has to accept the queen rather than the rook, as these variations show:

1) 25 gxf4 (this exposes the weakness of White's 20th move) 25...♗xf4+ 26 ♘xf4 (or 26 ♔d4 ♕f2+ 27 ♔c3 ♕c5#) 26...♘xc2+ and Black wins.

2) 25 ♘xf4 ♘xc2+ is also a disaster for White.

| 25 | ♖xh2 | ♖f3+ |
| 26 | ♔d4 | ♗g7! |

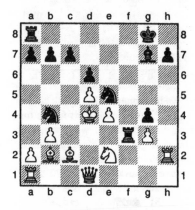

A whole queen down, Nezhmetdinov produces a deadly quiet move. The main threat is the simple 27...b5, followed by 28...♘ec6#. Many defences have been suggested, but none are sufficient, e.g.:

1) 27 ♘g1 ♖xg3 28 ♘e2 ♖f3 29 ♘g1 ♘ed3+ 30 ♔c4 (30 e5 ♗xe5+ 31

♔c4 ♖f4+ 32 ♗d4 ♖xd4+ 33 ♔c3
♘xd5+ 34 ♔d2 ♗f4+ 35 ♔e2 ♖e8+
36 ♔f1 ♘e3+ is complete carnage)
30...♘xb2+ 31 ♔xb4 ♗c3+ 32 ♔a3
b5! and now Steve Giddins provided
the variations 33 ♕d4 ♗xd4 34 ♘xf3
♗c3 35 b4 ♘c4+ 36 ♔b3 ♗xa1 37
♘g5 g3, winning for Black, and 33 b4
a5 34 bxa5 ♘c4+ 35 ♔b3 ♘xa5+ 36
♔a3 ♘c4+ 37 ♔b3 ♖a3#.

2) 27 ♗d3 ♘exd3+ 28 ♔c4 ♘xb2+
29 ♔xb4 ♘xd1 30 ♖xd1 ♖e8 and
Black will be two pawns up.

3) 27 ♖f2 c5+ 28 dxc6 ♘ed3+ 29
♔c4 b5+ 30 ♔xb5 ♖b8+ 31 ♔a4 (31
♔a5 ♘xc6+ 32 ♔a4 ♖b4+ 33 ♔a3
♗xb2#) 31...♘xb2+ 32 ♔a3 ♘xd1 33
♖xf3 ♘xc2+ 34 ♔a4 ♘b2+ 35 ♔a5
gxf3 and once more Black wins.

4) 27 ♘c3 ♘ed3+ 28 e5 (28 ♔c4
♘xb2+ 29 ♔xb4 ♗xc3+ 30 ♔a3 b5
31 b4 a5 is similar to variation "1b")
28...♗xe5+ 29 ♔c4 ♘xb2+ 30 ♔xb4
♗xc3+ 31 ♔a3 ♘xd1 32 ♖xd1 ♖xg3
33 ♖xh7 ♖g2 and Black's material advantage is sufficient.

Polugaevsky's move allows the
prettiest finish. It prevents ...b5, but
doesn't stop the mate.

27	a4	c5+
28	dxc6	bxc6
29	♗d3	♘exd3+
30	♔c4	

Or 30 e5 ♗xe5+ 31 ♔c4 d5#.

30	...	d5+
31	exd5	cxd5+
32	♔b5	♖b8+

| 33 | ♔a5 | ♘c6+ |

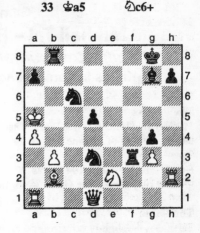

0-1

After 34 ♔a6 Black has the luxuri-
ous choice of three dmates in one.

Lessons from this game:

1) When facing a strong centre, it's
vital for any development advantage
to be exploited immediately, before
the opponent has a chance to consolidate his position. Here Nezhmetdinov's 9...♘g4 and 10...♕h4 is an
excellent example of active play versus a solid structure.

2) Sometimes keeping an attack
going can be a good practical choice
over cashing in for material. This was
Nezhmetdinov's thinking with 12...f5,
instead of 12...♘g4.

3) Massive king-hunts often involve one silent but deadly move. Here
it was the preparatory 26...♗g7!.

Game 41

Mikhail Tal – Robert Fischer

Candidates tournament, Zagreb 1959

King's Indian Defence, Petrosian System

The Players

Mikhail Tal (1936–92) was World Champion 1960–1, and one of the greatest attacking players of all time. See Game 39 for more information.

Robert Fischer (born 1943) was World Champion 1972–5, and arguably the greatest player ever. See Game 38 for further details.

The Game

Tal makes the slightly surprising decision to try to outplay his young opponent in a heavy strategic battle, meeting Fischer's King's Indian with the Petrosian System, which aims to stifle Black's activity. Fischer responds with a methodical, logical system, but one that just doesn't give enough counterplay. Tal responds forcefully, and is set to besiege Black on the centre and kingside, when suddenly Fischer grabs a pawn, opening the position. Tal is shocked by this, his intuition telling him that it is a terrible idea. For a few moves the game becomes totally unclear, but one weak move from Fischer lands him in deep trouble, and he is quickly routed. Black's situation towards the end of the game is quite pitiful: he is almost unable to move anything, while the white pieces have all the time in the world to weave a mating net around the black king.

1	d4	♘f6
2	c4	g6
3	♘c3	♗g7
4	e4	d6
5	♗e2	0-0
6	♘f3	e5
7	d5	

This move, particularly when linked with the subsequent ♗g5, is known as the Petrosian System. It is one of the toughest positional lines against the King's Indian, by which White does his utmost to stifle Black's counterplay.

7 ...   **♘bd7**

7...a5 is the modern preference, while 7...♘a6 is regarded as more accurate if Black wishes to head for a

traditional set-up. Fischer's move is characteristic of the way the King's Indian was handled in the 1950s.

8 ♗g5

White's idea is to follow up with ♘d2, cutting out any ...♘h5 ideas, whereupon Black will find it very hard to generate counterplay.

| 8 | ... | h6 |
| 9 | ♗h4 | a6 |

Fischer spends a move preparing to step out of the pin by ...♕e8 (by cutting out ♘b5 as a reply), but allows White the convenient regrouping with ♘d2. The alternative is to seek counterplay at the cost of weaknesses, by 9...g5 10 ♗g3 ♘h5, which was later analysed extensively, with Keres's 11 h4!? regarded as the critical line. However, in 1959, the Petrosian System was still quite new, and Fischer clearly didn't trust a line that left such weaknesses in his position. "It is not in the style of the youthful, but cautious American grandmaster to decide on such a continuation without extreme necessity" – Tal.

10 0-0 ♛e8
11 ♘d2

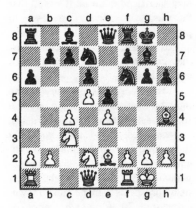

11 ... ♘h7

As so often in King's Indian positions of this type, 11...♘xe4 works tactically, but not positionally. In other words, 12 ♘dxe4 f5 regains the piece, but gives White a firm grip on the vital e4-square.

12 b4 ♝f6

Fischer had prepared this odd-looking more for this game. "After the game it was revealed that the young American had spent 10 hours analysing this variation. Alas, it did not improve the variation, but it left Fischer tired." – Tal. Earlier in the same tournament he had reached the same position against Tal, and played 12...♘g5

but the standard ...f5 push did not prove too effective as the knight rather got in the way. Instead 12...f5 13 exf5 forces 13...♖xf5 (as 13...gxf5? 14 ♝h5 wins an exchange for virtually nothing), which is positionally horrible for Black. White dominates the e4-square and Black has none of the piece activity he would need to have to contemplate taking on this structure.

13 ♝xf6

Although this is an exchange of White's "good" bishop for Black's "bad" bishop, there is no point in White spending time avoiding the trade. Black has by now activated his bishop (after 13 ♝g3 ♝g5 it would be a good "bad" bishop), so White does best to try to exploit the loss of time.

13 ... ♘hxf6
14 ♘b3 ♛e7
15 ♛d2

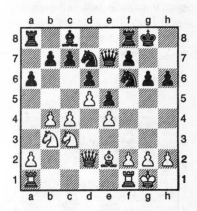

15 ... ♚h7
16 ♛e3

16 ♖ac1 was afterwards suggested by Tal as more accurate, simply intending to play c5, and not for now committing the queen.

16 ... ♘g8

Tal praised this move, which defends the queen in preparation for the tactical exchanges that are about to occur when Black plays ...f5.

Instead, 16...♖g8 intending ...g5 and ...♘f8-g6 was suggested by Petrosian.

17 c5   f5

White, in general, has several methods of meeting this move in the King's Indian:

1) Ignore it, and recapture on e4 with a piece;

2) Play f3, inviting Black to push on with ...f4;

3) Exchange on f5 and attack on the light squares (with pieces and/or by f3 and g4);

4) Exchange on f5 and meet ...gxf5 with f4.

In cases where Black's dark-squared bishop has been exchanged, the fourth option is normally best, as the opening of the long diagonal constitutes no drawback from White's viewpoint.

18 exf5   gxf5
19 f4   exf4
20 ♕xf4

It is remarkable how even top-class players can differ so fundamentally in their views on a position. Here, for instance, Tal felt that this move was a suicidal concession, rupturing Black's queenside, and hardly worth consideration, regardless of any small material gains Black might make. Fischer, he quite reasonably presumed, thought the move good and that Tal had missed that it was possible. One of Fischer's great qualities was his willingness to take sacrificed material if he felt that this was the objectively correct way to proceed, even if it entailed an arduous defensive task. His opponents knew they couldn't afford to take liberties against him.

Such differences of opinion can only be resolved by hard analytical facts, and here the note to Black's 21st move suggests that Fischer was right in this case. Even if the murky complications in that note are not advantageous for Black, they certainly offer better prospects than the move Tal was expecting, 20...♘e5, whereupon he intended 21 ♖ae1 followed by ♘d4 and a kingside attack.

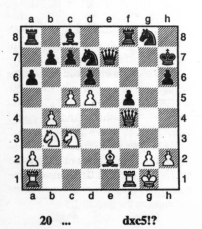

20 ...   dxc5!?

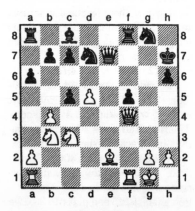

21 &d3!?

Tal spent quite a while analysing 21 bxc5 ♘xc5 22 ♖ac1 &d7 23 ♕xc7 ♖ac8 24 ♕f4 ♘xb3 25 axb3 ♖xc3 26 ♖xc3 ♕xe2 27 ♖c7 ♕e7 28 d6 ♕e6 but couldn't see a decisive continuation.

21 ... cxb4?!

21...♕g7! is the critical move for the assessment of both sides' play. Black hits the c3-knight, gets the queen out of the line of fire, and quickly prepares to bring the g8-knight knight into useful service via e7 and g6. 22 &xf5+ ♔h8 23 ♘e4 (23 ♕xc7 looks good at first, but 23...c4 keeps things very unclear; 23 ♕d2 cxb4 24 ♘e4 ♘e5!) and then:

1) 23...♘e7!? is interesting and logical.

2) 23...♘e5 24 ♘g3 ♘e7 25 ♖ae1 ♘d3?? (25...♘5g6 is tougher, but not 25...&xf5?? 26 ♕xe5) 26 ♖xe7, winning for White, was the line cited by Tal.

3) 23...c4! looks best, e.g. 24 ♘bd2 ♘b6 25 ♘g3 ♘e7 26 ♘h5 ♖xf5 27 ♘xg7 ♖xf4 28 ♖xf4 ♔xg7 (Nunn) is a sample line that is very good for Black.

However, these lines are all terribly unclear, and absolutely anything could have happened if 21...♕g7 had been played in the game.

22 ♖ae1 ♕f6?!

22...♕d6 23 &xf5+ ♔h8 24 ♕d4+ ♕f6 (24...♘df6!? gives Black more play) 25 ♕xb4 ♕b6+ 26 ♕d4+ ♕xd4+ 27 ♘xd4 (Tal) gives White a fine position, but Black has survival chances.

23 ♖e6 ♕xc3

23...♕g5 24 ♕xb4 keeps the pressure on.

24 &xf5+ ♖xf5

25 ♕xf5+ ♔h8
26 ♖f3 ♕b2

26...♕g7 27 ♖g3 forces the win of Black's queen, as 27...♕h7 (27...♕f8 28 ♕xf8 ♘xf8 29 ♖e8) 28 ♖e8 is instantly terminal.

After 26...♘df6 27 ♖xc3 bxc3 White would win in the long run.

27 ♖e8 ♘df6
28 ♕xf6+ ♕xf6
29 ♖xf6 ♔g7
30 ♖ff8!?

30 ♖f3 is also very strong.

30 ... ♘e7
31 ♘a5

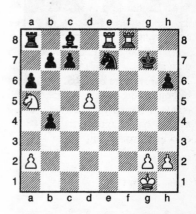

A famous position has arisen. Black is completely helpless, and virtually in zugzwang. The c-pawn cannot move as White's d-pawn would then cause havoc; the bishop is pinned to the rook, and the knight is tied to the defence of the bishop. And the rook? Can the rook move to a7 perhaps? Sadly not; the rook is tied to maintaining the tactical defence of the knight; thus if 31...♖a7, 32 ♖f3 wins a whole piece.

31 ... h5
32 h4

When the opponent is in zugzwang, the most sensible thing is to maintain it – especially if it possible to construct a mating net simultaneously!

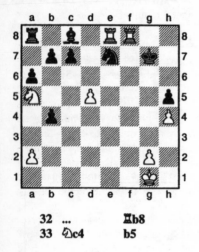

| 32 | ... | **Rb8** |
| 33 | **Nc4** | **b5** |

After 33...Ra8 34 Ne5 Rb8 the knight's improved position permits a mate: 35 Rf7+ Kh6 36 Rh8#.

| **34** | **Ne5** | **1-0** |

Lessons from this game:

1) Sometimes it is more important to create counterplay than it is to avoid weaknesses. Wounds need not be fatal, but suffocation normally is.

2) In a difficult position it is far more important to activate pieces than it is to grab pawns. While Fischer's 20th move was right, this was only because it disturbed the smooth flow of White's initiative; his "in for a penny, in for a pound" 21st move proved disastrous.

3) Immobilizing and pinning down the opponent's pieces is a very convincing way to round off a game.

Boris Spassky – David Bronstein
USSR Championship, Leningrad 1960
King's Gambit

The Players

Boris Spassky was the last of the string of post-war Soviet World Champions before Fischer's brief reign. He was born in 1937 in Leningrad and was, by the standards of the time, a prodigy. He qualified for the Interzonal at the age of 18 and made an impressive debut in the USSR Championship in 1955, receiving his grandmaster title in the same year. However, in the next few years his progress seemed to stall. He had difficulty finding a trainer who could both inspire and encourage him, and these problems were mirrored in his personal life, as his marriage ended in divorce. Around 1960 he went through a creative crisis: he began to play wild, sacrificial chess, and although this phase undoubtedly broadened his chess horizons and pleased the spectators greatly, it was no recipe for sustained success at the highest level.

Eventually he found in Bondarevsky the ideal trainer, and so began his remorseless progress to the world championship. He dominated the 1965 Candidates cycle, but lost narrowly to Petrosian in 1966. He qualified again and in 1969 beat Petrosian convincingly.

Spassky has always been a cultured, kind-hearted man, without the obsessive streak that has characterized many chess champions. It is therefore a little ironic that it was this very normal man who was called upon to defend the Soviet grip on the world championship against the super-energy drive of Bobby Fischer. Up until 1972 Spassky had an excellent personal score against Fischer, but he did not seem able to devote himself to the fanatical hard work that was needed to give himself the best chance of victory. His lingering self-doubts re-emerged during the match – in several games he made serious blunders, and ended up losing heavily to Fischer. Nevertheless he fought hard to the end, making it a classic match.

During the 1970s Spassky continued to play at top level, and made determined efforts in each Candidates cycle, but was edged out, first by Karpov and then by Korchnoi. In his later career, he became very peaceably inclined, with short draws a standard feature of his tournament practice. Nowadays he plays occasionally, most notably in the annual Ladies vs Veterans competitions.

David Bronstein (born 1924) was the challenger for the world championship in 1951, and is an extremely imaginative player. For more information see Game 37.

The Game

Spassky surprises his opponent with a King's Gambit, which quickly takes an unusual course. Bronstein fails to play actively enough, allowing White to seize space and build up a powerful attacking position. To quicken the pace of his attack, Spassky makes a sensational rook sacrifice. Bronstein stumbles under the pressure, and is quickly routed.

| 1 | e4 | e5 |
| 2 | f4 | |

An interesting choice. Spassky has used the King's Gambit occasionally throughout his career, mostly as a surprise weapon. Here he tries it against one of his few grandmaster colleagues who also experiments with this old gambit from time to time.

2	...	exf4
3	♘f3	d5
4	exd5	

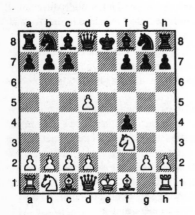

| 4 | ... | ♗d6 |

A somewhat unusual move. Normally Black plays 4...♘f6, often with ...♗d6 to follow shortly.

| 5 | ♘c3 | |

Spassky makes no real attempt to refute Black's 4th move.

1) 5 ♗b5+ is a natural alternative, both speeding up White's kingside development and keeping his centre pawns mobile, for example 5...♗d7 (5...c6!? is a more ambitious reply) 6 ♗xd7+♘xd7 7 0-0 ♘e7 8 c4 0-0 9 d4.

2) 5 d4 with possible ideas of c4-c5 seems more critical. 5...♘f6 6 c4 0-0 and then:

2a) 7 c5?! (this immediate push is unconvincing) 7...♖e8+ 8 ♗e2 ♗f8 and now 9 ♘c3 ♘xd5 10 ♘xd5 ♕xd5 11 ♗xf4 ♘c6 12 ♗xc7 ♗g4 13 0-0 ♘xd4! 0-1 was the dramatic conclusion of Gons – Van Hofwegen, correspondence game 1986.

2b) 7 ♘e5?! ♖e8 8 ♗xf4 c5! (a thematic blow to White's centre) 9 dxc6 (not exactly the move White wants to play, but there is no decent way to meet the threat of ...cxd4) 9...♘xc6 and Black will regain his pawn while blowing open the centre.

2c) 7 ♗e2 ♖e8 8 0-0 c5 9 ♘c3 (9 b4!?) 9...♗g4 10 ♔h1 is considered good for White by King's Gambit expert Joe Gallagher.

| 5 | ... | ♘e7 |

Bronstein reveals the point of his move-order, giving the knight a more flexible role than it would have on its natural square, f6. From e7 the knight eyes both the g6- and f5-squares, but is a less robust defender of the kingside.

5...♘f6 leads back to standard positions after 6 ♗b5+ or 6 ♗c4.

| 6 | d4 | 0-0 |
| 7 | ♗d3 | ♘d7 |

7...♗f5 is a more consistent follow-up to ...♘e7, seeking to exchange off White's aggressive bishop.

| 8 | 0-0 | h6? |

Black cannot afford this weakening pawn move. Black's game will stand or fall depending on how much influence his pieces can exert, and for this purpose one of the following would be more appropriate:

1) 8...♘f6 9 ♘e5 (9 ♘g5!? is an interesting idea) 9...♘exd5 10 ♘xd5 ♘xd5 11 ♕h5 (11 ♗xf4 ♘xf4 12 ♖xf4 ♕g5) 11...g6 (or 11...♘f6) 12 ♕h6 ♕f6 is equal – Spassky.

2) 8...♘g6 9 ♘e4 ♘f6 10 ♘xd6 ♕xd6 11 c4 ♗g4.

9 ♘e4!

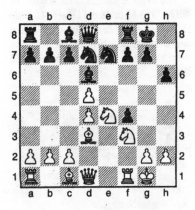

Now, when his pieces are fully developed and his king is safe, Spassky prepares to advance his c-pawn. True, this move surrenders the d5-pawn, but in return White gains some precious tempi.

9 ...   ♘xd5
10 c4   ♘e3

It is logical to make White give up his dark-squared bishop for the knight; otherwise White has a solid positional advantage:

1) 10...♘5f6?! 11 ♘xd6 cxd6 12 ♗xf4 gives White a space advantage, better development, the bishop-pair and the superior structure.

2) 10...♘b4 11 ♗b1 leaves the black knight out on a limb without inconveniencing White's attacking forces.

11 ♗xe3   fxe3
12 c5   ♗e7

White has surrendered the bishop-pair, and it seems that he will need to spend a couple of moves rounding up the e3-pawn – and in that time Black will be able to activate his forces. However, it turns out that Spassky has a far more daring scheme in mind.

Instead 12...♗f4? 13 g3 ♗g5 14 ♘fxg5 hxg5 15 ♕h5 gives White a decisive kingside attack.

13 ♗c2!

Playing directly for a kingside attack. 13 ♕e2?! ♘f6 (13...f5 intending ...f4 is rather too greedy) 14 ♕xe3 ♘d5 leaves Black well positioned; it will be hard for White to drum up attacking chances.

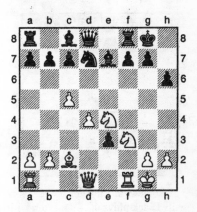

13 ...   ♖e8

It appears a little unnatural to move away the main defender of the sensitive f7-pawn, but Bronstein wishes to coordinate his defences by bringing the knight back to f8, whereupon the queen's bishop can also participate. Instead 13...♘f6 14 ♘xf6+ (14 ♕d3 should be met by 14...♖e8!? rather than 14...♘xe4, when 15 ♕xe4 f5 16

♕xe3 followed by ♘e5 secures a substantial superiority for White) 14...♗xf6 15 ♕d3 g6 (15...♖e8!? could be tried) 16 ♕xe3 gives White the better prospects.

14 ♕d3   e2

Rather than continue with the intended ...♘f8, Bronstein chooses to flick in this disruptive little pawn move. However, Spassky's staggering reply has ensured that this game will be remembered for a long, long time.

Instead 14...♘f8 15 ♘e5 ♗e6 (not 15...f6?? 16 ♘g5!! hxg5 {16...fxg5 17 ♕h7+ is the same} 17 ♕h7+! ♘xh7 18 ♗b3+ and ♘g6# follows – we see this theme later in the game) 16 ♖ae1 is clearly better for White.

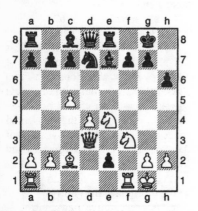

15 ♘d6!?

Objectively, this move is hardly necessary. Instead 15 ♖f2 keeps an excellent position, but psychologically the impact of this surprise was enormous, with Bronstein immediately going seriously wrong.

15 ...   ♘f8?

Bronstein nonchalantly decides to press ahead with his intended defensive plan, even though his attempt to distract the white queen from the b1–h7 diagonal has failed. This turns out to have drastic consequences.

Instead 15...exf1♕+ 16 ♖xf1 is no improvement because 16...♘f8 transposes to the game continuation, while 16...♘f6 17 ♖xf7! ♔xf7 18 ♘e5+ (18 ♗b3+ also wins) 18...♔g8 (18...♔f8 19 ♗b3) 19 ♕h7+! ♘xh7 20 ♗b3+ ♔h8 21 ♘g6# is a pretty mate.

The critical line is 15...♗xd6! 16 ♕h7+ ♔f8 17 cxd6 exf1♕+ (17...cxd6 18 ♖f2 ♘f6 19 ♕h8+ gives White a decisive attack while Black does not even have a rook for his troubles) 18 ♖xf1:

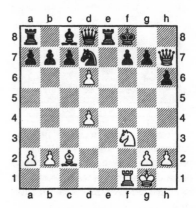

1) 18...♘f6? 19 ♕h8+ ♘g8 20 ♘e5 (threatening mate and so forcing Black's reply; 20 ♗h7 ♕xd6 is less convincing) 20...f6 21 ♗h7 ♗e6 22 d7! ♗xa2 (22...♖e7 23 ♗xg8 ♗xg8 24 ♖xf6+! gxf6 25 ♕xf6+ ♗f7 26 ♘g6+ ♔g8 27 ♕h8#) 23 ♗xg8 ♗xg8 24 dxe8♕+ ♕xe8 25 ♖xf6+! gxf6 26 ♕xf6+ wins the black queen, since 26...♗f7 27 ♘g6+ ♔g8 28 ♕h8# is mate.

2) 18...cxd6 19 ♕h8+ ♔e7 20 ♖e1+ ♘e5 21 ♕xg7 ♖g8 22 ♕xh6 ♕b6 23

♔h1 ♗e6 24 dxe5 d5 leads to quite an unclear situation. Black has survived the initial onslaught, but White has a pawn for the exchange and continuing pressure against the black king, which has long-term problems finding a shelter, and against Black's isolated d- and f-pawns. Bronstein would undoubtedly have gone in for this if he had seen White's 16th move.

16 ♘xf7!

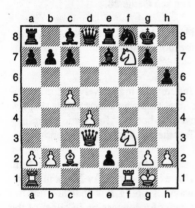

16 ... exf1♕+

Given that White will not be distracted from his attack, Black might as well eat the rook and pray for salvation.

17 ♖xf1 ♗f5

Or:

1) 17...♔xf7 allows a pretty forced mate: 18 ♘e5++ ♔g8 19 ♕h7+ ♘xh7 20 ♗b3+ ♔h8 21 ♘g6#.

2) 17...♕d7 loses to 18 ♘3e5.

3) 17...♕d5 18 ♗b3 ♕xf7 (White also wins after 18...♕h5 19 ♘xh6++ ♔h8 20 ♘f7+ ♔g8 21 ♘7g5+ ♔h8 22 ♗f7) 19 ♗xf7+ ♔xf7 20 ♕c4+ ♔g6 21 ♕g8! ♗f6 (21...♗e6 22 ♘e5+ ♔h5 23 ♕xg7 forces mate) 22 ♘h4+ ♗xh4 23 ♕f7+ ♔h7 24 ♕xe8 wins.

18 ♕xf5 ♕d7

By returning a bishop Black has gained a little time to defend.

19 ♕f4 ♗f6
20 ♘3e5

20 ♘xh6+ is a perfectly good way to win material, but Spassky is after bigger game.

20 ... ♕e7

20...♗xe5 21 ♘xe5 ♕e7 (21...♖xe5 just leaves Black a pawn down) 22 ♕e4, with threats of 23 ♖xf8+ and 23 ♗b3+, is decisive.

21 ♗b3 ♗xe5

21...♘e6 22 ♘xh6+! gxh6 23 ♕xf6 and White picks off the e6-knight too.

21...♔h7 22 ♕f5+ g6 23 ♕xf6 forces an ending with a huge material advantage.

22 ♘xe5+ ♔h7
23 ♕e4+ 1-0

There will follow 24 ♖xf8(+). This finish was used in a famous scene at the start of the James Bond film *From Russia With Love*, but with the white pawns absent from c5 and d4 – perhaps the director felt they obscured some shot. The fictitious version of the game was between Kronsteen and McAdams.

Lessons from this game:

1) A preventative pawn move in front of the castled king may just prove to waste time and create a weakness.

2) Don't automatically recapture material if doing so distracts you from your attack.

3) "Flashy" moves aren't necessarily good, and tend by their nature to randomize the position – but they can be very useful for secret agents in a hurry!

Mikhail Botvinnik – Mikhail Tal

World Championship match (game 6),
Moscow 1960
King's Indian Defence, Fianchetto Variation

The Players

Mikhail Botvinnik (1911–95) was World Champion 1948–57, 1958–60 and 1961–3. For an account of Botvinnik's career, see Game 28.

Mikhail Tal (1936–92) was World Champion 1960–1, and one of the greatest attacking players of all time. See Game 39 for more information.

The Game

Tal adopts an unusual strategy in a King's Indian: playing actively on the queen-side in preparation for kingside play. Objectively his play seems a little suspect, but it was enough to confuse Botvinnik over the board. After some complications, including a famous ...♘f4 sacrifice, Tal emerges with a winning endgame.

1	c4	♘f6
2	♘f3	g6
3	g3	♗g7
4	♗g2	0-0
5	d4	d6
6	♘c3	♘bd7
7	0-0	e5
8	e4	c6
9	h3	

As Tal put it, "White intends to develop his pieces harmoniously in the centre, and if he should succeed sooner or later in forcing his opponent to exchange on d4, he will gain the opportunity to put pressure on the weak pawn at d6." Thus White will try to maintain the central tension as long as possible, while Black will encourage him to release it (i.e. to play either d5 or dxe5). His main method of doing so is by threatening to play ...exd4 at a moment when, generally for tactical

reasons, this is favourable for him. However, the trick for Black is to find ways of doing this that are not too much of a concession in either of the scenarios after White releases the tension. For instance, the relatively crude procedure of playing ...♖e8 can often be advantageously met by d5, when the rook can do little from e8, and tends to get in the way of the other pieces.

9 ♗e3, as in Game 35, had by now been abandoned by Botvinnik.

9 ... ♛b6

This aggressive move has quite a good theoretical reputation, and has been used in recent years by Kasparov. The immediate threat is 10...exd4 11 ♘xd4 ♘xe4!.

10 d5

While of course not bad, this move rather falls in with Black's plans. 10 c5 is a sharp and critical move, which has been subjected to detailed analysis in the 1990s.

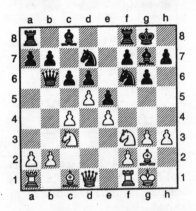

10 ...   cxd5

10...♘c5, followed by exchanging on d5, may be slightly more accurate, as it denies White the additional possibility mentioned in the note to White's 12th move (i.e. 10...cxd5 11 cxd5 ♘c5 12 ♘d2). Here, of course, 11 ♘d2? is just a mistake in view of 11...♘d3, robbing White of his important dark-squared bishop. Moreover, by exchanging immediately on d5 Black foregoes two interesting possibilities: 10...♘c5 11 ♕e2 ♕a6 and 10...♘c5 11 ♘e1 ♕b4.

11 cxd5

In King's Indian positions, White virtually always recaptures on d5 with the c-pawn rather than the e-pawn. The reason for this is that since White has made quite a lot of pawn moves in the opening to stake out a space advantage, he should be trying to keep Black's pieces bottled up, cramping Black's game.

11 ...   ♘c5
12 ♘e1

12 ♕c2, 12 ♕e2 and 12 ♖e1 are alternatives, while 12 ♘d2 ♗d7 (but not 12...♘d3?? 13 ♘c4 ♕d4 14 ♘xd6) 13 ♘b3 is the additional possibility mentioned above. While it may not pose a huge threat to Black, it greatly reduces his chances of developing counterplay.

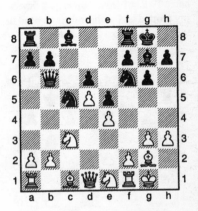

12 ...   ♗d7
13 ♘d3   ♘xd3
14 ♕xd3   ♖fc8

It seems as if Black is intending to play exclusively on the queenside. Indeed, this is what Tal wanted Botvinnik to think. In fact, he had already conceived a scheme whereby play on both wings would act in harmony.

15 ♖b1

Botvinnik believes that the queenside is to be the main focus of the battle; otherwise he might have preferred 15 ♕e2!?, which also prepares ♗e3, but would additionally prevent ...♘h5 followed by ...f5.

15 ...   ♘h5
16 ♗e3   ♕b4

16...♕d8?! 17 ♘b5 forces 17...♗xb5 18 ♕xb5.

17 ♕e2

17 ♕d1 ♖c4 18 ♔h2 ♖ac8 19 ♗f3
♘f6 20 a3 ♕a5 21 ♕b3 b5 22 ♗e2
was possibly a tiny bit better for White
in Panczyk – Wojtkiewicz, Czesto-
chowa 1992.

17 ...   ♖c4

17...f5?! 18 exf5 ♗xf5 (positionally the "wrong" capture, but forced
here) 19 ♖bc1 leaves Black just thrash-
ing around and with suffering ahead in
view of his kingside weaknesses.

18 ♖fc1

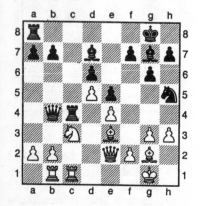

Intending ♗f1. Mass exchanges
would give White an excellent ending,
as the g7-bishop would be a poor piece,
and the h5-knight difficult to activate.

18 ...   ♖ac8

19 ♔h2

19 ♗f3 and 19 ♗f1 would both be
met by 19...f5.

19 ...   f5

Tal finally launches the combinative idea that has been in his mind
since his 14th move.

20 exf5   ♗xf5

21 ♖a1?!

White had an important, and apparently very strong alternative here, viz.
21 a3! ♕b3 22 ♘e4 and now:

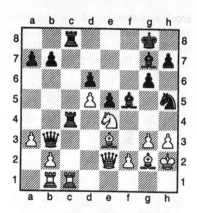

1) 22...♗xe4 23 ♗xe4 ♖xc1 24
♖xc1 ♖xc1 25 ♗xc1 ♘f6 26 ♗d3 is
the type of ending Tal has been trying
to avoid.

2) 22...♗f8 23 ♘d2 ♖xc1 24 ♘xb3
(24 ♖xc1? ♕xb2) 24...♖xb1 25 g4
wins a piece for not very much.

3) 22...♖c2 23 ♖xc2 (23 ♕d1!?
♘f4) 23...♖xc2 24 ♕d1 ♘f4 (24...♗h6
is answered by 25 ♘d2) "with incal-
culable complications" – Tal. Let us
try to calculate them: 25 ♖c1 ♘xg2 26
♖xc2 (threatening ♖c8+) and then:

3a) 26...♗f8? succeeds in shield-
ing the king from a check, but does not
protect it against a decisive mate
threat: 27 ♘f6+ ♔h8 28 ♖c7!.

3b) 26...♕a2 27 ♗g5 ♗xe4? (after
27...h6 28 f3 White has a clear extra
exchange) 28 ♖c8+ and White forces
mate: 28...♔f7 (28...♗f8 29 ♗h6 ♔f7
30 ♖xf8+ ♔e7 31 ♕a4) 29 ♕a4.

3c) 26...♕b5 27 ♗g5 ♗xe4 28
♖c8+ ♔f7 29 ♕c1 ♗f5 (29...♕a5 30
♗d8!) 30 ♕c7+ forces an exchange of
queens and therefore a won ending.

After the text-move, 21 ♖a1, it appears as if the threat of 22 g4 forces a
retreat from Black, whereupon White
will start to push Black back on all

fronts and make good use of the e4-square that he has been handed. That would make a nonsense of Black's play so far. But now the key point of Tal's plan is revealed.

21 ...   ♘f4!?

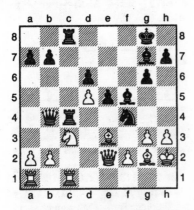

"The controversy provoked by this move was really rather pointless. It is a good move, in that all other continuations are bad, and if the knight sacrifice is incorrect, then the question mark should be attached not to Black's 21st move, but, say, to his 17th." – Tal. Suddenly all Black's pieces become active, and White must analyse some very concrete and intricate variations. If there is an advantage for White, it will be due to some specific tactical points, rather than a clear positional edge in an easy position.

22 gxf4   exf4
23 ♗d2

Instead 23 a3 (23 ♗xa7? ♕a5 and Black regains the piece with advantage) 23...♕b3 24 ♗xa7 ♗e5 (threatening ...f3+) is a critical line for the evaluation of Black's knight sacrifice. Tal makes an interesting comment: "It is hardly worth trying to convince the

reader that Black calculated every variation in detail, and decided that the sacrifice of the knight at f4 was correct. Rather, the move 21...♘f4 was a purely positional sacrifice." Here are some variations from this "positional" sacrifice:

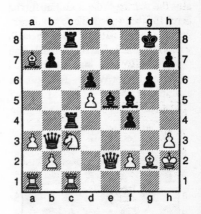

1) 25 ♗f3? and now:

1a) 25...b6 26 ♕d1 ♕xb2 27 ♖a2 ♖xc3 28 ♖xb2 ♖xc1 29 ♕e2 (29 ♕d2? ♗e4! 30 ♔g2 ♗xf3+ 31 ♔xf3 ♖8c3+ 32 ♔e4 ♖c4+ 33 ♔f3 ♖1c3+ 34 ♔e2 f3+ 35 ♔d1 ♗f4) 29...♖8c3 and Tal comments "Black's material deficit is for the moment unimportant". This seems an odd assessment: White is queen for rook up, and 30 ♖xb6 both prepares to attack Black's king and brings the a7-bishop back into the defence of f2.

1b) 25...♖a8! 26 ♗b6 (26 ♘b5 ♖xc1 27 ♖xc1 ♗d3) 26...♕xb6 is the way for Black to continue, for example 27 ♕xc4? ♕xf2+ winning.

2) 25 ♔g1 b6 (Black is threatening 26...♖4c7) 26 a4! (26 ♕d1 ♕xb2 27 ♖a2? ♖xc3!) 26...♖8c7 (26...♖4c7? 27 ♖a3 ♕b4 28 ♕b5) 27 ♗f1 f3 28 ♕d1 (rather than 28 ♕xf3 ♖h4 with

an attack) and Black's case is not proven.

3) 25 f3! b6 26 a4! (26 ♕f2? is met by 26...♗d4 followed by ...♗e3; 26 ♕d1 allows Black to sacrifice his queen to exploit the bricking-in of the g2-bishop: 26...♕xb2 27 ♖a2 ♖xc3 28 ♖xb2 ♖xc1 29 ♕d2 ♗xb2 30 ♕xb2 ♖1c2 31 ♕d4 ♖e8 32 ♕xf4 ♖ee2) 26...♗xc3 (26...♖8c7 27 ♖a3 ♕b4 28 ♘a2) 27 ♖xc3 ♖xc3 28 bxc3 ♖a8 (28...♕xc3 29 ♖e1 ♕a5 30 ♕e7 ♖a8 31 ♕b7 wins for White – Ragozin, for example 31...♕xa7 32 ♖e8+) 29 ♕e7 is strong.

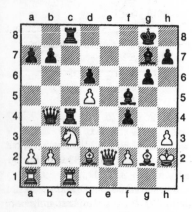

23 ...　　　　♕xb2?

Tal misses a chance to secure a good game by 23...♗e5!:

1) 24 ♔g1 ♕xb2 25 ♖ab1 (25 ♘d1?? ♖xc1) 25...♗xb1 26 ♖xb1 ♕c2 27 ♖c1 (27 ♗e4? ♖xe4) 27...♕f5 28 ♕f3 ♕h5 and White's queenside is on the verge of collapse.

2) 24 ♗f3 ♕xb2 25 ♘d1 ♕a3! 26 ♖xc4 ♖xc4 (threatening both 27...♖c2 and 27...♖e4) 27 ♕xc4 ♕xf3.

3) 24 f3 ♕xb2 gives Black excellent play, e.g. 25 ♘d1! ♕d4 26 ♖xc4 ♖xc4 27 ♖c1 ♖xc1 28 ♗xc1 ♕xd5 29

♗f1 was considered roughly equal by Tal.

24 ♖ab1!

24 ♘d1? ♕e5! 25 ♕f3 (25 ♕xe5 ♗xe5 leaves White defenceless against the various threats) 25...♗e4 26 ♕xe4 ♕xe4 27 ♗xe4 ♗xa1 is good for Black.

24 ...　　　　f3

Not 24...♗xb1 25 ♖xb1 ♕c2 26 ♗e4!.

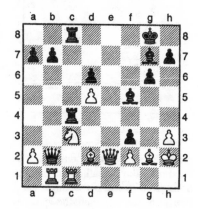

25 ♖xb2?

Botvinnik could have exploited his opponent's inaccurate 23rd move by 25 ♗xf3! ♗xb1 (25...♗e5+ 26 ♔g2 ♗xb1 27 ♖xb1 ♕c2 28 ♗e4! ♖xe4 29 ♘xe4 ♕xb1 30 ♘xd6! with a decisive counterattack: 30...♗xd6 31 ♕e6+ ♔g7 32 ♕d7+) 26 ♖xb1 ♕c2 and now:

1) 27 ♖c1 ♕b2 (27...♕f5 28 ♗g4 ♕e5+ 29 ♕xe5 ♗xe5+ 30 f4 ♖xc3 was a line Botvinnik feared, missing that it fails to 31 ♗xc8) 28 ♖b1 repeats.

2) 27 ♗e4! (Flohr) 27...♖xe4 (if 27...♗e5+, then 28 ♔g2) 28 ♘xe4! (28 ♕xe4? ♗e5+) 28...♕xb1 (28...♗e5+ 29 ♔g2 ♕xb1 is the same as the line 25...♗e5+ earlier in this note) 29 ♘xd6 ♖f8 30 ♕e6+ ♔h8 31 ♘f7+ ♖xf7 32

♕xf7 with a favourable ending for White.

25	...	fxe2
26	♖b3	♖d4!
27	♗e1	

27 ♗e3? ♖xc3 28 ♖bxc3 ♖d1 wins.

27	...	♗e5+
28	♔g1	♗f4

28...♖xc3! 29 ♖bxc3 ♖d1 wins.

29	♘xe2	

29 ♖a1? ♖xc3 30 ♖xc3 ♖d1 wins.

29	...	♖xc1
30	♘xd4	

30 ♘xc1 is answered by 30...♖d1.

30	...	♖xe1+
31	♗f1	♗e4
32	♘e2	

32 ♖xb7 drops a piece to 32...♗d3.

32	...	♗e5
33	f4	♗f6
34	♖xb7	

Or 34 ♔f2 ♗h4+.

34	...	♗xd5
35	♖c7	

35 ♖xa7? ♖xe2! 36 ♗xe2 ♗d4+.

35	...	♗xa2

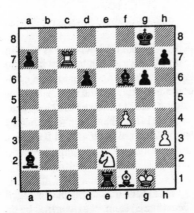

36	♖xa7	♗c4

Not 36...♖xe2? 37 ♖a8+. After the text-move, Black catches the white

pieces in a deadly pin. White can never break it by ♔f2, due to ...♗h4+.

37	♖a8+	♔f7?!

37...♔g7! gives Black a smoother path to victory, for example 38 ♖e8 (38 ♖a7+ ♔h6) 38...♗d4+!? (alternatively, 38...d5).

38	♖a7+	♔e6?

38...♔f8 39 ♖a8+ ♔g7 was better, returning to the 37...♔g7 line.

39	♖a3	

White gains some counter-chances, as his rook can reach the e-file.

39	...	d5
40	♔f2	♗h4+
41	♔g2	♔d6
42	♘g3	

White liberates himself at last, but the outcome is a lost rook ending.

42	...	♗xg3
43	♗xc4	dxc4
44	♔xg3	♔d5
45	♖a7	c3
46	♖c7	♔d4

0-1

47 ♖d7+ was the sealed move, but Botvinnik resigned without resuming.

Lessons from this game:

1) What Tal's play here may have lacked in soundness, it more than made up for in originality and surprise value. These are powerful weapons in practical chess – inducing errors is an important part of the game.

2) A weakness on one side of the board can sometimes justify a tactic on the other side.

3) If the opponent has sacrificed to gain the initiative, look for ways to sacrifice material back to go on the offensive yourself – especially if there are weaknesses in the opponent's position waiting to be exploited.

Game 44

Nikolai Krogius – Leonid Stein

Russian Republic – Ukraine match, Kiev 1960

King's Indian Defence, Petrosian System

The Players

Nikolai Krogius (born 1930) is a Soviet grandmaster who achieved some modest over-the-board successes in the 1960s. He qualified seven times for the USSR Championship, but did not distinguish himself in this event. In the 1970s he began to move into chess administration and became a functionary in the Soviet Chess Federation.

Leonid Stein (1934–73) was a leading player of the late 1960s who died while at the peak of his powers. Born in the Ukraine, Stein's early progress was slow and it was not until 1961 that he qualified for the USSR Championship, in which he finished an excellent third equal. In the remainder of the 1960s he won one tournament after another, including three Soviet Championships, but he was less fortunate in World Championship cycles. In 1962 and 1964 he would have qualified as a Candidate except for a rule (today widely regarded as having been unfair) restricting the number of Candidates from one country. In 1967 he again failed to reach the Candidates; this time he was eliminated on tie-break after an inconclusive play-off with Hort and Reshevsky. By 1970 he was rated in the world top ten, and his greatest successes seemed yet to come. However, on 4th July 1973 he collapsed and died in a Moscow hotel, under circumstances that are still not entirely clear.

The Game

Stein adopts a rather dubious line in the King's Indian Defence, and is soon in some difficulties. His response, typically, is to throw caution to the winds and risk everything on a do-or-die sacrificial attack. Analysing at home with computer assistance reveals where Krogius could have refuted the attack, but it is never easy finding the right defence while sitting at the board with the clock ticking. Eventually Krogius slips up, and the response is a brilliant queen sacrifice by Stein. White could perhaps still have drawn by superbly accurate defence, but a shell-shocked Krogius collapses.

1	d4	♘f6
2	c4	g6
3	♘c3	♗g7
4	e4	0-0
5	♗e2	d6
6	♘f3	e5

7 d5

This move introduces the so-called Petrosian System, characterized by d5 coupled with ♗g5. It is still widely played today.

| 7 | ... | h6 |

However, this idea has completely disappeared; today nobody believes that it is worth spending a whole tempo just to prevent ♗g5. 7...a5, 7...♘a6 and 7...♘bd7 (see Game 41) are the accepted continuations.

8 0-0

There cannot be anything wrong with this natural developing move. 8 ♘d2 is quite a good alternative, intending to restrain ...f5 by playing g4.

	8 ...	♘h7
	9 ♘e1	♘d7

If we compare this position with that arising in the standard line 7 0-0 ♘c6 8 d5 ♘e7 9 ♘e1 ♘d7, the only difference is that Black's pawn is on h6 instead of h7 and his knight is on h7 instead of e7. It is clear that this difference favours White. When the knight is on e7, it can easily participate in the coming kingside attack by ...g5 and ...♘g6-h4, whereas on h7 its future is much less certain. It might eventually move to g5 if Black can play ...g5, ...h5 and ...g4, but that is a big "if".

10 ♘d3

10 ♗e3 f5 11 f3 is also possible, again with a normal position except for Black's misplaced knight.

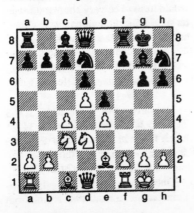

10 ...	f5
11 f3	

11 exf5 is an interesting idea, since in the position with the knight on e7 Black normally replies ...♘xf5. Here he is forced to play 11...gxf5, but after 12 f4 e4 13 ♘f2 a5 the position may not be so bad for him, as his knights end up quite harmoniously placed on c5 and f6.

11 ...	f4
12 b4	

Black normally has to play ...♘df6 at some stage, when White can continue c5 without spending a tempo on the preparatory b4. Thus 12 ♗d2 may appear a more natural move; however, White has a specific idea in mind which requires the speedy advance of the c-pawn.

12 ...	♖f7
13 c5	♘df6
14 c6!	

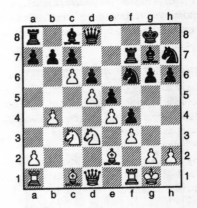

A very strong move, whereby White emphasizes another defect of having the knight on h7 – Black has less control over the key central squares c6 and d5.

14 ...	bxc6

This move is an unpleasant necessity. After 14...b6 15 b5! (not 15 a4? a6, when White cannot open lines on the queenside) 15...g5 16 a4 h5 17 a5 ♖b8 18 axb6 axb6 19 ♖a7 g4 20 ♘b4, followed by ♘a6, Black's queenside crumbles long before he can generate real threats on the kingside.

15 dxc6　　　♗e6
16 b5

The best move, preparing the manoeuvre ♘b4-d5. After 16 ♘b2 (after 16 ♘d5 Black can reply 16...♗xd5 17 exd5 ♘xd5) 16...♕b8! 17 b5 (not 17 ♗c4 ♗xc4 18 ♘xc4 ♕xb4) 17...a6 Black has sufficient counterplay.

16 ...　　　♗f8
17 ♘b4　　　d5!?

A good practical decision. If White is allowed to play ♘bd5 then Black will be strategically lost (advanced queenside majority and control of d5). In this desperate situation Black resolves to muddy the waters as much as possible; his immediate intention is to activate his dark-squared bishop at c5.

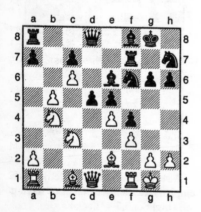

18 ♘bxd5

White retains the advantage after this move, but 18 exd5! is clearer:

1) 18...♗f5 19 ♘a6! (not 19 ♘d3? ♘h5 20 ♗b2 ♗xd3 21 ♗xd3 ♗c5+ 22 ♔h1 ♘g3+ 23 hxg3 fxg3 mating) when White prevents the bishop reaching c5. On a6, unlike d3, it is very hard for Black to exchange the knight off.

2) 18...♗c5+ 19 ♔h1 with another branch:

2a) 19...♘h5 20 dxe6 ♘g3+ (the lines 20...♖f5 21 ♕xd8+ ♖xd8 22 g4 and 20...♕h4 21 exf7+ ♔f8 22 h3 are also winning for White) 21 hxg3 ♕g5 22 exf7+ ♔g7 23 ♕d7! and the queen comes back to h3.

2b) 19...♗f5 20 ♘d3! (here 20 ♘a6? ♗d4 21 ♕b3 ♘h5 gives Black a very strong attack) 20...♗d4 21 ♗b2 ♘h5 (21...♗xc3 22 ♗xc3 ♘xd5 23 ♕b3 ♘xc3 24 ♕xc3 with a large advantage for White) 22 ♘e4 ♗xe4 (other lines also lose: 22...♘g3+ 23 ♘xg3 fxg3 24 ♗xd4 exd4 25 hxg3, 22...♕h4 23 ♗xd4 exd4 24 ♕e1, 22...♕xd5 23 ♘xe5 and 22...♗e3 23 ♘xe5 ♕h4 24 ♕e1) 23 fxe4 ♘g3+ 24 hxg3 fxg3 25 ♗g4 and White defends.

It is perhaps not surprising that Krogius did not go in for this continuation; ideas such as ♕d7-h3 in line "2a" above are not obvious, and one would have to be very confident to enter such a line, knowing that the slightest slip would lead to a rapid mate.

18 ...　　　♗c5+
19 ♔h1　　　♘h5

Threatening to sacrifice on g3.

20 ♕e1

The only move, since 20 h3 ♗xh3 21 gxh3 ♕h4 and 20 ♘a4 ♘g3+ 21 hxg3 fxg3 22 ♘f4 ♕h4+ 23 ♘h3 ♗xh3 are winning for Black.

20 ...　　　♘g3+!

Once having started along the sacrificial path, Black must not shrink from giving up more material to maintain the momentum of his attack. In fact this is quite an easy decision – everything else is hopeless, so Black must try the knight sacrifice whether it is sound or not.

21 hxg3   ♕g5

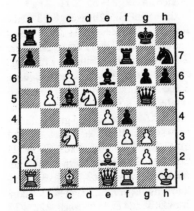

22 g4   h5

With the threat 23...hxg4, followed by either 24...g3 or 24...♘f6 and 25...♖h7+.

23 g3!

White finds the correct plan, which is to free g2 for his king. After 23 ♖f2 (23 ♘a4 hxg4 24 ♘xc5 ♕h5+ 25 ♔g1 g3 mates) 23...hxg4 24 fxg4 ♕h4+ 25 ♔g1 ♘g5 Black has a very strong attack, for example 26 ♗d1 (the threat was 26...♗xd5, winning after 27 ♘xd5 ♘xe4 or 27 exd5 ♖h7) 26...♔g7 27 ♔f1 ♕h1+ 28 ♔e2 ♗xg4+ 29 ♔d2 ♗e3+ 30 ♘xe3 ♘xe4+ 31 ♘xe4 ♖d8+ 32 ♔c2 ♕xe1 33 ♗xg4 fxe3 34 ♖xf7+ ♔xf7 and here Black has a clear advantage.

23 ...   hxg4
24 ♔g2

24 fxg4 ♗xg4 (24...♕h6+ 25 ♔g2 ♘g5 26 ♖h1 wins for White) 25 ♔g2

♖af8 is also strong for White, as it would transpose into the next note.

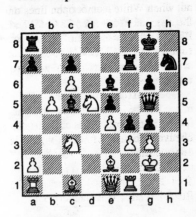

24 ...   ♖af8
25 ♗d2?!

White starts to make life difficult for himself. The best line is 25 fxg4 ♗xg4 and now:

1) 26 ♗xf4 exf4 27 ♘xf4 (27 ♖xf4 ♗e6 28 ♖xf7 ♖xf7 leads to an unclear position) 27...♗xe2 28 ♘cxe2 ♕e5 29 ♘c3 ♗d4 30 ♖f3 ♘g5 31 ♖d3 ♘xe4 32 ♕xe4 ♕xe4+ 33 ♘xe4 ♗xa1 34 ♘xg6 ♖e8 with a likely draw.

2) 26 ♘xf4! exf4 (26...♗xe2 27 ♘cxe2 exf4 28 ♘xf4 ♕e5 29 ♖b1 ♘g5 30 ♗b2 and White wins) 27 ♖xf4 (27 ♗xf4 ♗xe2 28 ♘xe2 ♕g4 is dangerous for White) 27...♖xf4 28 ♗xf4 ♕h5 29 ♗xg4 ♕xg4 with a further branch:

2a) 30 ♘d5 ♘g5 (30...g5 31 ♖c1 gxf4 32 ♖xc5 ♘g5 33 ♘e7+ ♔h7 34 ♕h1+ ♔g7 is murky) 31 ♗xg5 ♕xg5 32 ♖d1 ♖f2+ 33 ♕xf2 ♗xf2 34 ♔xf2 ♕e5 35 ♔f3 ♕h5+ with a near-certain draw.

2b) 30 ♕d2 ♘g5 31 ♕d5+ ♘e6 gives Black enough counterplay for the two pawns.

2c) 30 ♕f1! (the key move; White's queen arrives on the a2–g8 diagonal, but d5 is left clear for the knight) 30...♘g5 31 ♕c4+ ♘e6 32 ♘d5! and Black's attack runs out of steam, for example 32...♖f7 33 ♖f1 g5 34 ♘e3 ♗xe3 35 ♗xe3 ♖xf1 36 ♔xf1 and White wins.

One must say that none of the missed wins is particularly straightforward, and perhaps it is only at move 28 that criticism of White's play is really justified.

25 ...   ♕h6

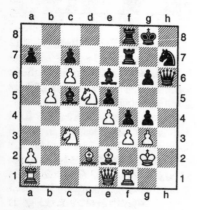

26 ♖h1

Once again, the capture on g4 would have tipped the balance in White's favour: 26 fxg4 ♘g5 (26...♗xd5 27 ♘xd5 ♘g5 28 ♖h1 defends) 27 ♖h1 f3+ (27...♕g7 28 gxf4 exf4 29 ♗f3 ♘xf3 30 ♔xf3 ♕d4 31 ♕e2 and the attack collapses) 28 ♗xf3 ♕xh1+ (or 28...♘xf3 29 ♗xh6 ♘xe1+ 30 ♖hxe1 ♖f2+ 31 ♔h3) 29 ♕xh1 (but not 29 ♔xh1? ♖h7+ 30 ♔g2 ♘xf3 and Black wins) 29...♗xg4 (29...♘xf3 30 ♗h6 wins) 30 ♕h6! ♗xf3+ 31 ♔h2 ♗g4 (31...♗h5 32 ♕xg5 ♖f2+ 33 ♔h3 defends) and now:

1) 32 ♘e3 ♖f2+ 33 ♔h1 (33 ♘g2? ♖xg2+ 34 ♔xg2 ♖f2+ 35 ♔g1 ♘f3+ 36 ♔h1 ♗h5 mates) 33...♗f3+ 34 ♔g1 and now:

1a) 34...♖xd2 35 ♕xg6+ ♔h8 36 ♕xg5 ♖g2+ 37 ♔f1 ♗xe4+ 38 ♔e1 wins for White.

1b) 34...♖g2+ 35 ♔f1 ♖xg3 36 ♕xg6+ ♔h8 37 ♕h6+ ♔g8 38 ♘e2! ♗xe4+ 39 ♕xf8+ wins.

1c) 34...♘h3+! 35 ♕xh3 ♖xd2 36 ♖e1 ♗d4 and the position is rather unclear; after 37 ♘cd5 ♗xe4 38 ♕g4 ♗xd5 39 ♕xg6+ ♔h8 40 ♕h6+ ♔g8 White has no more than perpetual check.

2) 32 ♗e3! ♖f2+ (32...♗xe3 33 ♘xe3 ♖f2+ 34 ♔h1 wins) 33 ♔h1! (33 ♔g1 ♗xe3 34 ♕xg6+ ♔h8 35 ♕h6+ ♔g8 36 ♘xe3 ♘h3+ 37 ♔h1 ♗f3+ 38 ♘g2 ♖xg2+ 39 ♔h2 ♗f1+ draws) 33...♗f3+ 34 ♔g1 ♖g2+ 35 ♔f1 and Black cannot continue his attack.

26 ...   ♕g7

Now White faces the problem that he cannot play fxg4 without allowing ...f3+, while Black threatens 27...fxg3.

27 gxf4

The best way to meet Black's threat. Here are some lines which illustrate the dangers White faces if he does not take on f4:

1) 27 ♕d1 g5 28 gxf4 exf4 29 ♔f1 gxf3 30 ♗xf3 g4 31 ♗e2 f3 with a very strong attack.

2) 27 ♘a4 ♗d4 28 ♗c3 gxf3+ 29 ♗xf3 fxg3 30 ♗xd4 exd4 31 ♘xc7 ♖xf3 32 ♘xe6 ♖f2+ 33 ♔g1 ♕e5! 34 ♘xf8 (34 ♖xh7 ♕xe6 35 ♖h6 ♕g4, followed by 36...♕f3, wins for Black) 34...♘g5 35 ♕d1 ♕xb5! (threatening 36...♕f1+) 36 ♖h4 ♕xa4 37 ♔h1 ♘f3 with decisive threats.

27 ... **exf4**

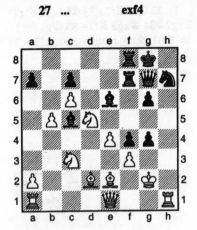

At first sight the worst is over for White, because Black's only threat is the relatively slow 28...g5, followed by ...gxf3+ and ...g4. On the other hand this threat, while slow, is certainly deadly when it does arrive.

28 Rd1?

Krogius finds an ingenious defence which only fails due to Stein's even more ingenious reply. This was the last moment when White could have refuted Black's attack and, in contrast to some of the earlier missed wins, this one involves rather natural moves: 28 ♘a4! (the elimination of the dangerous dark-squared bishop is the key) 28...♗d4 (28...♗d6 29 ♗c3) 29 ♗c3 and now:

1) 29...g5 30 ♗xd4 ♕xd4 31 ♕d1 ♕xd1 32 ♖axd1 gxf3+ 33 ♗xf3 (33 ♔xf3 g4+ 34 ♔f2 g3+ 35 ♔g1 f3 36 ♗c4 ♘g5 is dangerous for White) 33...g4 34 ♗xg4 ♗xg4 35 ♖dg1 and White emerges a pawn up with a good position.

2) 29...♗xd5 30 exd5 ♘g3 31 ♕d2 ♖e7 32 ♕xd4! (32 ♗xd4 ♖e2+ 33 ♕xe2 ♕xd4 34 ♕d1 gxf3+ 35 ♔f1

♕c4+ is at least equal for Black after either 36 ♔f2 ♖e8 or 36 ♔g1 ♖f5) 32...♖xe2+ 33 ♔f1 ♕xd4 34 ♗xd4 gxf3 35 ♖e1 and Black does not have enough compensation for the piece (35...♖xa2? 36 ♖e7).

28 ... **g5**

29 e5

Practically forced, as White must free a square for his bishop to flee from the advancing black pawns.

29 ... **♕xe5**

29...gxf3+ 30 ♗xf3 g4 31 ♗e4 f3+ is tricky, for example 32 ♔f1? g3 33 ♗xh7+ ♕xh7 34 ♕xg3+ ♖g7 35 ♘e7+ (35 ♖xh7 ♖xg3 36 ♗e3 ♗xe3 37 ♘xe3 ♔xh7 38 ♘e4 is unclear) 35...♗xe7 36 ♖xh7 ♗c4+ 37 ♔f2 ♗c5+ 38 ♗e3 ♗xe3+ 39 ♔xe3 ♖xg3 40 ♘e4 ♔xh7 41 ♘xg3 ♗xb5 42 ♖d7+ ♔g8 43 ♖xc7 f2 with a likely draw. All very entertaining, but unfortunately 32 ♔g3! ♕xe5+ 33 ♗f4! squashes the attack.

30 fxg4

There is nothing better, for example 30 ♗c1 ♗d4 31 ♕d2 (31 ♖xd4 ♕xd4 is also unclear) 31...♗e3 32 ♘xe3 fxe3 33 ♕d3 gxf3+ 34 ♗xf3 g4 is complex and double-edged.

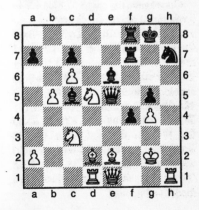

The text-move appears to cause Black serious problems, for example:

1) 30...♗xd5+ 31 ♘xd5 ♕xd5+ 32 ♗f3 ♕xa2 33 ♖xh7 ♖xh7 (33...♔xh7 34 ♕e5 wins for White) 34 ♕e5 ♕c2 35 ♕xg5+ ♔h8 36 ♕e5+ ♔g8 37 ♕d5+ ♔g7 38 ♖c1 and Black loses his bishop.

2) 30...f3+ 31 ♗xf3 ♕xe1 32 ♖hxe1 ♖xf3 33 ♖xe6 ♖f2+ 34 ♔h1 ♖f1+ 35 ♖xf1 ♖xf1+ 36 ♔g2 ♖f2+ 37 ♔g3 ♖xd2 38 ♔f3 and the ending should be a win for White.

Stein's brilliant reply not only eliminates Black's difficulties but even poses problems for White.

30 ...   ♕xe2+!

31 ♕xe2

Krogius correctly decides to return the queen. After 31 ♘xe2 ♗xd5+ White can try:

1) 32 ♔f1 ♖xh1! (32...f3 33 ♘d4 ♗xd4 34 ♗e3 f2 35 ♕b4 ♗xh1 36 ♗xd4 is less clear) 33 ♖c1 and now:

1a) 33...f3 34 ♖xc5 and White can hang on after 34...fxe2+ 35 ♔xe2 or 34...f2 35 ♕a1 ♗g2+ 36 ♔xg2 f1♕+ 37 ♕xf1 ♖xf1.

1b) 33...♗b6! 34 ♗c3 f3 35 ♘d4 ♗g2+ 36 ♔f2 ♘f6 37 ♕e6 (37 ♔g1 ♘d5 also wins) 37...♖e8 38 ♕c4 ♘e4+ 39 ♔g1 ♘xc3 and Black wins.

2) 32 ♔h3 ♘f6 33 ♘g3 (33 ♘xf4 gxf4 34 ♗xf4 ♖h7+ 35 ♔g3 ♖xh1 wins for Black) 33...fxg3! (33...♖h7+ 34 ♘h5 ♘xh5 35 gxh5 ♖xh5+ 36 ♔g4 ♖xh1 37 ♕e5 ♖xd1 38 ♕xg5+ is equal) 34 ♗xg5 ♖h7+ 35 ♗h4 (35 ♔xg3 ♘e4+ wins) 35...♗f2 36 ♖xd5 (36 ♕e2 g2 37 ♕xf2 gxh1♕+ 38 ♖xh1 ♗xh1 is clearly better for Black) 36...♗xe1 37 ♖g5+ ♔f7 38 ♖xe1 ♖fh8 39 ♔xg3 ♖xh4 and again Black has a distinct advantage.

31 ...   f3+

32 ♕xf3   ♖xf3

White's material advantage has been cut to a pawn, and since he must meet the threat of 33...♖f2+ he cannot save the pawn on g4. Indeed, the activity of Black's bishops and rooks is such that White can hardly avoid losing the exchange. However, that is not the end of the story. White's advanced queenside pawns, his well-placed knight on d5 and Black's out-of-play knight on h7 are positional assets which can counterbalance the loss of the exchange, provided that White defends accurately.

33 ♖hf1?

The prolonged tactical battering finally takes its toll and Krogius makes a disastrous blunder losing immediately. White could still have held the draw by 33 ♗e1! ♗xg4 with various possibilities:

1) 34 ♗g3 ♘f6! (activating the knight is the first priority; 34...♖3f7 35 ♖d3 ♗f3+ 36 ♖xf3 ♖xf3 37 ♘e4 gives White enough play for the exchange) 35 ♘xf6+ (35 ♖h6 ♘h5) 35...♖3xf6 36 ♖d3 ♗f3+ 37 ♖xf3

♖xf3 38 ♘e4 ♗b6 and Black has winning chances.

2) 34 ♘xc7 ♖e3! 35 ♘a6 ♗f3+ 36 ♔h2 ♘f6 37 ♖g1 ♘g4+ 38 ♖xg4 ♗xg4 39 ♖d5 ♗e7 and Black's attack is more dangerous than the c-pawn.

3) 34 a4! (Black does not have a serious threat, so White can afford to advance his majority) 34...♖3f5 (White also has no problems after 34...♖3f7 35 ♖d3 ♗f3+ 36 ♔xf3 ♖xf3 37 ♘e4 or 34...♘f6 35 ♖h6 ♘xd5 36 ♖xd5 ♔g7 37 ♖h2 ♖3f5 38 ♖xf5 ♖xf5) 35 ♖d3 ♗d6 (35...♗f3+ 36 ♔xf3 ♖xf3 37 ♘e4 is similar) 36 ♖h6 ♗f3+ 37 ♔xf3 ♖xf3 38 ♖g6+ ♔h8 39 ♘e4 ♗e5 40 ♖e6 and White's active pieces give him full compensation for the exchange.

The remarkable feature of these lines is that White is saved by the positional assets he acquired as long ago as move 14 and which have persisted through all the complications.

33 ...   ♗xg4

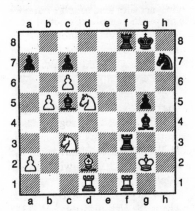

34 ♘e4?!

White cannot avoid shedding material, but it wasn't necessary to lose a whole rook! 34 ♖xf3 ♗xf3+ 35 ♔h2 ♗xd1 36 ♘xd1 ♖f5 37 ♘5c3 ♘f6 was a better chance, but Black should win comfortably as White's pieces are very passively placed.

34 ...   ♗h3+

The end.

35	♔h2	♖xf1
36	♖xf1	♗xf1
37	♘xc5	♖f2+
38	♔g1	♖xd2
39	♘xc7	♗h3
40	a4	♖g2+
41	♔h1	♘f6
42	a5	♘g4
43	♘e4	♖e2

0-1

Lessons from this game:

1) Once you are committed to a sacrificial attack there is no turning back.

2) It is important to recognize that it is difficult to conduct a prolonged defence against a vicious attack. Even though you may feel that it is objectively correct to grab material and weather the storm, you should take into account the human factor.

3) It very often happens that one error leads to another. The realization that something has gone wrong can easily prove a distraction and lead to a loss of concentration. Be especially careful after you have made a mistake – another one may be lurking just round the corner.

Game 45
Robert Fischer – Mikhail Tal
Leipzig Olympiad 1960
French Defence, Winawer Variation

The Players

Robert Fischer (born 1943) was World Champion 1972–5, and arguably the greatest player ever. See Game 38 for further details.

Mikhail Tal (1936–92) was World Champion 1960–1, and one of the greatest attacking players of all time. See Game 39 for more information.

The Game

Tal springs a surprise on Fischer by playing an unusual line of the French Defence. There arises a complicated position, which becomes a remarkable tactical shoot-out. The players trade blows until a perpetual check is inevitable.

1	e4	e6

Tal only played the French a handful of times in his career, when he felt it would prove a good surprise weapon against particular opponents. In 1974 Tal himself wrote of the French, "One of my most unsuccessful openings. Almost all the games in which I chose it ended in defeat – fortunately there weren't all that many of them. ... I feel these losses were not accidental. Black, in the French, has to play with great accuracy, and this is a quality which I never had a great measure of, neither now nor in my earlier days."

2	d4	d5
3	♘c3	♝b4

Fischer's performances against the Winawer were never quite so convincing as his games in the Ruy Lopez or Sicilian, with which Tal had been fortunate to survive in earlier games against Fischer.

4	e5	c5
5	a3	♝a5

This is an unusual deviation from the standard line of the Winawer, 5...♝xc3+. It is generally considered somewhat dubious, but many lines are very unclear. Those who specialize in this system and are familiar with its idiosyncrasies tend to score quite well with it.

6	b4

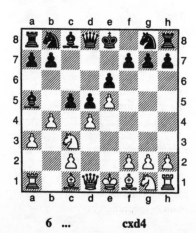

6	...	cxd4

6...cxb4 7 ♘b5 is regarded as a good pawn sacrifice, by which White blows open lines on the queenside.

7 ♕g4   ♘e7

7...♔f8 defends the pawn, but is unwise in view of the reply 8 bxa5 dxc3 9 a4 followed by ♗a3+.

8 bxa5

8 ♘b5 is an alternative.

8   ...   dxc3
9 ♕xg7   ♖g8
10 ♕xh7

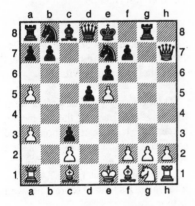

10 ...   ♘bc6

Tal improves over 10...♘d7 11 ♘f3 ♘f8 (11...♕c7 12 ♗b5 a6 13 ♗xd7+ ♗xd7 14 0-0 d4 15 ♘xd4 ♕xe5 16 ♕d3 is good for White – Fischer) 12 ♕d3 ♕xa5 13 ♗g5, which gave Black a difficult position in Smyslov – Botvinnik, World Championship match (game 9), Moscow 1954.

11 ♘f3

11 f4 is an alternative, but rather slows White's development. 11...♕xa5 12 ♘f3 ♗d7 13 ♘g5 0-0-0! 14 ♘xf7 ♘f5 15 ♘xd8 ♕xd8 16 ♕h3 ♘cd4 is a good reply, but this line is the domain of specialists in opening theory.

11 ...   ♕c7

11...♕xa5 12 ♘g5! ♖f8 13 f4 followed by the advance of the h-pawn ties Black up – Fischer.

12 ♗b5!?

12 ♗f4 ♗d7 13 ♗d3 0-0-0 14 ♗g3, as played by Dolmatov, might be a shade better for White, but gives Black plenty of play.

12 ...   ♗d7

12...♖xg2? 13 ♔f1! ♖g8 14 ♖g1! ♖xg1+ 15 ♔xg1 and now, according to Fischer, "Black's king remains hemmed in the centre while White merely marches his h-pawn to victory".

13 0-0

13 ♗xc6? ♗xc6 14 0-0 d4! 15 ♘g5 ♕xe5 16 ♕xf7+ ♔d7 with advantage to Black – Fischer.

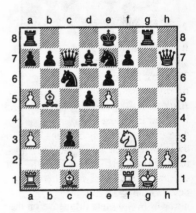

13 ...   0-0-0

13...♘xe5! was Petrosian's suggestion, and is interesting despite Fischer's condemnation. 14 ♘xe5 ♕xe5 15 ♗xd7+ ♔xd7 16 ♕d3! and now:

1) 16...♖ac8 17 ♖b1 ♔c7 (Black should consider 17...♖c7!?) 18 ♖b5! (18 ♖b4!? is also promising) 18...♔b8 19 ♗e3 is good for White – Tal.

2) 16...♔c7 is also met by 17 ♖b1.

3) 16...♘c6 is a natural move.

4) 16...♕e4 (? – Fischer) 17 ♕xe4 dxe4 and then:

4a) 18 ♖b1 b6 19 axb6 axb6 20 ♖xb6 ♖gb8 was played in an obscure correspondence game, and is quite satisfactory for Black. White's position is awkward and it is difficult to advance either of his passed pawns to good effect.

4b) 18 f3! wins a pawn (Fischer), but Moles and Wicker dispute the claim that this is good for White after 18...exf3 19 ♖xf3 f5 (19...♗f5?! can be met by 20 ♗f4 or 20 ♖d3+) 20 ♗f4 (20 ♖xc3 ♖ac8) 20...♘d5 21 ♗e5 ♔e7.

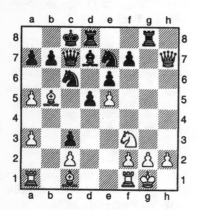

14 ♗g5?!

Fischer condemns this move on the basis that 14 ♗xc6 is better:

1) 14...♘xc6 15 ♖e1 followed by ♗g5 and h4 with a decisive bind – Fischer.

2) 14...♕xc6 15 ♗g5 d4 16 h4!.

3) 14...♗xc6 (the strong German player Karsten Müller has played this position as Black, though his opponent, GM Lengyel, did not adopt Fischer's 15 ♕xf7) 15 ♕xf7 d4 (15...♖xg2+?

16 ♔xg2 d4 17 ♔g1 ♖g8+ 18 ♘g5) 16 ♕xe6+ ♗d7 (16...♔b8 17 ♘g5) 17 ♕xe7 ♖xg2+ 18 ♔xg2 ♗h3+ 19 ♔xh3 ♕xe7 20 ♗g5 "consolidating to victory" – Fischer.

14 ... ♘xe5!

15 ♘xe5!

15 ♗xe7?? ♘xf3+ 16 ♔h1 ♖h8.

15 ♗xd7+ ♖xd7 16 ♘xe5 (16 ♗xe7 ♘xf3+ 17 ♔h1 ♕xh2+!) 16...♕xe5 17 ♗xe7 ♖h8! 18 ♖ae1 ♖xh7 19 ♖xe5 ♖xe7 is good for Black.

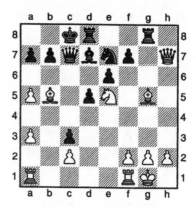

15 ... ♗xb5!

15...♕xe5 16 ♗xe7 ♖h8 (16...♗xb5 17 ♗xd8 ♖h8 18 ♖ae1 ♕xe1 19 ♖xe1 ♖xh7 20 ♗f6) 17 ♖fe1! (17 ♖ae1? ♕b8!) 17...♕xe1+ 18 ♖xe1 ♖xh7 19 ♗xd8 ♔xd8 (19...♗xb5? 20 ♗f6!) 20 ♗xd7 ♔xd7 21 ♖e3! (bails White out – Fischer) 21...d4 (21...♖h4!? is a better try for activity) 22 ♖e4 with some advantage for White – Tal.

16 ♘xf7

16 ♗xe7 ♕xe7 (not 16...♕xe5? 17 ♖fe1) 17 ♖fe1 was Fischer's suggestion to keep the game going; then after 17...♕g5 White would play 18 ♕h3, rather than 18 g3? ♖g7 19 ♕h3 ♕d2, when Black has all the chances.

16 ...   ♗xf1!

16...♖df8 17 ♗h6 (17 ♖fb1 ♗c6 18 ♘d6+! ♕xd6 19 ♕xe7 is about equal – Fischer) 17...♗xf1 18 ♗xf8 ♖xg2+ (18...♗xg2?? loses to 19 ♘d6+! ♕xd6 20 ♗xe7 or 19 ♗xe7!) 19 ♔xf1 (19 ♔h1 ♖xf2) 19...♖xh2 20 ♕d3 ♕f4 (20...♖h1+ 21 ♔e2 ♖xa1 22 ♗xe7 is messier) gives Black good play.

17 ♘xd8   ♖xg5
18 ♘xe6

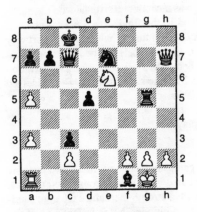

18 ...   ♖xg2+!
19 ♔h1!

Not 19 ♔xf1? ♖xh2! 20 ♕f7 (20 ♘xc7 ♖xh7) 20...♖h1+! with a winning attack.

19 ...   ♕e5!

19...♕c4 20 ♕xe7 and now:

1) 20...♖g8? 21 ♘f4! d4 (and not 21...♕xf4? 22 ♕e6+ ♔c7 23 ♕xg8) 22 ♕e4 (22 f3 is also good) and Black's pieces, in particular the f1-bishop, turn out to be ineffectively placed, while White has built up his attack methodically.

2) 20...♖g1+ 21 ♔xg1 ♕g4+ 22 ♔xf1 ♕c4+ is a safe draw, as Black has a perpetual check: 23 ♔e1 ♕e4+ 24 ♔d1 ♕h1+ 25 ♔e2 ♕e4+, etc.

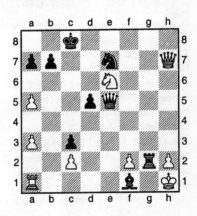

20 ♖xf1   ♕xe6

20...♖g6 21 ♕xe7 ♖xe6 22 ♕f8+ (22 ♕c5+ ♔b8 23 a6! and "White would be able to draw without difficulty" – Tal) 22...♖e8 23 ♕f3 is in White's favour – Fischer.

21 ♔xg2   ♕g4+
½-½

Lessons from this game:

1) The Winawer French can lead to positions that are extremely difficult for both sides to play.

2) All Black's counterplay sprung from the fact that he had an open file against the white king, which he exploited to the full.

3) Perpetual check is a common outcome when neither king has much protection and there are rooks and queens flying around the board.

A. Rubezov – Georgy Borisenko

USSR Correspondence Championship 1960–3

Sicilian Defence, Sozin Attack

The Players

Georgy Borisenko was born in 1922 in the Kharkov region of the Ukraine. He played in the final of the USSR Championship (over-the-board) eight times in the period 1950–67, his best result being 9/19 in 1955. His performance in the 4th correspondence world championship was most impressive: he won his qualifying group with 8½/10, and came second in the final with 8½/12, unbeaten throughout. He fared less well in the 5th Championship, withdrawing part way through, with bad positions in many of his games. There are two opening variations named after him, the most notable being the Borisenko-Furman Variation of the Queen's Gambit Accepted (1 d4 d5 2 c4 dxc4 3 ♘f3 a6 4 e4). He received the correspondence grandmaster title in 1966.

A. Rubezov is a Soviet correspondence player.

The Game

This is the first of three correspondence games in this book. In a sharp opening line that was topical at the time, White misses what is now considered the best chance for an advantage. Black replies with a strong, thematic exchange sacrifice. Black then makes what appears to be a blunder, but is in fact a carefully worked-out sequence, whereby he temporarily goes a whole rook down but chases the white king around the board. After White misses the best path he is hunted down mercilessly.

	1	e4	c5
	2	♘f3	♘c6
	3	d4	cxd4
	4	♘xd4	♘f6
	5	♘c3	d6
	6	♗c4	

This move characterizes the Sozin Attack, a more overtly aggressive system than 6 ♗g5, the Richter-Rauzer Attack, which we saw in Games 36 and 39. By putting the bishop on c4 White sets up tactical possibilities on the a2–g8 diagonal. Immediately there are some ideas against f7, and after

Black plays ...e6 White has the possible plan of f4-f5, with threats against both the e6-pawn and the kingside.

	6	...	e6
	7	0-0	♗e7
	8	♗e3	0-0
	9	♗b3	

9 ♔h1 a6 10 f4 ♕c7 11 ♗b3 is an alternative line.

| | 9 | ... | ♘a5?! |

This move is generally considered a little suspect since, although his motives are well-founded, Black is neglecting the centre. 9...a6 10 f4 ♘xd4

11 ♗xd4 b5, 9...♗d7!? and 9...♕a5!? are more normal.

10 f4

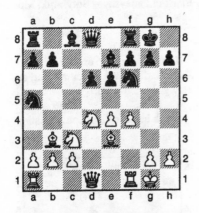

10 ...   b6

Black secures the right to exchange off the b3-bishop at the most appropriate moment, but weakens his control of e5 and leaves the d4-knight in its strong centralized post.

10...♘xb3 11 axb3 b6 is not a good way for Black to try to avoid the problems seen in the next note: 12 e5 dxe5 13 ♘c6 ♕c7 14 ♘xe7+ ♕xe7 15 fxe5 ♘d5 (15...♗d7 16 ♕f3 ♖b8 17 ♖xa7; 15...♘e8 16 ♗xb6) 16 ♘xd5 exd5 17 ♗xb6 and White wins a pawn for not very much.

11 g4?!

Other moves:

1) 11 f5? e5 12 ♘de2 ♘xb3 13 axb3 ♗b7 14 ♘g3 d5! (Kasparov and Nikitin) gives Black everything he might ever want in a Sicilian position.

2) 11 ♕f3 ♗b7 12 g4 transposes to the game.

3) 11 e5! ♘e8 12 f5 dxe5 13 fxe6! is the critical test of Black's system, and has put largely put players off this line since the early 1960s.

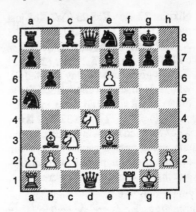

3a) 13...f6 fails to 14 ♘f5 ♘xb3 15 ♘d5!.

3b) 13...♘xb3 14 ♘c6! ♕d6! 15 ♕xd6! (not 15 ♘d5? ♗h4 16 exf7+ ♖xf7 17 ♖xf7 ♘xa1! 18 ♕f1 ♗f6 19 ♘xf6+ ♘xf6 0-1 Bilek – Petrosian, European Team Championship, Oberhausen 1961) 15...♗xd6 16 axb3 ♗xe6 and now White has a choice:

3b1) 17 ♖xa7 ♖c8 18 ♘e7+ ♗xe7 19 ♖xe7 b5 may give Black enough play.

3b2) 17 ♘b5 ♗d7 (or 17...a6!?) 18 ♘cxa7 ♗c5 19 ♖xc5 bxc5 20 ♖a4 and now Black should try 20...♗d6!?.

3b3) 17 ♗xb6 a6 18 ♖fd1 f6 (perhaps 18...f5!?) 19 ♘b5 ♗d7 20 ♘ba7 ♗xc6 21 ♘xc6 ♖c8 looks OK for Black.

3b4) 17 ♘xa7! ♖b8 (17...♘f6 18 ♗xb6) 18 ♖a6 (18 ♘e4 threatens 19 ♘xd6 ♘xd6 20 ♘c6 winning a pawn – Mednis) 18...♘f6! (18...♗c7 19 ♘cb5 had been analysed in a 1958 theoretical article by the Polish master Kostro) 19 ♖xb6 (19 ♗xb6?? ♖xb6 20 ♖xb6 ♗c5+) 19...♖xb6 20 ♗xb6 ♖b8 21 ♗f2 ♘g4 22 ♘ab5 (now "Black has no compensation for the sacrificed pawn and should lose" – Kasparov and

Nikitin; 22 ♘c6 ♖c8 23 ♘a7 ♖b8 just repeats) 22...♗b4 23 ♗a7 ♖b7 24 h3 ♗xc3 25 bxc3 ♖xb5 26 hxg4 ♗xg4 27 c4 ♖b7 28 ♖a1 ♗f5 29 c5? (29 ♖a2! ♖d7! is given as best play by Mednis, who feels Black has enough activity to draw) 29...♗xc2 30 c6 ♖xb3 and now:

3b41) 31 g4?? ♖g3+ 32 ♔f2 ♖xg4 33 c7 ♗f5 led to a win for Black (four connected passed pawns always win against a minor piece) in Fischer – Korchnoi, Candidates tournament, Curaçao 1962.

3b42) 31 c7 ♗f5 (31...♖c3?? 32 ♗c5!) 32 ♗f2 h5 33 ♖a8+ ♔h7 34 c8♕ ♗xc8 35 ♖xc8 should be a draw.

3c) 13...exd4 is perhaps the best try, and the only one that has enjoyed any success in recent practice. 14 exf7+ ♔h8 15 fxe8♕ ♕xe8 16 ♗xd4 ♘xb3 17 axb3 ♖xf1+ 18 ♕xf1 ♗b7 gives Black some compensation for the pawn in view of his bishop-pair and slight exposure of the white king, though whether this should be enough is another matter. 19 ♖e1 ♕d7 20 ♖d1 (20 ♘b5!?) 20...♕c6 21 ♕e2 ♕g6 22 ♖d3 ♗d6 23 ♖e3 ♖d8 24 ♖e6 ♕f7 25 ♗f2 ♗c6 26 ♗g3?? ♗c5+ 27 ♔h1 ♖d2! 28 ♖xc6 ♖xe2 0-1 Renet – Relange, French Championship, Toulouse 1995.

11	...	♗b7
12	♕f3	♖c8
13	g5	♖xc3!

A thematic Sicilian exchange sacrifice. Although it is more common in the Dragon, the theme cuts across all lines where Black's play is directed against the e4-pawn.

14 gxf6

14 bxc3? ♘xe4 15 ♕g4 ♕c8 16 ♖f3 ♘xb3 17 axb3 f5! 18 ♕h4 (18 gxf6!? ♖xf6 19 f5 exf5 20 ♘xf5 ♗f8

intending ...♖g6 – Chekhov) 18...e5 19 ♖h3 h6 20 ♕h5 ♕xc3 21 ♖d1 exd4 22 ♗d2 ♕c6 led quickly to a win for Black in Padevsky – Botvinnik, Moscow 1956.

| 14 | ... | ♖xe3 |
| 15 | ♕xe3 | |

15 fxe7? ♖xf3 16 exd8♕ ♖xf1+ 17 ♖xf1 ♖xd8 leaves Black a clear, and very good, pawn up.

15 ... ♗xf6

Black has excellent compensation.

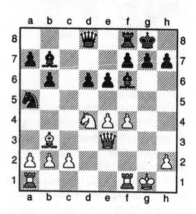

16 ♖ad1

16 c3 is an alternative way for White to try to glue his position together.

16 ... ♘xb3

16...♕e7 is more cautious, but gives White more freedom to manoeuvre, e.g. 17 c3 g6 18 ♘f3 ♗g7 19 ♕d3 ♗h6 20 ♘e1 ♕e8 21 ♘c2 ♕c6 22 ♘e3 ♘xb3 23 axb3 ♖d8 24 ♘g4 ♗g7 25 ♘f2 and White managed to hold his game together in Jankovec – Smejkal, Czechoslovak Championship, Trinec 1972.

17 axb3 a6

Allowing White a tempting tactical idea. Borisenko, however, has seen that he will also get some open lines.

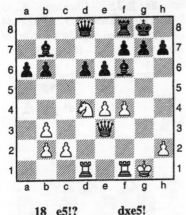

18 e5!?   dxe5!
19 ♘xe6!?

This move has been criticized, but its objective merit depends on the note to White's 21st move.

19 fxe5 ♗g5 20 ♕g3 and now:

1) 20...♕d5? 21 ♕xg5! (21 ♖d3 ♗c1!?) 21...f6 22 ♕g4! ♕h1+ 23 ♔f2 fxe5+ 24 ♔e2 ♕xh2+ 25 ♔d3 ♖d8 26 ♕xe6+ ♔h8 27 ♕xb6 is no good for Black, since 27...♖xd4+ loses to 28 ♕xd4 exd4 29 ♖f8#.

2) 20...♕e7 is the safe, sensible move, giving Black an absolutely secure position, in which his chances are probably slightly for preference.

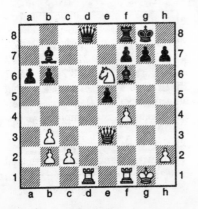

19 ...   ♕c8
20 ♘xf8   ♕c6!

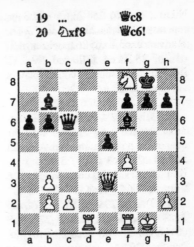

21 ♔f2?

With this, White loses his last opportunity of emerging with a decent game.

21 ♖d2 (not 21 ♕g3?? losing to 21...♗h4!) was the best move:

1) 21...♕h1+?! 22 ♔f2 ♗h4+ 23 ♔e2 ♕g2+ 24 ♖f2 ♗xf2 25 ♕xf2 ♕e4+ 26 ♔f1! (avoiding the repetition, which is possible after 26 ♔d1 ♕h1+ 27 ♔e2 {not 27 ♕e1?? ♗f3+} or 26 ♕e3 ♕g2+ 27 ♕f2 ♕e4+) 26...♕h1+ 27 ♕g1 ♗f3+ 28 ♔e1 (28 ♖f2?? ♕d1#) 28...♕e4+ 29 ♖e2 (29 ♔d1 ♔xf8) 29...♕xf4 30 ♕e3 forces an ending where White has good winning chances.

2) 21...♗h4 22 ♖f3 (this is forced) 22...♕xf3 (22...exf4 23 ♕xf4 ♕xf3 24 ♕xf3 ♗xf3 25 ♘d7 doesn't look convincing, e.g. 25...♗g5 26 ♖d3 ♗e4 27 ♖c3 and 28 ♘xb6) 23 ♕xf3 ♗xf3 24 ♘d7 and then:

2a) 24...e4 25 ♘e5 is unconvincing for Black, as 25...♗h5 (25...e3? 26 ♖d3) 26 ♘c4 followed by ♘e3 slows him down significantly.

2b) 24...exf4 25 ♘xb6 and even though Black's pawns are not as quick to advance as it might appear at first glance, 25...♗e4 followed by ...f3 gives Black reasonable counterplay in a complex ending.

    21 ...   **♕g2+**

21...♗h4+ 22 ♔e2 ♕g2+ is less effective as the king escapes into the open without serious mishap. After 23 ♔d3 e4+ 24 ♔c3 ♗f6+ 25 ♔b4:

1) 25...♕xc2?! is unconvincing: 26 ♕xb6 ♗e7+ 27 ♔a4 (27 ♔a5 ♕xb2 28 ♕xb7 ♕a3+ 29 ♔b6 ♕c5+ 30 ♔xa6 ♕a3+ is perpetual check) 27...♕c8 (27...♕xb2 28 ♖a1 ♗c8 29 ♖fb1) 28 ♘e6 fxe6 29 b4.

2) 25...♗e7+ 26 ♔c3 ♗f6+ repeats.

    22 ♔e1   **♗h4+**
    23 ♖f2   **♗f3!**

Tying White up. Black has a strong attack.

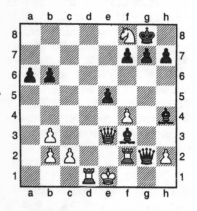

    24 ♖d8!

White find the best chance, forcing Black to find a very precise sequence.

    24 ...   **♕g1+**
    25 ♔d2   **♕d1+**
    26 ♔c3   **♕xd8**

    27 ♖xf3

27 ♕xf3?? ♕d4#.

    27 ...   **e4!**

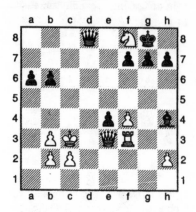

A striking move. Black, a whole rook down, gives up this pawn just to open the diagonal from f6 to c3 and to make sure it stays open.

    28 ♖h3

28 ♕xe4 ♗f6+ 29 ♔c4 b5+ 30 ♔c5 ♗e7+ 31 ♔c6 ♕c8+ 32 ♔b6 ♗c5+ 33 ♔a5 ♕c7+ 34 ♔xa6 ♕b6# neatly corners the king.

    28 ...   **♗f6+**
    29 ♔c4   **♕c7+!**

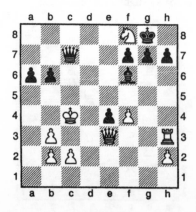

| 30 | ♔d5 | ♕b7+ |
| 31 | ♔d6 | ♔xf8 |

Finally, when the white king has been driven into a wholly untenable position, Black captures the knight.

| 32 | ♖xh7 | ♗e7+ |
| 33 | ♔e5 | f6+ |

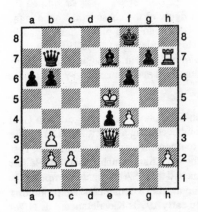

34 ♔e6

34 ♔f5 ♕c8+ is the same thing.

After 34 ♔d4 Black wins the white queen by 34...♗c5+.

34	...	♕c6+
35	♔f5	♕c8+
36	♔xe4	♕xc2+
37	♔d5	

37 ♕d3 f5+! 38 ♔e3 ♗c5+ drives the king away from the defence of the queen.

| 37 | ... | ♕xh7 |

0-1

Lessons from this game:

1) Decentralizing, even to eliminate a key attacking piece, is a risky venture.

2) It is well worth sacrificing an exchange to dislocate the enemy pawn structure and deny the hostile king long-term safety.

3) Any line of play that drags the enemy king up the board deserves careful analysis, even if there is a substantial sacrifice involved.

Eduard Gufeld – Lubomir Kavalek

Student Olympiad, Marianske Lazne 1962
Ruy Lopez (Spanish), Cordel Gambit

The Players

Eduard Gufeld (born 1936) is a colourful figure of the chess world, who is famous for his bold attacking chess. This Ukrainian-born player has played in many Soviet Championships and received his grandmaster title in 1967. His best results include first equal at Tbilisi in 1974 and first at Tbilisi in 1980. Also a chess journalist, Gufeld's own career is illustrated in his famous book *My Life in Chess*.

Lubomir Kavalek (born 1943) is a Czech-born player who emigrated to Germany, before settling in Washington DC and becoming a US citizen. During the 1970s he was a very active and successful tournament player, with numerous first places, including an outright victory in the US Championship in 1978. He has represented both his native Czechoslovakia and the USA in chess Olympiads. In the 1980s Kavalek concentrated more on organizing tournaments and promoting the Grandmasters Association, and in the early 1990s Kavalek acted as Nigel Short's trainer. With Kavalek's help, Short fulfilled his potential by defeating both Karpov and Timman in Candidates matches. This led to Short's challenge to Kasparov for the world title in 1993.

The Game

In an extremely original encounter, Kavalek correctly sacrifices a piece in the opening, finally obtaining four powerful pawns in return. Just when it looks as if Gufeld is getting back into the game, Kavalek ups the stakes with another amazing sacrifice. Now a rook up, Gufeld looks for a way to prevent Black's stampeding pawns from running down the board. He finds an ingenious way to do so, but Kavalek is ready with one final sacrifice. At the end Kavalek has no pieces left. Gufeld still has a rook, but is still forced to resign.

1	e4	e5
2	♘f3	♘c6
3	♗b5	♗c5
4	c3	f5!?

With this extremely sharp continuation, known as the Cordel Gambit, Black attempts to snatch the initiative from White's grasp at a very early stage. It can be compared to the more popular Schliemann Defence (1 e4 e5 2 ♘f3 ♘c6 3 ♗b5 f5!?). Both lines are known to be extremely risky, but such is the complexity of the variations that they are also difficult for White to meet unless he is well prepared. In this game Gufeld is caught out.

5	d4	fxe4
6	♘g5	

These days the accepted continuation is 6 ♗xc6 dxc6 7 ♘xe5, which is known to be better for White.

   6   **...**   **♗b6**

   7   **d5**

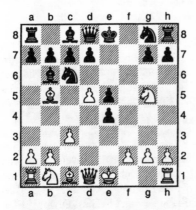

   7   **...**   **e3!**

Gufeld had played his last move quickly, hoping for 7...♘ce7? 8 ♘e6!, neatly trapping the black queen. Only after this move did Gufeld realize that he had fallen into a trick that he already knew. The whole line had been shown to him by Konstantinov. Meanwhile, the members of the Prague Chess Club, to which Kavalek belonged, had also discovered this tactical idea.

   8   **♘e4**   **♕h4**

   9   **♕f3**   **♘f6**

In *My Life in Chess* Gufeld criticizes this move, preferring 9...♘ge7, although he doesn't give any more details. After 10 dxc6 bxc6 11 g3 ♕h6 12 ♗e2 exf2+ 13 ♔d1 ♕g6 Black has three pawns and dangerous play for the piece.

   10 **♘xf6+**   **gxf6**

   11 **dxc6**   **exf2+**

   12 **♔d1**

Faced with a difficult decision, White makes the wrong choice. Gufeld likes 12 ♔f1, giving the line 12...bxc6 13 ♗e2 d5 14 ♗e3!, with advantage to White. Black should probably try instead 12...dxc6, immediately opening up his c8-bishop. Now 13 ♗xc6+ commits hara-kiri after 13...bxc6 14 ♕xc6+ ♔e7 15 ♕xa8 ♕c4#. This leaves us with 13 ♗e2 ♖g8 14 ♕h5+ ♕xh5 15 ♗xh5+ ♔e7, when we reach a position very similar to the actual game, the only difference being that the white king is on f1 rather than d1. This little difference affects the assessment of the position in White's favour, as the king on f1 lends vital support to the sensitive g2-pawn. That said, even here Black retains reasonable play for the piece after 16 ♘d2 ♗f5 17 ♗e2 e4.

   12 **...**   **dxc6**

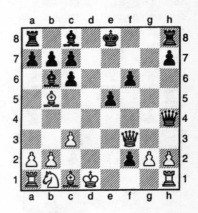

   13 **♗e2**

Once more White can hardly contemplate 13 ♗xc6+ bxc6 14 ♕xc6+, as after 14...♔f7 15 ♕xa8 ♗g4+, the queen is lost.

With 13 ♗e2 White plans to relieve the pressure by exchanging queens.

He does succeed in trading queens, but Black keeps a rampant initiative.

13   ...   ♗e6

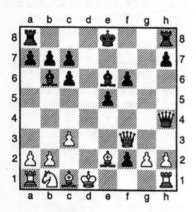

14	♕h5+	♕xh5
15	♗xh5+	♔e7
16	b3	♗d5
17	♗a3+	♔e6
18	♗g4+	f5
19	♗h3	♖hg8
20	♘d2	♗xg2
21	♗xg2	♖xg2

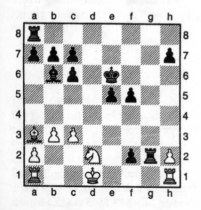

22   ♖f1

White would like to run back into the action with his king, but after 22

♔e2 Black can continue 22...f1♕+! 23 ♔xf1 ♖xd2, regaining the sacrificed piece. After 22 ♖f1 Black's four pawns outweigh White's extra piece. His central pawns are particularly dangerous.

22   ...   ♖d8
23   ♔e2

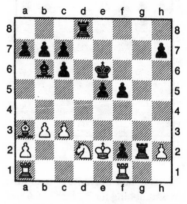

23   ...   ♖xd2+!!

"There are critical moments in a chess player's life when he is inspired. That is when brilliant masterpieces are born, recorded in the scanty !lines of chess notation. It seems that my opponent had a moment of inspiration." – Gufeld.

Black's only desire is to retain the dark-squared bishop, which can shepherd the central pawn-mass to the eighth rank. 23...♖xd2+ is a radical, but justified way to prevent its exchange with ♘d2-c4. It has to be said that even without this brilliant concept, Black's position is winning. Central pawn operations, starting with 23...e4! also promise returns, e.g.:

1) 24 ♖ad1 d3! (threatening to play ...♖e3#) 25 ♘c4 ♖g1 and now White can try:

1a) 26 ♖d2 f4 27 ♘xb6 (or 27 ♖xf2 f3+) 27...f3+ 28 ♔xf2 ♖g2+ 29 ♔e1 ♖dxd2 and Black wins.

1b) 26 ♖c1 f4 27 ♘xb6 f3+ 28 ♔xf2 ♖g2+ 29 ♔e1 ♖e2# is a attractive mate (see diagram).

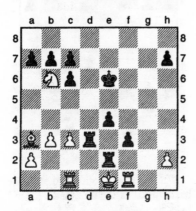

2) 24 ♘c4 is White's main idea, but after 24...f4 25 ♘xb6 f3+ 26 ♔e3 ♔f5! (this intermezzo, which threatens ...♖d3#, is very important) 27 ♖ad1 ♖xd1 28 ♖xd1 ♖g1! 29 ♔xf2 ♖xd1 30 ♘c4 ♖a1 and this endgame is winning for Black.

24 ♔xd2 e4

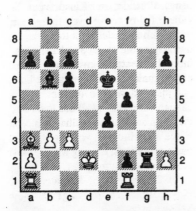

Black's threats are beginning to loom, e.g. 25 h4 f4 26 c4 ♗d4 27 ♖ad1 f3 28 ♔c2 e3 29 ♖xd4 e2 30 ♖dd1 ♖g1! 31 ♖xg1 fxg1♕ 32 ♖xg1 f2 and the pawns promote (see diagram).

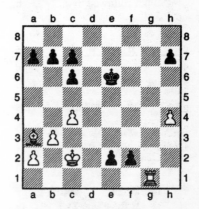

25 c4, planning c5, is met simply by 25...♗d4 26 ♖ad1 f4 27 ♔c2 ♔e5 28 ♗c1 c5! and White can do nothing to prevent the steady procession of Black's pieces and pawns down the board.

With his next move Gufeld had seen an ingenious way of exchanging off the dark-squared bishops, but it seems that Kavalek was ready even for this.

25 ♗f8 f4
26 b4! ♖g5!
27 ♗c5?

Consistent, but this move allows Black to carry through his concept to its logical conclusion. 27 c4 would force Black to work harder for the full point. Probably the best way forward for Black would be 27...♗e3+ 28 ♔c2 (alternatively, 28 ♔e2 ♗d4 29 ♖ab1 f3+) 28...♖g2 29 ♗c5 ♗xc5 30 bxc5 ♔f5 and now:

1) 31 ♖ab1 ♔g4 32 ♖xb7 ♔f3, followed by ...e3-e2 wins.

2) 31 ♔d2 e3+ 32 ♔d3 ♖xh2 33 ♖ab1 b6 34 cxb6 cxb6 and despite having the extra rook, White is absolutely paralysed. Nothing can be done about the eventual advance of the h-pawn to h3, followed by ...♖g2, ...h2 and ...♖g1.

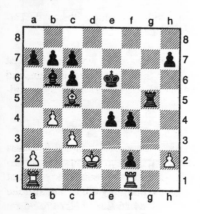

| 27 | ... | ♖xc5! |

Of course!

28	bxc5	♗xc5
29	♖ab1	f3
30	♖b4	

Resourceful until the end, White attempts to distract the bishop from its main role, with no joy. Passive defence also fails, e.g. 30 ♖h1 ♔e5 31 ♖xb7 e3+ 32 ♔d3 e2 33 ♖bb1 ♗e7! 34 h3 ♗h4 and ...e1♕ leaves Black with an easily won position.

| 30 | ... | ♔f5 |

| 31 | ♖d4 | ♗xd4 |
| 32 | cxd4 | ♔f4 |

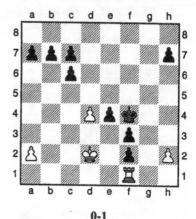

0-1

White can do nothing to stop the basic threat of ...e3-e2, and 33 ♖xf2 loses to 33...e3+.

Lessons from this game:

1) It pays to remember what you've been told! Here Gufeld forgot about 7...e3, and was rewarded with a lousy position.

2) Sometimes one piece dominates the entire game. Here it's the dark-squared bishop, and Kavalek put the value of this above everything else, with dramatic results!

3) Winning a nice game is one thing, but winning while retaining all of your pawns is something else!

Game 48

Mikhail Tal – Hans-Joachim Hecht

Varna Olympiad 1962

Queen's Indian/Nimzo-Indian Hybrid

The Players

Mikhail Tal (1936–92) was World Champion 1960–1, and one of the greatest attacking players of all time. See Game 39 for more information.

Hans-Joachim Hecht was born in 1939 in Luckenwalde in what became East Germany. For many years he was a mainstay of the (West) German team, and used to play regularly for the Bayern Munich club. He was awarded the grandmaster title in 1973.

The Game

Tal played as second reserve for the Soviet team at the Varna Olympiad. This was not just due to the extreme strength of Soviet chess, but because Tal was recovering from major illness, with his participation itself being only subject to stringent medical approval. Despite this, he still managed, in his own words, to "play quite well" including the following game, which "was unofficially judged to be the most brilliant played in the Olympiad." It is an extremely complex game, with some spectacular sacrifices leading not to mate but to a better ending. In the mass of complications Hecht has just one fleeting chance to achieve a draw.

1	d4	♘f6
2	c4	e6
3	♘f3	b6
4	♘c3	♗b4
5	♗g5	♗b7
6	e3	h6
7	♗h4	♗xc3+

This voluntary exchange (i.e. without waiting for White to play a3) may seem a little odd, but in this line White has no intention of playing a3. Therefore if Black wishes to inflict doubled pawns on White, then he needs to do so quickly, or else White may play ♕c2 and remove the possibility entirely. For example, 7...0-0 8 ♕c2 d6 9 ♗d3 ♘bd7 10 ♘d2! c5 (grabbing the g2-pawn would suicidally open the

g-file for White's attack) 11 0-0 gives White a pleasant edge.

7...g5 8 ♗g3 ♘e4 is the main alternative, which we see later in the book, in Game 81, Miles – Beliavsky.

8	bxc3	d6
9	♘d2	e5
10	f3	♕e7
11	e4	♘bd7
12	♗d3	♘f8!?

A logical move, intending ...♘g6 hitting the bishop and eyeing the inviting f4-square, but rather provocative.

13 c5!?

This is not just a typical Tal pawn sacrifice, opening lines to try to exploit Black's delay in castling, but is also highly thematic in this structure.

Since it is undoubtedly somewhat speculative, and leads to profoundly unclear play, in modern practice the more methodical 13 ♘f1 has been preferred, e.g. 13...♘g6 14 ♗f2 ♘f4 15 ♘e3 g6 16 ♗c2 0-0 17 ♗h4 with good kingside prospects for White, Seirawan – Browne, USA Championship, Key West 1994.

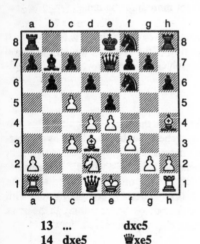

	13	...	dxc5
	14	dxe5	♕xe5
	15	♕a4+	c6

There were two important alternative ways to parry the check:

1) 15...♘8d7 and then:

1a) 16 ♕c2? ♘d5!.

1b) 16 0-0? ♕xc3.

1c) 16 ♗xf6 "and Black has to lose a few tempi before castling" – Tal and Koblencs. However, after 16...♕xf6 it isn't clear how much of a problem this really is to Black. White must take care of the threat of ...♕xc3, not just for the sake of saving the pawn, but because from c3 the queen hits several pieces and gains access to d4. I think White needs to find a less crude way to exploit the lack of convenient squares for the knights.

1d) 16 ♖c1 0-0 17 ♗g3 (17 0-0? ♕f4) 17...♕g5 18 f4 and ideas of e4-e5 give Black plenty to think about.

2) 15...♘6d7 keeps the unpinned knight more active, but delays castling further. 16 ♕c2 seems the best reply, with reasonable attacking chances. Instead 16 ♖c1 ♕e6 17 0-0 ♗c6 18 ♕a6 ♘e5 19 ♗c2 g5 20 ♗g3 ♘fg6 gave Black a reasonable game in Gilb. Garcia – O'Kelly, Capablanca memorial, Havana 1963.

16 0-0!

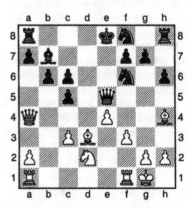

Defending the c-pawn would now be rather too slow, since Black has kept both his knights active. Tal sees that he can justify sacrificing the pawn thanks to the newly-created weakness on d6.

16 ...   ♘g6

16...♕xc3 was nevertheless well worth considering. 17 ♘c4 and now:

1) 17...b5? 18 ♘d6+ ♔d7 (18...♔e7 19 ♘f5+) 19 ♘xb5! ♕b4 (19...cxb5 20 ♗xb5+ leads to a rout) 20 ♕c2 (20 ♕xb4 cxb4 21 e5 suffices for an edge) 20...cxb5 21 ♖ab1 must be a winning attack, for example 21...♕d4+ 22 ♗f2 ♕d6 23 ♗xb5+ ♔c8 24 ♖fd1.

2) 17...♕xd3? 18 ♖fd1 b5 (after 18...♕e2 White can play 19 ♘d6+ ♔e7 20 ♘f5+) 19 ♖xd3 bxa4 20 ♘d6+ ♔e7 (20...♔d7 21 ♘xb7+ ♔c7 22 ♖b1 and the attack continues) 21 ♘f5+ ♔e8 22 ♘xg7+ ♔e7 23 ♘f5+ wins.

3) 17...♘g6 looks like a decent try, e.g. 18 ♘d6+ ♔f8 19 ♗xf6 ♕xd3 20 ♘xb7 gxf6 21 ♕xc6 and although Black's kingside is still very shaky, he has survival chances.

17 ♘c4 ♕e6

Black threatens both ...♘xh4 and ...b5, and so might have been forgiven for thinking that White would now have to find a way to bale out.

Instead 17...b5? loses to 18 ♘xe5 bxa4 19 ♘xg6 fxg6 20 e5 while 17...♕xc3 transposes to line "3" of the note to Black's 16th move.

18 e5!

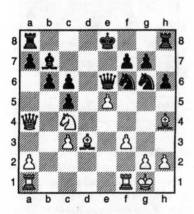

With this astonishing move, Tal commits himself to the sacrifice of at least a piece, and in many lines much more than that. In making such a choice, Tal would have been guided by a fair amount of specific analysis, and an intuitive feel that this was the right follow-up to his previous play.

18 ... b5!

18...♘xh4 19 ♘d6+ ♔f8 20 ♖ae1 (20 ♕xh4 ♕xe5 is no good for White) keeps Black under pressure:

1) 20...♕d5 21 ♘xb7 ♕xd3 (after 21...♘e8 22 ♖d1 g5 23 ♖fe1 Black's position is thoroughly unpleasant) 22 exf6 leaves Black with serious defensive problems.

2) 20...♘xg2 21 ♔xg2 b5 22 ♕d1 and White wins a piece after 22...♘d5 23 ♘xb7 or 22...♗a6 23 ♗f5.

3) 20...g5 supports the knight and gives the king a square, but by playing 21 ♘xb7 ♘d5 22 ♘d6 ♔g7 (22...♘xc3 23 ♕xc6) 23 g3 White keeps a powerful initiative.

19 exf6

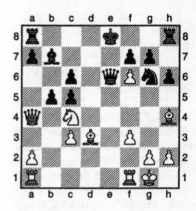

19 ... bxa4?!

After this move Black seems unable to avoid a difficult ending. 19...0-0! is best, but doesn't refute White's combination. The critical line is long, complicated, and rather fantastic. The correct result appears to be a draw. To avoid this note becoming too long, I shall just give the best lines for White: 20 ♖ae1 ♕xe1 21 ♖xe1 bxa4 22 ♗xg6 fxg6 23 ♖e7 g5 24 ♖xg7+ ♔h8 25

♗g3 (25 ♖g6 gxh4 26 ♘e5 may well
be enough to force a draw) 25...♗a6
26 ♗e5! ♗xc4 27 f7 h5 28 g4! hxg4
29 fxg4 ♖ad8 30 h4 and now:

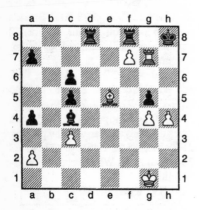

1) 30...gxh4? 31 g5 (White threatens mate by 32 ♖g6+ ♔h7 33 ♖h6#)
and now:

1a) 31...♖d5?? 32 g6.
1b) 31...♗xf7?? 32 ♖g6+ ♔h7 33
♖h6+ ♔g8 34 ♖h8#.
1c) 31...♖xf7 32 ♖g6+ ♖g7 33
♖xg7 ♖d5 34 ♗f6 and with g6 a threat,
and ♖xa7+ and ♖xa4 coming otherwise, White's a-pawn could quite unexpectedly become a major force.
34...♖d1+ (34...♖f5 35 ♖xa7+ ♔g8
36 ♖xa4) 35 ♔g2 ♖a1? 36 g6 wins.
1d) 31...♖d1+ 32 ♔h2 ♖d2+ 33
♔h3 ♗e6+ 34 ♔xh4 ♖h2+ 35 ♔g3
♖h3+ 36 ♔g2 ♖h5 37 g6 ♖xf7 38
♖h7++ ♔g8 39 ♖xh5 ♖g7 40 ♗xg7
♔xg7 41 a3 (probably clearer than 41
♖h7+ ♔xg6 42 ♖xa7 ♗xa2 43 ♖xa4)
41...♗d5+ 42 ♔f2 ♔xg6 43 ♖h4 ♗b3
(43...c4 44 ♔e3 wins easily) 44 ♔e3
with a simple win by either ♔e4-e5, or
♔d3, c4 and ♖h8-a8.

2) 30...♗xf7?! 31 ♖xf7+ ♔g8 32
♖g7+ ♔h8 33 ♖xa7+ ♔g8 34 ♖g7+

♔h8 35 hxg5 ♖d1+ 36 ♔g2 ♖e1 37
♖e7+ ♔g8 38 g6 ♖e2+ 39 ♔g3 gives
White winning chances.

3) 30...♖d1+! is a clear-cut draw.
The plan is to keep checking on d1, d2
and d3 until the white king moves to
the f-file; then ...♗xf7 draws: 31 ♔g2
(31 ♔h2 ♖d2+ 32 ♔g3 ♖d3+ 33 ♔f2
♗xf7; 31 ♔f2 ♗xf7) 31...♖d2+ 32
♔f3 ♗xf7 33 ♖g6+ (33 ♖xg5+? ♔h7
34 ♖g7+ ♔h6 35 g5+ ♔h5 36 ♖h7+
♔g6 37 ♖h6+ ♔f5 and Black wins)
33...♔h7 34 ♖g7+ ♔h8 (not 34...♔h6??
35 hxg5#) with a forced repetition of
moves.

20 fxg7　　　♖g8

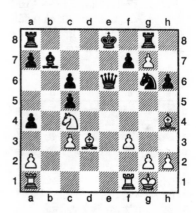

21 ♗f5!!

Although practically forced, this
move nevertheless has a magical quality. White, a bishop for a queen down,
leaves three pieces *en prise*!

21 ♗xg6 fxg6 (21...♕xc4? 22
♖fe1+ ♔d7 23 ♖e7+; 21...♕xg6? 22
♖fe1+ ♔d7 23 ♘e5+; 21...♗a6!? also
looks OK) 22 ♖fe1 would be a less effective continuation:

1) 22...♔f7? 23 ♖xe6 ♔xe6 24
♖e1+ ♔d5 (24...♔d7 25 ♖e7+ ♔d8 26
♗f6! mates) 25 ♘e3+ ♔d6 26 ♗g3+

♔e6 (26...♔d7 27 ♘g4! and ♘f6 wins)
27 ♘g4+ ♔f7 (27...♔d5 28 ♖e4) 28
♗e5 and ♘(x)h6(+) wins.

2) 22...♗c8! 23 ♘d6+ ♔d7 24 ♖xe6
♔xe6 25 ♘e8 ♔f7 26 ♖e1 g5 looks
good for Black.

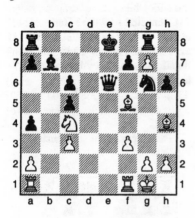

21 ...   ♘xh4

Or:

1) 21...♕xc4? 22 ♖ae1+ ♕e6 23
♖xe6+ fxe6 24 ♗xg6+ ♔d7 25 ♖d1+
is a rout. Black's king must go back to
the first rank, whereupon ♗f6 and
♗f7 will leave White a piece up. If
Black refuses to retreat, then 25...♔c7
26 ♗g3+ ♔b6 27 ♖b1+ ♔a6 28 ♗d3+
♔a5 29 ♗c7# is a pretty mate.

2) 21...♕xf5 22 ♘d6+ ♔d7 23
♘xf5 ♘xh4 24 ♖ad1+ ♔c7 25 ♘xh4
♖xg7 26 ♖fe1 leaves Black with his
standard problem: an ending where all
his pawns are horribly weak. Compare
the game continuation.

3) 21...♗a6 22 ♗xe6 fxe6 (the alternative 22...♘xh4 transposes to the
game) 23 ♘d6+ ♔d7 24 ♘e4 saves
White's piece and leads to another
ending where Black will suffer due to
his shattered pawns.

22 ♗xe6   ♗a6

22...fxe6 23 ♘d6+ ♔e7 24 ♘xb7
would be yet another miserable ending for Black.

23 ♘d6+   ♔e7
24 ♗c4

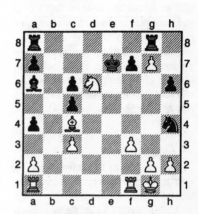

A beautiful move, rescuing White's
pieces. Black is now forced into a miserable ending. The amazing thing
about Tal's play here is that all this
brilliance and all these sacrifices have
been "just" to isolate Black's pawns.

24 ...   ♖xg7
25 g3   ♔xd6
26 ♗xa6   ♘f5

26...♖b8 is a better try.

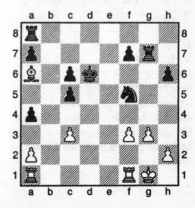

27	♖ab1	f6
28	♖fd1+	♔e7
29	♖e1+	♔d6
30	♔f2	

Tal disliked the characterization of him as a brilliant attacker but a poor endgame player. Though he sometimes joked about his shortcomings in the technical areas of the game, there was no doubting his skill in the endgame. Here he gives his opponent no chances, and realizes his advantage systematically and accurately.

30	...	c4
31	g4	♘e7
32	♖b7	

Making use of his active pieces to tie Black down and prevent any counterplay.

32	...	♖ag8
33	♗xc4	♘d5
34	♗xd5	cxd5
35	♖b4	

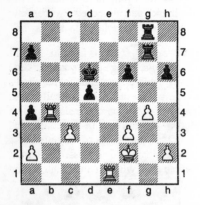

White has clarified his advantage. He will eventually create a passed pawn on the kingside, while making sure that Black's queenside pawns remain feeble or disappear altogether.

35	...	♖c8
36	♖xa4	♖xc3
37	♖a6+	♔c5
38	♖xf6	h5
39	h3	

Connected pawns are far more effective that disconnected ones. 39 gxh5? would throw away the positional gains made by his earlier brilliant play.

39	...	hxg4
40	hxg4	♖h7
41	g5	

"Passed pawns must be pushed", as they say.

41	...	♖h5
42	♖f5	♖c2+
43	♔g3	♔c4
44	♖ee5	d4
45	g6	♖h1
46	♖c5+	♔d3
47	♖xc2	♔xc2
48	♔f4	♖g1
49	♖g5	1-0

After 49...♖xg5 50 ♔xg5 d3 51 g7 d2 52 g8♕ d1♕ 53 ♕b3+ White forces the exchange of queens and then promotes his f-pawn.

Lessons from this game:

1) It is worth sacrificing a pawn to activate your pieces and catch the enemy king in the centre.

2) No matter how many pieces are being sacrificed, they can only be taken one at a time!

3) Connected pawns are far more valuable than isolated pawns in the endgame.

Game 49

Viktor Korchnoi – Mikhail Tal
USSR Championship, Erevan 1962
Modern Benoni

The Players

Viktor Korchnoi (born 1931) has been one of the world's leading players for nearly forty years, and can be counted among the strongest players never to become World Champion. He has been a Candidate many times and came closest to winning the world title when he fought back from 5–2 down to 5–5 against the defending champion Karpov in Baguio City in 1978, before Karpov won the final game. He was less convincing in a similar challenge to Karpov in 1981, this time going down by the score of 6–2. Since then he has remained one of the top players. Korchnoi is known for his intense fighting spirit. He has a high percentage of decisive games and very few end in short draws. Korchnoi is an extremely strong defensive player, always willing to grab material and be prepared ride the storm. He writes "If a player believes in miracles he can sometimes perform them."

1962 was not one of Mikhail Tal's better years. He was forced to withdraw from the Curaçao Candidates tournament due to ill health, when he had scored just 7/21, but he did recover sufficiently to win a board prize for the USSR team at the Varna Olympiad. The next major event for Tal was this Soviet Championship.

The Game

Korchnoi had set a startling pace at this event, scoring 9 points from his first 11 games. His next two opponents were his main rivals, Boris Spassky and Mikhail Tal. He defeated Spassky in an excellent game, which meant that Tal required a win to keep any chance of a gold medal alive. In the event he was not really given any chance at all. Some inaccurate opening play by the Latvian leads him into a very difficult situation early on. Korchnoi breaks through in the centre and reaches a winning position by move 25. Korchnoi then eases off slightly and a slip allows Tal a single opportunity back into the game. This is missed, however, and from that moment on Korchnoi takes a firm grip, winning a very interesting endgame by marching his king up the board.

1	d4	♘f6
2	c4	c5
3	d5	e6
4	♘c3	exd5
5	cxd5	d6
6	♘f3	g6

Tal's games provided the main impetus behind the surge in popularity of the sharp Modern Benoni in the 1960s. The pawn structure dictates that, as Black has an extra pawn on the queenside, he will attempt to take over the initiative there. White, on the other hand, tries to use his extra central pawn to create a central pawn-roller.

>   7 g3   ♗g7
>   8 ♗g2   0-0
>   9 0-0

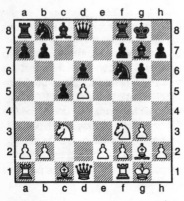

>   9 ...   ♘a6

In *Viktor Korchnoi's Best Games*, Korchnoi adorns this move with a question mark. Nevertheless, it has proved to be a playable alternative to the more common 9...a6 10 a4 ♘bd7.

10 h3

This move prepares to play the central advance e2-e4, without allowing Black the possibility of exchanging his bishop with ...♗g4, which is a common idea for Black to rid himself of the "problem bishop". White can also start a typical Benoni manoeuvre with 10 ♘d2. After 10...♘c7 White doesn't even need to prepare the occupation of c4 with 11 a4, as after 11 ♘c4, 11...b5 can be answered with 12 ♘xd6! ♕xd6 13 ♗f4 ♕b6 14 d6, when White wins material.

>   10 ...   ♘c7?!

I suspect this move is the real culprit in Black's opening play. Black does

nothing to prevent White from carrying out his central advance. 10...♖e8 makes more sense. Then 11 ♖e1 may be answered with the simplifying 11...♘e4!. White's other plan of occupying c4 is less effective now. After 11 ♘d2 ♘c7 12 ♘c4 Black can play 12...b5. The trick 13 ♘xd6 isn't nearly so powerful now, since the h3-pawn hangs at the end. Following 13...♕xd6 14 ♗f4 ♕b6 15 d6 ♘e6 16 ♗xa8 ♘xf4 17 gxf4 ♗xh3 18 ♗g2 ♗xg2 19 ♔xg2 ♖d8 White's shaky kingside gives Black excellent compensation for the exchange.

>   11 e4   ♘d7

Black can hardly think about expanding on the queenside when he has so many problems in the centre. 11...b5 is punished by 12 e5, when 12...dxe5 13 d6 is very strong. Black can play 12...♘fe8, but 13 ♖e1 retains a solid advantage for White.

>   12 ♖e1

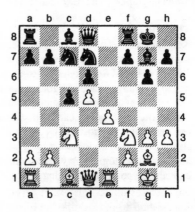

>   12 ...   ♘e8

Black's fiddling with his knights has effectively meant the loss of two tempi over normal lines (the knights could have reached these squares after three moves instead of five). This is hardly likely to go unpunished. Nonetheless 12...b5 is still premature after either Taimanov's 13 &f4 ♘e5 14 ♘xe5 dxe5 15 &e3, or Korchnoi's 13 e5 ♘xe5 14 ♘xe5 &xe5 15 ♖xe5! dxe5 16 d6. Korchnoi also gives 12...♖e8 13 &f4 ♘e5 14 ♘xe5 dxe5 15 &e3 as good for White. It's usually a sign that things have gone wrong for Black if he has to capture on e5 with his d6-pawn, but 14...&xe5 (instead of 14...dxe5) 15 &xe5 ♖xe5 16 f4 is also obviously very pleasant for White.

| 13 | &g5 | &f6 |
| 14 | &e3 | |

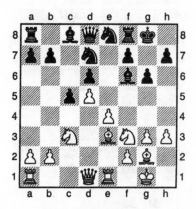

| 14 | ... | ♖b8 |

Perhaps Korchnoi's suggestion of 14...b5 is Black's last real chance of activity. He gives the variation 15 &h6 ♘g7 16 ♘xb5 ♕b6 17 ♘a3 ♕xb2 18 ♘c4 ♕xa1 19 ♕xa1 &xa1 20 ♖xa1 and assesses this as unclear. It's true that the vital d6-pawn drops, but Black does have a rook for a bishop. 17 ♕a4! looks stronger, however, with the point that 17...a6 18 ♘a3 ♕xb2 19 ♘c4 ♕b5 20 ♕c2! &xa1 can be answered with 21 ♖b1, winning the queen.

After 14...♖b8 Korchnoi is able to snuff out Black's attempt at counterplay with ...b5.

15	a4	a6
16	&f1!	♕e7
17	♘d2	♘c7
18	f4	

18 ♘c4 is also very strong, because 18...b5 can be met by 19 ♘a5, coming into the c6-outpost.

| 18 | ... | b5 |

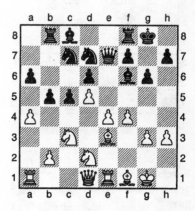

19 e5!

A classic Benoni central breakthrough. White's pieces can flood into the space vacated by the pawns and create major threats. In particular Black will have to deal with ideas involving d5-d6.

| 19 | ... | dxe5 |
| 20 | ♘de4 | ♕d8 |

After 20...♘e8 White has many promising continuations. In his notes to this game from *The Soviet Championships* Taimanov gives 21 ♘xf6+ ♘exf6 22 fxe5 ♘xe5 23 &f4 ♘fd7 24 d6 as one of many ways to keep a large plus.

| 21 | ♘xf6+ | ♘xf6 |
| 22 | d6! | |

Keeping on the right track. Material grabbing by 22 ♗xc5 ♖e8 23 fxe5 ♘fxd5 24 ♘xd5 ♘xd5 25 ♗d6 is punished severely with 25...♕b6+ 26 ♔h2 ♗b7 27 ♗xb8? ♕f2+ 28 ♔g2 ♘c3!! and Black wins. This was analysed by Grandmaster Andor Lilienthal.

22	...	♘e6
23	fxe5	b4
24	♘d5	♘xd5
25	♕xd5	♗b7
26	♕d2	♕d7
27	♔h2	

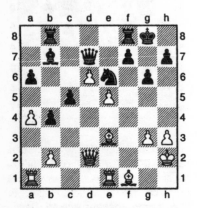

The smoke has cleared, leaving White with an unquestionable advantage, due to his extra space, bishop-pair and strong protected passed pawn on d6. Added to this Black is extremely weak on the dark squares around his king. With Black's next move, Tal is signalling his intentions that he will not wait around to be squashed, but instead will try to distract White with a demonstration on the queenside. Notice that the active 27...f6 28 exf6 ♖xf6 29 ♗c4 only serves to emphasize the power of the two bishops.

27	...	b3
28	♖ac1	♕xa4

29	♗c4	♗c8

After 29...♗c6 White can win with 30 ♗h6, e.g.:

1) 30...♖fe8 31 ♖f1 ♗b5 32 d7! ♗xd7 (or 32...♖ed8 33 ♗xe6 ♗xf1 34 ♗xf7+! ♔xf7 35 ♕d5+ mates) 33 ♖xf7! ♔xf7 34 ♕f4+ ♔g8 35 ♕f6 winning Black's queen or mating.

2) 30...♘d4 31 ♖f1 ♖b4 32 ♕f4 ♖xc4 33 ♕f6 ♘e6 34 ♗xf8.

Even after 29...♗c8 White can play the same way, e.g. 30 ♗h6 ♘d4 31 ♖f1 ♖b4 32 ♕f4 ♖xc4 33 ♕f6 ♘e6 34 ♗xf8.

30	♖f1	♖b4

31 ♗xe6?

Giving Black a chance to get back in the game by reviving his inactive pieces. Taimanov gives 31 ♕d3 ♗d7 32 ♗h6, when it is unlikely that Black will survive for too long.

31	...	♗xe6
32	♗h6	♖e8?

Missing the only chance. 32...♖fb8! is stronger, as it doesn't allow White a later tactic involving d6-d7. Taimanov gives 33 ♕f2 ♖e4 34 ♖ce1 as good for White, but after 34...♖xe1 35 ♖xe1 ♕d4! Black is holding his own. After

36 ♕f6 ♕xb2+ 37 ♔g1 ♕d4+ White cannot escape the perpetual check.

    33   ♕g5   ♖e4

    34   ♖f2!

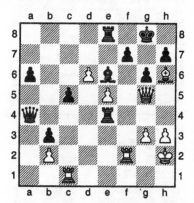

Now the defence 34...♕d4 doesn't work, as after 35 ♕f6 ♕xe5 White has 36 d7!. Then 36...♗xd7 37 ♕xf7+ ♔h8 38 ♕f8+ ♖xf8 39 ♖xf8# is mate, as is 36...♕xf6 37 dxe8♕#.

    34   ...   f5

    35   ♕f6!

It's much more important to keep possession of the pair of passed pawns. After 35 exf6? ♗f7 Black can erect a blockading defence.

    35   ...   ♕d7

    36   ♖xc5   ♖c4

    37   ♖xc4   ♗xc4

    38   ♖d2   ♗e6

    39   ♖d1   ♕a7

    40   ♖d2   ♕d7

    41   ♖d1   ♕a7

    42   ♖d4!

Korchnoi found this clever move in his adjournment analysis. White blocks out the queen and prepares the advance of his king. The rook also proves to be very useful on the fourth rank. White's position is winning, but it still

requires some very accurate play to finish the job off, especially against a tactician such as Tal, who would grab the slightest chance of counterplay with both hands.

    42   ...   ♕d7

    43   g4   a5

    44   ♔g3!

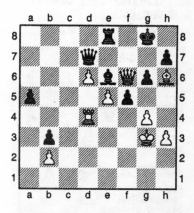

The king safely marches up the dark squares in order to enhance White's final assault. With his next move Black prepares ...♕f7, which cannot be played immediately due to 45 d7!.

    44   ...   ♖b8

    45   ♔h4   ♕f7

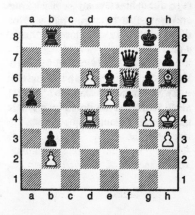

46	♔g5!	fxg4
47	hxg4	♗d7
48	♖c4	a4
49	♖c7	a3

This is Black's last throw of the dice, but Korchnoi has everything under control. The other try, 49...♕xf6+ 50 ♔xf6 a3, also leads to a white win after 51 e6 axb2 52 exd7 ♖f8+ 53 ♔g5 b1♕ 54 ♖c8!.

50	♖xd7	♕xd7
51	e6	

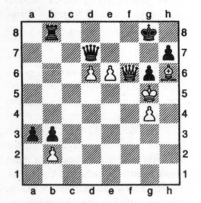

The culmination of White's strategy. Two connected passed pawns sit proudly on the sixth rank, while all of the dark squares around the black king are controlled by white pieces. Not surprisingly, all moves lose for Black, e.g.:

1) 51...♕b7 52 ♕e5 ♕b5 53 ♕xb5 ♖xb5+ 54 ♔f6 followed by d7 and e7.

2) 51...♕b5+ 52 ♔h4 ♕b7 53 ♕f1! axb2 54 d7 and the threat of ♕f7+ is too much for Black.

51	...	♕a7

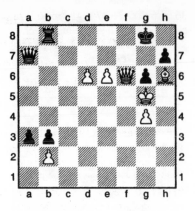

52	♕e5	axb2
53	e7	♔f7
54	d7	1-0

It is mate after 54...b1♕ 55 e8♕+ ♖xe8 56 dxe8♕#, or 54...♕xd7 55 ♕f6+ ♔e8 56 ♕f8#.

Lessons from this game:

1) In a cramped position, it is normally useful to seek to ease the congestion by exchanges. This is why 10...♖e8, intending ...♘e4, would have been a good idea for Black. Conversely, when one has more space, it makes sense to avoid exchanges. This is the reason for White's early h3.

2) When fianchettoing your king's bishop, always be very wary about exchanging this piece later on, as trading it will undoubtedly lead to a weakening of the kingside. Of course, in this game, Tal hardly had any choice in the matter.

3) A pair of connected passed pawns on the sixth rank, and in the centre, is a priceless weapon!

Robert Byrne – Robert Fischer
USA Championship, New York 1963/4
Grünfeld Defence, Fianchetto Variation

The Players

Robert Byrne (born 1928) is a former college lecturer, who gave up his post in the late 1960s to concentrate on chess playing and writing. He was winner of the US Open Championship in 1960, and also won the more prestigious closed Championship in 1972, after a play-off with Reshevsky and Kavalek. He came third in the 1973 Leningrad Interzonal, becoming a Candidate for the World Championship in the process, but lost his first Candidates match against Spassky. Byrne represented the USA at the 1952 Olympiad, the first of many appearances for his country.

For Bobby Fischer (see Game 38 for career details), 1963 proved to be an eventful year on and off the board. Past squabbles caused him to boycott FIDE qualifying tournaments, while another dispute caused him to pass up an invitation to play in the Piatigorsky Cup, despite a considerable first prize being on offer. When he did play, he let his chess do the talking. There was some excitement prior to the 1963/4 US Championships. Fischer had only just managed to win the previous year's event, and he was apparently a little rusty. In the event, the chess public were right to get excited, but for different reasons. Fischer destroyed the opposition, scoring a perfect 11/11. At the end Fischer was a mighty 3½ points ahead of the second-placed player, Larry Evans. International Arbiter Hans Kmoch duly congratulated Evans on winning the real tournament, and Fischer for winning the exhibition!

The Game

Perhaps one of the most amazing features of this brilliancy is that Fischer manages to win in only 21 moves from an incredibly dull-looking opening position, and without White making any obvious mistakes. This ability to extract something from nothing separates the outstanding from the merely very good. The complexity of Fischer's final combination was such that, at the point when Byrne resigned, grandmasters in the commentary room were casually informing the audience that White had a won position!

1	d4	♘f6	6	♘c3	♗g7
2	c4	g6	7	e3	0-0
3	g3	c6	8	♘ge2	♘c6
4	♗g2	d5	9	0-0	b6
5	cxd5	cxd5	10	b3	♗a6

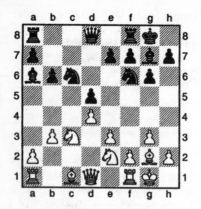

11 ♗a3   ♖e8
12 ♕d2

In *My 60 Memorable Games* Fischer gives 12 ♖c1 as a good alternative. It certainly would have prevented the tactical fireworks that we see in the game. After 12 ♖c1 the advance 12...e5 would probably be too risky. Following 13 dxe5 ♘xe5 14 ♖c2! (but not 14 ♘xd5? ♘xd5 15 ♗xd5 ♗xe2, when Black wins a piece) 14...♗b7 15 ♖d2! the queen and rook are very effectively lined up on the d-file, strongly pressurizing the weak d5-pawn. Instead of 12...e5, Black should probably be content with the more restrained 12...e6, leading to an equal position.

A rather drastic way of stopping Black advancing his e-pawn would have been 12 f4?!, but this advance compromises White's pawn structure and leaves the e4-square very weak. Fischer explains that with 12...e6, followed by ...♗f8 and an eventual doubling on the c-file, Black would obtain the advantage.

12 ...   e5!

"I was amazed at this advance, which seems to leave Black's queen's pawn a hopelessly weak isolani," admitted Byrne in *Chess Life*. It's true that after this advance the game hangs on a knife edge. Black has to play both extremely actively and accurately in order to offset the weakness of d5. Of course, similar considerations apply to White.

13 dxe5

Accepting the challenge. Fischer notes that White can accept a passive position after 13 ♖ac1 exd4 14 exd4 ♖c8 15 f3, although Black would have problems in breaking through. It could be added that instead of 15 f3, the more active 15 ♖fe1 looks OK, as the tactical line 15...♗xe2 16 ♖xe2 ♘xd4 17 ♖xe8+ ♕xe8 18 ♖e1! (but not 18 ♕xd4 ♘e4) 18...♘e4 19 ♘xe4 dxe4 20 ♖xe4 actually favours White, who keeps the pair of bishops.

13 ...   ♘xe5

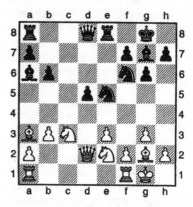

14 ♖fd1?

This is very much a case of "the wrong rook". One can understand Byrne's desire to break the pin on the e2-knight, but this turns out to be less important than other considerations. Fischer spends a lot of time and energy analysing the superior 14 ♖ad1!, but still comes to the conclusion that Black can keep the advantage. Here is a summary of the analysis:

1) 14...♖c8 15 ♘xd5 ♘xd5 16 ♗xd5 ♗d3 17 ♗g2 ♖c2 18 ♕xc2! and White wins a pawn.

2) 14...♘d3? 15 ♕c2! with a clear plus to White. In this particular variation we see the point of 14 ♖ad1 as opposed to 14 ♖fd1: there is no sacrifice on f2 here.

3) 14...♕d7 15 ♕c2 and again the weakness of d5 begins to tell. After 15...♖ac8 White can side-step with 16 ♕b1!.

4) 14...♕c7 15 ♕c1! ♘e4!? 16 ♘xd5! ♕xc1 17 ♘xc1 ♗xf1 18 ♗xe4 ♗a6 19 ♘e7+ ♔h8 20 ♗xa8 ♖xa8 21 f4 and White keeps his extra pawn.

5) 14...♘e4 was Fischer's original "refutation" of 14 ♖ad1. After 15 ♘xe4 dxe4 16 ♗xe4 ♕xd2 17 ♖xd2 ♘c4 18 ♗xa8 ♘xd2 19 ♖d1 ♘c4 20 bxc4 ♖xa8, Black picks up the weak c4-pawn and remains better in the endgame due to the bishop-pair. However, Yuri Averbakh's suggestion of 20 ♗c6! puts a spanner in the works. Following 20...♘xa3 21 ♗xe8 ♗xe2 22 ♖d7 it is White who has all the winning chances.

6) 14...♕c8! was the move that Fischer finally settled upon. The queen removes itself from the d-file and eyes the weak light squares around the white king. Some of the variations stemming from this line have great depth, but it does seem as if Black keeps the advantage, or at the very least, his game is easier to play in a practical sense:

6a) 15 ♖c1 ♕d7! 16 ♖cd1 ♖ad8 and Black's little jig with his queen has gained a valuable tempo.

6b) 15 ♗b2 ♕f5 and Black keeps the initiative on the light squares, although Fischer considers this line to be relatively best for White. It's worth mentioning here that after 16 ♘xd5 ♘xd5 17 ♗xd5 ♘f3+ 18 ♗xf3 ♕xf3 19 ♘d4 ♕h5 20 ♖fe1 ♗b7 Black's light-square control has reached dominating proportions, giving him excellent compensation for the pawn.

6c) 15 ♕c1 ♘e4 16 ♘xd5 ♗xe2 17 ♗xe4 ♔h8! and Black wins the exchange, e.g. 18 ♕xc8 ♖axc8 19 ♘e7 ♖c7 20 ♖c1 ♖d7 21 ♖fe1 ♗f3!, or 18 ♘e7 ♕h3 19 f3 ♗xf1 20 ♖xf1 ♖ad8.

6d) 15 ♘xd5!?, grabbing the d-pawn on offer, has to be the most critical test of 14...♕c8.

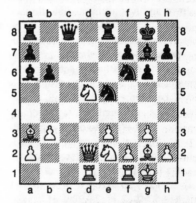

Fischer gives 15...♘xd5 16 ♗xd5 ♖d8 17 f4 (forced as Black has many threats, involving ...♘f3+) 17...♖xd5! 18 ♕xd5 ♗b7, when the meek 19 ♕d8+ ♖xd8 20 ♖xd8+ ♖xd8 21 fxe5 ♗xe5 gives Black a clear endgame plus. Against the more testing 19 ♕d2 Fischer gives the line 19...♕h3! 20 ♘d4 ♘g4 21 ♘c2 (21 ♖fe1 ♘xe3! should win) 21...h5 with a strong attack. At first I was slightly sceptical about this line, as I thought that White could improve on 21 ♘c2 with 21 ♘f3!, which is not mentioned by Fischer.

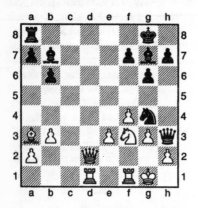

Black is the exchange and a pawn down and has no immediate threats. Added to this Black also has to be careful of white ideas such as ♘g5 or even ♕d8+. Nevertheless after the quiet 21...h6! Black's active pieces maintain a slow-burning pressure. This will be augmented by ...♖e8, hitting the e3-pawn. Incredibly, it is extremely difficult for White to do anything active. The most obvious try is 22 ♖c1, but after 22...♖e8 White seems to be in some trouble, e.g. 23 ♖ce1 ♗xf3 24 ♖xf3 ♗c3! 25 ♕xc3 ♕xh2+ 26 ♔f1 ♕h1+ 27 ♔e2 ♕g2+ 28 ♔d1 ♕xf3+ 29 ♔c1 ♖xe3, or 23 ♕d7 ♖xe3 24 ♕xb7 ♖xf3 25 ♖xf3 ♗d4+ and mate. Finally there is 23 ♖c7, but even here Black has some fun with 23...♘xe3 24 ♖f2 ♗xf3! 25 ♖xf3 ♗d4!, threatening 26...♘g4+ 27 ♕xd4 (27 ♔h1 ♖e1+!) 27...♖e1+ and mate. The only way to prevent this is with 26 ♖c1, but now Black maintains the advantage with 26...♘c2+ 27 ♔h1 ♕h5 28 ♕xc2 ♕xf3+ 29 ♕g2 ♕xg2+ 30 ♔xg2 ♖e2+

and 31...♖xa2. This last line brings up a surprisingly common occurrence, that is an incredibly long line of tactics finishing with one side "just a pawn up" in the endgame.

Finally it can also be added that if a defensive improvement is found for White in that last variation, then Black can content himself with the safer continuation 19...♕c6 (instead of Fischer's 19...♕h3). Now 20 ♘d4 ♕h1+ 21 ♔f2 ♕xh2+ 22 ♔e1 ♕xg3+ 23 ♕f2 ♕xf2+ 24 ♖xf2 ♘g4 25 ♖e2 ♗a6! is better for Black, while 20 ♕d5 ♕xd5 21 ♖xd5 ♗xd5 22 fxe5 ♗xe5 also gives Black an endgame edge.

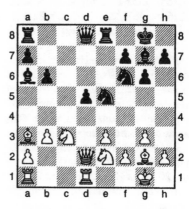

14   ...   ♘d3!
15   ♕c2

Fortunately some of the variations now become slightly simpler. Fischer gives 15 ♘d4 ♘e4 16 ♘xe4 dxe4 17 ♗b2 ♖c8, when the knight on d3 promises Black some advantage, and 15 ♘f4 ♘e4 16 ♘xe4 dxe4 (but not 16...♗xa1? 17 ♘d6) 17 ♖ab1 ♖c8 18 ♘xd3 ♗c3! 19 ♕e2 ♗xd3 20 ♕g4 f5 21 ♕h3 ♗xb1! 22 ♖xd8 ♖exd8 23 ♗f1 ♖d1 (threatening ...♗d3) 24 ♔g2 ♗d3! 25 ♗xd3 exd3, when Black's d-pawn cannot be stopped. He also mentions the line 15 f3 ♗h6 16 f4 (16 ♘f4? d4!) 16...♗g7!, when we have arrived back at the same position, except White has weakened himself with f2-f4.

15 ...   ♘xf2!!

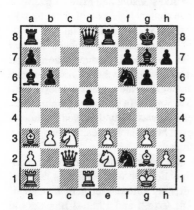

Without this move, all of Black's previous play would have been pointless, but as Fischer points out "The complete justification for this sac does not become apparent until White resigns!"

16 ♔xf2   ♘g4+

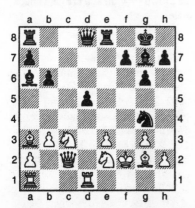

17 ♔g1

The only move. 17 ♔f3 allows total carnage after 17...♖xe3+ 18 ♔xg4 (18 ♔f4 ♗h6+ 19 ♔xg4 ♗c8+) 18...h5+ 19 ♔h3 (19 ♔f4 ♗h6#) 19...♗c8+ and mate next move, while following 17 ♔e1 ♘xe3, Black will capture on g2.

17 ...   ♘xe3

Known in the trade as a "family fork". White has to move the queen.

18 ♕d2

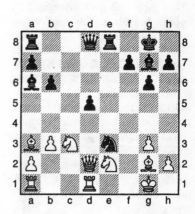

18 ...   ♘xg2!

Another outwardly surprising move, which takes the game onto a higher plane. Grabbing the rook by 18...♘xd1 19 ♖xd1 would have allowed White right back into the game. Instead Black removes the key defender of the light squares.

19 ♔xg2   d4!

And now the lines are cleared for the deadly force of the two bishops. Once more the materialistic 19...♗xe2 20 ♘xe2 ♗xa1 21 ♖xa1 would have favoured White.

20 ♘xd4   ♗b7+
21 ♔f1

White has no defence, as the following lines prove:

1) 21 ♔g1 ♗xd4+ 22 ♕xd4 ♖e1+!
23 ♔f2 ♕xd4+ 24 ♖xd4 ♖xa1 and
Black is the exchange up. Fischer continues with 25 ♖d7 ♖c8 26 ♖xb7 (or
26 ♗b2 ♖h1) 26...♖xc3 27 ♖b8+ ♔g7
28 ♗b2 ♖xa2 and Black wins.

2) 21 ♔f2 ♕d7! and now:

2a) 22 ♖ac1 ♕h3 23 ♘f3 ♗h6 24
♕d3 ♗e3+ 25 ♕xe3 ♖xe3 26 ♔xe3
♖e8+ 27 ♔f2 ♕f5!, winning the knight
on f3.

2b) 22 ♘ce2 isn't mentioned by
Fischer, but Black wins comfortably
with 22...♕h3 23 ♘f3 (or 23 ♔e1 ♕xh2
24 ♕b2 ♗a6) 23...♗xa1 when both 24
♘eg1 ♕f5 25 ♖xa1 ♖ad8 26 ♕b2 ♖d3
and 24 ♖xa1 ♖ad8 25 ♕c2 ♕e6 end
White's resistance.

21 ...   ♕d7!

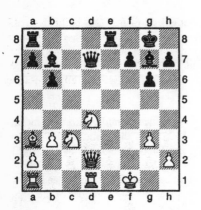

0-1

A sudden end. Fischer was "bitterly
disappointed" by this resignation,
which prevented him from taking the
game to its logical conclusion with 22
♕f2 (22 ♘db5 ♕h3+ 23 ♔g1 ♗h6 and
...♗e3+) 22...♕h3+ 23 ♔g1 ♖e1+!!
24 ♖xe1 ♗xd4, and mate on g2.

Lessons from this game:

1) Accepting an isolated d-pawn
can be a double-edged sword. You
have to weigh up the activity it can give
you against the actual weakness of the
pawn itself. In this game Fischer's decision was fully justified, although
even here Black's position hangs by a
thread.

2) Be sure to look for stronger continuations before reclaiming material
after an initial sacrifice. Instead of
18...♘xg2! and 19...d4! Black could
have easily spoilt things by 18...♘xd1
or 19...♗xe2.

3) Chess history is full of too many
premature resignations in drawn or
even won positions. In this game
White is actually lost in the final position, but it would have been nice for
the crowd to witness a brilliant checkmate.

Game 51
Vasily Smyslov – Mikhail Tal
USSR Team Championship, Moscow 1964
English Opening

The Players

We have already met Vasily Smyslov in Games 34 and 35. The time of this game coincided with a purple patch for the ex-World Champion. After winning the Moscow Tournament in 1963, Smyslov went on a run of seven further successive tournament victories.

Mikhail Tal had a very busy year in 1964. He began it at the legendary Hastings International, which he won, while he also took first place later in the year at the Amsterdam Interzonal, to qualify once more for the Candidates stages of the World Championship. He went on to defeat Portisch and Larsen, before losing to the rising star Boris Spassky. For more information see Game 39.

The Game

Smyslov plays the opening in an insipid fashion, allowing Tal to build up an initiative with the black pieces. The "Magician from Riga" doesn't need any more encouragement. Forceful middlegame play leads to a surprising queen sacrifice. Smyslov immediately returns the material to head for his forte, the endgame. However, on this occasion the odds are stacked against him. Tal duly scores the point in exemplary fashion.

	1	c4	g6
	2	♘c3	♗g7
	3	g3	c5
	4	♗g2	♘c6
	5	b3	

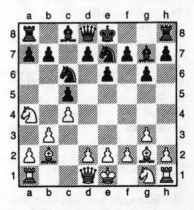

Smyslov showed a fondness for the double fianchetto in this opening, although with this move White is merely looking to achieve a playable middlegame position, rather than seeking any theoretical edge, for which he could aim after the more critical 5 ♘f3 or even 5 a3. Smyslov's actual choice puts Black under no immediate pressure.

	5	...	e6
	6	♗b2	♘ge7
	7	♘a4	

Once more this is rather an extravagance. For the pleasure of obtaining the exchange of the dark-squared bishops White expends some time and is left with an offside knight. Black will achieve a very easy position from the opening.

7	...	♗xb2
8	♘xb2	0-0
9	e3	d5
10	♘f3	♘f5

It is important to prevent, or at least dissuade, White from making the d2-d4 advance. Tal gives 10...b6 11 0-0 ♗b7 12 d4 as slightly better for White. The position after 12 d4 is almost symmetrical, but following the exchange of pawns the white knights will sit nicely on c4 and d4.

11	0-0	b6
12	♘a4	

In the classic book *Learn from the Grandmasters* Tal writes "Summing up the results of the opening, one can say that both sides have completed their development, but Black's pieces are the more harmoniously developed. Possibly only White's bishop can be said to be a better piece than its opposite number, and this, only if Black gets a weakness at d5."

White can try to fix the d5-pawn with 12 d4, but Black simply becomes too dynamic. Tal gives 12...cxd4 13 ♘xd4 (or 13 exd4 ♕f6 14 ♘a4 ♗a6 15 ♖e1 ♘fxd4 16 ♘xd4 ♘xd4 17 cxd5 ♖ac8) 13...♘cxd4 14 exd4 ♗a6 15 ♖e1 ♕f6 16 cxd5 ♖ad8 and Black will capture on d4, when his pieces are much more active.

12	...	♗b7
13	cxd5	exd5
14	d3	

Tal once again dismissed 14 d4 with 14...cxd4 15 g4 ♘h4 16 ♘xd4 ♘xd4 17 ♕xd4 ♘xg2 18 ♔xg2 ♖e8 19 ♘c3 ♖c8, when the threat of ...♖xc3 is very annoying. Even after 20 ♖ac1 Black can still play 20...♖xc3, as 21 ♖xc3 ♖e4 22 ♕d1 d4 promises Black unpleasant threats against the white king.

With 14 d3, White hasn't given up on the idea of d4, but wishes to be in a stronger position before carrying out the advance.

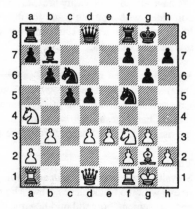

14	...	♕f6
15	♕d2	♖ad8
16	♖fd1	♖fe8
17	♖ab1	

Tal thought this move, preparing b4, was too optimistic, preferring 17 ♖ac1. Note that 17 d4 is still no good after 17...cxd4 18 ♘xd4 ♘fxd4 19 exd4 ♘xd4! 20 ♕xd4 ♖e1+, winning material.

17	...	♘d6
18	♘e1	d4!

The right time for this advance. White is virtually forced to block the centre, but Black is well placed to strike out with ...f5. It must have been around this time that Tal spotted the stunning idea which he executed on move 24.

19	e4	♕e7
20	♘c2	f5

| 21 | exf5 | ♘e5 |
| 22 | f4 | ♘f3+! |

The correct method. Tempting is 22...♗xg2, which works after 23 fxe5 ♗a8 24 exd6 ♕b7 and White will be mated. Unfortunately White has the simple 23 ♕xg2, which leaves Black rather embarrassed.

| 23 | ♗xf3 | ♗xf3 |
| 24 | ♖e1 | |

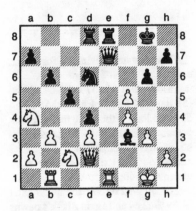

| 24 | ... | ♕e2!! |

This was the only logical way forward, and I suspect that the idea was totally overlooked by Smyslov. White has to accept the offer, but feels obliged to return the material immediately.

| 25 | ♖xe2 | ♖xe2 |
| 26 | ♕xe2 | |

If White holds on to the queen with 26 ♕c1, Black continues 26...♖g2+ 27 ♔f1 ♖xh2 28 ♘e1 ♗d5 29 ♖b2 ♖h1+ 30 ♔f2 ♖e8 and, despite the material advantage, White is completely tied up.

26 ♕xe2 results in an endgame where White's weakness on d3 gives Black a definite advantage.

| 26 | ... | ♗xe2 |
| 27 | ♘b2 | gxf5 |

28	♖e1	♗h5
29	♘c4	♘xc4
30	bxc4	♖e8
31	♔f2	♖xe1
32	♔xe1?	

Tal criticized this move, stating that 32 ♘xe1, with the idea of transferring the knight to e5 as soon as possible, would have been stronger. White would still be suffering, but he would keep good drawing chances.

32	...	♔f8
33	♔d2	♔e7
34	♘e1	a6
35	a4	a5

It is important to fix this pawn on a light square. It could be won immediately with 35...♗e8, but 36 a5 bxa5 37 ♘f3 allows the white knight to get to e5.

36	♔c2	♗e8
37	♔b3	♗c6
38	♔a3	♔f6
39	♔b3	♔g6
40	♔a3	♔h5
41	h3	

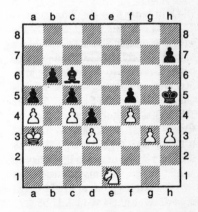

This was the adjourned position. Black's advantage lies in his better minor piece, plus White's weak pawns on a4 and d3. Even so, to win the game requires some masterly technique.

41	...	♔g6
42	♔b3	♔g7
43	♔a3	♔f6
44	♔b3	♗e8
45	♘g2	

White soon gets into zugzwang after 45 ♘f3 ♗h5 46 ♘e5 ♗d1+ 47 ♔a3 ♔e6! 48 ♘c6 ♗e2 49 ♘e5 h6! 50 g4 ♗f1 (or 50...♗d1).

45	...	♗h5
46	♔c2	♗e2
47	♘e1	♗f1
48	♘f3	

White will not be provoked into weakening his kingside. Following 48 h4 Black wins easily by transferring his bishop back to c6 and then penetrating on the kingside with his king, e.g. 48...♗e2 49 ♔d2 ♗h5 50 ♔c2 ♗e8 51 ♔b3 ♗c6 52 ♘c2 ♔g6 53 ♘e1 ♔h5 and White can already resign.

48	...	♗xh3

There was an alternative win to be had with 48...h6 (preventing ♘g5) 49 ♘e5 ♗xh3:

1) In *Learn from the Grandmasters* Tal cites analysis of 50 ♔d2 by the Moscow master Shatskes. The black bishop has problems extricating itself, but this proves to be irrelevant after 50...♔e6 51 ♔d1 ♗g4+! (Tal's original analysis had run 51...♗g2 52 ♔e2 ♗b7 53 ♔d2 ♗c8 54 ♔c2 ♗d7 55 ♘xd7! ♔xd7 56 ♔d2 ♔e6 57 ♔e2 ♔f7 58 ♔f3 ♔g6 59 ♔g2 ♔h5 60 ♔h3 and White draws as Black has no tempo moves with his pawns; this is why Tal left his pawn at h7) 52 ♘xg4 fxg4 53 ♔e1 h5 54 ♔d2 ♔d7 55 ♔e2 ♔d8!! and the black king is perfectly placed for the pawn breaks and races that are to follow.

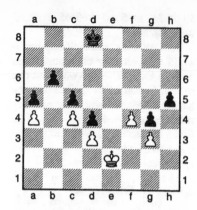

This endgame is winning for Black, e.g.:

1a) 56 ♔e1 b5! 57 cxb5 c4! 58 b6 (58 dxc4 h4 59 gxh4 g3 and 58 f5 h4 59 f6 h3 lead to the same result: Black promotes first) 58...h4 59 gxh4 c3 60 h5 g3 61 h6 g2 62 ♔f2 c2 63 h7 g1♕+! 64 ♔xg1 c1♕+ and the extra queen will mop up.

1b) 56 ♔d2 b5 57 cxb5 h4 58 gxh4 g3 59 ♔e2 c4 and again Black's pawns are faster. In these variations speed is paramount, not the number of pawns!

2) White can also try 50 ♘d7+:

2a) White is still in the game after 50...♔e6 51 ♘xb6 ♗g2 52 ♘c8 ♗c6 53 ♔b3 ♗d7 54 ♘a7!.

2b) 50...♔g6 51 ♘xb6 ♔h5 52 ♘d7 ♔g4 53 ♘xc5 ♔xg3 54 ♘e6 ♗g2 55 ♘xd4 and it's not over.

2c) The most accurate move-order is the paradoxical 50...♔e7! 51 ♘xb6 ♔d8!, when the knight has no future, for example 52 ♘d5 ♗g2 with another branch:

2c1) 53 ♔b3 ♗xd5! 54 cxd5 ♔d7 55 ♔c4 ♔d6 56 ♔b5 ♔xd5 57 ♔xa5 c4 and Black wins the king and pawn ending after 58 ♔b4 (or 58 dxc4+ ♔c5 and the d-pawn promotes) 58...cxd3

59 ♔b3 ♔e4 60 a5 ♔e3 61 a6 d2 62 ♔c2 ♔e2.

2c2) White's final chance is to avoid the exchange of minor pieces with 53 ♘f6. Nevertheless, Black can still get the knight, it's just that he won't have to lose the bishop in the process! After 53...♔e7! 54 ♘g8+ ♔e6 55 ♘xh6 ♗h3! 56 ♔d2 ♔f6 the knight is well and truly corralled and will have to give itself up for a pawn.

That said, Tal's move is also quite sufficient for victory.

>   49　♘g5　　♗g2
>   50　♘xh7+　♔g7
>   51　♘g5　　♔g6
>   52　♔d2

Perhaps White's biggest problem in this endgame is that the knight is just not mobile enough to stop any passed pawns that Black obtains. This is seen in the variation 52 ♘e6 ♔h5 53 ♘c7 ♔g4 54 ♘d5 ♔xg3 55 ♘xb6 ♔xf4 56 ♘d7 ♔e3 57 ♘xc5 f4 and there is nothing White can do to stop the f-pawn promoting.

>   52　...　　　♗c6
>   53　♔c1

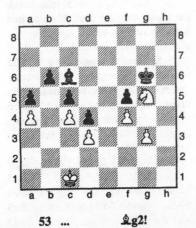

>   53　...　　　♗g2!

Excellent technique. It would be easy to grab the a-pawn, but 53...♗xa4 54 ♘f3 allows the knight of its box and complicates the victory. 53...♗g2 prepares the decisive advance of the black king.

>   54　♔d2　　　♔h5

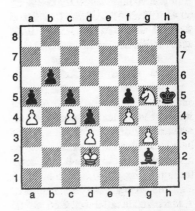

>   55　♘e6

White has other choices, but all roads eventually lead to Rome:

1) 55 ♔e2 ♔g4 56 ♔f2 ♗c6 57 ♘f7 ♗xa4 58 ♘h6+ ♔h5 59 ♘xf5 ♗d7 60 ♘d6 a4 61 ♘e4 a3 62 ♘d2 ♗a4 and the a-pawn promotes. This is another striking demonstration of the power of a bishop over a knight when there are pawns on both sides of the board.

2) 55 ♘f7 ♔g4 56 ♘h6+ ♔xg3 57 ♘xf5+ ♔xf4 58 ♘e7 ♔e5 59 ♘c8 (or 59 ♔c2 ♔e6 60 ♘g6 ♗c6 61 ♔b3 ♔f6 62 ♘f4 ♔f5 and the black king reaches e3) 59...♗c6 60 ♘xb6 ♔d6 61 ♔e2 ♔c7 62 ♘d5+ ♗xd5 63 cxd5 ♔d6 64 ♔d2 ♔xd5 65 ♔c2 c4 66 dxc4+ ♔xc4 67 ♔d2 ♔b4 68 ♔d3 ♔xa4 69 ♔xd4 ♔b3 and the a-pawn goes through.

>   55　...　　　♔g4

56	♘c7	♝c6
57	♘d5	♚xg3
58	♘e7	♝d7!

Once again Black's approach is faultless. Keeping the f-pawn is more important than keeping the b-pawn, so 58...♝d7 is stronger than 58...♝xa4, after which Tal gives 59 ♘xf5+ ♚xf4 60 ♘e7 ♚e5 61 ♘c8 ♝d7 62 ♘xb6 ♝c6 63 ♚c2 ♚d6? 64 ♚b3 ♚c7, when White has the saving 65 ♘a4.

59	♘d5	♝xa4
60	♘xb6	♝e8

A slight inaccuracy, as Tal pointed out. 60...♝c6! 61 ♘d5 ♚f3 62 ♘e7 ♝d7 63 ♘d5 a4 leads to a quicker win.

61	♘d5	♚f3
62	♘c7	♝c6
63	♘e6	a4
64	♘xc5	a3
65	♘b3	

Once again after 65 ♘e6 a2 66 ♘xd4+ ♚xf4 67 ♘c2 ♝a4 68 ♘a1 ♚g3 the knight cannot cope with both passed pawns.

The rest of the game is relatively straightforward. The f-pawn proves decisive.

65	...	a2
66	♚c1	♚xf4
67	♚b2	♚e3
68	♘a5	♝e8
69	c5	f4
70	c6	♝xc6!
71	♘xc6	f3
72	♘e5	f2

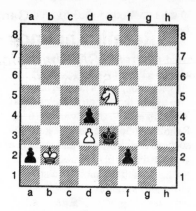

0-1

After 73 ♘g4+ ♚e2 74 ♘xf2 ♚xf2 75 ♚xa2 ♚e2 Black takes on d3 and promotes the d-pawn.

Lessons from this game:

1) There's a difference between playing solidly and playing passively. In this game Smyslov was ultimately punished for his overly quiet opening play.

2) Knights are not very good at stopping passed pawns in the endgame, especially ones near the edge of the board. Even if they are able to block the pawn, they are tied down to this function and cannot influence events elsewhere.

3) Tal was renowned as a tactical wizard, but this game demonstrates that he could also play a mean positional game.

Ratmir Kholmov – David Bronstein

USSR Championship, Kiev 1964

Sicilian Defence, Najdorf Variation

The Players

Ratmir Kholmov (born 1925) is a Lithuanian grandmaster who had a long and successful career without reaching the absolute top level of Soviet chess. He competed in 16 Soviet Championships from 1948 to 1972, his best result being joint first with Spassky and Stein in 1963 (although Stein won the play-off). His direct attacking style sometimes led to severe defeats, but on his day he could be dangerous to anybody, as this game proves.

David Bronstein (born 1924) came within a whisker of gaining the world championship in 1951, and is one of the most imaginative players of all time. For more details see Game 37.

The Game

Bronstein adopts the Najdorf Variation of the Sicilian, already a provocative choice against an attacking player such as Kholmov, and then goes into an especially risky line of it. Kholmov responds with an unexpected pawn sacrifice. This was later shown to be incorrect, but in the game Bronstein immediately slips up with a natural but erroneous pawn-push. Kholmov is in his element and simply blows Bronstein away with a stream of elegant tactics.

1	e4	c5
2	♘f3	♘f6
3	♘c3	d6
4	d4	cxd4
5	♘xd4	a6
6	♗g5	e6
7	f4	♗e7
8	♕f3	♕c7
9	0-0-0	♘bd7
10	g4	b5
11	♗xf6	gxf6

By far the most common move today is 11...♘xf6. The risky text-move was introduced by Fischer, who astonished everybody by following it up with ...0-0. At first sight suicidal, it turns out that it is not so easy for

White to attack Black's king. Nevertheless, the position is poised on a knife-edge and a slight slip by Black can easily prove fatal.

12	f5	♘e5

In return for White's pressure on e6 and attacking chances, Black has one major asset – the rock-solid knight on e5.

13	♕h3	

The traditional move, as used by Fischer's opponents. The alternative 13 ♕g3 was introduced in the 1990s.

13	...	0-0

A critical moment for White. In the early games with this line White favoured direct attacking moves such as

14 ♖g1 or 14 ♕h6. These days more positional methods are preferred, for example 14 ♗e2, 14 ♗d3 or 14 ♘ce2.

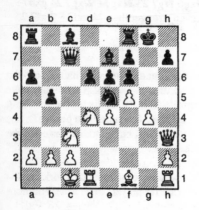

14 g5!?

This move, a remarkable attempt to refute Fischer's line completely, was played for the first and last time in this game.

14 ...   b4?

A natural reply which allows White to gain the advantage with a dazzling combination. Analysis after the game revealed that Black at least equalizes with the correct response 14...fxg5! 15 fxe6 (White can play for the attack with 15 ♖g1, but this is very unconvincing after 15...b4 16 ♘ce2 exf5) 15...fxe6 16 ♘xe6 ♕d7 (not 16...♕b7 17 ♘d5) 17 ♘d5 (17 ♘xf8 ♕xh3 18 ♗xh3 ♗xh3 and the knight is trapped) and now:

1) 17...♕xe6 18 ♕xe6+ ♗xe6 19 ♘xe7+ ♔f7 20 ♘f5 (20 ♘d5 ♗xd5 favours Black) 20...d5 21 ♗g2 with equality.

2) 17...♗d8 18 ♘xd8 ♕xh3 19 ♗xh3 ♗xh3 20 ♘b7 is unclear.

3) 17...♖f3 18 ♕h6 (after 18 ♘b6 ♖xh3 19 ♘xd7 ♗xd7 20 ♗xh3 g4

Black wins material, while 18 ♕h5 ♕xe6 19 ♕e8+ ♗f8 20 ♕xe6+ ♗xe6 21 ♘c7 ♖c8 22 ♘xe6 g4 is slightly better for Black) 18...♕xe6 19 ♕xe6+ ♗xe6 20 ♘xe7+ ♔f7 21 ♘f5 ♗xf5 22 exf5 ♖d8 looks promising for Black, but with accurate play White can draw: 23 ♗g2! ♖xf5 24 ♗e4 ♖f2 25 ♗xh7 ♖h8 26 ♗e4 with general liquidation.

15 gxf6   ♗xf6
16 ♖g1+   ♔h8
17 ♕h6   ♕e7

After 17...♕d8 the knight sacrifice played in the game is even more effective: 18 ♘c6! ♘xc6 19 ♖xd6 ♕e7 20 e5 ♘xe5 (20...♗xe5 21 f6 ♗xf6 22 ♗d3 ♗g5+ 23 ♖xg5 f6 24 ♗xh7 fxg5 25 ♗f5+ ♔g8 26 ♖xe6 ♗xe6 27 ♗xe6+ ♔f7 28 ♘d5 ♕xe6 29 ♕xe6 is winning for White) 21 ♘e4 ♘g6 22 ♘xf6 ♕xf6 23 ♗g2! ♖a7 24 fxg6 fxg6 25 ♖f1 ♕xf1+ 26 ♗xf1 ♖xf1+ 27 ♔d2 and White should win.

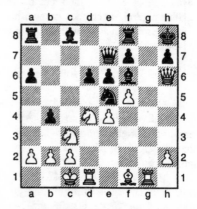

18 ♘c6!!

A truly incredible sacrifice. The logic is that Black's kingside is hanging by a thread, but this state of affairs will exist for only one move. If Black could play ...♗b7 and ...♖g8 then he would have a large advantage thanks to his two active bishops. Thus White must take instant action and the point of this sacrifice is simply to remove the knight from e5 for a moment. Then White has the chance to play e4-e5 and free e4 for his knight. It all looks a bit unbelievable, but analysis shows that White gains the advantage in every line.

18 ...   ♘xc6
19 e5!

After 19 ♖d3, the simplest reply is 19...♗g5+ 20 ♖xg5 f6, followed by 21...bxc3.

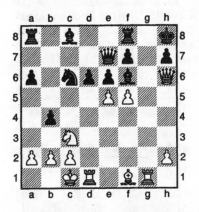

19 ...   ♗g5+?!

This leads to a forced loss. The alternatives offered more defensive chances, although Black has no really satisfactory option:

1) 19...♖g8 20 ♖xg8+ ♔xg8 21 exf6 ♕f8 22 ♕g5+ ♔h8 23 ♘a4 is very good for White, e.g. 23...d5 24 ♘b6 ♖b8 25 ♘xc8 ♖xc8 26 fxe6 fxe6 27 ♗xa6 and Black is a pawn down with a bad position.

2) 19...♘xe5 20 ♘e4 and now:

2a) 20...♕d7 21 ♖xd6 ♖g8 (White wins after 21...♗e5 22 f6 ♗xf6 23

♖xd7) 22 ♖xg8+ ♔xg8 23 ♖xd7 ♗g5+ 24 ♘xg5 ♕xd7 25 f6 and mates.

2b) 20...♘g6 21 ♘xf6 ♕xf6 22 fxg6 ♕g7 23 ♕xg7+ ♔xg7 24 gxh7+ (even stronger than 24 gxf7+ ♔xf7 25 ♖xd6) 24...♔h8 (24...♔xh7 25 ♖d4 and mate) 25 ♖xd6 ♗b7 26 ♗d3 with a large advantage for White.

3) 19...♗xe5 (the best chance) 20 f6! ♗xf6 21 ♗d3 ♗g5+ 22 ♖xg5 and now:

3a) 22...f6 with a final branch:

3a1) 23 ♗xh7 fxg5 24 ♗e4+ ♔g8 25 ♖g1 is a draw after 25...bxc3 26 ♖xg5+ ♕xg5+ 27 ♕xg5+ ♔f7 28 ♗g6+ ♔g8 or unclear after 25...♖a7 26 ♘d5 ♕g7 27 ♖xg5 ♕xg5+. Not, however, 25...♖f7?, when 26 ♘d5! ♕d8 (26...exd5 27 ♖xg5+ ♕xg5+ 28 ♕xg5+ ♔f8 29 ♕xd5 ♗d7 30 ♕xd6+) 27 ♖xg5+ ♕xg5+ 28 ♕xg5+ ♖g7 29 ♘f6+ ♔f7 30 ♕f4 wins for White.

3a2) 23 ♖g3! f5 (23...♖f7 24 ♘e4 d5 25 ♖dg1 ♗b7 26 ♘d6 wins) 24 ♖dg1 ♖a7 25 ♘e4! fxe4 26 ♗xe4 ♕f7 (26...♘d4 27 ♗xh7 is an immediate win for White) 27 ♗xc6 (threatening 28 ♖f3) 27...♕e7 (27...d5 28 ♕e3! also wins) 28 ♗e4 with a decisive attack.

3b) 22...f5 23 ♖dg1! ♖a7 24 ♘e2! (24 ♘e4 fxe4 25 ♗xe4 ♘d4 26 ♗xh7 ♕xg5+ 27 ♖xg5 ♖f1+ 28 ♔d2 ♖xh7 29 ♕g6 ♘f3+ 30 ♔e2 ♘xg5 31 ♔xf1 is slightly better for Black) and White's attack is worth more than Black's two extra pawns. The pressure along the g-file ties Black down and it is hard to find an answer to the simple threat of ♘f4-h5 followed by ♖g7. One line runs 24...♘e5 25 ♘f4 ♕f7 (25...a5 26 ♘h5 ♘g4 27 ♖5xg4 fxg4 28 ♗xh7 wins) 26 ♗e2! (the immediate 26 ♘h5 is met by 26...♘g4) 26...♖c7 27 ♘h5

♘g4 28 ♗xg4 fxg4 29 ♖5xg4 and
White wins.

20 ♖xg5   f6

Black regains his extra piece, since
21 exf6 ♖xf6 attacks the queen, but
Kholmov has everything under control.

21 exd6   ♕f7
22 ♖g3!   bxc3

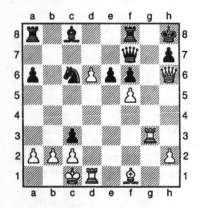

23 ♗c4!

Not 23 ♗e2 ♖d8! 24 ♖dg1 ♖a7 25
♗h5 ♕f8 26 ♕xf8+ ♖xf8 27 ♖xc3
♘d4 with an unclear ending.

After the text-move, there is no real
answer to the threat of taking twice on
e6, followed by either ♕g7# or ♕xf8#.

23 ...   cxb2+
24 ♔b1   ♘d8

Other moves also lose:

1) 24...♖g8 25 ♖xg8+ ♕xg8 (or
25...♔xg8 26 fxe6 ♗xe6 27 ♗xe6
♕xe6 28 ♖g1+) 26 d7 ♗xd7 27 ♖xd7
♕g1+ 28 ♔xb2 ♖b8+ 29 ♗b3 wins.

2) 24...♖e8 25 d7 ♗xd7 26 ♖xd7
♖e7 27 fxe6 ♖b8 (a nice try, but unavailing) 28 ♖c7 wins.

3) 24...♖d8 25 fxe6 ♕f8 26 e7
♘xe7 27 dxe7 ♖xd1+ 28 ♔xb2 ♖b8+
29 ♔c3 and mates.

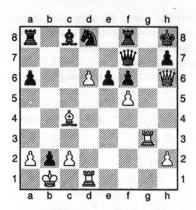

25 ♖dg1?!

25 d7 ♗xd7 (25...♗b7 26 fxe6
♘xe6 27 ♗xe6) 26 ♖xd7 would have
been a simpler win, but this slip makes
no difference to the result.

25 ...   ♖a7

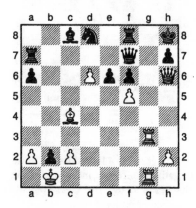

26 d7!

A neat finish, based on a problem
theme – the so-called Novotny interference. Black's rook must guard the
second rank, or else ♖g7 wins, and his
bishop must guard e6, or else White
wins by taking twice on e6. By dropping a unit on the intersection point of
the two guard lines, White forces Black

to block one or the other. White could also have won boringly but efficiently by 26 ♗e2 and 27 ♗h5.

26 ...	♖xd7

26...♗xd7 fails to 27 ♖g7.

27 fxe6	♘xe6
28 ♗xe6	

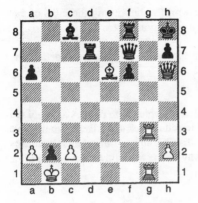

28 ...	♖d1+

The only move, but it merely prolongs the game a little.

29 ♖xd1	♗xe6
30 ♔xb2	♖b8+

Or 30...♗xa2 31 ♖d7 ♖b8+ 32 ♔a3! and wins.

31 ♔a1	♗xa2
32 ♖gd3	

Black cannot both counter the threat of 33 ♖d8+ and defend his bishop.

32 ...	♛e7
33 ♔xa2	♛e6+
34 ♖b3	1-0

Lessons from this game:

1) Broken pawns in front of a castled king spell danger.

2) When defensive pieces are overburdened, look for a tactical solution.

3) Outrageous-looking moves do sometimes work – but not very often!

Game 53
Efim Geller – Vasily Smyslov
Candidates match (game 5), Moscow 1965
Grünfeld Defence, Classical Exchange Variation

The Players

Efim Geller (born 1925) was among the world's elite during the most of the 1950s and 1960s. See Game 31 for more information.

Vasily Smyslov (born 1921) was World Champion 1957–8. For career details see Game 34.

The Game

A sharp and dynamic line of the Grünfeld, with which both players are very familiar, becomes a race between White's kingside attack and Black's attempts to destroy White's centre. Geller manages to fuel his attack somewhat better, finding some subtle touches to smooth the way. Some brilliant tactics round off a powerful performance.

1 d4	♘f6
2 c4	g6
3 ♘c3	d5

This move characterizes the Grünfeld Defence, named after Ernst Grünfeld (see Game 20). We have already seen (in Games 38 and 50) Fischer employing minor forms of this opening, i.e. opting for it only when White has foregone the most critical replies. Here Geller is given the possibility, which he takes up, of playing the most aggressive and double-edged system of all, the Exchange Variation.

4 cxd5	♘xd5
5 e4	♘xc3
6 bxc3	♗g7

White has set up a big pawn-centre, which Black will try to destroy, or at least immobilize and weaken. White's task is to keep the pawns mobile and strong, or else to use them as cover for an attack.

7 ♗c4

At the time this was considered White's only reasonable move, on the basis that the knight needed to come to e2, since on f3 it would be subject to an annoying pin by ...♗g4. However, perceptions of these things change over the years, and 7 ♘f3 c5 8 ♖b1 is today considered the most critical test of Black's resources.

7 ... c5

This is an absolutely standard lever against White's pawn-centre in the Exchange Grünfeld. Quite often the tension between the d4- and c5-pawns will be maintained for several moves. Black does not generally exchange on d4 until there is something specific to be gained from doing so – he may instead prefer to keep the position closed, pushing the pawn on to c4 in some cases. White, meanwhile, is unlikely to want to take on c5 even if there are no tactical problems with the c3-square, as the capture leaves his pawn-centre as just a collection of weaknesses. It is more normal for White to consider pushing on in the centre with d4-d5, after due preparation. Generally, as in this game, both sides develop rapidly before changing the central structure.

12 f4

With this extremely aggressive move White aims to take advantage of the fact that Black has left f7 rather weak. 12 &f4 is more popular nowadays, and has scored so well for White that this whole system has lost its popularity for Black, at top level at least.

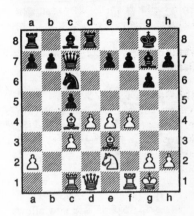

8	♘e2	0-0
9	0-0	♘c6
10	&e3	♕c7

This is known as the Smyslov System, so it comes as no surprise that Smyslov plays it! There are two other Smyslov Variations in the Grünfeld, which gives you some idea how much of an expert Smyslov was in this opening, and therefore how great Geller's achievement in this game.

10...&g4 11 f3 ♘a5 is the main line, when play normally continues 12 &d3 (12 &xf7+ ♖xf7 13 fxg4 is Karpov's speciality, but few others are willing to take on White's rather awkward position) 12...cxd4 13 cxd4 &e6, when in order to keep the initiative White tends to sacrifice a pawn (14 ♖c1) or the exchange (14 d5).

| 11 | ♖c1 | ♖d8 |

| 12 | ... | e6 |

12...&g4 is a more ambitious and critical response. Then 13 f5 gxf5 14 h3 leads to very sharp and complex play, in which Black seems able to hold his own.

13 &h1!

Geller shows an excellent understanding of the position. One of Black's main ideas in this line is to play ...f5 (after suitable preparation, such as ...b6, ...&b7 and ...♘a5 to force the bishop off the a2–g8 diagonal). This flexible and useful king move prepares the manoeuvre ♘g1-f3-e5, exploiting the fact that Black would then have no pawns capable of evicting the knight from e5. It is also often useful for the e3-bishop to be able to drop back to g1, for example if Black's knight comes in to c4 at some point.

Instead, 13 f5 exf5 14 ♗g5 ♖f8 15 exf5 ♗xf5 is unclear – but this idea is worth bearing in mind, as White can seek an improved version of it.

    13 ...   **b6**
    14 f5!

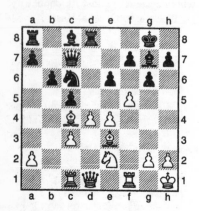

    14 ...   **♘a5**

14...exf5 15 ♗g5 ♖f8 now allows White a pleasant choice of dangerous continuations:

1) 16 d5 ♘a5 (16...♘e5 17 d6) 17 d6 ♕d7 18 ♗d5 ♗b7 19 exf5 is quite good for White, e.g. 19...♗xd5 20 ♕xd5 ♖ae8 21 f6 ♖xe2 22 fxg7 ♖fe8 23 ♕f3 possibly followed by ♗e7.

2) 16 ♘f4!? and then:

2a) 16...h6 17 ♘d5 ♕b7 18 ♗b5 ♗d7 (18...♔h8!?) 19 ♘f6+ ♗xf6 20 ♗xf6 gives Black an awkward defensive task, e.g. 20...fxe4 21 ♕d2 ♔h7 22 ♖f4 ♖ae8 23 ♖h4 e3 24 ♕e1 h5 25 ♖xh5+ gxh5 26 ♕h4 forcing mate.

2b) 16...♘a5 17 ♘d5 ♗b7 18 exf5 is good for White.

2c) 16...fxe4 looks like Black's best chance, but 17 ♘d5 offers White good play for the pawn(s).

    15 ♗d3   **exf5**
    16 exf5   **♗b7**

    17 ♕d2!

17 ♗g5? ♖e8 18 ♘f4 cxd4 19 cxd4 ♕d6 gave Black the advantage in a later game Razuvaev – Haag, Polanica Zdroj 1972. Razuvaev hadn't been studying his (modern) classics! Geller's approach is more subtle, amassing his forces for a kingside attack without letting his centre disintegrate any quicker than it has to.

    17 ...   **♖e8**
    18 ♘g3   **♕c6**

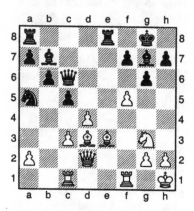

    19 ♖f2!

A multi-purpose move, both preparing to double on the f-file, and covering g2 so as to free the queen for more productive work further up the board.

    19 ...   **♖ad8**

19...♖xe3 20 ♕xe3 cxd4 21 ♕f4 dxc3 22 f6 ♗f8 23 ♘f5 ♔h8 (23...♕e6 24 ♘h6+ ♔h8) 24 ♘h6 ♕e6 25 ♖xc3 denies Black sufficient compensation for the exchange, since 25...♕e1+ 26 ♖f1 ♕xc3 27 ♘xf7+ ♔g8 28 ♘e5 gives White a strong attack, for example 28...♕c5 (28...♕b4 29 f7+ ♔h8 30 ♕f6+ ♗g7 31 ♘xg6+ hxg6 32 ♕xg6 ♕h4 33 ♖f5) 29 f7+ ♔h8 30 ♕f6+

♗g7 31 ♘xg6+ hxg6 32 ♕xg6 ♗xg2+ 33 ♕xg2 ♖c6 34 ♗e4 wins.

	20	♗h6	♗h8
	21	♕f4	♖d7
	22	♘e4	c4

22...♕c7 23 ♖e1 ♗xe4 removes the dangerous knight.

	23	♗c2	♖de7

Black is generating enormous pressure on the e-file and the a8–h1 long diagonal. White would be unable to maintain his knight on e4 by normal means, but he turns out to have sufficient tactical resources.

	24	♖cf1!	♖xe4
	25	fxg6!	f6

Forced. Instead 25...♖xf4?? allows 26 gxh7#, while 25...♕xg6? 26 ♗xe4 ♗xe4 27 ♕xf7+ ♕xf7 28 ♖xf7 wins for White.

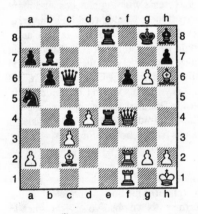

26 ♕g5!

Threatening 27 g7. The queen is invulnerable due to the mate on f8.

	26	...	♕d7
	27	♔g1!	

Now White intends 28 ♖xf6 ♗xf6 29 ♕xf6 hxg6 30 ♕xg6+ ♔h8 31 ♗g5 ♖4e6 32 ♗f6+ ♖xf6 33 ♖xf6!, when 33...♖e1+ would be just a "spite" check. White could not play this immediately because after 27 ♖xf6 ♗xf6 28 ♕xf6 hxg6 29 ♕xg6+ ♔h8 30 ♗g5 ♖4e6 31 ♗f6+ ♖xf6 he would have to recapture with the queen, 32 ♕xf6+ (32 ♖xf6?? allows 32...♖e1+ mating), when 32...♕g7 is good for Black.

	27	...	♗g7

Black turns out to be quite powerless in the face of White's plan.

	28	♖xf6	♖g4

28...♗xf6 29 ♕xf6 hxg6 30 ♕xg6+ ♔h8 31 ♗g5 ♖4e6 32 ♗f6+ ♖xf6 33 ♖xf6! carries out the threat mentioned above, winning.

	29	gxh7+	♔h8
	30	♗xg7+	♕xg7
	31	♕xg4	1-0

31...♕xg4 32 ♖f8+ ♖xf8 33 ♖xf8+ ♔g7 34 h8♕#.

Lessons from this game:

1) A big pawn-centre can be used as cover for an attack. Even if the centre cannot survive indefinitely, it may buy enough time to launch the offensive successfully.

2) King safety is an important positional factor. Here we saw Black's pressure down the e-file and on the long diagonal coming to nought because of a "local problem" on the kingside.

3) If there is some tactical problem with your intended line of play, don't give up on it, but try to find a way to circumvent the difficulty (here Geller's 27 ♔g1 not only gave him a threat, but made it completely irresistible).

Game 54
Mikhail Tal – Bent Larsen
Candidates match (game 10), Bled 1965
Sicilian Defence, Classical Variation

The Players

Mikhail Tal (1936–92) was World Champion 1960–1, and one of the greatest attacking players of all time. See Game 39 for more information.

Bent Larsen was one of the first Western players to mount a serious challenge to the Soviet domination of post-war chess. He was born in north-west Jutland, Denmark, in 1935. He learned to play chess at the age of 12, while recovering from illness. He quickly made progress, and gained his international master title in 1955, and the grandmaster title the next year, when he made the best score on top board in the Moscow Olympiad. He soon established himself as clearly the best Western European player. During the 1960s he was a regular and successful tournament competitor, regularly winning international events ahead of the leading Soviet players. His success was founded on his provocative style; he would happily take risks to disturb the balance and create winning chances, and more often than not his fighting spirit and resourcefulness would prevail. However, in match play this strategy proved less successful. His disastrous loss in the Candidates semi-final to Fischer in 1971 brought to an end his hopes of becoming world champion, though he continued to play at top level until the late 1980s, and to this day he continues to play occasionally. He is a prolific chess journalist, and also assisted Zsuzsa Polgar in her quest for the Women's World Championship in the mid-1990s. Although he no longer lives in Denmark, preferring both the climate and tax laws in South America, he has inspired a great deal of enthusiasm for chess in his native land, where he remains a household name.

The Game

This was the last scheduled game of the match, in which the score stood level at 4½–4½. In this extremely tense situation, Tal burns his boats completely, going all-out for the win with a speculative sacrifice. As we observe several times in this book when Tal storms a fundamentally sound position, there is a fleeting chance for the defender to hold his position together. Here it is on move 17 that Larsen misses a chance to secure a good game. Thereafter it is one-way traffic and Tal scores a brilliant victory.

1	e4	c5
2	♘f3	♘c6
3	d4	cxd4
4	♘xd4	e6

5	♘c3	d6
6	♗e3	♘f6
7	f4	♗e7
8	♕f3	0-0

9 0-0-0

While preparing for this game, Tal and his trainer Koblencs had correctly guessed Larsen's choice of opening and played the following game from this position (with Tal playing White): 9 ♗e2 ♗d7 10 0-0-0 ♘xd4 11 ♗xd4 ♗c6 (11...♕a5 12 e5 dxe5 13 fxe5 ♗c6 14 exf6 ♗xf3 15 fxe7 ♖fe8 16 gxf3) 12 g4 ♕a5 13 g5 ♘d7 14 ♖hg1 b5 15 ♕h5 b4 16 ♖d3! bxc3 17 ♗xc3 ♕xa2? (17...♕a4) 18 ♖h3 ♗xe4 19 g6 ♗xg6 20 ♕xh7+! 1-0.

One positive result of the training game was the text-move, which they considered more energetic than 9 ♗e2.

9 ... ♕c7

This move is directed against White's intended g4.

After 9...♗d7, 10 ♖g1!? has scored well for White in recent practice, e.g. 10...♘xd4 11 ♗xd4 ♗c6 12 g4 ♕a5 13 g5 ♘d7 14 ♕h5 ♖fc8 15 ♖g3 ♘f8 ("you can't get mated with a knight on f8" – an old chess saying that doesn't always apply) 16 f5 exf5 17 ♗c4 ♗e8 18 ♘d5 ♗d8 19 ♘f6+ 1-0 Ulybin – Van den Doel, Leeuwarden 1995.

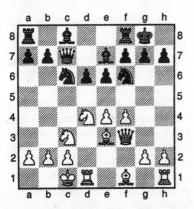

10 ♘db5

However, with this move, gaining time on the queen to cut out ...♘xd4 ideas, White nevertheless achieves the g4 advance.

10 g4?! ♘xd4 11 ♗xd4 (11 ♖xd4 e5 12 ♖c4 ♗xg4!) 11...e5 is similar to the note to Black's 13th move, but with the black queen more actively placed, but also more exposed, e.g. 12 g5 (12 fxe5 dxe5 13 ♕g3 has been White's choice whenever this line has occurred in high-level practice, but it is none too convincing for White) 12...♗g4 (12...exd4! is probably better still) 13 ♕g3 and then:

1) 13...♗xd1 14 gxf6 ♗xf6 and now there is no 15 ♘d5 because of 15...♕xc2#, but White can play 15 fxe5 dxe5 16 ♘xd1.

2) 13...exd4 14 ♖xd4 (14 gxf6 dxc3 15 fxe7 cxb2+ followed by ....♗xd1 is not good for White here) 14...♘xe4 (14...♗e6 15 gxf6 ♗xf6 16 ♘d5) and White has a choice between 15 ♖xe4 and 15 ♘xe4, with fairly unclear play.

10 ... ♕b8
11 g4 a6
12 ♘d4 ♘xd4
13 ♗xd4 b5

Both players felt that this was a critical moment. Larsen wrote that it would be theoretically important to establish what would happen after 13...e5, while Tal argued that Black has to try the move, since after 13...b5 "it is immediately easy to see that White's attack threatens to break through more quickly, which is of decisive significance in such positions."

After 13...e5 Tal's analysis ran 14 g5 ♗g4 15 ♕g3 and now:

1) 15...exd4 16 gxf6 dxc3 17 fxe7 cxb2+ 18 ♔b1 ♗xd1 and "the position is simplified, and Black has good

defensive chances" – Tal. Nunn provides the continuation 19 ℤg1 g6 20 exf8♕+ ♕xf8 21 ♗c4 ♗h5 22 ♗d5, with the better chances for White.

2) 15...ℤxd1 16 gxf6 ♗xf6 17 ♘d5 is very good for White, for example: 17...♔h8 18 ♘xf6 gxf6 19 ℤg1 ℤg8 20 ♕h4; 17...exd4 18 ♘xf6+ ♔h8 19 ℤg1; 17...♕d8 18 ♗b6 exf4 19 ♕a3; or 17...♗d8 18 fxe5 ♗h5 19 e6 ♗g6 20 e7.

14 g5   ♘d7

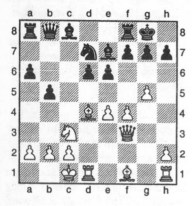

15 ♗d3

15 a3 was Tal's first thought here, preventing the knight being displaced from c3. However, he was attracted by a sacrificial idea (15 ♗d3 b4 16 ♘d5), and after some analysis of the two lines, including seeing the game continuation as far as move 18, had to make a decision. He recounts that in the end the decision was made by the thought "Misha, if you lose the match in the end, in no way will cowardice have been the reason for your defeat", and he went for the knight sacrifice. After 15 a3, 15...b4 16 axb4 ♕xb4 17 ♕h5 ℤb8 18 ℤd3 ♕xb2+ 19 ♔d2 seemed promising to Tal – this has

certain similarities to the training game cited in the note to White's 9th move above, though Black has more counterplay here.

15 ...   b4

Of course, whenever Black plays this move in the Sicilian, the ♘d5 sacrifice is an idea to be considered. Perhaps Larsen did not imagine in this instance it was to be taken very seriously, otherwise he might have preferred 15...♗b7. Tal would have met this by 16 a3, when Black no longer has the option of playing ...b4 and recapturing with the queen.

16 ♘d5!?

This is the sacrifice that has made this game rightly famous.

16 ...   exd5
17 exd5

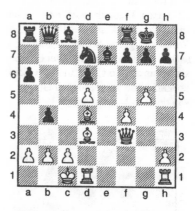

To quote Tal again: "The 16th move was a purely positional sacrifice. The black pieces stand crowded together on the queenside (rook on a8, queen on b8, bishop on c8) and it will not be easy for them to hurry to the aid of their king. The open e-file acts as a barrier and both white bishops are aimed at the enemy king." That said,

White also has some distinctly tactical threats: the "routine" double bishop sacrifice, i.e. 18 ♗xh7+ ♚xh7 19 ♕h5+ ♚g8 20 ♗xg7! ♚xg7 21 ♕h6+ ♚g8 22 g6, winning, and the simple double attack 18 ♕e4. These threats are easy enough to parry, but, however Black chooses to do so, further weaknesses will be created, adding to White's "purely positional" compensation.

This game provides a fine example that the distinction so often made between positional and tactical play is artificial. In reality the two go completely hand-in-hand: positional play needs to be backed up by accurate tactics, and here we see Tal launching a vicious sacrificial onslaught, yet he is motivated by positional factors.

17 ...   f5

"Larsen attempts to defend h7 ... but in doing so he increases the scope of White's dark-squared bishop" – Tal.

17...g6! has been the subject of considerable analysis over the years, and appears to be quite acceptable:

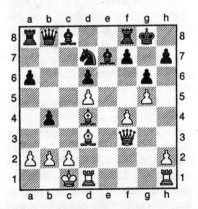

1) 18 ♕h3?! ♘f6 19 ♕h6 ♘h5 20 f5 (what else?) 20...♗xf5 returns the

piece in order to trap the queen: 21 ♗xf5 ♖e8 and ...♗f8.

2) 18 h4 ♘c5 19 ♗xc5 (19 h5 may be met by 19...♘xd3+ followed by ...♗f5) 19...dxc5 20 h5 ♖a7 defends well enough.

3) 18 ♖de1 ♗d8 (18...♖e8 19 ♗f6 wins back the piece with advantage) 19 ♕h3 is a critical moment:

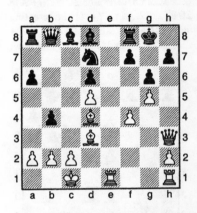

3a) 19...♘f6? is now no good since the queen will be safe on h6 for long enough: 20 ♕h6 ♘h5 21 ♗e2 wins, e.g. 21...♗b6 22 ♗f6.

3b) 19...♘c5? 20 ♕h6 ♘xd3+ (or 20...f6 21 ♗xg6!) comes to the same thing as 19...♘e5 20 ♕h6 ♘xd3+?.

3c) 19...♗b6! 20 ♗xg6! and White forces mate in at most six more moves: 20...♘f6 21 ♕h6 fxg6 (21...♗xd4 22 gxf6) 22 ♖e7 ♖f7 23 gxf6 ♗f5 24 ♖xf7 ♚xf7 25 ♕g7+ ♚e8 26 ♕e7#; or 20...fxg6 21 ♖e7 ♖f7 (21...♘f6 22 ♕h6 transposes to the 20...♘xf6 line) 22 ♕e6 ♘e5 23 ♕xf7+! ♘xf7 24 ♖e8#.

3d) 19...♘e5! 20 ♕h6 ♗b6! (this is the deeply concealed resource that questions the correctness of Tal's sacrifice; the chances of any opponent finding this over the board while deciding on his 17th move are remote; 20...♘xd3+? 21 cxd3 ♕c7+ 22 ♔b1 f6 23 gxf6 {threatening ♖e7} 23...♕f7 24 ♕g7+! ♕xg7 25 fxg7 will leave White the exchange up since the f8-rook cannot move for fear of ♖e8+) 21 fxe5 (21 ♗xb6 ♘xd3+; 21 ♗xe5 dxe5 22 fxe5) 21...♗xd4 22 ♖e4 ♕a7 (22...♗xe5 23 ♖h4 ♖e8 24 ♕xh7+ ♔f8 25 ♖f1; 22...♗f2!? is also interesting and unclear) 23 ♖h4 f5 24 exf6 ♗e3+ (24...♗f5 25 ♖xd4) 25 ♔b1 and now:

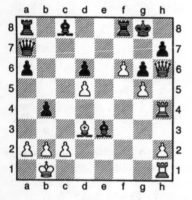

3d1) 25...♗f5 26 ♗xf5 gxf5 27 ♖h3 (threatening ♖xe3, and angling for g5-g6 if the bishop moves) 27...♖f7 28 ♖e1 ♗d2 29 ♖d1 ♕f2 30 ♕h5 ♖c7 31 g6 h6 (31...♗h6?? 32 f7+ ♔h8 33 g7+) 32 ♕f3 (simplification is now White's best course) 32...♕xf3 33 ♖xf3 ♗g5 34 ♖xf5 ♖f8 35 ♖df1 ♖c4 and Black seems to be OK.

3d2) 25...♖xf6! 26 ♖e1 ♗f5 27 ♖xe3 ♖f7 (27...♕xe3?? 28 ♕xh7+ ♔f8 29 ♕h8+ ♔e7 30 gxf6+ forces mate; 27...♗xd3?? 28 gxf6) 28 ♖e1 ♕f2 and Black has a good counterattack, while White's pieces are tied up on the h-file.

18 ♖de1

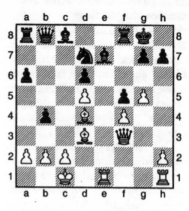

18 ... ♖f7

The drawback to this move is that White is likely to be able to open the g-file, with gain of time on the rook, with g6 at some point.

After 18...♗d8 Tal intended 19 ♕h5 ♘c5 20 ♗xg7! ♘xd3+ 21 ♔b1! (21 cxd3? ♕c7+) and now:

1) 21...♘xf4? 22 ♕h6 ♕b7 23 ♗xf8 is considered under 21...♕b7 22 ♗xf8 ♘xf4? 23 ♕h6.

2) 21...♘xe1? 22 g6! ♔xg7 23 ♕xh7+ ♔f6 and now 24 g7 wins due to the pretty mate 24...♖f7 25 g8♘#. 24 ♕h6 is, as Fritz will point out after a few seconds' thought, a slightly quicker forced mate – it doesn't matter though!

3) 21...♔xg7? 22 ♕h6+ ♔g8 23 g6 ♕c7 24 ♖hg1 wins.

4) 21...♕b7 22 ♗xf8 ♘xe1 (not 22...♘xf4? 23 ♕h6 ♕f7 24 ♗xd6 ♘xd5 {24...♘g6 25 h4} 25 ♖hg1 intending g6) 23 ♖xe1 ♕f7 24 ♗xf7+ ♔xf7 25 ♗xd6 with an interesting ending, in which White has three pawns for a piece.

19 h4 ♗b7!

19...♘c5 20 h5 ♘xd3+ 21 ♕xd3 ♗f8 22 g6 ♖e7 23 ♖xe7 ♗xe7 24 h6 leaves Black defenceless.

19...♘f8 shows once more that passive defence doesn't work: 20 h5 ♕c7 21 g6 ♖f6 (21...hxg6 22 hxg6 ♘xg6 23 ♕h5) 22 h6! smashes through on the kingside.

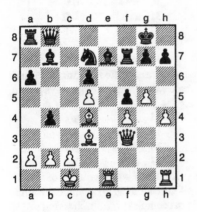

20 ♗xf5!?

White even has the luxury of alternatives by this point:

1) 20 h5 looks promising. Certain sources then claim that 20...♘e5 21 fxe5 ♗xg5+ 22 ♔b1 dxe5 is good for Black, but after 23 ♖xe5 there is nothing decent apparent for Black.

2) 20 g6!? hxg6 21 h5 g5! (an excellent resource to keep lines closed) 22 ♗xf5 (22 h6? g4 23 hxg7 ♗f6) and now:

2a) 22...♖xf5? 23 ♖xe7 ♘e5 24 h6!, e.g. 24...♘xf3 25 h7+ ♔f8 26 ♖xg7 forcing mate.

2b) 22...♘f8 23 h6 ♗f6 (23...g6? 24 h7+ wins) 24 ♕h5! should win for White.

2c) 22...♗f6! (Tal could not see a forced win after this move) 23 ♗e6 and now:

2c1) 23...♗xd4 24 fxg5 (intending g6 – Tal implied this won on the spot; 24 ♗xf7+ ♔xf7 25 ♕e4 is also possible) 24...♕e8 25 ♕g4 ♘c5 26 g6 ♘xe6 27 gxf7+ ♔xf7 28 ♖hf1 and White should be better, but there is plenty of work left to do.

2c2) 23...♕f8 and although Tal was convinced this position ought to be winning, he made the practical decision not to get involved in analysing long variations, given that he had a simpler, and very good alternative. 24 ♗xf6 g4 25 ♕xg4 ♘xf6 26 ♕g5 (intending h6 and ♖eg1) 26...♔h8 27 ♗xf7 (27 h6 ♘h7) 27...♕xf7 28 h6 g6 29 f5 ♘h7 (29...gxf5? 30 ♕g7+ ♕xg7 31 hxg7+ ♔xg7 32 ♖e7+) 30 ♕xg6 ♗xd5 is one sample line – Black may yet hang on.

20 ...   ♖xf5

20...♘f8 21 ♕e4 threatens ♗xh7+ followed by g6.

21 ♖xe7   ♘e5

21...♖f7 is passive. Then 22 ♖xf7 ♔xf7 23 g6+ hxg6 24 h5 opens up the black king.

22 ♕e4   ♕f8

22...♖f7 is refuted by 23 ♖xf7 ♘xf7 24 g6!.

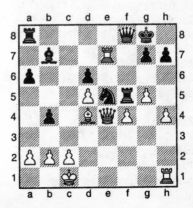

| 23 | fxe5 | ♖f4 |
| 24 | ♕e3 | ♖f3? |

It will come as no surprise that following the pounding he has received so far in this game, Larsen was in time-trouble by this point, and with this error makes White's task easier.

A more resilient line was 24...♗xd5 25 exd6 ♖xd4 26 ♕xd4 ♗xh1 27 b3:

1) 27...♖e8? is neatly refuted by the spectacular move 28 ♕xg7+!! (it is strange that Tal missed this relatively simple trick when writing his notes to the game) 28...♕xg7 29 ♖xe8+ ♔f7 (29...♕f8 30 d7!) 30 ♖e7+ ♔f8 31 ♖xg7 ♔xg7 32 d7 and the pawn promotes.

2) 27...♖c8 28 h5 intending h6.

3) 27...♗f3 (to stop h5, but this means returning the extra piece) 28 ♕c4+ ♔h8 29 ♖f7 ♕xd6 30 ♖xf3 gives Black some chances of saving the game, according to Tal.

25	♕e2	♕xe7
26	♕xf3	dxe5
27	♖e1	♖d8

27...♖f8 28 ♖xe5 ♕xe5 29 ♕xf8+ ♔xf8 30 ♗xe5 ♗xd5 31 ♗d6+ picks off the b4-pawn, with a clearly won ending for White.

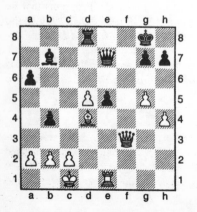

| 28 | ♖xe5 | ♕d6 |
| 29 | ♕f4! | |

With this neat piece of tactics, White secures his two-pawn advantage. The game is decided.

| 29 | ... | ♖f8 |

29...♗xd5? loses the queen to 30 ♖e8+.

30	♕e4	b3
31	axb3	♖f1+
32	♔d2	♕b4+
33	c3	♕d6
34	♗c5!?	

A nice sacrifice to finish, though there were plenty of other ways to win, e.g. 34 b4.

34	...	♕xc5
35	♖e8+	♖f8
36	♕e6+	♔h8
37	♕f7	1-0

Koblencs wrote proudly of his pupil's creation "In my opinion this is the most complex game in chess history on the theme of the sacrifice for the initiative. Is this the chess of the future?" It is tempting to respond "Maybe, but only if there is another Mikhail Tal born in the future!"

Lessons from this game:

1) It takes a lot of courage to sacrifice a piece on the basis of general considerations, but if a sacrifice seems justified and there is no obvious defence for the opponent, it may very well prove successful.

2) Defence demands just as much creativity as attack. In this game Black needed to find some tricky tactics to have a chance of surviving.

3) When mopping up after a successful attack, don't get obsessed with trying to force mate – just concentrate on finding an efficient way to win.

Yakov Estrin – Hans Berliner

5th Correspondence World Championship 1965–8

Two Knights Defence, Berliner Variation

The Players

Yakov Estrin (1923–87) was born in Moscow, and was a lawyer by profession. His over-the-board successes were relatively modest, but in the slower form of the game he excelled. He competed in the final of the World Correspondence Championship five times, emerging as Champion in the 7th contest (1972–6). He loved sharp gambit play. His games often featured "Romantic" gambits, and he wrote extensively on the subject.

Hans Berliner was born in Berlin in 1929, but when he was 8 years old his family emigrated to the USA, where he lives to this day. He learned to play when he was 13 years old and enjoyed considerable success in over-the-board play, representing the USA at the 1952 Olympiad. When he turned to correspondence chess in 1955, his results were phenomenal. He won every event in which he competed, and throughout his career lost only one game, and didn't concede too many draws either. He won the 5th Correspondence World Championship with the fantastic score of 14/16. He did not compete again. The effort involved in these events is phenomenal, and he had proved his dominance beyond any doubt.

His success was based on extremely deep analysis and fantastic opening preparation. He developed a whole new method of decision-making in chess, which he is to expound in print for the first time in late 1998 in a book called *The System: A World Champion's Approach to Chess*.

He has worked extensively with chess-playing computers. Programs that he helped develop won world computer championships in 1985 and in 1989, in the latter year tying for first with Deep Thought (the forerunner to Deep Blue), despite its more advanced hardware.

We would like to thank Dr Berliner for contributing some unpublished analysis of this game from his forthcoming monograph *From the Deathbed of the Two Knights Defense 4 ♘g5*.

The Game

Berliner introduces a brand-new idea in an opening in which Estrin was an expert. It leads to immense and chaotic complications, which Berliner had analysed in painstaking detail prior to the event. Estrin fails to find the right path, and is eventually forced to accept a bad ending, which Berliner plays to perfection to haul in the full point.

1	e4	e5
2	♘f3	♘c6
3	♗c4	♘f6

This move brings about the Two Knights Defence. It is rather rare at grandmaster level, but quite common amongst club players, and among some correspondence players. In this game, Berliner had prepared to play it especially against Estrin, who was regarded as an expert on the opening. This wasn't just bravado – he felt that Estrin's published analysis was unconvincing, and that the 4 ♘g5 line could be refuted.

4 ♘g5

A controversial move. White attacks the f7-pawn, which Black has left rather open. Black will argue that White's loss of time will tell against him.

4 ... d5

4...♗c5 is the only other reasonable move here, and leads to wild complications, with Black immediately sacrificing material.

5 exd5 b5

5...♘a5 is the standard move, with Black claiming compensation after 6 ♗b5+ c6 7 dxc6 bxc6 8 ♗e2.

6 ♗f1

This move looks very odd, but analysis has shown that this is the best square for the bishop, as the knight is unable to attack it, while eventually the threat to take on b5 will need to be addressed.

6 ♗xb5 ♕xd5 is reckoned to be OK for Black.

6	...	♘d4
7	c3	♘xd5
8	♘e4	♕h4!

This move characterizes the Berliner Variation. The alternative 8...♘e6

9 ♗xb5+ ♗d7 10 ♗xd7+ ♕xd7 11 0-0 denies Black sufficient compensation, Spassky – Shamkovich, USSR Championship, Leningrad 1960.

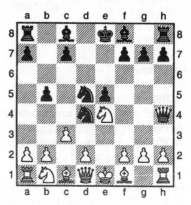

9	♘g3	♗g4
10	f3	e4!

The key discovery made by Berliner in his analysis. 10...♘f5 11 ♗xb5+ ♔d8 12 0-0 ♗c5+ 13 d4! exd4 14 ♘e4 is good for White.

11	cxd4	♗d6
12	♗xb5+	♔d8

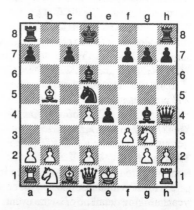

Now the game enters a phase of pure tactics. There is very little scope for strategic planning here – it is mainly calculation that is needed. It would be hardly possible to play such a position well in anything other than a correspondence game.

13 0-0

Or:

1) Not 13 fxg4? ♗xg3+ 14 hxg3 ♕xh1+ 15 ♗f1 ♘b4 16 ♘c3 ♘d3+ 17 ♔e2 ♕g1 18 ♘xe4 ♕xd4 19 ♔f3 ♘e5+ 20 ♔f4 h6 and Black wins.

2) 13 ♕b3 ♗xg3+ 14 ♔d1 ♗e6 15 ♗c6 exf3 16 ♖xd5 (16 ♗xa8? fxg2 17 ♖g1 ♕g4+ wins) 16...fxg2 (16...♕h5? 17 ♕xf3 ♗g4 18 ♗xa8! is good for White) 17 ♕xg3 ♕xg3 18 hxg3 ♗xd5 19 ♖g1 ♖e8! 20 ♘c3 ♗f3+ 21 ♔c2 ♖b8 22 d3 ♖b6 23 ♗f4 (23 ♗d2 ♖g6 24 ♗e1 ♖h6! with a small advantage for Black) 23...h5 was a main line of Berliner's analysis, which he considered about equal.

13 ...   exf3

14 ♖xf3

There were some major alternatives here:

1) 14 ♕e1 fxg2 15 ♖xf7 is an intriguing possibility, but Black should be doing well after 15...♖b8, e.g.:

1a) 16 a4? ♖xb5 17 axb5 ♖e8 wins for Black: 18 ♕f2 ♗xg3 19 ♕xg3 ♖e1+ 20 ♔xg2 ♗h3+ 21 ♔f2 (21 ♕xh3 ♖e2+) 21...♖f1+ 22 ♔e2 ♕e4+.

1b) 16 ♗c6 ♘b4! hits the bishop and prepares to invade on c2 or d3.

1c) 16 ♗a4 ♘f4 17 ♖xf4 (not 17 ♕e4?? ♘e2+) 17...♗xf4 is very dangerous for White, e.g. 18 ♕f2 ♗xg3 19 ♕xg3 ♕f6 20 ♔xg2 ♗f8 and Black wins.

2) 14 ♕b3 was put forward, even years after the game, by Estrin as the refutation of Berliner's idea, though he failed to take into account some

ideas that had been analysed in detail by his opponent prior to their game:

2a) 14...fxg2 15 ♖f2 ♗e6 16 ♕f3 ♖b8 17 ♗c4 ♕xd4 18 d3 and White wins – Estrin.

2b) 14...♘f4 15 ♖xf3 ♖b8 16 ♖xf4 ♖xb5 (16...♗xf4 17 ♕d5+ ♗d6 18 d3 is good for White) 17 ♕xb5 ♗xf4 18 ♕d5+ ♗d7 19 ♘f1 ♗xh2+ 20 ♘xh2 ♕e1+ 21 ♘f1 ♕xc1 22 ♕c5 ♕e1 23 b3 ♖e8 24 ♘c3! ♕xa1 25 ♘d5 gave White a winning position in Estrin – J. Nielsen, 7th Correspondence World Championship 1972–5.

2c) 14...♘b4!! was Berliner's intention:

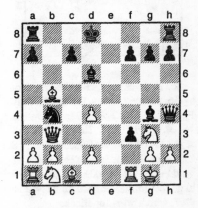

2c1) 15 a3 ♖b8! and now:

2c11) 16 ♗c4 ♗xg3 17 hxg3 ♕xg3 18 ♖f2 ♖e8 19 ♗f1 (19 axb4 ♖e1+ 20 ♗f1 ♖xf1+ 21 ♔xf1 fxg2+ wins the white queen) 19...♖e1! 20 ♕xf7 ♖xf1+ 21 ♔xf1 ♘d3 22 ♕g8+ ♔d7 23 ♕d5+ ♔c8 24 ♕g8+ ♔b7 25 ♕b3+ ♔a8 26 ♕d5+ ♖b7 27 ♕d8+ ♗c8 28 ♕xc8+ ♖b8 and the checks run out, whereupon White is mated.

2c12) 16 axb4 ♖xb5 (threatening ...♖h5) 17 ♖a5! (17 ♖xa7 ♖h5 18 ♖xf3 ♕xh2+ 19 ♔f1 ♗xg3 20 ♖a8+

♗c8 21 ♖xg3 ♖e8 wins for Black)
17...♖xa5 18 bxa5 ♖e8 19 ♕b8+ (19
♖xf3 loses against 19...♗xf3 20 ♕xf3
♕xd4+) 19...♗c8 20 ♖xf3 ♖e1+ gives
Black a winning attack.

2c2) 15 ♖xf3 c6!! was again part
of Berliner's preparation:

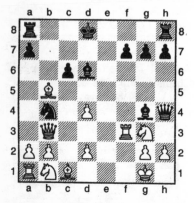

2c21) 16 ♗xc6? should be met not
by 16...♘xc6?, when White can play
17 ♕d5!? or 17 ♖xf7!?, but rather
16...♗xf3! 17 ♗xf3 ♖e8 18 ♘a3 (18
♗xa8 ♕xd4+ 19 ♔f1 ♘d3 mates; 18
♘f1 ♖c8 19 ♘c3 ♗xh2+ 20 ♘xh2
♕xd4+ 21 ♔f1 ♘d3) 18...♗xg3 19
hxg3 ♕xg3 20 ♘c2 ♘xc2 21 ♕d5+
♔e7, which wins for Black.

2c22) 16 ♗e2 ♗xf3 17 gxf3 (Black
wins after either 17 ♗xf3 ♖e8 or 17
♕xf3 ♕xd4+ 18 ♔h1 ♗c5 19 ♕f1
♘c2 20 ♘f5 ♕f2) 17...♗xg3 18 hxg3
♕xg3+ 19 ♔f1 gives Black a draw at
least.

2c23) 16 a3!? ♗xf3 17 ♕xf3 ♖e8
and then:

2c231) 18 ♘c3 ♖e1+ 19 ♔f2 (19
♗f1 ♕xd4+ 20 ♕f2 ♗c5! 21 ♕xd4+
♗xd4+ 22 ♔h1 ♘d3) 19...♘c2! 20
♘e2 ♗xg3+ 21 ♕xg3 ♕xg3+ 22 hxg3
cxb5 wins for Black.

2c232) 18 ♕f2 ♘c2 19 ♗xc6 ♖e1+
20 ♕xe1 ♘xe1 21 ♗xa8 ♕xd4+ 22
♔f1 ♗xg3 23 hxg3 ♘d3 and Black
wins.

2c233) 18 axb4! ♖e1+ 19 ♗f1 (19
♔f2 ♖xc1) 19...♕xd4+ 20 ♔h1 (20
♕f2 ♕xf2+ 21 ♔xf2 ♖xc1) 20...♗xg3
21 hxg3 and here:

2c2331) 21...♖xc1 22 ♕xf7 ♕xb2
23 ♖a3! ♕xb1 (23...♕f6? 24 ♖d3+
♔c8 25 ♕e8+ ♔b7 26 ♖d7+ ♔b6 27
♕e3+ wins) 24 ♕f3 is good for White.

2c2332) 21...♕c4 22 ♘a3 ♕xf1+
23 ♕xf1 ♖xf1+ 24 ♔h2 and Black
should be OK in the ending since his
pieces are active and White's pawns
weak.

14 ...   ♖b8

The rook will head for the kingside
via b6 or b5 with gain of tempo. This
rook-lift is an essential part of Black's
scheme.

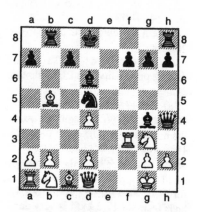

15 ♗e2?

With this move White starts to go
seriously downhill. Some of the most
interesting lines, from White's viewpoint, were possible here:

1) 15 ♗c6 ♘b4 with a large advantage for Black.

2) 15 ♗f1 ♖e8 16 ♘c3 ♘f6 is analysed by Berliner to a win for Black, for example 17 d3 ♗xf3 18 ♕xf3 ♘g4 19 h3 ♗xg3 20 ♕xg4 ♗f2+! 21 ♔h2 ♕xg4 22 hxg4 ♖e1 23 ♗e2 ♖b6 24 ♗d1 ♗xd4 or 17 ♘ce2 ♗xf3 18 gxf3 ♘h5 19 ♕e1 ♖b6 20 ♕f2 ♖xe2! 21 ♘xe2 ♗xh2+ 22 ♕xh2 ♖g6+, etc.

3) 15 ♘c3 (an attempt to give back some material to get the queenside developed) 15...♘xc3 (15...♗xf3 16 ♕xf3 ♕xd4+ 17 ♔h1 ♗xg3 18 ♕xg3 ♖xb5 19 ♘xb5 ♕c4 20 d3 ♕xb5 21 ♕xg7 and ♗g5+; 15...♗xg3 16 hxg3 ♗xf3 17 gxh4 ♗xd1 18 ♘xd5 ♖xb5 19 ♘c3) 16 dxc3 requires an accurate response by Black:

3a) 16...♗xf3?! 17 ♕xf3 ♖xb5 18 ♕a8+ ♔d7 19 ♕xh8 ♖h5 20 ♕xg7 ♕xh2+ and Black has no convincing continuation.

3b) 16...♖xb5 17 ♕d3 ♖h5 (not 17...♗xf3? 18 ♕xb5 ♗xg3 19 ♗g5+) and now:

3b1) 18 ♗f4? ♕xh2+ 19 ♔f2 ♗xf3 20 ♕xf3 ♖b5.

3b2) 18 ♖xf7?! is the interesting move, but as Hans Berliner himself indicated, the key to the position is the move ...♗e6. He gave 18...♕xh2+ 19 ♔f2 ♗e6, which is OK, but I prefer the immediate 18...♗e6!, for example 19 ♘xh5 ♗xh2+ 20 ♔f1 ♗xf7 21 ♕b5 (what else?), when the simple 21...h6, stopping ♗g5+, is very good for Black – if White grabs the h8-rook, he is mated by ...♗c4#.

3b3) 18 ♘xh5 ♕xh2+ 19 ♔f2 ♕xh5 is equal.

4) 15 a4 a6! 16 ♗f1 (16 ♗xa6 ♖e8 17 ♘c3 ♗b4 {17...♗xf3!? 18 ♕xf3 ♕xd4+ 19 ♔h1 ♖e1+ 20 ♗f1 is unclear} 18 ♗f1 ♗xf3 19 ♕xf3 ♘c2 20 ♖b1 ♖e1 21 d3 ♕xd4+ 22 ♔h1 ♕xc3!

23 bxc3 ♖xb1 24 ♗d2 ♖ed1 25 ♗f4 ♘e3! 26 ♗xd6 ♘xf1 and White must force a perpetual check) 16...♖e8 17 ♘c3 c6 18 d3 (18 ♘xd5 cxd5 19 ♗xa6 ♗xf3 20 ♕xf3 ♕xd4+ was good for Black in Kuzhanov – Limonikov, correspondence game 1994) 18...f5! and then:

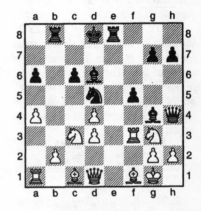

4a) 19 ♗d2 and now:

4a1) 19...♖xb2?! (the only move cited by Berliner) should be met by 20 ♘xd5!? ♗xf3 21 ♗a5+ ♔d7 22 ♕xf3 ♕xd4+ 23 ♔h1 ♕xd5 24 ♕xd5 cxd5 25 ♘xf5 ♖f8 26 ♘xd6 ♔xd6, reaching an ending where Black's active king and rooks may save him, though it is never easy to fight with a rook against two bishops.

4a2) 19...♗xf3! 20 ♕xf3 (20 gxf3 ♗xg3 21 hxg3 ♕xg3+ 22 ♗g2 ♘f4 23 ♗xf4 ♕xf4 and White's material advantage is now minute, while Black remains better coordinated) 20...♖xb2 21 ♘xd5 ♖xd2 is an improved version of line "4a1" – here the d2-bishop does not have time to escape the rook.

4b) 19 ♗e2 ♗xf3 20 ♗xf3 ♘e3 21 ♗xe3 ♖xe3 22 ♘ce2! ♖xb2! with the branch:

4b1) 23 ♕c1 ♖exe2 24 ♘xe2 (24 ♗xe2 ♕xd4+ 25 ♔h1 ♗xg3 is at least OK for Black) 24...♖xe2 25 ♗xe2 ♗xh2+ 26 ♔f1 ♗f4 and the result is a draw.

4b2) 23 ♖b1 ♖bxe2 24 ♘xe2 ♖xe2 25 ♗xe2 ♕xh2+ 26 ♔f1 (26 ♔f2?? ♗g3+ 27 ♔f3 ♕h4 and Black forces mate) 26...♕h1+ 27 ♔f2 ♕h4+ with a perpetual check.

4c) 19 ♘ce2 ♖e6 20 ♖f2 g5 21 ♕d2 ♘e3 was given as clearly better for Black by Berliner. This seems to be a critical line. There is no immediate prospect of Black regaining material, nor of White untangling his pieces. In such instances, the normal verdict would be "unclear".

15	...	♗xf3
16	♗xf3	♕xd4+
17	♔h1	

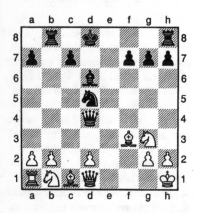

17	...	♗xg3!
18	hxg3	♖b6!
19	d3	♘e3

By blocking off the bishop's guard over h6, Black brings about a major defensive crisis for White.

20	♗xe3	♕xe3
21	♗g4!	

White failed to regain the exchange and went down quickly in Visser – Koster, Netherlands 1996: 21 ♘c3? ♖h6+ 22 ♗h5 g6 23 g4 gxh5 24 g5 ♕xg5 25 ♕f3 ♖g8 26 ♖f1 ♕h4+ 27 ♔g1 ♖xg2+ 28 ♕xg2 ♖g6 29 ♖xf7 ♖xg2+ 30 ♔xg2 ♕g5+ 31 ♔h3 ♕d2 0-1.

21	...	h5!
22	♗h3	g5

Black has accurately worked out that White cannot save the bishop and that the outcome is a better ending for Black.

23	♘d2	g4
24	♘c4	♕xg3
25	♘xb6	gxh3
26	♕f3	hxg2+
27	♕xg2	♕xg2+
28	♔xg2	

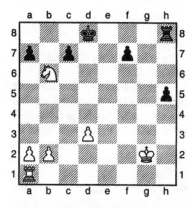

It seems ironic that after all the crazy complications the game ends up in a very normal-looking ending.

28	...	cxb6!!

"To win, Black needs to penetrate with his king to the queenside without allowing White to reduce the number of pawns with the plan a4-a5." – Sowray. Thus 28...axb6 29 a4 intending a5 should be sufficient for White to hold the draw.

29 Rf1

It is surprising, to say the least, that the moves up to this point occurred in a subsequent over-the-board game. Lopukhin – Semeniuk, Cheliabinsk 1975 deviated here with 29 ♔h3 Re8 30 Rf1 Re3+ 31 ♔h4 ♔e7 32 ♔xh5 ♔e6 33 ♔g5 Rg3+ 34 ♔f4 Rxd3 35 Re1+ ♔f6 36 Rc1 Rd4+ 37 ♔e3 Ra4 38 a3 ♔e5 39 Rc8 f5 40 Re8+ ♔d5 41 ♔d3 Rd4+ 42 ♔c3 Rc4+ 43 ♔d3 Rc7 44 Rf8 ♔e5 45 ♔e3 Rc2 46 Re8+ ♔d5 47 Ra8 a5 48 b4 Rc3+ 49 ♔f4 Rxa3 50 bxa5 Rxa5 0-1. If we assume that White did not enter this ending deliberately, then this does suggest that Estrin's moves to reach this position have been very natural.

29	...	♔e7
30	Re1+	♔d6!
31	Rf1	Rc8!
32	Rxf7	Rc7!

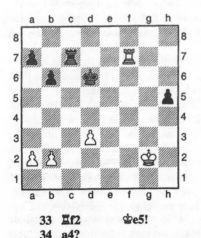

33	Rf2	♔e5!
34	a4?	

This move simplifies Black's task. The critical line was 34 ♔g3! ♔d4 35 ♔h4 ♔xd3 36 ♔xh5 Rc2! and now:

1) 37 Rf3+ ♔d2! 38 b3! (38 b4 Rc3! 39 Rf2+ ♔e1) 38...♔c1! 39 a4 Rb2! 40 a5 b5 41 a6 b4 42 ♔g4 ♔c2 43 Rf7 Rxb3 44 Rxa7 Ra3 45 Rb7 b3 46 a7 b2 wins for Black.

2) 37 Rf7 Rc5+! 38 ♔g4 Ra5 39 Rf3+! ♔d2!! (39...♔c2 40 Rf2+ is less clear) 40 a3! (40 b3 Ra3! stops 41 a4; 40 Rf2+ ♔e1) 40...♔c2 41 Rf2+ ♔b3 42 ♔f4 Rb5! 43 ♔e4 ♔a2! 44 Rf7 a6 45 Ra7 Ra5! 46 Rb7 b5 and Black wins.

34	...	♔d4
35	a5	♔xd3
36	Rf3+	♔c2
37	b4	

37 axb6 axb6 38 Rf6 Rb7 makes sure that the b-pawn can safely advance.

37	...	b5!
38	a6	Rc4
39	Rf7	Rxb4
40	Rb7	

40 Rxa7 is met by 40...Ra4, when Black's b-pawn can move forward, whereas the a-pawn is going nowhere.

40	...	Rg4+
41	♔f3	b4
42	Rxa7	b3

0-1

There could follow 43 Rc7+ ♔b1 44 Rc5 Ra4!.

Lessons from this game:

1) Successful correspondence chess requires extremely detailed, accurate analysis.

2) It can be worth sacrificing material to retard the opponent's development, especially if in the meantime you can attack his king.

3) In the endgame, the more pawns remain on the board, the more winning chances there are.

Tigran Petrosian – Boris Spassky
World Championship match (game 10), Moscow 1966
King's Indian Defence, Fianchetto Variation

The Players

Tigran Petrosian (1929–84) was World Champion 1963–9. He was born in Tbilisi, Georgia, to Armenian parents. He learned to play chess, amongst other board games, when he was young, and found solace in chess after his parents died when he was 16 years old. He enjoyed considerable local success, winning the championship of Armenia, where he had relocated, for the first time in 1946. His first results in higher-level competitions were unimpressive. His debut in the USSR Championship, in 1949, was very shaky: 7½/19, having started in the first round with a 13-move loss. Over the next few years he almost reinvented his game, adopting methods that suited his own skills and temperament. The result was a unique playing style that opponents found very hard to handle. Often it wasn't even clear what they were fighting against, as Petrosian's deeply prophylactic play would be preventing ideas that had not even occurred to them. Once his opponent's active possibilities were neutralized, Petrosian would squeeze relentlessly. His results in the early 1950s were spectacular. A second place in the 1951 USSR Championship was followed by second in the Saltsjöbaden Interzonal (without loss – presaging his future "invincibility") in 1952, the year in which he gained the grandmaster title. In the 1953 Candidates tournament he finished an impressive fifth.

However, he was not yet ready to challenge for the world title; Smyslov and then Tal, in particular, were ahead of him. His seized his chance by winning the 1962 Curaçao Candidates tournament – by just half a point, but undefeated. He went on to beat Botvinnik convincingly in 1963. In 1966 he managed to defend his title against the challenge of Boris Spassky. Hooper and Whyld, in *The Oxford Companion to Chess*, make the interesting point that this was the first time since the days of Steinitz that a world champion had defeated his closest rival in match play – the intervening champions had either drawn, lost, been prevented from playing by circumstances, or avoided a match altogether! In 1969 though, Spassky's dynamism and aggression proved too much, and Petrosian was defeated. Throughout the rest of his career, Petrosian played at a high level, and was frequently a Candidate, but never again challenged for the world title. Cancer brought his life to a premature end in 1984.

The fabled invincibility of "Iron Tigran", as he became known, is perhaps best illustrated by his overall score in the ten Olympiads in which he played: 79 wins, 50 draws, and only one loss.

Boris Spassky (born 1937) was World Champion 1969–72. For more information see Game 42.

The Game
Seeing his opponent's desire to play aggressively for a win, Petrosian plays a few slightly odd moves to tempt Spassky to over-reach a little. Spassky reacts with an ambitious central advance. It is OK in itself, but no more than that. Petrosian keeps on giving Spassky a little more rope, and eventually he oversteps the mark with his winning attempts. Two exchange sacrifices lay bare the black king and a beautiful and famous combination rounds off the game.

1	♘f3	♘f6
2	g3	g6
3	c4	♗g7
4	♗g2	0-0
5	0-0	♘c6
6	♘c3	d6

Spassky invites a transposition to a King's Indian rather than going in for a quieter line of the English that his opponent has offered him. Petrosian, a great connoisseur of the King's Indian, is happy to oblige.

7	d4	a6

This is known as the Panno Variation, with which Black prepares to chip away at White's centre by means of the ...b5 advance. White's next move brings about a standard transposition into another line, called the Yugoslav Variation, the "official" move-order of which sees Black playing first ...c5, and then ...♘c6, meeting White's d5 with ...♘a5. However, in modern practice, this is more often reached from the Panno move-order (...c5 is played after the knight has been driven to a5), so the whole issue of naming these variations is rather messy.

8	d5	♘a5
9	♘d2	c5
10	♕c2	e5

10...♖b8!? intending ...b5 is the normal line, which has been extensively

analysed – as far as an ending in quite a few variations.

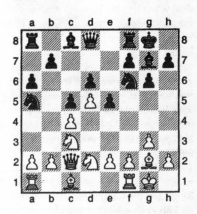

11 b3

Tal prefers the more direct 11 a3, preparing b4, which is a good way to exploit the fact that Black has voluntarily cut out some tactical ideas on the long dark-squared diagonal:

1) 11...b6 12 b4 ♘b7 13 ♖b1 with good queenside play.

2) 11...♕c7 12 b4 cxb4 13 axb4 ♘xc4 14 ♘b5 ♕b6 15 ♘xc4 ♕xb5 16 ♖a5 ♕e8 17 ♘xd6 ♕d8 18 ♘c4 is good for White.

11	...	♘g4
12	e4	

Other possibilities include 12 ♗b2 f5 13 ♖ae1!? and 12 a3 b6 13 b4 ♘b7.

| 12 | ... | f5 |
| 13 | exf5 | gxf5 |

15...♘h6 followed by queenside play is a safe and good alternative.

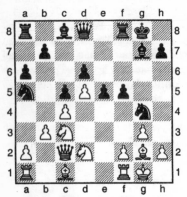

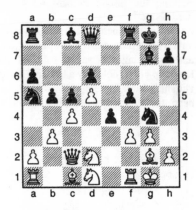

14 ♘d1!?

Typical Petrosian – rather than play the most active moves, he entices the opponent into attacking him. 14 ♗b2! ♗d7 15 ♖ae1 b5 16 ♘d1 is a logical way to prepare for active play in the centre.

14 ... b5

Black could instead try 14...f4!?, while 14...e4 is possible too, provided that after 15 ♗b2 he avoids 15...♗d4? (15...♗xb2 is better) 16 ♗xd4 cxd4 17 b4, when White wins the wayward knight.

15 f3?!

This move takes provocation a little too far. 15 ♗b2 ♖b8 16 f3 ♘f6 17 ♗c3 ♗h6 18 ♖e1 would be a rational course.

15 ... e4!?

Spassky, behind in the match, succumbs to temptation, and tries to punish Petrosian's seemingly careless play. However, White's position cannot be knocked over so easily, and meanwhile Black is starting a fight in which not all his pieces are ready to participate.

16 ♗b2

Petrosian was not only a great connoisseur of exchange sacrifices, but also an expert in the subtleties of the King's Indian, so rejects 16 fxg4 ♗xa1 17 gxf5 ♗xf5 18 ♘xe4, since Black retains his key dark-squared bishop.

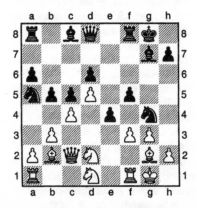

| 16 | ... | exf3 |
| 17 | ♗xf3 | |

White should avoid 17 ♘xf3? ♗b2 18 ♕xb2 bxc4.

17 ... ♗xb2

17...♘e5 looks more natural, keeping more tension in the position, and retaining the king's faithful bodyguard on g7.

  18 ♕xb2   ♘e5
  19 ♗e2

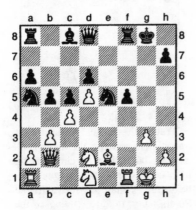

  19 ...   f4?!

19...♖a7!? 20 ♘e3 (20 cxb5 axb5 21 ♗xb5 would be an inappropriate pawn-grab: it loosens White's position and leaves the d5-pawn untenable in the long term) and now:

1) 20...♖g7 is a reasonable idea.

2) 20...f4 21 ♖xf4 ♖xf4 22 gxf4 ♖g7+ 23 ♔h1 ♕h4 24 fxe5 ♕f2 25 ♘f3 (or 25 ♕c3!) 25...♕xe3 26 e6 ♗b7 27 ♕f6 and it is White who exploits the open g-file.

3) 20...♕f6 21 ♕c2 ♖g7 22 ♘g2 ♘g6 with ideas of ...f4 looks best, e.g. 23 ♔h1 f4 24 ♘xf4? (24 ♘e4!? is correct) 24...♘xf4 25 gxf4 ♗h3 (Tal) leaves White in some trouble.

  20 gxf4

Petrosian is still playing on the psychology of the situation, aiming to lure his battle-hungry, less experienced opponent into overstepping the mark. Objectively, White ought to choose 20

♖xf4 ♖xf4 21 gxf4 ♘g6 (21...♖a7 22 ♘e3 ♖g7+ 23 ♔h1 ♗h3 24 fxe5 ♕g5 25 ♘g4 ♗xg4 26 ♘e4 wins for White) 22 ♘e4 ♘xf4 23 ♘e3! (23 ♘df2 ♖a7) 23...♖a7 24 ♘f6+ ♔f7 25 ♖f1 ♕xf6 26 ♕xf6+ ♔xf6 27 ♖xf4+, but Black's active king may yet save this difficult ending. However, it is clear that in this line Black would not get carried away trying to complicate the struggle, but would fight grimly to survive.

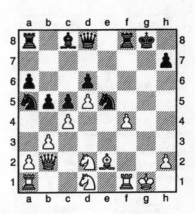

  20 ...   ♗h3?

Petrosian's second, Alexei Suetin, wrote: "This is it, the psychological crisis of the struggle. Almost without a thinking, Black embarks on a previously worked out plan, forgetting for the moment concrete analysis. And in such positions, concrete analyses spell death for general considerations."

Instead 20...♖xf4 21 ♘e3 (21 ♖xf4 ♕g5+ 22 ♔h1 ♕xf4) 21...♕g5+ 22 ♔h1 ♖xf1+ 23 ♘dxf1 ♗h3 (23...♖a7 is also possible) is quite OK for Black.

  21 ♘e3!

An essentially forced, but strong exchange sacrifice. White cannot play 21 ♖f2? due to 21...♖xf4.

  21 ...   ♗xf1

After 21...♖xf4 22 ♖xf4 ♕g5+ 23 ♖g4! ♘xg4 (23...♗xg4 24 ♘xg4 comes to the same thing) 24 ♘xg4 ♗xg4 25 ♗xg4 ♕xg4+ 26 ♔h1, now that the kingside is wide open, the sidelined knight on a5 proves ineffective. Black would have to continue 26...♕d4 27 ♖g1+ ♔h8 28 ♕xd4+ cxd4 with some survival chances in the ending.

22 ♖xf1

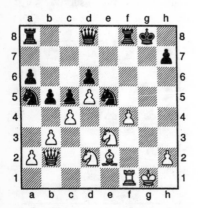

22 ...   ♘g6

22...♘d7 23 ♗g4 ♘f6 (23...♕f6 24 ♗e6+ ♔h8 25 ♕c1 does not solve Black's problems either) 24 ♗e6+ is easy to play for White.

23 ♗g4!

23 ♘g4 threatens mate, but 23...h5! solves the problem easily, and gives Black a decent game.

23 ...   ♘xf4?

Or:

1) 23...♖xf4? 24 ♗e6+ ♔f8 25 ♖xf4+ ♘xf4 26 ♕h8+ ♔e7 27 ♘f5#.

2) 23...♕f6? 24 ♗e6+ ♔h8 25 ♕xf6+ ♖xf6 26 f5 ♘e5 27 ♘e4! wins material.

3) 23...h6 was perhaps the best chance, but 24 ♘f5 is still very uncomfortable for Black.

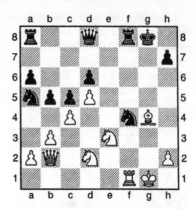

24 ♖xf4!

"Yet another exchange sacrifice. To a specialist, perhaps, the finale is elementary, but to the wide circle of chess lovers, the concluding stages are as beautiful as they are instructive." – Suetin.

24 ...   ♖xf4
25 ♗e6+   ♖f7

25...♔f8 26 ♕h8+ ♔e7 27 ♕xh7+ ♔f6 (after other king moves White picks off the rook with a few queen checks) 28 ♕h6+ ♔e5 29 ♕g7+ ♕f6 30 ♕g3 wins heavy material.

26 ♘e4   ♕h4

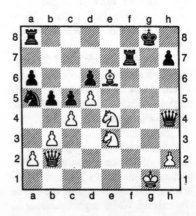

After 26...♖aa7, 27 ♘f5 ♕f8 28 ♕f6! wins.

27   ♘xd6   ♕g5+

27...♕e1+ 28 ♔g2 ♕xe3 loses Black his queen: 29 ♗xf7+ ♔f8 30 ♕h8+ ♔e7 31 ♘f5+ ♔xf7 (31...♔d7 32 ♗e6+) 32 ♕g7+ ♔e8 33 ♘xe3.

28   ♔h1   ♖a7

28...♕xe3 29 ♗xf7+ ♔f8 30 ♕h8+ ♔e7 31 ♘f5+ ♔xf7 32 ♕g7+ ♔e8 33 ♘xe3 is by now a familiar pattern.

29   ♗xf7+   ♖xf7

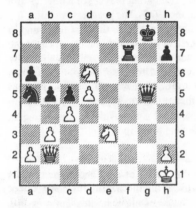

Now for one of the most famous moves in world championship history:

30   ♕h8+!!   1-0

"The tenth game was one of the shortest games of the match, but was also one of the richest, both in content and dramatic psychology." – Suetin.

This finish is remarkably similar to the end of the following game of Petrosian's, played ten years earlier:

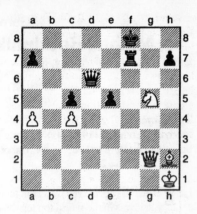

Petrosian – Simagin
*Match (game 5), Moscow
Championship 1956*

**44   ♕a8+ ♔g7 45 ♗xe5+!! ♕xe5
46 ♕h8+!! ♔xh8 47 ♘xf7+ ♔g7 48
♘xe5 1-0**

Lessons from this game:

1) Be very wary of "going for the win" as Black. Your chances of doing so are best if you adopt a measured approach and at least equalize first.

2) The exchange sacrifice is a powerful weapon. Rooks can be clumsy pieces in defence, especially when the king is being attacked along diagonals.

3) The more combinational patterns you are familiar with, the easier it will be to recognize the possibilities for them at the board. Here Petrosian could not help but be aware of the ♕h8+ idea!

Mikhail Botvinnik – Lajos Portisch
Monte Carlo 1968
English Opening

The Players

Mikhail Botvinnik (1911–95) was one of the great World Champions, holding the title from 1948 to 1963 with two short breaks (1957–8 and 1960–1). For more details see Game 28.

Lajos Portisch (born 1937) was the leading Hungarian player for a quarter of a century and was in the world top ten during the 1970s. His progress was slow but steady; in 1958 he won the Hungarian Championship for the first time, and in 1961 he became a grandmaster. In the course of a long and successful career he has qualified for the Candidates no fewer than eight times, won more than twenty major international tournaments and has played for his country in nineteen Olympiads stretching from Moscow 1956 to Erevan 1996. He is famed for hard work and excellent preparation; indeed, his systematic approach extends to all the activities he engages in. His clear positional style results in many elegant games, but he does occasionally have a tactical blind spot.

The Game

Botvinnik's opening strategy is based on the power of his fianchettoed king's bishop operating on the long diagonal. Portisch commits a minor inaccuracy, and after only a few more moves his queenside comes under unpleasant pressure. Seeking to relieve the pressure, Portisch decides to regroup his pieces. This allows Botvinnik to make a lightning switch to attack Portisch's king; aided by the sacrifice of both rooks, the offensive crashes through. The final attack is conducted on the light squares, with the fianchettoed bishop offering excellent support.

1	c4	e5
2	♘c3	♘f6
3	g3	d5
4	cxd5	♘xd5
5	♗g2	♗e6
6	♘f3	♘c6
7	0-0	♘b6

The position is a reversed Sicilian Dragon with White having an extra tempo. As in the Dragon proper, the play revolves around the power of the fianchettoed bishop. Black would like to exchange it off, but this is more easily said than done.

On the subject of reversed openings generally, it often happens that the extra tempo is of less help than one might imagine. A structure which is suitable as a black defence may not be easy to convert into one appropriate for gaining the advantage, even with a move in hand.

8 d3   ♗e7
9 a3

White plans queenside expansion by b4-b5. This will not only threaten Black's e-pawn, but also increase the scope of the g2-bishop.

9 ...   a5

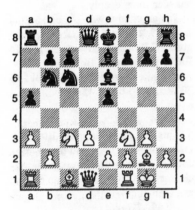

The simplest response; Black directly prevents the intended advance of the b2-pawn. However, it does have the defect of weakening his queenside pawn-structure. The protruding a-pawn can itself become weak after the a8-rook has moved to the centre, and the square b5 is available for occupation. These days the straightforward 9...0-0 is more common.

10 ♗e3   0-0
11 ♘a4

White attempts to exchange the b6-knight and so leave the b7-pawn vulnerable to attack along the b-file.

11 ...   ♘xa4?!

This falls in with White's plans too easily; now White's queen comes directly into play and Black's queenside pawns start to come under serious pressure. 11...♘d5 12 ♗c5 b6 13 ♗xe7 ♘dxe7 is a better approach as Black's

queenside is more solid and White's knight on a4 will sooner or later have to return to c3. In Gheorghiu – Mariotti, Interzonal tournament, Manila 1976, Black had more or less equalized after the further moves 14 b4 axb4 15 axb4 ♕d6 16 b5 ♘a5.

12 ♕xa4

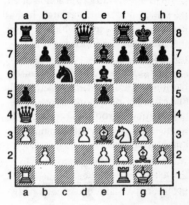

12 ...   ♗d5

The unpleasant nature of this position is only confirmed by the game Forintos – Sapi, Hungarian Championship 1968, when after 12...♕d7 13 ♖fc1 ♖fd8 14 ♗c5 ♗d5? White gained a pawn by 15 ♘xe5! ♘xe5 16 ♕xd7 ♖xd7 17 ♗xd5 ♗g5 18 ♗xb7 ♖b8 19 f4 ♖xb7 20 fxg5 ♖xb2 21 ♖ab1 ♖xb1 22 ♖xb1. It is interesting to note that White had a second and highly thematic way to gain the advantage in this line: the exchange sacrifice 14 ♖xc6 ♕xc6 15 ♕xc6 bxc6 16 ♘xe5 ♗d5 17 ♖c1. White will definitely win the c6-pawn and with two good pawns for the exchange he has a definite advantage. An exchange sacrifice on c6 is a common motif in this line and Portisch takes steps to defend c6 and so rule it out.

13 ♖fc1   ♖e8

Black continually has to worry about the possibility of ♕b5, both attacking the b7-pawn and setting up tactical tricks based on ♘xe5. He therefore decides to move the knight from c6 and then play ...c6. This would both prevent ♕b5 and set up a small pawn-chain b7-c6 to restrict the action of the g2-bishop. First of all, though, he has to defend the e5-pawn, which explains this move and the following one.

14 ♖c2

The immediate 14 ♕b5 is ineffective after 14...♗f6, when 15 ♕xb7 fails to 15...♘d4. Botvinnik therefore decides to double rooks in order to frustrate Black's plan of moving the knight from c6.

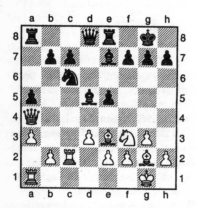

14 ...   ♗f8

The tactical line 14...b5 15 ♕xb5 ♖b8 16 ♕a4 ♗b3 fails to 17 ♕xc6. However, since the move played proves unsatisfactory it would have been better to try 14...♗d6 15 ♕b5 ♘e7 16 ♘d2 ♗xg2 17 ♔xg2 ♕b8, followed by ...c6, although White retains an advantage due to his more active pieces.

15 ♖ac1   ♘b8

Black continues with his plan despite White's pressure along the c-file. It looks risky to retreat all but one of Black's pieces to the first rank, but Portisch thinks that White cannot take the pawn on c7 for tactical reasons. However, it turns out that Botvinnik has seen more deeply.

The alternative was 15...e4 16 dxe4 ♗xe4 17 ♖d2 ♕f6 (17...♗d6 18 ♗c5 gives White a clear advantage) 18 ♗f4 ♖ac8, as given by Botvinnik. However, White can continue 19 ♗h3! ♗f5 20 ♗xf5 ♕xf5 21 ♕b3, winning a pawn.

16 ♖xc7   ♗c6

This is Portisch's idea: Black attacks both the queen and the c7-rook and so White must surrender the exchange. The refutation is both elegant and thematic.

17 ♖1xc6!

First of all Black's light-squared bishop is eliminated. Now there will be nothing to counteract the power of the g2-bishop.

17 ...   bxc6

After 17...♘xc6 18 ♖xb7 White has a large positional advantage as well as two pawns for the exchange.

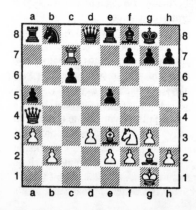

18 ℤxf7!

White blows Black's kingside apart. Note how both White's sacrifices take place thematically on light squares, which White was already aiming to dominate when he fianchettoed his bishop on g2.

18 ...　　h6

The g2-bishop plays its part in the line 18...♔xf7 19 ♕c4+ ♔g6 (Black cannot interpose his queen because of ♘g5+, uncovering the bishop) 20 ♕g4+ ♔f7 21 ♘g5+, when Black must give up his queen to avoid mate.

19 ℤb7

The rook has done its job and quietly retires, leaving Black's position an utter wreck. The move ...h6 and the disappearance of the f7-pawn have left him with crippling light-square weaknesses on the kingside. In addition Black's development is non-existent, so we can safely state that White is winning.

19 ...　　♕c8

20 ♕c4+　　♔h8

After 20...♕e6 21 ♘xe5 White makes off with another pawn.

21 ♘h4!

White's position is so strong that he has many ways to win, for example 21 ℤf7 (threatening 22 ♘h4) 21...♗d6 (so as to meet 22 ♘h4 with 22...♕e6) 22 ♗xh6 gxh6 23 ♕e4 is decisive. However, the move played is both effective and neat. Black has no way of defending his light squares, so he may as well accept the new rook offer.

21 ...　　♕xb7

22 ♘g6+　　♔h7

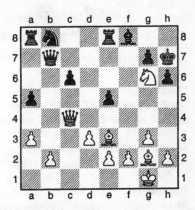

23 ♗e4　　♗d6

24 ♘xe5+　　g6

Or 24...♔h8 25 ♘f7+ ♔g8 26 ♘xd6+ winning the queen.

25 ♗xg6+　　♔g7

26 ♗xh6+!　　1-0

Black loses his queen following 26...♔xh6 27 ♕h4+ ♔g7 28 ♕h7+ ♔f6 (28...♔f8 29 ♕xb7) 29 ♘g4+ ♔e6 (29...♔g5 30 ♕h5#) 30 ♕xb7.

Lessons from this game:

1) A fianchettoed bishop can exert tremendous pressure on a long diagonal. It is often advisable to exchange it or, failing that, restrict it by means of a suitable pawn-chain.

2) The thematic Dragon exchange sacrifice (normally ...ℤxc3 by Black) can also occur with colours reversed!

3) Unless the position is blocked, retrograde manoeuvres should be carefully checked for tactical flaws.

Game 58

Lev Polugaevsky – Mikhail Tal
USSR Championship, Moscow 1969
Queen's Gambit Declined, Semi-Tarrasch Defence

The Players

Lev Polugaevsky (1934–95) was one of the world's top grandmasters from the late 1960s to the early 1980s. For further details see Game 40.

Mikhail Tal (1936–92) was World Champion 1960–1, and one of the greatest attacking players of all time. See Game 39 for more information.

The Game

Polugaevsky steamrollers Tal using a powerful piece of opening preparation. The demonstration starts with a logical pawn sacrifice, to which Tal replies in the most natural and ambitious manner, seeking to eliminate the pieces that support the advance. Polugaevsky sacrifices a piece to open up the black king in standard fashion. Two brilliant pawn moves (21 h4 and 25 e6) are the subtle touches that make the whole thing work. Tal can see nothing better than going into bad ending, which Polugaevsky wins efficiently.

1	d4	♘f6	
2	c4	e6	
3	♘f3	d5	
4	♘c3	c5	

This move characterizes the Semi-Tarrasch Defence, in which Black aims to exploit the fact that the move ♘f3 exerts less pressure on Black's position than ♗g5 (as in the normal lines of the Queen's Gambit) by playing ...c5, but without accepting the structural weaknesses inherent in the Tarrasch Defence (see Game 77). The main drawback of the Semi-Tarrasch is that White can set up a big pawn-centre, and Polugaevsky, not one to avoid critical opening lines, takes full advantage of this.

5	cxd5	♘xd5	
6	e4	♘xc3	
7	bxc3	cxd4	

8	cxd4	♗b4+	
9	♗d2	♗xd2+	
10	♕xd2	0-0	

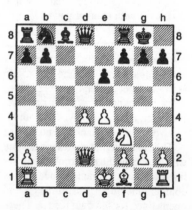

Early in 1969 Polugaevsky analysed this position together with Spassky, who was then preparing for his second match against Petrosian. Their work proved fruitful, and they devised a plan that is to this day considered a critical test of Black's resources. Spassky indeed scored a win against Petrosian. However, it was left to Polugaevsky to demonstrate the main line of their analysis.

11	&c4	&c6
12	0-0	b6
13	&ad1	&b7
14	&fe1	&a5

Tal plays the most natural and active move, doubtless intended as an improvement over 14...&c8, when 15 d5 exd5 16 &xd5 gave White a useful advantage in Spassky – Petrosian, World Championship match (game 5), Moscow 1969.

15	&d3	&c8

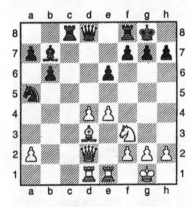

16 d5!

This is a thematic pawn sacrifice with this central structure. White closes lines for his opponent, reducing his counterattacking possibilities, and opens lines for his own pieces. There are obvious parallels with the pawn sacrifice seen in Game 6, though here the black king is better defended, but

White also has an e-pawn to help in the attack. White's score of 83% from this position (a statistic compiled from the games on ChessBase's MegaBase 98) speaks volumes about the power of this move.

16 ... exd5

Declining the pawn by 16...&d6 is no fun either. After 17 &g5 (17 &e2 and 17 dxe6 should suffice for an edge) 17...exd5 18 exd5, Black felt obliged to take the queens off by 18...&h6 19 &xh6 gxh6 in Jasnikowski – Przewoznik, Polish Team Championship, Bydgoszcz 1990, but after 20 d6 &cd8 21 &h4 &g7 22 &f5+ &f6 23 h4 &c8 24 &g3 &g7 25 &f5 his position proved untenable.

17 e5!

For the pawn, White has blunted the b7-bishop and gained the d4- and f5-squares together with the possibility of e5-e6.

17 ... &c4

Black could set up a stouter defence, but Tal wished to bring the game to an immediate crisis. Other moves:

1) 17...g6 18 &h6 favours White – Polugaevsky.

2) 17...&e7 18 &f4! (18 &d4 g6!) 18...f5 19 &d4 g6 20 h4! &c6 21 &b5 &e6 22 h5 &cd8 23 hxg6 hxg6 24 &e3 &d7 25 &c2! gave White much the better game in Bagirov – Zhuravliov, USSR 1974.

3) 17...h6 18 &f4 &c6 19 &f5 g6 20 &g4 gave White powerful attacking chances in N. Popov – Rumiantsev, USSR 1978.

4) 17...d4 18 &g5 h6 19 &h7 &c4 has been played with success (i.e. Black drew) in a couple of games, but 20 &f4 &b2 21 &f6+! &h8 22 &d2 is good for White:

4a) 22...②xd3 23 罩xd3 罩c3 (to neutralize White's threat of 罩h3) 24 罩xd4 gives White the advantage.

4b) 22...②c4 23 奥xc4 罩xc4 24 罩d3 奥c8? (24...罩c3 transposes to "4a") 25 g4! (preparing 罩h3) 25...罩c3 26 罩xd4 is now winning since the queen has no decent square.

18 豐f4

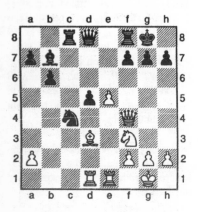

18 ...   ②b2

This allows, indeed encourages, the familiar bishop sacrifice on h7. Of course, to Tal the 奥h7+ sacrifice was an absolutely routine matter of attacking technique, so he must have felt that it ought not to work. Otherwise he would have played a more defensive move, e.g.:

1) 18...h6 and now 19 e6 fxe6 20 豐g4 gives White some attacking prospects on the light squares, while Polugaevsky's suggestion 19 豐f5 g6 20 豐h3 含g7 21 e6 looks good.

2) 18...g6 appears ugly, but how should White refute it? 19 h4 is one idea, while 19 豐h6 is inconclusive:

2a) 19...f6 20 奥xg6 is good for White since 20...hxg6? 21 豐xg6+ 含h8 22 罩d4 wins on the spot.

2b) 19...豐d7 20 ②g5 f5 21 exf6 罩xf6 22 奥xc4 罩xc4 23 ②xh7 罩e6 (23...豐xh7 24 罩e8+ 含f7 25 豐f8#) 24 罩xe6 豐xe6 25 ②g5 and White wins easily.

2c) 19...f5 is best, for example 20 exf6 (probably wrong) 20...豐xf6 21 ②g5 罩c7 22 ②e6 豐xf2+ 23 含h1 罩e7 isn't too clear, for example 24 豐xf8+ (24 罩f1 豐xf1+ 25 罩xf1 罩xf1+ 26 奥xf1 罩xe6) 24...豐xf8 25 ②xf8 and then 25...含xf8 or 25...罩xe1+ 26 罩xe1 含xf8.

19 奥xh7+!   含xh7
20 ②g5+   含g6

20...含g8 21 豐h4 豐xg5 22 豐xg5 ②xd1 23 罩xd1 does not give Black enough for his queen.

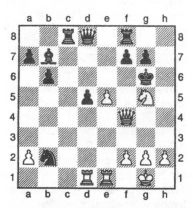

"The first impression is that nothing comes of White's attack, but he has at his disposal a prepared move of terrible strength." – Polugaevsky.

21 h4!!

This brilliant move, threatening 22 h5+ 含xh5 (22...含h6 drops the queen) 23 g4+ 含g6 (or 23...含h6 24 豐h2+) 24 豐f5+ 含h6 25 ②xf7+ 罩xf7 26 豐h5#, was part of Polugaevsky's and Spassky's preparation.

"I think that it was only here that Tal realized that he was battling under unequal conditions, but there was already no way out." – Polugaevsky.

21 ...   &c4

Or:

1) 21...f6 allows White's threat.

2) 21...f5 is met by 22 &d4 intending 23 h5+ or 23 ♕g3.

3) 21...&xd1 is Fritz's initial preference (and has occurred in practice a few times), grabbing some material in the hope of being able to give some back to stave off the mating threats, but there then follows 22 h5+ &h6 23 &e6+ g5 (23...&h7 24 &xd8) 24 hxg6+ &xg6 25 ♕g4+ &h6 26 ♕g7+ &h5 27 &f4+ &h4 28 g3#.

4) 21...♕d7 22 e6 fxe6 23 ♕g4 &f6 24 &xe6+ &h6 25 &e5 ♕f7 (or 25...g6 26 ♕g5+) 26 &h5+ ♕xh5 27 ♕xg7# (1-0) was Dimov – Tsolov, Bulgarian Correspondence Championship 1990.

5) 21...♕e7 22 h5+ &h6 (22...&xh5 23 g4+ &g6 24 ♕f5+ &h6 25 ♕h7+ &xg5 26 ♕f5+ &h6 27 ♕h5#) 23 &xf7+ &h7 24 e6 (24 ♕f5+ &g8 25 e6 &xf7) 24...♕f6 25 ♕xf6 gxf6 is the same as the game continuation, except that Black has substituted the move ...&h8-h7 for ...&c8-c4. This certainly doesn't solve his main problems.

22 h5+

22 &d4 also proved effective in Linna – Huuskonen, Finnish Correspondence Championship 1992 after 22...♕e7 23 h5+ &h6 24 &e6+ &h7 25 &xf8+ ♕xf8 26 &xc4 &xc4 27 e6 f6 28 ♕f5+ &g8 29 e7 ♕e8 30 h6 &d6 31 ♕g4 1-0.

22 ...   &h6

22...&xh5 23 g4+ &g6 (23...&h6 24 ♕h2+ &xg5 25 ♕h5+ 1-0 was the

finish of de la Vega – Gonzales, Argentina 1970; it is mate next move) 24 ♕f5+ &h6 25 &xf7+ &xf7 26 ♕h5#.

23 &xf7++

Note that if Black's 21st move had not attacked the white queen, then 23 &e6+ would have been decisive.

23 ...   &h7

23...&xh5 runs into 24 g4+ &g6 25 ♕f5#.

24 ♕f5+   &g8

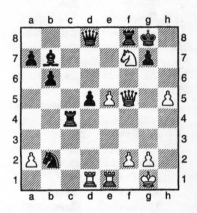

25 e6!!

Polugaevsky had been analysing this position before the game, and had predicted to Grandmaster Efim Geller that it would occur on his board that day! Geller was understandably astonished when this prediction came true.

White now threatens 26 e7 and 26 &xd8. The move is far better than 25 &xd8? &xf5 26 e6 &c8 27 e7 &d7, when Black stops the pawn at the cost of a "mere" bishop.

25 ...   ♕f6

25...♕e7 26 h6! wins: 26...&h4 27 &d4 &xh6 (27...&xd4 28 h7#) 28 &xh6+ gxh6 29 &g4+ &h8 30 ♕g6 ♕f6 31 e7.

26 ♕xf6   gxf6

27 Rd2

This move is good enough to win, and so can hardly be criticized. However, 27 ♘d6 has been claimed to be stronger, even by Polugaevsky himself, but it is not clear if this is so. The move was tried in Naumkin – Nevanlinna, Jyväskylä 1993, when 27...♘xd1 28 e7 ♖c1 29 h6 ♖b8 30 ♘xb7 ♖e8 31 ♘d6 ♖xe7 32 ♖xe7 ♘e3+ 33 ♔h2 ♘g4+ 34 ♔g3 ♘xh6 led to a draw.

27 ...   Rc6

27...♖b4 is no better since after 28 a3 the rook is overloaded: it cannot defend both the knight and the d4-square. White wins after either 28...♘c4? 29 ♖d4 or 28...♖b3 29 ♖d4 ♖xa3 30 ♖g4+ ♔h7 31 e7 ♖e8 32 h6.

27...♘a4 28 ♘d6 also leaves White much better.

28 Rxb2   Re8

28...♗c8 was "slightly the lesser evil" according to Polugaevsky.

29 ♘h6+   ♔h7
30 ♘f5   Rcxe6
31 Rxe6   Rxe6
32 Rc2   Rc6
33 Re2!

White is now clearly winning. His pieces are far more effective than Black's, and his knight is secure on f5, and consequently so is the powerful pawn on h6.

33 ...   ♗c8

Tal tries desperately to dislodge the knight, but it now finds an even better square.

34 Re7+   ♔h8
35 ♘h4   f5
36 ♘g6+   ♔g8
37 Rxa7   1-0

"It goes without saying that an innovation lasting 25 moves is a rarity, but it once more emphasizes what a great return – both competitive and creative – a player can expect from searching, and from experimenting. In itself, such a success far exceeds the disappointment from other, less successful attempts, and it is quite capable of inspiring a player, as the game with Tal inspired me in that USSR Championship." – Polugaevsky.

Lessons from this game:

1) Deep, original opening analysis leads to competitive success and creative satisfaction – as long as you correctly predict your opponents' choices!

2) If the logical plan in the position is kingside attack, you must pursue this goal with the utmost energy. A single inappropriate move can render the attack ineffective.

3) Sometimes an attack cannot be successfully pursued using pieces alone. Pawns are often needed as additional attacking units.

Game 59
Bent Larsen – Boris Spassky
USSR vs Rest of the World, Belgrade 1970
Nimzowitsch-Larsen Attack

The Players

In 1970 Boris Spassky was enjoying life as World Champion, having defeated Tigran Petrosian the previous year. He was representing the Soviet Union on board 1 in the "Match of the Century" against the Rest of the World. For more details see Game 42.

Bent Larsen had been in a rich vein of form from 1967 to early 1970, scoring eight tournament wins out of nine (he was second at Palma in 1968), and so it was not unreasonable that he took first board for the Rest of the World ahead of Bobby Fischer, who had been relatively inactive in those years. Later on in 1970 Larsen came second to Fischer at the Palma Interzonal, but defeated the American in their individual encounter. See Game 54 for more information.

The Game

In a brilliant miniature Spassky fully exploits Larsen's rather extravagant opening play with an imaginative attack on the kingside. An excellent piece sacrifice is followed on move 14 by one of the most incredible moves of all time. This game is essential viewing!

1	b3	e5
2	♗b2	♘c6
3	c4	♘f6
4	♘f3?!	

This move, attacking the e5-pawn and beckoning it forward, is typical of Larsen's provocative style, although on this occasion it seems to overstep the bounds of respectability. More prudent is 4 e3, which would probably lead to a reversed Sicilian set-up after 4...d5 5 cxd5 ♘xd5.

4	...	e4
5	♘d4	♗c5
6	♘xc6	

This capture is the only way forward for White. After 6 e3? ♗xd4! 7 exd4 d5, the b2-bishop is a very poor piece.

6	...	dxc6!

It is normal to capture towards the centre of the board, to increase one's control of the central squares. Chess is a game full of contradictions, however, and on this occasion Spassky is able to break the "rules" to great effect. The point is that after 6...dxc6, Black has opened a line for his c8-bishop, thus enabling him to develop very quickly indeed. Added to this, he now has a half-open d-file on which to operate. The presence of the pawn on e4 means that White's own d-pawn is rendered backward and is therefore a liability. Black's position is already more comfortable to play.

7	e3	♗f5
8	♕c2	♕e7
9	♗e2	0-0-0
10	f4?	

Even by Larsen's standards, this move is excessive. I suppose White is trying to claim some space on the kingside, but such matters as development should really be addressed first of all. With this in mind, it would have been more sensible to play 10 ♘c3 or possibly 10 ♗xf6 ♕xf6 11 ♘c3, hoping to gang up on the slightly vulnerable e4-pawn.

| 10 | ... | ♘g4! |

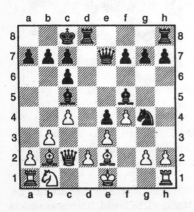

Immediately exploiting the weakness created by White's tenth move. I imagine Larsen either missed or underestimated the strength of this move. The main strength of 10...♘g4 is that it prevents White from smoothly completing his development.

11 g3

This move has the merit of preventing ...♕h4+, but on the other hand it gives Black another target to latch onto, one which Spassky is quick to exploit. However, there were no good alternatives:

1) The natural 11 0-0 allows the powerful sacrifice 11...♖xd2!, when 12 ♕xd2 loses the queen to 12...♗xe3+, while 12 ♘xd2 ♘xe3 13 ♕c1 ♘xf1+ 14 ♔xf1 ♕h4! 15 g3 ♕xh2 16 ♔e1 e3 leads to total annihilation. Given that 11 0-0 fails, White is already scrambling for a useful move.

2) 11 ♗xg4 ♕h4+ 12 g3 ♕xg4 leaves White pathetically weak on the light squares.

3) 11 ♗xg7 would be taking optimism to the extreme. 11...♖hg8 12 ♗b2 ♗xe3! would be a effective way to punish the gluttony: Black wins nicely after 13 dxe3 ♘xe3 14 ♕c3 ♕h4+ 15 g3 ♖xg3 or even more pleasingly after 13 ♗xg4 ♖xg4 14 dxe3 ♕h4+ 15 ♔f1 ♖xg2!! 16 ♕xg2 (16 ♔xg2 ♗h3+ 17 ♔g1 ♕e1#) 16...♖d1+ 17 ♔e2 ♗g4+.

11 ... h5!

The superiority of Black's position has already reached the stage where sacrifices such as 11...♖xd2 have to come into serious consideration. Following 12 ♘xd2 ♘xe3 13 ♕c3 ♖d8 Black has a very strong attack, but then again, there's no need to go overboard with sacrifices – not just yet anyway!

12 h3

In contrast to the last note, after 12 ♘c3 Black should take the plunge with 12...♖xd2:

1) 13 ♔xd2 ♗xe3+ 14 ♔d1 ♖d8+ 15 ♔e1 ♗f2+ 16 ♔f1 ♘e3+ and Black wins.

2) 13 ♕xd2 is a better try, but 13...♗xe3 14 ♕d1 ♘f2! 15 ♕c2 ♘xh1 16 ♘d1 ♗g1! looks winning for Black. White's lack of coordination means there is no way of exploiting Black's unusual occupation of the eighth rank, e.g. 17 ♗f1 ♕d7 18 ♗g2 e3!.

12 ...   h4!

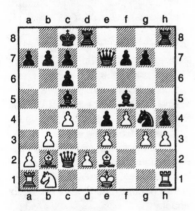

In his book *Boris Spassky: Master of Tactics*, Bernard Cafferty writes "After this fine move the hall with over two thousand spectators bubbled over with enthusiasm. B.H. Wood and I, who were sitting in the front rows, feverishly analysed the acceptance of the offer on a portable set, especially the variation beginning 13 ♗xg4. After some initial scepticism our conclusion was that Black should win, but I must admit in all honesty that we did not find Spassky's *coup de grâce* at move fourteen."

It is incredibly difficult even to visualize Black's spectacular move at this stage, never mind work it out to a forced win. But this is exactly what Spassky does.

13 hxg4

The other way to accept the sacrifice is with 13 ♗xg4, although the lines tend to be similar to the game. After 13...♗xg4 14 hxg4 hxg3 15 ♖g1 Black has two ways to win:

1) 15...♖h1 16 ♖xh1 g2 17 ♖g1 ♕h4+ and then:

1a) 18 ♔e2 loses to 18...♕xg4+ 19 ♔e1 ♕g3+ 20 ♔e2 (or 20 ♔d1 ♕f2 21 ♕xe4 ♕xg1+ 22 ♔c2 ♕f2) 20...♕f3+ 21 ♔e1 ♗e7.

1b) 18 ♔d1 is a better try, although Black's two queens should be sufficient following 18...♕f2 19 ♕xe4 ♕xg1+ 20 ♔c2 ♕f2 21 ♕f5+ ♔b8 22 ♕xc5 g1♕ 23 ♕e7 ♖c8 24 ♗xg7 ♕xg4.

2) The less flashy 15...♖h2 may be even more straightforward. After 16 ♕c3 ♕h4 Black wins after either 17 ♘a3 ♕xg4 or 17 ♔d1 ♖h1 18 ♖xh1 ♕xh1+ 19 ♔c2 g2 20 ♘a3 ♕xa1 21 ♗xa1 ♗xa3! and ...g1♕. Note that 16 ♖xg3 ♕h4 also wins quickly for Black.

13 ...   hxg3
14 ♖g1   ♖h1!!

This move elevates the game onto an altogether different plane. Black sacrifices a rook simply to gain one tempo to push his g-pawn. The one tempo, however, makes all the difference. That said, it should be mentioned that Black can also win in a more mundane manner with 14...♕h4 15 ♖g2 ♕h1+ 16 ♗f1 ♗xg4 17 ♕xe4 ♖he8 18 ♗e5 (18 ♕c2 loses to 18...♗xe3! 19 dxe3 ♖xe3+) 18...f6, but as well as being harder work (Larsen hoped to put up some resistance by 19 ♘c3), that would have been far less eye-catching.

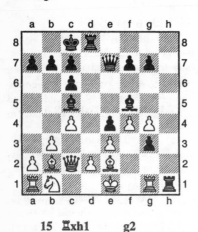

15   ♖xh1   g2

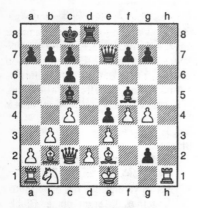

16   ♖f1

Black also wins after 16 ♖g1 ♕h4+ 17 ♔d1 ♕h1 18 ♕c3 ♕xg1+ 19 ♔c2 ♕f2 20 gxf5 and now both the simple promotion 20...g1♕ and 20...♕xe2 21 ♘a3 ♗b4! win for Black. In the

second line White loses his queen, as 22 ♕xb4 allows 22...♕d3+ 23 ♔c1 g1♕#.

16   ...   ♕h4+
17   ♔d1   gxf1♕+

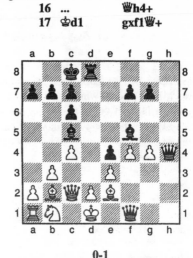

0-1

It is forced mate after 18 ♗xf1 ♗xg4+ 19 ♔c1 ♕e1+ 20 ♕d1 ♕xd1#.

Lessons from this game:

1) Development matters! It doesn't matter how strong a player you are, if you fail to register some development in the opening, then you are asking for trouble.

2) Knowing when to break the "rules" in chess is a very powerful attribute. Here Spassky flouted conventional wisdom as early as move six and was handsomely rewarded. Of course, Larsen also broke some development rules, and his reward was rather smaller!

3) Promoting a pawn, especially before move twenty, usually brings success!

Game 60
Robert Fischer – Oscar Panno
Buenos Aires 1970
Sicilian Defence, King's Indian Attack

The Players

By 1970 most people believed Robert Fischer to be the best player on the planet. He was certainly exhibiting World Championship class. Fischer destroyed the opposition in Buenos Aires, scoring 3½ points more than the second-placed player, the same margin of victory as he enjoyed at the Palma Interzonal later in the year. For more information see Game 38.

Oscar Panno (born 1935) won the World Junior Championship in 1953 and two years later qualified as a Candidate by finishing in third place at the Gothenburg Interzonal. Panno, a civil engineer, has represented Argentina on several occasions, making his debut in 1954 and making the best second-board score at the Havana Olympiad in 1966.

The Game

A forceful game from the World Champion-to-be. Fischer plays unpretentiously in the opening, but then capitalizes on a minor slip by the Argentinean on move 10 to set up a bind in the centre. Panno immediately realizes that this cannot be challenged, and attempts to gain counterplay on the queenside. However, it soon becomes apparent that Fischer's kingside attack is the most important feature of the position. Panno tries to regroup and defend his king, but misses a stunning sacrifice, which is the straw that breaks the camel's back. In the final attack Black's kingside is torn to shreds.

1	e4	c5
2	♘f3	e6
3	d3!?	

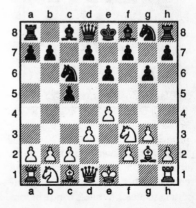

Fischer often employed this quiet system when he didn't fancy facing the rigours of an Open Sicilian. Indeed, he became possibly the world's leading expert on this King's Indian with colours reversed, hardly a surprise giving his skills in playing the King's Indian Defence with Black.

3	...	♘c6
4	g3	g6
5	♗g2	

Interestingly, White can actually consider the paradoxical 5 d4 here. It may look ludicrous to move this pawn again after seemingly committing it to d3, but in fact 5 d4 is an ambitious attempt to exploit the weak dark squares in the black position.

5	...	&g7
6	0-0	&ge7
7	&e1	

White can also consider the immediate 7 c3.

| 7 | ... | d6 |
| 8 | c3 | 0-0 |

There's nothing wrong with this move, but most players now prefer 8...e5, which eliminates any immediate worries about White advancing in the centre with d3-d4. As with 5 d4, the extra tempo spent moving the e-pawn is less important than the amount it achieves.

| 9 | d4 | cxd4 |
| 10 | cxd4 | |

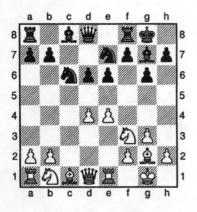

10 ...   d5?!

This move allows White to set up an ideal position, whereas Black's game remains rather lifeless. It is very important to attack White's centre before

he consolidates. For this reason it seems that the most critical move here is 10...&b6!, forcing White into a decision about the d4-pawn. As 11 &e3 allows Black to snatch the b2-pawn, White must instead advance the d4-pawn, which allows Black some freedom. After 11 d5 &d4 (the complicated 11...&xb2!? is also possible; then 12 &xb2 &xb2 13 dxc6 &xa1 14 &b3 &xc6 15 &c3 &d4! 16 &xa1 &xb3 17 axb3 &d7 was equal in Dorfman – Gorelov, Volgodonsk 1981) 12 &c3 exd5 13 exd5 &xf3+ 14 &xf3 &f5 15 &g2 &d7 16 &e2 &fe8 Black had a very active position in Chikovani – Sideif-Zade, Rostov-on-Don 1976.

11 e5   &d7

It's quite surprising how ineffective Black's queenside play becomes. In hindsight one could recommend immediate action in the centre with 11...f6, hoping for 12 exf6 &xf6 13 &h6 &e8, when Black's dark-squared bishop comes to life and the d4-pawn may become weak. Unfortunately for Black, instead of the meek 12 exf6 White should support the e5-pawn with 12 &f4! and follow up with &d2 and &c3.

12	&c3	&c8
13	&f4	&a5
14	&c1	b5
15	b3	b4
16	&e2	&b5
17	&d2	&ac6
18	g4	

A critical moment. White's attack is gradually gathering momentum and with 18 g4 White vacates the g3-square for the knight currently on e2. Black now has to make one of those difficult decisions in chess. He has one chance to exchange his b5-bishop for this knight. Panno chose not to, but this was probably the wrong decision. The game proves that the attacking qualities of the knight outweigh the defensive ones of the bishop. Perhaps Panno was hoping to sneak this bishop to d3 at some point, where it would give some added protection to the kingside, but this proves to be a forlorn hope. After 18...♗xe2 White would still hold the advantage. He could re-route his bishop via f1 to d3 to add extra impetus to the attack. Nevertheless Black would still have better chances to survive than in the actual game. On general principles, exchanging is a good idea when you have a cramped position.

18	...	a5?!
19	♘g3	♛b6
20	h4	♘b8
21	♗h6	

Planning to exchange bishops. The weakness of the dark squares around the black king is emphasized by this trade.

21	...	♘d7
22	♛g5	♖xc1
23	♖xc1	♗xh6

| 24 | ♛xh6 | ♖c8 |
| 25 | ♖xc8+ | ♘xc8 |

At last Black has achieved some exchanges, but at a certain cost. White still has enough pieces for a direct attack on the black king, and Black's pieces are not ideally placed to defend against this.

| 26 | h5 | ♛d8? |

Notwithstanding the last note, Black should not have been in a hurry to retreat this queen. On b6 it was Black's last semblance of counterplay, keeping a watchful eye on d4. After the superior defence 26...♘f8! White cannot win by direct means, for example 27 ♘g5? ♛xd4 28 ♘xh7 ♘xh7 29 hxg6 ♘f8! and White has gone too early. However, it is difficult to see how White can so powerfully punish this mistake.

| 27 | ♘g5 | ♘f8 |

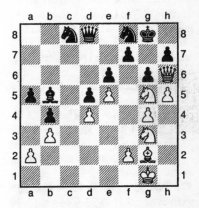

| 28 | ♗e4!! | |

A bolt from the blue! This bishop wants to get on the b1–h7 diagonal, so it does. There is now no way to defend against all of White's threats.

White could sacrifice by 28 ♘xh7!? ♘xh7 29 hxg6 fxg6 30 ♛xg6+ ♚h8

31 ♕xe6 ♘e7 32 ♘f5, but 28 ♗e4 leads to a much clearer finish.

28   ...   ♕e7

Black cannot capture the bishop; after 28...dxe6 29 ♘3xe4 ♕e7 30 ♘f6+ ♔h8 31 ♘gxh7, mate cannot be prevented.

28...♗e8 puts up more resistance, but after 29 hxg6 hxg6 30 ♘h5 gxh5 White can win in two ways:

1) 31 ♘h7 ♘xh7 32 ♗xh7+ ♔h8 33 ♗d3+ ♔g8 34 ♕h7+ ♔f8 35 ♕h8+ ♔e7 36 ♕f6+ ♔d7 37 gxh5! and a very agreeable position is reached. Black's extra piece is useless in the fight against White's h-pawn. If Black swaps queens then he cannot prevent the promotion of the pawn, while after 37...♕b6 38 h6 ♕xd4 39 ♗b5+ ♔c7 40 ♗xe8 ♕g4+ 41 ♔h2 ♕h5+ 42 ♔g3 the checks run out and White wins.

2) 31 ♗h7+ is also sufficient to win after 31...♘xh7 32 ♘xh7 f6 33 ♘xf6+ ♔f7 34 ♘xh5! (threatening mate on g7) 34...♔e7 35 ♕g7+ ♗f7 36 ♕f6+ ♔e8 37 ♘g7+ ♔d7 38 ♕xf7+ and White's two extra pawns are sufficient.

29   ♘xh7   ♘xh7
30   hxg6   fxg6
31   ♗xg6   ♘g5

31...♗e8 loses to 32 ♗xh7+ ♕xh7 33 ♕xe6+.

31...♘f8 leads to a similar ending to the game after 32 ♘h5 ♘xg6 (or 32...♘d7 33 g5 a4 34 ♘f6+ ♘xf6 35 gxf6 ♕c7 36 f7+) 33 ♘f6+ ♔f7 34 ♕h7+ ♔f8 35 ♕g8#.

32   ♘h5   ♘f3+

33	**♔g2**	**♘h4+**
34	**♔g3**	**♘xg6**
35	**♘f6+**	**♔f7**
36	**♕h7+**	

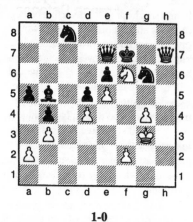

1-0

Black is mated after 36...♔f8 37 ♕g8#.

Lessons from this game:

1) A strongpoint pawn on e5 (or e4 for Black) is often an excellent basis for a kingside attack. Here Fischer cemented the strongpoint at move 11 and it remained there until the end of the game, supporting the knight on f6 in the final mating pattern.

2) Knowing when to exchange and when not to exchange is a vital part of the game. On this occasion Panno gets it wrong on move 18.

3) Panno survived longer in this game than at the Palma Interzonal where the game Fischer – Panno went 1 c4 1-0!

Game 61
Robert Fischer – Bent Larsen
Candidates match (game 1), Denver 1971
French Defence, Winawer Variation

The Players

Robert Fischer (born 1943) was World Champion 1972–5, and arguably the greatest player ever. See Game 38 for further details.

Bent Larsen (born 1935) was one of the world's leading players in the period 1960 to 1980. For more information see Game 54.

The Game

Fischer plays the opening strongly, and Larsen feels the need to grab a "hot" pawn to avoid coming under immense pressure. Fischer whips up a powerful initiative, and refuses to be bought off by Larsen's attempts to give back the pawn. Eventually Larsen finds an imaginative way to regain the initiative at the cost of giving up two bishops for a rook. He then misses what appears to be a saving resource, and goes instead for the white king. Fischer responds with a series of fine blows, leading by force to an interesting ending that is greatly in his favour.

Both players deserve great credit for the quality of their play in this game. It is still hard to believe that it was the first game of a 6–0 whitewash!

1	e4	e6
2	d4	d5
3	♘c3	♗b4

Larsen used many sharp opening systems, and often tailored his choices to suit his opponents. Throughout his career, Fischer had seemed to experience certain problems when playing against the Winawer.

4	e5	♘e7
5	a3	♗xc3+
6	bxc3	c5
7	a4	

Fischer firmly believed Black's opening to be positionally unsound, and so he usually met it with this solid positionally-orientated move, rather than getting involved in the tactical excesses of 7 ♕g4. The bishop will come to a3, exerting pressure along the a3–f8 diagonal, emphasizing Black's weakness on the dark squares. By pushing his a-pawn, White also rules out any ideas Black may have had of playing ...♕a5-a4, bottling up White's queenside.

7	...	♘bc6
8	♘f3	♗d7
9	♗d3!?	♕c7

9...0-0 is no good because of the standard sacrifice 10 ♗xh7+ ♔xh7 11 ♘g5+ ♔g6 (11...♔g8? 12 ♕h5 ♖e8 13 ♕h7+ ♔f8 14 ♕h8+ ♘g8 15 ♘h7+ ♔e7 16 ♗g5+ forces mate) 12 h4 with a very strong attack.

10	0-0	c4
11	♗e2	f6
12	♖e1!	

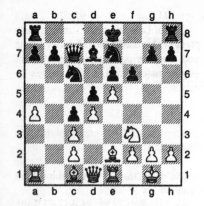

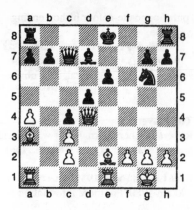

White places his rook on the e-file, not so much to support the e5-pawn, but to maximize his initiative if Black tries to grab it.

12 ...   ♘g6

After 12...fxe5 13 dxe5, Black cannot contemplate 13...♘xe5?? in view of 14 ♘xe5 ♛xe5 15 ♗h5+.

12...0-0 13 ♗a3 ♖f7 14 ♗d6 gives White good play.

13 ♗a3!   fxe5

This is certainly a risky decision, but not necessarily a bad one. In any case, it is typical of Larsen's provocative style – a style that has brought him many fine victories.

14 dxe5   ♘cxe5
15 ♘xe5   ♘xe5

After 15...♛xe5?! 16 ♗xc4 ♛xc3 17 ♗xd5 0-0-0 18 ♖e3 Black's king will now come under attack on the queenside.

16 ♛d4   ♘g6

16...0-0-0 is poor: 17 ♛xa7 ♘c6 18 ♛a8+ ♛b8 19 ♛xb8+ ♔xb8 20 ♗d6+ ♔a7 21 f4 with a substantial positional advantage, as Black will find it virtually impossible to activate his pieces.

16...♘c6?? is even worse: 17 ♗h5+ ♔d8 18 ♛xg7 wins.

17 ♗h5!

Fischer is more interested in dominating the key central squares than in regaining his pawn by taking on g7, which would cost him the initiative. 17 ♗f3!? is an interesting alternative, since 17...0-0-0 18 ♛xa7 is similar to the next note, while 17...♔f7 invites the sacrifice 18 ♗xd5 exd5 19 ♛xd5+ ♔f6 20 ♗c5, when it is not easy for Black to defend.

17 ...   ♔f7

Or 17...0-0-0 18 a5! (intending ♗c5; 18 ♛xa7 b6 19 ♛a8+ ♛b8 20 ♛xb8+ ♔xb8 21 ♗d6+ ♔b7 doesn't give White much) 18...a6 19 ♗c5, and then:

1) 19...♖de8 looks passive, but now ...e5 is a more appealing idea for Black, when it isn't simple for White to increase the pressure, for example 20 ♖ab1?! (20 ♗b6 is sensible) 20...e5 21 ♛xd5? ♘f4.

2) 19...e5 20 ♛xd5 ♘f4 21 ♛e5 ♛xe5 22 ♖xe5 ♘xh5 23 ♖xh5 leads to an ending with rooks and opposite-coloured bishops, in which Black has decent drawing chances. Note, however, that the presence of rooks makes this far less safe for Black than a

"pure" opposite-colour bishop ending would be.

18 f4!

White sets up possible threats involving f4-f5. In general it is obviously logical to play on the f-file, given that the black king has just taken up residence there.

18	...	♖he8
19	f5	exf5
20	♕xd5+	♔f6

This is better than 20...♖e6? 21 ♕xf5+ ♔f6 22 ♖e7+ or 20...♗e6? 21 ♖xe6 ♖xe6 22 ♕xf5+ ♖f6 23 ♕d5+ ♖e6 24 ♖f1+, when the e6-rook falls.

21 ♗f3!?

This move has been criticized, but the suggested alternatives aren't necessarily more convincing:

1) 21 g4 ♕b6+ 22 ♗c5 ♕c6 23 ♕d4+ (23 ♕xc4, threatening h4, could be tried) 23...♔g5!? might survive.

2) 21 ♗d6 ♕d8 (21...♕c6 22 ♕d4+ ♔f7 23 ♗f3, followed by ♗d5+, is good for White) 22 ♗f3 (22 g4 ♕b6+) 22...♗c6 23 ♕d4+ ♔f7 24 ♗xc6 bxc6 25 ♕xc4+ ♔f6 26 ♕xc6 ♕b6+ and White's weak pawns reduce his winning chances in the ending.

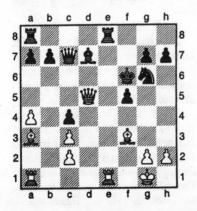

21 ...   ♘e5!

One of Larsen's great strengths as a player is his ability to find tricky twists and turns in positions where others might instead resign themselves to merely trying to put up stubborn resistance. Such is the case here. With this knight move Larsen brings about a position where, albeit at the cost of some material, he has managed to regain the initiative and create some real threats to the white king. Others are less of a problem for White:

1) 21...♗e6 22 ♕d4+ ♔f7 23 ♖ab1 (or 23 ♗d6 and 24 ♖ab1) 23...♖ad8 24 ♕xa7 ♗c8 25 ♖xe8 ♔xe8 (25...♖xe8 26 ♗d5+ ♔f6 27 ♕d4+) 26 ♕c5! ♕xc5+ 27 ♗xc5 gives White a promising ending thanks to his superbly active pieces.

2) 21...♖xe1+ 22 ♖xe1 ♖e8 23 ♕d4+ ♔f7 24 ♖b1! b6 25 a5 gives White a dangerous, board-wide attack.

22 ♕d4!

Now 23 ♗d6 is a powerful threat. Instead 22 ♖xe5? ♖xe5 23 ♕d4 ♕b6! not only saves Black, but gives him a decisive advantage.

22 ...   ♔g6

Certainly not 22...♖ad8? 23 ♗d6 ♕a5 24 ♗d5, when Black's position falls apart.

23 ♖xe5   ♕xe5

23...♖xe5? 24 ♗d6 will leave White a piece up.

24 ♕xd7   ♖ad8

After 24...♕xc3, 25 ♕d6+ forces 25...♕f6 (and not 25...♔g5?? 26 h4+ ♔xh4 27 ♕f4#), when Black fails to create counterplay. "Normal service" would then be resumed, with White's two bishops overpowering Black's position.

25 ♕xb7

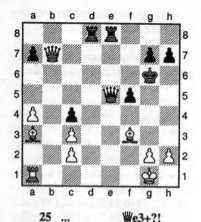

25 ...   Ⓦe3+?!

This extremely tempting move ultimately turns out not to work. Instead 25...Ⓦxc3 might very well have saved Black:

1) 26 Ⓦb1 Ⓡe5! (a move found by Yakov Murei) 27 ♗b4 (27 ♗b2? Ⓦe3+ 28 ♔h1 Ⓡb8) 27...Ⓦe3+ 28 ♔h1 c3.

2) 26 Ⓦc6+ ♔g5 and then:

2a) 27 h4+?! ♔xh4 28 Ⓦc7 Ⓦxa1+ 29 ♔h2 (29 ♗c1? Ⓦxc1+ 30 ♔h2 is an attempt to sacrifice most of White's pieces to give mate; the snag is that after 30...Ⓡd6! 31 Ⓦxd6 ♔g5 there is no mate, and Black is still material up) 29...♔g5 (rather than 29...Ⓦe5+ 30 Ⓦxe5 Ⓡxe5 31 ♗c1 f4 32 ♗xf4 Ⓡg5 33 g3+ Ⓡxg3 34 ♗xg3+ with a difficult ending for Black) and White's attack does not seem sufficient, e.g. 30 ♗e7+ Ⓡxe7 31 Ⓦxe7+ Ⓦf6.

2b) 27 ♗c1+ f4 (27...♔h4 28 g3+ ♔h3 29 ♗g2+ ♔g4 30 h3+ ♔xg3 31 Ⓦc7+ Ⓦe5 32 Ⓦxe5+ Ⓡxe5 33 ♗g5! neatly corners the black king – he can only avoid mate, e.g. by Ⓡf1-f3#, at great material cost) 28 h4+ ♔f5 29 g4+ fxg3 30 ♔g2 Ⓦd4 (30...Ⓦxa1 31 ♗g4+ allows White more dangerous play, since his king is more secure

against checks from the black queen) 31 ♔xg3 Ⓦxa1 32 ♗g4+ ♔e5 33 Ⓦc5+ ♔f6 34 Ⓦf5+ ♔e7 35 ♗g5+ ♔d6 36 ♗f4+ and White only has a draw.

26 ♔f1

The king must come out from under its pawn-cover, of course, since 26 ♔h1 Ⓦe1+ forces mate.

26 ...   Ⓡd2

Black's counterattack has apparently reached truly frightening proportions. However, a beautiful, flowing sequence of power moves from Fischer shows that this is just an illusion.

27 Ⓦc6+   Ⓡe6

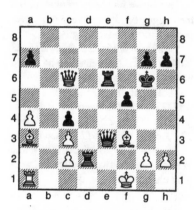

28 ♗c5!

The exclamation mark is just for the aesthetic appeal of the move, leaving the queen *en prise* and calmly allowing a double check – there are no viable alternatives.

28 ...   Ⓡf2+

29 ♔g1

Fischer has foreseen that the best Black can get out of this position is an ending where the black queen is inferior to White's rook and two bishops.

29 ...   Ⓡxg2++

30	♔xg2	♛d2+
31	♔h1	♖xc6
32	♗xc6	♛xc3

Play against the exposed black king now helps White to coordinate his scattered pieces.

33	♖g1+	♔f6
34	♗xa7	

It is very important that White has managed to secure a passed pawn, which he is able both to protect and advance.

| 34 | ... | f4 |

34...g5 35 ♗b6 g4 36 a5 ♛b2 37 ♗d8+ ♔g6 38 a6 also sees White pushing his pawn towards promotion.

35	♗b6	♛xc2
36	a5	♛b2
37	♗d8+	♔e6
38	a6	

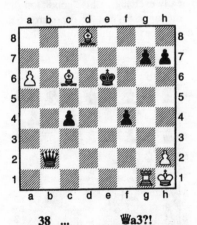

| 38 | ... | ♛a3?! |

In a position with so many loose pieces and both kings exposed, it is not surprising that the moves leading up to the time-control are not too accurate. 38...♛d4!? (centralization!) is more resilient. For example, 39 ♗c7 (39 ♖e1+ ♔d6) 39...♛c5 40 ♖e1+ ♔f7 41 ♗e8+ ♔f8 42 ♗xf4 ♛a5 and

White's a-pawn falls, greatly reducing his winning chances.

| 39 | ♗b7 | |

39 ♖e1+!? also coordinates White's pieces: 39...♔f5 (39...♔d6?? 40 ♗e7+; 39...♔f7 40 ♗d5+ ♔g6 41 ♗e7 and the threat to the black king – ♖g1+ will drive it to the h-file – and the idea of advancing the a-pawn are too much) 40 ♗e4+ ♔g4 (after 40...♔e5 41 ♗b6 the pawn runs through) 41 ♖g1+ ♔h5 42 ♖xg7 (threatening mate in two by 43 ♖xh7+ ♔g4 44 ♖h4#) 42...♛a1+ 43 ♖g1 ♛xa6 44 ♗f3+ ♔h6 45 ♗c7 corners the king: 45...♛f6 46 ♖g4 ♛a1+ 47 ♔g2 ♛b2+ 48 ♔h3 and ♗xf4+ follows.

| 39 | ... | ♛c5?! |

39...♛b2 40 ♖e1+ ♔d6 41 ♗g5 only prolongs the game.

40	♖b1	c3?!
41	♗b6!	**1-0**

Since the a-pawn is unstoppable, e.g. 41...c2 42 ♖e1+ ♛e5 and now 43 ♖xe5+ ♔xe5 44 a7 is the simplest; after 44...c1♛+ 45 ♗g1 and a8♛ White is two bishops up with a safe king.

Lessons from this game:

1) By all means choose an opening that you think will unsettle the opponent, but it is at least as important not to unsettle yourself in the process.

2) When you have sacrificed material for the initiative, don't rush to win it back when there are still ways to crank up the pressure and force more concessions.

3) Decision-making in a messy ending can often be simplified by considering which are the dangerous pawns – the "big" pawns that are heading for promotion – and how to advance one's own and stop the opponent's.

Game 62
Robert Fischer – Tigran Petrosian
Candidates match (game 7), Buenos Aires 1971
Sicilian Defence, Kan Variation

The Players
Robert Fischer (born 1943) was World Champion 1972–5, and arguably the greatest player ever. See Game 38 for further details.

Tigran Petrosian (1929–84) was World Champion 1963–9. For more information see Game 56.

The Game
In a crystal-clear positional masterpiece, Fischer starts off by saddling his opponent with some weak pawns. He refuses to give Petrosian even a sniff of the initiative in return – this is to be a torture session. Adeptly exchanging the right pieces off, he establishes a large and durable advantage. At the point when the assembled grandmasters in the press room are wondering how he is to make further progress, Fischer shocks them by paradoxically exchanging his "good" knight for Petrosian's "bad" bishop. It quickly becomes apparent that this is no error, but rather the move of a genius, as his remaining pieces make quick work of Black's position.

1	e4	c5
2	♘f3	e6
3	d4	cxd4
4	♘xd4	a6
5	♗d3	

This is the most flexible reply to Black's system, retaining the possibility of playing c4, putting a bind on the d5-square. Ordinarily the move ♗d3 (instead of ♘c3) would be a little slow at this stage of an Open Sicilian, and allow Black to generate play in the centre with a quick ...d5 or pressure against the d4-knight, but Black's ...a6, while a thematic and generally useful move, is also rather slow.

5	...	♘c6
6	♘xc6	bxc6
7	0-0	d5

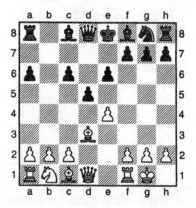

8 c4!?

A strong positional move. Black has achieved a substantial pawn-presence in the centre, but as yet it is not supported by his pieces. If Black is granted time to provide it with such support, then he would stand quite well. Therefore Fischer makes use of his development advantage to attack the pawns immediately.

8 ♘d2 had been Spassky's choice in this position against Petrosian in their 1969 world championship match, but he made no impression on Black's position. Fischer's choice is much more to the point.

8 ...   ♘f6

Instead, capturing on either c4 or e4 would leave Black with a dreadful pawn-formation and nothing to show for it.

8...d4 was mentioned by Stean as a plausible alternative, though "yet another non-developing move must be regarded with some suspicion". One practical example bears out this suspicion: 9 e5 c5 10 ♖e1 ♘e7 11 ♗g5 ♕c7 12 ♗xe7 ♗xe7 13 ♘d2 ♖b8 14 b3 g6 15 ♘f3 0-0 16 ♕d2 with a positional advantage for White, J. Enevoldsen – Moe, Esbjerg 1972.

9 cxd5   cxd5
10 exd5   exd5

Petrosian chooses to accept an isolated pawn now, while there are still plenty of pieces left on the board with which he can hope to generate counterplay. The other captures are unattractive:

1) 10...♕xd5 11 ♘c3 ♕c6 12 ♗e2 emphasizes Black's poor development.

2) After 10...♘xd5, 11 ♗e4! makes sure that Black will have an isolated d-pawn:

2a) 11...♖a7 12 ♗xd5 (12 ♕f3 ♖d7 13 ♘d2, intending ♘c4-e5, is R. Byrne's suggestion) 12...♕xd5 13 ♕xd5 exd5 14 ♗e3 ♖c7 15 ♘c3 ♗e6 16

♖fd1 gave White a comfortable advantage in G. Kuzmin – Schendel, Yalta 1995.

2b) 11...♗e7 12 ♘c3 ♗b7 13 ♕a4+ ♕d7 14 ♕xd7+ ♔xd7 15 ♖d1 actually won the pawn immediately in Averbakh – Taimanov, USSR Championship, Leningrad 1960.

11 ♘c3   ♗e7

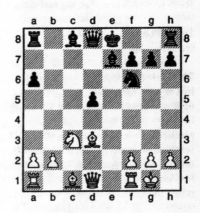

12 ♕a4+!

"A deep move. Given time to castle, play ...♗b7 and ...d4, Black would be happy. Remember, weak pawns are only a handicap if they result in the pieces being driven to bad or passive squares in order to defend them." – Stean, writing in *Simple Chess*.

12 ...   ♕d7?!

Petrosian decides that drastic measures are called for, and, typically, offers an exchange sacrifice. While it would be too much to call the idea a trap, Black would get a good deal of activity, and Fischer is wise to decline the offer and continue positionally.

Instead the obvious move 12...♗d7 gives White a pleasant choice:

1) 13 ♕c2 keeps some advantage, but Black gets a playable game after

either 13...0-0 14 ♗g5 d4, 13...♗e6 14 ♗g5 h6 15 ♗xf6 ♗xf6 16 ♕a4+ ♔f8 or 13...d4!? 14 ♘e2 (and not 14 ♘e4?! ♘xe4 15 ♗xe4 ♖c8 and 16...♗b5).

2) 13 ♕d4! is best, keeping the queen powerfully centralized, and eyeing dark squares (on which Black is particularly vulnerable) on both sides of the board. It would then be very difficult for Black to create any real counterplay. Byrne gives the continuation 13...♗e6 14 ♗f4 0-0 15 ♖ac1.

13   ♖e1!

Fischer's play is a picture of simplicity. He is sees that his positional advantage is far more valuable than a mere exchange – especially when offered by the master of the exchange sacrifice. 13 ♗b5?! axb5 14 ♕xa8 0-0 is described by Speelman as "extremely messy". Speelman is a specialist in messy positions, so we can trust his judgement, which is borne out by the continuation 15 ♕a5 d4 (15...b4!? is another way to create confusion) 16 ♘xb5 (16 ♖d1!? is a better attempt to disrupt Black's plans, though White's position remain shaky) 16...♗b7 threatening 17...♖a8 and 17...♗xg2. A perpetual check is quite a likely outcome.

13   ...   ♕xa4

13...d4? simply loses the pawn after 14 ♕xd7+ ♗xd7 15 ♘e2 ♗b4 16 ♖d1 ♗c5 17 ♗f4 followed by 18 ♗e5.

14   ♘xa4

The exchange of queens has hardly eased Black's game. Indeed, the a6-pawn is now more of a glaring weakness than it was with queens on the board.

14   ...   ♗e6
15   ♗e3   0-0

Black has no time to stop White's imminent invasion on c5 – his sluggish

development is still hampering his game. Instead 15...♘d7 16 f4! g6 17 ♗d4 0-0 18 ♖ac1 gives White a very pleasant game – Black's pieces have very little scope.

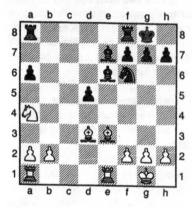

16   ♗c5!

Fischer knows exactly what he should be aiming for. Black's dark-squared bishop is his only piece that cannot be tied down to defending his weak pawns, which are fixed on light squares. White's own dark-squared bishop is the right piece to exchange it for, since White's knight will, following the exchange, be able to exert a paralysing grip on Black's position from the c5-square. Less convincing alternatives:

1) 16 ♘c5 a5! 17 ♗d4 ♗xc5 18 ♗xc5 has allowed Black an extra tempo (...a6-a5) by comparison with the game. Although Black's game remains difficult, this difference certainly lightens his load.

2) 16 ♘b6 is an admittedly crude attempt to grab material, and, though not bad, gives Black better drawing chances than the game continuation: 16...♖ab8 17 ♗xa6 ♘g4!? (17...♗d8

18 ♘a4 d4 "gives Black the initiative" according to Botvinnik, but things are not too rosy for Black if we extend this line a little further: 19 ♗xd4 ♖b4 20 ♗xf6 ♗xf6 21 ♘c5 ♖xb2 22 ♘xe6 fxe6 23 ♗c4 ♗d4 24 ♖xe6 ♔h8 and Black has certain drawing chances) 18 ♗d4 (18 ♘a4 ♖a8) 18...♗f6 (18...♗d8 allows 19 ♖xe6! fxe6 20 ♘d7) 19 ♗c5 ♖fd8 and White's pieces have lost some of their coordination.

16	...	♖fe8
17	♗xe7	♖xe7

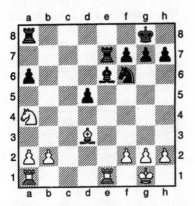

18 b4!

Fischer does not rush to use the c5-square. First he secures the outpost, and prepares to meet an ...a5 advance by playing b5, creating a mighty passed pawn. This move therefore fixes the pawn on a6, where it is most easily attacked. Indeed, now when White plays ♘c5, it will cause an immediate crisis in Black's game. Stean makes an interesting point here: "Whether you approach the position from the point of view of outposts or weaknesses, the move 18 b4! cries out to be played." That, of course, is the way it should be. Thinking about a position from

two different but wholly valid angles should lead to the same conclusion about the objectively most effective move (if there is one).

18	...	♔f8

Preparing a defence for the a6-pawn and improving the king's position, however slightly.

19	♘c5	♗c8
20	f3!	

White stops Black using the e4-square and gives the king a fast-track to the centre. Stean makes the point that 20 ♖xe7? ♔xe7 21 ♖e1+ ♔d6 would solve most of Black's problems at a stroke, as his king is well-placed to coordinate the queenside defence.

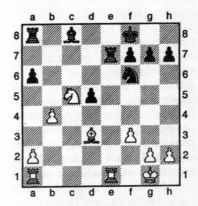

20	...	♖ea7?

This odd-looking move, attempting to develop the bishop by ...♗d7-b5, does not work. Instead Black had to try 20...♖xe1+ 21 ♖xe1 ♘e8 22 ♔f2 ♘c7 23 ♔e3 ♔e7 24 ♔d4+ ♔d6 "and the worst is behind Black once the knight is on c7" – Botvinnik. Instead, 20...♘d7 21 ♘b3 (White avoids piece exchanges) 21...♘e5 22 ♗f1 ♗d7 (intending ...♗b5) fails, as Stean indicates, because of the weakness of the d5-pawn: 23 ♖ed1! and Black must abandon his plan.

21 ♖e5!   ♗d7

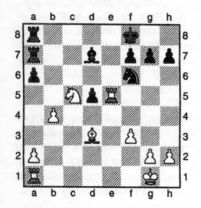

22 ♘xd7+!!

This is one of the most talked-about moves in chess history. It looks extremely unnatural to exchange off the strong, beautifully-placed knight for Black's bad, awkward bishop. Yet it wins the game quickly and efficiently. Is there something wrong with the principles that would lead many players not even to consider the move? Not really. Nine times out of ten (if not more frequently) it would be wrong to exchange a good knight for a bad bishop. The problem is if a useful general principle takes on the status of a hard-and-fast rule, rather than it always being governed by the proviso, "unless the specifics of the position demand another move". Speelman explains the logic as follows: "...although it was 'bad', the bishop was holding together the black position. After its exchange, the white rooks can show their paces in a way which was not possible before." To put it another way, Fischer has transformed the

advantage of the superior minor piece into the advantage of greater rook activity. Given that the rooks have plenty of targets, this is a good trade. Nevertheless, the move came as a complete surprise to the assembled grandmasters in the press room, with the impulsive Najdorf immediately criticizing it as a mistake.

22 ...   ♖xd7
23 ♖c1

Threatening 24 ♗xa6 in view of Black's weak back rank.

23 ...   ♖d6

Black prevents ♖c6, but at the cost of allowing the rook into c7. After 23...g6, 24 ♖c6 wins material.

24 ♖c7   ♘d7
25 ♖e2

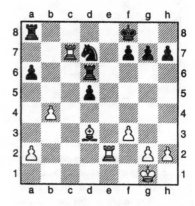

Black is quite seriously tied up, and close to being in zugzwang.

25 ...   g6

Or:

1) 25...♘b6 would allow White to play 26 ♖ee7.

2) 25...a5 loses to, amongst other moves, 26 ♗b5.

3) After 25...♖e8 Stean gave the amusing line 26 ♖xe8+ ♔xe8 27 ♖a7

♘b8 28 b5! axb5 29 ♗xb5+ ♔f8
(29...♘d7 30 ♔f2 ♔d8 31 ♖xd7+
♖xd7 32 ♗xd7 ♔xd7 33 ♔e3 is a trivially won king and pawn ending for
White in view of his outside passed
pawn) 30 ♖b7, dominating the b8-
knight and tying the rook to its defence, and in turn restricting the black
king. Following 30...♖d8 31 ♔f2 White
puts his king in front of the d-pawn
and promotes his a-pawn.

26 ♔f2   h5

26...♖b8 27 a3 a5 was Botvinnik's
suggestion, but 28 bxa5 (28 b5 a4 was
the idea) looks awkward to meet.

After 26...♖e8 27 ♖xe8+ ♔xe8 28
♖a7 ♖b6 29 a3 ♘b8 30 ♔e3 the white
king will penetrate, given suitable care
to circumvent a ...♘c6+ fork.

27 f4

White now plans ♔g3-h4-g5 and
f5.

27 ...   h4

27...♘b6 28 ♖ee7 ♖f6 is a better
way to stir up at least some trouble.

28 ♔f3!

The simple threat of ♔g4 and ♔xh4
obliges Black now to weaken more
squares in his position.

28 ...   f5
29 ♔e3   d4+

Petrosian desperately tries to keep
the white king out, but the price is that
the bishop's scope is greatly increased.
After 29...♘f6 30 ♔d4 ♘e4 31 ♖ec2
White "oozes" in.

30 ♔d2

Black is in a sort of zugzwang, except that White has active plans, such
as ♗c4, ♔d3, ♖e6, etc.

30 ...   ♘b6

If the a8-rook moves, 31 ♖a7 follows, while 30...♖d5 loses to 31 ♖e6.

30...a5 31 bxa5 ♖xa5 32 ♖c8+ ♔g7
33 ♗c4 ♔f6 34 ♖ce8 ♘c5 puts up
more resistance, but 35 ♖f8+ ♔g7 36
♖f7+ ♔h6 37 ♖ee7 ♘e4+ 38 ♔d1
♘f6 39 ♖f8 g5 40 ♖e5 is good enough.

31 ♖ee7   ♘d5
32 ♖f7+   ♔e8
33 ♖b7   ♘xf4

33...♖b6 34 ♖xb6 ♘xb6 (34...♔xf7
35 ♗c4) 35 ♖g7 ♔f8 36 ♖xg6 ♘d5 37
♗c4 wins.

33...♖b8 34 ♖a7 ♖a8 (34...♘xf4 35
♖h7 ♘e6 36 ♗c4) 35 ♖xa8+ ♔xf7 36
♗c4 ♔e6 (otherwise the a-pawn drops
after an exchange on d5) 37 ♔d3 and
Black is completely helpless.

34 ♗c4   1-0

White's mating ideas with 35 ♖h7
are decisive.

Lessons from this game:

1) Pawn weaknesses can cost you
the game – if you accept them, be sure
that you have enough activity to compensate.

2) If the pawn position is in your
favour, keep it that way! Stamp out
possible pawn breaks for the opponent
and secure key outposts.

3) "Good" and "bad" are only formal terms for bishops. If the specifics
of the position make your opponent's
"bad" bishop an effective piece, either
offensively or defensively, you should
have few qualms about exchanging it
for your own "good" bishop or a
"strong" knight.

Game 63
Dragoljub Velimirović – Ljubomir Ljubojević
Yugoslav Championship, Umag 1972
Sicilian Defence, Najdorf Variation

The Players

Dragoljub Velimirović (born 1942) is a Yugoslav grandmaster who comes from a chess-playing family – his mother was Yugoslavia's first women's champion. Velimirović won the Yugoslav Championship twice, in 1970 (jointly) and 1975. Although he has never reached the higher echelons of world chess, Velimirović is a dangerous attacking player who occasionally produces beautiful sacrificial games.

Ljubomir Ljubojević (born 1950) was ranked third in the world in 1983 and was Yugoslavia's leading player from the mid-1970s to the late 1980s. During this period he won many major international tournaments, but he made little impact in world championship cycles and has never qualified for the Candidates. He has played less often in the 1990s, but still takes part in a few tournaments each year and is quite active in club chess. "Ljubo", as he is universally known, is full of energy and is famous for his rapid-fire conversations in several languages. Ljubo has retained his Serbian nationality although, like many other leading players, he now lives in Spain. Ljubo is also a dangerous attacking player, as Game 69 (Ljubojević – Andersson) demonstrates.

The Game

At first the game follows a standard line of the Najdorf, but at move 12 Velimirović introduces a stunning novelty, sacrificing a piece. After many years of analysis this sacrifice was proved incorrect, but Ljubojević was faced with a difficult task over the board. Ljubojević makes two small slips and the sacrificial onslaught breaks through.

1	e4	c5
2	♘f3	d6
3	d4	cxd4
4	♘xd4	♘f6
5	♘c3	a6
6	♗g5	e6
7	f4	♗e7
8	♕f3	♕c7
9	0-0-0	♘bd7
10	♗d3	b5
11	♖he1	♗b7

This is a standard position of the Sicilian Najdorf and at the time this game was played, 12 ♕g3 was the most popular move (it is regarded as strongest today). Rather than follow the conventional line, Velimirović uncorks an incredible piece sacrifice.

12 ♘d5!?

It was years before the correct reply was discovered, so this was certainly an excellent practical bet!

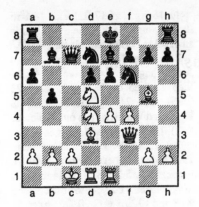

12   ...   ♘xd5

One can hardly criticize Ljubojević for not finding the difficult refutation. Readers should refer to a book on opening theory for the full details, but the main line runs 12...exd5 13 ♘f5 ♚f8 14 ♕g3 dxe4 15 ♗xe4 ♗xe4 16 ♖xe4 ♕c5! 17 ♗h6 ♘xe4! 18 ♕xg7+ ♚e8 19 ♕xh8+ ♚f8 20 ♗xf8 ♗xf8 21 ♕xh7 ♖c8 and Black has the advantage. The move played appears natural, but there is a stunning surprise in store.

13   exd5   ♗xg5

More or less forced, as 13...♗xd5 (13...♘f6 14 ♗xf6 ♗xf6 15 ♗e4 e5 16 fxe5 ♗xe5 17 ♘c6 0-0 18 ♘xe5 dxe5 19 ♕h3 h6 20 d6 is also very good for White) 14 ♕xd5! exd5 15 ♖xe7+ ♚f8 (15...♚d8 16 ♖xf7+ ♚c8 17 ♗f5 wins) 16 ♗f5 h6 (or 16...♖d8 17 ♗e6 f6 18 ♖f7+ ♚e8 19 ♖xg7 fxg5 20 ♗f7+ ♚e7 21 ♗h5+ ♚f6 22 ♖f7#) 17 ♖xd7 ♕c4 18 ♗e7+ ♚g8 19 ♗xd6 ♕xa2 20 ♘c6 gives White a winning position.

14   ♖xe6+!

This further rook sacrifice is the only way to maintain the attack's momentum. After 14 ♘xe6 (14 fxg5 ♘e5

15 ♕h3 ♗xd5 16 g6 0-0-0 also favours Black) 14...fxe6 15 ♕h5+ ♚f8 16 fxg5 ♘e5 17 g6 (17 ♖xh7 ♕c4 18 b3 ♕f4+ 19 ♚b1 ♗e7) 17...h6 18 ♖xe5 dxe5 19 ♖f1+ ♚e8 20 ♖f7 ♕c5 21 ♕xe5 ♗xd5 22 ♕xg7 ♖f8 White runs out of steam.

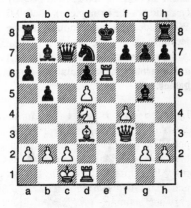

14   ...   fxe6

Once again, Black does not have much choice, e.g.:

1) 14...♗e7 15 ♘f5! g6 (15...fxe6 16 ♘xg7+ ♚f7 17 ♘xe6 ♕a5 18 ♕h5+ ♚g8 19 ♕g4+ ♚f7 20 ♕g7+ ♚e8 21 ♗g6+ hxg6 22 ♕xg6#) 16 ♖xe7+ ♚d8 (16...♚f8 17 ♖de1 gxf5 18 ♕h5 wins) 17 ♖xf7 gxf5 18 ♗xf5 ♗c8 19 ♕g4 ♕a7 20 ♕g5+ ♚c7 21 ♗xd7 ♕e3+ 22 ♚b1 ♗xd7 23 ♖e7, followed by 24 ♖xd7+ and 25 ♕g7+, with a winning position.

2) 14...♚d8 15 fxg5 ♘e5 16 ♖xe5 dxe5 17 ♘c6+ ♚e8 18 ♗f5 with a massive attack in return for a minimal material investment.

15   ♘xe6!

Once again White chooses the most dangerous move. After 15 ♕h5+ g6 16 ♗xg6+ hxg6! (not 16...♚e7 17 ♕xg5+ ♘f6 18 ♘f5+! ♚d7 19 dxe6+

♔c6 20 ♖xd6+ ♕xd6 21 ♘xd6 ♔xd6 22 ♕e5+ ♔c6 23 b4 ♕d5 24 ♗e4 and White wins) 17 ♕xh8+ (or 17 ♕xg6+ ♔d8 18 ♘xe6+ ♔c8 19 ♘xc7 ♗xf4+ 20 ♔b1 ♔xc7 and Black has too many pieces for the queen) 17...♘f8 18 ♘xe6 ♗xf4+ 19 ♘xf4 (19 ♔b1 ♕f7 20 ♖f1 ♗xd5 21 ♖xf4 ♕xe6 22 ♕xf8+ ♔d7 consolidates the extra piece) 19...0-0-0 White does not have enough for the piece.

After the text-move Black faces a crucial choice: where should he move his queen?

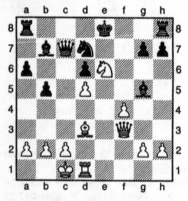

15   ...   ♕a5?!

White's main threat is to play his rook to the e-file, lining up against the enemy king, which is trapped in the centre. Hence this move appears most natural, since it not only prevents ♖e1 but also attacks the a2-pawn. However, in such a position it is dangerous to rely on general principles. It turns out that the alternative 15...♕b6! is more accurate. The queen is more actively placed on b6, and a later ...♕e3+ will prevent ♖e1 with gain of tempo. In response to this move White may try:

1) 16 fxg5? g6 17 ♖f1 ♘e5 18 ♕f6 ♖g8 favours Black – the e5-knight is an excellent defensive piece.

2) 16 ♖e1? ♗f6 17 ♕h5+ g6 18 ♗xg6+ hxg6 19 ♕xg6+ ♔e7 20 ♘g7+ ♗e5 21 fxe5 dxe5 22 d6+ ♔d8 23 ♘e6+ ♔c8 24 ♕g7 ♖d8 25 ♘xd8 ♕xd8 and White has run out of pieces.

3) 16 ♕h5+ g6 and now:

3a) 17 ♗xg6+ ♔e7 18 ♕xg5+ ♘f6 19 ♗h5! (the alternatives all win for Black: 19 ♗f5 ♖ag8, 19 ♘d4 hxg6 20 ♕xg6 ♘e8! 21 ♖e1+ ♔d8 22 ♘e6+ ♔c8 and 19 ♖e1 ♕f2 20 ♔d1 hxg6 21 ♕xg6 ♖ag8 22 ♘g7+ ♔d7 23 ♕xf6 ♔c8 24 ♘f5 ♔b8) 19...♕e3+ 20 ♔b1 ♖ag8 21 ♘g7 ♗c8 22 ♕h4 ♖xg7 23 ♖e1 ♕xe1+ 24 ♕xe1+ ♔d8 and Black is slightly better in this complex position.

3b) 17 ♕xg5 ♕e3+ 18 ♔b1 ♔f7 (18...♘e5 19 ♕f6 ♘f7 20 ♘c7+ ♔f8 21 ♘e6+ is an immediate draw) with a final branch:

3b1) 19 ♕h6 ♖ag8! (if Black plays 19...♗xd5 White can at any rate force a draw by 20 ♕g7+ ♔xe6 21 f5+ gxf5 22 ♗xf5+ ♔xf5 23 ♖f1+ ♔e4 24 ♕g4+ ♔e5 25 ♕g7+) 20 ♘g5+ ♔e8 21 ♕h4 ♔d8 22 ♖e1 ♕b6 23 ♘f7+ ♔c8 24 ♘xh8 ♖xh8 25 ♗xg6 ♕d8!, forcing the exchange of queens, after which Black has a clear advantage.

3b2) 19 ♕h4! (the best chance) and now Black has the choice between forcing a draw by 19...♖ae8 20 ♖e1 ♕d2 21 ♘d8+ ♖xd8 22 ♕e7+ ♔g8 23 ♕e6+ or playing for a win with the unclear 19...♗xd5 20 ♘c7 ♕c5 21 ♘xa8 ♘f6 22 f5 gxf5 23 ♖f1 ♗e6 24 ♘c7 ♕xc7 25 ♗xf5 ♗xf5 26 ♖xf5 ♕e7 27 ♕h5+ ♔e6 28 ♕h3.

Previous annotators have dismissed Black's position as lost following

15...♕a5?!, but I believe that the fatal error only occurs later. What is clear, however, is that after 15...♕b6! White is struggling for a draw whereas after 15...♕a5?! it is Black who must play (very) accurately to save the game.

16 ♕h5+   g6

17 ♕xg5

Not 17 ♗xg6+? ♔e7 18 ♕xg5+ ♘f6 and the attack falters.

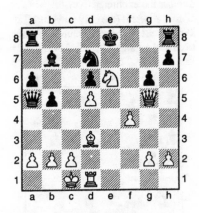

17 ...   ♖g8!

Other defences are inferior:

1) 17...♖f8 18 f5 ♖f6 (18...♖g8 19 fxg6 h6 20 ♕xh6 ♗xd5 21 ♗f5 ♗xa2 22 ♕e3 and 18...♗xd5 19 ♘xf8 ♘xf8 20 fxg6 ♕xa2 21 gxh7 win for White) 19 fxg6 h6 20 ♕xh6 ♗xd5 21 ♘g7+ ♔d8 22 ♘h5! ♕xa2 23 ♘xf6 ♘xf6 24 ♕f8+ ♘e8 25 ♖e1 ♗c6 26 g7 and wins.

2) 17...♘f8 18 ♕f6 ♘xe6 (White also wins after 18...♗xd5 19 ♗e4 ♗xe4 20 ♕xh8 ♔e7 21 ♘g5) 19 dxe6 ♖f8 20 ♕g7 0-0-0 (20...♗c6 21 ♕xh7) 21 e7 and White will be a pawn up with a good position.

18 ♖d2!

The rook finds an alternative path to the e-file. It is astonishing that

White, a whole rook down, can afford this relatively leisurely manoeuvre, but Black's king cannot easily flee from the e-file.

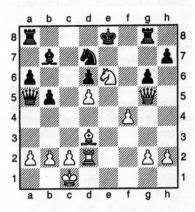

18 ...   ♘f8?

The key moment of the whole game. Faced with the unrelenting pressure, Ljubojević makes a serious error which loses by force. The alternatives are:

1) 18...♕xa2 19 ♖e2 ♔f7 20 ♕h6 ♗xd5 21 ♕xh7+ ♔f6 22 ♘f8! and White wins.

2) 18...♖a7 19 ♖e2 ♔f7 20 ♕h6 ♘f8 21 ♘g5+ ♔f6 22 ♘xh7+ ♔f7 23 ♕g5 with a decisive attack.

3) 18...♘b6 19 ♖e2 ♔d7 (19...♔f7 20 ♘d8+ ♖gxd8 21 ♗xg6+ mates) 20 ♕h6 ♘xd5 21 ♕xh7+ ♔c6 22 ♗e4 ♕b6 23 c4! bxc4 24 ♖d2 ♔b5 25 ♗xd5 ♗xd5 26 ♘c7+ ♔a4 27 ♘xd5 and Black's king is too exposed.

4) 18...♔f7 (the most obvious move, but it is bad) and now:

4a) 19 ♕h6 with two lines:

4a1) 19...♘f8 20 ♖e2 ♗xd5 21 ♘g5+ ♔f6 22 ♕h4! ♕xa2 (22...♔g7 23 ♖e7+ leads to a quick mate) 23 ♘xh7+ ♔g7 24 ♖e7+ ♗f7 25 ♕f6+ ♔xh7 (25...♔h6 26 ♘xf8 ♖axf8 27

♕g5+ ♔h7 28 ♕h5+ ♔g7 29 ♕xg6+ ♔h8 30 ♕h7#) 26 ♖xf7+ ♕xf7 27 ♕xf7+ ♖g7 28 ♕f6 with a winning position for White.

4a2) 19...♗xd5! 20 ♕xh7+ ♔xe6 21 ♗xg6 ♖xg6 22 ♕xg6+ ♘f6 23 ♖e2+ ♔d7 24 ♕xf6 ♕xa2 and Black is slightly better.

4b) 19 ♖e2! (this is the correct move-order; White defends the d5-pawn for one more move and so cuts out the defence of line "4a2") 19...♘f6 (19...♕xa2 20 ♕h6 transposes to the winning line "1" above) 20 ♕h6 ♔e7 (20...♔e8 21 ♕h4! ♔e7 22 ♘c5+ ♔f7 23 ♖e6 wins) 21 ♘d4+ does win, but it requires accurate play:

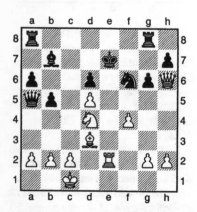

4b1) 21...♔f7 22 ♘f3 ♖g7 23 ♖e7+ ♔xe7 24 ♕xg7+ ♔e8 25 ♕xb7 and Black's position is hopeless.

4b2) 21...♔d8 22 ♕h4 ♖f8 (or 22...♕xa2 23 ♕xf6+ ♔c8 24 ♖e7 ♗xd5 25 ♕xd6 ♕a1+ 26 ♔d2 ♕a5+ 27 c3 ♕d8 28 ♕c5+ ♔b8 29 ♗e4 ♗xe4 30 ♕e5+ ♔c8 31 ♕xe4 and Black loses) 23 ♘e6+ ♔d7 24 ♕h3! ♖fb8 25 ♘c5+ ♔d8 (25...♔c7 26 ♖e7+) 26 ♕e6 ♔c7 27 ♕e7+ ♔b6 28 ♕xd6+ ♔a7 29 ♕xf6 wins.

4b3) 21...♔d7 22 ♕h3+ ♔c7 (after 22...♔d8 23 ♕e6 ♕xa2 24 ♕xf6+ we transpose to "4b2") 23 ♖e7+ ♔b8 24 ♕e6 ♕d8 25 ♕xf6 ♗xd5 26 ♕g5 ♗b7 27 ♗xb5! ♕b6 (27...axb5 28 ♖xb7+ ♔xb7 29 ♕d5+ ♔b6 30 ♕xb5+ wins the queen) and now one very promising line is 28 ♗c6! ♗xc6 29 ♕a5 ♕xa5 30 ♘xc6+ ♔c8 31 ♘xa5 with two pawns and an excellent position for the exchange.

5) 18...♘c5! (the only move) 19 ♖e2 and now Black probably has two ways to save the game:

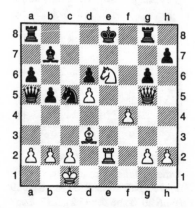

5a) 19...♔d7? 20 ♗f5!! ♗xd5 (or 20...gxf5 21 ♘xc5+ dxc5 22 ♖e7+ ♔d8 23 ♖g7+ wins) 21 ♘xc5+! (21 ♘d4+ gxf5 is less clear) 21...♔c6 22 ♗d7+!! (a superb move) 22...♔xc5 23 ♕e7 (the ♕e7-e3 manoeuvre is reminiscent of a chess problem) 23...♔b6 24 ♕xd6+ ♔a7 25 ♕xd5 with a large advantage for White.

5b) 19...♗xd3+! 20 cxd3 ♔f7 21 ♕h6 ♗xd5 22 ♕xh7+ ♔f6 23 ♕h4+ ♔f7 24 ♘g5+ ♔f6 (24...♔f8? 25 ♕h6+ ♖g7 26 ♕h8+ ♗g8 27 ♘e6+ wins) 25 ♘h7+ ♔g7 26 ♖e7+ ♗f7 and now 27 ♖xf7+ ♔xf7 28 ♕f6+

♔e8 29 ♕e6+ ♚d8 30 ♕xg8+ ♚c7 31 ♕xa8 ♕e1+ 32 ♚c2 ♕e2+ 33 ♚c3 ♕e1+ 34 ♚b3 ♕d1+ 35 ♚b4 ♕d2+ 36 ♚a3 ♕xd3+ 37 b3 b4+ 38 ♚xb4 ♕d2+ unexpectedly leads to perpetual check. The only alternative is 27 ♘g5 ♖h8 28 ♖xf7+ ♚g8 29 ♖h7 ♕c7+! 30 ♖xc7 ♖xh4, but in view of White's poorly-placed knight it is doubtful if he can claim any advantage.

5c) 19...♘xe6! 20 dxe6 (20 ♕f6 ♗xd5 21 ♖xe6+ ♗xe6 22 ♕xe6+ is a draw) with a position so complicated as almost to defy analysis:

5c1) 20...♖c8?! is probably bad after 21 f5 ♕xa2 22 ♕f6 ♖c7 23 fxg6 ♕a1+ 24 ♚d2 ♕a5+ 25 c3 ♕a2 (otherwise 26 ♕f7+ wins) 26 c4 ♕a5+ 27 ♚c2 ♕a4+ 28 b3 ♕a2+ 29 ♚c1 ♕a3+ 30 ♚d1 ♕xb3+ 31 ♗c2 ♕xc4 32 gxh7, when White wins.

5c2) 20...♕xa2 21 ♗xb5+ axb5 22 ♕xb5+ ♚f8 23 ♕d7 (23 ♕xb7 ♕a7 24 e7+ ♚e8 25 ♕c6+ ♚f7 26 ♕c4+ is a draw) 23...♕a1+ 24 ♚d2 ♕a5+ 25 ♚c1 looks like a draw.

5c3) 20...♗c6 21 f5 ♕xa2 22 f6 ♕a1+ 23 ♚d2 ♕xb2 24 f7+ ♚f8 25 ♕f4 ♖h8 26 ♕xd6+ ♚g7 27 ♕xc6 ♖ac8 is very unclear.

19 ♘xf8

This simple capture wins by force.

19 ... ♕d8

19...♖xf8 20 ♖e2+ ♚f7 21 ♗xg6+ hxg6 22 ♖e7+ leads to mate and 19...♚xf8 20 ♕f6+ ♚e8 21 ♖e2+ ♚d7 22 ♕f7+ is dead lost for Black.

20 ♘xh7 ♕xg5
21 fxg5 ♚f7

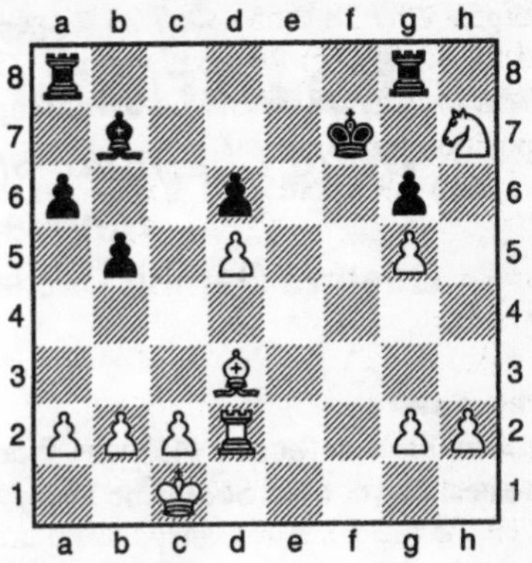

22 ♘f6

White not only has three pawns for the exchange, but his dominating knight on f6 prevents Black from activating his rooks. Black's position is "resignful", as Ljubo might say.

22	...	♖h8
23	g3	♗c8
24	h4	♗f5
25	♗xf5	gxf5
26	h5	♖a7
27	♖f2	**1-0**

Lessons from this game:

1) A surprise move has an undoubted psychological effect. If you are on the receiving end, the number one priority is to stay calm.

2) In ultra-sharp positions, general principles can be a useful guide, but there is no substitute for analysis based on concrete variations.

3) Even very strong players tend to go wrong when subjected to an unrelenting attack.

Robert Fischer – Boris Spassky

World Championship match (game 6),
Reykjavik 1972

Queen's Gambit Declined, Tartakower Defence

The Players

Robert Fischer (born 1943) was World Champion 1972–5, and arguably the greatest player ever. See Game 38 for further details.

Boris Spassky (born 1937) was World Champion 1969–72. For more information see Game 42.

The Game

This game occurred at a crucial stage of the match. Fischer had just drawn level by winning the fifth game as Black, but had been shaky in his previous game as White. The opening was a great surprise: Fischer had never played it before, while Spassky had a wealth of experience on the black side. Nevertheless, Fischer wins a positional masterpiece, tying Black up on both sides of the board before moving in methodically for the kill. The rot starts when he manages to fix Black's hanging c- and d-pawns as a weakness with his instructive play on moves 18–20.

1 c4

This came as a considerable surprise. Although he had dabbled with alternatives to 1 e4, in particular at the Palma de Mallorca Interzonal in 1970, Bobby's favourite move had always been 1 e4. However, the fourth game of the match had seen Spassky reach a very promising position as Black in a Sicilian, so this was a good time for Fischer to reveal not just the depth, but also the breadth of his preparation.

1	...	e6
2	♘f3	d5
3	d4	♘f6
4	♘c3	♗e7
5	♗g5	

By transposition, the game has reached the main-line position of the

Orthodox Queen's Gambit. The defence Spassky now employs is generally named after Tartakower, although in Russian literature it is linked with the names Bondarevsky and Makogonov.

5	...	0-0
6	e3	h6
7	♗h4	b6

It is odd that before the match it had been Fischer's opening repertoire that had been criticized as too predictable! Here Fischer's task in switching from 1 e4 was made substantially easier by the fact that Spassky tended to use the Tartakower Defence to the Queen's Gambit, especially when facing the English Opening move-order (1 c4).

Nevertheless, one can understand why Spassky placed his faith in this system. A few facts: Spassky had never lost from this position prior to this game, having used it many times, his opponents including Smyslov, Larsen and Petrosian. In fact he has only lost twice in his subsequent career from this opening position, to Karpov and Korchnoi. Fischer, on the other hand, had never before played a Queen's Gambit of any type as White in tournament or match play.

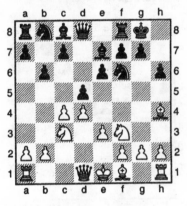

8	cxd5	♘xd5
9	♗xe7	♕xe7
10	♘xd5	exd5
11	♖c1	♗e6

This is a standard theme in the Tartakower Variation. Just because Black has played ...b6 doesn't mean he must fianchetto the bishop if a better square becomes available.

12	♕a4	c5
13	♕a3	♖c8
14	♗b5!?	

Furman's idea. It puts more pressure on Black than the other possibilities here, since Black does not want to let White exchange his bishop for the knight, but in the final analysis does not pose insuperable problems.

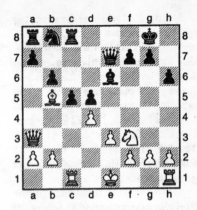

| 14 | ... | a6 |

Alternatives:

1) 14...♔f8 15 dxc5 ♖xc5 16 ♖xc5 ♕xc5 worked out well for Black in an obscure correspondence game Zelinskis – Sichov, 1971.

2) 14...♕b7 15 dxc5 bxc5 16 ♖xc5 ♖xc5 17 ♕xc5 ♘a6! 18 ♗xa6 ♕xa6 19 ♕a3 ♖c4 20 ♔d2 ♕g4 21 ♖g1 d4! 22 ♘xd4 ♕h4 23 ♖e1 ♕xf2+ 24 ♖e2 ♕f1 led to a win for Black in Timman – Geller, Hilversum AVRO 1973. This has put most players off Furman's 14 ♗b5.

| 15 | dxc5 | bxc5 |

15...♖xc5?! would not lead to a hanging pawn position, since White would simply reply 16 0-0.

| 16 | 0-0 | ♖a7?! |

Commentators have been universal in criticizing this move, but in far less agreement as to how Black should improve:

1) 16...♘c6 17 ♗xc6 ♖xc6 18 ♘e5! ♖c7 19 ♘d3 is good for White, who has achieved an ideal set-up to attack Black's pawns.

2) 16...♘d7 17 ♗xd7 ♗xd7 18 ♘d4 followed by ♘b3 puts pressure on c5.

3) 16...♛b7 removes the annoying pin of the c5-pawn against the queen, and so gives White fewer opportunities to bring his knight to a good square. Nevertheless, 17 ♗a4! (as Seirawan points out, White's strategic aim is still to take off the knight if it ventures out from b8; 17 ♗e2 ♞d7 leaves Black with fewer problems) 17...♛b6 18 ♞e5 a5 19 f4! f6 20 f5 ♗f7 21 ♞xf7 ♚xf7 22 ♖fd1 is good for White – Andersson.

4) 16...♛a7! (a refinement of line "3", and best according to Seirawan) 17 ♗e2 (17 ♗a4 a5! {intending to continue ...♞a6-b4} 18 ♗b5 ♞d7 19 ♗xd7 ♗xd7 followed by ...♗e6 and ...d4 gives Black an equal game – Seirawan) 17...♞d7 18 ♖c3 (or 18 ♖fd1) 18...a5 and Black can secure counterplay on the b-file against the b2-pawn.

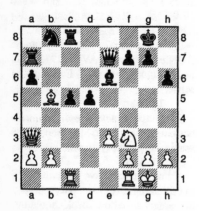

17 ♗e2

Here White is happy to drop the bishop back to e2, since Black will now find it hard to keep his various exposed pawns safe.

17 ...   ♞d7

17...c4 (Petrosian) gives up the d4-square, of course, but as we saw in Game 13, this idea has long been part of Black's armoury. After 18 ♛xe7 (18 ♛c3 allows Black to create play on the b-file) 18...♖xe7 19 ♞d4 ♞c6 Purdy suggested that 20 ♞xe6 fxe6 21 b3 ♞a5 22 bxc4 ♞xc4 23 e4 would give White the advantage.

17...a5 18 ♖c3! ♞d7 19 ♖fc1 ♖e8 20 ♗b5 gave White a definite plus in Furman – Geller, USSR Championship, Riga 1970.

18 ♞d4!

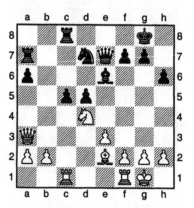

Iivo Nei, a member of Spassky's team for the match, admitted quite simply that "Black should not have allowed this knight move". Apart from the unwieldy structure that Black is given, the disappearance of a pair of minor pieces lessens the cramping effect of the hanging pawns and gives White more freedom to attack them.

18 ...   ♛f8

Spassky wishes to resolve the tension by forcing White's knight to declare its intentions, but he surely underestimated the power of White's 20th move. 18...♞f6 (Euwe mentioned 18...♞f8) 19 ♞b3 c4 (19...♞e4 is met by 20 f3! c4 21 ♛xe7 ♖xe7 22 ♞d4

♘c5 23 b3; 19...♘d7 20 ♖c3 followed
by ♖fc1 puts heavy pressure on the
c5-pawn and along the c-file) 20 ♕xe7
♖xe7 21 ♘d4 a5! is Seirawan's suggestion, seeking counterplay along the
b-file.

19 ♘xe6!

As normal, Fischer opts for the clearest solution to the position. We are
about to see him again use a bishop to
good effect versus a knight.

19 ... fxe6

In playing this, Spassky may have
been envisaging ...c4 and ...♘c5. However, he never gets the time.

20 e4!!

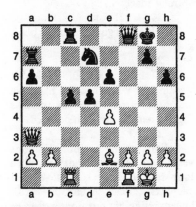

Fischer immediately attacks the
pawns, giving Black a choice of rotten
strategic options.

20 ... d4

This move has come in for a great
deal of criticism, with Botvinnik even
placing it alongside moves by Spassky
from other games by which he actually blundered material. Undoubtedly
Spassky did not enjoy playing this move,
which allows the hanging pawns to become weak and immobile, but he only
had a choice of evils by this point:

1) 20...♘f6 21 e5! ♘d7 (21...♘e4?!
22 f3 ♘d2? 23 ♖fd1 ♕f4 24 ♕c3) 22
f4 puts Black under heavy kingside
pressure.

2) 20...dxe4 21 ♖c4 ♘f6 22 ♖fc1
and White regains his pawn, while
Black's structure has been annihilated.

3) 20...c4 21 ♕h3! ♕f7 (21...♘c5
22 b4!? cxb3 23 axb3 liquidates the
c4-pawn and keeps the pressure on
Black) and now:

3a) 22 ♗g4 ♖e8 23 exd5 (23 ♗h5
is met by 23...g6) 23...exd5 24 ♖fe1
and now 24...♘e5 25 ♗h5 g6 26 ♕g3
♖ae7 27 f4 ♘d3 (27...♔h7 is more resilient) 28 ♖xe7 ♖xe7 29 ♗xg6 ♕xf4
30 ♗f7++! ♔xf7 31 ♖f1 ♕xf1+ 32
♔xf1 ♖e1+ 33 ♕xe1 ♘xe1 34 ♔xe1
gives White a won king and pawn ending – this line is analysis by Tal. However, 24...♖xe1+ 25 ♖xe1 ♘f8 gives
Black a decent game.

3b) 22 exd5 exd5 23 ♗f3 followed
by ♖fe1 is good for White.

3c) 22 ♗h5! ♕e7 (22...g6? 23 ♗g4!
picks off a pawn) 23 ♗g4! (23 exd5
exd5 24 ♖fe1 ♕c5!?) 23...♖e8 24 ♖fe1!
forces major concessions from Black.

21 f4

Now that Black's pawn-majority
has been crippled, White prepares to
use his own. The immediate threat is
♗c4 and f5.

21 ... ♕e7

21...♔h8 22 ♗c4 e5 23 fxe5 ♕e7
24 e6 ♘e5 doesn't work because of 25
♕g3! ♘xc4? 26 ♖f7, winning – Timman.

After 21...e5? 22 fxe5 ♕e7 23 e6
Black's "temporary" pawn sacrifice
doesn't look such a good idea!

22 e5!

A multi-purpose move. White fixes
the weak pawn on e6, denies the knight

some squares and keeps lines open for his bishop. He will be able to play around Black's passed d-pawn. Moreover, Black's d4-pawn is now robbed of the possible support of the e-pawn, so a further idea for White appears – to undermine this pawn by means of b4. Although Fischer never actually adopts this plan, it is nice to have active play on both sides of the board.

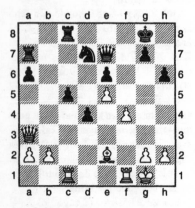

22 ...   ♖b8

After 22...♘b6 23 ♕b3 (23 f5 c4 24 ♕a5 ♕c5 25 b4 ♕b5 26 a4 ♘xa4 27 ♖xc4 ♖xc4 28 ♕d8+ ♔h7 29 f6 ♖c8! isn't at all clear, and might even be winning for Black) 23...♘d5 24 f5! ♖b7 and now:

1) 25 ♕h3 (this switch to the kingside seems premature) 25...♖xb2 26 ♗c4 and now Black can go for counterplay with either 26...♖d8 27 fxe6 ♖b6 (not 27...♘e3? 28 ♖f7, when White has a winning attack) 28 ♖b1 ♖xb1 (not 28...♖xe6? 29 ♖b7! ♕e8 30 ♗xd5 ♖xd5 31 ♖b8!) 29 ♖xb1 ♕g5 or the immediate 26...♕g5!?.

2) 25 ♕a3! aims to cause more problems on the queenside before a possible switch to the kingside, e.g.

25...♖cb8 26 f6 gxf6 27 exf6 ♘xf6 28 ♕g3+ ♔h8 29 ♕e5 ♖f8 30 ♖xc5 ♖xb2 31 ♖c6, etc.

23   ♗c4

Naturally, the bishop makes use of this beautiful square.

23 ...   ♔h8

23...♘b6 24 ♕xc5 (24 ♕b3 has been claimed to be winning, but is not so clear after 24...♘d7 25 ♗xe6+ ♔h8 26 ♕d5 ♖xb2) 24...♘xc4 25 ♕xc4 ♖xb2 26 ♕xd4 is very good for White, since if Black tries to regain the pawn with 26...♖xa2 he is hit by 27 f5 ♕g5 (forced) 28 ♕e4 (defending g2 and threatening ♖c8+) 28...♖d2 29 f6 with a strong attack.

24   ♕h3!

Now White is gunning for the black king.

24 ...   ♘f8

24...♖xb2 25 ♗xe6 ♘f8 26 ♗c4 is winning for White because his pawn majority is extremely mobile, whereas Black's remains firmly blockaded.

25   b3

Solidifying the position. White is very clearly better, but the win is still a long way off.

25 ...   a5

Improving his position as best he can. This move hopes to turn a target into a battering-ram, albeit a small one.

26   f5

Fischer is not one to play unnecessary defensive moves, so he ignores Black's a-pawn and goes for the throat.

26 ...   exf5

Allowing f6 would be unthinkable.

27   ♖xf5   ♘h7

An odd place for the knight, but the one square where it could generate any sort of threat is g5. Instead 27...♘g6? 28 ♖f7 ♕xf7 29 ♗xf7 ♖xf7 30 ♕e6 costs Black more material than he intended.

28   Rcf1!

28 Rf7?? loses to 28...Ng5.

28   ...   Wd8

29   Wg3

The threat is now simply 30 e6, opening the fifth rank and the h2–b8 diagonal to add to Black's woes.

29   ...   Re7

30   h4!

Denying Black's pieces use of the g5-square.

30   ...   Rbb7

31   e6!   Rbc7

32   We5!   We8

32...Nf6? is asking for 33 Rxf6 gxf6 34 Rxf6, which forces mate.

33   a4

Now Fischer plays this move, emphasizing Black's total helplessness.

33   ...   Wd8

Waiting for the blow to fall, but there was nothing active for Black to undertake.

34   R1f2   We8

35   R2f3   Wd8

36   Bd3

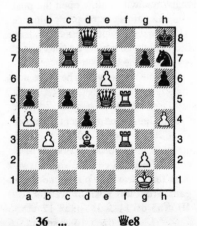

36   ...   We8

36...Wg8 37 Rf7 Rxf7 38 exf7 Rxf7 39 Bc4 makes decisive material gains.

37   We4

37 Rf7 is another way to make progress.

37   ...   Nf6

37...Rxe6 allows mate in three: 38 Rf8+ Nxf8 39 Rxf8+ Wxf8 40 Wh7#.

38   Rxf6!   gxf6

39   Rxf6   Kg8

40   Bc4!?

There were plenty of ways to win, but this is attractive, stopping the e7-rook moving for fear of e7+.

40   ...   Kh8

41   Wf4   1-0

White will mate shortly.

Lessons from this game:

1) Knowing which pieces you want exchanged is a great help in finding the right moves. With the structure that existed from move 13 to 17, Fischer knew that if he could exchange his king's bishop for Black's queen's knight, he would reach a position in which his knight would prove more effective than Black's bishop. As things worked out, Spassky avoided this by delaying the development of his knight, but, ironically, landed in a position where he had a poor knight against a strong bishop!

2) If your opponent has a mobile pawn-centre, the best way to fix it is to attack it, particularly with pawns. Here, as soon as Fischer forced Black's d-pawn to advance, he was able to play around Black's pawns without difficulty.

3) A pawn-majority, unless it is crippled, can generate a passed pawn. This fact can be as useful in the middlegame as it is in the endgame.

Boris Spassky – Mikhail Tal

Tallinn 1973

Nimzo-Indian Defence, Leningrad Variation

The Players

Boris Spassky (born 1937) was World Champion 1969–72. For more information see Game 42.

Mikhail Tal (1936–92) was World Champion 1960–1, and one of the greatest attacking players of all time. See Game 39 for more information.

The Game

Spassky comes out fighting with a sharp line against the Nimzo-Indian, to which Tal replies with a logical but somewhat speculative pawn sacrifice to gain a central majority. A slightly careless move from Spassky allows Black's initiative to become quite dangerous, and Tal finds an interesting combination to give himself a small material advantage. Spassky appears to be coordinating his rooks to create serious counterchances, but suddenly gets blown away by a bishop sacrifice that rips the defences from his king.

1	d4	♘f6
2	c4	e6
3	♘c3	♗b4
4	♗g5	

This unusual line has been a favourite of Spassky's, on and off throughout his career. It is a sharp line, leading to unusual positions, where the player who better understands the specific nuances will tend to come out on top.

4	...	h6!

Black normally plays this move here, as after the bishop drops back to h4 it cannot easily return to defend the queenside if the need should arise. Black thereby gives the idea of ...c5 followed by ...♛a5 added punch. It is also tempting for Black to try the immediate 4...c5 followed by ...♛a5, as this creates a potential attack on the loose g5-bishop. However, experience

has suggested that this plan is less effective.

5	♗h4	c5
6	d5	b5!?

Tal responds in sharp fashion, sacrificing a pawn to blow open the position and gain a central predominance. It has a great deal in common with the Blumenfeld Gambit, 1 d4 ♘f6 2 c4 e6 3 ♘f3 c5 4 d5 b5.

Instead, 6...d6 would be more normal.

7	dxe6	

It makes sense to accept the pawn, since otherwise Black has simply struck a major blow against White's centre. Instead 7 e4 g5 8 ♗g3 ♘xe4 9 ♗e5 leads to sharp play. One recent game from this position went 9...0-0 10 ♛h5 d6 11 ♗d3 ♘xc3 12 ♛xh6 ♘e4+ 13 ♔f1 dxe5 14 ♗xe4 f5 15

♕g6+ with a draw by repetition, Yermolinsky – Shabalov, USA Championship, Parsippany 1996.

7 ... fxe6

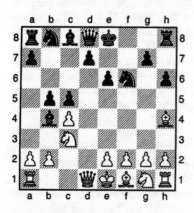

8 cxb5

8 e4 0-0 9 e5?! ♕a5 proved ineffective for White in Bareev – Gelfand, GMA Qualifier, Moscow 1990.

8 ... d5

8...0-0 9 e3 ♕a5 is perhaps a more modern way of handling the position, with Black developing pressure with his pieces rather than immediately setting up a big centre, which might become a target for counterplay. Whether it is any more effective is another matter.

9 e3 0-0

9...d4?! 10 a3 (10 exd4 cxd4 11 a3 ♗a5 12 b4 dxc3 13 bxa5 ♕xa5 is much less clear) 10...♗a5 (taking on c3 leaves White better) 11 ♗xf6 ♕xf6 12 ♕h5+ ♔d8 (otherwise ♕xc5) 13 0-0-0 turns out well for White.

10 ♘f3

10 ♗d3 d4 11 exd4 cxd4 12 a3 ♗a5 13 b4 dxc3 14 bxa5 ♗b7 15 ♘f3 ♕xa5 16 0-0 ♘bd7 17 ♕e2 ♗xf3 18 ♕xf3 ♘e5 19 ♕e2 ♘xd3 20 ♕xd3

♘d5, with equality, was played in a later game Spassky – Unzicker, European Team Championship, Bath 1973.

10 a3 is also suggested by Tal, cutting the Gordian Knot at some structural cost.

10 ... ♕a5

Black now threatens 11...♘e4.

11 ♗xf6 ♖xf6

12 ♕d2

In reply to 12 ♕c1 (so that a subsequent a3 has more bite as the rook will be defended) Tal suggested 12...c4.

12 ♖c1 ♕xa2 13 ♖c2 a6 14 ♘e5 axb5! 15 ♘d3 ♕a5 16 ♘xb4 ♕xb4 was analysed by Minev as very good for Black.

12 ... a6

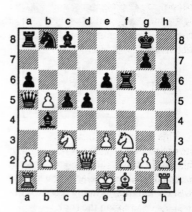

13 bxa6?!

Tal criticized this move, preferring 13 b6 or 13 ♗e2 axb5 14 0-0. The capture on a6 would be fine if Black had to reply with 13...♗xa6, as White would then be able to develop his kingside without loss of time, but Black is under no such compulsion.

13 ... ♘c6!

Now Black's initiative and development advantage are worth more than the pawn. He threatens 14...d4 15 exd4 ♖xf3!.

Instead 13...♗xa6?! 14 ♗xa6 ♕xa6 15 ♕e2 and 0-0 sees White developing his forces more smoothly.

14 ♗e2?!

14 ♕c1 is safer, planning to meet 14...d4 with 15 a3 ♗xc3+ 16 bxc3, when, according to Tal, "White would not have been in any immediate danger".

14 ...   d4!

15 exd4

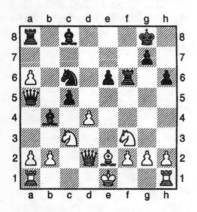

15 ...   ♖xf3!

This lovely exchange sacrifice leads to an advantage for Black. The logic is that the knight was doing more to control the centre than the rook.

15...cxd4 16 ♘xd4 ♘xd4 17 ♕xd4 ♗c5 18 ♕e4 ♗xf2+ 19 ♔d1 is less convincing; White's king is on the move, but Black's pieces are not well enough coordinated to take advantage.

16 ♗xf3   cxd4

17 0-0

17 ♖c1 ♗xa6 (17...dxc3 is no good, since after 18 bxc3 Black lacks a decent follow-up) 18 ♗xc6 ♖d8 19 ♕c2 dxc3 20 bxc3 ♕e5+ 21 ♗e4 and now,

at the board, Tal indulged in analysing some very unnecessary tactics:

1) 21...♗xc3+ 22 ♕xc3 ♕xe4+ 23 ♕e3 ♕xg2 24 ♕xe6+ ♔h8 25 ♕c6 ♕xc6?! (25...♕g5! wins on the spot: 26 ♖c4 ♕d2+ 27 ♔f1 ♖f8) 26 ♖xc6 ♗b7 skewering the rooks, for example 27 ♖xh6+ gxh6 with a couple of pretty mates if White tries to save material: 28 0-0 ♖g8# or 28 ♖g1 ♗f3 and ...♖d1#.

2) 21...♗d3 wins easily, without any fuss. Tal saw this, of course.

17 ...   dxc3

18 bxc3

18 ♕c2 ♘d4 19 ♕e4 ♘xf3+ 20 ♕xf3 ♕d5 will be a horrible ending for White: two bishops almost always make mincemeat of a rook.

18 ...   ♗xc3

19 ♕d6   ♖xa6

19...♗xa1?? loses to 20 ♕xc6.

20 ♗xc6

Otherwise 20...♘d4.

20 ...   ♗b4

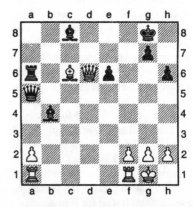

The final point of the combination Black started with his 14th move: the c6-bishop is lost. Black will therefore gain a material advantage of two bishops vs rook and pawn. However, his task of converting this into victory will not be at all straightforward. For the time being his pieces are not well co-ordinated, while White's queen and rooks can generate meaningful counterplay against the black king.

21	♕b8	♖xc6
22	♖ac1	♗c5
23	♖c2	

White's attempt to embarrass Black on the c-file will come to grief due to the weakness of his f2-square, well-defended though it appears to be.

| 23 | ... | ♕a4 |
| 24 | ♕b3 | |

24 ♖fc1?? ♗xf2+ means a catastrophic loss of material for White.

| 24 | ... | ♕f4 |

24...♕e4 was rejected by Tal on the basis of 25 ♖fc1 ♗b7 26 ♕xb7 ♗xf2+ 27 ♔f1 (27 ♔h1?? ♖xc2) 27...♕d3+ 28 ♔xf2 ♖xc2+ 29 ♖xc2 ♕xc2+ and although Black emerges with an extra pawn, it will be very difficult to make any real progress with it.

| 25 | ♕g3 | |

Or:

1) After 25 ♕f3 Black would consolidate with 25...♕d6 or 25...♕c7.

2) On 25 ♕b5 Tal intended to continue 25...♕d6 26 ♖fc1 ♗a6 with the point 27 ♕a5?? ♗xf2+.

3) 25 ♖d1 might have been better, but Spassky was intent on the theme of exploiting Black's apparent embarrassment on the c-file.

| 25 | ... | ♕f5 |

Black cannot, of course, exchange queens while the problem of the c-file pin remains unsolved.

| 26 | ♖fc1 | ♗b7 |
| 27 | ♕f3 | |

27 ♕b8+? ♔h7! 28 ♕xb7 (if White retreats, tail between his legs, by 28

♕g3, then 28...e5 followed by ...♖g6 punishes the waste of time) fails to the by now standard theme 28...♗xf2+.

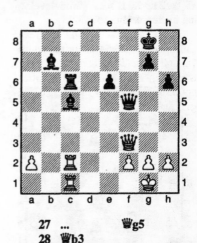

| 27 | ... | ♕g5 |
| 28 | ♕b3 | |

28 ♕g3? ♗xf2+! (although the variations are simple enough, a sacrifice on a square that is defended three times is always attractive) 29 ♕xf2 (29 ♔xf2 ♕f5+ and ...♖xc2) 29...♕xc1+ 30 ♖xc1 ♖xc1+ wins for Black, as 31 ♕f1 is forced.

28 ♕h3 would put up more stubborn resistance, but that is all. Black's rook could then at last step out of the pin, e.g. 28...♖d6, since 29 ♖xc5?? is impossible due to 29...♕xc5 30 ♖xc5 ♖d1#.

| 28 | ... | ♖c7 |
| 29 | g3 | |

Now Black lands the blow that has been in the air for so long, yet still comes as a surprise.

| 29 | ... | ♗xf2+!! |
| 30 | ♔xf2 | ♕f6+ |

30...♕f5+! 31 ♔g1 ♕e4 reaches the position that arises after Black's 35th move in the game, but without in the interim giving White a chance to save himself. However, the text-move does not as yet cost Black any of his advantage.

31 ⟨e1   ⟩e5+
32 ⟨f1

32 ⟨e2 ⟨xc1+ 33 ⟨d2 is no way out since 33...⟩g5+ keeps the booty.

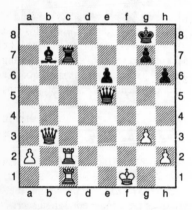

32 ...   ⟨a6+?

An unfortunate blemish on an otherwise near-perfect performance from Tal. 32...⟩f5+! 33 ⟨g1 ⟩e4 was the last chance to reach by force the winning position that arises in the game after Black's 35th.

33 ⟨g1   ⟩d4+
34 ⟨g2   ⟩e4+
35 ⟨g1?

35 ⟨h3? loses to 35...⟨xc2 followed by 36...⟨f1+, but 35 ⟨f2! puts up far more resistance: 35...⟨f7+ 36 ⟨g1 and then:

1) 36...⟨b7 37 ⟨c8+ ⟨xc8 (not 37...⟨h7?? 38 ⟩c2 and White will be material up in a simplified position; after 37...⟨f8? 38 ⟨xf8+ ⟨xf8 39 ⟨f2 only White has winning chances)

38 ⟨xc8+ and Black has the choice between a drawish rook ending and a drawish queen ending.

2) 36...⟨d3 37 h4 (37 ⟩c3? ⟩e3+ 38 ⟨g2 ⟨e4+ 39 ⟨h3 ⟩g5 wins for Black) 37...⟩f3 38 ⟨h2 (38 ⟨c8+? ⟨h7 leaves White defenceless) and here:

2a) 38...⟩e3 39 ⟩b2 is quite safe for White.

2b) 38...⟩g4 39 ⟨g2 (39 ⟨c8+? ⟨h7 40 ⟩b8 ⟨f2+ 41 ⟨g1 ⟩d4) 39...⟨f1 is drawish.

2c) 38...⟨xc2 39 ⟩xc2 ⟩e3 40 ⟩c8+ ⟨f8 41 ⟩c4 ⟨f2+ 42 ⟨h3 and White is still hanging on.

35 ...   ⟨b7

Now all is well again, and Black wins in short order.

36 h4   ⟩h1+
37 ⟨f2   ⟨f7+

37...⟩g2+ 38 ⟨e1 ⟩e4+ also brings the house tumbling down, but it is just a matter of taste by now.

38 ⟨e2   ⟩e4+

0-1

White is losing at least a rook.

Lessons from this game:

1) A mobile central pawn majority can be well worth a pawn, especially if the enemy king is still in the centre, as then this provides a target for further pawn advances.

2) Try to analyse forcing sequences right to the end – there may be a "sting in the tail".

3) Two bishops aiming at a king along adjacent diagonals are very powerful – it is difficult for the defender to avoid some sort of tactical blow, even if his position seems generally OK.

Game 66

Vladimir Bagirov – Eduard Gufeld

USSR Championship semi-final, Kirovabad 1973

King's Indian Defence, Sämisch Variation

The Players

Vladimir Bagirov was born in 1936 in Batumi, Georgia. He played in the final of USSR Championships nine times in the period 1960 to 1978, of which his first attempt turned out to be his most successful (fourth place). For many years he was based in Baku, Azerbaidzhan, and this coincided with the rise of the young Garry Kasparov, in whose early training Bagirov participated. He subsequently relocated to Latvia, where he also found some excellent pupils, notably Edwins Kengis.

His playing strength was never quite sufficient for him to be permitted to play in events outside the Soviet Union, so it has only been in his late career that he has participated freely in events in western Europe, which he does regularly and successfully. He is an expert in certain opening systems, including the English Opening and the Alekhine Defence. He achieved the grandmaster title in 1978.

Eduard Gufeld (born 1936) is a colourful figure of the chess world, who is famous for his bold attacking chess. For more details see Game 47.

The Game

This is Gufeld's "Immortal Game", about which he has waxed lyrical in his writings. A sharp Sämisch King's Indian leads to a position where the two sides are attacking on opposite wings. As Black cannot afford it to become a straight race, he finds some subtle moves to delay White on the kingside. Attack, defence and counterattack are then in approximate equilibrium. Bagirov, however, misses or spurns lines that should lead to a draw, and Black's counterattack gains new strength. Gufeld finds some tremendous line-opening sacrifices to channel his pieces rapidly towards the white king. A scintillating sacrifice to force mate rounds off the game.

1	d4	g6
2	c4	♗g7
3	♘c3	d6
4	e4	♘f6
5	f3	0-0
6	♗e3	♘c6

In this modern system against the Sämisch, Black exerts pressure on d4 so as to restrict his opponent's choices.

7	♘ge2	♖b8

A subtle move-order; 7...a6 is more normal. There are pros and cons for both move-orders, but they come to exactly the same thing if White's plan is kingside attack.

8 ♕d2

8 ♘c1 e5 (Black absolutely must hit the d4-square if White neglects it at

all – this is the strategic basis of the
...♘c6 line) 9 d5 ♘d4 10 ♘b3 c5 11
dxc6 bxc6 12 ♘xd4 exd4 13 ♗xd4
♖xb2 shows a point of Black's 7th
move.

8   ...   a6

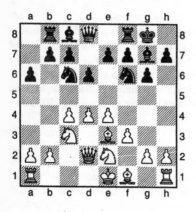

9 ♗h6

There are many other moves at this
point, of which 9 h4 is the most critical
and popular. The text-move, intending
a quick exchange of dark-squared bishops, was popular in the early days of
the ...♘c6 system, but is unpopular in
modern practice. The logic goes something like this: with 9 ♗h6 White is
spending time making the positional
concession of exchanging his "good"
bishop for Black's "bad" bishop. The
justification for this is that he hopes to
launch a kingside attack, aiming to
give mate or to force a major concession from Black to avoid mate. However, if Black can defend his kingside,
he has every reason to expect to
emerge with a positional advantage.
This opens up several possibilities for
Black. He can go for a "fortress kingside" policy, stoutly defending while
seeking to generate play gradually on

the queenside. Another is to make a
positional sacrifice to deaden White's
attack. Since he starts off with a positional advantage, this plan has a greater
chance of success than normal. What
Black must avoid is a straight race, in
which he spends no time defending his
own king and goes straight for counterplay against the white king. Black
would lose such a race.

This explains why White has sought
attacking plans that do not burn his
boats positionally. Strange as it may
seem, the advance 9 h4 is less committal, and keeps more options of playing
on other parts of the board, and so
gives Black a smaller choice of viable
plans.

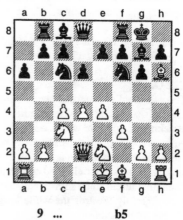

9   ...   b5

This is perhaps not the most effective, as it does not immediately seize
upon White's last move to enhance the
strengths of Black's position. 9...♗xh6
10 ♕xh6 e5 is another, more direct,
option, by which Black shows that he
has so much faith in his defences that
he is willing to draw the white queen
forward. One interesting possibility is
then 11 d5 ♘d4 12 0-0-0 c5 13 dxc6

bxc6 14 ♘xd4 exd4 15 ♖xd4 ♖xb2 16
e5!? ♘h5 17 ♔xb2?! ♕b6+ 18 ♘b5
axb5 19 ♖xd6 bxc4+, which led to a
brilliant victory for Black in Gelpke –
Lane, Heidelberg 1986.

10 h4   e5

As explained above, this is especially logical when the dark-squared
bishops are going to be exchanged. It
also gives Black ideas of defending
along his second rank, e.g. by ...♕e7,
meeting a subsequent h5 and hxg6
with ...fxg6.

11 ♗xg7   ♔xg7
12 h5

In such positions White does best to
get on with his attack. Instead 12 cxb5
axb5 opens lines and increases Black's
counterplay.

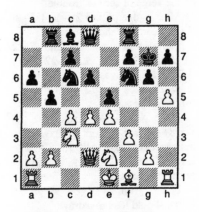

12 ...   ♔h8!?

A surprising idea, which crops up
quite often in such positions. Other
moves:

1) 12...♘xh5? 13 g4 ♘f4 (13...♘f6?
loses to 14 ♕h6+ and 15 ♘d5) 14 ♘xf4
exf4 15 cxb5 (here there is a specific
reason for this capture) 15...axb5 16
♗xb5 ♘e7 17 ♕xf4 ♘g8 18 g5 should
win for White.

2) 12...♘xd4 13 ♘xd4 exd4 14
♘d5! gave White a strong attack in
Ker – Spassky, Wellington 1988.

3) 12...bxc4 and now:

3a) 13 ♘d5?! ♘xd5 14 hxg6?! (14
exd5) 14...♘f6 (14...♘f4 15 ♘xf4
exf4 16 ♕xf4 hxg6 17 ♕h6+ ♔f6 18
♕h4+ and now 18...♔g7 19 ♕h6+ repeats, but Black can try for more with
18...g5!?) 15 ♕h6+ ♔g8 16 g7 ♖e8 17
♘g3 exd4 (17...♘xd4? 18 ♘h5) 18
♘h5 ♘xh5 19 ♖xh5 (after 19 ♕xh5
♔xg7 White does not appear to have
even a perpetual check, e.g. 20 ♕h6+
♔g8 21 ♕xh7+ ♔f8) 19...♗f5! 20
♖xf5 ♖e6 staves off the mating threats,
leaving Black better.

3b) 13 0-0-0 ♘g8 14 ♔b1 a5 15 d5
♘b4 16 ♘c1 ♗a6 17 g3 ♖b7 18 a3 c5
19 dxc6 ♘xc6 20 h6+ ♔h8 21 ♕xd6
♕a8, with compensation for Black, is
a line cited by John Watson in his superb opening monograph *6...♘c6 in
the Sämisch Variation, King's Indian
Defence.*

13 ♘d5

13 ♕h6 allows Black to demonstrate the main idea behind his 12th
move: 13...♘g8 followed by ...g5.

13 ...   bxc4
14 hxg6   fxg6
15 ♕h6

It has been claimed that White retains a slight advantage after 15 0-0-0
or 15 ♘xf6 ♕xf6 16 d5. However,
precisely what a "slight advantage"
means in such an unbalanced position
is not clear.

15 ...   ♘h5!

The best way to block lines. Sometimes Black can let White take on g6
for tactical reasons, but here it is not
possible: 15...♖f7? 16 ♕xg6 ♕g8 17
♕xf6+! and after 17...♖xf6 18 ♘xf6

White regains the queen with a large advantage.

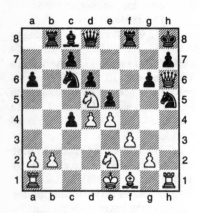

16 g4

16 ♘g3 was suggested by Petrosian, but 16 0-0-0 is the critical move:

1) 16...♘e7 17 ♘xe7 ♕xe7 18 g4 ♕g7 is one possible reply.

2) 16...♘xd4 gives White a pleasant choice between 17 ♘xd4 exd4 18 ♗xc4 c6 19 ♘f4! ♖xf4 20 ♖xh5 gxh5 21 ♕xf4 and 17 ♖xd4 exd4 18 ♘ef4 ♖xf4 (18...♖g8 19 g4 c6 20 gxh5 cxd5 21 ♘xg6+ ♖xg6 22 hxg6 ♖b7) 19 ♘xf4 ♕g8 20 ♘xg6+ ♕xg6 21 ♕f8+ ♕g8 22 ♕xg8+ ♔xg8 23 ♗xc4+ ♔g7 24 ♖xh5, with a comfortable advantage.

3) 16...♖f7 17 g4 ♘f6 18 ♕xg6 ♕g8! 19 ♕xg8+ ♘xg8 with roughly equal chances according to Gufeld, who gives the continuation 20 ♖h3 a5 21 ♘e3 ♗a6 22 d5 ♘b4 23 ♘c3 ♘d3+ 24 ♗xd3 cxd3 25 b3 ♘e7 26 ♔d2 ♘g6 27 ♘f5 ♘f4.

16 ...   ♖xb2!
17 gxh5   g5!

A standard idea in such positions. Black wishes at all costs to keep the h-file closed.

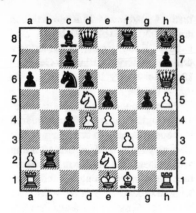

18 ♖g1   g4!
Still blocking the g-file.
19 0-0-0   ♖xa2
20 ♘ef4?!

This imaginative idea lands White on the verge of serious trouble.

After 20 dxe5 ♘xe5 21 ♘ef4 ♔g8! Black maintains the balance.

White's best try was 20 ♗h3! ♖xe2 21 ♗xg4 ♖f7 (21...♗xg4 22 ♖xg4 ♖f7 23 ♖dg1 gives White enough to draw) 22 ♗xc8 ♕xc8 23 ♘f6, with the following possibilities:

1) 23...♘xd4 24 ♖xd4 ♕f8 25 ♕xf8+ (25 ♖g8+ ♕xg8 26 ♘xg8 exd4 transposes to line "2c1") 25...♖xf8 26 ♖xc4 ♖xf6 27 ♖xc7 isn't advantageous for Black.

2) 23...♕b8 24 ♖g8+ ♕xg8 25 ♘xg8 should lead to a draw:

2a) 25...♔xg8? loses to 26 ♖g1+.

2b) 25...♘b4! (Black sets up the ...♘a2+, ...♘c3+, etc., drawing device) 26 ♖d2 ♖e1+ 27 ♖d1 (27 ♔b2? loses to 27...♖xf3) 27...♖e2 repeats.

2c) 25...♘xd4!? is a winning attempt, but only seems a more complicated way to draw:

2c1) 26 ♖xd4 exd4 27 ♘f6 (27 ♘e7? ♖xf3) 27...♖g7 28 ♘g4 d3 29

♕f6 c3 and now White must take a draw by 30 ♕f8+ ♖g8 31 ♕f6+.

2c2) 26 ♘e7 ♘b3+ (26...♖c2+?! 27 ♔b1 c3 28 ♖xd4 ♖b2+ 29 ♔c1 exd4 30 ♘g6+ ♔g8 31 ♘f4 and Black no longer has a clear draw) 27 ♔b1 c3 28 ♘g6+ ♔g8 29 ♘e7+ ♖xe7 (29...♔h8 30 ♘g6+ is a draw) 30 ♖g1+ ♔f7 31 ♖g7+ (31 ♕xh7+ ♔e8 32 ♕g8+ ♔d7 33 ♕xb3 ♖b2+ 34 ♕xb2 cxb2 35 h6 and White should avoid losing because of his dangerous h-pawn) 31...♔e8 32 ♖xe7+ ♔xe7 33 ♕xh7+ ♔d8 34 ♕g8+ ♔e7 (this is a draw as Black's king must stay near the h-pawn; not 34...♔d7?? 35 ♕xb3 ♖b2+ 36 ♕xb2 cxb2 37 h6) 35 ♕g7+ (35 ♕xb3?? ♖b2+ 36 ♕xb2 cxb2 and Black wins) 35...♔e8 with a draw by repetition.

20 ... exf4

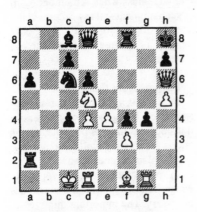

21 ♘xf4?

Bagirov needed instead to find a very precise sequence to make a draw: 21 ♗xc4 ♖a1+ (21...♖a4 22 ♗b3) 22 ♔b2 ♖xd1 23 ♖xd1 ♖g8! (23...gxf3? 24 ♖g1; 23...♘a5 24 ♗a2) 24 ♘f6 ♖g7 25 ♗g8! ♕e7 26 ♗xh7 ♖xh7 27 ♘xh7 ♕xh7 28 ♕f8+ ♕g8 29 ♕h6+ with a perpetual check.

21 ... ♖xf4!

Eliminating the possibility of ♘g6+ without wasting any time.

22 ♕xf4 c3!

"When the rook restricts the king to its first rank, there is always the possibility of using the pawn and knight in harmony with it (...♘b4). Though this threat is repelled, the c3-pawn remains a kind of bayonet put to the white king's throat." – Gufeld.

23 ♗c4

23 ♕f7 ♘b4 24 ♗d3 ♖a1+ 25 ♗b1 ♗e6! 26 ♕xe6 ♕g5+ forces mate.

23 ... ♖a3!

"The most difficult move of the game and perhaps my whole life." – Gufeld.

23...♖a4 24 ♗b3 ♘xd4 25 ♖xd4 ♖xd4 26 fxg4 gives White more counterplay.

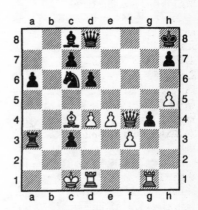

24 fxg4

24 ♔b1 is met by 24...♗e6!, when the threat of 25...♕b8+ wins.

24 ... ♘b4

25 ♔b1!

White has his own threats, and needs only a move or two's respite to move in for the kill. Black must therefore

operate with checks or absolutely forcing moves. He now needs to give check
with his queen on b8. There are two
pieces in the way, but with suitable ingenuity that is just a minor problem...

25 ...   Ձe6!!

Not 25...c2+? 26 ☗b2 cxd1♕ 27
☖xd1, when Black is in danger due to
the threat of 28 ☖f1.

26 Ձxe6   Ձd3!

Extreme precision is necessary.
26...Ձd5? 27 exd5 grants the king a
corridor to freedom: 27...♕b8+ 28
☗c2 ♕b2+ 29 ☗d3 c2+ 30 ☗e4 and it
is Black who will be mated.

27 ♕f7

27 ☖xd3 ♕b8+ mates.

27 ...   ♕b8+

28 Ձb3

28 ☗c2 Ձb4+ 29 ☗b1 ☖a1+ 30
☗xa1 Ձc2+ 31 ☗a2 ♕b2#.

28 ...   ☖xb3+

29 ☗c2

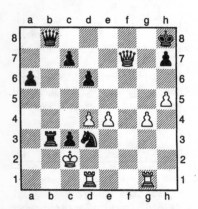

For a moment it seems that White
has survived and that Black's king will
come under fire. However, this illusion is swept away by a beautiful
forced mate in eight moves.

29 ...   Ձb4+!!

30 ☗xb3

30 ☗c1 ☖b1+! 31 ☗xb1 Ձd5+ 32
☗c2 ♕b2+, etc.

30 ...   Ձd5+

This discovered check blocks off
the white queen's access to, and control over, c4, b3 and a2.

31 ☗c2   ♕b2+

32 ☗d3   ♕b5+

0-1

There would follow a dance around
the c3-pawn culminating in mate: 33
☗c2 ♕e2+ 34 ☗b3 ♕b2+ 35 ☗c4
♕b5#.

"Every artist dreams of creating
his own Mona Lisa, and every chess
player of playing his own Immortal
Game. No game has given me as much
satisfaction as this one. To this day I
feel happiness when remembering it.
In such moments all my failures at the
chessboard are forgotten, leaving only
the joy of a dream come true." –
Gufeld.

Lessons from this game:

1) Even if your main plan is a direct attack, it is good to keep other options open as long as possible, as this
makes it more difficult for the opponent to plan the counterattack.

2) When attacking on opposite
wings, defensive moves are sometimes
necessary. The important thing to determine is whether the delay in the opponent's attack is greater than the time
spent on the defensive moves.

3) When a game becomes a straight
race, always look for the quickest possible way to bring the key pieces into
the attack – even if this means sacrificing other pieces.

Anatoly Karpov – Viktor Korchnoi
Candidates match (game 2), Moscow 1974
Sicilian Defence, Dragon Variation

The Players

Anatoly Karpov was born in 1951 in Zlatoust in the Ural Mountains. He learned to play chess when he was four years old and made steady progress until, at the age of thirteen, he came to the attention of the chess authorities in Moscow. He received some coaching from Botvinnik, and from Semion Furman (1920–78), who became Karpov's long-term trainer and mentor. Karpov won the European Junior Championship in 1967/8 and became World Junior Champion in 1969, in which year he also became a grandmaster. Already he was seen as a potential world champion, and his progress towards this goal was very smooth. During the 1973–4 world championship qualifying cycle he seemed to become stronger with each game, each new challenge enriching his play. In the Candidates semi-final against Spassky, he started shakily with a bad loss, but then took Spassky's measure with great assurance, winning the match 7–4 in the end – no less convincing than Fischer's victory over Spassky two years earlier, as Tal observed. The Candidates Final, against Korchnoi, was a long drawn-out affair, with many draws. Karpov took an early lead and a comeback by Korchnoi occurred too late to stop Karpov winning the match. Karpov's victory in this match turned out to be enough for him to become World Champion, as Fischer did not agree terms with FIDE for his title defence. Although to start with he may have been seen as a "paper champion", Karpov's impressive string of tournament victories in subsequent years left no doubt that he was a worthy champion.

He successfully defended his title twice against Korchnoi, but lost it to Kasparov in an exciting match in 1985, following a bizarre and controversial sequence of events with the termination of their original 1984/5 match. He contested further matches with Kasparov in 1986, 1987 and 1990, in each case narrowly failing to regain the title.

Following Kasparov and Short's breakaway from FIDE in 1993, Karpov regained the FIDE title, but second time around he really has been largely regarded as just a paper champion. Kasparov has remained a very active player, comfortably topping the rating list, and meanwhile several other players have moved ahead of Karpov. However, all this is hardly Karpov's fault – there is no reason why should he refuse FIDE's title just because other players have had disputes with that organization. Nor is it his fault if FIDE fails to organize a credible championship.

Karpov has remained at the very top level of world chess for more than a quarter of a century, and shows no sign of weakening. His career has been impressive indeed, and it is a shame that the "World Champion" label has proved so divisive.

Karpov is a small, unassuming man, who plays very efficient chess. He doesn't aim for complications, and, especially as Black, rarely burns his boats playing for a win. His opening knowledge has always been excellent, but he is no deep researcher in this field of the game. His play is based on restricting the opponent's possibilities and his phenomenal ability in technical positions. In his finest games, his pieces appear to dance on the board, always working in perfect harmony.

Viktor Korchnoi (born 1931) has been one of the world's leading players for nearly forty years, and is one of the strongest players never to become World Champion. For more details see Game 49.

The Game
Korchnoi decides to come out fighting against his young opponent in this second game of the match, playing one of the sharpest opening lines in his repertoire. Karpov replies with a powerful prepared novelty. Although Black has a deeply concealed path to survival, at the board Korchnoi's task is virtually impossible, and he succumbs to a volley of crisp tactical blows.

1	e4	c5
2	♘f3	d6
3	d4	cxd4
4	♘xd4	♘f6
5	♘c3	g6
6	♗e3	♗g7
7	f3	♘c6
8	♕d2	0-0
9	♗c4	

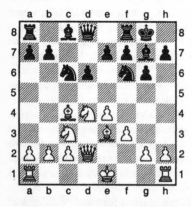

This move has three main ideas. One is to prevent the ...d5 advance, with which Black would open the centre, gaining counterplay and distracting attention from his king. The second is to discourage Black's queen's bishop from coming to its most active square, e6. The third is linked to White's attacking ideas. White's standard plans involve ♗h6 and the advance h4-h5. If Black is able to recapture on g6 with his f-pawn, then this gives his king greater chances of survival. By pinning the f7-pawn against the black king, White seeks to prevent this defensive idea. The drawback of the move 9 ♗c4 is that the bishop is now on an unstable square, from which it will undoubtedly be forced to move in the near future. The theory of the Dragon, and of 9 ♗c4 in particular, has been analysed in extraordinary detail, with whole books devoted not only to 9 ♗c4, but to subvariations arising from it.

9	...	♗d7
10	h4	♖c8

Black has two important and far-reaching strategic decisions to make in this line of the Dragon. Firstly, whether he shall meet h4 with ...h5, and which rook he shall bring to c8. In this game he decides not to block the advance of White's h-pawn, and to bring the queen's rook to c8. Other things being equal, Black would prefer to play ...♖fc8, as this means that the other rook is free to act on the a- or b-file, and that a subsequent ♗h6 by White can be met by ...♗h8, avoiding the exchange. However, the problem is that Black would first need to move his queen, and there are some tactical problems with this, as after 10...♕a5 the queen is a little exposed, both to a timely ♘b3 and to tricks with ♘d5.

11 ♗b3   ♘e5
12 0-0-0

12 h5 is also possible, denying Black a last chance to revert to lines with ...h5.

12 ...   ♘c4
13 ♗xc4   ♖xc4

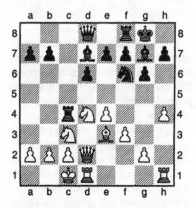

14 h5

14 g4 is an alternative, which after 14...♕a5 15 ♔b1 ♖fc8 leads to a position that can also be reached via 10...♕a5 11 0-0-0 ♖fc8 12 ♗b3 ♘e5

13 ♔b1 ♘c4 14 ♗xc4 ♖xc4 15 g4 ♖ac8.

14 ...   ♘xh5
15 g4   ♘f6

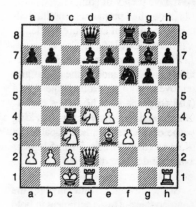

An extremely important position in the theory of the Dragon Sicilian has been reached. White has tried an enormous variety of moves here, many of which demand play of the utmost precision from Black, and without a clear favourite emerging. "Direct" moves include:

1) 16 ♗h6 ♘xe4 17 ♕e3 ♖xc3 18 bxc3 ♘f6 is an important line, which had occurred in the game Geller – Korchnoi, Candidates match (game 4), Moscow 1971. It is still a critical line in 1998, but as things stood in 1974, Korchnoi was prepared to repeat it as Black.

2) 16 e5 is a very sharp move, whereupon most lines fizzle out with very precise play to a draw, for example 16...♘xg4 17 fxg4 ♗xg4 18 ♖dg1 dxe5 19 ♖xg4 h5 20 ♖xh5 ♖xd4 21 ♗xd4 exd4 22 ♘d5 gxh5 23 ♖xg7+ ♔xg7 24 ♕g5+ ♔h7 25 ♕xh5+ ♔g7 26 ♕g5+ ♔h7 27 ♘xe7 d3! 28 ♕h5+ with perpetual check – but note that

this is only one line from a great forest of possibilities.

16 ♔b1 and 16 ♘b3 are quieter ways to handle the position, which both have plenty of sting.

Karpov had prepared something altogether different and more subtle...

16 ♘de2!?

With this cunning move, White reinforces the defence of the c3-knight, removes the knight from danger on d4 (and so prepares ♗h6), eyes the f4- and g3-squares (useful for attacking purposes) and creates the tactical threat of 17 e5 (then 17...dxe5 18 g5 knocks away the defence of the d7-bishop).

16 ... ♛a5

Black prevents e5 and plays for the counterattack. This is sufficient to hold the balance, but some of the variations are especially hair-raising. Then again, that is the nature of the Dragon.

16...♖e8 is a safer alternative which seems viable for Black. The key point is to avoid the exchange of dark-squared bishops: 17 e5 (17 ♗h6 ♗h8 18 e5 ♘xg4 19 fxg4 ♗xe5! 20 ♗f4 ♛a5 21 ♗xe5 ♛xe5 22 ♘d5 with complicated play, Klovans – Beliavsky, Leningrad 1977) 17...♘xg4! 18 fxg4 ♗xg4 19 e6!? ♗xe6 20 ♗d4 f6 21 ♘f4 ♗f7 22 ♛h2 h5 23 ♘xg6!? is messy, but not bad for Black.

17 ♗h6 ♗xh6

Or:

1) 17...♖fc8 transposes to the game after 18 ♗xg7 ♔xg7 19 ♛h6+ ♔g8, but with the move-number increased by one.

2) 17...♗h8 18 ♗xf8 ♔xf8 is the sort of exchange sacrifice that is well worth trying if more normal methods fail. Black averts any immediate disaster and obtains reasonable fighting

chances, even though with precise play White should be able to deny him full compensation. As the analysis below shows, it was not yet time for Black to give up on more "scientific" ways of holding the balance. One example after the exchange sacrifice is 19 ♛e3! ♖c5 20 ♘d4 ♗e6 21 ♔b1 b5 22 ♘xe6+ fxe6 23 ♘e2!, when Black did not have enough for the exchange in Kruppa – Golubev, USSR 1984.

18 ♛xh6 ♖fc8

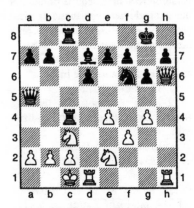

It appears that White is extremely close to breaking through to the black king, but in fact it is not at all straightforward, as Black also has some quite potent threats to the white king.

19 ♖d3!

This was a new move at the time of the game. Although it can be viewed as simply a good move to make an attack work, the ideas behind it go a little deeper than that. The factor that makes White's attack fail if he plays something violent to try to smash through to h7 is White's vulnerability to an exchange sacrifice (or two!) on c3. The rook move reinforces the protection of c3. Black will still be able to sacrifice

there, but he will not be left with
enough of an attacking force, and so
20 g5 ♘h5 21 ♘f4 is a real threat
again. However, the move 19 ♖d3 is
not just a "defensive" prophylactic
move; there are also active ideas with
the move itself, as we see in the lines
below following the reply 19...♕d8
(or one could say that it is also prophylaxis against Black's main defensive
idea, ...♕d8-f8, but that might be
stretching a point). Karpov's novelty
is therefore very much the product of
the strategic concept that has most
characterized his chess: active prophylaxis. The older moves, 19 ♖d5 and 19
g5, are not reckoned to give White any
advantage. Some sample lines:

1) 19 ♖d5 ♕d8 and then:

1a) 20 g5 ♘h5 21 ♘f4 ♕f8! 22
♕xf8+ ♖xf8 (22...♔xf8?! 23 ♘xh5
gxh5 24 ♖xh5 gives White an edge) 23
♘xh5 gxh5 24 ♖xh5 f5! is a little better for Black according to Gufeld.

1b) 20 e5 dxe5 21 g5 ♘h5 22 ♘g3
♕f8 23 ♖xh5 gxh5 24 ♖xd7 ♕xh6 25
gxh6 h4 and Black's strong passed h-
pawn gives him enough play.

2) 19 g5 (the most obvious move)
19...♘h5 and then:

2a) 20 ♘g3?? loses to 20...♖xc3!:

2a1) 21 bxc3 ♕a3+! 22 ♔b1 (22
♔d2 ♕xc3+ 23 ♔e2 ♗b5+ also mates)
22...♖c6 23 ♖d4 ♗e6 and Black forces
mate.

2a2) 21 ♘xh5 ♖xc2+ 22 ♔b1
gxh5 23 ♕xh5 (23 ♖xh5? ♖xb2+ 24
♔xb2 ♕c3+ 25 ♔b1 ♕c2+ 26 ♔a1
♕xd1+ 27 ♔b2 ♕c1+ 28 ♔b3 ♕c3#)
23...♕e5 and Black wins.

2b) 20 ♘f4?? ♖xc3! is similar.

2c) 20 ♖xh5 gxh5 21 ♘d5! ♖xc2+
22 ♔b1 ♔h8 (22...♕d8 23 ♘ef4 ♕f8
24 ♘xe7+ ♕xe7 25 ♘d5 ♖xb2+ 26

♔xb2 ♕e5+ 27 ♔b1 ♔h8 28 ♘f6
♕b5+ is also a draw) 23 g6 fxg6 24
♘ef4 and now Black can take a draw
by 24...♖c1+ 25 ♖xc1 ♖xc1+ 26 ♔xc1
♕e1+ 27 ♔c2 ♕f2+ 28 ♔c3 ♕e1+,
etc.

3) 19 ♘d5? loses to 19...♖xc2+ 20
♔b1 ♕b5!, since White has neither a
mate nor a perpetual: 21 ♘xf6+ exf6
22 ♕xh7+ ♔f8 and the king will be
quite safe on e7.

We shall now return to the position
after Karpov's 19 ♖d3.

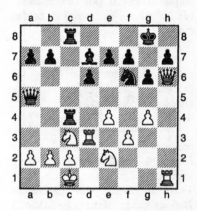

19   ...   ♖4c5?

As so often is the case, the reply to a
major opening novelty is a natural but
erroneous move. Black addresses the
immediate threat (20 g5), but fails to
penetrate to the heart of the position.

Here are the three most interesting
alternatives, in increasing order of
merit:

1) 19...♗a4? is a less effective way
of counterattacking than line "3":

1a) 20 g5?! ♘h5 21 ♘g3 ♖xc3 22
bxc3 ♖xc3 23 ♘xh5 ♖xc2+ 24 ♔b1
gxh5 (24...♕e5? 25 ♘f6+ exf6 26
♕xh7+ ♔f8 27 ♕h8+ ♔e7 28 ♕xf6+)
25 ♕xh5 ♕e5 26 ♕xh7+ ♔f8 27

♕h8+ ♕xh8 28 ♖xh8+ ♔g7 with an
interesting ending in prospect, which
is roughly level.

1b) 20 ♘f4! ♖xc3 (20...♕e5 21
♖d5) 21 bxc3 ♖xc3 22 ♘d5 ♖xc2+ 23
♔b1 gives White decisive threats.

2) 19...♕d8 (this allows White a
better game than the lines we considered above with 19 ♖d5 ♕d8):

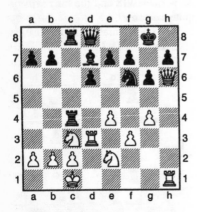

2a) 20 ♘d5 ♖xc2+ 21 ♔b1 ♗b5!
is quite OK for Black.

2b) 20 e5 dxe5 was analysed by
Botvinnik as satisfactory for Black: 21
g5 (21 ♘g3 ♕f8 22 ♕xf8+ ♖xf8! 23
g5 ♗c6 24 gxf6 exf6 and Black will
demonstrate "pawn power" in the ending) 21...♘h5 22 ♘g3 ♕f8 23 ♕xf8+
♔xf8 24 ♘xh5 ♗f5! 25 ♘g3 ♗xd3 26
cxd3 ♖f4 and Black probably has the
advantage in this sharp ending.

2c) 20 g5 ♘h5 21 ♘f4 ♕f8 22
♕xf8+ ♖xf8 (22...♔xf8 23 ♘xh5 gxh5
24 ♖xh5) 23 ♘xh5 gxh5 24 ♖xh5 and
here White has a useful edge. His rook
is better placed on d3 than it was on
d5, as it does not prevent the knight
dropping into its ideal square d5,
while the rook is flexibly placed for
action on either kingside or queenside.

3) 19...♗e6! 20 g5 ♘h5 21 ♘g3
♕e5! brings the queen to an ideal post,
from where it both attacks and defends:

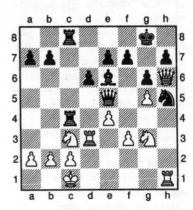

3a) 22 ♖xh5 gxh5 23 ♘xh5 ♖xc3
(after 23...♕h8?, 24 ♘f6+ exf6 25
gxf6 bricks the queen in, and wins) 24
bxc3 ♖xc3 25 ♘f6+ (25 f4 ♖xc2+ 26
♔xc2 ♕c5+ and the king cannot escape the checks) 25...exf6 26 gxf6
♕g3!! 27 ♖xc3 ♕g1+ 28 ♔b2 ♕b6+
29 ♖b3 ♕d4+ 30 ♔c1 ♕g1+ 31 ♔d2
♗xb3 32 axb3 ♕g6 with a probable
draw.

3b) 22 ♘xh5 gxh5 23 ♕xh5 ♔f8!
(run away!) 24 ♕h2 ♕xg5+ 25 f4 ♕f6
26 f5 ♖xc3 27 bxc3 ♗xa2 28 ♕xh7
♔e8 led to an equal ending in Nagor-
nov – Nesis, correspondence game
1976–8.

20 g5!

It turns out that Black's previous
move did not prevent g5 at all! True, it
does not immediately drive the knight
from f6, but forces a loss of coordination in Black's forces, and this in turn
allows White to achieve his goal by
another route.

20   ...   ♖xg5

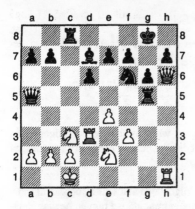

21 Rd5!

21 Nd5? Rxd5 leaves White with no way to remove the knight from f6, as so brings his attack to an end. Black would then have two good pawns for the exchange, and all the play.

21	...	Rxd5
22	Nxd5	Re8

22...Nh5 loses to 23 Nxe7+ Kh8 24 Nxc8.

22...Qd8 is too late now: 23 Nxf6+ (move-order is important here; 23 Nef4? e6 lets Black hang on) 23...exf6 24 Nf4! (intending Nd5, leading to a quick mate) 24...Rc5 (24...Re6 25 Qxh7+ Kf8 26 Nxe6+ fxe6 27 Qh8+ Ke7 28 Rh7#) 25 Qxh7+ Kf8 26 Qh8+ Ke7 27 Nxg6+ fxg6 28 Rh7+ wins easily.

23 Nef4

White now threatens Nxf6 and Nd5, mating.

23 ... Bc6

After 23...Be6 Karpov provides the line 24 Nxe6 fxe6 25 Nxf6+ exf6 26 Qxh7+ Kf8 27 Qxb7 Qg5+ 28 Kb1 Re7 29 Qb8+ Re8 30 Qxa7 (not 30 Rh8+?? Kg7, when Black actually wins, due to the threat of 31...Qg1#) 30...Re7 31 Qb8+ Re8 32 Qxd6+,

which he describes as a form of "windmill".

24 e5!

"Cutting off everything on the fifth rank. I was almost dazzled by the wealth of apparently effective possibilities, but only this continuation appears to be decisive." – Karpov.

24 Nxf6+ exf6 25 Nh5 does not work because of the typical device to take the queens off, 25...Qg5+! (this shows why White should block the fifth rank) 26 Qxg5 fxg5 27 Nf6+ Kg7 28 Nxe8+ Bxe8, with a tough ending in prospect.

24 ... Bxd5

After 24...dxe5 25 Nxf6+ exf6 26 Nh5, mate cannot be prevented.

25	exf6	exf6
26	Qxh7+	

26 Nh5?? Re1+ (26...gxh5 27 Rg1+ Kh8 28 Qg7# being White's idea) 27 Rxe1 Qxe1# shows that one must never, ever, assume that the opponent has no threats.

26	...	Kf8
27	Qh8+	1-0

27...Ke7 28 Nxd5+ Qxd5 29 Re1+ makes decisive material gains.

Lessons from this game:

1) If you play extremely sharp opening lines, you will occasionally lose games without even getting a fighting chance.

2) Even in the midst of an all-out attack, it is worth giving a thought to bolstering the defences, particularly when normal methods of continuing with the attack are failing because of the opponent's counterattacking ideas.

3) When you are moving in for the kill at the end of a successful attack, don't allow a back-rank mate!

Game 68
Dragoljub Minić – Albin Planinc
Rovinj/Zagreb 1975
Ruy Lopez/Spanish, Arkhangelsk Variation

The Players

Dragoljub Minić was born in 1937 in Titograd, which is now called Podgorica, in Montenegro, Yugoslavia. He won the Yugoslav Championship in 1962 and received the international master title in 1964.

Albin Planinc was born in 1944 in Briše, Yugoslavia and was a successful tournament competitor in the 1970s. An extremely imaginative player, he was capable of spectacular results and often played brilliant attacking games. However, his play was always too erratic for him to break through to the higher echelons of world chess. He was awarded the grandmaster title in 1972.

The Game

A sharp line of the Ruy Lopez explodes into life as Planinc gives up his queen to create threats based on a far-advanced passed pawn, together with White's weak back rank and exposed king. In a very complex position, it is not clear whether Minić should be playing for a win or for a draw, and he goes wrong, allowing Planinc a spectacular victory.

1	e4	e5
2	♘f3	♘c6
3	♗b5	a6
4	♗a4	♘f6
5	0-0	b5
6	♗b3	♗b7

This is known as the Arkhangelsk Variation, named after the Russian town. However, many players refer to it as the "Archangel", making it the only opening line named after a minor deity.

6...♗c5 is a related idea that has proved popular amongst top players in the 1990s.

7	d4	♘xd4
8	♘xd4	exd4
9	e5	♘e4
10	c3	

10 ♕xd4?? c5, followed by ...c4 trapping the bishop, is a form of the so-called Noah's Ark Trap.

10 ♕f3 would be met by 10...♕e7.

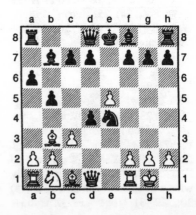

10 ...   d3!?

10...dxc3 11 ♕f3 is seen more often nowadays:

1) 11...♕e7 12 ♘xc3 with the possibilities:

1a) 12...♕xe5? 13 ♗f4 ♕f5 (or 13...♘xc3 14 ♕xb7) 14 ♘xe4 ♗xe4 15 ♖fe1 wins a piece, as after 15...d5 16 ♗xd5 ♕xd5 17 ♖xe4+ Black's queen is lost.

1b) 12...♘xc3? 13 ♕xb7 ♘e2+ 14 ♔h1 ♖d8 and Black's position is a wreck.

1c) 12...♘c5 13 ♘d5 ♗xd5 (not 13...♕xe5?? 14 ♗f4 ♕f5 15 ♖fe1+ wins; 13...♔d8 avoids immediate disaster, but is fairly miserable for Black in the long run) 14 ♗xd5 ♖b8 (14...c6? 15 ♗xc6) 15 ♗e3 ♘e6 (15...♘d3 16 ♗a7 ♘xe5 17 ♕g3) 16 ♖fd1 puts Black under great pressure – this is worth more than Black's very shaky extra pawn.

2) 11...d5 12 exd6 ♕f6 13 ♖e1 (13 d7+ ♔d8!) 13...0-0-0 is the critical line.

11 ♕f3   ♕e7
12 ♘d2

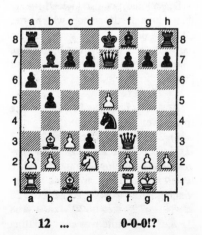

12 ...   0-0-0!?

12...♘c5 is answered by 13 ♗d5 c6 (13...♗xd5 14 ♕xd5 c6) 14 ♘e4!, when 14...cxd5? fails to 15 ♘d6+ ♔d8 16 ♗g5, so Black should go in for 14...♘xe4 15 ♗xe4.

13 ♘xe4   ♕xe5
14 ♖e1   f5

14...d5? 15 ♗f4 dxe4? 16 ♕h3+ costs Black his queen.

15 ♕g3!

This "elastic band" move seems to keep an extra piece. However, there is a surprise coming.

15 ...   ♕e8!

15...♕xg3?? 16 ♘xg3 is an easily winning ending for White.

16 ♘d6+

Naturally White accepts the queen sacrifice. 16 ♗f4 fxe4 17 ♗xc7 ♕g6 enables White to win the exchange, but in the ending that results, Black's protected passed d-pawn will be a major force, while the white rooks will have problems becoming active – there are no open files for them.

16 ...   ♗xd6
17 ♖xe8   ♖hxe8

17...♗xg3 18 ♖xd8+ ♖xd8 19 hxg3 c5 is an interesting ending, though Black would be fighting for a draw.

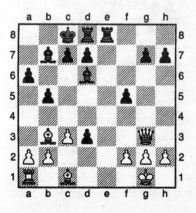

18 ♗f4

The alternative 18 f4 was Minić's preference afterwards, and he may well be right. 18...♖e2 19 ♗e3 (19 ♗d1 ♗c5+ 20 ♔f1 ♗xg2+ 21 ♕xg2 ♖xg2 22 ♔xg2 ♖e8 gives Black three pawns for the piece and a route in for his rook, via g6) and now:

1) 19...g5 20 ♗f2 d2 is unconvincing after either 21 ♕xg5 or 21 ♖f1.

2) 19...♖xg2+ 20 ♕xg2 ♗xg2 21 ♔xg2 gives Black three pawns for the piece, but since he is unable to enforce the advance ...c5-c4, it is not clear that this is good enough for him: 21...♖e8 22 ♔f3 or 21...c5 22 c4.

18 ...　　　　　 d2
19 ♖f1

19 ♔f1 ♖e4 20 ♗xd6 ♖de8 21 f3 ♖e1+ 22 ♖xe1 dxe1♕+ 23 ♕xe1 ♖xe1+ 24 ♔xe1 cxd6 is a safe alternative for White; Black's extra pawn is doubled and isolated and does not give him any winning chances.

19 ...　　　　　 ♖e1

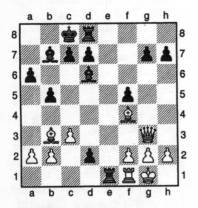

20 ♗xd6　　　 ♖de8!

Here we see the key point of Black's plan. He has only a rook and two pawns for queen and bishop, but his mating threats and powerful d-pawn provide enough compensation.

21 f3

21 ♕d3? ♖xf1+ 22 ♕xf1 cxd6 23 f3 (23 f4 ♖e1 is similar) 23...♖e1 24 ♔f2 ♖xf1+ 25 ♔xf1 ♗d5! is good for Black. In the king and pawn ending, Black's extra pawn will have some value, while 26 ♗c2 ♗c4+! (26...♔xa2 27 ♔e2 is less convincing) 27 ♔f2 f4 28 g3 g5 29 b3 ♗d3 stamps out White's activity completely.

21 ...　　　　　 ♗d5!!

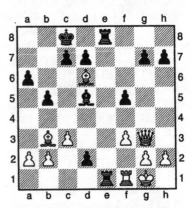

Sensational, but also logical! Rather than taking the d6-bishop, which after all isn't doing him any immediate harm, Planinc targets the b3-bishop, which is holding up his big passed pawn.

22 ♕f4?

22 ♗f4! is better, and enables White to survive:

1) 22...♗c4 23 ♗xc4 d1♕ 24 ♗d3 ♖xf1+ 25 ♗xf1 ♖e2 has been suggested as a winning attempt, but when tested in practice it appeared unconvincing: 26 a4 bxa4 27 ♕xg7 ♖xb2 28 ♕g8+ ♔b7 29 ♕c4 d6 30 ♕xa6+ ♔b8 31 ♗e3 and White was consolidating

in Antunes – Lugo, Capablanca Memorial, Holguin 1989.

2) 22...♖xf1+ 23 ♔xf1 ♗c4+ 24 ♔f2 ♖e2+ 25 ♔g1 (25 ♔f1 ♖e1++ is equivalent) 25...♖e1+ 26 ♔f2 ♖e2+ is a perpetual check.

22 ...   ♗c4

Now Black is winning.

23 h4   ♖xf1+
24 ♔h2   ♖e2
25 ♗xc7

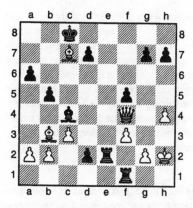

a b c d e f g h

25 ...   ♖ff2

This move has been unjustly criticized, with 25...♖g1 suggested as a winning move, but the continuation 26 ♔xg1 ♗xb3 27 ♗a5 d1♕+ 28 ♔h2 d6 29 ♕g5 seems to give White enough play to draw.

26 ♕d6

26 ♗d1! ♖xg2+ 27 ♔h1 (not 27 ♔h3?, when 27...♗e6!!, threatening 28...♖h2+ 29 ♕xh2 f4#, leaves White defenceless, for example 28 ♗xe2 ♖xe2 29 ♗b6 d6 and White can't even try to start counterplay since his queen is frozen in place on f4) is a better try, but still seems to lose:

1) 27...♖h2+?? 28 ♕xh2 ♖e1+ 29 ♔g2 ♖xd1 30 ♕d6 and White wins.

2) 27...♖gf2 28 ♔g1 ♖g2+ repeats (and not 28...♗d5?? 29 ♗b6).

3) 27...♗d5! (threatening 28...♖gf2 29 ♔g1 ♗xf3, e.g. 30 ♕xf3 ♖xf3 31 ♗xe2 ♖d3! and the less destructive but also serious 28...♖h2+ 29 ♕xh2 ♗xf3+ 30 ♔g1 ♖xh2 31 ♔xh2 ♗xd1 32 ♗f4) 28 ♕xf5 ♖gf2 29 ♔g1 ♗xf3 30 ♕f8+ ♔xc7 31 ♕c5+ ♔b7 and the checks immediately run out.

26 ...   ♖xg2+
27 ♔h3   ♖h2+

27...f4 also wins neatly (e.g. 28 ♕xf4 ♗xb3), but there is nothing quite like chasing the opponent's king up the board to its doom.

28 ♔g3   ♖eg2+
29 ♔f4   ♖xh4+
30 ♔xf5   ♖h6

0-1

White cannot deal with the threats to his king and queen, and from the d2-pawn.

Lessons from this game:

1) Bold, imaginative play, posing the opponent all sorts of problems, is likely to be well rewarded in practice.

2) A far-advanced passed pawn, well supported by pieces, is an immensely powerful weapon.

3) When you are under pressure, don't panic! Tackle each problem in turn, and don't be in a hurry to try to solve all your difficulties in one fell swoop – such a solution may not exist.

Game 69
Ljubomir Ljubojević – Ulf Andersson
Wijk aan Zee 1976
Sicilian Defence, Scheveningen Variation

The Players

Ljubomir Ljubojević (born 1950) was ranked third in the world in 1983 and was Yugoslavia's leading player from the mid-1970s to the late 1980s. See Game 63 for more details.

Ulf Andersson (born 1951) became a grandmaster in 1972 and in the 1970s and early 1980s he won a number of strong tournaments; for much of this period he was one of the top dozen players in the world. Andersson has a unique and individual style involving the accumulation and exploitation of very small advantages, a strategy he conducts with phenomenal patience. In addition to his endgame skill, Andersson is also a very accomplished defender. He played relatively little chess in the early 1990s and only returned to active play in the mid-1990s but he has found it hard to match his earlier achievements, partly due to a tendency to fall into time-trouble. Unusually for an over-the-board grandmaster, Andersson has also been very successful in correspondence chess.

The Game

After a standard opening, Ljubojević starts the fun with an unexpected pawn sacrifice. For several moves the two players display incredible ingenuity, Andersson in defence and Ljubojević in attack, and both sides avoid possible drawing lines in their all-out attempts to win. At move 24 Ljubojević takes a huge gamble; Andersson misses his chance and is the one to crack under the pressure.

1	e4	c5
2	♘f3	e6
3	d4	cxd4
4	♘xd4	♘c6
5	♘c3	♛c7
6	♗e2	a6
7	0-0	♘f6
8	♗e3	♗e7
9	f4	d6
10	♛e1	0-0
11	♛g3	♗d7
12	e5!?	

A very surprising innovation. In earlier games White had prepared his kingside attack gradually, but Ljubojević doesn't believe in hanging around! Despite White's success in this game, few people believed in the objective merits of Ljubojević's innovation. However, this type of pawn sacrifice proved an important extra weapon for White against the Scheveningen, and it wasn't long before it was being tried in analogous positions (e.g. 12 ♔h1 b5 13 e5).

12	...	dxe5
13	fxe5	

There can be no backing out as 13 ♘xc6 ♗xc6 14 fxe5 ♘e4 15 ♘xe4

&xe4 16 c3 &c5 is at least equal for Black.

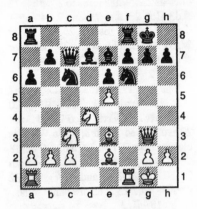

13 ...   ♘xe5

The only real test is to take the pawn. The alternative 13...♘xd4 (not 13...♕xe5? 14 ♘xc6 winning, while 13...♘e8 14 ♘xc6 &xc6 15 &d3 f5 16 &c4 &d7 17 ♖ad1 ♖d8 18 &b3 is slightly better for White) 14 &xd4 gives White an edge after 14...♘d5 15 ♘xd5 exd5 16 c3 or 14...♘e8 15 &d3 f5 16 exf6 &xf6 (16...♕xg3? loses to 17 fxe7) 17 ♕e3 &xd4 18 ♕xd4.

14 &f4   &d6
15 ♖ad1

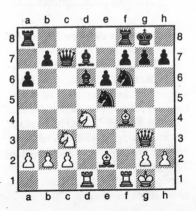

With the relatively slow threat of 16 ♘b3 followed by 17 ♖xd6.

15 ...   ♕b8!

Not an easy move to find, because it appears more natural to develop a piece. However, there is only one reasonable alternative:

1) 15...♘d5 16 ♘f5 exf5 17 ♘xd5 ♕c5+ 18 &e3 f4 (18...♕c6 19 ♘f6+ ♔h8 20 ♘xd7 wins a piece) 19 ♘f6+ ♔h8 20 ♕xf4 ♘g6 and now the unbelievable 21 ♕g3!! wins material.

2) 15...♘f3+ 16 ♖xf3 e5 17 &h6 ♘h5 18 ♕g5 exd4 19 ♘d5 &xh2+ 20 ♔h1 ♕e5 21 ♘f6+ ♔h8 22 ♘xh5 gxh6 23 ♕f6+ ♔g8 24 ♕xh6 f5 25 &c4+ ♔h8 26 ♖h3 and White wins.

3) 15...♖ad8!? (this is playable) 16 ♘b3 ♘d5 17 ♘xd5 (17 ♖xd5 exd5 18 ♘xd5 ♕b8 is unsound) 17...exd5 18 ♖xd5 f6 19 ♘d4 with perhaps an edge for White. Neurohr – Darga, 2nd Bundesliga 1994 continued 19...&c6? (19...♔h8 is better) 20 ♘e6 ♕e7 21 ♖xd6 ♖xd6 22 ♘xf8 ♕xf8 23 &xe5 ♖e6 and now White could have won a piece by 24 ♕b3! ♕c5+ 25 ♖f2 ♕xe5 26 &c4.

After the text-move 16 ♘b3 may be met by 16...&c7.

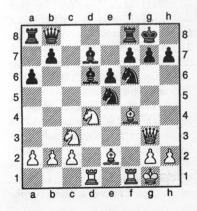

16 ♖d3!

An ingenious move, intending to attack the e5-knight again by 17 ♖e3.

16 ...   ♘e8

Defending the d6-bishop and so unpinning the knight on e5. The alternatives 16...♘c4 17 ♗xd6 ♕xd6 18 ♖xf6 ♕xg3 19 ♖xg3 and 16...♘xd3 17 ♗xd6 ♕a7 18 ♕xd3 are certainly good for White, but on the basis of computer analysis, it has been claimed that 16...♖c8 favours Black. This is not so:

1) 17 ♘b3? ♖xc3! 18 ♖xc3 ♘e4 is indeed very good for Black.

2) 17 ♖e3?! ♘c4 18 ♗xd6 (18 ♘e4 ♘xe4 19 ♖xe4 ♗xf4 20 ♖exf4 ♕e5 21 ♗xc4 ♖xc4 22 c3 f6 is good for Black) 18...♕xd6 19 ♗xc4 (19 ♘xe6 ♕xg3 20 ♖xg3 ♗xe6 21 ♗xc4 ♖xc4 22 ♖xf6 transposes) 19...♕xg3 20 ♖xg3 ♖xc4 21 ♘xe6 ♗xe6 22 ♖xf6, and the ending is promising for Black.

3) 17 ♘xe6! and now:

3a) 17...♘e8 18 ♘xg7 ♘xg7 19 ♖d5! regains the piece and breaks up Black's kingside.

3b) 17...fxe6 18 ♖xd6 ♕xd6 19 ♗xe5 ♕c5+ (19...♕b6+ 20 ♔h1 ♘e8 21 ♗h5 wins) 20 ♔h1 ♘e8 21 ♗d3 (threatening 22 ♕h4; 21 ♗h5 ♕e7 22 ♖f7 ♕xf7 23 ♗xf7+ ♔xf7 24 ♕d3 ♗c6 25 ♕xh7 may be slightly better for White but is far less convincing) 21...♕e7 22 ♕h3 h6 23 ♕g4 ♕g5 (23...♖xc3 24 bxc3 doesn't help Black) 24 ♕e4 g6 25 h4 ♕h5 26 ♕f4 ♘d6 27 ♕f6 and White wins.

3c) 17...♗xe6! 18 ♖xd6 ♕xd6 19 ♗xe5 ♕b6+ 20 ♔h1 ♘e8 and White's kingside threats are enough to hold the balance. 21 ♗d3!? f6 22 ♕h4 h6 23 ♕e4 is an interesting continuation, but if White wants to prove that he is not worse then 21 ♘e4 is simplest; the

draw is forced after 21...♖xc2 (21...♖c6 22 ♗xg7 ♘xg7 23 ♘f6+ is also a draw as 23...♔h8? loses to 24 ♕h4) 22 ♗d3 ♖c6 23 ♗xg7! ♘xg7 24 ♘f6+ ♔f8 (24...♔h8? loses to 25 ♕h4 h5 26 ♕g5) 25 ♘xh7+ ♔g8 (25...♔e7 26 ♕xg7 favours White) 26 ♘f6+, etc.

17 ♘e4   ♗c7

The line 17...♘xd3 18 ♗xd6 ♕a7 (not 18...♘xd6 19 ♘f6+ ♔h8 20 ♘xd7 ♕c7 21 ♘xf8 ♘c5 22 b4 ♖xf8 23 ♕c3 ♘de4 24 ♕e3, when White is clearly better) 19 c3 ♘xb2 20 ♗xf8 ♔xf8 is rather risky for Black as both 21 ♕f2 f6 22 ♘c5 and 21 ♘g5 f6 22 ♘xh7+ ♔e7 23 ♗h5 are dangerous.

18 ♖c3

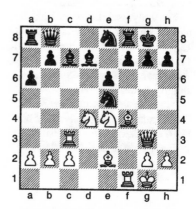

Now White's agile rook threatens to take on c7.

18 ...   ♘c6!

18...♗c6 is another supposed refutation of White's play. It is true that after 19 ♘g5 h6! (19...♗d6 20 ♘xc6 ♘xc6 21 ♕d3 g6 22 ♕h3 h5 23 ♗xd6 ♕xd6 24 ♗xh5 gxh5 25 ♕xh5 ♕d4+ 26 ♔h1 ♕g7 27 ♖g3 wins for White) 20 ♘gxe6 (20 ♘h3!? ♔h8 is not very convincing although White retains some attacking chances) 20...fxe6 21

Nxe6 Rxf4 22 Rxf4 Bd6! 23 Qf2 Qa7! Black has some endgame advantage, but as it turns out this line is irrelevant. White can improve by 19 Nxc6! Nxc6 (19...bxc6 20 Rb3 Qa7+ 21 Be3 c5 22 Bxc5 Nd7 23 Bxa7 Bxg3 24 Bc5 Nxc5 25 Nxc5 and 26 Nd7 wins) 20 Bxc7 Qxc7 (20...Nxc7 21 Nf6+ Kh8 22 Qh4 Qa7+ 23 Kh1 h6 24 Qe4 gxf6 25 Qf4 wins) 21 Nf6+ Kh8 22 Qxc7 Nxc7 23 Nd7 Nd5 24 Rg3 Nd4 25 Bd3 and in Delanoy – Lechtynsky, Kecskemet 1989 Black jettisoned the exchange by 25...f5 but lost in the end. The alternative of giving up the f-pawn may be a better chance, but this is in any case a miserable ending for Black.

18...f6 is also inferior as 19 Nc5! (not 19 Bg4 Qa7! 20 Nc5 Nxg4 21 Qxg4 Bxf4 22 Rxf4 e5 with advantage to Black) 19...Qa7 20 Kh1 gives White dangerous threats.

19 Bxc7 Nxd4

This tactical defence is the point of Black's play. 19...Qxc7? 20 Nf6+ Kh8 21 Qxc7 Nxc7 22 Nxd7 Nxd4 23 Rxc7 Nxe2+ 24 Kf2 would be very good for White.

20 Bd3 Qa7

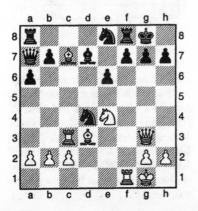

21 Nc5 Bb5!

One of the main critical moments of the game. Had Black been satisfied with a draw, then he could have forced one by 21...Nxc7, when White should take the perpetual check available with the neat combination 22 Bxh7+! (22 Qxc7 Bb5 leaves White struggling) 22...Kxh7 23 Qxg7+! Kxg7 24 Rg3+, etc. However, Black is quite justifiably trying to win.

21...Nf5?! is bad after 22 Bxf5 exf5 23 Be5 and now 23...b6 loses the exchange to the surprising 24 Bb8! Rxb8 25 Nxd7 Qxd7 26 Qxb8 Qd4+ 27 Kh1 Nd6 28 Rd3!, so Black should settle for 23...Be6 24 Bd4 Qb8 25 Qxb8 Rxb8 26 Be5 Rd8 27 Nxb7, although this is slightly better for White.

21...Nb5 is another claimed refutation (poor Ljubo, some people just don't believe his sacrifices...), but 22 Kh1! is at least equal for White:

1) 22...Nexc7 23 Nxd7! (23 Bxh7+ Kxh7 24 Qxg7+ Kxg7 25 Rg3+ is again a draw) 23...Nxc3 24 Nf6+ Kh8 25 Nxh7 (25 bxc3 Nd5 26 Nxh7 Qe3 defends) 25...N3d5 (25...Rg8? 26 Ng5 mates) 26 Nxf8 Kg8 27 Bh7+ Kxf8 28 Qd6+ Ne7 29 Qxc7 and White is slightly better.

2) 22...Nxc3 23 Nxd7 Nxc7 (or 23...Nd5 24 Be5 h6 25 c4 Nb4 26 Nf6+ and wins) 24 Nf6+ Kh8 25 Nxh7 is line "1".

3) 22...Bc6 23 Nxe6 Nxc3 (not 23...Nbxc7 24 Bxh7+! Kxh7 25 Qh4+ Kg8 26 Rh3 when both 26...f6 and 26...f5 are met by 27 Ng5! mating) 24 Nxf8 Bxf8 (24...Nd5 25 Bxh7+ Kxf8 26 Qa3+ Ne7 27 Re1 wins) 25 bxc3 Qc5 (25...Nxc7 26 Qxc7 is very good for White) 26 Be5 with an edge for White – his active bishops are

more important than the weakened queenside pawns.

4) 22...♗c8 (this looks very odd, but may be best) 23 ♗xh7+ ♔xh7 24 ♕h4+ ♔g8 25 ♖h3 f5! (25...f6 26 ♘d3 is more dangerous) 26 ♘d3 (26 ♗d8!? is unclear) 26...♖f6 (26...♕d4 27 ♕h7+ ♔f7 28 ♘e5+ ♔e7 29 ♖d3 ♕xd3 30 cxd3 ♘bxc7 31 ♘g6+ ♔f7 32 ♘e5+ is another draw) 27 ♘e5 ♖h6 28 ♕e7 ♖xh3 29 ♕xe8+ ♔h7 30 ♕g6+ ♔g8 31 ♖d1 ♘d4 32 gxh3 b5 and now White should take the perpetual.

    22 ♗e5   ♘c6

Not 22...♗xd3 23 ♗xd4 ♗xf1 24 ♘xe6, when 24...♕b8 25 ♘xg7 ♕xg3 26 ♖xg3 ♘xg7 27 ♖xg7+ ♔h8 28 ♖xf7+ ♔g8 29 ♖g7+ ♔h8 30 ♖g6+ mates, while 24...fxe6 25 ♗xa7 ♖xa7 26 ♕b8! costs Black material.

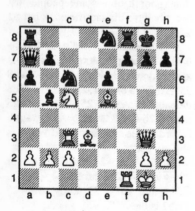

    23 ♗xh7+!

White must keep up the momentum. If he allows Black to exchange his light-squared bishop, then his attack will collapse.

    23 ...   ♔xh7
    24 ♖f4?!

Both players have shown remarkable fighting spirit, but objectively speaking this is one risk too many – on the other hand Ljubojević wouldn't have won the game without it! White could have forced a draw by 24 ♗xg7 ♘xg7 (24...♖g8 25 ♕h3+ ♔xg7 26 ♖xf7+! ♔xf7 27 ♕xe6+ mates) 25 ♕xg7+ ♔xg7 26 ♖g3+ and this would have been the scientifically "correct" outcome of the game. However, Ljubojević is very fond of the casino and puts the lessons he has learnt there to work on the chessboard. By now Andersson was short of time and Ljubo was betting on him missing the correct defence.

The text-move threatens 25 ♗xg7 ♘xg7 26 ♕xg7+ ♔xg7 27 ♖g3+ mating.

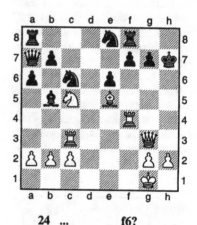

    24 ...   f6?

After this the correct result should again be a draw. The alternatives are:

1) 24...♖d8?! (a simple way to force a draw) 25 ♖h4+ (25 ♕h4+ ♔g8 26 ♖h3 ♖d1+ 27 ♔f2 ♕xc5+ and Black wins with checks) 25...♔g8 26 ♕h3 ♖d1+ 27 ♔f2 ♖f1+ 28 ♔g3 f5 29 ♖h8+ ♔f7 30 ♕h5+ ♔e7 31 ♕g5+ ♔f7 and White must take the perpetual.

2) 24...♘xe5! 25 ♖h4+ ♔g8 26 ♕xe5 and now:

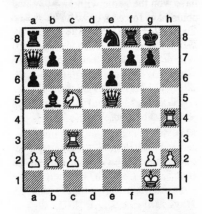

2a) 26...♕b6 27 a4 f6! 28 ♕e3 (28 ♕xe6+ ♕xe6 29 ♘xe6 ♗c6 30 ♘xf8 ♔xf8 is better for Black) 28...♗xa4 29 ♖xa4 ♕xb2 and after 30 ♘xe6 ♕b1+ 31 ♔f2 ♖f7 or 30 ♖b3 ♕xc2 31 ♕xe6+ ♖f7 32 ♘xb7 ♘c7 Black has some advantage.

2b) 26...♗d7! (defending e6 so as to meet ♖ch3 by ...f6) 27 ♔f1 (27 ♖ch3 f6 and 27 ♔h1 b6 28 ♖ch3 f6 29 ♕e4 ♔f7 30 ♘xd7 ♖d8 are hopeless for White) 27...f6! (27...b6 28 ♖ch3 f6 29 ♕e4 ♔f7 30 ♘xd7 ♕xd7 31 ♕xa8 ♕d1+ 32 ♔f2 ♕xc2+ 33 ♔g3 ♘d6 34 ♕a7+ ♔e8 35 ♕b8+ ♔e7 is only a draw) 28 ♕e3 (or 28 ♕e4 f5) 28...♖d8 29 ♕h3 ♕b6 30 ♖h8+ ♔f7 31 ♕h5+ ♔e7 and the attack collapses.

3) 24...f5! (also very strong) 25 ♖h4+ (25 a4 ♘xe5 26 ♖h4+ ♔g8 27 ♕xe5 ♗d7 28 ♔f1 b5 29 ♖d4 ♘f6 30 ♘xe6 ♖f7 31 ♖c7 ♕b6 defends) 25...♔g8 26 ♕g6 ♘xe5 27 ♕xe6+ ♖f7 28 ♕xe5 ♖d8 29 ♖ch3 is the critical line and now Black wins with the stunning 29...♖e7!! 30 ♕xe7 (30 ♖h8+ ♔f7 31 ♕xf5+ ♘f6 32 ♖xd8 ♖e1+ 33

♔f2 ♖f1+) 30...♖d1+ 31 ♔f2 ♖f1+ 32 ♔e3 (32 ♔g3 ♕b8+ mates) 32...♖e1+.

25 ♖h4+   ♔g8

26 ♕h3

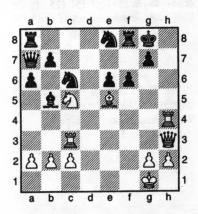

26 ...   ♘d8

Black could have forced a draw by 26...f5 27 ♖h8+ ♔f7 28 ♕h5+ ♔e7 29 ♕g5+ ♔f7 since the combination 30 ♗xg7? ♘xg7 31 ♖h7 ♖g8 32 ♔h1 is refuted by 32...♘d8! 33 ♘e4 ♕d4 34 ♖c7+ ♗d7. However, the move played should also lead to a draw.

27 ♗d4

Threatening 28 ♖h8+ ♔f7 29 ♖xf8+ ♔xf8 30 ♘xe6+.

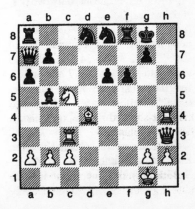

27 ...   b6

Forced, because White wins after 27...♕b8 28 ♘xe6 ♘xe6 29 ♕xe6+ ♖f7 30 ♖ch3.

28 ♘xe6   ♘xe6
29 ♕xe6+   ♕f7

Not 29...♖f7 30 ♖ch3.

30 ♕e4

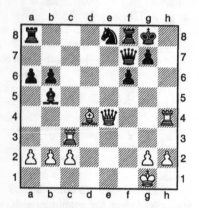

Threatening mate on h7 and the rook on a8.

30 ...   g5?

The losing move. Black could still have drawn by 30...♖xa2!, setting in motion a counterattack which makes use of the otherwise rather offside bishop on b5. White has only two possible replies:

1) 31 ♕xa8 and now previous annotators have given 31...g5 32 ♖g4 ♘d6 33 ♕f3 ♕b1+ 34 ♔f2 ♕f1+ 35 ♔g3 ♘f5+ 36 ♔h3 ♔f7 as winning for Black, although White can continue 37 ♕b7+ ♔g6 38 ♖c8! ♗e2 (38...♗e8 39 ♗xf6!) 39 ♖xg5+! ♔xg5 40 ♗e3+! ♘xe3 41 ♕g7+ ♔f4 42 ♕c7+ with perpetual check. However, Black can win either by 36...♕xf3+ 37 ♖xf3 ♗d7 in this line, which leads to

a winning ending, or by direct attack with 31...♕b1+! 32 ♔f2 ♕f1+ 33 ♔g3 ♕e1+ 34 ♗f2 (34 ♔f3 ♗e2+ and 34 ♔h3 ♗d7+ 35 g4 g5 36 ♕d5+ ♗e6 37 ♕xg5+ fxg5 38 ♖h8+ ♔f7 39 ♖f3+ ♔g6 40 ♖hxf8 ♗xg4+ also win) 34...♕e5+ 35 ♔h3 ♕e6+ 36 ♔g3 (36 ♖g4 f5 37 ♖f4 g5 wins) 36...♘d6 37 ♖h8+ (37 ♕a7 ♘f5+ 38 ♔h3 ♘xh4+ 39 ♔xh4 g5+ wins) 37...♖xh8 38 ♕xf8+ ♔h7 and White's king is too exposed.

2) 31 ♕h7+! (taking the perpetual check is best) 31...♔f7 32 ♕h5+ ♔g8 (not 32...g6? 33 ♕h7+, when White wins after 33...♘g7 34 ♖c7+ ♗e6 35 ♕xg7 ♕b1+ 36 ♔f2 ♕f1+ 37 ♔g3 or 33...♔e6 34 ♖e4+ ♔f5 35 ♖ce3) 33 ♕h7+, etc.

31 ♖h6

31 ♖g3, threatening 32 ♖xg5+, would also have been decisive.

31 ...   ♖a7

Black has no defence to the threat of 32 ♖ch3.

32 ♖ch3   ♕g7
33 ♖g6   ♖af7
34 a4   1-0

As 34...♗xa4 35 ♖xg7+ ♖xg7 36 ♗xb6 ♗d7 37 ♖a3 leaves White too far ahead on material.

Lessons from this game:

1) Tactics are not the sole preserve of the attacker and can also be used defensively.

2) Rooks can be fed horizontally into a kingside attack along the third or fourth ranks (or both, as here).

3) The defender should not assume an unnecessarily passive frame of mind and should be on the lookout for counterattacking possibilities.

Game 70

Samuel Reshevsky – Rafael Vaganian

Skopje 1976

French Defence, Tarrasch Variation

The Players

Samuel Reshevsky (1911–92) was born in Poland and learned the game at a very early age. By the time he was six years old he had established himself as one of the strongest child prodigies of all time, and was already famous for giving simultaneous displays around Europe against 20 or more players. Reshevsky's family later settled in America, where Reshevsky continued his exhibitions, attracting large, admiring crowds.

In 1935, having qualified as an accountant from Chicago University, Reshevsky began to take his chess career more seriously, and for the next twenty years he was one of the top players in the world. Many tournament successes followed, including first at Margate ahead of Capablanca, and four consecutive US Championships between 1936 and 1942. The nearest Reshevsky came to the world title was when he shared third place in the World Championship match-tournament in 1948.

Rafael Vaganian (born 1951) is an Armenian grandmaster from the same generation as Anatoly Karpov. A popular player with a distinctive attacking style, Vaganian came to prominence by tying for the European Junior Championship and then winning the prestigious Vrnjačka Banja tournament at the age of 19, thus securing his GM title. Many tournament victories have followed, including the Soviet Championship in 1989. Vaganian has also qualified for the Candidates matches on two occasions, but lost both times in his first match.

The Game

Despite the peculiar meandering of the white king in this game, you have to believe me when I say that Reshevsky is merely following the theory at the time! This, however, proves to be an unfortunate idea against an inspired Vaganian. After sixteen moves the Armenian has already sacrificed two pieces, but on the other hand the white king has arrived on the half-way line. Five moves later Black has recuperated his material with interest, and the rest of the game is merely mopping up.

	1	e4	e6
	2	d4	d5
	3	♘d2	♘f6
	4	e5	♘fd7
	5	f4	

This move introduces White's most ambitious plan against 3...♘f6. White bolsters the e5-pawn and plans to develop his pieces behind an impressive centre, before slowly squashing Black on the kingside. The drawback of 5 f4 (when compared to the more popular 5 ♗d3) is that it doesn't contribute towards White's development. Consequently, Black can obtain quicker and more dangerous counterplay against the d4-pawn. Another point of this line is that White is often forced to go on a little walk with his king, which is not to the taste of everyone.

5	...	c5
6	c3	♘c6
7	♘df3	♕a5

The most fashionable move at the time, this has now been replaced by 7...♕b6, putting pressure on the d4-pawn.

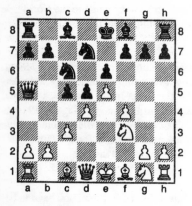

8 ♔f2

The reason for the virtual disappearance of 7...♕a5 is the move 8 ♗e3!. Then 8...cxd4 9 ♘xd4 ♘xd4 10 ♗xd4 gives White a comfortable edge. For a while the critical line for Black was to attack the white pawn-chain with 8...b5 9 dxc5 b4, but then the important novelty 10 ♘d4! was discovered, which presents Black with too many opening problems. The following continuations were enough to put most players off

adopting the black side of this variation:

1) 10...♕xc5 11 ♕a4 bxc3 12 ♕xc6 cxb2 13 ♖b1 ♕a3 14 ♔f2 ♖b8 15 f5 ♗b7 16 ♕c7 ♗a6 17 ♕xa7 ♕xa2 18 ♘gf3 ♗c4 19 ♕xa2 ♗xa2 20 ♗b5 ♗a3 21 fxe6 fxe6 22 ♘xe6 ♗xb1 23 ♖xb1 ♔e7 24 ♘ed4 ♖hc8 25 ♘c6+ ♖xc6 26 ♗xc6 was winning for White in Adorjan – J. Watson, Edward Lasker Memorial, New York 1981.

2) 10...♗b7 11 a3 bxc3 12 b4 ♕d8 13 ♘gf3 a6 14 ♘xc6 ♗xc6 15 ♘d4 ♕c7 16 ♖c1 h5 17 h4 ♘b8 18 ♖xc3 and White already has a won position, as in Tseshkovsky – Vaganian, Vilnius 1975.

8	...	♗e7
9	♗d3	♕b6
10	♘e2	f6
11	exf6	♗xf6

Keeping up the theme of attacking d4. After the alternative 11...♘xf6 White has time to complete his development with 12 ♖e1 and 13 ♔g1. Now he faces a tough dilemma on how to consolidate his position and exploit his bind in the centre.

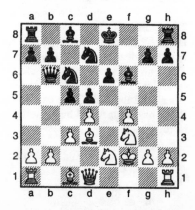

12 ♔g3!?

A very bold decision, some would say a little foolish, especially against someone with the attacking prowess of Vaganian. Objectively, however, it's not necessarily a mistake, as the real error comes later. White feels obliged to remove his king from the critical g1–a7 diagonal, preventing Black from freeing himself with the advance ...e5. Nevertheless, it is possible to allow ...e5, for example 12 ♖f1 and now Black can try:

1) 12...cxd4 13 cxd4 e5 14 ♘c3! (hitting d5 is the way to answer ...e5; 14 fxe5? ♘dxe5 15 ♘xe5 ♗xe5 is clearly good for Black) 14...♘b4 15 ♘a4 ♘xd3+ 16 ♕xd3 ♕a5 17 dxe5 ♕xa4 18 exf6 ♘xf6 19 ♖e1+ ♘e4+ 20 ♔g1 and White is probably a bit better.

2) 12...0-0 13 ♔g1 cxd4 14 cxd4 e5 15 ♘c3 ♘xd4 16 ♘xd5! ♘xf3+ 17 ♔h1 ♕d4 18 ♕xf3 with a roughly level position.

12	...	cxd4
13	cxd4	0-0
14	♖e1?	

This is the really bad move. 14 h3, preparing ♔h2, was the only way to consolidate. Now the fireworks start.

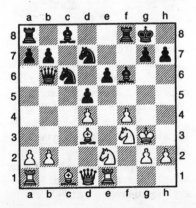

14	...	e5!
15	fxe5	♘dxe5
16	dxe5	

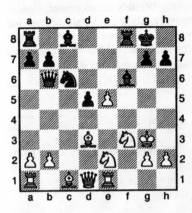

| 16 | ... | ♗h4+!! |

This move and the next one are the most striking of the entire game. The natural 16...♗xe5+ falls short after 17 ♗f4 (but not 17 ♘xe5? ♕f2#). After 16...♗h4+ the white king travels to the heady heights of the fourth rank, though at least White does have a lot of extra material for his trouble. In any case, White has no choice because 17 ♘xh4 ♕f2# is mate.

| 17 | ♔xh4 | ♖xf3! |

Perhaps Reshevsky was expecting 17...♕f2+ 18 ♘g3 ♕xg2, when 19 ♗f1! gives back one piece to force an endgame.

The text-move cuts off the white king's route back to the relative safety of the third rank. Taking the rook with 18 gxf3 allows mate after 18...♕f2+ 19 ♔g5 (or 19 ♘g3 ♕xh2+ 20 ♔g5 ♕h6#) 19...h6+ 20 ♔g6 ♘e7+ 21 ♔h5 ♕xh2#. White can eliminate the h-pawn with 18 ♗xh7+ ♔xh7 and then capture with 19 gxf3, but Black still wins with 19...♕f2+ 20 ♔g5 ♘xe5, threatening 21...♘f7+ 22 ♔f4 g5#, and the simple 21...♘xf3+.

18 ♖f1   ♕b4+
19 ♗f4

White continues to walk on hot coals. 19 ♘f4 ♕e7+ 20 ♔h5 ♕xe5+ 21 ♔h4 ♕f6+ 22 ♔h5 ♕h6# is another pretty mating pattern.

19 ...   ♕e7+

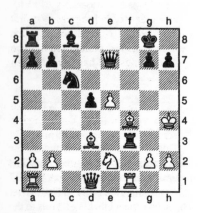

20 ♗g5

The only move to stay in the game. Another checkmate arises after 20 ♔h5 ♕e6 21 gxf3 ♕h3+ 22 ♔g5 ♕h6#.

20 ...   ♕e6!

Threatening mate in two ways forces White to give up his remaining extra piece and effectively ends the game as a contest. Black remains a pawn up, while the white king still suffers from fear of open spaces. The two threats cannot be parried in any other way, e.g. 21 ♕a4 ♖h3+! 22 gxh3 ♕xh3#, or 21 h3 ♖xh3+! 22 gxh3 ♕xh3#.

21 ♗f5   ♖xf5
22 ♘f4

After having to offload his two extra pieces, White does not even have the consolation of grabbing a pawn. After 22 ♖xf5 ♕xf5 23 ♕xd5+ ♗e6

24 ♕f3 ♕xe5 25 ♗f4 Black wins with 25...g5+! 26 ♗xg5 ♕xh2+.

22 ...   ♕xe5
23 ♕g4   ♖f7
24 ♕h5   ♘e7

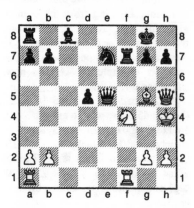

Threatening ...♘f5+ and ...♘g6+. There is no defence, e.g. 25 ♗xe7 ♖xf4+ 26 ♖xf4 ♕xf4+ 27 g4 ♕xh2+ 28 ♔g5 h6+ 29 ♔g6 ♕c2+. Black need only bring up his reserves.

25 g4   ♘g6+
26 ♔g3   ♗d7
27 ♖ae1   ♕d6
28 ♗h6

A little joke before resigning.

28 ...   ♖af8

0-1

Lessons from this game:

1) Ambitious plans are often the most risky ones. White's 5 f4 is a case in point. White aims for everything, but ends up with a severe beating!

2) Be very careful when wandering around with your king in the opening, even if it is all theory!

3) Unexpected moves have a great effect. One can only imagine Reshevsky's reaction to 16...♗h4+!!.

Smbat Lputian – Garry Kasparov
Caucasus Youth Games, Tbilisi 1976
King's Indian Defence, Sämisch Variation

The Players

Smbat Lputian was born in 1958 in Erevan, Armenia. After some good results in junior events, his first major success at senior level was his second place at Erevan 1977, a good IM-standard performance. He made steady progress, and first played in the final of the USSR Championship in 1980/1. His best result in this event was 5th place in 1984. In that same year he became a grandmaster. Since then he has occupied a high place in the world rankings, but has never broken through to the very highest levels.

Garry Kasparov is the greatest player of modern times. He was born in 1963 in Baku, Azerbaidzhan. He was originally named Garry Vainshtain, but following the death of his father when Garry was 7 years old, he adopted his mother's maiden name.

It was clear from an early age that he was a gifted child. He learned to read and add when he was very young, and apparently solved a chess problem at the age of 6 without ever having been taught how to play the game. His early trainers were astonished by his memory and ability to concentrate. Garry made rapid progress, and by the age of 9 he had reached first category (strong club player standard). He was already developing a spectacular style of play; his first chess "hero" was Alekhine. In 1973 he was invited to the Botvinnik Chess School. Botvinnik helped to inspire Kasparov and to bring more discipline into his play. Kasparov continued to make rapid progress, and in 1976 became the youngest ever USSR Junior Champion. 1978 saw more impressive steps forward. In his first senior international tournament, at Minsk, he dominated a strong field, to finish first with 13/17, and then qualified for the final of the USSR Championship, in which he achieved a 50% score. In 1979, he annihilated a world-class field at Banja Luka while he was still without a title or international rating. This result, fully consistent with super-grandmaster status, prompted the magazine *Chess* to announce in a headline *New Soviet Chess Volcano!* This turned out to be no exaggeration. Over the next few years Kasparov established himself as heir apparent to Karpov. In 1980 he completed his grandmaster title and won the World Junior Championship, and in 1981 won the USSR Championship for the first time. In 1982–3 he confidently overcame each hurdle on the way to a world championship match, all the time retaining an exceptionally aggressive, enterprising playing style. This made him a great favourite with the public. He started poorly in the 1984/5 world championship match, but grimly hung on, denying Karpov the sixth win he needed for overall match victory. After 48 games, with the score Karpov 5 wins vs Kasparov's 3, the match was controversially terminated, and a rematch ordered. Kasparov had learned a great deal from the 48 games, and seemed fully Karpov's equal in the 1985 match, which he won narrowly but convincingly. He hung on to his title through a whole string of defences against Karpov in the second half of the 1980s.

Kasparov has completely dominated tournament chess in the 1990s, and his aggressive style and thorough preparation have set the standards that other players have had to follow if they wish to get to the top. His chess is a synthesis of raw talent, scientific research and grim determination. Opponents find his physical presence at the board intimidating.

Kasparov has been extremely active in chess politics too, but here his aggressive style has borne less fruit. He has founded a series of organizations to challenge FIDE's grip on world chess. While this has undoubtedly weakened FIDE, each rival organization has in turn disintegrated. Kasparov's 1993 and 1995 title defences were held under the auspices of the Professional Chess Association (PCA), a body which no longer exists. At the time of writing, he is trying to arrange a title defence under a new organization.

Although the new generation of players are close on his heels, Kasparov remains firmly the world number one, and will undoubtedly be a major figure in world chess for a long time.

The Game

"The following game, with its scintillating series of sacrifices, reminds one of the famous Donald Byrne – Fischer game from the 1956 Rosenwald Tournament, coined 'The Game of the Century'. In both games the young protagonists display wonderful command of the black pieces, never allowing the white king to find a happy haven." – Pritchett and Kopec, in *Best Games of the Young Grandmasters*. There is little to add to that, except that Kasparov shows great expertise in an opening system which was to become one of his trademarks.

1	d4	♘f6
2	c4	g6
3	♘c3	♗g7
4	e4	d6
5	f3	♘c6?!

Kasparov chooses a highly provocative system, hoping for an improved version of the lines following 5...0-0 6 ♗e3 ♘c6, which is the standard move-order. The following variations are pertinent to our featured game:

1) 7 d5 is not effective here, since 7...♘e5 8 h3 (8 f4 is met by 8...♘eg4) 8...e6 (8...♘h5!?) 9 f4 ♘ed7 is good

for Black as White has wasted too much time.

2) 7 ♕d2 a6 8 ♖b1 (8 ♘ge2 is more normal) 8...♖b8 9 b4 would transpose to the game.

6 ♗e3?!

6 d5 is a more critical test of Black's move-order, since after 6...♘e5 White can play 7 f4.

| 6 | ... | a6 |
| 7 | ♕d2 | |

In an earlier game, Korchnoi had tried to take advantage of Black's unusual move-order in another way: 7

♘ge2 ♖b8 8 ♘c1 e5 9 d5 ♘d4 10 ♗xd4 exd4 11 ♕xd4 (this pawn-grab is only possible because Black has not already castled; however, surrendering the dark-squared bishop for the knight is suspicious on general principles) 11...0-0 (threatening ...♘xe4!) 12 ♕d2 c5 13 a4 ♘h5 14 g4 ♕h4+ 15 ♔d1 ♘f6 16 ♕e1 ♕xe1+ 17 ♔xe1 ♘d7 18 ♗e2 ♘e5 19 ♖g1 f5 with excellent play for Black, Korchnoi – Kasparov, simultaneous display, Leningrad 1975.

7 ...   ♖b8

8 ♖b1!?

8 ♘ge2 b5 (8...0-0 returns to normal lines, as in Game 66) was apparently Garry's intention, though after the natural 9 cxb5 axb5 10 d5 followed by ♘d4, it is not clear how Black should continue.

8 ...   0-0

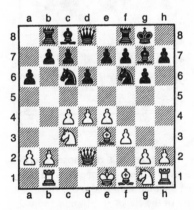

9 b4!?

Instead 9 ♘ge2 leads back to more normal lines. One possibility is then 9...♖e8 10 b4 ♗d7 11 ♘c1 e5 12 d5 ♘d4 13 ♘b3! (13 ♘1e2?! c5! 14 dxc6 bxc6 15 ♘xd4 exd4 16 ♗xd4 c5 17 bxc5?! ♘xe4 18 fxe4 ♕h4+ is similar to the game, but even worse for White),

when Black does not seem to have any tactical solution to the position, and should go in for 13...♘xb3 14 ♖xb3 ♘h5, but White must be a little better here.

After the text-move Garry sank into thought for 25 minutes in search of a way to take advantage of White's particular set-up. By that age, he was already an expert in the subtleties of King's Indian positions, and was aware of the "tools" at his disposal – the tactical motifs and standard plans – but finding a way to use them in the most appropriate way in an unfamiliar setting is never easy. Kasparov's trainer at the time, Nikitin, comments that for the next 15 moves, with all their complexities, Garry spent just 15 minutes, so it is clear how well he had mapped out the play from here. However, in this type of position, Black's choice is often simplified by the lack of decent alternatives. Black pieces together a logical jigsaw to determine what is the best way to strike at White's position, and then plays it. If it doesn't work because of some subtle tactical resource 12 moves down the road, then that is just bad luck!

9 ...   e5

Normally Black would play this move only after White had played ♘ge2 and then moved his knight from e2. Thus it could be argued that here White will save two tempi compared to lines where he plays ♘ge2-c1, and then meets ...e5 by d5, and then ...♘d4 with ♘1e2. However, the two tempi "gained" (♖b1 and b4) are not terribly useful if the position gets blown open, and could even turn out to be weakening.

10 d5   ♘d4!

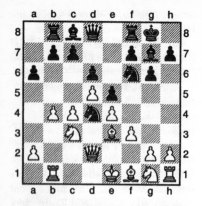

As we observed in Game 66, this possibility is the central theme of the ...♘c6 system against the Sämisch.

11 ♘ge2

White should avoid 11 ♗xd4? exd4, when 12 ♕xd4?? loses catastrophically to 12...♘xe4 13 ♕xe4 ♖e8. 12 ♘ce2 is necessary, but even if White manages to win the d4-pawn, Black still has more than enough compensation – compare the note to White's 7th move.

11 ...   c5!

11...♘xe2 12 ♗xe2 gives White a comfortable advantage.

12 dxc6   bxc6!
13 ♘xd4   exd4
14 ♗xd4

Black has a development advantage and tactical counterchances against White's exposed king in return for the sacrificed pawn. However, it is not yet time for a violent solution to the position.

14 ...   ♖e8!

After 5 minutes' thought, Kasparov decided that he needed to bring up the reinforcements, seeing that the immediate 14...c5 15 bxc5 ♘xe4 16 fxe4 ♕h4+ 17 ♔d1! ♖xb1+ 18 ♘xb1 ♕xe4

19 ♗xg7 ♕xb1+ 20 ♕c1 ♗g4+ 21 ♔d2 ♕xc1+ 22 ♔xc1 ♔xg7 23 cxd6 ♖d8 24 c5 ♖c8 25 ♗xa6 ♖xc5+ 26 ♔b2, when White's rook finally enters the game, gives White a good ending thanks to his outside passed pawn.

15 ♗e2

It seems natural after Black's last move to block the e-file, so as to discourage ...d5, but this move allows Black to demonstrate his main idea – an improved version of the previous note. Instead 15 ♗d3 d5 16 cxd5 cxd5 is absolutely OK for Black, but also permits White to emerge from the opening in one piece.

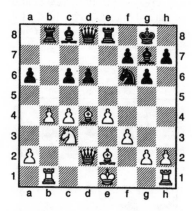

15 ...   c5!

The start of a grandiose combination to exploit the one tactical defect of the plan with ♖b1 – the vulnerability of the rooks on b1 and h1 to being forked by a queen on e4. For anyone coming to this position "cold", this statement appears ludicrous, as it seems highly implausible that Black will have time to arrange such a situation for a long time, while White is just one move away from castling. As so often in chess, it is a case of knowing what the thematic tactical blow is, and then seeking by whatever devious means are necessary to make it a reality.

16 bxc5

16 ♗xf6 ♗xf6 17 ♘d5 was probably necessary, and if Lputian had seen what was about to hit him, he would surely have tried this. However, giving up the dark-squared bishop is the sort of major strategic concession that neither side in a Sämisch tends to make unless it is completely forced.

16 ...   ♘xe4!!

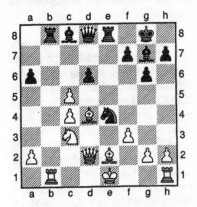

A really beautiful move. White's reply is forced.

17 fxe4

17 ♘xe4 is impossible owing to 17...♖xb1+. This is the reason Black had to open up the b-file first of all.

17 ...   ♕h4+

18 g3?!

Instead:

1) 18 ♔d1? ♖xb1+ 19 ♘xb1 ♕xe4 and now:

1a) 20 ♕d3 ♕xg2 21 ♖g1 (21 ♖e1 ♗f5) 21...♕xh2 22 ♘c3 ♗f5 23 ♕d2 ♗h6 24 ♕b2 (after 24 ♕e1 ♕f4 Black forces mate) 24...dxc5 25 ♗xc5 ♗g7

completely overloads White's fragile defences.

1b) 20 ♗xg7 ♕xb1+ 21 ♕c1 ♕xc1+ 22 ♔xc1 ♔xg7 23 ♗d3 dxc5 gives White an ending with a solid extra pawn and the better bishop – more than enough to win.

2) 18 ♗f2 ♗xc3 19 ♗xh4 ♖xb1+ 20 ♔f2 ♗xd2 21 ♖xb1 dxc5 22 ♖b8 was indicated by Nikitin as White's best chance of survival, e.g. 22...♗c3 23 ♗f3 ♗d4+ 24 ♔f1 ♗e5 25 ♖a8 ♗xh2 26 ♗e7!.

3) 18 ♔f1 is a natural try, but has gone unmentioned by previous commentators. 18...♖xb1+ 19 ♘xb1 ♕xe4 20 ♗xg7 ♕xb1+ and now:

3a) 21 ♗d1?! ♔xg7 and then:

3a1) 22 ♕d4+? f6 23 cxd6 ♖e4 24 ♕d2 ♗e6 and Black wins, e.g. 25 d7 (25 c5 ♕b5+) 25...♗xc4+ 26 ♔f2 ♕b6+ 27 ♔g3 ♖d4.

3a2) 22 cxd6 ♖e6 is good for Black since 23 d7? allows 23...♖xd7! 24 ♕xd7 ♕f5+ 25 ♗f3 ♖e1+ 26 ♔xe1 ♕xd7.

3b) 21 ♕d1 ♕f5+ 22 ♗f3 ♔xg7 23 cxd6 and while Black is certainly not worse, it is not clear how he can establish a meaningful advantage.

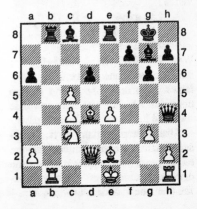

18	...	**Rxb1+**
19	**♔f2**	

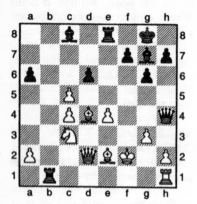

Black is an exchange up, but has a queen and a rook attacked, and no effective checks. In fact, it might appear that Black has got himself into some trouble. However, he has a brilliant move that confirms his clear advantage.

19	...	**Rb2!!**

Whether Kasparov had seen this idea several moves ago, or went into this position intuitively believing that there must be something that would work, it is an impressive feat of chess vision.

20	gxh4	**Rxd2**
21	**♗xg7**	**♔xg7**
22	**♔e3**	**Rc2**
23	**♔d3**	**Rxc3+!**

The clearest and most effective way. Black goes into a rook and bishop ending in which White is much worse owing to his shattered kingside pawns and bad bishop. In many ways, a combination that yields an advantage due to the pawn weaknesses it leaves the opponent is more aesthetically pleasing than one that leads to a massacre –

it suggests that the opponent had only gone slightly wrong, and the combination extracted the appropriate penalty for a "minor infringement". Compare Game 48 in this book.

Instead 23...Rb2 24 cxd6 ♗b7 25 ♗f3 (25 Rd1 is also interesting) 25...f5 is far more messy, and not necessarily advantageous for Black.

24	**♔xc3**	**dxc5**
25	**♗d3**	**♗b7**
26	**Re1**	

26 Rb1 ♗xe4 27 ♗xe4 Rxe4 28 Rb6 f5 sets Black's passed pawn in motion – compare the game continuation.

26	...	**Re5!**

Again Kasparov proceeds with ruthless efficiency, blockading the e-pawn before attacking it with his f-pawn. Nikitin gives the line 26...f5?! 27 e5 ♗e4 (27...f4 is a better try, but Black has lost control of the game) 28 ♗xe4 Rxe5 29 ♔d3 ♔f6 30 Re2 fxe4+ 31 Rxe4 ♔f5 32 Rxe5+ ♔xe5 33 ♔e3 h6 34 h5! as leading to a draw. This appears to be true: 34...g5 (34...gxh5 35 h4!) 35 h3! and Black can make no progress: White has the opposition, and ...a5 can always be met by a4.

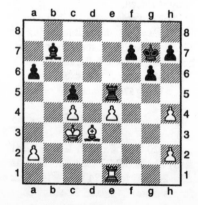

27 a4

Lputian hopes that he might be able to create some counterplay on the queenside, but there is little chance of this amounting to much.

After 27 ♖e2 Black attacks the other weak pawns: 27...♖h5! 28 e5 ♗c8 (stopping e6, which might cause some confusion) 29 ♖e4 ♗f5 and White must yield one of his pawns.

27 ... f5

Rather than being distracted by the h-pawns, Kasparov strikes at the heart of the matter.

28 ♖b1 ♗xe4
29 ♖b6 f4!

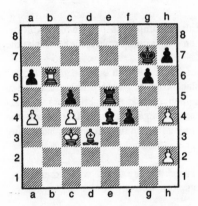

The endgame is all about pushing passed pawns, and this is the most effective method here.

30 ♖xa6 f3
31 ♗f1 ♗f5!
32 ♖a7+ ♔h6

33 ♔d2 f2

Black's pieces have admirably supported this pawn, and now it is the pawn's turn to support the pieces: ...♖e1 is threatened.

34 ♗e2 ♗g4!

A final series of tactical blows commences.

35 ♗d3 ♖e1
36 ♖f7 ♗f5!
37 a5 ♗xd3!
38 ♖xf2 ♖f1!

Black not only rescues his pieces, but also activates them so as to render White's a-pawn harmless.

0-1

39 ♖xf1 ♗xf1 40 ♔c3 ♔g7 41 a6 ♔f6 42 a7 ♗g2 is an easy win.

Lessons from this game:

1) If you have a good understanding of the openings you play, you should be able to find good responses even if your opponent surprises you.

2) If you see a potential tactical drawback in your opponent's set-up, pay particular attention to ideas that exploit it – and if they don't work look for improved versions – for example after a preparatory move or with a different move-order.

3) When you have secured a particular advantage, try to focus the game around that advantage – don't create any more mess than you need to, as this can help the opponent find counterplay.

Game 72
Anatoly Karpov – Yosif Dorfman
USSR Championship, Moscow 1976
Sicilian Defence, Keres Attack

The Players

Anatoly Karpov (born 1951) has been FIDE World Champion 1975–85 and from 1993 onwards. See Game 67 for more details.

Yosif Dorfman (born 1952) is a Russian player who has now settled in France. He first came to prominence in the mid-1970s, in particular with his excellent showing in the 1976 USSR Championship, and his victory in the 1977 event. He became a grandmaster in 1978. Although he has never broken through to the top levels of world chess, he maintains a high rating and is a respected trainer.

The Game

This was one of the decisive games of the Championship, in which Karpov, newly crowned World Champion, faced an even younger player who was at the top of his form.

After a sharp opening, Karpov seizes the initiative with a piece sacrifice, for which he gets two pawns and gives the black king long-term problems. After an intricate struggle, with many unusual manoeuvres and fine tactical points, Karpov eventually emerges on top, and manages to regain the material and consolidate his position. Thereafter, the black king, still with no safe home, is a sitting duck.

1	e4	c5
2	♘f3	d6
3	d4	cxd4
4	♘xd4	♘f6
5	♘c3	e6

This move brings about the Scheveningen Variation, which we have already seen in Game 71.

6 g4

Keres introduced this aggressive move, now known as the Keres Attack, in 1943. It takes advantage of the one tactical drawback of Black's 5th move (as opposed to the Najdorf, 5...a6 or the Classical, 5...♘c6), i.e. that Black does not control g4. Karpov

used it many times, with excellent results.

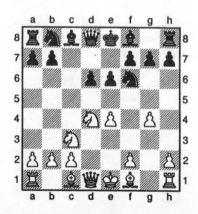

6 ... ♗e7

6...h6 is a more popular move, but this is largely a matter of taste and fashion. The text-move allows White to advance more quickly but also refuses to weaken his kingside.

7 g5 ♘fd7
8 h4 ♘c6
9 ♗e3 a6
10 ♕e2!?

Black must now watch out for sacrifices with ♘d5 or ♘f5.

10 ♕d2 is a more standard place for the queen but leaves it more vulnerable to attack from a black knight coming to c4 or f3.

10 ... ♕c7?!

This move is criticized by Kasparov and Nikitin, who propose 10...♘xd4 11 ♗xd4 0-0 12 0-0-0 b5 as leading to more double-edged play, e.g. 13 a3 ♗b7 14 f4 ♖c8.

11 0-0-0 b5
12 ♘xc6!

Seeing that he would have to sacrifice a piece to keep the initiative, Karpov sought the best way to do so. Dragging the queen to c6 means that the sacrifice on d5 will gain additional time. Instead 12 ♘f5 b4! (12...exf5 13 ♘d5 ♕d8 14 exf5) 13 ♘d5 exd5 14 exd5 ♘de5! leads to "immense complications" according to Karpov – indeed this does not look too convincing for White. Also 12 f4 b4 obliges White either to give up the initiative or sacrifice a piece by 13 ♘d5.

12 ... ♕xc6
13 ♗d4! b4

Dorfman decides to bring matters to a head. Instead:

1) 13...e5 leaves the d5-square seriously weak after the simple reply 14 ♗e3.

2) 13...0-0 was obviously not to Dorfman's liking, and Karpov did not even mention the possibility in his notes, but subsequent practice has shown that Black's position is viable, e.g. 14 ♖g1 ♗b7 (14...b4?! 15 ♘d5!) 15 h5 b4 16 g6 (16 ♘d5 exd5 17 exd5 ♕c7 shows one standard idea for Black versus the ♘d5 sacrifice: after 18 ♕xe7 ♖fe8 the queen is trapped, although here 19 ♗b6 saves White from disadvantage) 16...♗f6!? 17 gxh7+ ♔h8 (a typical theme: the king uses an enemy pawn as a shield) 18 ♗xf6 ♘xf6 19 e5 ♘e8 is somewhat unclear, as in Hawelko – J. Adamski, Naleczow 1985.

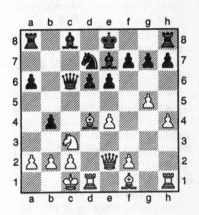

14 ♘d5!

This is a familiar sacrifice in the Open Sicilian, of a type we have seen in Games 54 and 63, although the follow-up ideas have been quite different in each case. Here White's main aim is to prise open the e-file and to gain enough time to disrupt Black's kingside by taking on g7. The upshot of this is that White gains a prolonged attack against Black's exposed king. As he has not sacrificed too much (it boils down to a piece for two pawns), if White can pick up another pawn or two or an exchange, then he can contemplate going into an ending.

    14 ...   **exd5**

    15 ♗xg7

15 exd5?? is no good since after 15...♕xd5 16 ♗xg7 ♕xh1 17 ♖e1 ♘e5 18 ♗xe5? dxe5 19 ♕xe5 Black can castle out of all danger: 19...0-0!.

    15 ...   **♖g8**

    16 exd5   **♕c7**

    17 ♗f6

17 ♖e1 is less effective, since the rook is needed on the d-file, as shown after 17...♘e5 18 ♗xe5 dxe5 19 f4 exf4, when White does not have any support for the deadly advance 20 d6.

    17 ...   **♘e5**

Black threatens ....♗g4. Other moves are less good:

1) 17...♘b6? 18 ♖e1 ♘xd5 19 ♗g2 wins.

2) 17...♘c5 18 ♖e1 ♖a7 19 ♗h3 (19 ♗xe7 ♕xe7 20 ♕d2 wins in simple fashion) 19...♗xh3 (19...♔f8 20 ♗xc8 ♗xf6 21 ♕e8+ ♔g7 22 gxf6+ ♔h8 23 ♕xg8+ ♔xg8 24 ♖e8# is an "amusing helpmate" – Karpov) 20 ♖xh3 and ♖e3 follows.

    18 ♗xe5

Best, as the tempting 18 f4? would be met by 18...♗g4 – the condemned knight supports the counterattack.

    18 ...   **dxe5**

    19 f4

White must keep up the pressure. Now, although his attack is unlikely to end in mate, he can hope to obtain a mighty pair of passed centre pawns to compensate for his sacrificed piece.

    19 ...   **♗f5**

19...e4? loses to 20 d6 ♗xd6 21 ♕xe4+, exploiting Black's loose pieces.

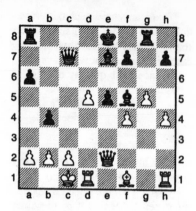

    20 ♗h3

20 fxe5 is an interesting alternative, but if Black responds accurately his chances are no worse than in the game continuation:

1) 20...b3? 21 axb3 ♕a5 22 ♕f3 ♕a1+ (22...♗b4 is met by 23 ♔b1 followed, if necessary, by ♗c4 to block the c-file) 23 ♔d2 ♗b4+? 24 ♔e2 wins.

2) 20...♖c8 21 ♖h2 and then:

2a) 21...♗c5? 22 ♔b1 ♗g1 23 ♗h3 (23 ♖g2 ♕c5) 23...♗xh2 24 ♗xf5 ♕xe5 25 ♕xe5+ ♗xe5 26 ♗xc8 is a winning ending.

2b) 21...♕a5! is best. Then 22 ♕f3 b3! 23 ♕xb3 (23 ♕xf5?? bxa2 24 ♕xc8+ ♗d8 and Black wins) 23...♖g6 gives counterplay, while 22 ♕xa6 ♕xa6 23 ♗xa6 ♖c5 reaches a complicated ending.

    20 ...   **♗xh3**

    21 ♖xh3   **♖c8**

    22 fxe5

22 b3 is also enough for an advantage, e.g. 22...e4 (22...f6? 23 gxf6 ♗xf6 24 fxe5 ♗xe5 25 ♖e3) 23 ♕xe4 ♔f8 24 f5 and White's three pawns are here more than enough for the piece.

    22 ...   **♕c4!**

"This manoeuvre, which is closely linked with the whole of Black's subsequent play, is a tribute to Dorfman's ingenuity." – Karpov.

23   Rdd3

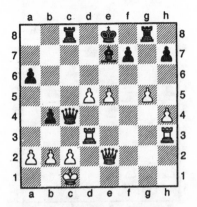

It is worth noting that from here until move 39 Karpov has to keep a constant eye upon his back rank. Until then he simply cannot afford to spend the tempo it would cost to remove the danger by playing b3, since every move is precious as he battles to keep the initiative.

23   ...   Wf4+!

There were two interesting, but ultimately less effective, alternatives:

1) 23...Wxa2 24 d6 Rc6 25 We4 Wc4 26 Rxc4 Rxc4 27 dxe7 is good for White.

2) 23...Rxg5 24 hxg5 Wxa2 25 d6 (25 Rhg3 Wa1+ 26 &d2 Wxb2 27 Wd1 is very good for White) 25...&xg5+ 26 Rhe3 and then:

2a) 26...Rc4? 27 d7+! (this wins quite simply, but was missed by Karpov, who analysed 27 e6 in detail) 27...&d8 28 Wf3 wins.

2b) 26...&f8 27 d7 Rd8 28 Wg4 &xe3+ 29 Rxe3 is good for White.

2c) 26...Rc5 (best) 27 Wg2! offers White some advantage. Instead 27 d7+ is ineffective: 27...&d8 28 Wf3 &xe3+ 29 Wxe3 Rd5, showing the key difference from line "2a".

24   &b1   Rc4!

Black finds an interesting way to activate his major pieces along his fifth rank.

25   d6   Re4
26   Rhe3   Rxe3

26...Rxg5? loses to 27 hxg5 &xg5 28 d7+ &d8 29 Wg2! (29 Rd1 also wins) 29...f5 30 exf6.

27   Rxe3   Wxh4

27...Rxg5 28 hxg5 &xg5 29 d7+ is good for White: Black is routed after 29...&e7 30 Wd3 or 29...&d8 30 Wxa6, while 29...&xd7 gives White time to cover c1 while rescuing his rook.

28   Wf3!

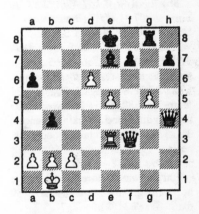

28   ...   Wxg5

As Karpov's analysis showed, this is the best of the three possible captures on g5, but he failed to consider an alternative by which Black delays this capture:

1) 28...Rxg5 29 Wc6+ &f8 30 dxe7+ &xe7 31 a3! and White frees

his king, while his opposite number remains in great peril.

2) 28...♗xg5 29 e6 fxe6 30 ♖xe6+ ♔d8 (30...♗e7 31 ♕c6+ ♔f7 32 ♕d5! wins; 30...♔d7 31 ♕f7+ ♔c6 32 d7+ and mates) 31 ♕c6 wins on the spot – Black has no way to exploit White's vulnerable back rank.

3) 28...♗d8!? (against most replies intending ...♖xg5, when both Black's major pieces are active; it is not so easy for White to relieve the threats to his king: 29 a3 ♖xg5 or 29 b3 ♖xg5) and then:

3a) 29 e6 fxe6 30 d7+ (30 ♖xe6+?! ♔d7 31 ♕f5 ♕xg5 32 ♖e7+ ♔c6!) 30...♔xd7 31 ♕b7+ ♔e8 32 ♕c6+ ♔f8 33 ♕d6+ ♔g7 34 ♕e5+ ♔g6 35 ♕xe6+ ♔g7 and White certainly has a draw, but it is not clear how he might try for a win.

3b) 29 d7+ ♔xd7 (29...♔e7 30 ♕f6+ ♔xd7 31 ♕xf7+ transposes) 30 ♕xf7+ (30 ♕b7+ ♔e8 31 e6 – see variation "3a") 30...♔c8 (30...♗e7? 31 ♖d3+ ♔c6 32 ♕e6+ ♔b5 33 a4+ gives the king some *luft* with tempo, when White wins easily; 30...♔c6 31 ♕e6+ ♔b7 32 ♕d5+ followed by a3 gives White good attacking chances) 31 a3 and White retains good prospects.

29 ♖e1!?

Karpov wants more than the edge he could get by 29 ♕c6+ ♔f8 30 dxe7+ ♕xe7 31 ♕h6+ ♖g7.

29 ...   ♕g2

29...♕g4!? 30 ♕c6+ ♔d7 31 ♕e4!? (31 ♕xd7+ ♔xd7 32 dxe7 is drawish) 31...♗d8 32 ♕xh7 ♖f8 leaves Black somewhat tied up.

30 ♕f5   ♖g6

Black safeguards his h7-pawn and prevents e6 ideas.

After 30...♕g4 31 ♕xh7 ♗h4 32 ♖f1 ♖g7 (32...♗f2? 33 e6) 33 ♕d3 White wins "at least one more pawn" according to Karpov.

31 ♖f1   ♕d5

32 dxe7

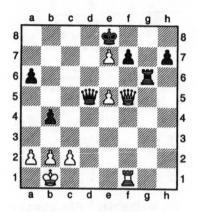

32 ...   ♔xe7

After 32...a5 33 ♕h5 h6 34 e6!! ♖f6 (34...♕xe6 35 ♕xa5 and Black's queenside dissolves) 35 exf7+ ♖xf7 (35...♕xf7? 36 ♕b5+ ♔xe7 37 ♕c5+ wins) 36 ♕g6 ♕e6! 37 ♕g8+ ♔xe7 38 ♖d1 White retains a powerful attack.

33 ♕f4!   a5

34 ♕h4+   ♔e8

35 ♕xh7   ♕f3

Again Black tries to make something of White's back rank, but little comes of it.

36 ♕h8+   ♔e7

36...♔d7 is powerfully answered by 37 e6+!:

1) 37...♔xe6?? loses the queen, e.g. 38 ♕c8+ ♔d6 39 ♕b8+ ♔e6 (39...♔d7 40 ♕a7+ and 41 ♖xf3) 40 ♕b6+ ♔e5 41 ♕c5+ ♕d5 42 ♖e1+.

2) 37...♖xe6 38 ♕d4+ ♔e8 39 ♖d1 and White's attack will prevail.

3) 37...fxe6 38 ♕d4+ ♔d5 39 ♕a7+ ♔d6 40 ♕b6+ ♔d7 41 b3! "and Black has no useful move" – Karpov.

37	♕h4+	♔e8
38	♕c4!	♕b7
39	b3	

"Now that he has finally made some *luft* for his king, White can attack without constantly having to think about his back rank." – Karpov.

39	...	♖e6
40	♖g1	♖xe5
41	♖g8+	♔e7
42	♕h4+	♔d7

Not 42...♔e6?? 43 ♖e8+.

| 43 | ♕f6! | |

43 ♖d8+ ♔c7 44 ♕d4 ♖e1+ 45 ♔b2 ♕c6 46 ♖d5 a4! gives Black some chances of survival.

| 43 | ... | ♖e7 |

43...♕c7 44 ♕xf7+ ♔c6 45 ♖g6+! ♔b7 46 ♕f3+ ♔a7 47 ♕f1! wins. 43...♕h1+ 44 ♔b2 ♖e7 45 ♕b6 is also annihilation.

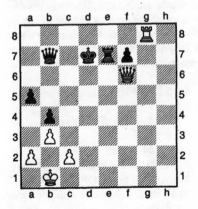

| 44 | ♕f5+ | ♔d6 |

44...♔c6 is best met by 45 ♕xa5 – there is nothing more to be gained by further checks for the moment.

| 45 | ♕xa5 | |

"A check is a check, but a pawn is a pawn." – Karpov. Now that he is a pawn up, simplifying to a technical ending becomes one possible way for White to bring the game to a successful conclusion.

| 45 | ... | ♖e5 |

45...♕e4 46 ♕b6+ ♔e5 47 ♕c5+ ♔f4?! 48 ♕g5+ ♔f3 49 ♕g3+ ♔e2 50 ♕h2+ ♔e3 51 ♖g3+ ♔d4 52 ♖d3+ ♔c5 53 ♕d6+ wins.

46	♕d8+	♔e6
47	♔b2!	f6
48	♖f8	♕g7
49	♕c8+	♔d5
50	♕c4+	1-0

Lessons from this game:

1) If you play either side of the Sicilian, study the ♘d5 sacrifice: when it works, when it doesn't, what it eats for breakfast, etc.

2) A sacrificial attack doesn't have to lead to mate. A prolonged initiative can provide enough compensation, especially when it is possible to pick off a few pawns without losing the initiative.

3) If you have a weak back rank and can't afford a tempo to give the king some *luft*, at each turn you should make sure you are not allowing a tactical trick.

Game 73

Jan Timman – Anatoly Karpov

Montreal 1979

English Opening

The Players

Jan Timman was born in 1951 in Amsterdam, and has been the Netherlands' leading player since the mid-1970s. From the early 1980s to the mid-1990s he was among the world's elite, and was for much of that time regarded as the best "western" player. He was a Candidate on several occasions, reaching the final on two occasions. Following the PCA breakaway in 1993 he contested a FIDE title match with Karpov. He remains a top-class player, but is no longer a regular in super-GM events.

His style is dynamic, aggressive and "positionally correct". Chess for Timman is very much a search for truth – one gets the impression that he believes that top grandmasters are capable of playing near-perfect chess.

Anatoly Karpov (born 1951) has been FIDE World Champion 1975–85 and from 1993 onwards. See Game 67 for more details.

The Game

Timman walks into an idea that had been intended to be used against Korchnoi in the previous year's world championship match. He is immediately in trouble, and as early as move 14, as White, he has to offer Karpov a chance to force a draw. Karpov correctly wants more, and some interesting tactics follow, in which a black knight wreaks havoc in White's kingside. The game ends in a rout, as Timman's king is dragged across the board to its doom.

1	c4	♘f6
2	♘c3	e5
3	♘f3	♘c6
4	e3	

4 g3 had been Korchnoi's choice in his 1978 match against Karpov. Against the text-move, Karpov had some unused preparation which he was able to demonstrate in this game.

4	...	♗e7

This seemingly modest move is connected with some nice tactical points. 4...♗b4 is the more obvious move, when at the time 5 ♕c2 0-0 6

♘d5 ♖e8 7 ♕f5 was a new and sharp line.

5	d4	exd4
6	♘xd4	

6 exd4 leaves White's centre ripe for 6...d5!, when it will be difficult for him to get a good IQP position, e.g. 7 cxd5 ♘xd5 8 ♗b5 0-0 with good play for Black.

6	...	0-0
7	♘xc6?!	

The effect of Karpov's novelty in this game was such that 7 ♘xc6 did not even rate a mention in the second edition of Volume A of the *Encyclopaedia of Chess Openings*! The main line is now 7 ♗e2 when Black can continue:

1) 7...♖e8 8 0-0 ♘xd4 9 ♕xd4 ♗d6!?, intending ...♗e5, establishes a solid central presence.

2) 7...d5! is good, and Karpov's intention – apparently Tal had drawn Karpov's attention to this move while preparing for the Baguio match. However, the move is no novelty, having been introduced by Keres in 1940. After 8 ♘xc6 bxc6 9 0-0 play transposes to the game, while 8 cxd5 ♘b4! 9 0-0 (9 e4?! ♘xe4! is the key tactical point: the idea is 10 ♘xe4?! ♕xd5 11 ♗f3 ♕xd4 12 ♕xd4 ♘c2+) 9...♘bxd5 10 ♘xd5 ♕xd5 is approximately equal, e.g. 11 ♘b5 ♕e5 (11...c6!? was Keres's choice, and possibly a better winning attempt) 12 ♗d2 ♘e4 13 ♗e1 c6 14 ♕d4 ♕xd4 15 ♘xd4 ♗f6 led to a comfortable draw in Seirawan – Nunn, Hastings 1979/80.

7	...	bxc6

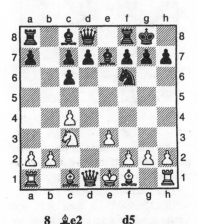

8	♗e2	d5
9	0-0	♗d6
10	b3	

10 cxd5 cxd5 is probably necessary, but undoubling Black's c-pawns removes most of his positional problems at a stroke – although White keeps a slight structural advantage, Black's active piece-play easily compensates.

10	...	♕e7
11	♗b2	

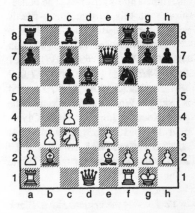

At the time, this position was regarded as favouring White – indeed the first edition of the *Encyclopaedia of Chess Openings, Volume A*, gave no hint that Black might have any active possibilities, let alone a forced sequence leading to advantage.

"Karpov's simple but paradoxical reply forces this evaluation to be radically changed. Right to the end of the tournament the grandmasters analysed this continuation, seeking equality for White. Perhaps someone managed to do this, but during the game Timman did not succeed in equalizing." – Tal, writing in the tournament book.

11	...	dxc4!

This move introduces Karpov's new plan. It looks horrendous to leave the doubled c-pawns isolated, but if Black is to justify his opening play, then it is by making use of his piece activity. He has already accepted some pawn weaknesses in order to fight for the centre and activate his pieces, so he is already committed to this path. The first gain Black makes is that White dare not recapture on c4 with his bishop, as this would remove one of the few defenders from White's kingside. The consequence of this is that the b-file is opened for immediate use by Black.

The old line went: 11...♖d8 12 cxd5 cxd5 (12...♕e5 13 g3 ♗h3 14 ♖e1 ♗b4 15 ♕c2 ♗f5 16 ♕c1 cxd5 17 ♗f3 ♕e7 18 a3 ♗a5 19 b4 ♗b6 20 ♘xd5! is clearly to White's advantage, as in the game Keene – Jansson, Haifa Olympiad 1976) 13 ♘b5 ♗a6 14 ♘d4! ♗xe2 15 ♕xe2 ♕e5 16 g3 ♖e8 17 ♖ac1 with a slight advantage for White – Taimanov.

12 bxc4?

12 ♗xc4 is the critical move. Black can then take a draw, but it is not clear whether he has anything better:

1) 12...♗xh2+ 13 ♔xh2 ♘g4+ 14 ♔g3 (14 ♔g1?? ♕h4) 14...♕g5 15 f4 ♕g6 16 ♗d3 f5 17 ♔f3 isn't a convincing attack for Black.

2) 12...♕e5 13 g3 ♗h3 14 ♖e1 is rather an unclear position.

3) 12...♘g4 13 g3 (13 h3? ♕e5 14 g3 ♘xe3 wins, e.g. 15 ♘d5 ♕xd5) 13...♘xh2 14 ♔xh2 ♕h4+ 15 ♔g1 ♗xg3 16 fxg3 ♕xg3+ 17 ♔h1 ♕h3+ with a perpetual check.

12 ...   ♖b8!

13 ♕c1

The queen must defend the bishop, but this in turn takes the guard off g4.

13 ♖b1? loses to 13...♖xb2 14 ♖xb2 ♕e5!, while 13 ♕c2 would be met in the same way as the text-move.

13 ...   ♘g4!

Black is able to channel his pieces quickly and effectively towards White's king. 13...♖e8, as played in Sande – Svenneby, Norway 1977 (so Karpov's 11...bxc4 wasn't technically a novelty!), is somewhat less effective.

14 g3

14 ♗xg4 ♗xg4 15 ♖fe1 ♖b4! keeps the pressure on White – Kholmov.

14 h3? walks into 14...♕e5 15 g3 ♘xe3!.

14 ...   ♖e8

Now 15...♘xh2 is threatened, since after 16 ♔xh2 ♕h4+ 17 ♔g2 ♕h3+ 18 ♔g1 ♗xg3 19 fxg3 ♕xg3+ 20 ♔h1, the rook enters the attack with decisive effect: 20...♖e6, etc.

The immediate 14...♘xh2 15 ♔xh2 ♕h4+ only forces a draw.

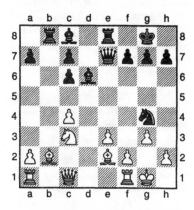

15 ♘d1?

There are a couple of possible improvements, but nothing looks really satisfactory for White at this point:

1) 15 ♗f3 and now:

1a) 15...♘e5 16 ♗e2 ♗e6 puts useful pressure on c4.

1b) 15...♕f6 16 ♗xg4 (16 ♗g2 is bad: 16...♕h6 17 h3 ♘e5!) 16...♗xg4

17 f3 ♗h3 18 ♖f2 ♕g6 with a strong initiative for Black – Karpov.

2) 15 c5 ♗xc5 16 ♘d1 has been suggested as the way for White to fight on, but it does not look very attractive.

15 ...   ♘xh2!!
16 c5

16 ♔xh2 ♕h4+ 17 ♔g2 (17 ♔g1 ♗xg3) 17...♕h3+ 18 ♔g1 ♗xg3 19 fxg3 ♕xg3+ 20 ♔h1 ♘e4! (20...♖e6 21 ♗f6) 21 ♖f4 ♖xf4 (21...♗h3 22 ♗f1 ♗xf1 also wins) 22 exf4 ♕e1+ 23 ♔g2 ♕xe2+ wins.

16 ...   ♘xf1!
17 cxd6

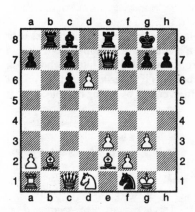

17 ...   ♘xg3!

It was this surprising move that Timman had missed.

18 fxg3

18 dxe7 ♘xe2+ 19 ♔f1 ♘xc1 is immediately disastrous for White.

18 ...   ♕xd6
19 ♔f2

19 ♔g2 ♕h6 20 ♘f2 (20 g4 loses to 20...♕g5) 20...♖xe3 21 ♗f3 c5 22 ♕d1 ♗h3+ 23 ♘xh3 ♖xb2+ 24 ♘f2 ♕f6 0-1 Panizzi – Lotti, Italian Correspondence Championship 1992.

19 ...   ♕h6
20 ♗d4

After 20 ♕c3 ♕h2+ (20...♖e6 is strong too) 21 ♔e1 (21 ♔f3 ♗g4+ 22 ♔xg4 ♕xe2+) 21...♕xg3+ 22 ♔d2 ♖d8+ 23 ♔c1 ♗f5 White is lost.

20 ...   ♕h2+
21 ♔e1   ♕xg3+

The game is decided. Black has a rook and four pawns for two pieces and his army is far better coordinated. The threats to the white king mean that the end is not far off.

22 ♔d2   ♕g2!
23 ♘b2   ♗a6
24 ♘d3

24 ♕f1 would be met by 24...♕h2 intending ...c5.

24 ...   ♗xd3!
25 ♔xd3   ♖bd8
26 ♗f1   ♕e4+
27 ♔c3   c5!
28 ♗xc5   ♕c6
29 ♔b3   ♖b8+
30 ♔a3   ♖e5
31 ♗b4   ♕b6
0-1

Lessons from this game:

1) If you have opted for activity rather than structure, don't be afraid to carry this policy to its logical conclusion by accepting structural horrors to hurl your pieces toward the enemy king.

2) If the opponent plays an unexpected move in the opening, try to assess it objectively. If it is strong and you need to bale out, it is best to start immediately.

3) When you have several undefended units and enemy knights are hovering around, be especially vigilant!

Game 74
Lev Polugaevsky – Eugenio Torre
Moscow 1981
Queen's Gambit Declined, Semi-Slav Defence

The Players

Lev Polugaevsky (1934–95) was one of the world's top grandmasters from the late 1960s to the early 1980s. For further details see Game 40.

Eugenio Torre was born in 1951 in Illcilo City, Philippines, and is the strongest player to have emerged from his country. He became a grandmaster in 1974, and from the mid-1970s to the mid-1980s he competed regularly in top-level events. In 1982 he qualified for the Candidates matches, but lost in the quarter-final to Ribli.

The Game

Torre plays a sharp and provocative opening, to which Polugaevsky replies with a tremendous novelty, which is based on a concept of stunning originality: a chain of pawns will brick in an enemy rook. Meanwhile White, a whole rook down, will calmly play in the rest of the board as if material is level and he has heavy positional pressure. Torre escapes to an ending by giving up a piece, but it shouldn't be sufficient to save the game.

1	d4	d5
2	c4	c6
3	♘f3	♘f6
4	♘c3	e6
5	♗g5	dxc4

With this move Black initiates one of the most bizarrely complex opening systems of all. It is known alternately as the Anti-Meran Gambit or the Botvinnik System.

| 6 | e4 | b5 |

This is essential, as otherwise White will have gained a fine pawn-centre for nothing.

| 7 | e5 | |

White pushes on in the centre. Other moves are possible but amount to somewhat speculative gambits.

| 7 | ... | h6 |

| 8 | ♗h4 | g5 |

In this way Black saves his piece, but White has some tactics at his disposal.

| 9 | ♘xg5 | |

This temporary piece sacrifice decimates Black's kingside pawn structure. On the other hand it gives Black open lines.

9	...	hxg5
10	♗xg5	♘bd7
11	exf6	♗b7

So, White is a pawn up and Black's king has nowhere safe to go. What is going on? As Black sees it, the f6-pawn can be rounded up whenever Black feels like. For the time being it is convenient to leave it on f6, where it gets in the way of White's pieces.

White's d4-pawn is weak and isolated. Meanwhile the black king can find a home on the queenside. Although his queenside pawns have advanced, they still provide a lot of cover, and besides Black's pieces will protect the king too. The open g- and h-files will give Black attacking chances against the white king. Therefore, somewhat surprisingly, the long-term factors are against White, and it is he who must act swiftly to make something happen before Black can organize his position. In this game Polugaevsky manages to do so brilliantly.

12 g3

Experience has shown that if White wishes to fight for the initiative, then his bishop must go to g2. Torre's reply seeks to take advantage of the momentary weakening this move causes.

12 ...   c5
13 d5   ♘b6?!

This is now thought suspect due to White's reply in this game. The main alternative is 13...♛b6 14 ♗g2 0-0-0 15 0-0 – see Games 95 and 98, while 13...♗h6 (Game 89) and 13...♘xf6 have also enjoyed spells of popularity.

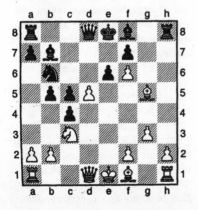

14 dxe6!

It is highly thematic that White's reply is based on making use of the advanced f6-pawn that Black spurned to capture.

14 ...   ♛xd1+

Some analysts decided that this was the fatal error and that 14...♗xh1 15 e7! ♛d7 was the way forward for Black. However, 16 ♛xd7+ ♘xd7 17 ♘xb5 ♗xe7 18 fxe7 f6 19 ♗e3 ♔xe7 20 h4 is good for White, who has more than enough for the exchange, e.g. 20...♗f3 21 ♗xc4 ♖hc8 22 ♖c1 ♘e5 23 ♘a3 ♖ab8 24 b3 ♖b4 25 ♗f1 ♔f7 26 ♘c4 and Black's position fell apart, starting with the c5-pawn, in Ionov – R. Scherbakov, Rostov-on-Don 1993.

15 ♖xd1   ♗xh1
16 e7

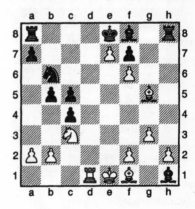

16 ...   a6

Torre plays the move that was recommended by theory at the time, and is hit by a bombshell. Instead:

1) 16...♗h6? loses to 17 ♘xb5 ♖c8 18 ♘c7+ ♖xc7 19 ♖d8#.

2) 16...♗c6 is far more resilient, and has never been properly analysed:

2a) 17 ♗g2 (this is just a blunder) 17...♗xg2 18 ♘xb5 was apparently given by Harding, but with no indication of what was supposed to happen after 18...♘d5, e.g. 19 ♘d6+ ♔d7 20 ♘xf7 ♖xh2.

2b) 17 ♖d6 looks best:

2b1) 17...♖c8 18 h4 ♗h6 (18...b4 19 ♗h3) 19 f4 (borrowing an idea from Polugaevsky!) 19...b4 20 ♗h3 ♖b8 21 ♖xc6 bxc3 22 bxc3 and White wins.

2b2) 17...♗d7 18 ♘e4 ♗xe7 19 fxe7 f5 20 ♘xc5 favours White.

2b3) 17...b4 18 ♖xc6 bxc3 19 ♖xb6 axb6 20 ♗xc4 ♔d7 21 bxc3 ♗h6 22 h4 ♗xg5 23 hxg5 is an interesting ending. White threatens 24 ♗xf7, while 23...♖h7 allows 24 ♗b5+ ♔e6 25 e8♕+ ♖xe8 26 ♗xe8.

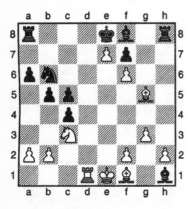

17 h4!!

Polugaevsky had cooked up this astonishing idea in his "laboratory" at home. Polugaevsky was a hard worker, and had doubtless spent many hours trying to refute Black's opening. 17 exf8♕+ ♔xf8! 18 ♖d6 ♖b8 19 ♗e3 ♖h5 20 ♗e2 ♖e5 21 ♘d1 ♔g8 22 ♗f4 ♖ee8 23 ♘e3 ♗e4! gave Black the better chances in Beliavsky – Bagirov,

Moscow 1981 – this was the "latest word" of theory in this line at the time of the Polugaevsky – Torre game.

17 ...   ♗h6
18 f4!!

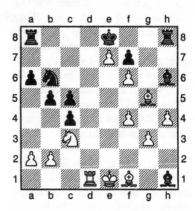

"Having given up a rook, White has no intention of regaining the lost material, but contents himself with the fact that the rook on h8 is not destined to come into play for some time." – Polugaevsky. The line of pawns from g3-h4-e7 is quite unlike anything normally seen in actual play. Indeed, if it occurred in a composed position, there would doubtless be comments that it looked artificial! The pawns constitute a prison-wall for the h8-rook, the king stuck on e8, himself in mortal peril, sealing off the escape route. White has no way of actually winning the rook, but can play quite normally, as though he isn't really a rook down.

18 ...   b4
19 ♖d6!   ♖b8!

19...bxc3 20 ♖xb6 cxb2 21 ♖xb2 (21 ♗xc4!? is also good) and now Pachman gave two sample lines:

1) 21...♗d5 22 ♖d2 ♗e6? 23 ♗g2 ♖c8 24 ♗c6+ and mate next move.

2) 21...♔d7 22 ♗xc4 ♗xg5 23 fxg5 (of course!) 23...♖hb8 24 ♖xb8 ♖xb8 25 ♗xf7, etc.

20	**♘d1**	**♗xg5**
21	**fxg5**	**♘d5!**

Black decides to give up a knight to free his rook. This is a good idea, but it gives White time to take some of Black's dangerous queenside pawns and thus secure a favourable ending. 21...♗d5 22 ♘e3 (intending ♘f5) 22...♗e6 (22...♗e4 23 ♗g2! ♗xg2 24 ♘f5 ♖g8 25 ♘g7+ ♖xg7 26 ♖d8+! ♖xd8 27 exd8♕+ ♔xd8 28 fxg7 and the pawn promotes) 23 ♗g2 (threatening to force mate by 24 ♗c6+) 23...♗d7 24 ♗e4 intending ♘f5, when the mate threat on g7 will force ...♗xf5, whereupon Black's king will become fatally vulnerable to a bishop check on the a4–e8 diagonal.

22	**♗xc4**	**♘xe7**
23	**fxe7**	**♔xe7**

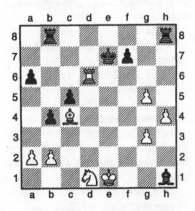

24 ♖f6!

24 ♖xa6 ♖he8! 25 ♖f6 ♔f8+, intending ...♖e7, was given by Polugaevsky. Other analysts extended this line as follows: 26 ♔f2 ♖e7 27 g6 ♖d8 28 ♘e3 ♖d2+ 29 ♔e1 ♖xb2 30 ♖xf7+

♖xf7 31 gxf7 ♗e4 32 ♘g4 ♗f5 33 ♘e5 ♖h2 34 ♗d5 giving this position as unclear, but Black still seems to be in trouble. 35 g4 is a big threat, overloading the bishop, and 34...♔g7 35 g4 ♗h3 36 ♔f2 is no help to Black.

24	**...**	**♖hf8**
25	**♘e3**	**♗e4**
26	**♖xa6**	

In return for the exchange, White has two pawns and his pieces are more active.

26	**...**	**♖bd8**
27	**♖f6**	

27 h5!? ♖g8 (27...♗d3? 28 ♖a7+ ♔e8 29 ♘d5; 27...♖d6 28 ♖a7+ ♖d7 29 ♖xd7+ ♔xd7 30 ♘g4 is very good for White) 28 g6 is also good, since 28...fxg6? loses to 29 ♖e6+!.

27	**...**	**♖d6**
28	**♖f4**	**♖d4**
29	**h5**	**♗d3!**
30	**♘d5+!**	**♔d6**
31	**♖xd4**	**cxd4**

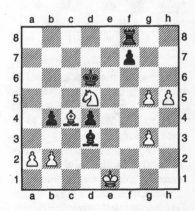

32 ♗b3?!

Sadly, after his magnificent play so far, Polugaevsky starts to misplay the ending slightly. However, there is no real damage done as yet.

32 ♗xd3! ♔xd5 33 h6! is a clear-cut win: 33...♔g8 (33...♖h8 34 ♔f2 ♔d6 35 ♔f3 ♔e7 36 ♔g4 f6 37 ♔h5) 34 h7 ♖h8 35 ♔d2 ♔d6 36 ♔c2 ♔e7 37 ♔b3 ♔f8 38 ♔xb4 ♔g7 39 ♔c4 (Polugaevsky).

32 ...   ♗c2!
33 ♗xc2   ♔xd5
34 ♗b3+?

34 h6! still wins – compare the note to White's 32nd move.

34 ...   ♔e5
35 g4

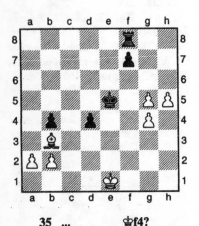

35 ...   ♔f4?

In time-trouble, Black misses his chance. It is not yet clear where his king will be most effective – this depends on how White chooses to advance his kingside pawns – but it is clear that his pawn will be more dangerous the further advanced it is. Therefore 35...d3! was the most logical move, with a likely draw:

1) 36 ♔f2 ♔f4! gives White nothing, e.g. 37 g6 fxg6 38 hxg6 ♖e8!? 39

g7 d2 and the d-pawn proves to be very strong.

2) 36 ♔d2 ♔d4! 37 ♗a4 (37 h6? ♖e8 38 h7 ♖e2+ 39 ♔d1 ♖h2 40 ♗xf7 ♔e3! wins for Black) 37...♖a8!? doesn't seem to give White anything better than 38 ♗b3.

3) 36 g6 fxg6 37 hxg6 ♔f6 38 ♗f7 ♖d8 39 ♔d2 doesn't give White winning chances either.

36 g6!

Now, after his slight hiccup, White is winning again.

36 ...   ♔e3

36...♔g5 is no good now: 37 ♗xf7 ♔h6 38 g5+ and the pawns go through.

36...fxg6 37 hxg6 ♖e8+ 38 ♔d2 and Black cannot stop the pawn, e.g. 38...♖e7 39 ♗f7!.

37 g7   ♖c8
38 ♔f1

38 h6?? lets Black survive after 38...♖c1+ 39 ♗d1 d3 40 g8♕ d2+ 41 ♔f1 ♖xd1+ 42 ♔g2 ♖g1+ 43 ♔xg1 d1♕+.

38 ...   d3

38...♔f3 is met by 39 ♗d1+ followed by h6.

39 ♔g2   ♔f4
40 h6   1-0

Lessons from this game:

1) Some openings require detailed specialist knowledge and to play them without such expertise would be suicide.

2) A piece permanently locked out of play is as good as lost.

3) Pawns are powerful and versatile pieces!

Game 75
Igor Kopylov – Sergei Koroliov
USSR Correspondence Championship 1981–3
Sicilian Defence, Nimzowitsch Variation (2...♘f6)

The Players

Igor Kopylov (born 1939) is a correspondence grandmaster. He won the 17th USSR Correspondence Championship in 1986–8.

Sergei Koroliov (born 1937) is a correspondence grandmaster, who is currently among the highest-rated postal players in the world.

The Game

A double-edged opening triggers early complications which leave both kings stranded in the centre. Imaginative play by both sides leads to a highly unusual position in which one of White's bishops is in danger of being trapped on h8(!). An apparently insignificant error by Black at move 21 gives Kopylov the chance he needs. The result is an amazing king-hunt across all eight ranks.

| | 1 | e4 | c5 |
| | 2 | ♘f3 | ♘f6 |

An opening line which is unfashionable today.

	3	e5	♘d5
	4	♘c3	e6
	5	♘e4	

5 ♘xd5 exd5 6 d4 is currently reckoned the strongest, but the line White chooses here is also dangerous.

| | 5 | ... | ♘c6 |
| | 6 | c4 | ♘db4 |

6...♘b6 and 6...♘f4 are playable alternatives.

| | 7 | a3 | ♕a5 |

This allows Black to maintain his knight on b4 for the moment. The danger is that it will eventually be forced to retreat to a6, where it will be out of play.

| | 8 | ♕b3 | |

8 ♗e2 and 8 ♘c3 are also possible, with the latter idea being the current

preference. The move played intends ♖b1 without allowing the reply ...♘a2.

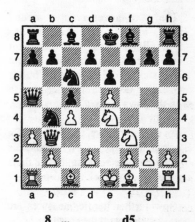

| | 8 | ... | d5 |
| | 9 | exd6 | e5 |

9...f5 was recommended by Kopylov himself; after 10 ♘xc5 ♕xc5 11 axb4 ♕xb4 White has only a very slight advantage. With the text-move,

Black aims to improve his pawn-structure before regaining the pawn on d6. The danger with such a strategy is that it may not in fact turn out to be so easy to regain the pawn, in which case the advanced d-pawn will be a thorn in Black's flesh, preventing the development of the f8-bishop.

10 ⧄b1   ⧄a6

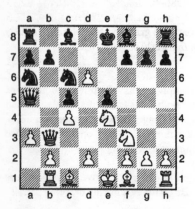

The next moves revolve around White's efforts to maintain the d6-pawn. If Black manages to recapture it then White will be worse on account of his backward d-pawn, so White is prepared to take extreme measures to keep the pawn alive.

11 g4

An amazing move, preventing ...f5. Black cannot take on g4, because his own b7-pawn is hanging, but he finds another way to attack the d6-pawn.

11 ...   ⧄d8

Now further heroic measures are necessary to retain the pawn.

12 d4!?   exd4

A difficult decision, as there were two other plausible moves:

1) 12...cxd4 13 c5 ⧄xc5 14 ⧄xc5 ⧄a5+ 15 ⧄d2 ⧄xc5 16 ⧄g5 ⧄xd6 17

⧄xf7+ (not 17 ⧄xf7? ⧄g6 and Black wins) 17...⧄d8 18 ⧄c4 ⧄e8 and now White can either repeat moves or play 19 ⧄g2. In the latter case his light-squared pressure and Black's centralized king provide good compensation for the exchange.

2) 12...⧄xd6 13 d5 ⧄d4 14 ⧄xd4 exd4 15 ⧄b5+ ⧄f8 leads to an unclear position. Black has been forced to move his king, but White's own king-side has been weakened and can be attacked by ...h5.

13 ⧄f4   ⧄d7

13...⧄a5 14 ⧄c2 ⧄xg4 is far too greedy: retribution would come in the shape of 15 ⧄e5 ⧄f5 (15...⧄e6 16 ⧄a4+ ⧄c6 17 ⧄xc6 ⧄d7 18 ⧄g2 ⧄c8 19 ⧄g5 and 15...⧄d7 16 ⧄e2 are also very good for White) 16 ⧄e2 ⧄b6 17 ⧄h5 ⧄e6 18 ⧄h3 with a decisive attack.

14 ⧄g3

White side-steps the skewer after ...⧄xg4. 14 h3 would be too slow because of 14...f5, and after an exchange on f5 White's minor pieces would be forked.

14 ...   h5

Black cannot afford to decentralize his queen by 14...⧄xg4 15 ⧄fg5 ⧄h5, for example 16 ⧄h3 ⧄xh3 (16...b6 17 ⧄a4 ⧄b7 18 d7+ ⧄d8 19 ⧄d1 wins for White after 19...⧄g6 20 ⧄f3 or 19...⧄xd1+ 20 ⧄xd1) 17 ⧄xb7 ⧄c8 18 ⧄xh3 ⧄xh3 19 ⧄xa6 and Black's inability to develop his kingside will almost certainly prove fatal.

15 ⧄d2!

Certainly not 15 gxh5? f5 16 ⧄h3 ⧄xh5 and White's position falls apart. White is prepared to offer his g-pawn in order to bring his rook to the open e-file.

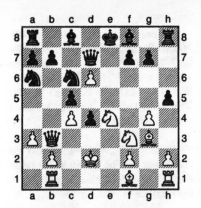

15 ... **hxg4**
16 ⟨Re1 **⟨Kd8**
17 ⟨ℂe5 **⟨ℂxe5**

Forced, since 17...Wf5 18 ⟨ℂxc6+ bxc6 19 Wa4 (threatening 20 Wxc6 and 20 Wa5+) 19...⟨ℂb7 20 Wa5+ ⟨ℂc8 21 h3! wins, e.g. 21...gxh3 22 ⟨Rxh3 ⟨Rg8 (or 22...⟨Rxh3 23 ⟨ℂxc5) 23 ⟨Rh4 g5 24 ⟨ℂh3 g4 25 ⟨Rh5! Wxh5 26 d7+ ⟨ℂxd7 27 ⟨ℂf6+ mating.

18 ⟨ℂxe5 **Wc6**

If 18...f5, then 19 ⟨ℂf6 Wc6 20 ⟨ℂd5 ⟨ℂxd6 21 ⟨ℂxg7 ⟨Rxh2 22 ⟨ℂf6+ ⟨ℂd7 23 ⟨ℂd3 ⟨Rxf2+ 24 ⟨ℂd1 gives White a decisive attack.

19 ⟨ℂg5 **⟨Rh5!**

Avoiding 19...Wxh1 20 ⟨ℂxf7+ ⟨ℂd7 (20...⟨ℂe8 21 ⟨ℂxh8) 21 ⟨ℂxh8 ⟨ℂxd6 (or else Black has no extra material to balance White's attack) 22 ⟨ℂxd6 ⟨ℂxd6 23 Wg3+ and Black loses.

The move played looks like an oversight as White can continue 20 ⟨ℂxf7+. However, Black would reply 20...⟨ℂe8! and the discovered checks are not dangerous, while the knight on f7 is trapped.

20 ⟨ℂxg7!

An equally creative response. With both rook and knight already under

attack, White also puts his bishop *en prise*.

20 ... **⟨ℂxd6**

Black finally removes the menacing pawn. Alternatives are worse:

1) 20...⟨ℂxg7 21 ⟨ℂxf7+ ⟨ℂd7 22 ⟨Re7#.

2) 20...Wxh1 21 ⟨ℂxf7+ ⟨ℂd7 22 ⟨ℂxf8 with a quick mate.

3) 20...⟨ℂe6 21 ⟨ℂxf8 Wxh1 22 f3 Wxh2+ (22...⟨ℂc8 23 Wb5) 23 ⟨ℂd1 b6 24 Wb5 ⟨ℂb8 25 ⟨ℂxe6+ fxe6 26 ⟨Rxe6 ⟨ℂd7 27 Wc6 and wins.

4) 20...⟨Rxg5 21 ⟨ℂxf8 Wxh1 22 ⟨ℂe7+ ⟨ℂd7 23 ⟨Rxg5 and White has a very strong attack.

21 ⟨ℂxf7+

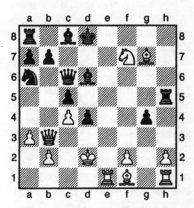

21 ... **⟨ℂc7?**

The most natural move, as it avoids blocking in the c8-bishop, but this mistake allows a crucial queen check on g3 later on. Black should have played 21...⟨ℂd7! 22 ⟨ℂxd6 and now:

1) 22...Wxh1? 23 ⟨ℂe4 Wxh2 (not 23...⟨Rf5 24 Wg3 winning) 24 ⟨ℂf6+ ⟨ℂc7 25 ⟨ℂxh5 Wxh5 26 ⟨ℂe5+ ⟨ℂd7 (26...⟨ℂd8 27 ⟨ℂf6+ ⟨ℂc7 28 Wg3+) 27 Wb5+ ⟨ℂd8 28 ⟨ℂxd4 with a clear advantage for White – Black's king is

more exposed and his a6-knight is off-side.

2) 22...♛xd6 23 ♕g3 (23 ♗g2 ♖g5 24 ♗h8 ♕h6 is fine for Black because there is no check on g3) 23...♕xg3 24 fxg3 ♔d6 25 ♗g2 ♖b8 26 b4 ♗e6 27 bxc5+ ♘xc5 28 ♗xd4 ♗xc4 and White's two bishops give him a slight edge, but in view of the reduced material a draw is by far the most likely result.

22 ♘xd6   ♕xd6

23 ♗g2

Here 23 ♕g3 ♕xg3 24 fxg3 is totally harmless as the c8-bishop is free to move.

23 ...   ♖g5

Positionally speaking, Black is in a bad way. White's two bishops are potentially very powerful, while Black's king is exposed and the a6-knight is out of play. The only positive factor is the temporarily bad position of White's dark-squared bishop, so Black must try to exploit this before White extracts the bishop and consolidates his advantage.

The alternative is 23...♖f5, but then 24 ♖e8! ♖xf2+ 25 ♔e1 ♖f5 (25...♖xg2 26 ♗e5 ♔d7 27 ♗xd6 ♔xe8 28 ♔f1 ♖d2 29 ♗f4 is also lost) 26 ♖f1! ♖xf1+ (26...♕d7 27 ♖xc8+) 27 ♔xf1 ♕f4+ 28 ♔e2 is winning for White.

24 ♗h8   ♕h6

If Black tries to repeat moves by 24...♖h5, then 25 ♖e8 ♖b8 26 ♕g3 ♕xg3 27 hxg3 ♖xh1 28 ♗xh1 leads to a winning ending for White.

The move played seems very strong as it both attacks the h8-bishop and threatens a deadly discovered check.

25 ♕g3+

A vital check which is only possible thanks to Black's slip at move 21.

25 ...   ♔b6

The only move, because 25...♔d8 26 ♔d1 ♕xh8 27 ♕d6+ ♗d7 28 ♕e7+ ♔c7 29 ♕xg5 costs the exchange while 25...♔d7 26 ♕f4 ♖g6 27 ♗e5 ♕xf4+ 28 ♗xf4 ♘c7 29 ♗e5 ♖b6 30 ♖he1 ♘e6 31 ♖d5+ ♔e7 32 ♔c2 gives White a winning ending.

26 ♔d1

White must avoid the discovered check, but now he threatens to rescue the bishop by ♗e5; thus acceptance of the sacrifice is virtually forced.

26 ...   ♕xh8

27 ♕d6+

The king-hunt begins in earnest.

27 ...   ♔a5

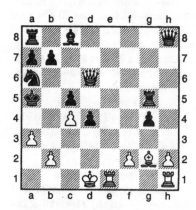

28 ♔d2!

Surprising, because the king has only just moved from d2 to d1. However, it introduces the threat of 29 b4+ ♔a4 30 ♗c6+ bxc6 31 ♕xc6+ followed by mate with the rooks.

28 ...   ♗f5!

Opening up the long diagonal by 28...d3 does not halt the attack: 29 b4+ ♔a4 30 ♗c6+ bxc6 31 ♕xc6+ ♔b3 32 ♖b1+ ♔a2 (32...♔xa3 33 ♖a1+ ♔b3 34 ♖hb1+ ♔xc4 35 ♖c1+ ♔d4 36

♕d6+ ♔e4 37 ♖c4+ ♕d4 38 ♖xd4+ cxd4 39 ♖e1+ ♔f5 40 ♖e5+ ♔f4 41 ♖e6+ mates) 33 ♕a4 ♕b2+ 34 ♖xb2+ ♔xb2 35 ♖b1+ ♔xb1 36 ♕b3+ ♔a1 37 ♔c3 cxb4+ 38 axb4 also mates.

29 ♗xb7

The point of Black's previous move is revealed if White continues 29 b4+ ♔a4 30 ♗c6+ bxc6 31 ♕xc6+ ♔b3 32 ♖b1+. Then 32...♗xb1 allows mate by 33 ♖xb1+ ♔xc4 (33...♔a2 34 ♕a4 ♔xb1 35 ♕b3+ ♔a1 36 ♔c1) 34 ♕e6+ ♔b5 35 a4+ ♔xa4 36 ♕xa6#, but 32...♔a2! 33 ♕a4 ♕h3! unexpectedly stymies the attack. The black pieces, operating from a distance, cover just enough squares to save the king.

The text-move attacks a6 and forces Black's reply.

29 ... ♖g6

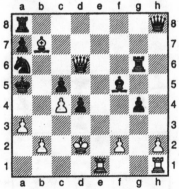

30 b4+ ♔a4

30...cxb4 31 axb4+ ♔a4 32 ♖a1+ ♔b3 33 ♕g3+ d3 34 ♖hb1+ ♔xc4 35 ♕f4+ ♔b5 36 ♕xf5+ and wins.

31 ♗c6+

Thanks to White's 29th move, this check is possible without sacrificing the bishop.

31 ... ♔b3

The most resilient defence since 31...♔xa3 fails to 32 ♕g3+ d3 (or 32...♔b2 33 ♖b1+ ♗xb1 34 ♖xb1+ ♔xb1 35 ♕b3+ ♔a1 36 ♕a3+ ♔b1 37 ♗e4+) 33 ♖a1+ ♔b3 34 ♖hb1+ ♔xc4 35 ♕f4+ ♕d4 36 ♖c1+ ♔b3 37 ♗d5+ ♕xd5 38 ♖cb1#.

32 ♕g3+ ♔b2

White wins on material after 32...d3 33 ♖b1+ ♔a2 34 ♖a1+ ♕xa1 35 ♖xa1+ ♔xa1 36 ♕e5+ ♔a2 37 ♗xa8, while 32...♔a2 33 ♖a1+ ♔b2 prolongs the game by just one move.

33 ♖b1+!

A superb final combination.

33 ... ♗xb1
34 ♖xb1+ ♔xb1
35 ♕b3+ ♔a1

Now 36 ♔c2 doesn't work, because after 36...d3+ followed by 37...♕b2 the black queen saves the day.

36 ♔c1! 1-0

The final finesse decides the game. After 36...♕h6+ 37 ♔c2 Black's queen has been drawn off the long diagonal and the pawn check no longer saves Black: 37...d3+ (after 37...♕d2+ 38 ♔xd2 White picks up the a8-rook) 38 ♕xd3 ♕g7 39 ♕d1+ ♔a2 40 ♕b1+ ♔xa3 41 ♕b3#.

Lessons from this game:

1) It is normally a good idea to castle early on, but bear in mind that it is not compulsory – in exceptional circumstances leaving the king in the centre may be the best plan.

2) An enemy pawn firmly embedded in one's position is like a fishbone in the throat – something best avoided!

3) Even when you have driven the opposing king up the board mate may not be automatic, especially if the opposing pieces control vital squares.

Game 76

Garry Kasparov – Lajos Portisch

Nikšić 1983

Queen's Indian Defence

The Players

Nikšić was Garry Kasparov's last main tournament before his Candidates match with Viktor Korchnoi in London. Korchnoi shocked the favourite by winning the first game with the black pieces, but Kasparov eventually overcame the old warrior by the score of 7–4. For more about Kasparov see Game 71.

The 1980s was a less successful period for Lajos Portisch than the previous decade, but he was still scoring some notable successes. See Game 57 for more information.

The Game

This is a performance typical of Kasparov at his very best. First-class opening preparation, sublime attacking play, powerful sacrifices and combinations, all encapsulated by Kasparov's incredible desire to win. This lethal cocktail proves to be too much, even for a resourceful Portisch.

1	d4	♘f6
2	c4	e6
3	♘f3	b6
4	♘c3	♗b7
5	a3	

A favourite idea of Kasparov's against the Queen's Indian. White expends a tempo on this little pawn move in order to prevent Black from developing his f8-bishop actively on b4. White's plan is to press forward in the centre with d4-d5, followed by e2-e4, blocking out the fianchettoed bishop. Indeed, this is such an effective plan that Black prevents it with his very next move. However, in doing so, Black is forced to give up Nimzowitsch's ideal of controlling the centre with pieces.

5	...	d5
6	cxd5	♘xd5

7	e3

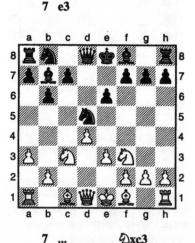

7 ...	♘xc3

Later on in the same year Korchnoi surprised Kasparov in the first game in their Candidates semi-final match with the interesting move 7...g6. Following

8 ♗b5+ c6 9 ♗d3 ♗g7 10 e4 ♘xc3 11 bxc3 c5! 12 ♗g5? ♕d6 13 e5 ♕d7 14 dxc5 0-0! 15 cxb6 axb6 16 0-0 ♕c7 17 ♗b5 ♗xe5! Korchnoi went on to win.

8	bxc3	♗e7
9	♗b5+	c6
10	♗d3	c5
11	0-0	♘c6
12	♗b2	♖c8
13	♕e2	0-0
14	♖ad1	♕c7

Perhaps Black should consider the immediate exchange with 14...cxd4, as then 15 exd4?! (15 cxd4 is stronger) 15...♘a5! 16 c4? ♗xf3 forces White to capture with the g-pawn in order to avoid dropping the pawn on c4.

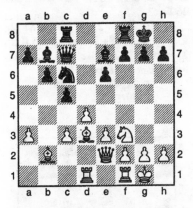

White has a potentially mobile pawn-centre, which may become a real asset, as it can help White to initiate an attack on the kingside. On the other hand, Black has no weaknesses, and can hope to attack the centre with his pieces. In an earlier game Polugaevsky – Portisch, European Team Championship, Plovdiv 1983, White played 15 e4. Portisch replied with 15...♘a5 and drew quickly. Obviously he had no objection to repeating this line

against Kasparov, but an improvement was awaiting him.

15 c4! cxd4

15...♗f6 is met by 16 d5!, when 16...♗xb2 17 dxc6 wins a piece, while 16...♘e5 17 ♘xe5 ♗xe5 18 ♗xh7+! ♔xh7 19 ♕h5+ ♔g8 20 ♗xe5 wins a pawn for White. Now White is left with the "hanging pawns" (see also Games 13 and 64). In this case, however, White is also well placed for an immediate breakthrough in the centre.

16 exd4 ♘a5
17 d5!

Now the action begins. Both the bishop on d3 and its colleague on b2 are now released for action. Black can already begin to sweat, as the bishops point like guided missiles towards the king.

17 ... exd5

After 17...♘xc4 White can start an attack with 18 ♕e4 g6 19 ♗xc4 ♕xc4 20 ♕e5. Following the forced sequence 20...f6 21 ♕xe6+ ♗f7 22 ♖c1 ♕a6 Kasparov originally gave (in his notes to the game in *Informator*) 23 d6, with the point that 23...♖xc1 24 ♖xc1 ♗d8 fails to the brilliant combination 25 ♘g5! fxg5 26 ♖c7! ♗xc7 27 ♕e8+ ♖f8 28 ♕e5 and White mates on the dark squares. However, the suggestion by Volgin of 23...b5! leaves the situation more unclear, e.g. 24 ♖fd1 ♖xc1 25 ♗xc1 ♗f8, so in *Fighting Chess* Kasparov preferred 23 ♘d4, when White's threats remain.

18 cxd5 ♗xd5
19 ♗xh7+ ♔xh7
20 ♖xd5 ♔g8

Black intelligently nudges his king back, where it's not exposed to any checks. Trying to ease the position through simplification with 20...♕c2 backfires after 21 ♖d2 ♕c5 22 ♘e5, when Black cannot deal with the many threats.

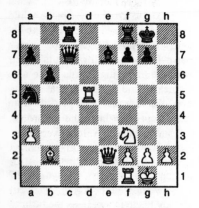

However, Black's sensible play is not enough to deny Kasparov. As he comments in *Fighting Chess*, "Now, although White's pieces are ideally poised, there's nothing that is obviously decisive. I pondered ... I felt I had to play actively. But how? To go ♘g5 or ♘e5? On g5 the knight does nothing, e.g. 21 ♘g5 ♕c2. 21 ♘e5 does not look bad, but the bishop on b2 would be blocked. What else? Yes! Yes! Sacrifice!"

In fact, Nunn points out in *The King-Hunt* that after 21 ♘g5 ♕c2 White can continue 22 ♕xe7 ♕xb2 23 ♕e4! g6 24 ♕h4 ♕g7 25 ♖d7 with a dominating position. He therefore prefers 21...♗xg5 22 ♖xg5 f6, when White's advantage is minimal.

21 ♗xg7!!

In this situation it's worth giving up the bishop to remove another pawn from the king's shield. Now the black king has no place to hide, and White's queen, rook and knight form a formidable team. Also, as Kasparov points

out, Black's knight on a5 takes time to get back into the game, and this proves vital for the success of White's attack.

21 ...   ♔xg7
22 ♘e5   ♖fd8

Other moves fail to conjure up a defence:

1) 22...f5 23 ♖d7 ♕c5 24 ♘d3 wins the bishop on e7.

2) 22...♖h8 23 ♕g4+ ♔f8 24 ♕f5 f6 25 ♖e1 ♘c6 (25...♕c1 loses to 26 ♖dd1 while 25...♘c4 26 ♘g6+ gives the same result) 26 ♘d7+ ♔f7 27 ♖xe7+! ♘xe7 28 ♕xf6+ and it's all over.

3) 22...♕c2 23 ♕g4+ ♔h7 24 ♖d3! ♖c3 (or 24...♖c6 25 ♕f5+ ♔g7 26 ♖g3+ ♔h8 27 ♘xf7+) 25 ♕h3+ and 26 ♖xc3.

4) 22...♖cd8 23 ♕g4+ ♔h7 24 ♘d7 f5 25 ♘xf8+ ♖xf8 26 ♖xf5 ♖xf5 27 ♕xf5+ ♔g7 28 ♖e1 and Black has little chance of survival.

23 ♕g4+   ♔f8
24 ♕f5

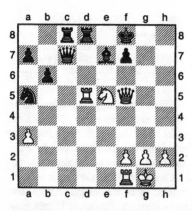

24 ...   f6

Black's only other try is 24...♗d6, but Kasparov refutes this defence very efficiently with 25 ♕f6! and now:

1) 25...♔g8 26 ♕g5+ ♔f8 27 ♕h6+ ♔g8 (27...♔e8 28 ♖e1 is convincing) 28 ♘g4 ♗e7 29 ♖h5 ♕c3 30 ♕h7+ ♔f8 31 ♖e5 f6 32 ♘h6 mating.

2) 25...♘c4 26 ♘g6+ ♔e8 27 ♖e1+ ♔d7 28 ♖e7+ ♔c6 29 ♖xc7+ ♔xc7 30 ♕xf7+ ♔b8 31 h4. Black's king has managed to escape to the queenside, but he is hopelessly behind on material.

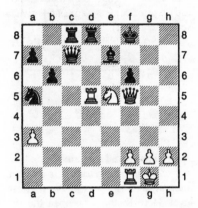

25   ♘d7+

25 ♘g6+ is enticing, as 25...♔e8? 26 ♕h5 ♖xd5 27 ♘e5+ forces mate. However, Kasparov gives 25...♔g7 as a stronger defence. Now 26 ♘f4 ♖xd5 27 ♕g6+? ♔h8 28 ♘e6? is refuted by 28...♕g5!, so after 27...♔h8 White has nothing better than a perpetual check with 28 ♕h6+. However, it should be said that 25 ♘g6+ isn't actually a bad move, as after 25...♔g7 26 ♘f4 ♖xd5 White should simply recapture with 27 ♘xd5 ♕c5 28 ♘xe7, when he has a pawn advantage. Looking once more at the position, we discover that Black's most accurate defence to 25 ♘g6+ is 25...♔f7!, preparing to answer 26 ♘f4 with 26...♕xf4!. Then White should play 26 ♘e5+ ♔f8 and we are back to

square one. White can then play 27 ♘d7+ as in the game.

25   ...   ♖xd7
26   ♖xd7   ♕c5
27   ♕h7

Kasparov states that 27 ♕h3 is more accurate, preparing to meet 27...♖c7 with 28 ♖d3. Now Black can lay a sneaky trap.

27   ...   ♖c7!
28   ♕h8+!

The queen vacates the hazardous seventh rank. 28 ♖d3? looks very natural, but then White would be stunned by the retort 28...♕xf2+!!. Then 29 ♖xf2?? ♖c1+ 30 ♖f1 ♗c5+ leads to mate, but even after 29 ♔xf2 ♗c5+ 30 ♔g3 ♖xh7 31 ♖xf6+ the position is only about equal.

28   ...   ♔f7
29   ♖d3   ♘c4
30   ♖fd1!

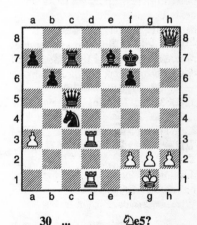

30   ...   ♘e5?

Black's only chance is 30...♗d6. In his original notes Kasparov gives 31 ♖d5, when 31...♕xa3? loses to 32 ♖xd6 ♘xd6 33 ♕h7+ and 34 ♕xc7. A more stubborn defence is 31...♕c6, but after the advance of the h-pawn starting with 32 h4 White is still better. Nunn gives 31 ♖h3!, which looks even stronger than 31 ♖d5, e.g. 31...♖c8 32 ♖h7+ ♔e6 33 ♕g7 ♘e5 34 ♖e1, or 31...♖e7 32 ♖h6. In either case Black's chances of survival are between slim and none.

Following 30...♘e5 the end is even swifter.

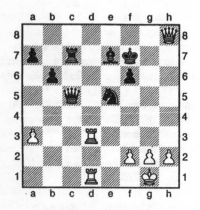

31   ♕h7+   ♔e6

31...♔f8 32 ♖d8+ mates, as does 31...♔e8 32 ♕g8+ ♗f8 33 ♕e6+ ♗e7 34 ♖d8#.

32   ♕g8+   ♔f5

Or 32...♘f7 33 ♖e1+ ♔f5 34 ♖f3#.

33   g4+   ♔f4

White also wins after 33...♘xg4 34 ♖f3+ ♔e5 35 ♖e1+ ♔d4 36 ♕xg4+.

34   ♖d4+   ♔f3
35   ♕b3+

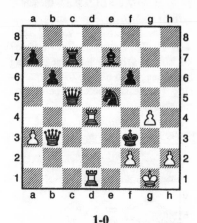

1-0

35...♕c3 36 ♕d5+ ♔e2 37 ♕e4+ ♕e3 38 ♕xe3#.

Lessons from this game:

1) Opening preparation is now an integral part of chess at the highest level. Here Kasparov reaped the rewards of a well-researched novelty at move 15.

2) Once more we see the attacking capacity of the hanging pawns, especially when they can be used for an instant breakthrough in the centre.

3) Kasparov is virtually unstoppable when he has the initiative!

Game 77
Anatoly Karpov – Garry Kasparov
World Championship match (game 9),
Moscow 1984/5
Queen's Gambit Declined, Tarrasch Defence

The Players

Anatoly Karpov (born 1951) has been FIDE World Champion 1975–85 and from 1993 onwards. See Game 67 for more details.

Garry Kasparov (born 1963) is the greatest player of modern times, and has been World Champion (of one sort or another) since 1985. For more information see Game 71.

The Game

Kasparov plays an opening that had served him extremely well in his Candidates matches, but Karpov shows his class by stamping out his opponent's activity and focusing attention on Black's isolated pawn. Kasparov then faces a grim defence for a draw. He skilfully reaches an ending where he still has only the one weakness, but then tries a little too hard to "force" a draw. Karpov seizes his chance with a stunning pawn sacrifice to gain entry with his king. The rest is agony for Black.

1	d4	d5
2	c4	e6
3	♘f3	c5
4	cxd5	exd5
5	g3	♘f6
6	♗g2	♗e7
7	0-0	0-0
8	♘c3	♘c6
9	♗g5	cxd4
10	♘xd4	h6
11	♗e3	♖e8

This position is one of the main battlegrounds of the Tarrasch. Black argues that his active pieces compensate for the weakness of the isolated central pawn. In tournament games and match play Kasparov had scored very well from this position, his opponents experiencing great difficulty in containing Kasparov's piece-play.

12	♕b3	

At the time this was slightly unusual, but is now a main line. The main idea is to drag Black's knight offside before putting the queen on its intended home, c2.

12	...	♘a5
13	♕c2	♗g4
14	♘f5	

This move had recently been introduced by Portisch, and has more bite than the older move 14 h3.

14	...	♖c8

14...♗b4 is more active. The critical line then runs 15 ♗d4 ♗xc3 16 ♗xc3 ♖xe2 17 ♕d1! d4! 18 ♘xd4

♖xf2 19 ♕a4 ♖xg2+ 20 ♔xg2 ♕d5+ 21 ♔g1 ♘c4, when Black has decent compensation for the exchange, Kasparov – Illescas, Linares 1990.

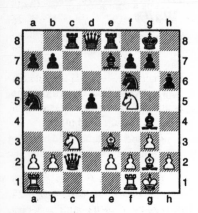

15 ♗d4

15 ♘xe7+ had been Karpov's preference in the seventh game of the match. Although he won that game, he did not consider that he had an advantage after 15...♖xe7 16 ♖ad1 ♕e8.

15 ...   ♗c5

A few other moves:

1) 15...♘e4? 16 ♘xg7 looks very good for White: 16...♘c6 (16...♘xc3 17 bxc3 ♘c6 18 ♖ad1 ♘xd4 19 ♖xd4 hits the g4-bishop; 16...♖f8 17 ♗xe4 dxe4 18 ♕xe4 rescues the knight) 17 ♖ad1 ♘xd4 18 ♖xd4 ♔xg7 (18...♗f6 19 ♖xd5) 19 ♗xe4 and White should win.

2) 15...♗xf5 16 ♕xf5 ♘c6 17 ♗e3 d4 18 ♖ad1 dxe3 (18...♕b6 19 ♗xc6 ♖xc6 20 ♗xd4) 19 ♖xd8 exf2+ 20 ♖xf2 ♖cxd8 followed by ...♗d6-e5 is considered to be only a little better for White by Kasparov.

3) 15...♘c6 16 ♘xe7+ ♕xe7 17 ♗xf6 ♕xf6 18 ♘xd5 wins a pawn for insufficient compensation.

16 ♗xc5   ♖xc5
17 ♘e3!

Here it is best to target the pawn directly rather than, in time-honoured fashion, simply aiming to blockade it. 17 ♘d4 ♘e4 18 e3 ♘xc3 19 bxc3 ♕c7 (Kasparov) is fine for Black, who has used the respite to create and attack a target of his own.

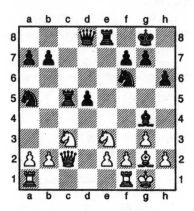

17 ...   ♗e6

17...d4? 18 ♖ad1 pins the pawn and prepares to round it up.

17...♕c8 18 ♘xg4 ♕xg4 19 e3 ♘c6 20 ♕d1! ♕e6 21 ♘e2 was cited by Kasparov as giving White an edge.

18 ♖ad1

White now threatens 19 ♘exd5 followed by 20 e4.

However, 18 ♖fd1 was the "right" rook according to Kasparov, since the queen's rook can in some lines perform good work on the c-file. However, it may come to much the same thing. His main line runs 18...♕c7 19 ♕a4 ♖d8 20 ♖d3 ♘c6 21 ♖ad1 with an edge for White.

18 b4? is the type of move that should never be forgotten about. It doesn't work here due to 18...♖c8 19

bxa5 d4, but Black must obviously keep an eye on this pawn.

18 ... ♛c8

After 18...♞c6 19 ♞exd5!? ♝xd5 20 ♝xd5 ♞b4 (20...♜xd5 21 e4 ♞cb4 22 ♛b3 wins material) 21 ♝xf7+ ♚xf7 22 ♛b3+ ♞bd5 23 e4 ♜xe4 24 ♞xe4 ♞xe4 25 ♛xb7+ ♛c7 26 ♛xc7+ ♞xc7 Black has drawing chances – Speelman.

18...♛c7 19 ♛a4 ♜d8, with a slight advantage to White, was best play according to Kasparov.

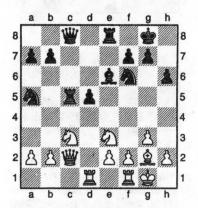

19 ♛a4

19 ♛b1!? ♜d8 20 ♜d3 is interesting, since 20...d4?! 21 ♜fd1 ♞c6 22 ♝xc6 wins the d-pawn for inadequate compensation.

19 ... ♜d8
20 ♜d3 a6
21 ♜fd1

21 ♛d1!? is an attempt to improve, by preventing the a5-knight from coming back into play via c4. 21...♞c4 (21...♛c6 would be the more passive alternative) and then:

1) 22 ♞exd5 ♞xd5 23 ♞xd5 ♝xd5 24 ♝xd5 ♞xb2 25 ♝xf7+! ♚xf7 26 ♜xd8 ♞xd1 27 ♜xc8 ♜xc8 28 ♜xd1

gives White a rook ending with an extra pawn, though Black may be active enough to survive.

2) 22 ♞xc4 ♜xc4 23 ♞xd5 (23 ♛d2 keeps a simple edge) 23...♞xd5 24 ♝xd5 ♝xd5 25 ♜xd5 ♜xd5 26 ♛xd5 ♜c2 27 ♛e5 and now Speelman suggests that Black should be OK with 27...f6 28 ♛e7 ♛c4.

In conclusion, 21 ♛d1 is probably not an improvement over the game continuation, given the assessment of the note to White's 23rd move.

21 ... ♞c4
22 ♞xc4

22 ♞exd5 ♞xd5 23 ♞xd5 ♝xd5 24 ♝xd5 ♜dxd5! 25 ♜xd5 ♜xd5 26 ♜xd5 ♞b6 (the point) 27 ♛d4 ♞xd5 28 ♛xd5 ♛c1+ 29 ♚g2 ♛xb2 enables Black to hold the position.

22 ... ♜xc4

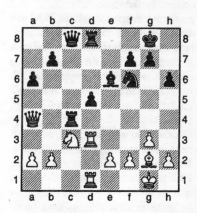

23 ♛a5

23 ♛b3! (Yusupov's idea) was considered better by Karpov: 23...d4? (otherwise White keeps firm control of the position) and now:

1) 24 ♛xb7 ♛xb7 25 ♝xb7 ♜b8 26 ♝xa6 dxc3 27 ♜d8+ (27 ♝xc4 c2 28 ♜d8+? is no good due to 28...♞e8!,

but White can solve this problem by switching his move-order) 27...Rxd8 (27...Ne8?? 28 Rxb8) 28 Rxd8+ Kh7 29 Bxc4 Bxc4 30 bxc3 Bxa2 gives Black excellent drawing chances.

2) 24 Qb6! wins a pawn, for example 24...Nd7 25 Rxd4!.

23 ...   Rc5

23...d4? fails to 24 Bxb7, overloading the queen, but 23...Rd7!? was successfully tried in Morović – Salazar, Zonal tournament, Santiago 1989: 24 Rd4 (24 Nxd5?! Bxd5! 25 Bxd5 Rc5 26 Bxb7 Rxb7 27 Rd8+ Kh7 28 Qxa6 Qc6 and Black's piece is at least as good as White's three pawns) 24...b5 (threatening ...b4) 25 Rxc4 (if White has nothing better than this, then Black really has solved his problems) 25...dxc4 26 Re1 Rd6 ½-½.

24 Qb6   Rd7
25 Rd4

Karpov suggested instead 25 h3 and 25 a3 as useful prophylactic moves, removing pawns from the second rank in preparation for a time when Black's defence is based on dropping a rook into c2. Compare the note to White's 27th move.

25 ...   Qc7

Black can now take the queens off because of the trick seen in the note to White's 27th move. It is notable that both players regard the exchange of queens as helpful to Black (Kasparov by going in for it, Karpov since he regards it as an inaccuracy to have allowed it), contrary to the general view that simplifications are unfavourable to the player with the static weakness. Clearly they see the ending as tenable for Black, and the queens being on the board as promoting White's chances of forcing a vital second weakness.

26 Qxc7   Rdxc7

27 h3

Karpov gives his king a flight-square and prepares to inch up the kingside.

27 Nxd5?! Nxd5 28 Bxd5 Bxd5 29 Rxd5 Rxd5 30 Rxd5 Rc2 draws, e.g. 31 Rd8+ Kh7 32 Rd7 Rxb2 33 Rxf7 Rxe2 is a line cited by Karpov.

27 e3 is another way to start improving White's pawn position, e.g.:

1) 27...g6?! 28 a3 Kg7 29 Nxd5 Nxd5 30 Bxd5 Bxd5 31 Rxd5 Rxd5 32 Rxd5 Rc2 33 b4 and we see why White has been shuffling his pawns up the board.

2) 27...Rc4 (Yusupov) is better, obliging White to "get on with it": 28 Nxd5 Nxd5 29 Bxd5 Rxd4 30 Rxd4 Bxd5 (30...Bh3? 31 Rc4) 31 Rxd5 Rc2 with drawing chances.

27 ...   h5!

Preventing g4 for now and in traditional fashion making it harder for White to advance without allowing exchanges of pawns, making a draw more likely.

28 a3   g6
29 e3   Kg7

30 ♔h2

Defending the h3-pawn and so introducing the threat of ♗f3, ♔g2 and ♘xd5. It is a slow plan, but Black must react.

	30	...	♖c4
	31	♗f3	b5
	32	♔g2	♖7c5
	33	♖xc4	

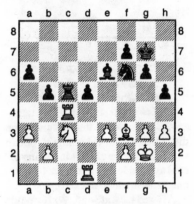

33 ... ♖xc4

Kasparov continues to rely on the principle that a single weakness isn't enough to lose a game. The alternatives are:

1) 33...dxc4? lets the white rook penetrate decisively: 34 ♖d6.

2) 33...bxc4 is not too bad, but still unpleasant with Black's pieces passive.

34 ♖d4

34 ♘xd5?! ♘xd5 35 ♗xd5 ♗xd5+ 36 ♖xd5 ♖c2 37 ♖d6 ♖xb2 38 ♖xa6 b4 eliminates the queenside pawns with a virtually certain draw.

	34	...	♔f8
	35	♗e2	♖xd4
	36	exd4	♔e7

36...♘e4 37 ♘a2 ♘d6 38 ♘b4 a5 39 ♘c6 ♘c4 would have given Black more chances to equalize, according to Karpov.

	37	♘a2	♗c8
	38	♘b4	♔d6
	39	f3	♘g8
	40	h4	♘h6
	41	♔f2	♘f5
	42	♘c2	f6

This move was sealed, and slightly complicates Black's task – as we are to see, there are some tactical problems with the plan of ...f6 and ...g5.

Instead 42...♘g7 43 g4 f6 44 ♗d3 g5 45 ♗g6! hxg4 46 h5 (Karpov) gives White a powerful passed pawn, but 42...♗d7 is more flexible, making no concessions on the kingside.

	43	♗d3	g5
	44	♗xf5	♗xf5

Now another factor emerges: White has a good knight against Black's somewhat bad bishop (the d5-pawn is fixed on a light square, while the b5- and h5-pawns are close to fixed).

45 ♘e3 ♗b1

45...♗g6 is safer.

46 b4

Apparently Kasparov and his analytical team had underestimated Karpov's possibilities with this move, considering that White's main winning chances were associated with possible king invasions via b4. This may account for his slightly careless reply, although it must be said that Karpov's 47th move came as a surprise to virtually everyone.

46 ... gxh4?

Black, by trying too hard to "force" the draw, allows White to penetrate. Other moves:

1) 46...♔e6 47 g4 hxg4 48 hxg5 fxg5 49 ♘xg4 ♗a2 holds, according to Speelman and Tisdall.

2) 46...♗g6 and, in Karpov's own words, "piercing a hole in the fortress would not have been so easy".

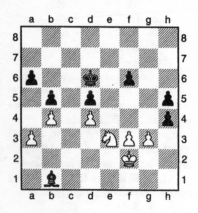

47 ♘g2!!

By sacrificing a pawn, White makes certain that his king will have a route into Black's position. Together with the fact that Black's bishop is now very "bad", this is quite enough to seal Black's fate. Instead 47 gxh4 would leave White with no real winning prospects. The f5-square is the only possible route by which White's pieces can penetrate, and this is easily enough defended.

47 ...   hxg3+

47...h3 48 ♘f4 and Black's pawns drop off.

48 ♔xg3   ♔e6
49 ♘f4+   ♔f5
50 ♘xh5

White has now regained the pawn and his pieces have plenty of room to invade. Meanwhile Black has no counterplay, so the rest of the game is extremely one-sided. Indeed Kasparov's position is already verging on resignable.

50 ...   ♔e6

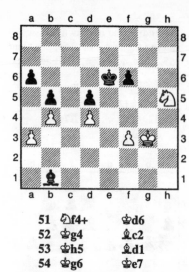

51 ♘f4+   ♔d6
52 ♔g4   ♗c2
53 ♔h5   ♗d1
54 ♔g6   ♔e7

Kasparov hopes that by giving up the d5-pawn now he might obtain some counterplay (his king gains access to the d5-square and the bishop's diagonals are less blocked).

After 54...♗xf3 55 ♔xf6 White will win the d5-pawn in any case.

55 ♘xd5+   ♔e6
56 ♘c7+   ♔d7
57 ♘xa6   ♗xf3
58 ♔xf6   ♔d6

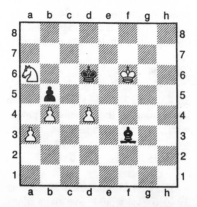

59	♔f5	♚d5
60	♔f4	♗h1
61	♔e3	♚c4
62	♘c5	

Sealing off the king's shortest route to the a3-pawn.

62	...	♗c6

62...♗g2 63 ♘d3 ♚b3 64 ♘f4 ♗b7 65 ♔d3 ♚xa3 66 ♔c3 is a line given by Karpov – Black is defenceless against the d-pawn's advance.

63	♘d3

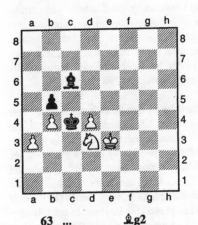

63	...	♗g2
64	♘e5+	♚c3
65	♘g6	♚c4
66	♘e7	♗b7

66...♚b3 67 d5 ♚xa3 68 d6 ♗h3 69 ♘d5 is the end of Black's counterplay.

67	♘f5	♗g2

67...♚c3 68 ♔f4 ♚b3 69 ♘e7 ♚xa3 70 d5 and either the bishop lets the pawn through or gives itself up for the d-pawn in such a way that White hangs on to his remaining pawn. This is not bad luck, of course, but a situation Karpov was able to bring about due to his large advantage.

67...♗c6 68 ♔f4 ♚b3 69 ♔e5 ♚xa3 70 ♔d6 ♗e4 71 ♘g3 and White consolidates.

68	♘d6+	♚b3
69	♘xb5	♚a4
70	♘d6	1-0

Lessons from this game:

1) This looked like a smooth win by Karpov. However, as the notes show, there were quite a lot of subtle tactical improvements for both sides along the way, and Black had various ways in which he could have lightened his burden. The moral? Don't despair and always look for hidden resources.

2) Taking queens off can be a help to a defender solidly holding on with just one weakness.

3) Don't be fooled by the principle that one weakness isn't enough to lose a game. A second "weakness" need only be very subtle – an active enemy king, a threat to create a passed pawn, etc.

4) When it is only a defensive wall that is stopping you breaking in to a diseased position, look for ways to sacrifice material in order to make inroads.

Alexander Beliavsky – John Nunn
Wijk aan Zee 1985
King's Indian Defence, Sämisch Variation

The Players

Alexander Beliavsky (born 1953) is a Ukrainian grandmaster who made an impact on the international scene at a relatively early age by winning the World Junior Championship in 1973. The following year saw another major success – joint first with Tal in the USSR Championship. Thereafter he became one of the regulars on the international circuit, achieving consistently good results and participating in many top tournaments, but without breaking into the very highest level of world chess. He has never achieved any particular success in world championship cycles, and is stronger in tournaments than in match play. After a few years of (for him) modest results in the early 1990s, he appears to have regained his form and he occupies joint 9th position on the January 1998 rating list.

John Nunn (born 1955) won several junior titles in Britain before his first international success – winning the European Junior Championship in 1974/5. He gained his grandmaster title in 1978 and won the British Championship in 1980. In 1981 he became a professional player, having previously been a mathematics lecturer at Oxford University. Since then he has won a number of international tournaments, including three victories at both Wijk aan Zee (one shared) and Hastings (twice shared). His best tournament results were in the 1988/9 World Cup cycle, in which he finished sixth. He has played for England in ten Olympiads, his best result being at Thessaloniki 1984 where he gained three individual gold medals. Recently, he has turned his energies more to writing and has twice won the British Chess Federation Book of the Year Award.

The Game

Black adopts a slightly unusual line against White's Sämisch King's Indian. Beliavsky, never one to shirk a confrontation, tries to refute it directly. Black's response is a surprising piece sacrifice which traps White's king in the centre of the board. Detailed analysis shows that the position is roughly level but, as so often, the defender is under more psychological pressure and is the first to crack. Black sacrifices another exchange and his pieces are soon swarming around White's hapless king.

1	d4	♘f6		
2	c4	g6		
3	♘c3	♗g7		
4	e4	d6		

5	f3	0-0
6	♗e3	♘bd7

The most common moves are 6...c5, 6...e5 and 6...♘c6, but after this game the 6...♘bd7 line became established as a genuine alternative, although it has never become as popular as the three main continuations.

7 ♕d2   c5
8 d5

A Benoni pawn-structure has arisen, in which Black's usual plan would be to chip away at White's centre by ...e6. However, this cannot be played immediately because the d6-pawn is hanging after the reply dxe6.

8 ...   ♘e5

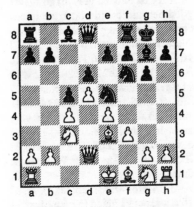

Not only covering d6 in anticipation of ...e6, but also preventing ♘h3 and ♘ge2 and so obstructing the development of White's kingside pieces.

9 h3?!

White cannot play 9 f4 because of 9...♘eg4, but now he threatens to drive the knight back with 10 f4. If White were to achieve this aim, then Black's plan would be exposed as a waste of time. However, it turns out that Black has adequate resources against this direct attempt to drive the e5-knight away. White soon turned to 9 ♗g5, again preparing f4, and this is considered the critical continuation today.

9 ...   ♘h5

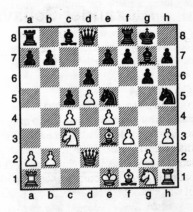

Taking aim at g3 and so immediately exploiting the slight dark-square weaknesses created by h3.

10 ♗f2

Probably best. 10 ♔f2 is unwise because of 10...e6, when ...♕h4+ is hard to stop, while after 10 ♕f2 e6! (the safest move, which enables Black to maintain the position of his knights) 11 f4 (11 g4 exd5 12 cxd5 ♗f6 13 h4 ♗xg4 14 fxg4 ♘xg4 leaves Black quite favourably placed, with three pawns and domination of the dark squares in return for his piece) 11...♗f6! and White has no good move, e.g. 12 g3 ♘xg3 13 fxe5 ♗h4 14 ♘f3 ♘xf1 15 ♘xh4 ♘xe3, 12 h4 ♘g4, or 12 ♘f3 ♘xf3+ 13 ♕xf3 ♘g3.

10 ...   f5

Other moves are too slow, for example after 10...e6 11 g4 Black's knights are driven back.

11 exf5

Better than 11 f4 ♗h6 12 g3 fxe4 13 ♘xe4 ♗f5 14 ♘g5 ♗xg5 15 fxg5 ♗e4 16 ♖h2 ♖f3 with advantage for Black.

11 ...   ♖xf5!

After 11...♗xf5? 12 g4 Black simply loses a piece for nothing, while 11...gxf5 12 f4 ♗h6 13 g3 does not provide the necessary activity: here the c8-bishop is shut in, and the threat of ♕e2 forces an immediate knight retreat.

12 g4

If the piece is declined, then ...♘f4 and ...♗h6 can follow and Black gets an aggressive position all the same.

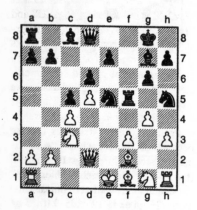

12 ...   **♖xf3**
13 gxh5

Again White cannot do better. If 13 0-0-0, then 13...♖f7! 14 gxh5 ♕f8 and Black regains his piece favourably, for example 15 ♘e4 ♗h6 16 ♗e3 ♗xe3 17 ♕xe3 ♖xf1.

13 ...   **♕f8**

Black's strong initiative and White's poor king position provide sufficient compensation for the piece, but no more. Now Beliavsky finds an excellent defensive plan.

14 ♘e4!

The alternatives are inferior:

1) 14 ♖h2 ♗h6 15 ♕d1 (15 ♕e2 ♘d3+ 16 ♕xd3 ♖xd3 17 ♗xd3 ♕f4 and 15 ♕c2 ♕f4 16 ♖g2 ♗f5 17 ♕d1 ♖xf2! 18 ♖xf2 ♕e3+ are also good for Black) 15...♕f4 16 ♖g2 ♗f5 with a strong attack, for example 17 ♗e2 ♖xf2 18 ♖xf2 ♕g3 or 17 ♘ge2 ♕xc4 18 ♘g1 ♕f4 and the loss of the c-pawn has only made White's situation worse.

2) 14 ♖d1 ♗f5 with the awkward threat of 15...♗h6. After 15 b3 (15 ♕e2 ♗d3 also wins) 15...♘d3+ 16 ♗xd3 ♖xd3 17 ♕xd3 ♗xd3 18 ♖xd3 ♕f5, followed by ...♗xc3+ and ...♕e4+, White loses too much material.

3) 14 hxg6 ♗f5 (14...hxg6 is less good because a little later the queen comes to bear on g6 – see the note to Black's 18th move) 15 gxh7+ ♗xh7! 16 ♖d1 (16 ♖h2 ♗h6 17 ♕d1 ♕f4! 18 ♖g2+ ♔h8 19 ♗e2 ♖xf2 20 ♖xf2 ♕g3 21 ♔f1 ♖g8 favours Black) 16...♗h6 17 ♕e2 ♗d3 18 ♕xe5 (18 ♖xd3 ♘xd3+ 19 ♕xd3 ♖xd3 20 ♗xd3 ♕f4 is very good for Black) 18...dxe5 19 ♘xf3 ♗xf1 20 ♘xe5 ♗g7 21 ♘g6 ♕f6 22 ♖xf1 ♕xg6 23 ♖g1 offers White some drawing chances.

4) 14 ♕e2 ♘d3+ 15 ♕xd3 ♖xd3 16 ♗xd3 ♗f5 17 ♖d1 (17 ♗e2 ♗xc3+ 18 bxc3 ♗e4 19 ♖h2 ♕f4 wins material, while after 17 ♗xf5 ♗xc3+ 18 bxc3 ♕xf5 19 ♘e2 ♖f8 20 ♗g3 ♕e4 21 ♖g1 ♖f3 White's pieces are too poorly coordinated to resist Black's attack) 17...♗xd3 18 ♖xd3 ♕f5 19 ♖f3 ♗xc3+ 20 bxc3 ♕b1+ 21 ♔e2 ♕e4+! 22 ♔d2 ♖f8 and Black wins.

These lines indicate the problems facing White: Black's enormously active pieces both prevent queenside castling and interfere with his normal development. White has no counterplay and must restrict himself to purely defensive moves, always a difficult situation in over-the-board play.

14 ...   ♝h6

After 14...♝f5 White can gain the advantage by 15 ♘g5 ♝h6 16 h4, taming one of the black bishops. Black may also attempt to dislodge the e4-knight by 14...♖f4, but after 15 ♕e2 ♝f5 16 ♝g2 ♘d3+! 17 ♕xd3 ♖xf2 18 ♝f3 ♖xb2 19 ♘e2 White is ready to castle kingside and Black is struggling for compensation.

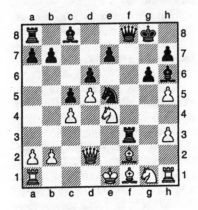

15 ♕c2?!

White is the first to slip up in the tactical *mêlée*. The best continuation is 15 ♕e2! ♘d3+ 16 ♕xd3 ♖xd3 17 ♝xd3 ♖f4 18 ♖d1! (the only move as 18 ♘e2? loses to 18...♕f3) 18...♝f5 19 ♘e2 ♕f3 20 ♘2g3 (again forced) 20...♝e3 21 ♖f1 ♝xe4 (this is the best Black can do) 22 ♘xe4 ♝xf2+ 23 ♖xf2 ♕xh5, and the game is roughly level.

15 ♕c2 is inferior because ...♝f5 will later be a pin and so Black can leave his rook *en prise* for one more move.

15 ...   ♕f4!

Sacrificing another exchange. A whole rook may seem like a large investment, but White's forces, which are mostly still on their original squares,

are not able to cover important squares in White's own camp. This means that Black's knight can hop in and out of White's ranks with impunity, wreaking havoc at every jump.

16 ♘e2

Or 16 ♘xf3 ♘xf3+ 17 ♔d1 (17 ♔e2 loses at once, to 17...♝f5 18 ♝g3 ♘d4+) 17...♝f5 18 ♝g3 (the countersacrifice 18 ♝d3 leads to nothing after 18...♘d4! 19 ♝xd4 ♕f3+ 20 ♕e2 ♕xh1+ 21 ♔c2 ♕xa1) 18...♝e3 19 ♝f2 ♕xe4 20 ♕xe4 ♝xe4 21 ♝g2 ♖f8 and Black already has one pawn for the exchange while the clumsy white rooks will be no match for his energetic bishops.

16 ...   ♖xf2

Black cannot go backwards now; after 16...♕f8 17 ♘2g3 White is ready to exchange on f5 if necessary, and the attack is on the wane.

17 ♘xf2   ♘f3+

17...♕h4? 18 ♕e4 and 17...♝e3? 18 ♝g2 ♝f5 19 ♕c1 are both bad.

18 ♔d1   ♕h4!

Again not 18...♝e3?, this time due to 19 ♘g4 ♝xg4 20 hxg4 ♕f2 21 ♝h3.

Here we can see the relevance of the comment in line "3" of the note to White's 14th move: had 14 hxg6 hxg6 been interposed before ♘e4, the black g-pawn would now be *en prise* with check!

19 ♘d3

The only way to save the knight without allowing mate at e1, as if the e2-knight moves, for example 19 ♘c3, then 19...♘d4 wins. The only other possibility is the counterattacking attempt 19 hxg6, but then 19...♕xf2 20 gxh7+ ♔h8 21 ♕g6 (21 ♕d3 ♝d7 22 ♖b1 ♖f8 wins) 21...♝d7 (threatening

22...♕e1+ 23 ♔c2 ♕d2+ 24 ♔b3 ♗a4+ 25 ♔xa4 ♕b4#) 22 ♗g2 (22 ♕xh6 ♕e1+ 23 ♔c2 ♗f5+ 24 ♔b3 ♕b4#) 22...♘d4 23 ♕d3 (23 ♖e1 ♕e3) 23...♕xg2 24 ♖g1 ♕f2 and Black wins easily.

19 ...   ♗f5

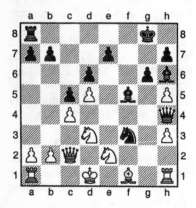

This time the threat is 20...♘e1 21 ♘xe1 ♗xc2+ 22 ♘xc2 ♕g5 and wins, because White's pieces are unable to defend d2.

20 ♘ec1!?

It is only at this point that White's position becomes definitely lost, although finding the following saving line over the board would be little short of a miracle. White should have played 20 ♕c3! ♗g7 21 ♕b3 ♗xd3 22 ♕xd3 ♕e1+ 23 ♔c2 ♕xa1 24 ♕xf3 ♕xb2+ 25 ♔d1 ♕a1+ (25...♖f8 26 ♕e3 ♕xa2 27 ♘c1 is unclear) 26 ♘c1 (if the king moves, two more pawns go, leaving Black with four against a knight) 26...♗h6 27 ♕a3 ♖f8 (threatens both 28...♖f3 and 28...♖f2) 28 ♗e2 (absolutely forced) 28...♖f2 29 ♖e1 ♖h2 (threatening 30...♖xh3) 30 ♔c2 ♗xc1 31 ♕xc1 ♕xa2+ 32 ♔d1 (32 ♕b2 ♕xc4+) and now:

1) Following 32...♖xh3 White survives with the amazing defence 33 hxg6! hxg6 (33...♖b3 34 gxh7+ ♔h8 35 ♖f1) 34 ♖f1!! ♖b3 35 ♗g4 ♖b1 36 ♗e6+, drawing by perpetual check as the pinned queen covers h6!

2) After 32...♕b3+ 33 ♕c2 ♕xc2+ 34 ♔xc2 gxh5 Black has five pawns for the bishop, but his pawns are so widely scattered that he cannot hang on to them.

Thus it seems that, thanks to an astounding defence, 20 ♕c3 would have kept the game alive. After the text-move Black's task is easier.

20 ...   ♘d2!

A strangely powerful move, threatening above all 21...♕e4 22 ♖g1 ♕e3, and if 23 ♖h1, then 23...♕f3+.

21 hxg6   hxg6

Not 21...♕e4? as White gets counterplay by 22 gxh7+ ♔h8 (22...♖xh7 23 ♖g1+ and 22...♔xh7 23 ♘e1! are also good for White) 23 ♕c3+ ♔xh7 24 ♘f2! ♕f4 25 ♘cd3 and suddenly White's knights have come alive.

The text-move renews the threat of 22...♕e4.

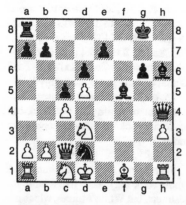

22 ♗g2

Despite White's extra rook, there is no defence:

1) 22 ♕xd2 ♗xd2 23 ♔xd2 ♕xc4, and with no knight at c3 the d-pawn disappears at once, since attempting to hold it by 24 ♗g2 loses to 24...♕d4 25 ♔e2 c4.

2) 22 ♖g1 is refuted by 22...♕d4 23 ♖h1 (23 ♘e2 ♕e3 24 ♕c3 ♘e4 wins) 23...♕e4 24 ♖g1 ♕e3.

3) 22 ♗e2 ♘xc4 23 ♕b3 ♘e3+ 24 ♔d2 c4 25 ♕xb7 ♘xd5+ 26 ♔c2 ♘e3+, followed by 27...♗e4, is catastrophic for White.

4) 22 ♕c3 ♗e4 23 ♖g1 ♘xc4 24 ♘f4 (24 ♖g3 ♕xg3 25 ♕xc4 ♕g5 26 ♕c3 ♖f8 27 ♗e2 c4 and Black wins) 24...♕f2 25 ♕xc4 ♕xg1 26 ♘e6 ♗g2 27 ♔e1 ♗xh3 28 ♘b3 (White is paralysed) 28...♗e3 wins for Black.

5) 22 ♘e2 and 22 ♘b3 are both met by 22...♘xc4, when the knight is heading for e3.

22 ...   ♘xc4

23 ♕f2

The only other possible attempt, 23 ♖e1, loses to 23...♕h5+ followed by 24...♘e3+.

23 ...   ♘e3+

Black is justified in playing for more than just a favourable endgame by 23...♕xf2 24 ♘xf2 ♘e3+.

24 ♔e2   ♕c4!

Now that the white queen has managed to crawl painfully across to f2, Black switches his own queen to the unguarded queenside. The chief threat is 25...♗xd3+ 26 ♘xd3 ♕c2+ 27 ♔e1 ♕xd3, etc.

25 ♗f3

25 ♕xe3 is met by 25...♕c2+ 26 ♔f3 ♗xe3.

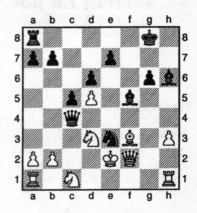

25 ...   ♖f8

There are now several routes to victory. 25...♗xd3+ 26 ♘xd3 ♕c2+ 27 ♔e1 ♕xd3 28 ♗d1 ♖f8 is equally effective.

26 ♖g1   ♘c2

Even stronger than 26...♗xd3+, because ...♘d4+ will win two pieces.

27 ♔d1   ♗xd3

0-1

Lessons from this game:

1) If your opening strategy depends on keeping the initiative, then you must keep going even at the cost of material sacrifice.

2) If you have sufficient attacking forces in play, it can be worth a piece to trap your opponent's king in the middle of the board.

3) If you play a game such as this, thinking of it will give you a warm glow for at least the next 13 years.

Anatoly Karpov – Garry Kasparov
World Championship match (game 16), Moscow 1985
Sicilian Defence, Taimanov Variation

The Players

Anatoly Karpov (born 1951) has been FIDE World Champion 1975–85 and from 1993 onwards. See Game 67 for more details.

Garry Kasparov (born 1963) is the greatest player of modern times, and has been World Champion (of one sort or another) since 1985. For more information see Game 71.

The Game

Kasparov repeats a daring gambit idea, in the full knowledge that Karpov and his team have had more than a week to prepare for it. This is either very brave or very foolhardy. The gamble turns out well, for Karpov happens to have underestimated the depth of Kasparov's scheme, and is dragged into a position where he has problems bringing his pieces into play thanks to the "octopus" knight that Kasparov establishes on d3. Karpov refuses to return the pawn to gain some freedom. This allows Kasparov, thanks to a number of brilliant tactical nuances, to tighten the bind to the point where Karpov is tied hand and foot. Kasparov finishes off his masterpiece with a burst of very one-sided tactics.

1	e4	c5
2	♘f3	e6
3	d4	cxd4
4	♘xd4	♘c6
5	♘b5	d6
6	c4	♘f6
7	♘1c3	a6
8	♘a3	d5?!

This is the aforementioned gambit.

9	cxd5	exd5
10	exd5	♘b4
11	♗e2!	

This is Karpov's new move, but Kasparov had a surprise ready.

11 ♗c4 ♗g4! had led to a short draw in the 12th game of the match.

Of course there are many possibilities in this sharp position, but Karpov decided the most prudent course was to return the pawn by 12 ♗e2 ♗xe2 13 ♕xe2+ ♕e7 14 ♗e3 ♘bxd5.

11	...	♗c5?!

Behind this move lies a fantastic idea, but unfortunately it has a tactical flaw.

Instead, the sensible 11...♘bxd5 12 0-0 (12 ♘xd5 ♘xd5 13 0-0 ♗e7 14 ♗f3 also gives White a useful advantage) 12...♗e7 (12...♗xa3? 13 ♕a4+) 13 ♘xd5 ♘xd5 14 ♗f3 ♗e6 15 ♘c2 is clearly better for White – Kasparov.

12	0-0?!	

12 ♗e3! ♗xe3 13 ♕a4+ is essentially a refutation of Black's idea. White keeps the extra pawn without falling into a bind. It is not clear whether Karpov missed this, or simply failed to perceive the need for it, thinking the game continuation to be good enough. In any case, he was all too happy to play this way a few weeks later in Karpov – Van der Wiel, Brussels 1986, when the Dutchman dared to play the Kasparov Gambit (as 8...d5 became known) against him. After 13...♘d7 14 ♕xb4 ♗c5 15 ♕e4+ White was clearly better, although a draw resulted in the end.

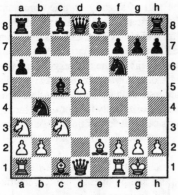

12 ...   0-0
13 ♗f3

After 13 ♗g5 ♘bxd5 14 ♘xd5 ♕xd5 15 ♗xf6 ♕xd1 16 ♖fxd1 gxf6 Black should draw without any particular difficulty – Kasparov.

13 ...   ♗f5!

Black prevents the a3-knight coming back into play via c2 and secures the d3-square as a possible resting place for his own knight. By all standard conventions this shouldn't be enough for a pawn, but some specific considerations swing the balance in Black's favour here.

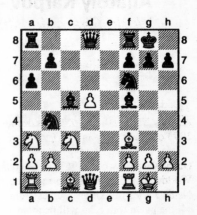

14 ♗g5

After 14 ♗e3 ♗xe3 15 fxe3 ♕b6:

1) 16 ♘c4 ♕c5 17 ♕d4 ♕xd4 18 exd4 ♗d3 19 ♘b6 ♗xf1 20 ♘xa8 ♗xg2 is an unclear ending – Kasparov.

2) 16 ♕d2 ♖fe8 targets the e3-pawn.

14 ...   ♖e8!

The smooth way in which Black's game unfolds disguises the need for great precision at each stage. Here for instance it was essential for Black to establish control of the e4-square. Instead 14...b5? 15 ♗e4! robs Black of all his compensation.

15 ♕d2

White should be looking for ways to return the pawn, but does not perceive the urgency. 15 ♘c4!? was one such way: 15...♗d3 16 a3 ♗xc4 (not 16...♗xf1? 17 axb4 ♗xc4 18 bxc5) 17 axb4 ♗xb4 18 ♖e1 (18 ♕d4? ♗xf1 19 ♕xb4 ♗b5!) 18...♖xe1+ 19 ♕xe1 reaches a "complicated position with chances for both sides" – Kasparov.

15 ...   b5!

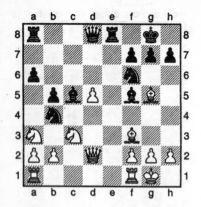

Now the knight is denied access to c4, and after the knight moves from b4, the pawn fork ...b4 will become a threat.

16 ♖ad1

Kasparov suggests that White should have considered 16 ♕f4 ♗g6 17 ♗xf6 ♕xf6 18 ♕xf6 gxf6 or 16 d6 ♖a7 17 ♖ad1, although neither line presents Black with problems.

16 ...   ♘d3!

17 ♘ab1?

Karpov is drifting into serious trouble. Had he foreseen what was to come (had "someone sent him a postcard of his position at move 21", as Michael Stean put it while commentating on British television), he would surely have seized a last chance with 17 d6, when Kasparov considered the exchange sacrifice 17...♕xd6! 18 ♗xa8 ♖xa8 to provide good compensation; ...♘g4 is a threat.

17 ...   h6!

It is a good time to nudge the bishop, as it cannot drop back to e3, and taking on f6 would be a concession.

18 ♗h4

18 ♗e3?! would give Black a pleasant choice between 18...♖xe3!? 19

fxe3 ♕b6 and 18...♗xe3 19 fxe3 ♕b6 20 ♗e2 ♖xe3 21 ♔h1 ♗g6.

18 ...   b4!

Now that he has been able to get in ...h6, this move exiles the knight to a4. It is fascinating how one little pawn-push on the kingside makes another one on the queenside so much more powerful.

19 ♘a4

19 ♘e2 is best met by 19...g5! 20 ♗xg5 (20 ♗g3 g4 21 ♘c1 ♘xc1 22 ♖xc1 gxf3 23 ♖xc5 ♘e4 wins material) 20...♘xf2 21 ♖xf2 (21 ♗xf6? ♘e4+) 21...♗xf2+ 22 ♔xf2 hxg5 23 ♕xg5+ ♗g6 which, in Kasparov's words "cannot satisfy White". This is the sort of slightly cryptic comment that writers often make when they don't want to commit themselves to a really precise evaluation. White has two pawns for the exchange, and after 24 ♘d2, parrying the threat of ...♘e4+ and intending ♘f4, Black will need to play energetically to expose the looseness of White's position.

19 ...   ♗d6

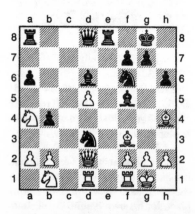

Kasparov writes that he had reached this position in his preparation. This is an extraordinary demonstration of the depth to which top-level players prepare (Karpov's 11th move had not been previously played), and also shows how well Kasparov had got to know Karpov's style of play. White has made quite a number of decisions along the way, with very few forced moves, but Kasparov had guessed correctly how his opponent would approach the situation. If we assume, for the sake of argument, that Karpov had three reasonable options on each of moves 12–19, then this makes 6,561 possible ways for White to have directed the game.

20 ♗g3

20 ♕c2? is bad since following 20...♖c8 21 ♕b3 ♘f4 22 ♖c1 (22 ♖d2 is no better, since after 22...g5 23 ♗g3 g4, 24 ♗d1 cuts off the defence of the b1-knight; thus 24...♗xb1) 22...♖xc1 23 ♖xc1 we encounter the recurring theme 23...g5! 24 ♗g3 g4, this time exploiting the f3-bishop's shortage of squares and White's weak back rank.

20 ...   ♖c8!

20...♘e4? allows 21 ♗xe4 ♗xe4 22 ♕e3, when White activates his queen, solving all his problems – the a4-knight even gets some squares.

20...♗xg3 was analysed by Kasparov as also leading to an advantage for Black, albeit in a somewhat simplified position. Therefore he preferred the more ambitious text-move, which aims to keep White completely bottled up.

21 b3

Now White intends ♘b2, when it seems he will slowly unravel his pieces. This gives Black a very concrete puzzle to solve with his next move: how to prevent this move?

21 ...   g5!!

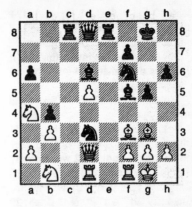

This is the first clear sign that things have gone horribly wrong for Karpov. Thanks to a little piece of tactics (there are some bigger tactical ideas with 21...g5 that we will see in a few moves), White cannot bring his knight to b2. Therefore he cannot dislodge the knight from d3, and hence he cannot move either of his rooks. Nor does his queen have any squares. To have deprived most of Karpov's pieces of any worthwhile moves on a full board, starting from a normal-looking position is a quite incredible feat.

22 ♗xd6

How else to give the f3-bishop a square?

1) 22 ♘b2? loses a piece after 22...♘xb2 23 ♕xb2 g4 24 ♗e2 ♖c2 and the e2-bishop drops off.

2) 22 ♗e2? ♘e4 23 ♕xd3 ♘xg3 wins a piece too.

3) 22 h4 is the only possible alternative:

3a) 22...g4? 23 ♗e2 ♘e4? (23...♘f4 24 ♗xf4 ♖c2 25 ♕d4 ♖exe2 is just unclear) 24 ♕xh6! ♗f8 (24...♘xg3? 25 fxg3 ♖xe2 26 ♖xf5) 25 ♕h5 ♘xg3 (or 25...♗g6 26 ♕xg4) 26 fxg3 ♗g6 27 ♕xg4 ♖e4 28 ♕f3 ♘e5 29 ♕f2

♗h6 30 ♘d2! ♗e3 31 ♘xe4 ♗xf2+ 32 ♘xf2 and White's rook, piece and pawns should outweigh the queen.

3b) 22...♘f4!? is interesting, but it is rather unthematic to abandon the d3-square so soon.

3c) 22...♘e4! 23 ♗xe4 ♗xe4 and now:

3c1) 24 ♗xd6 ♕xd6 25 hxg5 ♘f4 (thus far Kasparov's analysis) 26 ♖fe1 (26 f3? ♗xb1 and ...♖e2 was the only line cited by Kasparov) 26...♘xg2! 27 ♖xe4 ♖xe4 28 ♔xg2 ♖g4+ wins for Black: 29 ♔f3 ♕d7 30 ♕d3 ♖xg5; 29 ♔h3 ♕d7 30 ♘b6 ♕f5; 29 ♔h1 ♖h4+ or 29 ♔f1 ♕h2.

3c2) 24 ♕e3? fails to 24...♗f4! 25 ♕d4 gxh4 26 ♖xd3 hxg3.

3c3) 24 hxg5 ♗xg3 25 fxg3 ♕xd5 26 gxh6 (26 ♕e3? ♗xg2! 27 ♕xd3 ♕xd3 28 ♖xd3 ♗xf1 29 ♔xf1 ♖c1+) 26...♖e6 gives Black a strong attack (26...♖c6 was the move given in Kasparov's notes, but this is probably a typo, since then 27 ♕e3 gives White some significant counterchances, as the e4-bishop is pinned against the undefended e8-rook).

22   **...**   **♕xd6**

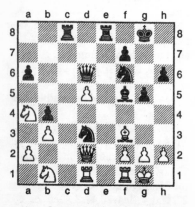

23 g3

Now Black is again faced with the task of preventing White from freeing himself by ♘b2. Note that he needed to have this worked out at least as early as his 21st move, as otherwise his play would not make much sense.

23 ♗e2 fails to shift the knight, now because Black can use the fact that his queen has just been given the chance to take part in the attack: 23...♘f4 24 ♗c4 ♘g4! 25 g3 ♖xc4! 26 bxc4 ♖e2 27 c5 (now Black can force mate, but 27 ♕d4 ♗e4 threatens mate in one, and so forces White to give up his queen) 27...♘h3+ 28 ♔g2 (28 ♔h1 ♘gxf2+ 29 ♖xf2 ♗e4+) 28...♗e4+ 29 ♔xh3 ♕g6 30 ♔g4 ♕f5+ 31 ♔h5 ♕h3#.

23   **...**   **♘d7!!**
24 ♗g2

24 ♘b2 ♕f6!! is good for Black:

1) 25 ♘xd3 ♗xd3 26 ♗g4 (26 ♕xd3 ♘e5! doesn't merely regain the piece, but wins the white queen – a truly sensational idea) 26...♘e5!.

2) 25 ♘c4 ♘7e5 and then:

2a) 26 ♘xe5 ♘xe5 27 ♗g2 (27 ♗e2 ♗d3!) 27...♗d3 and here:

2a1) 28 f4 ♖c2! 29 ♕e3 (29 fxe5 is met by 25...♕b6+) 29...♗xf1 30 ♖xf1 gxf4 and "Black must win" (Kasparov). 30...♘f3+!? 31 ♕xf3 ♖ee2 may well also lead to a win, in more striking fashion.

2a2) 28 ♖fe1 ♘f3+! 29 ♗xf3 ♕xf3 30 ♖xe8+ (not 30 ♕xd3?? ♖xe1+) 30...♖xe8 31 ♕xd3 ♖e1+ 32 ♖xe1 ♕xd3 and Black wins.

2b) 26 ♗e2 ♗h3 (Kasparov cuts off his analysis here, with the implication that Black is winning; after 26...♖xc4 27 bxc4 ♘xc4 28 ♕c2 ♘db2 29 ♗d3 White just about survives, but

Black is better) 27 ♘xe5 ♘xe5 (threatening 28...♞f3+) 28 f4 ♛b6+ 29 ♖f2 ♘g4 30 ♗xg4 ♗xg4 31 ♖e1 ♖xe1+ 32 ♛xe1 gxf4 33 gxf4 ♗f3!? 34 d6 ♗a8 and the long-range threats to the white king will be difficult to resist.

24   ...   ♛f6!

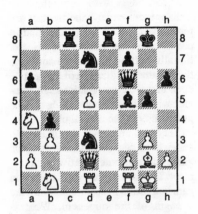

Black's masterplan is complete. White is reduced to a state of helplessness.

25   a3   a5
26   axb4   axb4
27   ♛a2

White's contortions speak volumes about his position. Transferring his queen to a2, where it does nothing, just to threaten to bring a knight to d2, is humiliating – especially when Black can stamp out even this meagre idea without difficulty.

27   ...   ♗g6!

Opening up a line of attack from f6 to f2, ready to refute White's only "active" idea.

28   d6

If White does nothing, then Black has no difficulty finding ways to make progress, e.g. an attack down the h-file. Other moves:

1) 28 ♗h3 ♖cd8 intending to continue ...♘7e5.

2) 28 ♘d2 ♖e2 and f2 collapses.

28   ...   g4!

Naturally Black is not interested in the d-pawn (28...♛xd6? 29 ♘d2), and prefers to nail down some light squares near the white king.

29   ♛d2

Back again, with its mission unaccomplished.

29   ...   ♚g7

Black simply defends his pawn. There is no rush; White can do nothing constructive.

30   f3

Karpov, short of time, short of a plan, sees nothing better than to try to break out at the expense of exposing his king, and inviting whatever fate has in store for him. 30 f4 is met by 30...♗f5, stopping the pawn moving any further, and calmly preparing to exploit the new weaknesses on the kingside.

30   ...   ♛xd6

Finally it is convenient to take this pawn, so as to free the d7-knight for more active service.

31   fxg4

Or:

1) 31 ♘b2 ♛d4+ 32 ♚h1 ♛xb2 33 ♛xb2+ ♘xb2 34 ♖xd7 ♖c2 35 fxg4 (or 35 ♖d2 ♖xd2 36 ♘xd2 ♖e2) 35...♖ee2 36 ♗d5 ♖f2 37 ♖xf2 ♖xf2 38 ♚g1 ♖c2 39 h4 ♚f6 40 h5 ♖c1+ 41 ♚g2 ♗xb1 42 ♖xf7+ ♚e5 and Black must win.

2) 31 ♛b2+ "is slightly more tenacious, but it would not have essentially changed anything" – Kasparov.

31   ...   ♛d4+
32   ♚h1   ♘f6!

Threatening 33...♘e4 or 33...♘xg4.

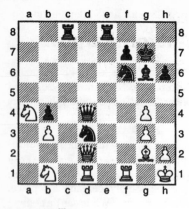

33 Rf4

33 h3 gives Black a choice:

1) After 33...Re3 White is unable to put up serious resistance, e.g. 34 Rf4 We5.

2) 33...♘e4 is condemned by Kasparov on the basis of 34 Wxd3 ♘f2+ 35 Rxf2 ♗xd3 36 Rfd2, but then Black has 36...We3 37 Rxd3 Rc1, an echo of the game continuation, making this an alternative, and more forcing win.

33 ...   ♘e4!

34 Wxd3

The knight had survived for 18 moves on d3, during which it played a major role in the downfall of White's whole position.

34 ...   ♘f2+

35 Rxf2

35 ♔g1 ♘h3++ 36 ♔h1 Wxd3 37 Rxd3 Re1+ 38 ♗f1 (38 Rf1 Rxf1+ 39 ♗xf1 ♗e4+ 40 ♗g2 Rc1+ and mate) 38...♘xf4 costs White most of his pieces.

35 ...   ♗xd3

36 Rfd2   We3!

37 Rxd3   Rc1!

38 ♘b2   Wf2!

39 ♘d2   Rxd1+

39...Re2! actually mates next move.

40 ♘xd1   Re1+

0-1

Kasparov wrote: "Such games are remembered for a long time, and in particular by the winner himself, after literally putting part of his soul into the sustained realization of his plan. ... none of my earlier creations can compare with this 16th game as regards the grandiosity of the overall plan.

"There is one other important reason why I can confidently call this game my supreme creative achievement. The value of any brilliantly won game increases in accordance with the strength of the opponent. What is noteworthy is the fact that this victory was achieved over such a super-class player as Karpov."

Lessons from this game:

1) Just as one poorly placed piece can make a whole position bad, so one really well-placed piece can make a whole position work.

2) Maintaining a bind is not a matter of smothering the opponent on all fronts, but rather identifying his active possibilities and providing a specific refutation to each.

3) Be prepared to return sacrificed material before you are getting strangled!

Game 80

Garry Kasparov – Anatoly Karpov

World Championship match (game 16),
London/Leningrad 1986

Ruy Lopez (Spanish), Flohr/Zaitsev Variation

The Players

Garry Kasparov (born 1963) is the greatest player of modern times, and has been World Champion (of one sort or another) since 1985. For more information see Game 71.

Anatoly Karpov (born 1951) has been FIDE World Champion 1975–85 and from 1993 onwards. See Game 67 for more details.

The Game

Like the 16th game of the previous match between Karpov and Kasparov, the 16th game of the 1986 return match also proved to be of decisive importance. Kasparov felt, going into the game, that a tempestuous battle lay ahead. He was sure that Karpov would make a supreme effort to get back into the match (he was trailing by one win to three), and to wipe out the memory of the 16th game from the previous match with a comprehensive victory. Of course, Kasparov is known to be somewhat superstitious, and quite possibly Karpov approached this as just another game.

In any event, Karpov had an interesting and sharp idea prepared, and Kasparov was filled with a lust for battle. The game turned out to be so complex and interesting that in his book on the match Kasparov devoted 20 large-format pages to its analysis. Both players indeed fought for victory with immense ferocity, and for several moves great forces held the game in a highly volatile equilibrium. When Karpov overstepped the mark with his winning attempts, the retribution was swift and severe.

1	e4	e5	11 ♘bd2	♗f8
2	♘f3	♘c6	12 a4	h6
3	♗b5	a6	13 ♗c2	exd4
4	♗a4	♘f6	14 cxd4	♘b4
5	0-0	♗e7	15 ♗b1	c5
6	♖e1	b5	16 d5	♘d7
7	♗b3	d6	17 ♖a3	c4
8	c3	0-0		
9	h3	♗b7		
10	d4	♖e8		

In the 1990 match between the same players, Karpov preferred 17...f5, breaking up White's centre at the cost of loosening the kingside, but it would take us too far afield to discuss the ramifications of this move.

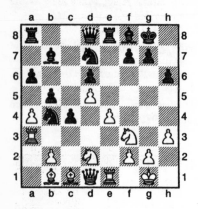

18 ♘d4

Kasparov deviates from the 14th game, where 18 axb5 axb5 19 ♘d4 ♖xa3! 20 bxa3 ♘d3 21 ♗xd3 cxd3 22 ♗b2 ♕a5 23 ♘f5 had occurred. Then 23...♘e5?! was played in the game, but 24 ♗xe5! forced 24...dxe5 25 ♘b3 ♕b6 26 ♕xd3, when Black was in some trouble. According to Kasparov, 23...g6! would have been fully OK for Black, e.g. 24 ♘b3 ♕a4 25 ♕xd3 ♘e5! 26 ♗xe5 ♖xe5 27 f4 ♖e8 28 ♘g3 ♗g7 with good compensation.

18 ... ♕f6

Karpov introduces a prepared novelty. He is prepared to sacrifice a pawn to cause congestion in the white position. A major point of his plan is to sink a knight into d3 – which indeed brings back memories of the 16th game from the 1985 match.

19 ♘2f3 ♘c5

Kasparov suggested the alternative idea 19...♘d3!?, which was eventually tested in practice in the mid-1990s, and proved its worth at the highest

level. 20 ♗xd3 (20 ♖xd3!? cxd3 21 axb5 also gives White compensation) 20...b4! 21 ♗xc4! bxa3 22 b3 leaves White with enough compensation for the exchange, but no more. The game Anand – Kamsky, PCA Candidates match (game 5), Las Palmas 1995 continued 22...♘c5 23 ♕c2 ♕g6 24 ♘h4 ♕f6 25 ♘hf3 ♕g6 26 ♘h4 ♕f6 ½-½.

20 axb5

Kasparov decides that he might as well have a pawn for his troubles.

20 ... axb5

21 ♘xb5

It would be a terribly bad idea to give Black the a-file: 21 ♖xa8? ♖xa8 22 ♘xb5 ♖a1 leaves White in serious trouble.

21 ... ♖xa3

22 ♘xa3

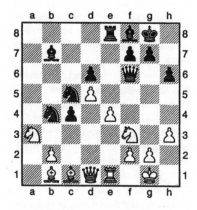

22 ... ♗a6

Karpov solidifies his grip on d3 before moving a knight there, challenging White to find a useful move in the meantime. The immediate 22...♘bd3?! eases White's task: 23 ♗xd3 ♘xd3 24 ♖e3! ♗a6! (this move turns out to be necessary in any case) 25 ♕a4 ♖a8 and now Kasparov's main line is 26 ♕c6! ♕d8 27 ♗d2 ♘xb2 28 ♘c2, returning the pawn to regain the initiative.

23 ♖e3

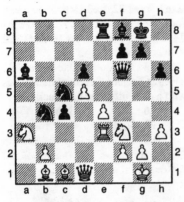

23 ... **♖b8!?**

Or:

1) 23...g6? is very well met by a pawn sacrifice: 24 ♗d2! ♕xb2 (otherwise 25 ♗c3 will make a nonsense of Black's 23rd move) 25 ♗c3 ♕xa3 26 ♕d4 ♖e5 27 ♘xe5 ♘b3 (27...♗g7 28 ♕d2!) 28 ♕a7! dxe5 29 ♖f3 f5 30 exf5 gives White a winning attack.

2) 23...♘cd3?! 24 ♗xd3 (24 b3!? is an interesting attempt to undermine the d3-knight) 24...cxd3? (24...♘xd3 transposes to the note to Black's 22nd move) 25 ♕a4 ♖b8 26 ♗d2! ♕xb2 27 ♖e1! and Black will suffer major losses on the queenside, where his pieces resemble a house of cards.

3) 23...♘bd3!? 24 ♗xd3 cxd3 25 b4 ♘xe4 26 b5 ♗b7 27 ♖xd3! ♖c8 (rather than 27...♘c3 28 ♗b2) is suggested by Kasparov, who feels that then White's extra pawn would not be relevant.

24 e5!

Kasparov senses that he must at all costs keep the initiative, as otherwise Black's occupation of d3, now that everything is ready, would leave White with a miserable position.

24 ♖c3? ♘bd3 25 ♘xc4? ♕xc3! 26 bxc3 ♖xb1 was one potential disaster that alarmed Kasparov at the board, and actually occurred in the game M. Pavlović – Cela, Ilioupolis 1995.

24 ... **dxe5**
25 ♘xe5

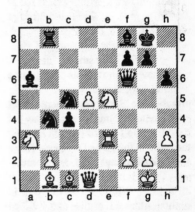

It is clear that Black should now plunge a knight into d3, but which one?

25 ... **♘bd3?**

It turns out that Karpov's choice is faulty, but that Kasparov failed to punish it.

25...♘cd3! is better because it keeps the c2-square covered. Play is then similar to that in the game (after the "exchange" of inaccuracies). 26 ♘g4! and now:

1) 26...♕b6? 27 ♖g3 ♗d6 (or 27...♗c5 28 ♘xh6+ ♔f8 29 ♕h5) 28 ♗e3 ♕c7 29 ♘xh6+ ♔f8 30 ♖xg7! ♔xg7 31 ♕g4+ ♔h7 32 ♘f5 with a winning attack.

2) 26...♕h4!? was played success-fully in Nunn – Psakhis, Hastings 1987/8: 27 ♖g3 ♔h8 28 ♗d2 ♗d6 29 ♖f3 ♘xb2 30 ♕e2 ♕e7 31 ♕xe7 ½-½.

3) 26...♕d4! puts the queen on a better square, rendering White's at-tack less effective and obliging him to continue in positional style: 27 ♘c2! (27 ♖g3 ♗d6! 28 ♗e3 ♕xb2 29 ♘xh6+ ♔f8 30 ♕h5 gxh6 31 ♖f3 ♘e5 and no decisive continuation for White is apparent) 27...♘xc2 (27...♕xd5?? 28 ♘f6+! gxf6 29 ♖g3+ and 30 ♕g4 wins) 28 ♗xc2 and now:

3a) 28...♗c5 was given by Kaspa-rov with the assessment "unclear". Given how much analysis of this game he published, we can certainly forgive him this one "lazy" assessment! How-ever, Gennady Timoshchenko may not have been so forgiving when he tried the move in the game Dvoirys – Timo-shchenko, Barnaul 1988, and immedi-ately found himself in big trouble after 29 ♕f3! – White threatens both 30 ♘xh6+ gxh6 31 ♕g3+ and 30 ♖e4 ♕xd5 31 ♘xh6+.

3b) 28...♗d6 has proved its worth in two games. 29 b3 ♕a1 30 bxc4 ♗xc4! (30...♘xc1 31 ♖e1 is more dan-gerous for Black) 31 ♗xd3 ♗xd3 32 ♖e1 (32 ♖xd3 ♖b1 33 ♘f6+ gxf6 34 ♕g4+ with a perpetual check, Kruppa – Titkov, USSR 1988) 32...♗g6 33 ♗d2 ♖b1 34 ♕e2 ♖xe1+ 35 ♕xe1 ♕xe1+ 36 ♗xe1 ♗e4 37 ♘e3 ♗c5 ½-½ Dvoirys – Timoshchenko, USSR Team Championship 1988. Black re-gains the pawn with dead equality.

26   ♘g4?

26 ♕c2! makes use of the fact that Black isn't covering c2 and "pins" the d3-knight against the mate on h7.

26...♖b4 (26...♘b3 27 ♘axc4 ♘bxc1 28 ♘xd3 ♘xd3 29 ♖xd3 and Black can hardly have enough for the pawns) 27 ♘c6 ♖b7 28 ♖e8 g5! (28...g6? loses to 29 ♗xh6) and then:

1) 29 ♘e5 ♖e7! 30 ♘g4 ♕d6 31 ♖xe7 ♕xe7 32 ♗e3 f5 isn't so clear, for example 33 d6!? ♕e6 (33...♕xd6? 34 ♘xc4) 34 ♗xc5 fxg4 35 d7 g3! with counterplay.

2) 29 f3! ♕d6 30 ♘xc4 ♕xd5 31 ♘4e5 is Kasparov's recommendation, with a difficult game for Black.

26   ...   ♕b6!
27   ♖g3

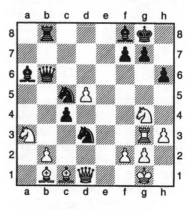

27   ...   g6!

Karpov chooses an ambitious move, doubtless feeling that he was fully jus-tified in hoping to win the game cleanly. In Kasparov's view this psychological factor comes into play at several points in the rest of the game, as Kar-pov rejects "messy" continuations in the search for a clear-cut win. Alas, there turns out to be no win for Black, clear-cut or otherwise, and it is in the messy lines that his salvation lies.

Kasparov analysed two interesting alternatives at this point:

1) 27...♔h8 28 ♘xh6 ♘e4 (not
28...gxh6? losing to 29 ♘xc4! ♗xc4
30 ♕g4 ♕g6 31 ♕xc4) 29 ♘xf7+ ♔g8
30 ♖e3 ♘exf2! 31 ♕h5 ♗c5 32 ♘g5
♗xe3 33 ♕h7+ ♔f8 34 ♕h8+ ♔e7 35
♕xg7+ ♔d6 36 ♕f6+ ♔d7 37 ♕f7+
♔c8 38 ♕e8+ ♔b7 39 ♕e7+ ♕c7 40
♕xe3 ♘xc1 and in this position Kasparov reckoned Black was not in danger.

2) 27...♘e4 28 ♘xh6+ ♔h7, aiming for an improved version of line
"1", was analysed in colossal detail by
Kasparov, whose conclusion was that
White had just about enough resources to secure a draw after 29 ♗e3
(29 ♖e3 ♘exf2 30 ♕f3 ♕f6!! is very
good for Black, as White cannot, in the
end, avoid losing material) 29...♕xb2
30 ♘xf7 ♘xg3 31 fxg3. His main
variation was now 31...♗e7 (31...♗xa3
32 ♗xd3+ cxd3 33 ♕h5+ ♔g8 34 ♘g5
forces a perpetual check) 32 ♕h5+
♔g8 33 d6 ♗f6 34 d7 ♖b7 35 ♗c2
♕xa3 (35...♖a8? 36 ♘g5) 36 ♕h8+
♔xf7 37 ♕xb8 ♕e7 38 d8♘+ ♔g6 39
♕xb7 ♕xe3+ 40 ♔h2 ♗xd4 41 ♕c6+
♗f6 42 ♕xc4 ♗d4! 43 ♗xd3+ ♔f6 44
h4 ♗e5 "with an obvious draw".

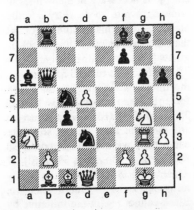

28 ♗xh6

"In the given instance the knight is
a much more valuable attacking piece
than the dark-squared bishop." – Kasparov. The future course of the game
certainly bears out this judgement.

28 ... ♕xb2
29 ♕f3!

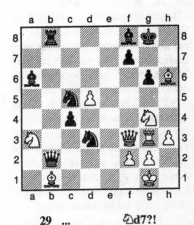

29 ... ♘d7?!

Here we see Karpov chasing the
elusive win. He wants to defend his
king, against both mating ideas and
threats of perpetual check, whereupon
he will take the a3-knight and White
can resign. The drawback of this move,
upon which White is able, with extremely inventive play, to seize, is that
Black now has less control over d3.
However, this move is by no means
disastrous in itself, but Black must
now play more accurately to survive.
Possible drawing lines:

1) 29...♕xa3 30 ♘f6+ ♔h8 31
♕h5 is one spectacular way for the
game to end in a draw: 31...♖xb1+
(31...gxh5?? 32 ♖g8#) 32 ♗c1+ ♔g7
33 ♘e8+ ♔g8 34 ♘f6+, etc.

2) 29...♗d6 30 ♗e3! ♗xg3 (not
30...f5? 31 ♘h6+ ♔h7 32 ♘xf5 ♕xa3

33 ♘xd6 ♖xb1+ 34 ♔h2 ♕a1 35 ♖xg6!
and White wins) 31 ♘f6+ ♔g7 32
♕xg3 ♔xf8 (32...♖h8!? is an interesting attempt to avoid the immediate
draw; 32...♕e5 33 ♘h5+! leaves White
in no danger) 33 ♗xd3 ♘xd3 34 ♕h4+
♔e5 35 ♕e7+ ♔xd5 36 ♕d7+ is a
draw.

30 ♗xf8   ♔xf8

Instead 30...♖xf8?! 31 ♘h6+ ♔g7
(31...♔h7? 32 ♘xf7) 32 ♘f5+ ♔h7 33
♕e3 gives White the better chances.

After the text-move it does not look
at all clear how White should proceed.
It is hard to make active tries work,
since Black has a variety of ways in reply to take pieces and/or make use of
checks to the white king. In fact,
White's attacking forces are well and
flexibly placed, and the one piece
whose position can definitely be improved is the king. This line of reason-
ing suggests White's next move.

31 ♔h2!

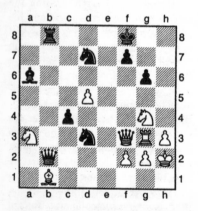

This is not everyone's idea of a
great attacking move, but it proves
highly effective here. ♔h2 is a move
White was going to have to play fairly
soon anyway, and now Black must

choose how he wishes to proceed, and
White can react accordingly, rather
than it being the other way around. In
other words, White makes sure that it
is his information that is greater by
one move, and not his opponent's.

31 ...   ♖b3!

This is undoubtedly the best move,
by which Black keeps his pieces coordinated, prepares to neutralize White's
major pieces on the third rank and gets
ready to grab the piece. To verify the
potency of White's ideas, let us take a
look at the alternatives:

1) 31...♕xa3? 32 ♘h6 wins for
White: 32...♕e7 (32...♘7e5 33 ♕f6;
32...♔e7 33 ♗xd3 cxd3 34 ♕xf7+
♔d8 35 ♖xg6) 33 ♖xg6 ♔e8 34
♗xd3! ♕e5+ (34...cxd3 35 d6 ♕e5+
36 g3 fxg6 37 ♕f7+ ♔d8 38 ♕g8+
and 39 ♘f7+) 35 g3 fxg6 36 ♗xg6+
♔e7 37 ♕a3+ and a knight fork wins
the black queen.

2) 31...♔g7? 32 ♘xc4! ♕xb1 33
♘d6 ♘3e5 (33...♖f8 34 ♕e3) 34 ♘xe5
♘xe5 35 ♕h5 ♕b2 36 ♘f5+ ♔g8 37
♕h6 and Black must give up his knight
to stop the mate.

3) 31...♕c1? 32 ♗xd3 (this exchange is necessary in many lines to
allow the white queen entry into the
black position; this is more important
than the passed pawn that Black is
granted) 32...cxd3 33 ♘f6! ♘e5 (or
33...♘xf6 34 ♕xf6 ♔g8 35 ♖g4! and
the threat of ♖h4 and mate on h8
forces Black to go passive) 34 ♕e4 d2
35 ♕xe5 d1♕ (Black is a queen up
and threatens mate in one, so White
had better have something good...) 36
♕xb8+ ♔g7 (36...♗c8 37 ♖e3!) 37
♘e8+! ♔h7 38 ♖e3 and White's army
turns out to be the more effective;
Black cannot regain the initiative by

38...♕g1+? 39 ♔g3 ♗f1 because after 40 ♘f6+ ♔g7 41 ♕g8+ ♔xf6 42 ♕h8+ ♔g5 White has a choice of mates in two.

32 ♗xd3!

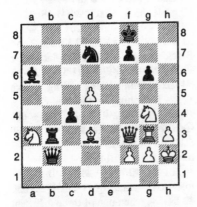

"By this point I had less than 10 minutes remaining on my clock, whereas Karpov had more than half an hour, but after 32 ♗xd3 I became absolutely calm, since I felt intuitively that White had nothing to fear." – Kasparov. Kasparov's analysis from here shows that Black still has a way to draw, but no more. Karpov undoubtedly saw that he could draw, but was convinced there was a way to win. Though unable to find a winning line, he couldn't bring himself to play a drawish line, and so wound up losing.

32 ... cxd3?!

This move leaves Black on the verge of being lost. Better moves:

1) 32...♖xd3 33 ♕f4 ♕xa3 34 ♘h6 ♕e7 35 ♖xg6 ♕e5 (this is one of Black's key defensive ideas and crops up in many variations) 36 ♕xe5 ♘xe5 37 ♖xa6 ♖xd5 and although White is a pawn up, the ending is likely to be drawn.

2) 32...♖xa3 33 ♕f4 ♖xd3 (for 33...cxd3? see line "1" in the note to Black's 33rd move) 34 ♕d6+ ♔g7 35 ♕xd7 ♖xg3 36 fxg3 ("in endings with queens it is important to keep the king screened from checks" – Kasparov) and now Kasparov gives as the best defence 36...♗b7 37 h4 ♗a8! (after 37...♕d4? 38 ♕xb7 ♕xg4 39 ♕b2+ White wins since the black king cannot become active) 38 ♕d8 ♕d4 39 ♕xa8 ♕xg4 40 ♕a1+ ♔f8! 41 d6 ♔e8 and here the king can approach the pawn, so Black should draw.

33 ♕f4

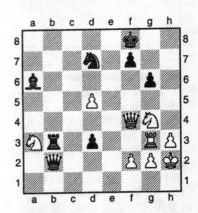

33 ... ♕xa3?

Now Black loses by force. Instead:

1) 33...♖xa3? also loses: 34 ♖f3 ♕b8 35 d6 ♕e8 36 ♖e3 ♕c8 37 ♖e7 ♗c4 38 ♕h6+ ♔g8 39 ♖xd7 and mate next move.

2) 33...d2! 34 ♘h6 ♘f6 35 ♖xb3 (35 ♕d6+ is analysed in great depth by Kasparov, whose main line ends in stalemate on move 57!) 35...♖xb3 36 ♕xf6 ♖xd5 and now:

2a) 37 ♘xf7 d1♕ (37...♔e8 38 ♘b1! d1♕ 39 ♘c3! forks two queens!) 38 ♘d6+ ♔g8 39 ♕xg6+ ♔f8 40

♕f6+ ♔g8 41 ♘f5! ♕xf5 42 ♕xf5 ♕d6+ and Black should hold the ending.

2b) 37 ♕h8+ ♔e7 38 ♘g8+ ♔d6 and now:

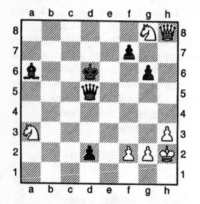

2b1) 39 ♕f6+ forces the black king to walk a tightrope to safety. Its destination is a8:

2b11) 39...♔c5? is implied by Kasparov to be good for Black, but this is most unconvincing after 40 ♕c3+, e.g.:

2b111) 40...♔d6 41 ♘c2 (41 ♘f6 ♕e5+ 42 ♕xe5+ ♔xe5 43 ♘g4+) 41...d1♕ 42 ♘e3 ♗b7 43 ♘f6 wins.

2b112) 40...♔b6 41 ♕b4+ ♔c7 (or 41...♔a7 42 ♘e7 ♕d7 43 ♘c6+ ♕xc6 44 ♕xd2) 42 ♘f6 ♕e5+ 43 f4 wins.

2b12) 39...♔d7 40 ♕e7+ ♔c8 (or 40...♔c6 41 ♘c2!) 41 ♘f6 ♕d4 42 ♕e8+ ♔b7 43 ♕xf7+ ♔a8 44 ♘d5 d1♕ (44...♕e5+ 45 f4; 44...♕c5 45 ♘c7+) 45 ♘c7+ ♔b8 (otherwise a discovered check picks up the d5-queen) 46 ♘xa6+ ♔a8 47 ♘b5 and White forces a won ending.

2b13) 39...♕e6? loses to 40 ♕d8+ ♕d7 41 ♕b6+ ♕c6 42 ♕b4+.

2b14) 39...♔c7! is best:

2b141) 40 ♕e7+ and then:

2b1411) 40...♕d7 41 ♕c5+ ♔b7 (41...♕c6? 42 ♕a5+) 42 ♘f6 ♕c7+ 43 ♕xc7+ ♔xc7 44 ♘d5+ ♔c6 45 ♘e3 ♗d3 46 ♔g3 ♔c5 47 ♔f3 ♔b4 48 ♘ac2+ (48 ♘d1 ♔xa3 49 ♔e3 ♗f1 50 g3 ♗xh3 51 ♔xd2 ♔b4) 48...♔c3 49 ♘a1 ♔b2 50 ♘d1+ ♔c1 (50...♔xa1 51 ♔e3 ♗f1 52 g3 ♗xh3 53 ♔xd2 and Black's king is very badly placed) 51 ♘b3+ ♔xd1 52 ♔e3 ♗f1 53 g3 ♗xh3 54 ♘xd2 with a tricky ending, where White is pushing for the win.

2b1412) 40...♔b8! 41 ♕b4+ (41 ♘f6 ♕d4 42 ♕e8+ ♗c8 43 ♕b5+ ♗b7 44 ♕e8+ is a draw) 41...♔a8! transposes to "2b142".

2b142) 40 ♕c3+ ♔b7! (40...♔d8? loses to the amazing 41 ♘b5!! ♗xb5? 42 ♕a5+, when one of three different knight forks will win the d5-queen; 40...♔b8? allows 41 ♕g3+! followed by 42 ♘b1! d1♕ 43 ♘c3) 41 ♕b4+ ♔a8! 42 ♘f6 (not 42 ♘e7? ♕d7) 42...♕d8 43 ♕e4+ ♔a7 only gives White a perpetual check.

2b2) 39 ♘f6 ♕e5+ 40 g3 ♕e2 (Kasparov) 41 ♕d8+ looks like White's best winning attempt:

2b21) 41...♔c6 42 ♕d7+ ♔b6 43 ♘d5+ ♔c5 44 ♘e3 ♕xf2+ (it is surprising that White can prosper by allowing this) 45 ♘g2 (threatening ♕a7+) 45...♕e2 (45...♔b4 46 ♘b1) 46 ♕c7+ ♔d5 47 ♘c2 should be winning for White.

2b22) 41...♔e6 42 ♕b6+ (42 ♘e4? d1♕) 42...♔e7 (42...♔f5 43 ♘d5) 43 ♘d5+ ♔f8 44 ♘b1 d1♕ 45 ♘bc3 wins a queen and leaves White with an extra pawn, but exploiting it will not be easy with Black's pieces active and the light squares around his king weakened. The general verdict on the ending of knight and three pawns vs bishop and two, with all the pawns on the same side of the board, is that it is a draw if the defender has no weaknesses, but provides excellent winning chances if there is the slightest chink in the defensive armour. The additional presence of queens means, again in general, that there are additional winning chances since an attack by the queen and knight can provoke weaknesses. However, if to safeguard his own king White needs to take queens off without provoking any weaknesses, then it will be a draw. We are close to this scenario here.

34 ♘h6

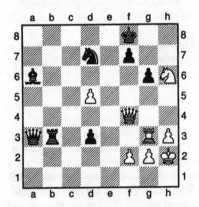

Now everything is fairly simple, thanks to Kasparov's diabolical 37th move.

34	...	♛e7
35	♖xg6	♛e5

35...♚e8 loses in simple fashion, also to 36 d6.

36	♖g8+	♚e7
37	d6+!	

Black will lose his queen, and could well resign here, but, in desperate time-trouble, Karpov plays a few more moves.

37	...	♚e6
38	♖e8+	♚d5
39	♖xe5+	♘xe5
40	d7	♖b8
41	♘xf7	

With time now to survey the wreckage, Karpov called it a day.

1-0

Lessons from this game:

1) When faced with an attempt to smother his position, Kasparov immediately blasted open the position and went for the opponent's king. This may not be the answer to every problem, but it beats getting squashed!

2) The initiative is an immensely powerful weapon. Here White had just enough initiative to do the highly improbable, and save his condemned knight on a3.

3) Don't get carried away trying to win a position where you have lost the thread and the wins are all proving elusive. Cut your losses!

Game 81

Tony Miles – Alexander Beliavsky

Tilburg 1986

Queen's Indian/Nimzo-Indian Hybrid

The Players

Anthony (Tony) Miles (born 1955) was the first English grandmaster, part of an English chess "explosion" during which the country was transformed from a relative chess backwater into a real powerhouse in less than a decade. Miles first sprung to prominence when he won the 1974 World Junior Championship by a margin of 1½ points. The following year Sheffield University gave him an honorary degree for his chess achievements, and he left without completing his studies to start as a professional chess player. His long and distinguished career has been littered with outstanding tournament victories. Miles is also renowned as a great fighter as well a creative openings expert. Bemused by Karpov's armoury against all the main openings, he once tried the eccentric St George's Defence (1 e4 a6!?) and won a fine game against the confused World Champion.

Despite his loss in this game Alexander Beliavsky further confirmed his status as one of the world's best players by winning this prestigious Tilburg event ahead of players such as Miles, Karpov, Korchnoi and Timman. For more information see Game 78.

The Game

When voting on the most important theoretical novelty in the second half of 1986, the nine judges for the chess periodical *Informator* gave this game a perfect 90/90. Bearing in mind that it is often difficult to get even two grandmasters to agree over anything, one can appreciate the strength of Miles's stunning 18th move, which virtually put a whole main-line opening variation out of business. Following his devastating novelty Miles played the rest of the game in a clinical fashion. After the initial blow, Beliavsky was never allowed the slightest chance to get back on level terms.

1	d4	♘f6
2	c4	e6
3	♘f3	b6
4	♘c3	♗b4
5	♗g5	♗b7

This variation, which is a hybrid of the Queen's Indian and Nimzo-Indian Defences, and can be reached from both openings, was extremely popular at the time of this game. Play can become extremely complex, as both sides play aggressively to fight for the initiative.

6	e3	h6
7	♗h4	g5
8	♗g3	♘e4
9	♕c2	d6
10	♗d3	♗xc3+

11 bxc3 f5!?

The most enterprising way to play the position. As in many variations of the Queen's Indian, Black attempts to keep control of the vital e4-square at all costs. However, such was the impact of this particular game that the more sober 11...♘xg3 began to take over as the main line.

12 d5!

White must play without restraint; otherwise he may well find himself on the defensive.

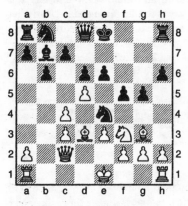

12 ... ♘c5

Accepting the pawn is not a good idea, as Black's own pawn-structure becomes very weakened. Following 12...exd5 13 cxd5 ♗xd5 14 ♘d4! ♕f6 15 f3 ♘xg3 16 hxg3 ♘d7 17 ♗xf5 White has regained the material and is clearly better. Tal – Vaganian, USSR Championship, Leningrad 1974 continued 17...0-0-0 18 ♕a4 a5 19 ♔f2 ♗b7 20 g4 ♕e7 21 ♘c6! and Black's weaknesses on the light squares were very prominent.

13 h4 g4
14 ♘d4 ♕f6
15 0-0 ♘xd3

After Miles's success in this game, players who were brave enough to venture down this line would try instead 15...♘ba6. After 16 ♘xe6 ♘xe6 17 ♗xf5 ♘g7 18 ♗g6+ ♔d7 19 f3 ♖af8 20 fxg4 ♕e7 21 e4, the consensus is that White's three pawns and safer king are worth more than the piece.

16 ♕xd3 e5
17 ♘xf5 ♗c8

This little bishop retreat is the point of Black's previous play. White's knight on f5 has no retreat-square. The obvious move for White here is 18 e4, but then Black's scheme is seen fully with 18...♗xf5! 19 exf5 ♘d7 and despite being a pawn down, Black has a reasonable game since his knight is strong in this blocked position, with numerous weak pawns to attack. Kasparov – Timman, Match (game 6), Hilversum 1985 saw instead 18 ♘d4!? exd4 19 cxd4 ♕f5 20 e4 ♕g6 21 ♕c3 0-0 22 ♖fe1 and White had compensation for the piece, but Miles's recipe, as well as being the most dramatic solution, is the most effective one too.

18 f4!!

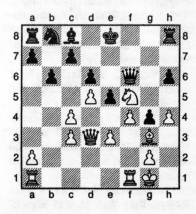

Totally ignoring the attack on f5. White simply plans to roll through with his central pawns.

18 ...   ♕xf5

Black runs into similar problems to the game after 18...♗xf5 19 e4 ♗h7 20 fxe5. The only other possibility is to decline the offer with 18...gxf3 19 ♖xf3, when Miles gives the following lines:

1) 19...♘a6 20 ♘e7!! (this fabulous move releases the queen and rook's potential, and attacks the bishop on c8; the black queen is lacking in squares, as is the black king) and now 20...♕g7 21 ♘xc8! ♖xc8 22 ♕f5 ♔d8 23 h5 is the end, while 20...♕xe7 21 ♕g6+ ♔d8 22 ♖f7 traps the queen.

2) After 19...♘d7 Miles once more gives 20 ♘e7!?, although this time it's not so effective after 20...♕xe7 21 ♕g6+ ♔d8 22 ♖f7 ♕e8 23 h5 (Miles stops here) 23...♗a6! 24 ♖xd7+ ♕xd7 25 ♕f6+ ♔c8 26 ♕xh8+ ♔b7 with a very unclear position, as the black king has somehow arrived into a totally safe position. Now 27 ♕xh6? allows Black to take over with 27...♖g8 28 ♗f2 ♕g4 29 g3 ♗xc4 and White is struggling badly on the light squares. In view of this White should be satisfied with 20 ♘d4 ♘c5 21 ♖xf6 ♘xd3 22 ♘b5 ♔d8 23 h5 with a clear advantage in this endgame.

3) 19...♗xf5 20 ♖xf5 ♕g7 21 ♗xe5!! (Nunn) 21...dxe5 22 d6! and now all lines favour White, e.g.:

3a) 22...♖g8 23 ♕e4 c6 24 ♖xe5+ ♔d8 25 ♖f1 ♘d7 26 ♖e7 ♕g4 27 ♕xg4 ♖xg4 28 ♖ff7 and the invasion of White's rooks on the seventh rank is decisive.

3b) 22...c6 23 ♕e4 ♘d7 24 ♕xc6 ♖d8 25 ♖af1 ♖g8 26 ♕d5 ♕g6 27

♖xe5+! ♘xe5 28 ♕xe5+ ♔d7 29 ♕e7+ ♔c6 30 ♕c7#.

3c) 22...♘d7 23 ♕d5 0-0-0 24 ♖f7 wins the queen, as 24...♕g6 25 ♕a8+ ♘b8 26 ♖xc7# is mate.

3d) 22...♕d7 23 ♖xe5+ ♔d8 24 ♖d1 and White's attack must win.

3e) 22...♘c6 (the best try) 23 ♕d5 ♕d7 24 ♖xe5+ ♔d8 (24...♘xe5? 25 ♕xe5+ ♔f7 26 ♖f1+ ♔g8 27 ♖f6 {Nunn} and Black has no defence, for example 27...♕h7 28 ♖e6 ♖he8 29 ♕f5+ ♔g8 30 ♖g6+) 25 ♖e6 ♖e8 26 ♖xh6 and although White has four pawns for the piece and is clearly better, there is no immediate forced win.

19 e4   ♕h5
20 fxe5   dxe5
21 c5!

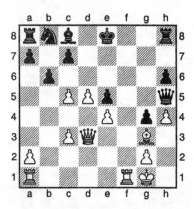

Breaking open the position before Black has any time to consolidate. Black's position is already teetering on the brink and the loss of the weak e5-pawn will be enough to push it over the edge. 21...♗a6 appears to gain a tempo for development, but following 22 c4 Black faces the daunting threat of ♖f5. After 22...♘d7 23 ♖f5 ♕g6 24 c6 ♘c5 25 ♖xe5+ ♔d8 26 ♕d4 Black has to play without his a8-rook. The greedy 21...bxc5 is met by 22 ♕b5+ ♘d7 (or 22...♔d8 23 ♕xc5 ♘d7 24 ♕c6 ♖b8 25 ♖f5 ♕e8 26 ♗xe5 and Black collapses) 23 ♕c6 ♖b8 24 ♖f5 and once more White crashes through on e5.

21	...	♔d8
22	d6	♕e8

Black would like to block the position, but cannot achieve his goal with 22...c6 as White can continue with 23 d7!, when White's queen, two rooks and bishop combine to give a decisive attack, e.g.:

1) 23...♗xd7 24 ♕d6 ♖g8 25 ♗xe5 ♘a6 26 ♖ad1 ♘xc5 27 ♕xc6 ♖c8 28 ♕f6+ ♔e8 29 ♗d6 and White mates.

2) 23...♘xd7 24 ♕d6 ♕e8 25 ♕xc6 ♖b8 26 ♖ad1 ♕e7 27 ♖f5 ♖e8 (or 27...♕xc5+ 28 ♕xc5 bxc5 29 ♗xe5, forking the two rooks) 28 ♖xe5 ♕xe5 29 ♗xe5 ♖xe5 30 ♕d6 and the threats of c6, ♕xe5 and ♕xb8 mean that more material will go.

23	dxc7+	♔xc7
24	♕d5	♘c6
25	♖f7+	♗d7
26	♖af1!	

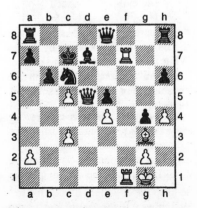

Bringing up the final reserves. This rook will find an ideal home on f6, adding even more pressure to Black's creaking joints. Black has no time at all to catch his breath and build a defence.

26	...	♖d8
27	♖1f6	♔c8
28	cxb6	axb6
29	♕b5	1-0

There is no way out:

1) 29...♘b8 30 ♗xe5! (Miles's 30 ♕xb6 also does the job) and Black is busted as 30...♗xb5 allows 31 ♖c7#, while otherwise White's next move is 31 ♖xb6.

2) 29...♕xf7 can be answered with the prosaic 30 ♖xf7 but Miles's 30 ♕a6+! ♔c7 31 ♗xe5+! ♘xe5 32 ♕a7+ ♔c8 33 ♖xb6 is a much classier finish.

Lessons from this game:

1) Playing ambitiously with the black pieces is a double-edged sword. Black's play, culminating in 17...♗c8, is rather provocative, to say the least. It's true that Miles's novelty is absolutely stunning, but it's also true that you expect White to have something in the position after 17...♗c8.

2) When one has sacrificed material, but has a lead in development, it's normal to open the position even more before the defender has a chance to consolidate. In this game this was achieved by the very direct 21 c5! and 22 d6!.

3) Games are often decided quickly once a vital pawn is captured. In many variations here Black loses his important e5-pawn and can resign immediately, as the white bishop is unleashed.

Mikhail Tal – Johann Hjartarson
Reykjavik 1987
Ruy Lopez (Spanish), Chigorin Variation

The Players

Mikhail Tal (1936–92) was World Champion for just one year (1960–1) but was at the top of world chess for some thirty years. For more details see Game 39.

Johann Hjartarson (born 1963) is an Icelandic player who gained the grandmaster title in 1985. In the following World Championship cycle he achieved considerable success, finishing joint first in the Szirak Interzonal of 1987 and thereby qualifying for the Candidates. In his first Candidates match, he defeated Korchnoi in a quick-play tie-break, but then lost a one-sided match against Karpov (1½–3½). This heavy defeat seemed to have an effect on his play, and his position on the rating list tumbled dramatically. However, by 1992 he had regained his form and re-established his position as a strong grandmaster. On the January 1998 rating list he occupied joint 37th position.

The Game

A standard opening line leads to a position with a blocked pawn centre and slow manoeuvring. At first White's ambitions appear to lie on the queenside, but after an inaccuracy by Black, Tal suddenly switches his attention to the black king. The result is an amazing stream of tactics embracing the whole board. The finale, with its breathtaking mate, is an appropriate finish to a magnificent game.

1	e4	e5		
2	♘f3	♘c6		
3	♗b5	a6		
4	♗a4	♘f6		
5	0-0	♗e7		
6	♖e1	b5		
7	♗b3	0-0		
8	c3	d6		
9	h3	♘a5		
10	♗c2	c5		
11	d4	♕c7		

The so-called Chigorin Variation, one of the oldest lines of the Closed Ruy Lopez. Black's strategy is to maintain his central pawn on e5.

12	♘bd2	♗d7

13	♘f1	cxd4
14	cxd4	♖ac8
15	♘e3	♘c6

By increasing the pressure against the d4-pawn, Black virtually forces White to close the centre. This relieves the central tension, but White can take consolation in his resulting space advantage.

16	d5	♘b4
17	♗b1	a5
18	a3	♘a6
19	b4	

Based on a tactical point, this aims to keep the a6-knight offside for several moves. Black cannot win a pawn

by 19...axb4 20 axb4 ♘xb4 because
21 ♗d2 traps the knight.

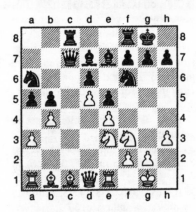

19 ...   g6

White's plan is to make progress on
the queenside, either by directly attacking the slightly weak b5-pawn or
by transferring a knight to a5. Black
normally tries to activate his pieces by
arranging ...f5 (for example, by ...♘e8-
g7) or by playing ...♗d8-b6. However,
these plans are by no means set in
stone. Indeed, if Black aims for ...f5,
White can often change direction and
try to exploit the loosening of Black's
kingside position.

20 ♗d2

Aiming to force Black to swap on
b4.

20 ...   axb4

Black can continue to delay taking
on b4, but the longer the delay, the
greater the chance that White will play
bxa5.

21 axb4   ♛b7

Black would like to play ...♘c7-
a8-b6, eventually arriving on a4 or c4,
while White would like to reach a5
with one of his knights.

22 ♗d3!

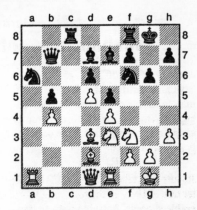

At the time a new move. Tal intends
to regroup his pieces on the queenside
to attack the b5-pawn and so make it
hard for Black to complete his knight
manoeuvre (because when the knight
arrives on b6, the b5-pawn will only
be defended once).

22 ...   ♘c7

The line 22...♘e8 23 ♛b3 ♘g7 24
♘g4! f5? 25 exf5 gxf5 26 ♘gxe5!
dxe5 27 ♘xe5, winning for White, is
an illustration of the dangers Black
faces if he tries to open the position up
too soon.

23 ♘c2!

The previous move freed c2 for the
knight. According to circumstances,
White will play either ♘a3 stepping
up the pressure on b5, or ♘a1-b3-a5.

23 ...   ♘h5

Black prepares ...f5 but, as mentioned above, he must take great care
before playing this move.

24 ♗e3

Threatening 25 ♖a7.

24 ...   ♖a8

25 ♛d2

One point of this move is to prepare
♖a5 followed by ♖ea1, so Black decides to swap rooks.

25 ...   Ixa1

Another point of White's previous move is that it prevents 25...f5 due to 26 ♗h6 ♖fb8 27 exf5 gxf5 28 ♘xe5! dxe5 29 d6 ♗xd6 30 ♕g5+ ♔h8 31 ♕xh5, restoring material equality but maintaining a clear positional advantage. With Tal, even in apparently quiet positions the tactics are only just below the surface.

26 ♘xa1!

Now the knight is only two moves away from a5.

26 ...   f5
27 ♗h6   ♘g7

This is forced, because 27...♖a8 fails to 28 exf5 gxf5 29 ♘xe5 dxe5 30 d6!, etc., as in the note to Black's 25th move.

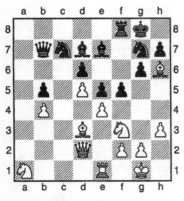

28 ♘b3   f4

Cutting off the bishop's retreat. Although the bishop appears oddly placed on h6, it actually turns out to be a thorn in Black's flesh and forms the basis for various tactical ideas.

29 ♘a5

The knight reaches its destination and from here can jump to an even more tempting outpost on c6.

29 ...   ♕b6
30 ♖c1

Tal points out that 30 ♘h2!?, followed by ♗e2-g4, was also a promising plan. If the light-squared bishops are exchanged then the knight invasion at c6 will become even more powerful. The text-move aims to occupy the c6-square more directly.

30 ...   ♖a8

If 30...♖c8?!, then White can set up an unusual pin by 31 ♕c2!, since 31...♘ce8 runs into 32 ♕xc8! ♗xc8 33 ♖xc8 ♗f8 (or 33...♔f7 34 ♘c6) 34 ♘c6 ♕a6 35 ♖b8 ♘c7 36 ♗xb5! ♕a1+ (36...♘xb5 37 ♘g5, followed by 38 ♘e7+ and mate) 37 ♗f1 ♘ge8 38 ♗xf8 ♔xf8 39 b5 ♕b1 40 ♘fxe5! dxe5 41 d6 and the passed pawns cannot be stopped.

31 ♕c2   ♘ce8
32 ♕b3   ♗f6

Black decides to eliminate the annoying bishop by ...♘h5 and ...♗g7, but this plan is quite time-consuming.

33 ♘c6   ♘h5

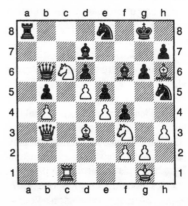

34 ♕b2!?

The immediate sacrifice 34 ♘fxe5 ♗xe5 (not 34...dxe5? 35 d6+ ♔h8 36

♕f7 ♘xd6 37 ♕xd7 ♘c4 38 ♗xc4 bxc4 39 ♕e6 and wins) 35 ♘xe5 dxe5 36 d6+ ♔h8 37 ♕d5 ♕xd6 38 ♕xa8 ♕xd3 39 ♕d8 ♕d6 40 ♖a1 leads to a very unclear position. Tal prefers to wait.

34 ...   ♗g7

After 34...♖c8, White continues 35 ♕a2 and then ♕a5, when the b5-pawn will be in trouble.

35 ♗xg7   ♔xg7?!

The line-up of white queen and black king is a danger sign, but Hjartarson can hardly be blamed for overlooking the brilliant method by which Tal exploits this. 35...♘hxg7 was better, although after 36 ♕e2 ♘c7 37 ♘h2, intending ♘g4, White retains an advantage thanks to his c6-outpost.

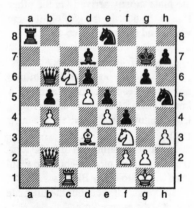

36 ♖c5!!

The obvious sacrifice is 36 ♘fxe5 dxe5 37 ♘xe5, but this is refuted by 37...♕f6. Instead Tal combines his queenside play against the b-pawn with tactics along the long diagonal.

36 ...   ♕a6

The best defence, forcing Tal to reveal the full depth of his combination. The lines 36...dxc5 37 ♘fxe5 ♔g8 38

♘xd7 ♕a6 39 bxc5 and 36...♗xc6 37 ♖xc6 ♕b7 38 ♘g5 lose straight away.

37 ♖xb5

White has to take with the rook, because after 37 ♗xb5 ♕a1+ 38 ♕xa1 ♖xa1+ Black will be able to take on c5.

37 ...   ♘c7

If Black first exchanges on c6, then White wins in a quite different way: 37...♗xc6 38 dxc6 ♘c7 39 ♖a5! ♕xc6 (39...♕xd3 40 ♖xa8 ♘xa8 41 ♕a1 ♘c7 42 ♕a7 also wins) 40 ♘xe5! dxe5 41 ♕xe5+ ♘f6 42 ♖c5 and the c7-knight falls.

After the text-move White's rook is pinned against the undefended bishop on d3.

38 ♖b8!

Instead 38 ♖a5 ♕xd3 39 ♖xa8 ♘xa8 40 ♘cxe5 dxe5 41 ♕xe5+ ♔g8 leads only to perpetual check (after 42 ♕b8+).

38 ...   ♕xd3

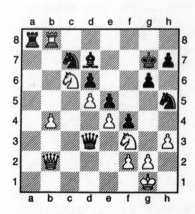

39 ♘cxe5!

Thanks to the rook on b8 this sacrifice, blowing open the long diagonal, is devastating.

39 ...   ♕d1+

White also wins after 39...dxe5 40 ♕xe5+ ♘f6 (or 40...♔h6 41 ♕g5+ ♔g7 42 ♕e7+ ♔h6 43 ♕f8+ ♘g7 44 ♕xf4+ mating) 41 ♕e7+ ♔h6 42 ♕f8+ ♔h5 43 ♕xf6.

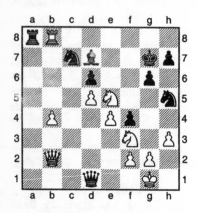

40 ♔h2   ♖a1

After 40...♖xb8 41 ♘xd7+ White will be two pawns up. With the text-move Black threatens mate himself, so White must mate with checks.

41 ♘g4+!

Even at this late stage White must be accurate. 41 ♘xd7+?? ♔h6 leads nowhere.

41 ...   ♔f7

42 ♘h6+

Again not 42 ♘g5+?? ♔e7.

42 ...   ♔e7

43 ♘g8+

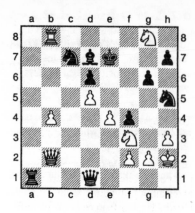

1-0

As 43...♔f7 44 ♘g5# is a beautiful mate with all White's remaining pieces taking part. The unique feature of this game is that the pieces participating in the mate mostly arrived via the other side of the board – the g8-knight came via a5 and the rook via c5 and b5.

Lessons from this game:

1) In closed positions, knight manoeuvres need special attention. A knight, once it has started on the wrong track, cannot easily switch to a new path.

2) Strategic aims can often be realized by tactical means – note how Tal used tactics to delay Black's ...f5.

3) Never forget about the ultimate target – the enemy king!

Jeroen Piket – Garry Kasparov
Tilburg 1989
King's Indian Defence, Classical Main Line

The Players

Jeroen Piket was born in 1969 in Leiden, the Netherlands. He was an extremely talented junior, competing regularly at grandmaster level while a teenager and achieving the GM title in 1989. Since then he has had an up-and-down career, periods of excellent results alternating with spells of inexplicable failure. He has an entertaining, dynamic style of play, with material imbalance and board-wide chaos a regular feature in his games.

Garry Kasparov (born 1963) is the greatest player of modern times, and has been World Champion (of one sort or another) since 1985. Tilburg 1989 was one of his best ever results, and took his rating for the first time higher than Bobby Fischer's record 2785 figure. In his next tournament, in Belgrade, he was in equally devastating form, taking his rating over 2800. For more information see Game 71.

The Game

A main-line King's Indian is set to become the standard race between wing attacks, when Kasparov introduces a novelty. It is more than a good new move; it is a whole new approach, which changes the entire landscape of the position. Completely adrift, Piket panics and grabs a rook, allowing Kasparov to smash through on the kingside. A striking finish follows.

1	d4	♘f6
2	♘f3	g6
3	c4	♗g7
4	♘c3	0-0
5	e4	d6
6	♗e2	e5
7	0-0	♘c6
8	d5	♘e7
9	♘e1	♘d7
10	♗e3	f5
11	f3	f4
12	♗f2	g5

The battle-lines are clearly drawn: Black will try to use his spatial plus on the kingside to launch a massive all-out attack, while White will aim to penetrate on the queenside. In itself Black's attack is the more dangerous, since if he achieves his aim – checkmate – the game is immediately over. However, this is rather an oversimplification, since White starts off with a slight lead, and once he has broken though on the queenside, he can very quickly start eliminating the back-up for Black's attack. In particular if he can force the exchange of the c8-bishop, this robs the attack of much of its potency, for the simple reason that this is the piece Black needs in a great many lines to sacrifice on h3 to crown his attack.

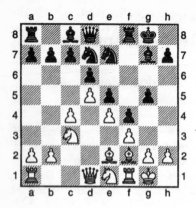

13 b4

Over the years White has tried a variety of moves here, all seeking to further his queenside attack while organizing his kingside defences as efficiently as possible. At the time of writing, the main moves are 13 a4 (intending 14 a5 and often playing 15 c5 as a pawn sacrifice) and 13 ♖c1 (also intending to sacrifice a pawn after 13...♘g6 14 c5). 13 b4 was the most popular in the 1980s, except for a brief vogue for 13 ♘b5 in 1987–8.

The most obvious way to prepare the c4-c5 advance is by 13 ♘d3, but this was discredited in the early days of the King's Indian. The problem is that the knight isn't very well placed on d3, where it gets in the way of the e2-bishop in particular. The classic example following this move is tremendously instructive, and highlights several themes that are relevant to our main game: 13...♘f6 14 c5 ♘g6 15 ♖c1 ♖f7 16 ♖c2 ♗f8 (...♖f7 and ...♗f8 is now an absolutely standard regrouping manoeuvre in many King's Indian lines) 17 cxd6 cxd6 18 ♕d2 g4 19 ♖fc1 g3! (a standard theme – Black is happy to sacrifice this pawn to open

lines) 20 hxg3 fxg3 21 ♗xg3 ♘h5 22 ♗h2 ♗e7 23 ♘b1 ♗d7 24 ♕e1 ♗g5 25 ♘d2 ♗e3+ 26 ♔h1 ♕g5 27 ♗f1 ♖af8 28 ♖d1 b5 29 a4 a6 30 axb5 axb5 31 ♖c7 ♖g7 32 ♘b3 ♘h4 33 ♖c2 ♗h3!.

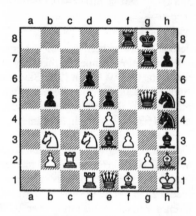

This bishop has been slumbering for much of the game but now lands the death-blow.

34 ♕e2 ♘xg2 35 ♗xg2 ♗xg2+ 36 ♕xg2 ♕h4 37 ♕xg7+ ♔xg7 38 ♖g2+ ♔h8 39 ♘e1 ♘f4 40 ♖g3 ♗f2 41 ♖g4 ♕h3 42 ♘d2 h5 0-1 Taimanov – Najdorf, Candidates tournament, Zurich 1953.

13	...	♘f6
14	c5	♘g6
15	cxd6	cxd6
16	♖c1	♖f7
17	a4	♗f8!?

This is Kasparov's new handling of the position. The old treatment was 17...h5 18 a5 ♗d7 19 ♘b5 ♗xb5 20 ♗xb5 g4 21 ♔h1 g3 22 ♗g1 gxh2 23 ♗f2. Black has indeed opened lines to the white king, but it is not easy for him to make further progress. He has had to surrender the light-squared bishop and his pawn on h5 occupies a square that his knights would like to use. If the pawn advances to h4, then it stops the queen coming to that square. Previously Black had seen this as just the price he had to pay to open up the kingside. Not Kasparov. He wanted to find a way to economize on this tempo, keep his light-squared bishop and still get in the kingside advance. The plan is to play as many useful moves as possible and to play ...g4 *unsupported by the h-pawn* when White's e4-pawn is inadequately defended – i.e. as soon as White plays ♘b5, which is a fundamental part of his plans. Although it might appear that the two sides are limbering up for an attack virtually independently of one another, the fates of these attacks turn out to be subtly linked, in the planning stage as well as when they are executed.

18 a5 ♗d7!

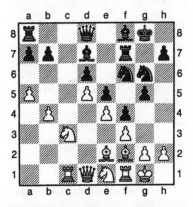

Posing White a dilemma. The next move on his programme is ♘b5, though this allows the "unsupported" ...g4. But what other useful moves does White have?

19 ♘b5?!

Piket decides to get on with it, and see what fate has in store for him. The popularity of this position for White plummeted after Kasparov's impressive display, but what later games there were featured 19 ♔h1!?:

1) 19...♕e8?! was a move Kasparov mentioned in his notes but it is unconvincing due to 20 ♘c2! h5 21 ♘a3 g4 (21...a6 stops a knight going to b5, but allows the knight to change route with great effect: 22 ♘c4 coming in to b6) 22 ♘cb5 ♗xb5 23 ♘xb5 g3 24 ♗xa7 gxh2 25 ♗f2 ♖b8 26 ♘c7 ♕e7 27 ♘e6 and Black was only able to thrash around in Van de Mortel – Cvitan, Oberwart 1994.

2) 19...♖g7 20 ♘b5 (20 ♖c2 {hoping for Black to play 20...h5} 20...♕e8 looks good now that White cannot play the ♘c2-a3 manoeuvre) 20...g4 21 ♘xa7 g3 22 ♗b6 ♕e8! 23 ♖c7 gxh2 24 ♖xb7 ♘h5 gave Black a good attacking position in Burgess – Badea, Prestwich 1990.

19 ... g4!

This move is best played immediately. Black need not, and should not surrender his light-squared bishop here. After 19...♗xb5?! 20 ♗xb5 g4 21 fxg4 ♘xe4 22 ♗d3 ♘f6 23 ♗f5, "the bishop becomes tremendously active" (Kasparov).

20 ♘c7

After 20 fxg4 ♘xe4 21 ♘c7 ♗a4 22 ♕xa4 ♖xc7 White's game is rather poor – his central phalanx is gone, and he has no prospects of establishing any sort of grip on the position.

After 20 ♘xa7, Black's accelerated kingside attack bears fruit: 20...g3! 21 ♗b6 ♕e7! (not here 21...gxh2+? 22 ♔xh2 ♕e7 23 ♖h1 ♘h5 24 ♔g1 ♘g3 25 ♖h2, which leaves White much better) 22 ♘b5 (22 ♖c7 gxh2+ 23 ♔xh2 ♘h5 does not give White time for

♖h1; 22 h3? ♗xh3 23 gxh3 ♕d7 gives Black an overwhelming attack, e.g. 24 ♗b5 ♕xh3 25 ♕d2 ♘h4 intending ...♖g7 and ...g2) 22...♘h5 23 ♔h1 gxh2 24 ♗f2 ♗xb5 25 ♗xb5 ♘g3+ 26 ♗xg3 fxg3 and although there is now a slight lull in the attack, Black will shortly move in for the kill – he has a large and stable advantage on the kingside.

20   ...   g3!

20...♗a4? 21 ♕xa4 ♖xc7 22 ♘d3 is very good for White, as Black has surrendered his light-squared bishop without any tangible rewards.

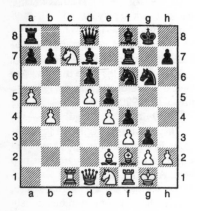

21   ♘xa8?

Piket panics and grabs the rook. It was not yet time for desperate measures – he should have gone in for 21 hxg3 fxg3! (21...♘h5?! 22 g4! ♘g3 23 ♘xa8 ♕h4 24 ♗xa7 and there is no obvious way to mate the white king; 24...♕h1+ 25 ♔f2 ♕h4 does not force a repetition either in view of 26 ♘d3 ♘xe4+ 27 ♔g1 ♘g3 28 ♘f2 ♗a4 29 ♕d2) 22 ♗xg3 ♗h6! (22...♘h5 23 ♗f2 ♘gf4 24 ♘e6! ♗xe6 25 dxe6 ♖g7 26 ♗c4 ♔h8 27 g4 is less clear – Kasparov) and now the time *has* come

to take the rook; he is to suffer in any event, and may need to give up some material to survive the attack:

1) 23 ♘e6 ♗xe6 24 dxe6 ♖g7 25 ♗c4?! d5!? (25...♔h8 26 ♖c3 ♘f4) 26 exd5 ♗xc1 gives Black a big advantage "for free".

2) 23 ♘xa8! ♘h5 and then:

2a) 24 ♗h2? ♗e3+ 25 ♖f2 (25 ♔h1?? ♕h4 forces mate) 25...♕h4 26 ♘d3 ♘gf4 27 ♖c2 (27 ♘e1 ♘xg2! 28 ♔xg2 ♖g7+ also mates; 27 ♕f1 ♘g3 28 ♗xg3 ♕xg3 wins as White cannot cope with the threats to f2 and g2, as well as the idea ...♖f6-h6) 27...♘h3+! 28 gxh3 ♕xh3 29 ♔h1 ♘g3+ 30 ♔g1 ♖g7 with an unavoidable mate.

2b) 24 ♗f2 ♘gf4 and now White can try:

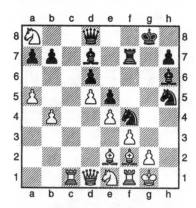

2b1) 25 ♖c7? ♗a4! 26 ♕xa4 (26 ♖c2 though humiliating, is probably best!) 26...♘xe2+ 27 ♔h1 (27 ♔h2? ♘hg3! 28 ♗xg3 ♗f4! wins cleanly) 27...♘hg3+ 28 ♗xg3 ♘xg3+ 29 ♔g1 ♗e3+ 30 ♖f2 ♖f4 wins since although 31 ♕d7 (31 ♖d7 blocks the queen's route to e8, and so 31...♕h4 wins) takes the queens off, it does not avoid mate after 31...♕xd7 32 ♖xd7 ♖h4.

2b2) 25 ♗c4 is a reasonable way to put up stubborn resistance. Black could probably take the a8-knight and then put the kingside under heavy siege, but the direct method, 25...♘h3+ 26 gxh3 ♖g7+ 27 ♔h1 ♗a4!, is more tempting. 28 ♕d3 (28 ♖c2 ♕c8 29 ♗h4 ♗e3 30 ♕d3 ♗xc2 31 ♕xc2 ♖g3 and Black wins; 28 ♕xa4? ♕c8) and now:

2b21) 28...♕c8? 29 f4 opens up some squares for the defending pieces to use.

2b22) 28...♘f4 29 ♕d2 ♕c8 30 ♗h4 (30 ♗e3? ♘h5) and it is not clear how Black should proceed.

2b23) 28...♗xc1 reduces the material deficit while keeping a strong attack.

2b3) 25 ♘d3! is the best defence:

2b31) 25...♘xg2?! (premature) 26 ♔xg2 ♖g7+ 27 ♔h2 (27 ♔h1? ♘g3+ 28 ♗xg3 ♖xg3 29 ♖f2 ♖h3+ 30 ♔g1 ♕h4 and Black wins) 27...♘g3! 28 ♗xg3 ♕g5?? (28...♖xg3 draws) 29 ♖g1 ♕h5+ 30 ♔g2 ♗e3 31 ♘f2 and White is winning.

2b32) 25...♖g7 and then:

2b321) 26 g4!? and now 26...♗a4!? is possibly more effective than the obvious continuation here, i.e. 26...♘xd3 27 ♕xd3 ♗xc1 28 ♖xc1 ♘f4, which is similar to the play following 26 ♘xf4 ♗xf4 27 g4, except that Black has lost a tempo.

2b322) 26 ♘xf4 ♗xf4 and here White has very little choice:

2b3221) 27 ♖c7? ♘g3! 28 ♖xd7? (28 ♕e1 ♕h4 29 ♗xg3 ♗xg3 30 ♕xg3 ♕xg3 31 ♖f2 doesn't give White enough for the queen) 28...♕h4! 29 ♖xg7+ ♔xg7 30 ♗xa7 ♘xe2+ 31 ♕xe2 ♗h2+ 32 ♔h1 ♗g3+ 33 ♔g1 ♕h2#.

2b3222) 27 ♖c3? allows a forced mate: 27...♖xg2+! 28 ♔xg2 ♕g5+ 29 ♔h1 ♘g3+ 30 ♗xg3 ♗xg3 and White is powerless against the queen's entry via h4.

2b3223) 27 g4! ♗xc1 28 ♕xc1 ♘f4 29 ♕e3 h5! "and Black's attack is very dangerous but it is possible to defend, for example 30 ♖c1 hxg4 31 fxg4 ♘xe2+ 32 ♕xe2 ♗xg4 33 ♕e3" – Kasparov.

21 ... ♘h5!

21...gxf2+ is far weaker, as the pace of Black's attack is greatly reduced. Specifically, White does not need to play the ♔g1-h1-g1 manoeuvre that we see in the game.

22 ♔h1

22 ♗xa7 ♕h4 23 h3 ♗xh3 (here we see an illustration of the role of this important bishop) 24 gxh3 (24 ♖f2 lasts longer) 24...♕xh3 25 ♖f2 gxf2+ 26 ♔xf2 ♘h4 27 ♘d3 ♕g3+ 28 ♔f1 ♘g2 (threatening 29...♘e3+, forcing mate) 29 ♕d2 ♕h2 30 ♗g1 ♘g3+ 31 ♔f2 ♘xe4+ 32 fxe4 ♕g3+ 33 ♔f1 ♘e3+ mating.

22 ... gxf2
23 ♖xf2 ♘g3+!

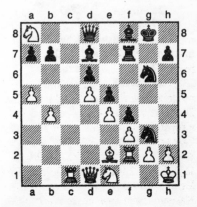

A wonderful way to exploit the fact that the king has gone to h1. The two tempi spent on ♔g1-h1-g1 are enough for Black to generate decisive threats.

24   ♔g1

24 hxg3? fxg3 forces mate.

24   ...   ♛xa8

Black's position can be considered winning since he has been able to open up lines to the white king without sacrificing; indeed he is slightly up on material.

25   ♗c4   a6!

Of course! Rather than the queen trying to find a way in via the kingside, the dark-square diagonal from a7 to g1 is now the ideal route.

26   ♛d3?!

White does not have to lose so quickly:

1) 26 ♘d3 ♛a7 27 ♘c5 ♗b5! 28 ♗xb5 axb5 29 hxg3 fxg3 30 ♖fc2 dxc5 31 bxc5 ♘f4 and before long the black queen will break through to the white king.

2) 26 hxg3 fxg3 27 ♖b2 and now that there is a check on h2, the queen reverts to its normal avenue of attack: 27...♛d8 28 ♔f1 (or 28 ♛d2 ♛h4) 28...♗h6 with a decisive attack.

26   ...   ♛a7

27   b5

27 ♖c2 is answered by 27...♗e7 followed by ...♗h4 and ...♘h1.

27   ...   axb5

28   ♗xb5   ♘h1!

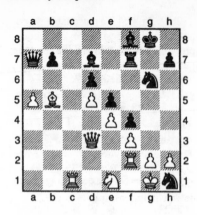

0-1

"The attack in this game reminds me of my young chess years. A pleasant memory!" – Kasparov.

Lessons from this game:

1) Really deep opening research has been a hallmark of Kasparov's domination of world chess. He does not just try to find new moves, but whole new plans and strategies.

2) Just because a particular move is an essential part of your strategic plan doesn't mean you have to prepare it by the crudest means available. Consider what your opponent is likely to want to do, and see if this gives you any additional ways to reach your goals.

3) If all else fails, fall back on stubborn defence, rather than lashing out in desperation.

Game 84
Ilia Smirin – Alexander Beliavsky
USSR Championship, Odessa 1989
Ruy Lopez, Breyer Variation

The Players

Ilia Smirin (born 1968) is one of the many Soviet émigrés (he was originally from Belarus) who now live in Israel. He made his big mark on the world chess scene with his impressive performances in the PCA Intel Grand Prix events throughout 1994 and 1995. He has represented Israel at Olympiads and other team championships since 1992.

Alexander Beliavsky's best achievement in 1989 was his tournament victory in Amsterdam, ahead of Speelman and Korchnoi, a success he was to repeat a year later. For more details of his career, see Game 78.

The Game

Alexander Beliavsky is a renowned expert on the super-solid Breyer Variation of the Ruy Lopez, and although his expertise is clear for everyone to see, one must regard this game as anything but solid! Smirin plays his part in an encounter which is a real slugfest, but it's Beliavsky who lands the final blow with a delicious double piece sacrifice and a king-hunt leading to inevitable mate.

1	e4	e5	13	♘f1	♗f8
2	♘f3	♘c6	14	♘g3	g6
3	♗b5	a6	15	♗g5	h6
4	♗a4	♘f6	16	♗d2	♗g7
5	0-0	♗e7	17	♕c1	
6	♖e1	b5			
7	♗b3	d6			
8	c3	0-0			
9	h3				

This is the main-line position of the Closed Spanish, and has occurred in many thousands of games. Black's next move, regrouping the knight for action via the d7-square, constitutes the Breyer Defence.

9	...	♘b8
10	d4	♘bd7
11	♘bd2	♗b7
12	♗c2	♖e8

A change from 17 a4!?, which we shall see in Fischer – Spassky, Match (game 1), Sveti Stefan 1992 (see Game 87).

With 17 ♕c1 White aims for kingside play and hopes to provoke a weakness in the black camp. Often this can be achieved through the Steinitzian advance of the h-pawn (see Game 5). The drawback is that, although the white queen and two bishops exert long-range pressure on the kingside, they also prevent White from connecting his rooks. Black may be able to exploit his more active pieces by opening the centre.

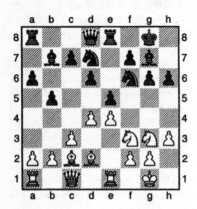

17 ...   ⌃h7

Varying from 17...h5, which occurred in another Smirin game from the same tournament: 18 ⌃h6 ⌃h7 19 ♕d2 ⌃xh6 20 ♕xh6 ♕f6 21 a4! ⌃df8 22 d5 c6 23 ♖ed1 c5 24 b4 ⌃d7 25 ⌃d3 c4 26 ⌃c2 ♖eb8 27 ♖a3! ⌃b6 28 ♖da1 and White's control of the a-file gave him a lasting initiative in Smirin – G. Georgadze, USSR Championship, Odessa 1989.

18 h4   d5!

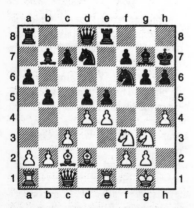

As mentioned before, Black's prospects of creating counterplay lie in meeting a wing attack with a classic break in the centre. More passive moves would allow White a free hand to attack on the kingside.

19 exd5

The main alternative is to press on for the attack with 19 h5. In his notes in *Informator* Beliavsky gives 19...dxe4 20 hxg6+ fxg6 21 ⌃xe4 exd4! (this is stronger than 21...⌃xe4 22 ⌃xe4 ⌃xe4 23 ♖xe4 exd4 24 ♖xe8 ♕xe8 25 cxd4 ♖c8 26 ♕c6 and White went on to win in Geller – Rubinetti, Siegen Olympiad 1970) and now 22 ⌃eg5+ doesn't work after 22...hxg5 23 ⌃xg5+ ⌃g8 24 ⌃xg6 ♖xe1+ 25 ♕xe1 ⌃f8 26 ⌃f7+ ⌃h8 27 f3 ⌃6h7. White can continue more conservatively with 22 ⌃xf6+ ♕xf6 23 ⌃xd4, but this is a situation where Black's active pieces in an open position give him the advantage. If, for example, 23...c5, one gets the distinct impression that White is getting pushed around the board.

19 ...   exd4

20 ⌃xd4?

It seems that initiative is more important than material here, and Beliavsky says as much when he gives a question mark to this natural recapture, preferring the pawn sacrifice starting with 20 h5!?, e.g. 20...dxc3 (it should be mentioned here that Black doesn't have to be so gluttonous; other moves certainly exist) 21 ⌃xc3 ⌃xd5 22 ⌃h4 when it is clear that, with the black structure on the kingside under some pressure, White has some compensation for the pawn. After 22...⌃f8 White can throw more wood on the fire with 23 ♖xe8 (Beliavsky gives the immediate 23 ⌃hf5 but it seems more accurate to exchange first, so that White's queen and dark-squared bishop remain on active diagonals) 23...♕xe8 24 ♘hf5!? gxf5 25 ♘xf5, when White has very dangerous threats. A sample variation is 25...♕d8 26 ♘e7+!? ♘e4 27 ♕d1! ♖xc3 28 ♘xd5 ♖xb2 29 ♗xe4+ ♔h8 and the position remains very unclear, although I suspect that White may be better.

Following 20 ♘xd4, however, Black is able to take over operations in the centre.

    20 ...   **♘e5!**

Black wants to capture on d5 with his queen, so as to set up powerful threats down the a8–h1 diagonal. Note that after ...♕xd5, mate on g2 will already be threatened.

    21 ♘e6!?   **♕xd5**
    22 ♘f4   **♕c6**

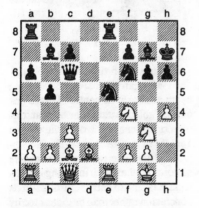

    23 h5

After 23 ♘e4 Black's pieces begin to dominate the board, e.g. 23...♘c4! 24 ♘xf6+ ♗xf6 25 h5 ♔g8! 26 hxg6 fxg6 27 ♖xe8+ ♖xe8 28 ♗xg6 ♖d8 (Beliavsky gives 28...♖e2, but this allows 29 ♗d3 ♖xd2 30 ♗xc4+) 29 ♗e1 ♗g5, when White is in big trouble.

After 30 f3 Black can simply cash in and win a piece with 30...♗xf4 31 ♕xf4 ♕xg6, as 32 ♕xc7 can be answered by the simplifying 32...♕b6+.

    23 ...   **♖ad8?**

After the more effective 23...♔g8!, removing the king from the pin and threatening ...g5, White begins to feel the heat, for example 24 hxg6 fxg6 25 ♗b3+ (or 25 f3 ♘xf3+! 26 gxf3 ♕xf3 27 ♖xe8+ ♖xe8 28 ♗e1 ♖e3 and Black wins) 25...♘c4 26 f3 g5 27 ♘fh5 ♘xh5 28 ♘xh5 ♗e5 and Black's more active pieces secure an advantage. If White tries the sacrifice 29 ♗xg5, hoping for 29...hxg5 30 ♕xg5+, then Black replies with 29...♕g6, hitting two pieces and winning one of them.

    24 hxg6+   **fxg6**
    25 ♕b1!

A fine move. White attacks the weakness on g6, surrendering the d2-bishop in the process. The character of the position changes once more, and Black has to be very careful.

    25 ...   **♖xd2**
    26 ♗xg6+   **♔g8**

Other moves leave White with a winning position, e.g.:

1) 26...♘xg6 27 ♕xg6+ ♔h8 28 ♘f5 ♖g8 29 ♖e6 ♕c5 30 ♖f1! and White has successfully met Black's threats, while White's own threats cannot be parried.

2) 26...♔h8 27 ♗xe8 ♘xe8 28 ♖xe5! ♗xe5 29 ♘g6+ ♔g7 30 ♘h5+ ♔h7 31 ♘xe5+ ♕e4 32 ♕xe4+ ♗xe4 33 ♖e1 ♗b7 34 ♘g4 and White has a healthy extra pawn in the endgame.

    27 ♗xe8   **♘xe8**
    28 ♕c1?

This mistake entitles Black to a spectacular finish, involving a double piece sacrifice followed by a good old-fashioned king-hunt. In his notes Beliavsky gives 28 ♕f5 ♘d6 29 ♕e6+ ♘df7 30 ♕xc6 ♗xc6 31 ♖e2, which is probably slightly better for Black, but that's not nearly as much fun, is it?

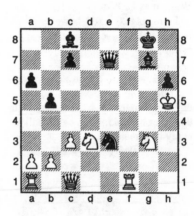

28	...	♖xf2!!
29	♔xf2	♘d3+
30	♘xd3	♕xg2+
31	♔e3	♘d6

Black threatens 32...♘c4+ 33 ♔f4 ♕f3#. If White protects the f3-square with 32 ♕d1 then Black continues 32...♗f6! and slowly quickly closes the net around the white king:

1) 33 ♕b3+ ♘c4+ 34 ♔f4 ♕f3#.

2) After 33 ♔f4 Black mates with 33...♗g5+ 34 ♔g4 ♗c8+ 35 ♔h5 ♕h3+ 36 ♔g6 ♗f5+ 37 ♘xf5 ♕xf5+ 38 ♔h5 ♗f6+ 39 ♔xh6 ♘f7#.

32	♖f1	♘c4+
33	♔f4	♕d5
34	♔g4	

There is no escape. 34 ♘f5 ♕e4+ 35 ♔g3 ♕xd3+ 36 ♔h4 ♕e4+! leads to another forced checkmate:

1) 37 ♔h5 ♕e2+ 38 ♔h4 ♕h2+ 39 ♔g4 ♘e5#.

2) 37 ♕f4 ♗f6+ 38 ♔g4 h5+! 39 ♔xh5 ♕e8+ and now:

2a) 40 ♔g4 ♕g6+ 41 ♔h3 ♕g2#.

2b) 40 ♔h6 ♕f8+ 41 ♔g6 (or 41 ♔h5 ♕f7+ 42 ♔g4 ♕g6+ – see "2a") 41...♕f7+ 42 ♔h6 ♕h7#.

34	...	♗c8+
35	♔h4	♕d8+
36	♔h5	♕e8+
37	♔h4	♕e7+
38	♔h5	♘e3

0-1

Lessons from this game:

1) Meet an offensive on the wing by an attack in the centre! This is one of the "golden rules" of chess and its importance cannot be overstated – see 18...d5! in this game.

2) Often when starting something as committal as Smirin's kingside attack, it is best to carry it through to its conclusion rather than be distracted by trifling matters. On this occasion the direct 20 h5! would have been much more troublesome for Black than the recapture 20 ♘xd4?.

3) Sometimes sneaky king moves can be very effective, even for the attacking player. 23...♔g8! (instead of 23...♖ad8) is an example of this.

Game 85

Vasily Ivanchuk – Artur Yusupov

Candidates match (game 9), Brussels 1991

King's Indian Defence, Fianchetto Variation

The Players

Vasily Ivanchuk (born 1969) is from the Ukraine and is one of the most talented players in modern chess. He encyclopaedic knowledge of chess openings is legendary, and his speed of thought equally remarkable. If he were able to make the most of his talent, he would surely be a real contender for World No. 1 spot, but he is a highly emotional player, who takes losses badly, tends to rush critical decisions when under pressure and sometimes lacks motivation. Nevertheless, he has comfortably maintained a position in the world's top eight players since 1990. However, he has never made much impact in world championship cycles, being knocked out by Yusupov in 1991 (as we are about to see), and by Kamsky in the 1994 PCA Candidates. Career highlights include: European Junior Champion 1986/7; winner of Linares 1991, beating both Kasparov and Karpov; winner of Wijk aan Zee 1996 and equal first at Belgrade 1997.

Artur Yusupov was born in 1960 in Moscow, but now lives in Germany. He was a pupil and subsequently a colleague of renowned trainer Mark Dvoretsky. Yusupov won the World Junior Championship in 1977, and was second in the USSR Championship at his first attempt, in 1979. He gained his grandmaster title in 1980. During the 1980s he established himself among the world's elite, but without ever looking a major threat to Karpov and Kasparov's dominance. He has reached the semi-final stage of the Candidates three times. In 1990 he survived a near-fatal shooting incident when he disturbed a robber, but still found the strength to continue with his matches. His chess is based on fine technique and a determined approach. In his writing he betrays an engaging and genuine modesty, which has made him an extremely popular author.

The Game

Yusupov had won the eighth game to tie the match. The rules were then that two rapid games would follow, with more games at faster time-limits being contested if the score remained level. Normally rapidplay games are somewhat scrappy affairs, with speed of the hands mattering as much as speed of thought. However, this one was a sacrificial masterpiece, on a par with Anderssen's games of the 1850s. Although Yusupov himself wasn't too impressed "It amused the audience", the game was published and highly praised around the world.

Yusupov's attack isn't quite sound, it must be said, but it is very close indeed. After Ivanchuk misses his one defensive chance, the finish is nothing short of magical.

1	c4	e5
2	g3	d6
3	♗g2	g6
4	d4	♘d7
5	♘c3	♗g7
6	♘f3	♘gf6
7	0-0	0-0

By a somewhat unusual move-order, the players have reached a Fianchetto King's Indian. This must have come as a considerable surprise to Ivanchuk because it is an opening that Yusupov hardly ever uses as Black.

8	♕c2	♖e8
9	♖d1	c6

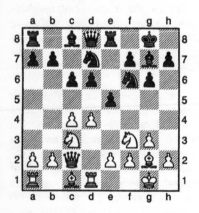

Neither player wants to release the central tension (...exd4 by Black or dxe5 by White), as this would be a strategic concession and reduce their winning chances.

10	b3	♕e7
11	♗a3	

11 e3 ♘f8 12 dxe5 dxe5 13 a4 is a quiet alternative which doesn't pose Black real problems.

11 e4!? (Seirawan) is a more ambitious way to handle the position, leading to more standard King's Indian play.

11	...	e4
12	♘g5	e3
13	f4?!	

13 f3 ♘f8 14 ♘ge4 is a better try for advantage; for details see a good opening book.

13	...	♘f8
14	b4	♗f5
15	♕b3	h6
16	♘f3	♘g4

Black prepares ...g5 and brings the knight within striking distance of the white king.

17	b5	

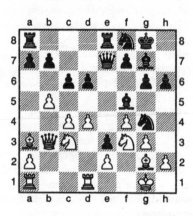

17	...	g5!

Yusupov bravely decides to press on with his kingside attack rather than spend time diverting forces to the defence of the queenside. Such decisions are never easy to make, and generally one must fall back on one's intuition, rather than make a decision based on analysis. Here Yusupov's judgement is vindicated.

18	bxc6	bxc6
19	♘e5!?	

19 fxg5 hxg5 20 ♘e5 is suggested by Dvoretsky as "more cautious", as it gives Black less to bite upon.

19	...	**gxf4**
20	**♘xc6**	**♕g5**
21	**♗xd6**	**♘g6**

21...♘xh2? 22 ♗xf4! (22 ♔xh2? ♕xg3+ 23 ♔h1 ♘g6 gives Black good attacking prospects) 22...♕h5 23 ♘d5 gives White the threats 24 ♘ce7+ and 24 ♘xe3.

22	**♘d5**

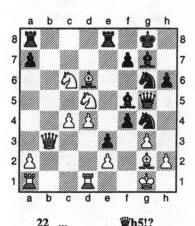

22	...	**♕h5!?**

This move has come in for some criticism that does not appear to be justified. Here are the supposed improvements:

1) 22...fxg3? is suggested by Dvoretsky as a strong and simple attacking method. 23 ♗xg3 h5 (intending ...h4) was strongly supported by Dvoretsky and Seirawan, but neither commentator (Dvoretsky gave no more analysis, while Seirawan considered only passive replies) spotted that 24 h4! forces a retreat since 24...♘xh4?? 25 ♗f4 wins the black queen (25...♕g6 26 ♘ce7+).

2) 22...♘xh2 and now:

2a) 23 ♘xf4? ♕xg3 24 ♘xg6 (or 24 ♘h5 ♕xd6) 24...♕xg6! is winning for Black.

2b) 23 ♔xh2 ♕xg3+ 24 ♔h1 gives Black at least a draw.

2c) 23 ♗xf4! puts the onus on Black to show that he has enough: 23...♕h5 (23...♘xf4? 24 gxf4) 24 ♕b7 (or 24 ♕b5 ♘g4) 24...♕g4 (24...♔h8? 25 ♘xe3) 25 ♘ce7+ ♘xe7 26 ♘xe7+ ♖xe7 27 ♕xe7 ♗f6 28 ♕b7 (otherwise 28...♕h2+ 29 ♔f1 ♗e4) 28...♖e8 may well be enough to draw, e.g. 29 ♕c6 ♖e6; 29 ♕b5 ♖d8 30 ♕c6 ♗c2; or 29 ♔f1 ♘h2+ 30 ♔g1 (30 ♔e1? ♗e4!) 30...♘g4 repeating.

23	**h4**	**♘xh4?**

"I should note that at this moment a mighty group of grandmasters (Karpov, Korchnoi, Short, M. Gurevich, ...) had gathered in the press centre. They all considered the sacrifice that Artur played to be totally incorrect." – Dvoretsky.

23...fxg3 24 ♗xg3 ♘xh4 was rejected by Yusupov because he thought it led to a repetition after 25 ♘f4 (25 ♘ce7+ ♔h7 26 ♘f4 ♕g5 keeps the pressure on White's position) 25...♕g5 26 ♘h3 ♕h5 but Black can instead play 26...♕f6!.

24	**gxh4**	**♕xh4**

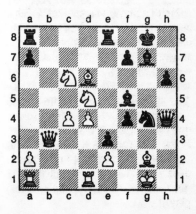

25 ♘de7+?

It is not at all clear why Ivanchuk chose to give check with this knight. White already has a large material advantage, and should be trying to find the best way to defend his king, and for this purpose the d5-knight is better placed than its colleague on c6. Actually, there are conflicting reports about this move. Seirawan claims that Ivanchuk simply picked up the wrong knight, whereas Dvoretsky puts forward a rational explanation for his decision. Both men were present at the match, but given that Ivanchuk's body language isn't the easiest to read, it is hard to know what to believe!

The analysis after 25 ♘ce7+! ♔h8 26 ♘xf5 ♕h2+ 27 ♔f1 ♗e5!? (Dvoretsky speculates that it was this possibility that encouraged Ivanchuk to give check with the other knight on e7, leaving the c6-knight to cover e5) is as follows:

1) 28 ♗xe5+? ♖xe5 29 dxe5 ♖g8 (threatening 30...♕h1+ 31 ♗xh1 ♘h2+ 32 ♔e1 ♖g1#) and then:

1a) 30 ♘dxe3? fxe3 31 ♘xe3 ♕f4+ 32 ♗f3 (32 ♔e1 ♘xe3 with a winning attack) 32...♘xe3+ 33 ♔e1 ♖g1+ 34 ♔f2 (34 ♔d2 ♕d4+ 35 ♕d3 ♘xc4+ and mate next move) 34...♘g4+ 35 ♔xg1 ♕h2+ 36 ♔f1 ♕f2#.

1b) 30 ♘g7!! ♖xg7?! (Black should take the draw by 30...♕g3 31 ♔g1 ♕f2+ 32 ♔h1 ♕h4+, etc.) 31 ♕b8+ ♖g8 32 ♕xg8+ ♔xg8 33 ♘f6+ ♘xf6 34 exf6 and Black is struggling to draw.

2) 28 dxe5! and then:

2a) 28...♖g8 (with the by now familiar threat of 29...♕h1+) 29 ♘dxe3! fxe3 (29...♘xe3+ 30 ♘xe3 fxe3 31 ♕b7 defends securely, and so wins) 30 e6! wins.

2b) 28...f3 29 exf3 e2+ 30 ♔xe2 ♕xg2+ 31 ♔d3 and now that the king has reached freedom, Black can resign.

Conclusion: 25 ♘ce7+ would have won.

Another idea for White is 25 ♗xf4 ♕f2+ 26 ♔h1, which should be met by 26...♕h4+, with a perpetual check.

25 ...   ♔h8
26 ♘xf5   ♕h2+
27 ♔f1

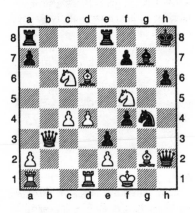

27 ...   ♖e6!

There are two alternatives, one bad and one reasonable:

1) 27...♖g8? 28 ♘xe3! ♗xd4 (not 28...♘xe3+? 29 ♕xe3) 29 ♖xd4 ♘xe3+ 30 ♔e1 ♖xg2 31 ♗e5+ ♔g8 32 ♕d3 leaves White substantially better.

2) 27...♗f6!? (planning both ...♖g8 and ...♗h4-f2) 28 ♖d3 (28 c5 ♖g8 29 ♕d5 ♕h1+!! 30 ♗xh1 ♘h2+ 31 ♔e1 ♖g1#) and now Black has two good continuations:

2a) 28...♖g8 29 ♖xe3 ♘xe3+ 30 ♘xe3 ♖ae8 31 ♘e5 ♗xe5 32 ♗xe5+ ♖xe5 33 dxe5 fxe3 34 ♕b7 h5!! (not 34...♖g4?, which loses to 35 ♕c8+), intending 35...♖g4, is good for Black.

2b) 28...♗h4!? 29 ♖xe3 ♗f2 30 ♖xe8+ ♖xe8 31 e4 ♕g1+ 32 ♔e2 ♕xg2 gives Black a powerful attack.

28 ♕b7?

It is probably too late to save the game, but Ivanchuk could certainly have made it far more difficult for Black:

1) 28 ♖d3 ♖g8! (this is stronger than 28...♖xd6 29 ♘xd6 f3 30 exf3 e2+ 31 ♔xe2 ♕xg2+ 32 ♔e1) 29 ♘ce7 ♗xd4 30 ♘xg8 ♖g6 31 ♗xf4 ♕xf4+ 32 ♔e1 ♗xa1 gives Black a strong attack for what is now a relatively small material deficit.

2) 28 ♘ce7! (the aim is to stop the black rook reaching the g-file) and then:

2a) 28...♖xd6? 29 ♘xd6 f3 and Black gets mated: 30 ♘xf7+ ♔h7 31 ♕d3#.

2b) 28...♗f6? loses to 29 ♕b7.

2c) 28...♖xe7 is a draw at best:

2c1) 29 ♘xe7 ♕g3 30 ♔g1 is a draw.

2c2) 29 ♖ab1?! ♖g8 30 ♕b8 (30 ♗xe7 ♗e5) 30...♖e4! (30...♗f8? 31 ♗xf4; 30...♖xb8 31 ♖xb8+ ♔h7 32 ♘xe7) 31 ♘e7 (31 ♖xa7? ♗f8! forces mate) gives Black two good options:

2c21) 31...♖xe7 32 ♗xe7 (32 ♗xf4 ♕h5) 32...♗f8 and the white king remains in considerable danger.

2c22) 31...♗f8 32 ♘g6+ (32 ♗e5+ ♘xe5 33 ♘xg8 ♕g3 34 ♔g1 f3) 32...fxg6 33 ♗xf8 f3 34 ♕xh2 ♘xh2+ 35 ♔g1 ♖xf8 36 ♔xh2 fxg2 is a promising ending for Black.

2c3) 29 ♗xe7 f3 30 exf3 e2+ 31 ♔e1!? (rather than 31 ♔xe2? ♕xg2+ 32 ♔d3 ♕xf3+) and it is not so easy for Black to justify his play.

2d) 28...♖g8!! seems to win, but it is very complicated:

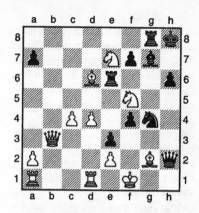

2d1) 29 ♘xg8 ♖g6 and now:

2d11) 30 ♘xe3? ♘xe3+ 31 ♔e1 (or 31 ♕xe3 ♕xg2+ 32 ♔e1 fxe3) 31...♖xg2 32 ♕d3 ♘f1 wins, e.g. 33 ♗e7 (to stop 33...♕h4+) 33...♖g3 34 ♕f5 f3!.

2d12) 30 ♕xe3 ♘xe3+ 31 ♘xe3 ♖xd6 32 ♘g4 ♕g3 33 ♘8xh6 ♗xh6 34 ♘e5 f3 35 exf3 ♗e3 36 ♘g4 ♗xd4 and Black wins.

2d2) 29 ♕d3 ♗f8 (29...♗f6?? 30 ♘xg8) 30 ♘xg8 ♖g6 31 ♘xe3 ♘xe3+ 32 ♔e1 ♗xd6 33 c5 f3! 34 ♗xf3 ♘c4! forces mate: 35 ♕xc4 ♗f4, etc.

2d3) 29 ♕b7 ♗xd4 30 ♘xg8 ♖g6 wins for Black.

2d4) 29 ♕b2!? and here:

2d41) 29...♗f8 30 d5+ ♔h7 31 ♘xg8 ♖g6 32 ♘f6+ ♘xf6 33 ♘xe3 ♗xd6 with an irresistible attack according to Dvoretsky, but 34 ♕xf6 ♖xf6 35 ♘g4 would certainly appear to resist!

2d42) 29...♘f2!? is a decent try, e.g. 30 ♘xh6 ♖xh6 or 30 ♖db1 ♘h3 31 ♔e1 ♕xg2, but the next line renders it irrelevant.

2d43) 29...♗e5!! 30 ♗xe5+ (30 ♘xg8 ♖g6) 30...♘xe5 31 ♘xg8 ♖g6 32 ♕b7 f3 forces mate.

28 ...   ℤg6!!

28...ℤg8? 29 ♘ce7 makes it difficult for a rook to stay on the g-file.

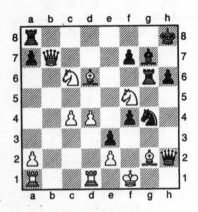

29 ♕xa8+   ♔h7

The threat is 30...♕h1+!! 31 ♗xh1 ♘h2+ 32 ♔e1 ℤg1#.

30 ♕g8+!

White must give up his queen to defend against the threatened mate.

After 30 ♘xe3? ♘xe3+ 31 ♔e1, the clearest win is 31...♘xc4, cutting off the king's flight-square d2.

30 ...   ♔xg8
31 ♘ce7+   ♔h7
32 ♘xg6   fxg6
33 ♘xg7   ♘f2!!

Not obvious, but very strong. Black simply threatens to mate by 34...♘h3.

34 ♗xf4   ♕xf4
35 ♘e6

35 ℤdb1 ♘h3+ 36 ♔e1 ♕h4+ 37 ♔d1 ♕xd4+ 38 ♔c2 ♕xc4+ 39 ♔b2 ♕xe2+ is utterly hopeless for White.

35 ...   ♕h2

36 ℤdb1   ♘h3
37 ℤb7+

37 ♔e1 ♕xg2 38 ♔d1 ♕e4 picks off the white knight.

37 ...   ♔g8
38 ℤb8+   ♕xb8
39 ♗xh3   ♕g3

0-1

Lessons from this game:

1) A policy of unrelenting aggression often pays off in chess, especially at fast time-limits.

2) If the enemy king is cut off from most of its potential defenders, it may be worth sacrificing a whole warehouse of material to attack it – it is a *local* superiority of force that a successful attack needs.

3) When you have correctly worked out which move is best, make sure you pick up the right piece!

Nigel Short – Jan Timman
Tilburg 1991
Alekhine Defence, Fianchetto Variation

The Players

Nigel Short (born 1965) is one of the strongest and most famous English players of all time and the only Englishman to challenge for an official World Championship. In 1980 he was second to Kasparov in the World Junior Championship. Two years later Short left school to concentrate solely on chess and he fully justified his decision by rapidly rising up the charts. In 1984 he achieved his grandmaster title and a year later became the first English player to reach the Candidates stage of the World Championship. He also qualified as a Candidate in the next cycle, although he was knocked out by fellow Englishman Jon Speelman. His third attempt as a Candidate proved much more successful. A revenge win against Speelman, followed by further successes over Gelfand, Karpov (Karpov's first match defeat by anyone other than Kasparov) and Timman catapulted the English GM to the role of challenger to Kasparov's title. The pair met in London in 1993, actually to battle for the PCA World Championship following their breakaway from FIDE, with Kasparov winning by a comfortable margin.

Jan Timman (born 1951) has been one of Western Europe's top grandmasters since the late 1970s. For more information see Game 73.

The Game

Playing with the white pieces, Short reaches a familiar opening and emerges with a comfortable advantage. After that, it's difficult to suggest a better way to conduct the attack on the black king than Short's own forceful method. The thing that makes the game remarkable, however, is Short's incredible king-march. Timman can only watch helplessly as Short's monarch joins in the fun and helps to set up a mating net.

1 e4	♘f6
2 e5	♘d5
3 d4	d6
4 ♘f3	g6
5 ♗c4	♘b6
6 ♗b3	♗g7
7 ♕e2	

Supporting the e5-pawn, which is used as a spearhead for any white attack in the future, and guarantees

White a healthy space advantage. 7 a4 is also popular, planning to harass the black knight with a4-a5. Black can either prevent this with 7...a5, which could well lead to the main game, or else delve into immense complications following 7...dxe5!? 8 a5 ♘6d7 9 ♗xf7+! ♔xf7 10 ♘g5+ ♔g8 11 ♘e6 ♕e8 12 ♘xc7.

7 ...	♘c6

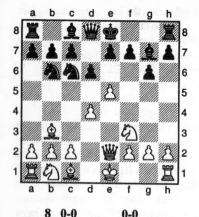

8   0-0   0-0

Black would like to pin the knight on f3, but the immediate 8...♗g4 allows 9 ♗xf7+! ♔xf7 10 ♘g5+ and 11 ♕xg4. Now White takes steps to prevent this.

9   h3   a5
10   a4!

This is a good move, which prevents Black from claiming extra space on the queenside by simply pushing his a-pawn up the board. For example, after 10 c3 a4! the white bishop is forced to move off its favourite diagonal. Indeed, following 11 ♗c2 Black can take over the diagonal himself with 11...♗e6!.

10   ...   dxe5
11   dxe5   ♘d4
12   ♘xd4   ♕xd4
13   ♖e1

Black has succeeded in exchanging a pair of minor pieces, which is generally a good idea in a slightly cramped position. However, not all of his problems have been solved. Black still has to find a suitable developing square for the c8-bishop. The f5-square looks a natural choice, but here it can be attacked with g2-g4. In this game Black

opts to close the a2–g8 diagonal, which has the value of blunting White's b3-bishop, but presents new development problems.

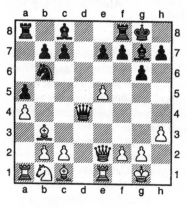

13   ...   e6
14   ♘d2

Nigel Short was already familiar with this position, having reached it four years earlier. Short – Hennigan, British Championship, Swansea 1987 continued 14...♗d7 15 c3 ♕c5 16 ♘f3 ♗c6 17 ♗e3 ♕e7 18 ♗g5 ♕c5 19 ♘d4 ♗d5 20 ♗xd5 ♕xd5 21 f4 ♕c4 22 ♕xc4 ♘xc4 23 b3 ♘b6 24 c4 ♖fc8 25 ♖ad1 ♗f8 26 ♘b5 ♗c5+ 27 ♔f1 c6 28 ♘d6! and Short nurtured this endgame advantage into a full point. One can only assume that Timman's divergence here was his attempt at an improvement over Hennigan's play, but it doesn't really have the desired effect.

14   ...   ♘d5
15   ♘f3   ♕c5
16   ♕e4   ♕b4
17   ♗c4   ♘b6
18   b3!

A revealing moment. White can play for a small plus with 18 ♗d3, but it has always been more in Short's character to gamble for a larger advantage. With 18 b3 White keeps the queens on the board, at the cost of accepting a split pawn-structure on the queenside.

 18 ...   **♘xc4**
 19 bxc4 **♖e8**

Black had to move this rook, as White was threatening a skewer with ♗a3. Given time, Black will attempt to unravel with ...♗d7-c6, so White takes steps to prevent this by seizing control of the open file.

 20 ♖d1   **♕c5**
 21 ♕h4   **b6**

Grabbing the e-pawn would be suicidal. After 21...♗xe5? 22 ♗a3 the queen would not be able to stay defending the bishop.

 22 ♗e3

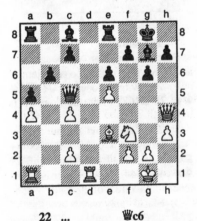

 22 ...   **♕c6**

With this move Black plans to line up his queen and bishop on the a8–h1 diagonal, which will make it very difficult for White to utilize his knight in the attack. More passive defence with 22...♕f8 allows White to build up a powerful attack with 23 ♘g5 h6 24 ♘e4!, when the knight has reached an aggressive outpost. Attempting to push away the queen with 24...g5 would run into a convincing refutation: 25 ♗xg5! hxg5 26 ♕xg5 ♔h7 (or 26...♕e7 27 ♘f6+ ♔f8 28 ♖d4! and ♖h4+) 27 ♕h5+! ♗h6 (27...♔g8 28 ♘f6+ ♗xf6 29 exf6 also wins for White as Black can do nothing to prevent ♖d3-g3 and mate) 28 ♘f6+ ♔g7 (28...♔h8 29 ♖d4, followed by ♖g4 and ♖g8+ wins) 29 ♖d4 ♕h8 30 ♖g4+ ♔f8 31 ♕xh6+!! ♕xh6 32 ♖g8+ ♔e7 33 ♖xe8#.

 23 ♗h6   **♗h8**

Capturing on h6 merely accelerates White's attack. After 23...♗xh6? 24 ♕xh6 ♗b7 25 ♖d4! White swings the rook to h4 and wins easily. With 23...♗h8 Black keeps his vital defensive bishop, but at a price. The presence of a white bishop on h6 makes Black's back rank extremely weak, a fact emphasized by Short's very next move.

 24 ♖d8!

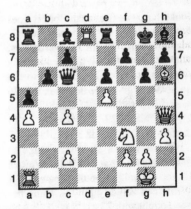

 24 ...   **♗b7**

Often when defending a difficult position it is worth sacrificing some material to relieve the pressure and

change the complexion of the position.
Here Timman could perhaps have tried
24...♗d7. White can then win Black's
queen for rook and bishop with 25
♘d4 ♖axd8 26 ♘xc6 ♗xc6, but his
position would be hard to break down.

25 ♖ad1

White's domination of the d-file is
very apparent. White now threatens
♕e7!, followed by ♖xa8 and then ♖d8,
after which Black's back rank defence
caves in.

25 ...　　　♗g7

Timman reverses his decision on
move 23 by offering the exchange of
bishops, but given the alternatives it
looks like he had no choice.

1) 25...♗xe5 fails to 26 ♖xa8 (but
not 26 ♘xe5?? ♕xg2#) 26...♗xa8 27
♖d8 ♗d6 (27...♗g7 28 ♕e7! ♗xh6 29
♕xe8+ wins for White, as does 27...f6
28 ♖xe8+ ♕xe8 29 ♘xe5 fxe5 30
♕f6) 28 ♖xd6! ♕xd6 29 ♕f6 and mate
on g7 can only be avoided by the loss
of the queen.

2) Grabbing a pawn with 25...♕xa4
looks far too extravagant, but it does
have its points: in particular the b7-
bishop comes to life. Nevertheless,
with accurate play White can reach a
winning position. In his notes to the
game Short gives the complex line 26
♕e7 ♗xf3 and now 27 ♖xa8!? ♗xa8
28 ♖d8 ♕a1+ 29 ♔h2 ♗xe5+ 30 f4
♗xf4+ 31 ♗xf4 ♖xd8 32 ♕xd8+ ♔g7
33 ♕xa8 with a clear advantage to
White. It's true that in this line White's
bishop outweighs the three pawns, but
White can actually put the game beyond doubt with 27 gxf3! ♕c6 28 ♗g5
(Short correctly points out that the immediate 28 ♖1d7 fails to 28...♕xd7 29
♕xd7 ♖exd8, but 28 ♗g5 now threatens 29 ♖1d7) 28...♔g7 (28...♗xe5 29

♖1d7 ♕xd7 30 ♕xd7 ♖exd8 31 ♗xd8
a4 32 ♕e8+ ♔g7 33 ♗f6+ ♔xf6 34
♕xa8 wins) 29 ♗f6+ ♔h6 30 ♖1d4!
(threatening ♖h4#) 30...g5 31 ♕xf7!
and White's attack crashes through,
for example 31...♕xf3 32 ♗xg5+ and
33 ♕xf3, or 31...♖axd8 32 ♗xg5+!
♔xg5 33 ♖g4+ ♔h6 34 ♕f4+ ♔h5 35
♕g5#.

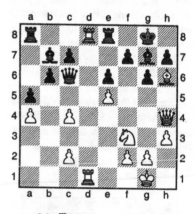

26 ♖8d7!

Black has only one way out after 26
♗xg7, but it proves to be sufficient:

1) 26...♔xg7? loses to 27 ♕f6+
♔g8 28 ♖1d7, when the f7-pawn is
lost.

2) 26...♖exd8?? is another case of
"the wrong rook". After 27 ♖xd8+
♖xd8 (27...♔xg7 28 ♕f6+ ♔h6 29
♖d4 and ♖h4#) 28 ♕f6! there is no defence to the threat of 29 ♗h6.

3) Black's only way is 26...♖axd8!
27 ♖xd8 (White could try 27 ♕f6, but
following 27...♖xd1+ 28 ♔h2 ♕c5 29
♗h6 ♕f8 30 ♗xf8 ♖xf8 Black's two
rooks fully compensate for White's
queen) 27...♔xg7! 28 ♕f6+ ♔g8 and
Black holds on.

With the text-move, 26 ♖8d7, White
threatens 27 ♗xg7 ♔xg7 28 ♕f6+.

26 ...   ♖f8

Timman's original intention had been 26...♕e4, but he then saw that White could win brilliantly with 27 ♖xf7!! ♕xh4 (27...♔xf7 28 ♘g5+) 28 ♖xg7+ ♔h8 29 ♘xh4, when White is a piece up. Note that 26...♗xe5 also allows 27 ♖xf7!, because 27...♔xf7 28 ♘xe5+ wins the queen.

27	♗xg7	♔xg7
28	♖1d4	♖ae8
29	♕f6+	♔g8
30	h4!	

The next stage. White intends to probe with h4-h5, inducing a further weakness in the black camp, as Black obviously cannot allow the pawn to reach h6. Black's next move prevents this, but Short has another, much more devious idea in mind.

30	...	h5
31	♔h2!!	

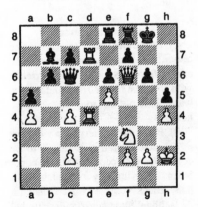

The start of an amazing concept. White's main idea is to march the king to h6 and deliver mate with ♕g7. Using the king in such an attacking fashion is very rare in chess, which makes it all the more startling when it does actually happen. In fact, Short is no stranger to such a king journey. He once performed a similar march to defeat Garry Kasparov.

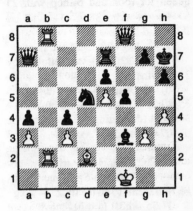

Kasparov – Short
"Speed Chess Challenge" (game 3), London 1987

Superficially Black's king looks to be in some trouble, but Short boldly ran into the open with 45...♔g6! 46 ♗c1 ♔h5! and suddenly his king was totally safe, while the World Champion's own king faced a vicious counterattack. After 47 ♖a8 ♕c5 48 ♖c8 ♕xa3 49 g4+ ♗xg4 50 ♖xc4 ♕a1 a bewildered Kasparov was forced to admit defeat.

We now return to Short – Timman.

31 ...   ♖c8

This move allows White to carry out the basic plan to its logical conclusion. A much stiffer defence is put up by 31...♗c8, attacking the d7-rook. However, White can still win in a brilliant way by 32 g4!:

1) 32...♗xd7 33 gxh5 ♔h7 (or 33...gxh5 34 ♕g5+ ♔h7 35 ♕xh5+ ♔g7 36 ♖g4#) 34 ♘g5+ ♔h6 (34...♔g8

35 h6 and ♕g7#) 35 ♘xf7+! ♖xf7 36 ♕xg6#.

2) 32...♗b7 33 ♖d3 hxg4 34 h5 gxh5 35 ♕g5+ ♚h7 36 ♕xh5+ ♚g7 37 ♕xg4+ ♚h6 38 ♕g5+ ♚h7 39 ♖3d4 and ♖h4#.

3) 32...hxg4 33 ♘g5! and now:

3a) 33...♗b7 34 ♘e4! followed by 35 h5 wins.

3b) 33...♗xd7 34 h5 g3+ (34...gxh5 35 ♕h6) 35 fxg3 ♕xa4 36 h6 ♕xc2+ 37 ♖d2! (deflecting the queen off the b1–h7 diagonal) 37...♕xd2+ 38 ♚h3 and mate on g7.

3c) 33...g3+ is the trickiest defence, but Jonathan Speelman's suggestion seems to do the trick: 34 ♚xg3 ♗xd7 35 ♚h2!! (a quiet move to set up deadly threats) 35...♕xa4 36 h5 gxh5 37 ♖h4 and Black has no good defence against ♖xh5 and ♖h8#.

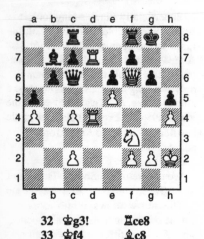

| 32 | ♚g3! | | ♖ce8 |
| 33 | ♚f4 | | ♗c8 |

34 ♚g5

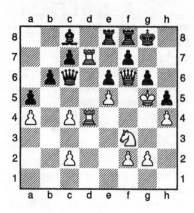

1-0

The only way to prevent 35 ♚h6 is by 34...♚h7, but then White has a choice of wins. Either 35 ♖xf7+ ♖xf7 36 ♕xf7+ ♚h8 37 ♚h6 or 35 ♕xg6+ ♚h8 36 ♕h6+ ♚g8 37 ♚f6 would do the job.

Lessons from this game:

1) Be careful about entering a line in which your opponent is already an expert. Short had previous experience with this line of the Alekhine and he was able to put this to good use at the board.

2) Pawn moves can play a vital part in an attack, even if it seems to be dominated by piece-play. Here Short's 30 h4! paves the way for the later brilliant attack.

3) Nigel Short is particularly lethal with his king!

Robert Fischer – Boris Spassky
Match (game 1), Sveti Stefan 1992
Ruy Lopez (Spanish), Breyer Defence

The Players

Robert Fischer (born 1943) was World Champion 1972–5, and arguably the greatest player ever. See Game 38 for further details.

Boris Spassky (born 1937) was World Champion 1969–72. For more information see Game 42.

The Game

The match was a major event in chess history: the long-awaited return of one of the lost legends of chess. Bobby Fischer had not played a competitive game since 1972 and had hardly been seen in public in the intervening time. It was as if he had reappeared out of a time capsule. Certainly it was distasteful that the match was played in war-torn Yugoslavia in violation of UN sanctions. Fischer's widely-reported extreme racism was also a cause for sadness. But these concerns were secondary to the joy that chess fans felt about Bobby being back.

Sadly, this was not the start of a true come-back. The world will never know how Bobby would have fared in a match against Kasparov or in a top-level tournament against all the young lions of the 1990s. Since winning this match against Spassky, Fischer has not played again, and at a press conference in 1995 to promote a form of "shuffle chess", he pronounced that chess was "dead".

The featured game is the first of the match. Spassky replies somewhat poorly to a new move from Fischer and never gets another look-in. A classic build-up on the a-file forces Black into a desperate sacrifice, whereupon Fischer opens the battle on all fronts and sacrifices the piece back to expose the black king.

1	e4	e5
2	♘f3	♘c6
3	♗b5	a6
4	♗a4	♘f6
5	0-0	♗e7
6	♖e1	b5
7	♗b3	d6
8	c3	0-0
9	h3	♘b8

This has for a long time been one of Spassky's standard openings.

10	d4	♘bd7

11	♘bd2	

11 c4 ♗b7 12 ♘c3 c6 is another reasonable line, but Bobby prefers the standard, classical approach.

11	...	♗b7
12	♗c2	♖e8
13	♘f1	

13 b4 was played in the tenth game of the Fischer – Spassky match in 1972.

13	...	♗f8
14	♘g3	g6

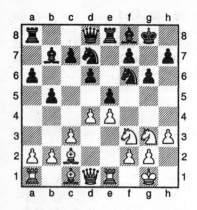

15 &g5

This excellent, probing move was actually introduced into top-level practice in 1966 by none other than Boris Spassky! 15 &d2 is an older move, with similar aims, but with the text-move White seeks to provoke a weakness.

15 ...   h6

In several other lines of the Closed Spanish in which the white bishop is still on b3, Black often feels obliged to play this move to stop ideas of ♘g5. Since White has already had to drop the bishop back to c2 to support the e4-pawn, a little trickery was needed here to achieve the same goal.

16 &d2

The fact that the pawn is on h6 rather than h7 may appear to be a minor point, but the game is likely to develop into a tense battle across the entire board. In that scenario, one chink in the armour can make all the difference: a tactic works that would not have done otherwise, Black's natural plan fails because it would leave his kingside light squares too weak, or whatever.

16 ...   &g7

16...exd4 17 cxd4 c5 was played in the third and fifth games of the match:

1) 18 &f4 was Fischer's odd and ineffective choice in the third game – after 18...cxd4 19 ♘xd4 ♘e5 20 b3 d5 Spassky blew open the centre, and Fischer was lucky to escape with a draw.

2) 18 d5 ♘b6 19 &a5! ♘fd7 20 b3 &g7 21 ♖c1 ♕f6 occurred in the fifth game. White is probably a shade better here, but he quickly allowed things to slide downhill.

17 a4!

A strong positional move, probing Black's queenside, and in effect "developing" the a1-rook. There is no actual threat against the b5-pawn as yet, but White can now threaten the pawn in just one move. Therefore Black will need to be that bit more vigilant. 17 ♕c1 was seen in Game 84, Smirin – Beliavsky.

17 ...   c5
18 d5   c4

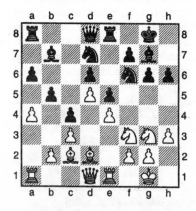

19 b4!

This was a new move at the time of this game. It forces an immediate and important decision from Black: does he open the queenside by capturing *en passant*, when his b5-pawn may prove weak, or does he accept that White has a space advantage and try to absorb the queenside pressure?

19 ...   ♘h7?!

Spassky, despite his immense experience in positions of this type, makes the wrong choice. White's queenside play, although he only has the a-file along which to operate, is very dangerous indeed, while Black's only real hope of counterplay, the ...f5 advance, is difficult to engineer in any satisfactory way. However, this is easy to say with hindsight. Other tries:

1) 19...a5?! is insufficient (no surprise since Black starts a skirmish in a part of board where he is outnumbered) in view of 20 axb5 axb4 21 cxb4 ♖xa1 22 ♕xa1 and now, as Suttles points out, 22...♕b6 fails to 23 ♗e3 ♕xb5 24 ♗a4 ♕a6 25 ♗c6!.

2) 19...♕e7 is Seirawan's preference if Black is to go for the solid approach. The plan is to bring the knight from f6 to c7 and the bishop from b7 to d7. This provides the b5-pawn with plenty of protection and so makes it difficult for White to smash through on the queenside. He gives the sample variation 20 ♕c1 ♕f8 21 ♖a3 ♖eb8 22 ♕b2 ♘e8! 23 ♖ea1 ♘c7 24 ♖1a2 ♗c8 25 ♕a1 ♘b6 26 ♗e3, when Black has still not equalized, but his position is far from desperate.

3) 19...cxb3 20 ♗xb3 and now:

3a) 20...bxa4?! 21 ♗xa4 and the complete opening of the queenside leaves Black in great trouble.

3b) 20...♖c8?! 21 axb5 axb5 22 ♕e2 ♕b6 23 ♖eb1 ♖a8 24 ♗a4 ♗a6 25 c4 is manifestly unacceptable for Black.

3c) 20...♘c5 isn't too bad for Black: 21 c4! (Chandler's idea, breaking open the queenside; 21 axb5 axb5 22 ♗c2 ♘fd7 23 ♕b1 is only a little better for White, as Black can hope to get decent piece-play) 21...bxa4 (or 21...bxc4 22 ♗xc4) 22 ♗xa4 ♖e7 23 ♗b4 with a positional edge for White after either 23...♖c8 or 23...♕c7.

20 ♗e3!

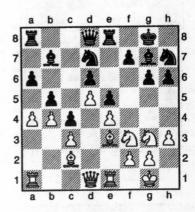

Attacking some squares on the queenside and preparing, with maximum efficiency, to build up the heavy artillery on the a-file.

20 ...   h5

This will be necessary after White's next move in any case. Note that Black's inability to play ...♔h7 is a consequence of his 19th move.

21 ♕d2   ♖f8

Angling for the ...f5 advance when the time is right. If the time will ever actually be right is another matter.

22 ♖a3   ♘df6

Turning away, for now, from the ...f5 plan. "Boris begins to wake up to the smell of frying bacon. His own! The text is an admission that ...f5 isn't happening." – Seirawan. If Black insists on counterplay with 22...h4 23 ②f1 f5, then 24 exf5 gxf5 25 ②g5 ②xg5 26 ♗xg5 ♗f6 27 ♗h6 ♗g7 28 ♗xg7 ♔xg7 29 f4 (Chandler) is one way for White to get a solid advantage. He is still well positioned to play on the kingside.

23	♖ea1	♕d7
24	♖1a2	♖fc8
25	♕c1	♗f8
26	♕a1	

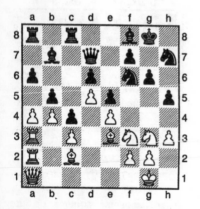

It was Alekhine who first brought it to the attention of the chess-playing public that the three major pieces are most effectively tripled with the queen at the back.

26	...	♕e8
27	②f1	♗e7
28	②1d2?!	

Starting an excellent plan of bringing the knight to b1, from where it threatens to go to a3 after the major pieces get exchanged off on the a-file. However, this move allows Black to drum up a little more counterplay than White need allow. Fischer could perhaps have kept a firmer grip on the game, while still implementing the same plan, by 28 ②3d2!? intending f3.

| 28 | ... | ♔g7 |

Suttles felt it was better to keep the king on its first rank by 28...♔h8, when he analysed 29 ②b1 ②g8 30 axb5 axb5 31 ♖xa8 ♗xa8 32 ♖a7 as good for White. Black's best chance is then probably 32...f5 33 exf5 g5, undermining the d5-pawn and hoping for some kingside play.

| 29 | ②b1 | |

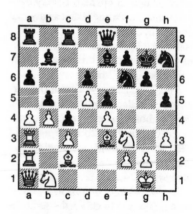

Demonstrating in stark fashion the problems Black faces. White intends simply to exchange on b5, take off all the major pieces on a8 and then play ②a3, when Black will have no way to defend the b5-pawn. It is very hard to counter this plan.

| 29 | ... | ②xe4!? |

Spassky, seeing that White's pieces are busy on the queenside, seizes his best chance of counterplay. Others:

1) 29...♖cb8 30 axb5 axb5 31 ♖xa8 ♗xa8 32 ♖a7, intending ♕a6 and ②a3, is miserable for Black.

2) 29...②d7 would allow White's main idea: 30 axb5 axb5 31 ♖xa8 ♖xa8 32 ♖xa8 ♕xa8 33 ♕xa8 ♗xa8 34 ②a3 and White wins.

| 30 | ♗xe4 | f5?! |

This active move, however, is asking too much of his position, though it is only thanks to White's magnificent 36th move that this becomes really clear. The recommended move was 30...♘f6 31 ♘bd2 ♘xe4 32 ♘xe4 ♗xd5 33 ♘ed2, though it is still hard to believe that Black has real chances of survival. Perhaps if Spassky had chosen 30...♘f6 and been gradually subdued in a lengthy struggle, 30...f5 would have been suggested as a better attempt to create some confusion.

31	♗c2	♗xd5
32	axb5	axb5
33	♖a7	

Fischer demonstrates that the moves 28...♔g7 and 30...f5 did not make a good combination.

33 ...   ♔f6

It is obvious that something has gone wrong when a king joins the fray like this.

34 ♘bd2   ♖xa7

34...f4 is met by 35 ♘e4+ ♗xe4 36 ♗xe4 ♖xa7 37 ♗xa7, when the bishop evades the pawn without having to retreat.

35 ♖xa7   ♖a8

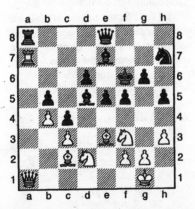

"I had been impressed by Bobby's handling of the pieces. But right now is his moment to shine. When I saw his next move, I knew that he was *good*. Bobby was *back*!" – Seirawan.

36 g4!!

There were other good moves at White's disposal, but this is very much to the point: White breaks up Black's kingside pawns and exposes his king.

| 36 | ... | hxg4 |
| 37 | hxg4 | ♖xa7 |

Or:

1) 37...fxg4 would be met by 38 ♘h2.

2) 37...f4 38 ♗e4! fxe3 (38...♖xa7 39 ♗xa7) 39 ♗xd5 ♖xa7 40 ♘e4+ ♔g7 41 ♕xa7 leaves White beautifully positioned to move in for the kill.

38 ♕xa7   f4

This allows a nice finish, but there was nothing better:

1) 38...fxg4 39 ♘h2 ♕c8 (39...♗e6 40 ♘e4+ ♔g7 41 ♘xd6) 40 ♘e4+ ♔e6 41 ♘xd6! ♗xd6 (41...♔xd6 42 ♗c5+) 42 ♕xh7 wins.

2) 38...♗c6 39 ♘h4 ♗d7 40 ♗h6 is terrible for Black.

39 ♗xf4!

Another great move. Fischer exploits Black's exposed king to the full. Instead 39 ♗b6 ♕c8! enables Black to put up resistance.

39 ...   exf4

40 ♘h4!!

White needs to conquer a few more light squares for his attack to become decisive. 40 ♕d4+ ♔e6 41 ♗f5+ gxf5 42 gxf5+ is a good deal less clear.

40 ...   ♗f7

40...♘f8 41 ♕d4+ ♔e6 (41...♔g5? 42 ♕xd5+) 42 ♘xg6! ♘xg6 43 ♗f5+ ♔f7 44 ♗xg6+ ♔xg6 45 ♕xd5 (Chandler) is winning for White. Although material is level, White's pieces are far better coordinated, while Black cannot defend his various loose pawns and his exposed king.

41 ♕d4+   ♔e6

41...♔g5? 42 ♕g7 forces mate.

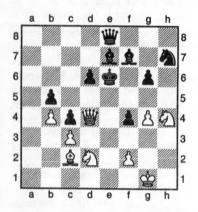

42 ♘f5!

The knight is immune here, and generates various threats, including the brutal ♘g7+.

42 ...   ♗f8

42...♔d7 43 ♕a7+ ♔d8 44 ♕b8+ ♔d7 45 ♕xb5+ wins at least a piece, for example 45...♔d8?! 46 ♕b8+ ♔d7 47 ♗a4+.

43 ♕xf4

Material is again level, but White's position is a picture of coordination, while Black's is a wreck. Black could perhaps have put up more stubborn resistance in the remainder of the game, but there is clearly no hope of salvation.

43 ...   ♔d7

43...gxf5 44 ♗xf5+ leaves White a pawn up after ♗xh7.

44	♘d4	♕e1+
45	♔g2	♗d5+
46	♗e4	♗xe4+
47	♘xe4	♗e7
48	♘xb5	♘f8
49	♘bxd6	♘e6
50	♕e5	1-0

Lessons from this game:

1) There are no general rules on whether to defend an awkward position by keeping the position blocked or by engaging in a hand-to-hand skirmish. It all comes down to analysing the specifics of the position.

2) Successful handling of semi-blocked positions depends on being able to manoeuvre the right pieces to the right squares quickly enough. Here Fischer's pieces were able to reach their ideal squares before Spassky's were ready to assume the right defensive posture.

3) Don't let the opponent dissuade you from attacking just because he has sacrificed. If your position is better, you still have the right to attack.

Boris Gelfand – Vishy Anand
Linares 1993
Queen's Gambit Accepted

The Players

Boris Gelfand was born in 1968 and is from Belarus. He became a very strong player in his late teens, winning the European Junior Championship in 1987/8, and was widely tipped as a potential world champion. He received the grandmaster title in 1989, and by 1990 had joined the super-grandmaster elite. However, his progressed seemed to stall, particularly following his loss to Nigel Short in their Candidates match in 1991. He reached the semi-final of the FIDE Candidates in 1995, but lost heavily to Karpov. Although he remains an exceptionally strong grandmaster, he has dropped a little in the world rankings. His chess is of a high technical quality, backed up by superb preparation, However, his choice of openings tends to be a little inflexible, and he does not always respond well to novelties, as we see in the featured game.

Viswanathan ("Vishy") Anand was born in Madras, India, in 1969, and is one of the top three players in the world. He learnt chess at the age of six from his mother and joined a chess club a year later. He played a lot of blitz chess in those years, frequently on a "winner stays on" basis. As his strength grew, he became famous for playing tournament games at breakneck speed. He won the Asian Junior Championship in 1984 and in 1985 gained the international master title and scored his first win against a grandmaster. His real breakthrough came in 1987, when he won the World Junior Championship and completed the requirements for the grandmaster title. His next major breakthrough came in 1990, when he qualified for the Candidates cycle, losing narrowly to Karpov in 1991. His outright victory at Reggio Emilia in 1991/2, beating Kasparov in their individual game, marked his graduation into the top level of the chess elite. He challenged Kasparov for the PCA Championship in 1995, and although he was in the lead after nine games, he then collapsed with four losses from the next five games. This experience seems to have toughened his chess, rather than disillusioning him. Since then his results have gained greater consistency and his rating has climbed inexorably. He won a string of tournaments in late 1997 and early 1998, and could fairly be said to be the best player in the world on current form. As we go to press, he is second on the FIDE rating list (May 1998), closing fast on Garry Kasparov.

Anand is a very "complete" player. He obviously has enormous talent, an exceptional speed of thought and a ferocious capacity for hard work. Though a natural attacking player, he is resourceful and resilient in defence, and rarely gets flustered under pressure. On a creative level his play retains its freshness and vitality, as we can see from his three victories featured in this book. It remains to be seen whether he will disprove those who consider him "too normal" ever to become World Champion.

The Game

In a sharp and topical opening, Anand produces an inspired novelty. Gelfand, both surprised and deeply impressed, fails to find a reasonable reply, and is soon in trouble. Anand plays the technical part of the game with great precision.

1	d4	d5
2	c4	dxc4
3	e4	c5
4	d5	♘f6
5	♘c3	b5

This extremely aggressive handling of the position was quite unusual at the time. Black tended instead to play the meek 5...e6, when after 6 ♗xc4 exd5 White has a pleasant choice between 7 exd5 and 7 ♘xd5. In either case Black must battle for equality.

The text-move instead aims either to smash White's pawn-centre to pieces, or else to generate play on the queenside with Black's pawn majority.

6 ♗f4

Prior to Linares 1993, this move, introduced by Beliavsky in 1988 (see next note) had put Black off the line with 5...b5. The alternative is 6 e5 b4 7 exf6 bxc3 8 bxc3 ♘d7 9 ♕a4!? exf6 10 ♗f4 ♕b6 11 ♗xc4 ♗d6 12 ♘e2 0-0 13 0-0, which tends to boil down to equality.

6 ... ♕a5!?

This move is Ehlvest's suggested improvement over Beliavsky–Ehlvest, World Cup, Belfort 1988, which continued 6...a6?! 7 e5 b4 8 exf6 bxc3 9 bxc3 ♘d7, whereupon 10 ♕a4! would have been strong.

7 e5

Two other moves at this point (7 a4 and 7 ♗d2) were tried in the same

event, and this has led to 5...b5 becoming known as the Linares Variation.

7	...	♘e4
8	♘e2	♘a6!

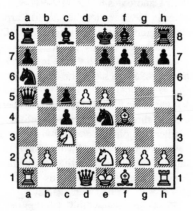

9 f3

9 a3 has been suggested, preventing the invasion on b4, but this rather passive move gives Black no problems after 9...♗b7 10 f3 ♘xc3 11 ♘xc3 ♘c7!. White's d-pawn is weak.

9 ... ♘b4!

This stunning novelty was described by Gelfand as one of the best he had ever had to face. Anand had prepared it as an improvement over an earlier game played in the same tournament: 9...♘xc3?! 10 ♘xc3 ♗f5 11 g4 ♗g6 12 a4 ♘b4 13 ♔f2 ♗d3 14 axb5 with an advantage for White, Beliavsky – Anand, Linares 1993.

10	fxe4	♘d3+
11	♔d2	g6!!

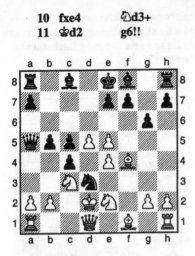

This is the key point of Anand's idea. He will play the position a piece down, with no prospect of regaining it, relying on the strength of the knight on d3, the obvious embarrassment of the white king, and his powerful queenside pawns. If White tries nothing radical, Black will continue ...♗g7, ...♘xe5 and advance his queenside pawns.

It takes considerable courage to play such an open-ended sacrifice directly from the opening, as there is no guarantee of success. In such cases, the important factor in weighing up the sacrifice is how many problems it poses the opponent. Here we see that White has an awkward series of problems to solve, with no emergency exits, and no clear light at the end of the tunnel. Therefore the sacrifice is a very good practical bet, even though there is no question of being able to prove its correctness by analysis.

Instead 11...♘f2?! 12 ♕e1 ♘xh1 13 g3 is good for White. On a pure head-count Black is not doing too badly, but he has nothing otherwise to show for the many tempi he has spent with his knights. Meanwhile White is substantially ahead in development and controls the centre very well.

"Gelfand sank into lengthy thought, during which he seems to have convinced himself that he was completely lost. This is an exaggeration, but I think Black is already slightly better. White's best lines lead to positions in which Black has something like two pawns and a dangerous attack for the piece." – Anand.

12 b3?

This move is definitely wrong, and leaves White in serious trouble. Let us investigate the lines that caused Gelfand such anguish:

1) 12 a4 b4 13 ♘b1 (13 ♘b5 a6 traps the knight) 13...♗g7 with "fantastic positional compensation for the piece" (Anand).

2) 12 ♗g3?! ♗h6+ 13 ♔c2 b4! and Black regains the piece with advantage, as 14 ♘b1? allows a forced mate: 14...b3+ 15 axb3 cxb3+ 16 ♔xb3 (16 ♔xd3 ♗a6#) 16...♖b8+ 17 ♔c2 ♖xb2+ 18 ♔xd3 ♗a6#.

3) 12 ♔c2 b4 (12...♗g7 is also possible) 13 ♕d2 (13 ♘b1?? loses to 13...b3+ 14 axb3 ♕xa1) 13...bxc3 wins back the piece with at least some advantage.

4) 12 ♕c2 should be answered by Black's standard plan of 12...♗g7 and ...♘xe5, etc.

5) 12 g3!? ♗g7 13 ♗g2 ♘xe5 avoids an immediate calamity for White, but does little to hinder Black's plan of creating counterplay by advancing his queenside pawns.

6) 12 d6!? would at least give Black some concrete problems to solve:

6a) 12...e6 is also interesting, with plans of activating both bishops on long diagonals (...♗b7 and ...♗g7), though White's d-pawn may prove annoying.

6b) 12...exd6 13 a4 and then:

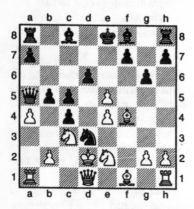

6b1) 13...♘xf4 14 ♘xf4 ♗h6 15 g3 (15 ♔c2!? ♗xf4 16 ♕xd6 is another way to return the piece to regain the initiative) 15...dxe5 16 ♔c2! exf4 17 ♕d6! (17 ♕d5?! 0-0! 18 ♕xa8 b4 works out very well for Black) gives White at least enough counterplay. Indeed it seems that an immediate draw should result: 17...♗e6 18 ♕c6+ ♔e7 19 ♕xc5+ ♔f6 20 ♕d4+ ♔e7, etc.

6b2) 13...b4! 14 ♘d5 ♗g7 and then:

6b21) 15 ♘f6+ ♗xf6 16 exf6 ♗e6 followed by ...0-0-0 gives Black excellent counterplay. Anand describes this as "a bit speculative", but I'm sure most players, given the choice, would much rather be Black here.

6b22) 15 exd6 0-0 is given by Anand as unclear – this seems a reasonable assessment!

7) 12 ♔e3 seeks to evacuate the king, while using it to defend his loose

minor pieces. However, there is an obvious risk in delaying development in order to move the king further up the board. 12...♗g7 and now:

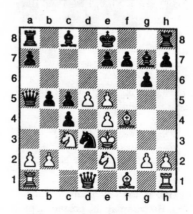

7a) 13 ♘c1? ♘xf4 14 ♔xf4 ♗e5+! 15 ♔xe5 (after 15 ♔f3 ♗xc3 16 bxc3 ♕xc3+ Black wins material due to the loose rook on a1) 15...g5! forces mate: 16 d6 f6+ 17 ♔d5 e6+ 18 ♔xc5 ♕b6+ 19 ♔b4 a5+ 20 ♔a3 ♕c5+ 21 b4 ♕xb4#.

7b) 13 ♘g3, intending ♗xd3, aims for an improved version of "7a" by keeping the a1-rook defended:

7b1) 13...g5 14 ♗xg5 ♘xb2 (not 14...♗xe5? 15 ♗xd3) 15 ♕c2 ♗xe5 and White must put a knight back on e2: 16 ♘ge2 (16 ♖c1?? ♗xc3 17 ♕xc3 ♘d1+; 16 ♘ce2 ♘d3 followed by ...♖g8) 16...♘d3 and Black keeps a grip on the position.

7b2) 13...♘xf4 14 ♔xf4 ♗xe5+:

7b21) 15 ♔xe5? g5! forces mate: 16 d6 allows the familiar mating sequence 16...f6+ 17 ♔d5 e6+ 18 ♔xc5 ♕b6+ 19 ♔b4 a5+ 20 ♔a3 ♕c5+ 21 b4 ♕xb4#; or 16 ♘h5 f6+ 17 ♘xf6+ exf6+ 18 ♔xf6 ♕d8+ 19 ♔g7 (19 ♔e5 ♕e7#) 19...♕e7+ 20 ♔xh8 ♗f5 and Black will give mate (by castling if permitted!).

7b22) 15 ♔e3 ♗d4+ 16 ♔d2 (16 ♔f3 h5 17 h3 ♗xc3 18 bxc3 ♖xc3+ 19 ♔f2 ♕f6+ 20 ♔g1 ♕e5 and Black is collecting a lot of pawns for his piece; 16 ♔f4 ♕c7+ 17 ♔f3 ♕e5) 16...b4 17 ♕a4+ ♕xa4 18 ♘xa4 ♗d7 regains the piece with some advantage.

7c) 13 g3 ♘xe5 gives Black good play according to Anand. Next will come ...0-0 and maybe ...f5.

12	**...**	**♗g7**
13	**bxc4**	**♘xf4**
14	**♘xf4?**	

14 cxb5 ♗xe5 15 ♕b3 ♘xe2 16 ♗xe2 0-0 is good for Black, but the text-move leads to disaster.

14	**...**	**♗xe5**
15	**♘fe2**	**b4**
16	**♕a4+**	

16 ♖c1 loses to 16...bxc3+ 17 ♘xc3 ♗f4+.

16	**...**	**♕xa4**
17	**♘xa4**	**♗xa1**
18	**♘xc5**	**0-0!**

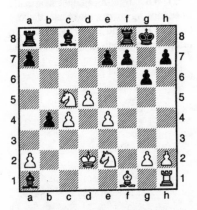

Black is now winning. 18...f5 is less clear-cut since 19 ♘f4 highlights the weakness of e6.

19	**♘d3**	**a5**

Black's technical task is a little tricky since White's pawn-centre could easily become menacing. With a variety of blows on both sides of the board Anand makes sure that the pawns never get the support they need.

20	**g3**	**♗g7**
21	**♗g2**	**♗a6!**
22	**c5**	**♖ac8**
23	**c6**	**♖fd8**
24	**♖c1**	

Anand mentions the line 24 ♘ec1 e6 25 ♘b3 exd5 26 exd5 ♗c4 27 ♘xa5 ♗c3+.

24	**...**	**♗h6+**
25	**♘ef4**	

25 ♘df4 loses to 25...e5 26 ♗h3 f5!.

25	**...**	**♗xd3**
26	**♔xd3**	**e5**
27	**♔c4**	**exf4**
28	**♖e1**	**fxg3**

28...f6? 29 ♖f1! g5 30 h4 illustrates the need for care.

29	**e5**	

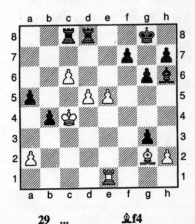

29	**...**	**♗f4**

The bishop finds a good spot from which to restrain the pawns. Slowly but surely, White's chances are being whittled away.

30 hxg3

Or: 30 ♖e4 g5; 30 d6 ♗xe5! 31 ♖xe5 ♖xd6.

| 30 | ... | ♗xg3 |
| 31 | ♖e3 | ♗f4! |

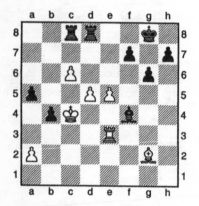

Anand makes the most of every tempo.

32	♖e4	♗h2
33	♗h3	♖c7
34	♖e2	♗g3
35	♖e3	♗f4
36	♖e4	g5
37	♔c5	♖e7

38 ♔d4

Black also wins after 38 d6 ♖xe5+ 39 ♖xe5 ♗xe5 40 ♗d7 h5! 41 c7 ♖f8 42 ♔d5 ♗f4.

38	...	f6!
39	d6	♗xe5+
40	♖xe5	♖xd6+

0-1

"I was extremely proud of this game and Gelfand was very sporting; he said that he didn't mind losing such a game and that I would have good chances to win both the best game and best novelty prizes in *Informator* (in fact I won neither!)." – Anand.

Lessons from this game:

1) It can be worth sacrificing material to cause prolonged disruption in the opponent's position.

2) If you have been hit by a surprising move, try to put some of the pressure back onto the opponent by giving him some difficult decisions, possibly by returning sacrificed material to regain the initiative.

3) When fighting against an armada of advancing pawns, make use of every tactical trick and every way to gain tempi to keep their progress in check.

Gata Kamsky – Alexei Shirov

World Team Championship, Lucerne 1993
Queen's Gambit Declined, Semi-Slav Defence

The Players

Gata Kamsky, an ethnic Tartar, was born in Siberia in 1974. His father, Rustam, a boxer, believed that any child could become a world champion in any field given sufficient hard work and chose that his son should become chess world champion. Young Gata, therefore, had a most unusual upbringing. Rustam defected, with Gata, to the USA in 1989. Although Gata's rating at the time was not exceptionally high, it was obvious that he was improving rapidly, and he shot up to 8th place in the world rankings in mid-1990. Although his initial results in super-grandmaster events were poor, he soon adapted to this level of play, and consolidated his position among the world elite. It is difficult to say much about Gata's personality, since his appearances at chess events were dominated by Rustam's aggression towards the organizers, Gata's opponents, and even his own team of assistants. Everywhere Kamsky played there was controversy and occasionally physical violence. Gata narrowly missed out on challenging for Kasparov's world title, but qualified for a crack at Karpov's FIDE title. Although Gata won some good games, Karpov emerged as clear winner. Kamsky subsequently announced his retirement from professional chess, at the age of 22, in order to become a medical doctor.

Alexei Shirov was born in 1972 in Latvia. An ethnic Russian, he has now settled in Spain. He was an immensely strong junior, and the first player ever to reach 2700-level before the age of 20. Allowing for a little inflation in the ratings, this put him on a par with Kasparov at the same age. His subsequent development as a player has not been so smooth though, but after some relatively patchy results in the mid-1990s, a run of success in early 1998 has re-established him as a serious contender for the world title. Perhaps the World Champion's characterization of Shirov in 1997 as "no more than an enthusiastic amateur" stung him into greater ambition.

Shirov is an enormously talented and creative player. His uncanny ability to whip up complications and to make daring sacrifices is strongly reminiscent of his great compatriot Mikhail Tal. His main weakness as a player is his nervousness, which was blamed for his failure to qualify as a Candidate for a world title, a status that the general level of his play so clearly merited.

The Game

Shirov introduces a surprising and powerful new idea in one of his favourite opening systems. Kamsky replies in a natural way, but is quickly in trouble. Shirov launches a ferocious attack against the white king, and although it seems that his own king is also in great danger, it turns out that Shirov has worked things out to perfection. The black king delicately tip-toes out of the minefield, whereas for his opposite number there is no reprieve.

1	d4	d5
2	c4	c6
3	♘c3	♞f6
4	♘f3	e6
5	♗g5	dxc4
6	e4	b5
7	e5	h6
8	♗h4	g5
9	♘xg5	hxg5
10	♗xg5	♞bd7
11	exf6	♝b7
12	g3	c5
13	d5	♝h6!?

In Game 74 we saw Torre trying 13...♞b6, and suffering badly. Here Shirov tries another alternative to the main line, 13...♛b6 (Games 95 and 98).

| 14 | ♗xh6 | ♜xh6 |
| 15 | ♕d2 | ♕xf6! |

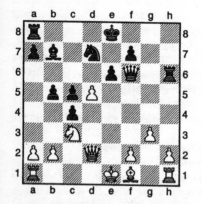

After Black found several surprising resources with this move, it had a period of great popularity in the early 1990s. The odd thing, though, is that

Shirov's interest in the move (and indeed the opening variation as a whole) stems from a game he played as *White* against Kamsky in a junior event in 1987. He subsequently analysed the game with Tal and Bagirov and, when he later took up the black side of the Semi-Slav, put into practice some of the ideas they developed.

16 0-0-0

Here is a sample of other possibilities:

1) 16 ♘e4!? ♕f3 (16...♕e5 17 0-0-0!) 17 ♘d6+ ♔e7 18 ♘xb7 and now:

1a) 18...♕xh1? 19 d6+ ♔e8 20 ♕xh6 ♕xb7? (20...♕e4+ doesn't help in view of 21 ♗e2 ♕h1+ 22 ♔d2 ♕xa1 23 ♕h8+ ♘f8 24 ♕f6 ♘g6 25 ♗f3) was played in the aforementioned game Shirov – Kamsky, USSR Junior Championship, Kapsukas 1987. Now Shirov indicates 21 ♕h4 as winning.

1b) 18...♜h5 19 ♜g1! (the alternative 19 d6+ ♔e8 20 ♜g1 c3! 21 bxc3 ♜e5+ 22 ♗e2 ♜xe2+ is reasonable for Black) 19...c3?! (19...♜xd5!? 20 ♗g2 ♜xd2 21 ♗xf3 ♜xb2 is Black's best try in this line) 20 ♕c2!! (20 bxc3 ♜e5+, etc., is less promising for White) leaves Black without a decent continuation, for example 20...♜e5+ (20...♕xd5 21 ♘a5) 21 ♗e2 cxb2 22 ♜b1 should win for White, as in Van Wely – Moll, Simultaneous display, Amsterdam 1994.

2) 16 ♗g2?! ♘e5 and then:

2a) 17 0-0?! 0-0-0 and now:

2a1) 18 ♕e3 walks into 18...♖xh2!:

2a11) 19 f4? fails to 19...♖xg2+ 20 ♔xg2 ♘d3.

2a12) 19 ♕xc5+? ♔b8 and Black should win: 20 ♔xh2? ♖h8+ 21 ♔g1 ♘f3+ 22 ♗xf3 ♕xf3 mates; 20 ♘xb5 ♖xg2+ 21 ♔xg2 ♖xd5! 22 ♕xa7+ ♔c8; or 20 f4 ♘d3 21 ♕xb5 ♖xg2+ 22 ♔xg2 exd5 23 ♖f3 a6 24 ♕a5 d4.

2a13) 19 ♗e4 is White's only hope of survival, but the open h-file will be a constant source of worry.

2a2) 18 f4 ♘d3 19 dxe6? (19 ♘xb5 exd5) 19...♕d4+ 20 ♔h1 and now Black forces mate in at most 12 moves, as the computer confirms: 20...♖xh2+! 21 ♔xh2 ♖h8+ 22 ♗h3 ♖xh3+ 23 ♔xh3 ♕h8+ 24 ♔g4 ♕g7+ 25 ♔h5 ♕g6+ 26 ♔h4 f5 27 ♕e2 ♕f6+ 28 ♔h5 ♗c6 and ...♗e8+. This variation combines some satisfyingly violent blows with a couple of more subtle, "quiet" moves.

2b) 17 ♘e4 ♘f3+ 18 ♗xf3 ♕xf3 19 ♘d6+ ♔d7 20 ♖g1 and here:

2b1) 20...c3 21 ♕xh6 is messy.

2b2) 20...♖xh2 (tempting, but the idea of directly targeting the white king does not appear to work) 21 dxe6+ (not 21 ♘xb7 exd5) 21...♔xe6 22 ♘xb7 ♖e8!? (22...♕xb7 allows 23 0-0-0) 23 ♘xc5+ ♔f6+ 24 ♔f1 ♕h5 25 ♕f4+ ♔g7 26 ♘e4 ♕h3+ 27 ♔e2 f5 28 ♕g5+ ♔h7 29 ♖ad1 ♖xe4+ 30 ♔f3 is good for White.

2b3) 20...♗xd5 21 ♕xh6 ♔xd6 is simplest and probably best; Black has excellent positional compensation.

16 ...   ♔f8!

16...♗xd5 had been played in an earlier game Yusupov – Shirov, Linares 1993. After 17 ♘xd5 exd5 18 ♗g2 ♘b6 Yusupov could have given Black difficulties by 19 ♗xd5 0-0-0

20 ♗b7+ ♔c7 21 ♕xd8+ ♕xd8 22 ♖xd8 ♔xd8 23 ♗a6.

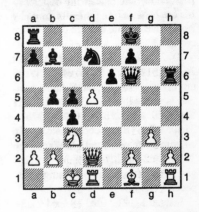

The text-move, 16...♔f8, was Yusupov's suggestion. The idea is to side-step future ideas with ♘e4 and ♘d6+ and so prepare 17...♘e5 as a reply to 17 ♗g2 and 17 dxe6.

17 f4

This move stops ...♘e5 but is a little too crude. After a few unsuccessful outings for this move, attention turned to 17 g4 and 17 f3. Unfortunately it would take us too far afield to examine the highly sophisticated body of theory that has grown up around these moves, except to mention that after 17 g4 (threatening 18 g5) 17...♖g6! 18 h3?! b4 19 ♘e4 c3! 20 bxc3 ♕f3 21 dxe6 ♗xe4 22 exd7 bxc3 23 d8♕+ ♔g7!! (Shirov) 24 ♕g5! (24 ♕d4+? was the only continuation he gave) forces Black to play extremely accurately, viz. 24...♖xd8 25 ♕e5+! and now:

1) 25...♕f6? 26 ♕xe4 ♖d1+ 27 ♔xd1 ♕xf2 28 ♕e5+ followed by ♗e2.

2) 25...f6?! 26 ♕c7+ ♔h6 27 ♖xd8 ♖g7 28 ♖h8+ ♔g6 29 ♕b8! c2 30

♕e8+ ♖f7 31 ♖g8+ ♔h6 32 g5+ fxg5
33 ♖h8+ ♔h7 (33...♗h7 34 ♕e6+ ♖f6
35 ♗d3!) 34 ♕e6+ ♗g6 35 ♗d3 ♕xd3
36 ♖xh7+ ♔xh7 37 ♕e7+ followed by
♕xc5 gives White enough dark-square
control.

3) 25...♖f6! 26 ♖xd8 ♕xf2 (not
26...♕xh1? 27 g5) 27 ♕xe4 (27 ♕xc3
might be a better try, but White's position is precarious) 27...♕b2+ 28 ♔d1
♕a1+ 29 ♔c2 ♕b2+ 30 ♔d3 ♕b1+
31 ♔e3 ♖e6 (Black could instead take
an immediate perpetual) 32 ♕xe6 fxe6
33 ♗g2 c2 34 ♖d7+ ♔f8 35 ♔d2 c4!
gives Black excellent winning prospects.

Instead 17 ♗g2 ♘e5 18 ♘e4 ♘d3+
19 ♕xd3 cxd3 20 ♘xf6 ♖xf6 21 ♖xd3
♖xf2 gives White difficult problems,
while 17 ♘e4 can be parried conveniently by 17...♕g6 now that there is no
check on d6. 18 dxe6 (18 ♘d6? ♗xd5)
18...♗xe4 19 exd7 ♖d8 is absolutely
OK for Black.

17 ...   ♘b6!
18 ♗g2   exd5

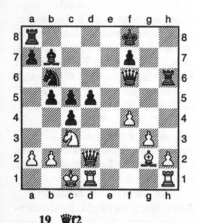

19 ♕f2

Shirov reckons that White is already in severe trouble:

1) 19 ♘xd5 ♗xd5 20 ♗xd5 ♖d8
21 ♕g2 c3 leaves White under heavy
attack with no worthwhile counterplay.

2) 19 ♘xb5 ♗c6 20 ♘c7 ♖d8 led
to a win for Black in Alterman – Kamsky, Tilburg 1993. This game was
played shortly after Kamsky – Shirov.
As can be imagined, 16...♔f8! quickly
found followers, including the move's
first victim.

19 ...   ♖c8!

Shirov parries the threat to the c5-
pawn while amassing his forces for
the attack. 19...d4?! would be reck-
less; after 20 ♗xb7 ♖b8 21 ♘e4 ♕e7
22 f5 the game is a real fight again.

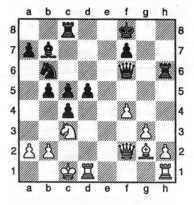

20 ♘xb5?!

Now the attack develops swiftly.
Alternatives:

1) 20 ♗xd5 ♘xd5 21 ♘xd5 ♕a6
and the attack breaks through.

2) 20 ♘xd5 ♗xd5 21 ♗xd5 c3 22
b3 c4! 23 bxc4?! c2 24 ♖d4 ♘xd5 25
cxd5 ♕a6 is a disaster for White.

3) 20 g4 was suggested by Shirov
as White's best chance for survival,
though 20...♖g6 21 h3 b4 22 ♘xd5
♗xd5 23 ♗xd5 c3 still gives Black
very dangerous attacking chances.

20 ...   ♘a4!

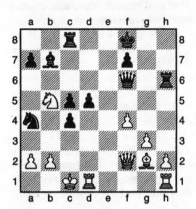

Black intends to rip open White's king with ...c3.

21 ♕c2

21 ♗xd5? ♗xd5 22 ♖xd5 ♕c6 23 ♘xa7 ♕xd5 24 ♖d1 ♕xd1+! 25 ♔xd1 ♖b8 wins for Black, e.g. 26 ♕d2 c3!.

21 ...   ♕a6!

22 ♘a3

22 ♘c3 fails to 22...♘xc3 23 ♕xc3 (23 bxc3 ♖b6) 23...♕xa2 24 ♖xd5 (not 24 ♗xd5? ♗xd5) 24...♗xd5 25 ♗xd5 ♖b8!, when White is material down and defenceless.

22 ...   c3!!

"Perhaps the most difficult move of the game." (Shirov). He perceives that 22...♖b6 23 ♕h7 gives real counterplay, whereas the game continuation, although hair-raising, only gives White visual counterplay.

23 ♗xd5

After 23 bxc3 ♕a5! 24 ♘b1 ♖b8 intending ...♗a8 and ...♖hb6, Shirov saw no defence for White, e.g.:

1) 25 c4 d4 26 ♗xb7 ♖xb7 doesn't help White.

2) 25 ♖he1 ♗a8! 26 ♖e3 d4! 27 cxd4 ♗xg2 28 ♖b3 (28 ♕xg2 cxd4)

28...♖xb3 29 axb3 ♗f3 and Black keeps a material advantage.

3) 25 ♗xd5 ♗xd5 26 ♖xd5 ♖hb6 and Black wins.

23 ...   ♘xb2

24 ♕f5

24 ♗xb7? loses to 24...♕xa3! 25 ♗c8 ♘c4+! (25...♗d3++ is actually a quicker mate, but less pretty) 26 ♔b1 ♖b6+ 27 ♔a1 ♕b2+! 28 ♕xb2 cxb2+ 29 ♔b1 ♘a3#.

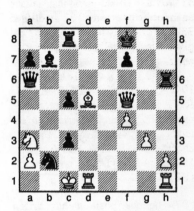

24 ...   ♖f6!?

24...♗xd5 25 ♖xd5 ♖b8 is an alternative, simpler win: 26 ♖d7 (26 ♘b1 ♕e2 27 ♘xc3 ♕e3+ 28 ♔c2 ♘c4) 26...♗d3+! 27 ♕xd3 ♕xa3+ 28 ♔d1 ♕xa2 29 ♖d8+ ♖xd8 30 ♕xd8+ ♔g7 31 ♕g5+ ♖g6 32 ♕e5+ ♔h7 33 ♕xc3 ♕d5+ wins the rook.

25 ♕h7

25 ♗xb7 loses to 25...♘d3+!: 26 ♕xd3 ♕xa3+ 27 ♔c2 ♕b2#; 26 ♔c2 ♕a4+ wins the queen at least; 26 ♔b1 ♕xb7+ wins the house.

25 ...   ♕xa3!

Interestingly enough, Shirov himself describes this as "the clearest way". Clarity is clearly a subjective matter.

25...♘xd1 26 ♖e1 ♘e3! 27 ♕h8+
(27 ♖xe3? ♕f1+ 28 ♔c2 ♕f2+; 27
♘c4? ♗xd5 28 ♖xe3 ♖h6) 27...♔e7
28 ♖xe3+ ♔d7 29 ♕h3+ ♔d6 30
♘c4+ ♔xd5 31 ♖xc3 ♔c6 32 ♘e5+
♔c7 33 ♖xc5+ ♔b8 34 ♘d7+ ♔a8 35
♖xc8+ ♗xc8 is another winning line
cited by Shirov.

26   ♕h8+   ♔e7
27   ♖he1+   ♔d7!

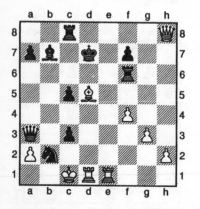

A famous position has arisen.
Black's king is running the gauntlet of
White's whole army, but there is nothing White can make of this – none of
the many discovered checks do him
any good. To go into such a position

willingly as Black demands nerves of
steel and considerable faith in one's
analytical abilities.

28   ♕h3+

Or: 28 ♗e6++ ♔c6; 28 ♗e6++
♔c6; 28 ♕xf6 ♘d3++ 29 ♔c2 ♘b4+
30 ♔b1 ♕b2#.

28   ...   ♔d6!
29   ♗xb7+   ♘xd1+
30   ♔xd1   ♕xa2
31   ♕g2   ♕b1+

0-1

White lost on time here, but he is
getting chopped to pieces anyway: 32
♔e2 ♖e8+.

Lessons from this game:

1) Subtle king moves can play a
role in the sharpest of positions if they
help evade the opponent's main attacking ideas.

2) Although Shirov's handling of
his king gets a strong "Don't try this at
home" warning, note the importance
of ascertaining which threats have real
substance, as opposed to those that are
no more than a few checks.

3) Only play either side of openings as sharp as the Anti-Meran Gambit in the Semi-Slav if you are very
confident of your tactical ability!

Game 90

Anatoly Karpov – Veselin Topalov

Linares 1994

English Opening

The Players

Anatoly Karpov (born 1951) has been FIDE World Champion 1975–85 and from 1993 onwards. See Game 67 for more details.

The Bulgarian GM Veselin Topalov (born 1975) is one of the strongest players in the world, with a string of tournament successes under his belt. He spent much of 1992 travelling around Europe, competing in open tournaments with such success that he catapulted himself into the limelight with a vastly improved rating the following year. His tough experience of the professional tournament circuit helped him to become a player of immense energy and fighting spirit. This, coupled with his excellent work-rate and preparation, makes him a fierce opponent.

The Game

Linares 1994 was one of Anatoly Karpov's greatest achievements. In one of the strongest tournaments of all time, Karpov destroyed the opposition, scoring an incredible 11/13, a full 2½ points ahead of second-placed Kasparov and Shirov. Kasparov now had cause to regret his declaration, "Whoever wins Linares can be considered the World Champion of tournament chess."

In the opening Karpov subdues his talented opponent by refusing lines that give him any counterchances, and then encourages Topalov to exchange knight for bishop, doubling Karpov's pawns to boot. It turns out that in this instance the structure gives White a firm bind on the kingside, stifling Black's bishop-pair and central majority. There follows a slow creep towards the black king, which explodes into a blaze of sacrificial tactics.

1	d4	♘f6	8	♘c3	0-0
2	c4	c5	9	0-0	d6
3	♘f3	cxd4	10	♗f4	♘h5
4	♘xd4	e6	11	e3!?	
5	g3	♘c6			
6	♗g2	♗c5			

Black is aiming for a solid "Hedgehog" formation, but before the bishop finds its home on e7, it hits the knight, forcing it to a less aggressive square than d4.

7	♘b3	♗e7

An interesting idea from Karpov; he voluntarily gives up the bishop-pair and accepts doubled pawns. More importantly, however, White further restrains the black central pawns so that they can be put under severe pressure. The pawn prongs on c4 and f4 are particularly effective in cramping the black position. Moreover, Black will always have to be wary of breaks involving c4-c5 and f4-f5.

The standard move for White is 11 ♗e3.

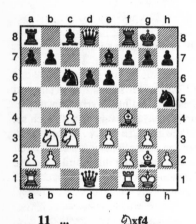

11 ...   ♘xf4

There seems nothing better than accepting the challenge. Otherwise, what is the knight doing on h5? White remains slightly better after 11...g6 12 ♗h6 ♖e8 13 e4 or 11...♘f6 12 e4.

12 exf4   ♗d7
13 ♕d2   ♕b8

A classic Hedgehog move. From b8 the black queen supports the advance on the queenside with ...a6 and ...b5, undermining one of White's prongs.

14 ♖fe1   g6

Allowing f4-f5 would not be a good idea. For example 14...♖d8 15 f5! ♗f8 16 fxe6 fxe6 17 f4 (one prong replaces another!) and the black pawn on e6 looks very vulnerable.

15 h4   a6
16 h5   b5?

The right idea, but the wrong timing. Before this advance, Black should play the useful 16...♖a7, which defends d7 and removes the rook from

the h1–a8 diagonal. Both these concepts are extremely important, as is seen very soon. Karpov gives 17 h6 b5 18 ♘d4, when White holds an advantage, but it is not as significant as in the actual game.

17 hxg6   hxg6

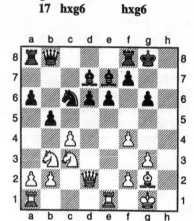

18 ♘c5!

Black has been careful to prevent White's pawn breaks, but this move proves even more potent. Black's only real alternative to capturing the knight is 18...♗e8, but this gives White the pleasant choice between the prosaic 19 ♘xa6 ♖xa6 20 cxb5 ♖b6 21 bxc6, when White has a clear extra pawn, and the more imaginative 19 ♘xe6!? fxe6 20 ♖xe6, when White has many threats, as shown by the following lines:

1) 20...♗f7 21 ♖ae1! and Black's light squares are shot to pieces.

2) 20...♖f6 21 ♖ae1 ♖xe6 22 ♖xe6 ♗f7 23 ♕e3 ♕c8 24 ♗xc6 is winning for White, a line given by Karpov.

One should also add that 18...♕c8 is not sufficient after 19 ♘xd7 ♕xd7 20 cxb5 axb5 21 ♘xb5 and again White has a healthy pawn advantage.

18	...	dxc5
19	♕xd7	♖c8

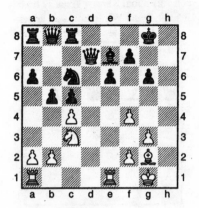

20 ♖xe6!!

Dismantling the flimsy pawn-cover around the black king, which has no easy ride for the rest of the game.

Topalov's defensive idea is seen after the obvious 20 ♗xc6, when Black regains his material with 20...♖a7, although White keeps an edge after 21 ♕d3 ♖xc6 22 cxb5 axb5 23 ♘xb5 c4 (or 23...♗b7 24 a4) and now the Linares bulletin gives 24 ♘xa7! cxd3 25 ♘xc6 ♕d6 26 ♘xe7+ ♕xe7 27 ♖ad1, when White has chances to win the endgame.

20	...	♖a7!

20...fxe6 21 ♗xc6 ♖a7 22 ♕xe6+ ♔g7 23 ♗e4 ♗f6 24 ♕g4 leaves White with a crushing position. Topalov's choice is more astute, as Black gains a tempo over the last line. This, however, is not enough to save his creaking position.

21 ♖xg6+!!

This "desperado" was obviously in Karpov's plans when he made his previous move.

21	...	fxg6

Black really does have to capture this time, as the alternatives lead to disaster, e.g.:

1) 21...♔f8 22 ♕h3 fxg6 23 ♕h8+ ♔f7 24 ♗d5#.

2) 21...♔h7 and now:

2a) 22 ♖g4!? is a flashy queen sacrifice mentioned by the bulletin. White plans to deliver checkmate with his two rooks. After 22...♖xd7 23 ♗e4+ ♔h6 White can do so by 24 ♔g2 and 25 ♖h1#. All seems completely lost for Black until Fritz spots the desperate 23...♔h8 24 ♔g2 ♗h4!. Even so, White can still win by means of 25 ♖h1 f5 26 ♗xf5 ♖cc7 27 ♗xd7 ♖xd7 28 ♖gxh4+ ♔g7 29 ♖h7+ and 30 ♖xd7. White's two rooks and extra pawns easily outweigh Black's queen.

2b) 22 ♕h3+! cuts out any nonsense, and therefore should be preferred. Karpov gives 22...♔xg6 23 ♗e4+, when after 23...♔g7 24 ♕h7+ White mates. 23...f5 prevents mate but 24 ♕xf5+ ♔g7 25 ♕h7+ ♔f8 26 ♕h6+ ♔e8 27 ♗xc6+ is a straightforward win.

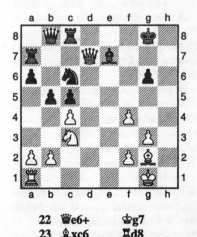

22	♕e6+	♔g7
23	♗xc6	♖d8

24 cxb5   ♞f6

Note that 24...axb5 loses immediately to the simple 25 ♞xb5, attacking the rook on a7, which would then not be able to maintain its defence of the bishop on e7.

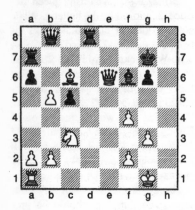

The smoke has cleared. White's knight and three pawns for a rook, together with Black's airy king and various pawn weaknesses give White a winning position. That said, there is still some work to be done, and Topalov characteristically puts up some stubborn resistance.

25 ♞e4   ♗d4

Black cannot grab the pawn. Following 25...♗xb2 26 ♜b1 ♗d4 27 b6 ♜f7 28 ♞g5 the black rook once more runs out of squares on the second rank, while after 28...♜f6, 29 ♕e7+ is immediately decisive.

26 bxa6   ♕b6

Black cannot allow White to play ♕e7+, for example 26...♜xa6 27 ♕e7+ ♚h8 28 ♞g5 ♜a7 29 ♞f7+ ♚g7 30 ♕xd8 ♕xb2 (Black seems to be getting some counterplay but now White has a forced winning sequence) 31 ♕h8+ ♚xf7 32 ♗d5+ ♚e7 33 ♜e1+

♚d6 34 ♕d8+ ♜d7 35 ♜e6+ ♚xd5 36 ♕xd7+ and finally White wins.

27 ♜d1   ♕xa6

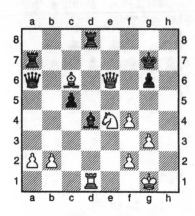

28 ♜xd4!

The third rook offer in only nine moves. Now Karpov has dominance over both the light squares and the dark squares. The rest of the game sees Black's king getting shoved from pillar to post, while the white queen picks off material at will, leaving the black defences totally bare.

28 ...   ♜xd4

28...cxd4 loses immediately to 29 ♕f6+ ♚h6 30 ♕h4+ ♚g7 31 ♕xd8 ♕xc6 32 ♕xd4+.

29 ♕f6+   ♚g8

Other moves also lose:

1) 29...♚h6 30 f5 ♜g7 31 ♕h4#.

2) 29...♚h7 30 ♞g5+ ♚g8 31 ♕xg6+ ♚f8 32 ♕e8+ ♚g7 33 ♞e6+ ♚f6 34 ♞xd4 cxd4 35 ♕f8+ ♜f7 36 ♕h8+ ♚g6 37 ♗e4+ ♜f5 38 g4 and Black can safely resign.

30 ♕xg6+   ♚f8

Again Black's choice is very limited. 30...♚h8 31 ♞f6 leads to mate, while 30...♜g7 31 ♕e8+ ♚h7 32 ♞f6+ ♚h6 33 ♕h5# is mate.

31	♕e8+	♔g7
32	♕e5+	♔g8
33	♘f6+	♔f7
34	♗e8+	♔f8

Topalov continues with dogged opposition. 34...♔g7 allows a convincing discovered check, with 35 ♘d7+ ♔g8 36 ♕g5+ ♔h8 37 ♕h5+ ♔g7 38 ♕f7+ ♔h6 39 ♕f8+ ♔h7 40 ♘f6+ and Black must surrender his queen.

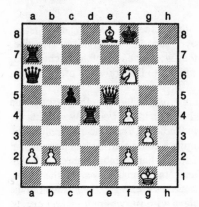

35	♕xc5+	♕d6
36	♕xa7	♕xf6

Black actually has a cheeky stalemate attempt here with 36...♖d1+ 37 ♔g2 ♖g1+!, hoping for 38 ♔xg1? ♕d1+ 39 ♔g2 ♕h1+!, when an unlikely draw is achieved. White can cut out this nonsense with 38 ♔h3 ♖h1+ 39 ♔g4. Instead Topalov captures the knight, but soon realizes it's better to reserve his energy for another game.

37	♗h5	♖d2
38	b3	♖b2
39	♔g2	1-0

Lessons from this game:

1) Be aware of ideas which involve a change of pawn structure. Karpov's 11 e3 and 12 exf4 proves to be a highly successful idea.

2) Desperado sacrifices can be powerful tools. Witness Karpov's 21 ♖xg6+!!.

3) Three rook sacrifices in one game is very unusual indeed!

Alexei Shirov – Judit Polgar

Sicilian theme tournament, Buenos Aires 1994

Sicilian Defence, Taimanov Variation

The Players

Alexei Shirov (born 1972) is originally from Latvia but has now settled in Spain. He is an enormously talented and creative player. For more information see Game 89.

Judit Polgar (born 1976) is the youngest of the three famous Hungarian sisters, who, particularly in the early 1990s, enjoyed superstar status due to their phenomenal chess-playing ability. Although they were given an intensive chess education from an early age, this was certainly not to the exclusion of everything else, as was the case with Gata Kamsky.

Judit started to play with some success at international level at the age of 9, and by 12 was already one of the highest rated women in the world. By winning the Hungarian Championship in 1991 (believed to be the first time a woman of any age had won a major national championship) she completed the requirements for the "men's" grandmaster title at the age of 15 years and 5 months, beating Fischer's all-time record. She has been the highest rated woman player since the January 1990 list, but rarely, if ever, plays in women's events. She is now among the top players in the world, and regularly plays with success in top-level events. However, she is yet to make any impact in world championship cycles. She has an exceptionally direct and aggressive style of play, based on thorough opening preparation.

The Game

Played in an event in which the Open Sicilian was a mandatory opening, the game starts in an unusual line of the Taimanov Variation for which both players were well prepared. However, it is Polgar who strikes first, with a powerful novelty, breaking up Shirov's impressive-looking pawn-front. Some spectacular tactics follow, including a queen sacrifice that White dare not accept. Shirov has no choice but to go into a hopeless ending.

	1	e4	c5
	2	♘f3	e6
	3	d4	cxd4
	4	♘xd4	♘c6

This move characterizes the Taimanov Variation of the Sicilian. It is a highly flexible system; Black has

various plans to generate quick queenside pressure, and can also play in the centre, based on such moves as ...♕c7 and ...♗b4. However, Black can also use it as a move-order trick to reach other variations while limiting White's options.

5 ♘c3

Probably the most critical test is to set up a type of Maróczy Bind with 5 ♘b5 d6 6 c4, but the slow play that results is hardly in keeping with Shirov's style.

5 ...   d6

With this move Black makes it clear that her aim is to reach a Scheveningen – 6 ♗e2 ♘f6 would now bring about a direct transposition. The true "Taimanov" move would be 5...♕c7, while 5...a6 can also lead to distinctive play.

6 g4

This move had not been taken seriously until Karpov played it against Kasparov in the 14th game of their 1985 World Championship match. While he undoubtedly played it as a stopgap while he was working out a reply to Kasparov's gambit continuation (5 ♘b5 d6 6 c4 ♘f6 7 ♘1c3 a6 8 ♘a3 d5 – see Game 79 in this book), he managed to show that the move had some bite. The idea is similar to the Keres Attack (see Game 72), except that here the knight is not yet on f6, so there is no threat of g5 as yet. However, it turns out not to be so easy for Black to find a good alternative to playing ...♘f6, while the move g4 is useful in a wide variety of Sicilian positions.

Moreover, there is a nice psychological side to the move 6 g4. Black's move-order shows that she wants to reach a Scheveningen. Then why did she not play the Scheveningen move-order (i.e. 4...♘f6 5 ♘c3 d6)? The answer must be that she did not want to face the Keres Attack. The text-move gives her again the problem of how to avoid that system.

6 ...   a6
7 ♗e3   ♘ge7
8 ♘b3

8 f4 was Shirov's choice in three subsequent games against Polgar. For example, 8...b5 9 g5 ♗b7 10 ♗g2 h6 11 gxh6 ♘g6 12 ♘xc6 ♗xc6 13 ♕d4 ♕h4+ 14 ♔d2 gxh6 led to sharp play in Shirov – J. Polgar, Madrid 1997.

8 ...   b5
9 f4

9 ♕e2!? is now considered a better try, e.g.:

1) 9...♘a5 10 ♗g2 ♗b7 11 ♘xa5 ♕xa5 12 f4 ♘c6 13 0-0 ♗e7 14 g5 ♕c7 15 ♕f2 ♗d8 16 ♘e2 gave White good kingside chances in Lanka – Yermolinsky, World Team Championship, Lucerne 1993.

2) 9...♗b7 10 f4 ♘a5 (Gallagher suggest that 10...g5!? might even be an idea here) 11 ♘xa5 ♕xa5 12 ♗g2 ♘g6?! (Gallagher proposes 12...♘c6 or 12...♖c8) 13 ♕f2! ♖c8 14 ♗b6 ♕b4 15 0-0-0! with good prospects for White, as in Gallagher – Vogt, Winterthur 1996.

9 ...   ♗b7

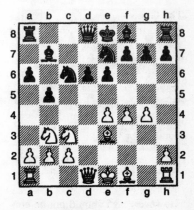

10 ♕f3?!

This move is rendered somewhat suspect by Polgar's excellent reply. 10 ♗g2 is considered an improvement, seeking to transpose to line "1" in the note to White's 9th move, though Black can avoid this by playing 10...♘g6.

10 ...   g5!

This is a thematic idea in many such positions. The e5-square is of such great significance that a pawn is a small price to pay for it – even more so if e5 can be occupied with gain of tempo, as is the case here.

Here is an example of what can happen if White is allowed to prepare his kingside attack undisturbed: 10...♘a5 11 0-0-0 ♘xb3+ 12 axb3 ♖c8 13 h4 ♘c6 14 g5 ♕a5 15 ♔b1 ♗b4 16 ♗d4 d5 17 f5! dxe4 and now, rather than 18 ♕h3?? ♗d6, which allowed Black to evacuate his king in Shirov – Kasparov, Novgorod 1994, Shirov analysed 18 ♕f4!!, preventing Black from organizing his defences, and giving White a large advantage, e.g. 18...♘d5 19 ♕e5! or 18...e3 19 fxe6 fxe6 20 g6! hxg6 21 ♕g4.

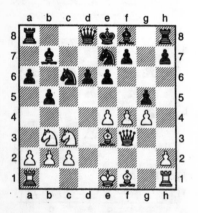

However, ...g5 should not be considered a universal panacea in such positions; in plenty of instances it would just open lines for White. Much depends on how stable Black's knight is on e5, and how much influence it has from there.

11 fxg5

11 0-0-0 gxf4 12 ♗xf4 ♘g6 13 ♘c5 ♕f6 14 ♘xb7 ♕xf4+ 15 ♕xf4 ♘xf4 16 ♘xd6+ ♔e7 is dangerous for White: his knight is in peril and his pawns are weak.

11 ...   ♘e5

12 ♕g2

Or:

1) After 12 ♕f6 Judit intended the exchange sacrifice 12...♘xg4 13 ♕xh8 ♘xe3 14 ♗d3 ♘g6 followed by rounding up the g5-pawn, with easy play.

2) 12 ♕e2 b4 13 ♘a4 ♗c6 14 ♘b6 ♗xe4, as given by Polgar, is good for Black, e.g. 15 ♗g2 ♗xg2 16 ♕xg2 ♖b8 or 15 ♘xa8 ♕xa8 16 ♖g1 ♘f3+.

12 ...   b4

13 ♘e2

Polgar considers 13 ♘a4 ♘d5! very strong for Black.

13 ...   h5!!

Far better than 13...♘c4 14 ♗d4 e5 15 ♘g3!, when White's pieces suddenly find some coordination.

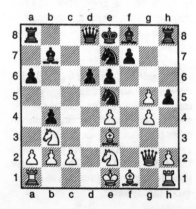

A key move, breaking open lines on the kingside. Polgar apparently had this position on her analysis board on the morning of the day this game was played. This shows not only a very good feel for which line the opponent would play, but also spot-on analysis of her new idea.

14 gxh5?

This lands Shirov in trouble. 14 gxh6 ♗xh6 (14...f5!? is very interesting too) 15 ♗xh6 ♖xh6 16 0-0-0 ♘7g6 was Polgar's preparation; Black's compensation is perfectly reasonable.

14 0-0-0 was Shirov's suggestion afterwards, for example 14...hxg4 15 ♘f4 ♘f5, though this is still not especially pleasant.

14 ...   ♘f5

15 ♗f2?

Perhaps 15 exf5 ♗xg2 16 ♗xg2 ♖xh5 offered better survival chances. Instead 15 ♗f4 is well countered by 15...♘h4 followed by 16...♗xe4.

15 ...   ♕xg5

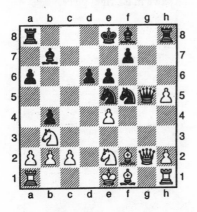

16 ♘a5?!

Or:

1) 16 ♘g3 ♘h4 17 ♕h3 is too horrible to contemplate.

2) 16 ♕xg5 ♘f3+ 17 ♔d1 ♘xg5 will give Black a material advantage due to the pin on the long diagonal.

3) 16 ♘ed4 ♘h4 17 ♕xg5 ♘hf3+ is similar.

After the text-move it seems for an instant (and indeed it was only an instant, for Polgar played her reply immediately) that all is well for White, but this illusion is shattered by Black's next move.

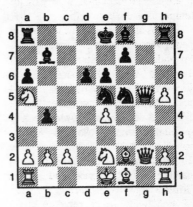

16 ...   ♘e3!!

A beautiful resource. The black queen is immune because of mate.

17 ♕g3

White has no decent option: 17 ♕xg5 ♘f3# is mate, while 17 ♗xe3 ♕xe3 18 ♘xb7 ♘f3+ wins the queen.

17 ...   ♕xg3

18 ♘xg3   ♘xc2+

19 ♔d1   ♘xa1

20 ♘xb7   b3!

This move frees the knight – a standard method of rescuing a cornered knight.

21 axb3

This lets the knight out without a fight, but there is no mileage in 21 a3 ♗h6 either.

| 21 | ... | ♘xb3 |

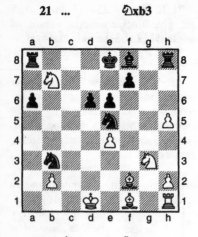

22	♔c2	♘c5
23	♘xc5	dxc5
24	♗e1	♘f3
25	♗c3	♘d4+
26	♔d3	♗d6
27	♗g2	

27 b4 ♔e7 28 bxc5 ♗xc5 29 ♗xd4 ♖hd8 30 ♘e2 e5 works nicely for Black.

| 27 | ... | ♗e5 |

| 28 | ♔c4 | ♔e7 |
| 29 | ♖a1 | ♘c6 |

29...♗xg3 30 hxg3 ♖xh5 is also good.

0-1

30 ♔xc5 would give Black a pleasant choice between 30...♘d4! and 30...♗xc3 31 bxc3 ♖hc8 – in either case Black is a clear exchange up and keeps enough pawns on the board to win without difficulty.

This game, over which Judit took just 48 minutes, won the prize for the most important theoretical novelty of the tournament (10...g5).

Lessons from this game:

1) It can be well worth sacrificing a pawn to gain firm control of a really important central square.

2) Be on the lookout for snap checkmates when two knights are hovering over an exposed king.

3) An apparently trapped knight in a corner can be freed with the help of one pawn in the right place.

Roberto Cifuentes – Vadim Zviagintsev
Open tournament, Wijk aan Zee 1995
Queen's Gambit Declined, Semi-Slav Defence

The Players

Roberto Cifuentes (born 1957) is a grandmaster from Chile, although he has now settled in Holland. He has a particular interest in computer chess and often writes on this subject.

Vadim Zviagintsev (born 1976) is a talented grandmaster from Russia who was a member of the Dvoretsky/Yusupov School. He was European Under-16 Champion in 1992 and shared first prize with Speelman at Altensteig 1994 (Category 12), but he really made a name for himself with the game below. Since then he has continued to improve, and on the January 1998 rating list he is ranked joint 24th in the world. In 1997 he took part in a number of strong events, finishing joint first at Calcutta and outright first at Portorož. He also took part in the 1997 knock-out Russian championship, reaching the quarter-finals before being eliminated by Dreev. He reached the last 16 in the 1997 FIDE world championship, his nemesis again being Dreev.

The Game

Cifuentes adopts a quiet opening, but starts to play ambitiously in the early middle-game. However, his plan of attacking on the kingside is soon proved ineffective, and it is Black who takes over the initiative on that part of the board. Soon the sacrifices start: first a piece, then the exchange, finally the queen, and White's king is chased up the board to its execution.

1	d4	e6
2	♘f3	d5
3	c4	♘f6
4	♘c3	c6
5	e3	♘bd7
6	♕c2	b6

An unusual plan in place of the almost universal 6...♗d6. Black intends to develop his pieces quietly and avoid the early central liquidation which often arises after 6...♗d6.

7	♗e2

Cifuentes adopts a solid response. 7 ♗d3 would position the bishop more actively, but of course this is largely a matter of taste.

7	...	♗b7
8	0-0	♗e7
9	♖d1	

It can be useful to put a rook opposite Black's queen, but here Black can simply side-step the danger by playing ...♕c7.

A more common plan, which offers greater chances for the advantage, is 9 b3 0-0 10 ♗b2.

9	...	0-0
10	e4	

White could still continue with 10 b3, but he decides to open the centre immediately.

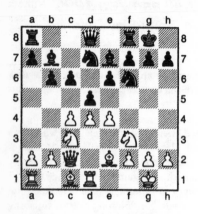

10   ...   dxe4
11   ♘xe4   ♕c7

It is dangerous to open the d-file while the queen is still on d8, for example after 11...c5 12 ♘xf6+ ♗xf6 13 dxc5 bxc5 14 ♗f4 Black's broken queenside pawns give White the edge.

12   ♘c3

If White tries to block in the b7-bishop by 12 ♘xf6+ ♘xf6 13 c5, then 13...bxc5 14 dxc5 a5 and the bishop can emerge at a6, while d5 is a very good square for the black knight.

The continuation 12 ♗g5 ♖fe8 13 ♘xf6+ ♘xf6 14 c5 ♘d7 15 ♖ac1 a5 16 h3 ♗a6 17 ♗xe7 ♖xe7 18 ♘g5 ♘f6 19 cxb6 ♕xb6 gave White an edge in J.Horvath – Payen, Paris 1995. Here Black made the mistake of allowing White to swap on b6 instead of taking on c5 himself. The result was a weak c-pawn on an open file.

12   ...   c5

Black plays to unbalance the game. After 12...e5 he could hope for no more than boring equality.

13   d5

An ambitious response. If White can maintain the pawn on d5 then Black's pieces will have less manoeuvring room, but there is an obvious danger that the advanced pawn will become weak. After 13 ♘b5 (13 ♗g5 is also possible) 13...♕b8 14 g3 cxd4 15 ♘bxd4 the position is roughly equal.

13   ...   exd5
14   cxd5   a6

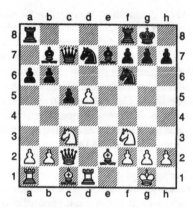

With a view to ...b5-b4, driving away a defender from the d5-pawn.

15   ♘h4!?

Further double-edged play. Black is more or less forced to reply ...g6, which slightly weakens his kingside, but if White's initiative comes to nothing, then the knight on h4 will have to retreat, with consequent loss of time.

15   ...   g6

After the immediate 15...♗d6 White could continue with 16 g3, as in the game, or he could play 16 ♘f5 ♗xh2+ 17 ♔h1 ♗d6 18 ♘e4 ♘xe4 19 ♕xe4 ♘f6 20 ♕h4, offering a pawn to enhance his kingside threats. Black prefers to play safe and simply stops the knight moving to f5.

16 ♗h6   ♖fe8

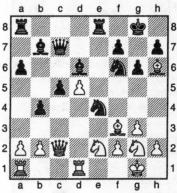

17 ♕d2?!

With this White raises the stakes, but the gamble does not pay off. He wants to utilize the knight's position on h4 and so introduces the possibility of ♘f5. Unfortunately the knight never reaches f5, while Black is given the chance to advance his queenside pawn majority.

White could have maintained equality by 17 a4 ♗d6 18 g3.

17 ...   ♗d6
18 g3   b5!
19 ♗f3

Suddenly it is clear that continuing the "attack" by 19 ♘f5 would backfire after 19...b4 20 ♘a4 (20 ♘xd6 ♕xd6 21 ♘a4 ♕xd5) 20...♘e4, followed by ...gxf5. White is therefore forced to reorganize his pieces to meet ...b4, but the knight is left out of play on h4.

19 ...   b4
20 ♘e2   ♘e4?!

20...♘e5 would have been more accurate, both preventing the h4-knight returning to the centre via g2 and introducing the idea of ...♘c4-b6, stepping up the pressure on d5.

21 ♕c2   ♘df6
22 ♘g2!

A good defensive move. Black's slight inaccuracy has given White a breathing space, and he correctly uses it to bring his knight back into the game. White might follow up with ♗f4 to exchange bishops, or with ♘e3, lending further support to the weak d5-pawn.

22 ...   ♕d7
23 ♘e3

The point of Black's last move lies in the line 23 ♗f4 ♗f8, when White has problems holding on to the d5-pawn as 24 ♘e3 g5 traps the bishop.

23 ...   ♖ad8
24 ♗g2?

This move leads to disaster for the seemingly innocuous reason that it leaves g4 insufficiently protected. After 24 ♖ac1! the position would be balanced. The combinative try 24...♘xf2 25 ♔xf2 ♕h3 fails to 26 ♗f4 ♕xh2+ 27 ♘g2 ♗xf4 28 ♘xf4 and the attack collapses, while 24...♕h3 25 ♗f4 leads to nothing. Black's problem is the b7-bishop, which remains inactive while the d5-pawn remains on the board.

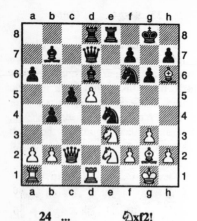

24 ... **♘xf2!**

This destructive sacrifice leads to an advantage for Black, even against perfect defence.

25 ♔xf2 **♖xe3!**

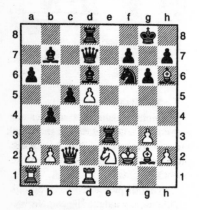

26 ♗xe3

When you are conducting a sacrificial attack, it is always pleasant to have an opponent who lets you show off the main points of your play. White could have bailed out with 26 ♔xe3 ♘g4+ 27 ♔d2 ♘xh6, but the resulting position clearly favours Black. In return for his very slight material investment, Black gains control of the dark

squares and White's king is left floating around in the middle of the board.

26 ... **♘g4+**
27 ♔f3 **♘xh2+**

There is no reason not to take the h-pawn before considering how to proceed.

28 ♔f2 **♘g4+**
29 ♔f3 **♕e6!**

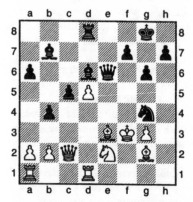

A neat move making use of the b7-bishop. The black queen attacks e3 while retaining its guard of the g4-knight. White's extra rook proves largely irrelevant as Black's pieces converge on the enemy king.

30 ♗f4

White is again cooperative and allows Black a brilliant finish. This time, however, there was nothing better:

1) 30 ♕e4 ♕xe4+ 31 ♔xe4 ♖e8+ wins.

2) 30 ♕d2 ♖e8 31 ♘f4 ♗xd5+! 32 ♘xd5 (32 ♕xd5 ♘h2+ 33 ♔f2 ♕xe3#) 32...♕e4+ and White loses all his pieces with check.

3) 30 ♗g5 ♖e8 is similar to the game.

4) 30 ♗c1 c4! (threatening both 31...♗xd5+ 32 ♖xd5 ♕xd5+ 33 ♕e4

♘h2+ 34 ♔f2 ♗c5+ 35 ♗e3 ♗xe3+ 36 ♔xe3 ♕c5+ 37 ♘d4 ♖xd4 38 ♕xd4 ♘g4+ 39 ♔e4 ♕f5# and the simple 31...♗c5 with an overwhelming attack) 31 ♕e4 (31 ♘f4 ♘h2+ 32 ♔f2 ♗c5+) 31...♕xe4+ 32 ♔xe4 ♘f2+ 33 ♔d4 ♘xd1 34 ♔xc4 ♖c8+ 35 ♔d3 ♗e5 with a won ending for Black.

30 ...   ♖e8

30...♗xf4 31 ♕e4 ♕xe4+ 32 ♔xe4 ♗e5 also wins, but Black is playing for mate. The immediate threat is 31...♗xd5+.

31 ♕c4

31 ♕d2 loses to 31...♗xd5+ 32 ♕xd5 ♕xe2#, but the move played allows a beautiful mate in six.

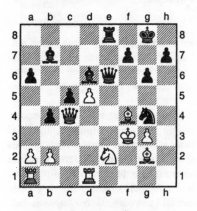

31 ...   ♕e3+!

Zviagintsev's brilliancy is completed by a queen sacrifice.

32 ♗xe3   ♖xe3+

33 ♔xg4   ♗c8+

34 ♔g5

Or 34 ♔h4 ♗e7#.

34 ...   h6+!

Not 34...♔g7 35 ♖h1, when White can prolong the game.

35 ♔xh6   ♖e5

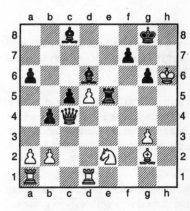

0-1

There is no defence to the twin threats of 36...♗f8# and 36...♖h5#.

Lessons from this game:

1) Making aggressive gestures usually entails a certain risk; if the attack fails to materialize, the "attacking" pieces may have to return with consequent loss of time.

2) Offside pieces should be brought back into play as quickly as possible.

3) A successful king-hunt is really satisfying.

Garry Kasparov – Vishy Anand

PCA World Championship match (game 10), New York 1995

Ruy Lopez, Open Variation

The Players

Garry Kasparov (born 1963) is the greatest player of modern times, and has been World Champion (of one sort or another) since 1985. For more information see Game 71.

Viswanathan ("Vishy") Anand (born 1969) was ranked number 3 in the world on the January 1998 FIDE rating list. He is the strongest-ever player from India and challenged unsuccessfully for the PCA World Championship in 1995, the event from which the current game is taken. For more details see Game 88.

The Game

After eight tense draws, the match exploded into life in the 9th game, when Anand played very smoothly to gain the first victory. The backlash was immediate and devastating. Kasparov won four of the next five games, effectively ending Anand's challenge. This game is the first, and hence the most important, of Kasparov's wins.

This encounter is an absolute triumph for opening preparation, which is becoming one of the most important factors in the modern game. Stung by an Anand novelty earlier in the match, Kasparov, aided by his vast team of helpers and his trusty computers, does his homework and confidently plays the same line four games later. Anand must have suspected some improvement by Kasparov, but he surely could not have envisaged the depth of the World Champion's idea. After 23 moves, despite frantic defence, the Indian GM can only reach a hopeless ending, which Kasparov converts into a win with ruthless precision. The depth of Kasparov's opening preparation is shown by his chilling press-conference quote "I spent two minutes during the game on the first 20 moves – but 48 hours beforehand."

1	e4	e5	8	dxe5	♗e6
2	♘f3	♘c6	9	♘bd2	♘c5
3	♗b5	a6	10	c3	d4
4	♗a4	♘f6	11	♘g5!?	
5	0-0	♘xe4			
6	d4	b5			
7	♗b3	d5			

This staggering move, an invention of Karpov's trainer Igor Zaitsev, caused a sensation when it was unleashed in game 10 of the Karpov – Korchnoi World Championship match in Baguio City in 1978. Apparently it just leaves a knight *en prise* to the black queen, but it's certainly not as simple as that.

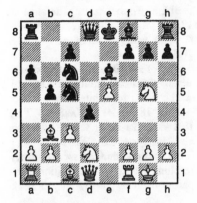

Variations after accepting the sacrifice are extremely complicated, for example after 11...♕xg5 12 ♕f3 0-0-0 13 ♗xe6+ fxe6 14 ♕xc6 ♕xe5 15 b4 ♕d5 16 ♕xd5 exd5 17 bxc5 dxc3 18 ♘b3 White has gone from a piece down to a piece up in just a few moves, as in Shirov – Timman, Wijk aan Zee 1996. Nevertheless, Black's mass of passed pawns still renders the position totally unclear. As well as the obvious 11...♕xg5, Black can also try 11...♗d5, or Anand's actual choice, the same as Korchnoi's back in 1978, which the Indian had played with some success four games earlier.

11	...	dxc3
12	♘xe6	fxe6
13	bxc3	♕d3

So far all of these moves had been played at great speed by both players. Now Kasparov unleashed his first surprise.

14 ♗c2!

Tal suggested this idea at the time of the Baguio match, without giving any further analysis. No doubt Anand and his team of seconds would have studied it, but it soon becomes apparent that they missed Kasparov's rook sacrifice. The 6th game saw Kasparov following Karpov's recipe from Baguio with 14 ♘f3, but Anand had improved on Korchnoi's play and after 14...0-0-0! (instead of 14...♕xd1) 15 ♕e1 ♘xb3 16 axb3 ♔b7 Black's active queen gave him a fully playable game, which ended in an eventful draw.

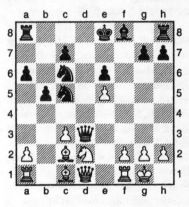

14 ... ♕xc3

Anand spent just four minutes on this move, suggesting that he was still following his pre-match preparation. After Kasparov's next move, however, Anand was left to his own devices.

15 ♘b3!!

Once more this was bashed out instantly by the defending champion. Anand pondered for a full 45 minutes before making the most obvious reply.

15 ... ♘xb3

It was subsequently discovered that Kasparov was not the first player to try 15 ♘b3. As the Australian grandmaster

Ian Rogers pointed out in a press conference after the game, an obscure correspondence game Berg – Nevesteit, 1990 continued 15 ♘b3 ♖d8 16 ♗d2 ♕xe5 17 ♖e1 ♕d5. Now Rogers' idea 18 ♕g4 seems to give White a very strong attack. Other ideas for Black are possible of course, but it's very difficult to decline a whole rook. In this line Kasparov suggests the counter-sacrifice 16...♖xd2!? 17 ♘xd2, as well as 15...♘b4 and 15...♗e7.

16 ♗xb3   ♘d4

The knight moves into the centre, attempting to exchange itself for the powerful b3-bishop.

The alternative is to take the rook immediately. Play after 16...♕xa1 is extremely complex:

1) After 17 ♕f3 Black can return the material by 17...♘d8! 18 ♕xa8 ♕xe5 19 ♕xa6 ♗d6 20 f4 ♕c5+ 21 ♔h1 0-0, with an unclear position.

2) Writing in the *New York Times*, Robert Byrne thought that 17 ♗xe6 had been Kasparov's intention, giving the enticing line 17...♖d8 18 ♗f7+ ♔xf7 19 ♕f3+ ♔e8 20 ♕xc6+ ♔f7 21 e6+ ♔g8 22 ♕xc7 ♕f6 23 ♗g5 ♗d6 24 ♕xd8+ ♕xd8 25 ♗xd8, with a winning endgame for White, although it looks as if Black can improve on this, e.g. 23...♖c8 24 ♕xc8 ♕xg5.

3) In fact, Kasparov had planned 17 ♕h5+!:

3a) Now 17...♔d7? loses after 18 ♗xe6+ ♔xe6 19 ♕g4+ ♔f7 (Black cannot move the king to a dark square, as a bishop check will discover a deadly attack on the black queen) 20 ♕f3+ ♔e6 (or 20...♔g8 21 ♕d5#) 21 ♕xc6+ ♗d6 22 exd6 ♕e5. In this position White has many promising

moves. Kasparov gives 23 ♗d2 ♕xd6 24 ♖e1+ ♔f7 25 ♕f3+ ♔g6 (or 25...♕f6 26 ♕d5+ ♔g6 27 ♖e6) 26 ♕g4+ ♔f7 27 ♗c3! and the white queen, rook and bishop combine to produce fatal threats.

3b) The most testing defence is 17...g6, when, having created a weakness, the white queen retreats with 18 ♕f3:

3b1) 18...0-0-0 19 ♕xc6 ♕xe5 20 ♕xa6+ ♔b8 (or 20...♔d7 21 ♗b2!) 21 ♗e3 is better for White.

3b2) 18...♘d4 19 ♕xa8+ ♔f7 20 ♖d1 ♘xb3 21 ♕f3+ ♔g8 22 ♗a3! is also clearly good for White.

3b3) With 18...♘d8 we are slowly reaching the truth of the position. Kasparov intended 19 ♕f6 ♖g8 20 ♗xe6!:

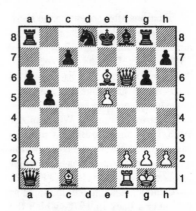

3b31) 20...♘xe6 21 ♕xe6+ ♗e7 22 ♕xg8+ and White wins easily.

3b32) 20...♗g7 21 ♗f7+! ♘xf7 22 ♕e6+ also wins after 22...♔f8 23 ♗a3+ or 22...♔d8 23 ♖d1+.

3b33) 20...♗e7 21 ♗d7+! ♔xd7 22 e6+ ♘xe6 23 ♕xa1 and White is clearly better, but there is still plenty of work to be done before this can be converted into a full point.

3b34) 20...♖g7 21 ♗a3 ♕xf1+ 22 ♔xf1 and all lines are good for White: 22...b4? 23 ♗xb4 ♗xb4 24 ♗d5 and White wins; 22...c5 23 ♗xc5 ♗xc5 24 ♕xg7 ♘xe6 25 ♕xh7 ♖d8 26 ♕xg6+ ♔e7 27 ♕f6+ ♔d7 28 ♕f3 and, according to Kasparov, White has excellent winning chances; 22...♗xa3 has been suggested, but instead of 23 ♕xg7 White should once again play 23 ♗d5!, with a winning position.

17	♕g4	♕xa1
18	♗xe6	

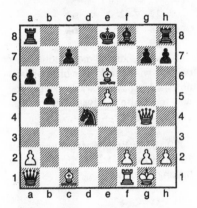

At this point Kasparov was still moving more or less instantly and was over an hour ahead on the clock. Meanwhile Anand was facing yet another tough decision...

18	...	♖d8

This move was actually played reasonably quickly by Anand, but there are important alternatives:

1) 18...♘xe6 19 ♕xe6+ ♗e7 20 ♗g5 is an easy win for White.

2) 18...♕c3! is the toughest defence. Kasparov merely mentions this move in *Informator*, while in *New in Chess*, he expands only a little with 19 ♗d7+ ♔f7 20 ♗e3 "and the rest is up

to you to find yourself". So what is the reality here? Black's position looks on the verge of collapse, but does White have to settle for an unhelpful assessment of "with good attacking chances" rather than the far more desirable "winning"? After 20...♗c5 (but not 20...c5? losing to 21 ♗xd4, when ♕e6 is coming) White has many enticing possibilities, such as 21 ♖d1 or 21 ♖c1 but it appears that Black still has defensive resources. The nearest White can get to a knockout is with 21 e6+ ♔g8 22 e7 g6 (the only move; 22...h6 23 ♗xd4 ♕xd4 24 ♕f5 and 22...h5 23 ♕e4 ♔f7 24 ♗xd4 ♕c4 25 ♕f5+ ♔xe7 26 ♗xc5+ are winning for White) 23 ♕e4! ♘e2+ 24 ♔h1 and now:

2a) 24...♔f7? 25 ♕d5+ ♔g7 26 ♗xc5 ♕f6 27 ♕d2! ♕e5 28 ♗e3!! leads to a very pleasing win, because 28...♕xe7 allows 29 ♗h6+ ♔f7 30 ♕d5+ ♔f6 31 ♗g5+, winning the queen, while 28...♔f7 29 e8♕+ ♖hxe8 30 ♗xe8+ ♖xe8 31 ♕xe2 leaves White a piece up.

2b) However, with the superior defence 24...♔g7! 25 ♗xc5 ♕xc5 26 ♕xe2 ♖he8 27 ♖e1 ♕d6 Black is still hanging on for dear life.

Back to the main game, which is much more clear-cut!

19   ♗h6!

Once again Kasparov bashed out this move with little thought. Anand now found the only way to carry on, as 19...♕xf1+ 20 ♔xf1 gxh6 21 ♕h5+ mates.

19	...	♕c3
20	♗xg7	♕d3

This is the only move to prevent immediate devastation around the black king. 20...♗xg7 21 ♕h5+ is mating again.

21 ♗xh8   ♕g6

Black's last chance to stay material ahead is by 21...♘e2+ 22 ♔h1 ♘g3+ 23 hxg3 ♕xf1+ 24 ♔h2, but with the black queen so far afield, Black is in no position to defend himself against White's queen, deadly bishops and rampant pawns, e.g.:

1) 24...♕xf2 25 ♗f6 ♕c2 26 ♗b3 ♕c5 27 ♕g8 and there's no way out of the net.

2) 24...♖d1 25 ♕h5+ mates after 25...♔d8 26 ♗f6+ ♗e7 27 ♗xe7+ ♔xe7 28 ♕f7+ ♔d8 29 ♕f8#.

3) 24...♕d3 is the most stubborn, but Black still has no chance of survival following 25 ♗f5! ♕c4 26 f4 ♕xa2 27 ♗xh7.

After 21...♕g6 Kasparov had his first long think, showing that he had finally left his home preparation. The result of all the fireworks is a technically winning position, but many accurate moves are still required before Black must finally throw in the towel. Kasparov's technique in this stage of the game cannot be faulted.

22 ♗f6   ♗e7
23 ♗xe7   ♕xg4

Black must exchange queens, as after 23...♔xe7 24 ♕h4+ ♔e8 25 ♗g4 the black king continues to feel the chill.

24 ♗xg4   ♔xe7
25 ♖c1!

A very important move, which nips any black counterplay in the bud. If Black is allowed to play the advance ...c5-c4 the situation would be much less clear. Black may still advance his queenside pawns, but the most dangerous one is stopped in its tracks.

25 ...   c6
26 f4   a5

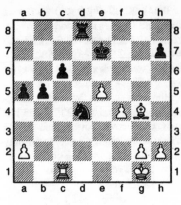

27 ♔f2   a4
28 ♔e3   b4
29 ♗d1

Another accurate move, combining defence with attack. The bishop holds up Black's pawns, while paving the way for White to advance his armada on the kingside.

29 ...   a3

29...b3 is simply premature. After 30 axb3 axb3 31 ♖b1 the b-pawn is lacking in support.

30 g4   ♖d5
31 ♖c4

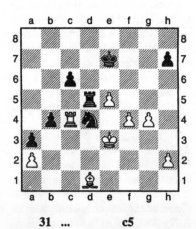

31 ...   c5

Black is fighting hard in this endgame but there is no real hope of survival. 31...♘f5+ loses trivially after 32 gxf5 ♖xd1 33 f6+ ♔d7 34 ♖xb4. Kasparov points out a trickier attempt in 31...♘e6 32 ♗b3 ♘c5, when the careless 33 ♖xb4 allows the trap 33...♖d3+ 34 ♔e2 ♖xb3!. However, White can avoid trouble with 33 ♗c2, when there are no more tricks.

32	**♔e4**	**♖d8**
33	**♖xc5**	**♘e6**

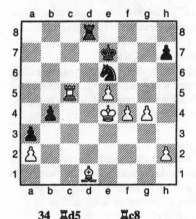

34 ♖d5   ♖c8

Black can eliminate the f-pawn after 34...♖xd5 35 ♔xd5 ♘xf4+, but White just takes Black's queenside pawns with 36 ♔c4, leaving an easy win. Kasparov also gives 34...♘c5+ 35 ♖xc5 ♖xd1 when White has many

ways to victory. Indeed, White's level of domination is shown by the World Champion's fantasy variation 36 ♖b5 ♖b1 37 ♖b7+ ♔d8 38 ♖xh7 b3 39 axb3 a2 40 ♖a7 a1♕ 41 ♖xa1 ♖xa1 42 h4, when the four kingside pawns should beat the black rook.

35	**f5**	**♖c4+**
36	**♔e3**	**♘c5**
37	**g5**	**♖c1**
38	**♖d6**	**1-0**

In fact White is drumming up a mating attack. Following 38...b3 39 f6+ ♔f8 40 ♗h5 ♖e1+ 41 ♔f3 ♘b7 42 ♖a6 ♘d8 43 ♖a8 ♖d1 44 e6 it's all over very quickly, and Anand had no wish to play this out.

Lessons from this game:

1) Kasparov is the absolute master of preparation. He has shown on numerous occasions that it's particularly dangerous to repeat a line against him. Anand learned his lesson the hard way!

2) The queen and two bishops are a lethal attacking force, especially in a wide-open position.

3) Technique is important. Often brilliant games are spoilt by inaccurate play in the endgame. This was certainly not the case here, as Kasparov gave the resourceful Anand no swindling chances whatsoever.

Veselin Topalov – Vladimir Kramnik
Belgrade 1995
Sicilian Defence, Sozin Attack

The Players

We have already met Veselin Topalov (born 1975) in Game 90. Although in 1994 he was an extremely strong grandmaster, by the time of our current game, in November 1995, he had established himself truly among the world's elite, a status he reinforced with a series of top-level tournament victories in 1996.

Vladimir Kramnik (born 1975) comes from Tuapse on the north-east coast of the Black Sea, in the deep south of Russia. He is one of the greatest stars of modern chess, and possibly the most serious threat to the World Number 1 status of Garry Kasparov, against whom he has an excellent personal score.

Kramnik has an all-round style: solid, aggressive, dynamic and pragmatic. He tends to play direct, classical opening systems with both White and Black, based on extremely deep preparation. This makes his games excellent models for ambitious chess players to study.

The Game

This spectacular and hard-fought battle is an excellent illustration of the fighting spirit typical of the top players of the 1990s. Both players display almost magical creativity: we see Kramnik conjuring up a deadly attack with very few pieces, and Topalov walking his king over the chess equivalent of hot coals.

The tactical shoot-out begins when both kings are forced to move after some ambitious opening strategy by Kramnik. With both players rejecting drawish possibilities, Topalov bravely and correctly marches his king into open space on the queenside. The outcome remains in doubt until he goes astray and allows Kramnik a decisive regrouping of his pieces. There is then no saving the beleaguered white king.

1	e4	c5	
2	♘f3	♘c6	
3	d4	cxd4	
4	♘xd4	♘f6	
5	♘c3	d6	
6	♗c4	♕b6	
7	♘db5		

7 ♘b3 had been played earlier in 1995 by Kasparov against Kramnik (Horgen 1995). White's knight retreat

leads to more standard Sicilian positions after the black queen drops back to c7. Topalov's choice is more critical.

7	...	a6	
8	♗e3	♕a5	
9	♘d4	♘e5	

The pawn-grab 9...♘xe4 10 ♕f3 leads to a treacherous position for Black.

10 ♗d3

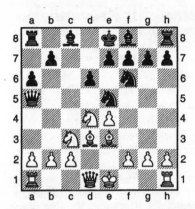

10 ...   ♘eg4

This is a new move, seeking to disrupt White's smooth development. 10...e6 is more sedate.

11 ♗c1

White must preserve this important bishop from exchange, and this is the correct square, since 11 ♗d2? ♕b6 12 ♘ce2 e5 13 h3 ♘xf2 14 ♔xf2 exd4 is obviously good for Black.

11 ...   g6

11...♕b6 is ineffective, since after 12 0-0 Black cannot take the knight (12...♕xd4?? loses to 13 ♗b5+).

12 ♘b3

White plans f4 followed by h3. After the immediate 12 f4, 12...e5 13 ♘b3 ♕b6 followed by ...exf4 will give Black's knight the e5-square, while 12 h3 ♘e5 is pointless for White, since although Black's ...♘e5-g4-e5 has "wasted" two tempi, so has White's queen's bishop, and he has played the rather useless h3 to boot.

12 ...   ♕b6

13 ♕e2!?

Topalov plays ambitiously, aiming to refute Black's plan. Instead, he could

develop routinely, but then Black would have a satisfactory position, e.g. 13 0-0 ♗g7 14 h3 ♘e5 15 ♗e3 ♕c7 16 f4 ♘c4 17 ♗xc4 ♕xc4 18 ♕d3.

13 ...   ♗g7

14 f4

White now threatens 15 h3, banishing the black knight to h6, and so making a nonsense of Black's play.

14 ...   ♘h5!

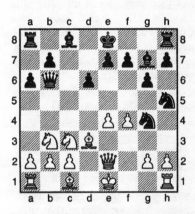

Although obviously risky, this is the only way to frustrate White's plan.

15 ♘d5

15 ♗d2!? is Kramnik's suggestion: 15...♗xc3 (15...0-0? 16 ♘d5 ♕d8 17 ♗a5 is White's idea) 16 bxc3 (not, of course, 16 ♗xc3? ♘xf4) 16...0-0 is a difficult position to assess. White's queenside is shattered, while it is not clear where his king shall find shelter. On the other hand, Black's king may well miss the protection of its dark-squared bishop if White can organize an attack.

15 ...   ♕d8

16 ♗d2

After 16 0-0 0-0 17 h3 ♘gf6 Black cunningly uses White's "active" knight on d5 to get his knights out of their tangle on the kingside.

16   ...   e6!

16...b6?! is a more obvious move, and appears safer, but fails to fight for the initiative; White has the advantage after 17 0-0-0.

17   ♗a5

Now total chaos breaks out over the whole board. 17 ♕xg4 exd5 18 ♕f3 leads to a more normal position; Black can then play for the initiative with 18...0-0! 19 0-0 (19 exd5 ♖e8+ catches the white king in the centre; 19 0-0-0 a5 gives Black good play on the queenside) 19...dxe4 20 ♗xe4 ♘f6, with approximate equality.

17   ...   ♕h4+
18   g3   ♘xg3

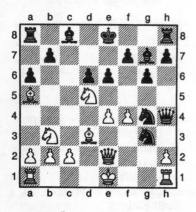

19   ♘c7+

After 19 hxg3, Black must avoid the obvious 19...♕xh1+? 20 ♔d2 ♕h3 21 ♘c7+, since although Black may well get several pawns, but they will be no match for White's active extra piece in the middlegame with Black's king so exposed. Instead the continuation 19...♕xg3+ 20 ♔d2 exd5 is promising for Black:

1) 21 exd5+ ♔d7 22 ♗b5+ (22 ♖af1 ♖e8 is no improvement) 22...axb5 23 ♕xb5+ ♔e7 24 ♖ae1+ ♘e5 25 fxe5 ♕g5+ 26 ♖e3 ♗xe5 and Black's extra pawn is sound enough.

2) 21 ♖af1!? ♘f6 22 exd5+ ♔f8 23 ♗b4 (23 ♖f3 ♕g4 24 ♗b4) 23...♗g4 24 ♗xd6+ ♔g8 and White will be hard-pressed to avoid simplification in Black's favour.

19   ...   ♔e7
20   hxg3   ♕xg3+
21   ♔d1   ♘f2+
22   ♔d2

22 ♔c1 ♘xh1 23 ♘xa8 ♕xf4+ is better for Black than the line in the note to White's 19th move above in which he got a few pawns for a piece, because White's rook is encased on a1, and the black pieces are more active.

22   ...   ♘xh1

The moves have all been practically forced since 17 ♗a5.

23   ♘xa8!?

This move brings about extreme complications, in which the white king must take a walk on the queenside. White had a safer option, namely to eliminate the h1-knight, which proves an effective attacking piece in the subsequent play, viz. 23 ☖xh1 ♕xf4+ (23...☖b8 is risky in view of 24 ♕f1) 24 ♔d1 ☖b8 25 ♗d2 ♕g3 26 ♗e1 ♕f4 27 ♗d2, repeating, is one possible way for the game to go.

23	...	♕xf4+
24	♕e3	♕h2+
25	♕e2	♕f4+
26	♕e3	♕h2+
27	♕e2	

Now Black has the option of taking an immediate draw by repetition. However...

27 ... ♗h6+

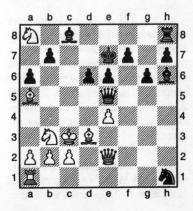

...Kramnik felt the position was too interesting for it to end immediately in a draw! Objectively this is a brave decision, since the situation that results is extremely unclear, and would have been impossible to evaluate with any certainty over the board. Doubtless Kramnik's intuition told him that the white king will be in trouble whether it runs to the queenside or stays nearer home, and so the gamble was a reasonable one.

28 ♔c3!

Topalov bravely and correctly advances his king into open space. 28 ♔d1? ♕g1+ 29 ♔e1 (not 29 ♗e1? e5 intending ...♗g4, when Black wins) 29...♕g4+ 30 ♗e2 (30 ♕e2? e5 again wins for Black, as 31...♕g4+ followed by 32...♗g4(+) is threatened, while 31 ♕xg4 ♗xg4+ 32 ♔e1 ☖xa8 gives Black three extra pawns) 30...♕xe4 31 ♘b6 ♗e3 (Kramnik's analysis) is good for Black, for example 32 ♕c3 ♘f2+ 33 ♔e1 ♕h4! (threatening the beautiful 34...♘d3++ 35 ♔d1 ♕e1+! 36 ♕xe1 ♘xb2# in addition to the simple threat of winning White's queen by 34...♘e4+) 34 ♕c7+ ♔f8 and now:

1) 35 ♕xc8+? ♔g7 36 ♕c3+ e5 leaves White with no decent reply, since after 37 ♕xe3 ♘g4+ 38 ♔d2 ♘xe3 39 ♔xe3 White's four uncoordinated minor pieces are no match for the black queen and flock of kingside pawns, which have the white king in their sights.

2) 35 ♗f3 ♘h3+ 36 ♔d1 ♕f2 and White is defenceless, e.g. 37 ♕xc8+ ♔g7 38 ♕c3+ (38 ♗c3+ ♔h6) 38...f6 39 ♕c7+ ♔h6 40 ♕c4 ♕xf3+ 41 ♕e2 ♘f2+ 42 ♔e1 ♕g3 and so on.

28 ... ♕e5+

29 ♔b4   ♘g3
30 ♕e1

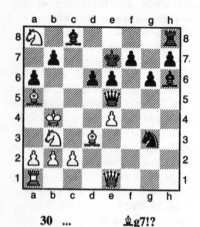

30 ...   ♗g7!?

This seems to be the best move, though there are two interesting alternatives:

1) 30...♕xb2 is an obvious move, but White can reply with 31 ♖b1 (31 ♗b6 is not clearly bad either) 31...♕e5 32 ♘b6 ♗g7 33 ♔a3, when Black has plenty of pawns for his piece, but White's forces have become coordinated. In fact, grabbing the b2-pawn has only given White an open b-file and provided his king with a possible route back.

2) 30...♗d7 was considered better by Topalov, but then Kramnik felt that 31 ♘b6 would be at least OK for White, while 31 ♔a3!?, threatening to exploit Black's loose pieces by ♗c3, looks better still. For example, 31...♖xa8 32 ♗c3 ♕f4 33 ♗d2 ♕h4 34 ♗xh6 overloads the black queen. Compare the next note.

31 ♘b6?

31 ♖b1 is necessary, and would both justify White's earlier play and cast some doubt over the wisdom of

Black's decision not to take the draw on move 27. Black would then have to rely on the strength of his kingside pawns, since the white king has at last found safety. For example, 31...♗d7 is answered by 32 ♔a3! with the idea of meeting 32...♖xa8 with 33 ♗c3, winning back the piece on g7. 32...f6 might be necessary, but is hardly what Black could have intended when playing 30...♗g7; still, he has three pawns for the piece while the black king remains better off than his white counterpart.

31 ...   d5!?

Black's idea is to open the f8–a3 diagonal so as to bring the g7-bishop into the attack. Now White has no time for the ♖b1/♔a3 defence we have seen in some lines above.

32 ♔a4

This move (threatening the cunning 33 ♗c3) has been condemned by some annotators as a blunder, but the suggested improvement is no better: 32 exd5 ♕d6+ 33 ♔c4 ♕f4+ 34 ♔c5 ♗d7 (34...♕d6+ 35 ♔c4 ♕f4+ repeats) 35 a4 is a position that has been claimed to be unclear, but Black wins as follows: 35...♗e5! (threatening mate in one) 36 ♘xd7 (36 ♘c4 ♖c8+ 37 ♔b4 b5 is hopeless for White) 36...♔xd7 (threatening 37...♖c8+; 36...♖c8+ 37 ♔b6 is far less clear) and now:

1) 37 ♔b6 ♗d4+ 38 ♘c5+ ♗xc5+ 39 ♔xc5 ♖c8+ mates.

2) 37 dxe6+ fxe6 and there is no escaping 38...♖c8+.

32 ...   ♗d7+!

This forcing check is definitely the best. Instead 32...dxe4? allows White finally to execute his main idea, viz. 33 ♗c3, while 32...♘xe4 33 ♗xe4! followed by ♗b4+ gives him enough counterplay.

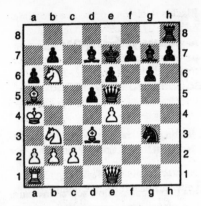

33 ♘xd7 b5+
34 ♔b4 ♔xd7

Black threatens 35...♗f8+.

35 ♗b6

Black wins after 35 ♘c5+ ♔c6 36 exd5+ ♔xd5 37 ♗e4 ♘xe4 38 ♕xe4 ♗f8.

35 ... ♕xb2?!

Instead after the tempting 35...♖c8? 36 ♗d4 ♗f8+ 37 ♔a5 the white king has reached an island of safety – it's not clear how Black should continue!

However, there was a neater way for Black to win, by 35...♘xe4! 36 ♗xe4 ♕xb2!! and now: 37 ♗d3 ♔c6!! threatens ...♗f8+ and is completely winning for Black; 37 ♗xd5 exd5 doesn't help White; 37 ♖b1 loses to the efficient 37...♕xa2 or the flashy 37...♖c8!? 38 ♗c5 ♗c3+! 39 ♕xc3 a5+; or 37 ♗c5 ♗c3+! 38 ♕xc3 a5+! wins the white queen.

36 exd5

Instead:

1) 36 ♕xg3?? allows mate in two.

2) 36 ♗xb5+ axb5 37 ♕xg3 ♖c8 38 ♖f1 f5! 39 exf5 ♕xc2 40 fxe6+ ♔e8! should win for Black, e.g. 41 ♖c1 ♗f8+ 42 e7 ♗xe7+ 43 ♗c5 ♕e4+! (43...♗xc5+? 44 ♘xc5 ♕xc1

45 ♕e5+ and White is saved) 44 ♔xb5 ♕e2+ 45 ♔b6 ♕e6+ 46 ♔b5 ♕c6+ 47 ♔b4 ♕b6+ and Black regains the piece, keeping two extra pawns.

36 ... ♖c8
37 dxe6+

Now what?

37 ... ♔e8!

Not 37...fxe6? 38 ♗xb5+, when 38...axb5? 39 ♖d1+ ♔e7 40 ♕xg3 should win for White.

38 ♗c5?

White had to try 38 ♗xb5+ axb5 39 exf7++ ♔xf7 40 ♕xg3 ♕c3+ 41 ♕xc3 ♗xc3+ 42 ♔xb5 ♗xa1 43 ♘xa1 h5, though Black's h-pawn is very fast, e.g. 44 a4 h4 45 a5 h3 46 ♗g1 ♖b8+ and 47...♖b1.

After 38 c4?, Black wins with the spectacular 38...♘e4!! White cannot take the knight due to instant mate, while 39 exf7+ ♔xf7 40 ♖c1 ♕xa2 41 cxb5 ♗f8+ 42 ♗c5 a5+! is a slaughter.

38 ... ♗c3+!
39 ♕xc3 a5+
40 ♔xb5 ♕xc3
0-1

Lessons from this game:

1) Delaying one's own development in order to disrupt the opponent's position is a very risky and committal strategy. Once started on this path, you must continue it to its logical conclusion, and be prepared to sacrifice (14...♘h5, 16...e6).

2) When both kings are exposed, be especially alert to "random" tactics and sudden counterattacks.

3) When defending against a powerful attack, try to spot any disharmony in the opponent's forces, and find a way to exploit it (Topalov's missed chance with 31 ♖b1 ♗d7 32 ♔a3).

Game 95
Vasily Ivanchuk – Alexei Shirov
Wijk aan Zee 1996
Queen's Gambit Declined, Semi-Slav Defence

The Players

Vasily Ivanchuk (born 1969) is one of the leading players of the younger generation. He is a phenomenally hard worker, but sometimes takes losses badly. For
more details, see Game 85.

Alexei Shirov (born 1972) is originally from Latvia but has now settled in Spain.
He is an enormously talented and creative player. For more information see
Game 89.

The Game

In a sharp main line of the Semi-Slav, Shirov plays an unusual variation, but is hit
by a big novelty from Ivanchuk. It leads to positions that are objectively very dif-
ficult to assess: White has two pieces for a queen, but Black's king is exposed and
White has some dangerous kingside pawns. The practical verdict is quite simple:
Black faces severe problems holding his position together. A few inaccuracies by
Shirov are all it takes for Ivanchuk to wrap up an impressive victory.

1	d4	d5
2	c4	c6
3	♘c3	♘f6
4	♘f3	e6
5	♗g5	dxc4
6	e4	b5
7	e5	h6
8	♗h4	g5
9	♘xg5	hxg5
10	♗xg5	♘bd7
11	exf6	♗b7
12	g3	c5
13	d5	♕b6

This move constitutes the heavily
analysed main line of the Anti-Meran
Gambit. We have already seen the alternatives 13...♘b6 and 13...♗h6 in
Games 74 and 89 respectively.

14	♗g2	0-0-0
15	0-0	b4

16	♘a4

16 ♖b1 is an important alternative,
which we shall see in Game 98.

16	...	♕b5
17	a3	

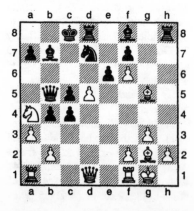

17 ...   exd5

17...♘e5 (17...♘b8 can be met in the same way) 18 axb4 cxb4 had once been considered satisfactory for Black, and was without doubt the main line, but the spectacular queen sacrifice 19 ♕d4! ♘c6 20 dxc6 ♖xd4 21 cxb7+, which first surfaced in 1994, changed all that. Perhaps Black can survive this position, but it is very difficult.

18 axb4   cxb4

18...d4!? is an extremely interesting alternative.

19 ♗e3   ♘c5
20 ♕g4+   ♖d7

Instead:

1) 20...♕d7?! 21 ♕xd7+ ♘xd7 22 ♖fd1 ♘xf6 23 ♗xa7 is good for White in view of his pressure on d5 and against the black king.

2) 20...♔b8?! 21 ♕d4!, with evil intentions on a7, left White substantially better in Agzamov – Chandler, Belgrade 1982.

3) 20...♔c7!? 21 ♗f4+ ♔c6 is suggested by Sadler, e.g. 22 ♘xc5 ♗xc5 intending ...♔b6 and ...d4. This idea is as yet untested in practice.

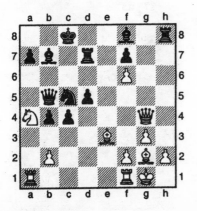

21 ♕g7!

This was Ivanchuk's amazing new idea, deflecting the bishop from the defence of c5 and generally disrupting the coordination of the black pieces. Nevertheless, the mind rebels against the idea that all this can be worth a queen. It is the sort of novelty that one automatically assumes was the product of many hours of painstaking work at home. However, according to Shirov, Ivanchuk was surprised by Shirov's choice of variation, and the queen sacrifice was over-the-board improvisation.

The mundane 21 ♘xc5 ♗xc5 22 ♗xc5 ♕xc5 was previously played. Black has compensation after 23 ♗h3 ♖hd8 24 ♕g7 ♔c7 25 ♗xd7 ♖xd7.

21 ...   ♗xg7

Black must accept the offer.

22 fxg7   ♖g8
23 ♘xc5

So, White has just two pieces for the queen! His pieces are well-placed, but can it be enough? Ivanchuk commented "Black's defence is very difficult, since he must parry White's threats on the queenside, but also waste some time eliminating the g7-pawn."

23 ...   d4?!

This move suffers from a tactical flaw. Black has at least one decent move here though:

1) 23...♗c6? loses to 24 ♘xd7 followed by ♖xa7.

2) 23...f5 24 ♖xa7! was felt by Shirov to give White a large advantage after either 24...dxg7 25 ♖fa1 or 24...♖gxg7 25 ♖fa1.

3) 23...♖c7 24 ♘xb7 and now:

3a) 24...♕xb7 25 ♖fd1! ♕c6 (not 25...♖xg7? 26 ♖xd5 and Black is defenceless) 26 ♖xd5 ♕e6 27 ♗f4 keeps a powerful initiative for White.

3b) 24...♖xb7 25 ♖fd1 ♖d7 (not 25...♖xg7? 26 ♖xd5) 26 ♗d4 is good for White – the plan is simply to push the h-pawn all the way up to h7. It is difficult for Black to do much about this.

4) 23...♖xg7!? is the best try:

4a) 24 ♖xa7 d4 (24...♖c7!? is interesting, e.g. 25 ♘xb7 ♖xb7 or 25 ♗h3+ ♔b8) 25 ♘xd7 ♗xg2 26 ♗xd4 ♗xf1! 27 ♘b6+ ♔b8 28 ♘d7+ ♔c8 29 ♘b6+ is a forced draw.

4b) 24 ♗h3!? f5! (24...♗c6? 25 ♖xa7) 25 ♗xf5 d4 (25...a6!? is also murky) 26 ♗xd4 and now 26...♖f7 isn't too clear. Instead 26...♕c6 27 ♘xb7 ♔xb7 28 ♖xa7+ ♔b8 29 ♖xd7 ♖xd7 30 ♗e5+ ♔b7 31 ♖e1 is very good for White.

4c) 24 ♗d4! f5 25 ♘xd7 ♖xd7 26 ♖xa7 "with a mess, although it may be easier for White to play this position than Black" (Sadler). This may well in fact be an appropriate assessment for the whole line with 21 ♕g7.

24 ♗xb7+   ♖xb7
25 ♘xb7!   ♕b6!

25...♔xb7 26 ♗xd4 defends g7 and attacks a7, whereupon White's rooks will move in for the kill.

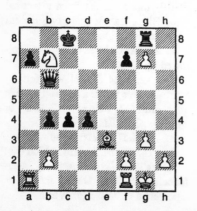

26 ♗xd4!!

After 26 ♗f4 ♔xb7 27 ♖fe1 a5! Black's queenside pawns are a force to be reckoned with; they defend the black king and offer real counterplay.

26 ...   ♕xd4
27 ♖fd1!

Better than 27 ♘a5.

27 ...   ♕xb2

Or:

1) 27...♕xd1+ 28 ♖xd1 ♔xb7 29 ♖d4 ♖xg7 30 ♖xc4 a5 31 ♖f4! ♔b6 32 h4 ♔b5 33 b3! is a won ending for White.

2) 27...♕xg7 28 ♖xa7 threatens to win on the spot by 29 ♘d6+, while 28...♔b8 29 ♖da1 ♖e8 (no better are 29...♕e5 30 ♘a5 and 29...♕d4 30 ♘a5!! ♕c5 31 ♖b7+ ♔c8 32 ♖xf7) 30 ♘d6 ♖e1+ 31 ♖xe1 ♔xa7 32 ♘xc4 is no use to Black since White can arrange his units to be defending each other against attack from the queen (pawn on b3, rook on the third rank) while his kingside pawns trundle up the board.

28 ♘d6+   ♔b8
29 ♖db1

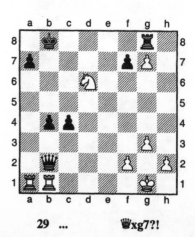

29 ...   ♕xg7?!

Or:

1) 29...♕c3 loses to 30 ♖xa7! ♔xa7 (30...♖xg7 31 ♖b7+ ♔a8 32 ♖7xb4 is completely terminal) 31 ♘b5+ ♔a6 32 ♘xc3 bxc3 33 ♖b4! assures White of a trivially won rook ending.

2) 29...♕d2 30 ♘xc4! ♕c3 31 ♖a4! b3 32 ♘a5! ♔a8 (32...b2 33 ♖b4+! wins the b-pawn, and with it goes Black's counterplay) 33 ♖a3! (33 ♖xb3 ♕e1+ 34 ♔g2 ♕d1!) 33...♕xg7 34 ♘c6 ♔b7 and now 35 ♘e7! is the neatest way to win, keeping all White's pieces well coordinated. Black will lose both his queenside pawns while his king remains exposed.

3) 29...♕e5 30 ♖xb4+ and then:

3a) 30...♔c7 31 ♖b7+ (31 ♖d1 was given by Ivanchuk, but 31...c3 isn't so clear) 31...♔xd6 32 ♖a6+ ♔c5 33 ♖a5+.

3b) 30...♔a8 31 ♖ba4 ♕c5 (or 31...♕xd6 32 ♖xa7+ ♔b8 33 ♖a8+ ♔b7 34 ♖xg8) 32 ♖a5 ♕b6 33 ♘xc4.

30 ♖xb4+   ♔c7

31 ♖a6!

White's pieces are beautifully coordinated. In this type of position the queen is wholly powerless against the rooks.

31 ...   ♖b8

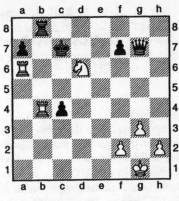

32	♖xa7+!	♔xd6
33	♖xb8	♕g4
34	♖d8+	♔c6
35	♖a1	1-0

Lessons from this game:

1) If you understand the logic of an opening really well, it is possible to work out good new ideas at the board.

2) Giving the opponent practical difficulties is just as important over the board as obtaining an objective advantage.

3) A queen can prove surprisingly feeble when facing a collection of smaller pieces that are well coordinated.

Deep Blue – Garry Kasparov
Match (game 1), Philadelphia 1996
Sicilian Defence, 2 c3

The Players

Deep Blue is IBM's supercomputer developed specifically with the aim of defeating Garry Kasparov in a match. Huge sums of money were poured into developing dedicated hardware that could calculate chess moves far faster than any other computer. In the first match, in 1996, the machine won the first game (featured here) in brilliant fashion, but in the end was convincingly defeated. The rematch in 1997 was an extremely odd event. It is very hard to say to what extent Deep Blue's victory was due to any real increase in its playing strength, as Kasparov seemed to suffer a bout of paranoia, and played well below his normal strength, losing the sixth and decisive game in ludicrous fashion.

After their publicity coup, IBM "retired" their machine from competitive play.

Garry Kasparov (born 1963) is the greatest player of modern times, and has been World Champion (of one sort or another) since 1985. For more information see Game 71.

The Game

Kasparov plays a new idea in a relatively quiet line of the Sicilian. However, all it takes is one minor inaccuracy for Deep Blue to gain the initiative. It plays a perfectly timed temporary pawn sacrifice to shatter Kasparov's structure. This prompts Garry to go all-out for a desperate attack, but the machine is then in its element, as it calculates a counterattack with great precision. This game, the first victory by a computer against a reigning World Champion at a normal time-limit, made headlines around the world.

1	e4	c5

At the time Kasparov was criticized by some commentators for not choosing a more closed opening against the computer. However, this criticism appears rather unjustified: if White is determined to open the game, then it is possible to find ways to do so no matter what Black does.

In the 1997 rematch, Kasparov tried playing more "anti-computer" systems, but with poor results.

2	c3	

A sensible choice. A main-line Sicilian (i.e. 2 ♘f3 followed by 3 d4), although sharp and tactical, would walk into Kasparov's lifetime of specialist knowledge and understanding.

2	...	d5
3	exd5	♕xd5
4	d4	♘f6
5	♘f3	♗g4
6	♗e2	e6
7	h3	♗h5

8	**0-0**	**♘c6**
9	**♗e3**	**cxd4**
10	**cxd4**	**♗b4**

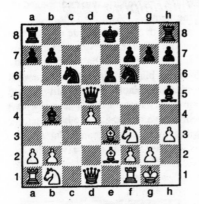

This was Kasparov's new idea. It ushers in a somewhat unusual manoeuvre, but is quite an effective way to develop the bishop.

11	**a3**	**♗a5**
12	**♘c3**	**♕d6**
13	**♘b5**	

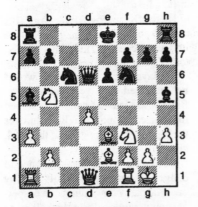

Deep Blue strives to keep the initiative. If left in peace for a move or two, Black could complete his development and start exerting unpleasant pressure against the isolated d4-pawn. Of course, the computer would not have seen the problem in those "verbal" terms, but rather the lines where it didn't force the pace were leading to poor evaluations. Therefore it played something forceful.

13 ...	**♕e7?!**

This gets Black into some trouble, as White has a strong plan for activating his pieces. Instead:

1) 13...♕b8 could be a better try: 14 ♘e5 ♗xe2 15 ♕xe2 0-0 (15...♘xe5 16 ♗f4 is good for White) 16 ♗g5 ♘xe5 17 dxe5 ♘d5 intending ...a6, since ♘d6 could be met without problems by ...♗c7.

2) 13...♕d5 was Kasparov's intended improvement when he repeated the same opening line in the third game of the match. Perhaps he considered this move during this game, but didn't want to allow a draw by repetition after 14 ♘c3 ♕d6 15 ♘b5. Instead, 14 ♗c4?! (when 14...♕xc4?? loses to the knight fork 15 ♘d6+) is well met by 14...♗xf3! 15 gxf3 ♕d7, so if White wants to make anything of the position, it must try the pawn offer 14 b4 ♗xf3 15 ♗xf3 ♕xb5 16 bxa5 ♘xa5 17 ♕e1, with compensation for White.

14	**♘e5!**	**♗xe2**
15	**♕xe2**	**0-0**
16	**♖ac1**	**♖ac8**
17	**♗g5**	

Black is now under considerable pressure. The pin on the f6-knight is particularly awkward. This shows the dark side of developing the king's bishop actively on the queenside, and why Black's decision on move 13 was so critical.

17 ...	**♗b6**

17...♖fd8 is a possible alternative; after 18 ♗xf6 gxf6 (18...♕xf6 19 ♘xc6 ♖xc6 20 ♖xc6 bxc6 21 ♘xa7 wins a pawn) 19 ♘c4, besides putting the bishop on b6 Black can choose between 19...♗c7 and 19...a6 20 ♘xa5 ♘xa5.

18 ♗xf6!   gxf6

Not 18...♕xf6?, when 19 ♘d7 picks up an exchange.

19 ♘c4!

Daniel King speculated that Kasparov may have overlooked this move, which holds on to the d-pawn based on the tactic 19...♘xd4 20 ♘xd4 ♗xd4 21 ♕g4+, and keeps the pressure on Black.

19 ...   ♖fd8
20 ♘xb6!   axb6

Now Black's queenside pawns are weak too.

21 ♖fd1   f5
22 ♕e3!

As we are about to see, the queen is superbly placed on e3. It is hard to give Black good advice. His pawns are weak and White's d4-d5 advance will shatter them completely.

22 ...   ♕f6
23 d5!

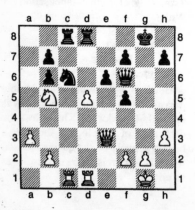

Kasparov wrote of this move: "...If I had been playing White, I might have offered this pawn sacrifice. It fractured Black's pawn structure and opened up the board. ... Although there did not appear to be a forced line of play that would allow recovery of the pawn, my instincts told me that with so many 'loose' black pawns and a somewhat exposed black king, White could probably recover the material, with a better overall position to boot."

23 ...   ♖xd5
24 ♖xd5   exd5
25 b3!

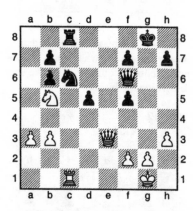

If played by a human, this would be described as a very calm move. Black's weaknesses cannot be solved in one free tempo, so White removes the b-pawn from the gaze of the black queen.

Seeing his pawns weakened and in danger of being picked off one by one, Kasparov now launches a desperate counterattack down the half-open g-file. However, this plays into the computer's strengths. Deep Blue replies in most unhuman fashion, allowing a lot of optical counterplay, but having accurately calculated that it does not work.

25 ... ♔h8?

This move is the final straw. Black's counterattack will just not work.

Black had to try to grovel into an ending: 25...♘e7 26 ♖xc8+ (or 26 ♕g3+ ♔h8 27 ♖xc8+ ♘xc8 28 ♕b8 ♔g7) 26...♘xc8 27 ♕e8+ ♔g7 28 ♕xc8 ♕a1+ 29 ♔h2 ♕e5+ 30 g3 ♕e2 regains the knight in view of the threat of perpetual check, but White will have a good queen ending in view of Black's shattered pawns. However, this would have been far more of a test for the computer, since in that ending understanding would matter more than pure calculating ability.

26	♕xb6	♖g8
27	♕c5	d4
28	♘d6	f4

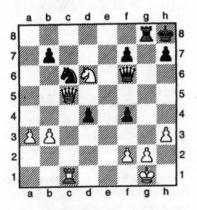

29 ♘xb7

This plan attracted a lot of comment in the media, with some being moved to draw analogies with American Civil War battles. However, the machine's number-crunching just happened to show that taking this pawn was a good way to win material and move the pieces into position for the counterattack. It didn't see a mate for Black, so had nothing to fear.

29	...	♘e5
30	♕d5	f3
31	g3	♘d3

Nothing works for Black, as Kasparov must have realized to his great agitation, e.g. 31...♕f4 32 ♖c8! ♕g5 33 ♖c5! is the end of Black's attack.

32	♖c7	♖e8
33	♘d6	♖e1+
34	♔h2	♘xf2
35	♘xf7+	♔g7
36	♘g5+	♔h6
37	♖xh7+	1-0

Black never gets to give his mate, as White's play comes first: 37...♔g6 38 ♕g8+ ♔f5 39 ♘xf3.

Lessons from this game:

1) It is possible to play normal chess against computers, but avoid really wild tactics.

2) When you have a static weakness, try to gain the initiative. Then you may be able to inflict some counterweaknesses or liquidate your own weakness altogether – ideally both.

3) If the opponent launches an artificial attack from a bad position, don't go into a defensive huddle, but find a way to knock the struts from his wobbly edifice.

Vasily Ivanchuk – Vladimir Kramnik
Dos Hermanas 1996
Sicilian Defence, Richter-Rauzer Attack

The Players

Vasily Ivanchuk (born 1969) is one of the leading players of the younger generation. He is a phenomenally hard worker, but sometimes takes losses badly. For more details, see Game 85.

Vladimir Kramnik (born 1975) was ranked second in the world on the January 1998 FIDE rating list and is widely seen as a potential challenger to Kasparov. For more details, see Game 94.

The Game

This game embodies the best elements of today's younger generation: a carefully prepared opening novelty involving a positional sacrifice; dynamic and aggressive play; refusal to be content with a draw; finally, exact calculation in an ultra-sharp position. Ivanchuk's efforts at counterplay are no less ingenious than Kramnik's attacking manoeuvres, but it takes only a small slip for White's king to succumb.

1	e4	c5	10	f4	♘xd4
2	♘f3	♘c6	11	♗xd4	b5
3	d4	cxd4	12	♕e3	♕c7
4	♘xd4	♘f6	13	e5	dxe5
5	♘c3	d6	14	♗xe5	

Many of the top younger players like to play the Classical Sicilian. It affords chances to play for a win with Black, but without involving excessive risks.

6 ♗g5

The Richter-Rauzer is White's most popular line against the Classical. White aims for queenside castling and double-edged positions are virtually guaranteed.

6	...	e6
7	♕d2	a6
8	0-0-0	h6
9	♗e3	♗e7

14 fxe5 ♘d7 15 ♘e4 is a major alternative, which may prove more attractive after the present game.

14 ... ♘g4!

This novelty is a remarkable idea. Black sacrifices the exchange, gaining in return some tempi and long-term pressure on the dark squares. It scarcely seems sufficient compensation, but it only takes one error by Ivanchuk for Black's threats to become really menacing.

Previously 14...♕a7 or 14...♕b7 had been played, with mixed results.

15 ♕f3

The only way to test Black's idea. After 15 ♗xc7 ♘xe3 16 ♖d3 ♘f5 Black has easy equality.

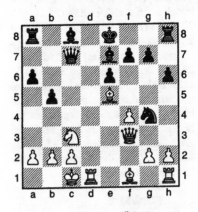

15 ...   **♘xe5**
16 ♕xa8   **♘d7**

Black cannot attempt to trap the queen by 16...♘c6? because of 17 ♘xb5!.

17 g3?

A mistake, as Black now gains a number of tempi. The best way to defend the f4-pawn was by 17 ♕f3 ♗b7 18 ♕g3, although after 18...b4 followed by 19...♗f6 Black obtains reasonable attacking chances on the queenside. Another idea is 17 f5, but after 17...♘b6 18 ♕f3 exf5 19 ♘d5 ♘xd5 20 ♕xd5 0-0 Black has sufficient compensation – one pawn and active bishops which can occupy good squares at e6 and f6.

17 ...   **♘b6**

Black must transfer his bishop to b7 immediately, or else White solves all his problems by playing ♗g2.

18 ♕f3   **♗b7**
19 ♘e4   **f5!**

Excellent judgement. Black is now deprived of the right to castle, which affords White certain chances for counterplay, but Kramnik is proved correct in his decision to continue pursuing the initiative.

20 ♕h5+   **♚f8**
21 ♘f2   **♗f6!**

Another powerful move, refusing to accept Ivanchuk's offer to return the exchange. If Black takes on h1, then the resulting position is roughly equal, since Black's queen and two remaining minor pieces are not enough to create decisive threats. Kramnik could also have forced a draw tactically by 21...♗c5 22 ♘h3 ♗xh1 23 ♘g5 hxg5 24 ♕xh8+ ♚f7 25 ♕h5+ with perpetual check, but he is playing to win. The b7-bishop is reserved to go to d5 or e4, supporting the attack against White's king.

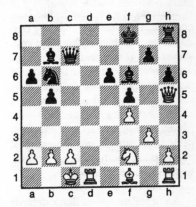

22 ♗d3

After 22 ♖g1 ♘a4 23 ♘d3 ♗e4 24 ♖g2 ♗xd3 (24...♘xb2 25 ♘xb2 ♕c3 26 ♘d3 is only a draw) 25 ♖xd3 ♗xb2+ 26 ♚b1 ♗f6 Black also has a dangerous attack. If 22 ♕e2, then 22...♚f7 brings the h8-rook into the attack.

22 ...   **♘a4**
23 ♖he1

White has no choice but to jettison his b-pawn as 23 b3 loses to 23...♗b2+ 24 ♔b1 ♗a3 25 ♖df1 ♗xh1 26 ♖xh1 ♕c3.

23 ...   ♗xb2+
24 ♔b1

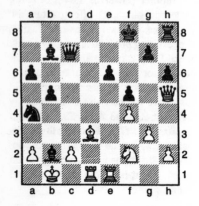

Amazingly, given that he had been confronted by a stunning opening novelty, Ivanchuk had at this stage consumed only 47 minutes on the clock and was almost an hour ahead of Kramnik. Such rapid play may indicate great self-confidence, but it can also be a sign of excessive nervousness – the player is unable to sit still and carefully work out the consequences of every option, but follows his intuition without detailed analysis.

24 ...   ♗d5!

An excellent move. Black defends the e6-pawn, while simultaneously increasing the pressure on White's queenside.

25 ♗xb5!

An ingenious defence making use of the somewhat exposed black king. 25 ♗xf5 is inferior due to 25...♗xa2+ 26 ♔xa2 ♕c4+ 27 ♔b1 ♘c3+ 28 ♔xb2 ♕b4+ and mate next move.

25 ...   ♗xa2+

Not 25...axb5 26 ♖xd5 and the rook is invulnerable because of mate at e8. The tempting 25...♘c3+ is also poor owing to 26 ♔xb2 ♘xd1+ (26...♘xb5 27 ♖d3 ♕b6 28 ♘d1 ♘c3+ 29 ♔xc3 ♕a5+ 30 ♔b2 ♕xe1 31 ♘c3 is also satisfactory for White) 27 ♘xd1 axb5 28 ♘c3 ♕a5 29 ♖e3 ♗c4 30 a3 b4 31 axb4 ♕xb4+ 32 ♔c1 ♗e7 (Black cannot win without the participation of his rook; 32...♔g8 33 ♕g6 does not help) 33 ♕h4+ g5 34 fxg5 ♕a3+ 35 ♔d2 ♖d8+ 36 ♖d3 ♗xd3 37 gxh6+ ♔d7 38 h7 and the h-pawn suddenly becomes a serious danger.

26 ♔xa2   axb5
27 ♔b1

Once again Ivanchuk finds the only move.

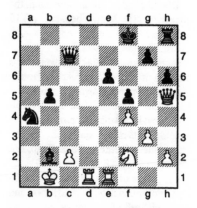

27 ...   ♕a5?!

By now Kramnik was down to his last five minutes (to reach move 40) and he commits an inaccuracy. He should have played 27...♕e7!, which also heads for the queenside but at the same time prevents ♖d7. Then 28 ♖d3 ♕b4 29 ♖d8+ ♔e7 30 ♖e8+ (30 ♖d7+ ♔xd7 31 ♕f7+ ♔c8 32 ♕xe6+ ♔b8 also wins) 30...Xxe8 31 Xxe6+ ♔xe6 32 ♛xe8+ ♔f6 33 ♛d8+ ♔g6 wins for Black.

28 ♘d3?

Surprisingly, 12 minutes' thought went into this error which allows Black to win easily. The best defence was 28 c3!, when despite appearances it is not so easy for Black to deliver mate. The obvious 28...♗xc3 29 Xd7 ♛b4+ 30 ♔c2 ♛b2+ 31 ♔d1 ♛b1+ 32 ♔e2 ♛xe1+ 33 ♔f3 leads nowhere because after 33...♔g8 34 Xd1! Black's queen is trapped. Instead he should continue 28...♘xc3+! 29 ♔xb2 ♘a4+ 30 ♔a2 ♛b4! 31 Xd8+ ♔e7 32 Xd7+ (Black also has good winning chances after 32 Xe8+ Xxe8 33 Xxe6+ ♔xe6 34 ♛xe8+ ♛e7) 32...♔xd7 33 ♛f7+ ♔c8 34 ♛xe6+ ♔b8 35 ♛e5+ ♔a8 36 ♛d5+ ♔a7 37 ♛d7+ ♔b8 38 Xe8+ Xxe8 39 ♛xe8+ ♔c7 40 ♛e5+ ♛d6 41 ♛xg7+ ♔b6 and the ending is very favourable for Black due to White's exposed king and the vulnerability of his knight to forks (if 42 ♘h3, then 42...b4 is very strong).

28 ...   ♗a3

Threatening mate in two.

29 ♔a2

Now 29 c3 ♘xc3+ 30 ♔c2 ♘xd1 is hopeless.

29 ...   ♘c3+
30 ♔b3   ♘d5

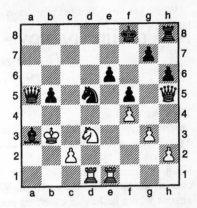

Although down to his last two minutes, Kramnik keeps a cool head. The white king cannot escape.

31 ♔a2   ♗b4+
32 ♔b1   ♗c3

0-1

Lessons from this game:

1) Exchange sacrifices for positional compensation occur surprisingly often and you should always bear them in mind.

2) If you need a particular minor piece for your attack, it may well be worth more than a rook on the other side of the board.

3) When conducting an attack, always consider whether it is possible to do so in such a way as to nullify the opponent's counterplay.

Veselin Topalov – Vladimir Kramnik
Dortmund 1996
Queen's Gambit Declined, Semi-Slav Defence

The Players

Veselin Topalov (born 1975) is one of the strongest players of the 1990s, and had a particularly good year in 1996. See Game 90 for more details.

Vladimir Kramnik (born 1975) is one of the greatest stars of modern chess, and possibly the most serious threat to the World Number 1 status of Garry Kasparov, against whom he has an excellent personal score. For more information see Game 94.

The Game

Both players acquit themselves well in this finely played and highly complicated draw. Kramnik is the first to deviate from previous play, with an improvement over a previous game of his own in a razor-sharp opening line. Topalov doesn't panic, but finds a way to keep enough play, in the face of a deficit of two rooks. The black king simply doesn't have enough shelter, and the game ends with a repetition of moves from which neither player dare deviate.

1	d4	d5
2	c4	c6
3	♘f3	♘f6
4	♘c3	e6
5	♗g5	dxc4
6	e4	b5
7	e5	h6
8	♗h4	g5
9	♘xg5	hxg5
10	♗xg5	♘bd7
11	exf6	♗b7
12	g3	c5
13	d5	♕b6
14	♗g2	0-0-0
15	0-0	b4
16	♖b1	

We have already seen 16 ♘a4 in Game 95.

The odd-looking text-move was first played by Uhlmann in the early

1980s, but it was not until the mid-1990s, when Kasparov introduced it into his repertoire, that it became popular. The idea is that this way White can keep the knight on c3 a little bit longer, thus keeping greater influence on the centre.

16 ...   ♕a6

16...♗h6 (too loosening) 17 ♗xh6 ♖xh6 18 b3! is good for White, showing another benefit of 16 ♖b1.

17 dxe6   ♗xg2

17...fxe6 18 ♘e4 is good for White; he has sacrificed nothing and Black's position is loose.

18 e7

A standard theme in such positions. The protected passed pawn on e7 often proves to be more powerful than a piece!

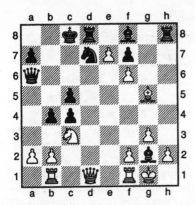

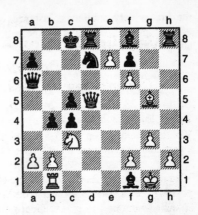

18 ...   &xf1

18...&a8?! 19 &d5 (White is in no hurry to cash in his big e7-pawn) 19...&b7 (this kind of pressure on the long diagonal can be very worrying at the board, but here it comes to nothing because White has the initiative) 20 exf8& &hxf8 21 &e7+ &c7 22 &f4+ &e5 23 &xe5+ &b6 24 f3 &xd1 25 &bxd1 is considered good for White in Peter Wells's superb book *The Complete Semi-Slav*. As we have seen in Game 95, the black queen can prove quite ineffective against an assortment of well-coordinated pieces. Having both to protect the exposed black king and to fend off an army of kingside pawns is an enormous task, even for a queen.

19 &d5

This move, a remarkable idea of Yermolinsky's, sparked off a major revival of 16 &b1. However, it appears to lead to a forced draw, although it is extremely complicated.

19 &xf1 is the move White must try if he wishes to keep any winning chances, though it seems Black has sufficient resources here too after 19...&c6!.

19 ...   &xe7

19...&h6 has also been extensively tested in practice, with the verdict currently being that it, too, is a draw with best play.

Instead 19...&d3?? loses to 20 &f4!! &b6 21 &a4 &b5 and now White forces mate: 22 &a8+ &b8 23 &xa7! &a6 (23...&b7 24 &b6+) 24 &b6+ &xb6 25 &xb6 and 26 &c6+.

20 fxe7

Black has a moment's respite here because &a8+ isn't such a deadly threat now that Black's rooks are connected.

20 ...   &d3!

This was Kramnik's improvement over 20...&dg8 21 &e4 &g6, which he had played against Kasparov. 22 &a8+! (22 &xf1?! &c6 23 &xc6+ &xc6 led to a draw in Kasparov – Kramnik, Intel Rapidplay, New York 1994) 22...&b8 23 &f4! (23 &xf1 was given by Kasparov as winning, but it is more complicated and less convincing) 23...&b7 24 &xb7+ &xb7 25 &xf1 &c6 26 &d1 &d7 and now Fritz3, when checking over Kasparov's annotations, pointed out that 27 &d6! was a clear-cut win. This was one of the first widely-publicized instances of a computer overturning competent analysis by a world champion.

21 ♘e4

21 ♕a8+? gets White into trouble after 21...♘b8 22 exd8♕+ ♖xd8 23 ♗xd8 (or 23 ♘d5 ♖xd5 24 ♕xd5 ♗xb1) 23...bxc3 24 bxc3 ♗xb1.

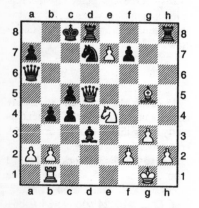

The knight was genuinely attacked, since opening the b-file for the rook is not a problem for Black when he is in a position is snap the rook off immediately!

21 ...　　♗xb1

Normally one would be suspicious of taking a relatively inactive rook when the enemy pieces are converging on one's king, but it makes sense to remove the reinforcements, and trust in the fact that White's army is now down to just queen, bishop and knight. Black has enough pieces around his king to avoid being mated, and if he needs to give back material, he has quite a lot in reserve. Instead 21...♖xe4? 22 exd8♕+ ♖xd8 23 ♕xe4 favours White, showing why the greedy approach is necessary.

22 ♘d6+　　♔c7

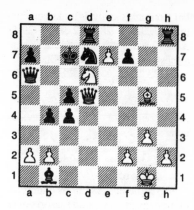

23 ♗f4!

White now threatens mate in five moves, starting with 24 ♘e8++.

Instead:

1) 23 ♘xc4? is well met by 23...f6 24 ♗f4+ ♘e5 (Sadler).

2) 23 ♘xf7? ♖c8 24 ♗f4+ ♔b6 leaves White with no decent continuation.

3) 23 exd8♕+?! ♖xd8 and now:

3a) 24 ♗f4 is similar to the game continuation, but with White having lost the option of keeping his pawn on e7; since Black has no time to save his rook, there seems no reason to surrender this possibility. In particular, note that the move doesn't threaten mate, unlike Topalov's choice in the game.

3b) 24 ♗xd8+? ♔xd8 25 ♘b7+ ♔c7 26 ♕xd7+ ♔xd7 27 ♘c5+ ♔d6 28 ♘xa6 doesn't work at all since after 28...c3 White doesn't even manage to give up his knight for the pawn: 29 ♘xb4 cxb2 or 29 bxc3 bxc3 30 ♘b4 a5.

3c) 24 ♘xf7 ♖e8 25 ♗f4+ ♔b6 (25...♔c8?? 26 ♕a8+ ♘b8 27 ♕xb8+ ♔d7 28 ♕c7+ ♔e6 29 ♘g5+ ♔f5 30 ♕f7+ wins everything) 26 ♕d6+ ♔a5 27 ♕xd7 is a controversial position, but Kramnik's analysis looks convincing: 27...♖e1+ 28 ♔g2 ♗e4+ 29 f3 ♗c6 30 ♕d8+ ♔a4 31 ♕d2 ♖a1 with a substantial advantage for Black.

23 ... ♔b6!

24 ♘xc4+

24 exd8♕+?! ♖xd8 25 ♘xf7 ♖e8 transposes to line "3c" of the previous note.

24 ... ♔b5

25 ♘d6+ ♔b6

26 exd8♗+

A completely gratuitous underpromotion, as there was no reason not to take a queen. Of course here Black has only one legal reply, so it doesn't matter, but in general unnecessary underpromotions are not a good idea!

26 ... ♖xd8

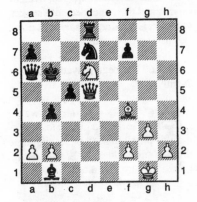

27 ♘c4+

27 ♘xf7!? ♖e8 is line "3c" of the note to White's 23rd move, but with the difference that there is no black pawn on c4. Then 28 ♕d6+ ♔a5 29 ♕c7+ (29 ♕xd7?? allows a forced mate, and shows a drawback of removing the pawn from c4: 29...♖e1+ 30 ♔g2 ♕f1+ 31 ♔f3 ♕e2+ 32 ♔g2 ♗e4+ 33 ♔h3 ♕h5#) 29...♕b6 30 ♕xd7 ♖e1+ 31 ♔g2 ♔a6! (instead 31...♗e4+?! 32 f3 ♗c6 33 ♕d2 is not so easy for Black here) is Ftačnik's recommendation, when it is not clear how White can hope to get more than a draw.

27 ... ♔b5

28 ♘d6+ ♔b6

29 ♘c4+

After 29 a4!? bxa3 (29...♗a2?! is suspect due to 30 a5+ ♔xa5 31 ♕xa2+ ♔b6 32 ♕d5) 30 ♘c4+ ♕xc4 31 ♕xc4 a2, Black's strong passed pawn makes it difficult for White to play for a win.

29 ... ♔b5

½-½

Lessons from this game:

1) **Don't be in a hurry to cash in your trumps** (such as the e7-pawn in this game). Doing so may simplify the opponent's decisions and improve the coordination of his pieces.

2) **Greed is sometimes a good idea!** It is important to evaluate which of the enemy pieces are the most dangerous and to eliminate them.

3) **A badly exposed enemy king** can compensate for an enormous material deficit; even if there is no mate, a perpetual check can save the day.

Game 99
Vishy Anand – Anatoly Karpov
Las Palmas 1996
Queen's Gambit Accepted

The Players
Viswanathan ("Vishy") Anand (born 1969) was ranked number 3 in the world on the January 1998 FIDE rating list. He is the strongest-ever player from India and challenged unsuccessfully for the PCA World Championship in 1995. For more details see Game 88.

Anatoly Karpov was World Champion from 1975–85 and FIDE World Champion from 1993 until the present day (1998). For more details see Game 67.

The Game
A rather unusual opening leads to an early liquidation of queenside pawns. Despite the almost symmetrical pawn-structure, White preserves an initiative because Black's queenside pieces are still on their original squares. Anand increases his advantage with subtle manoeuvres and then unexpectedly strikes on the other side of the board with a piece sacrifice. Even Karpov's famous powers of defence prove unable to cope with the ensuing onslaught.

1	♘f3	d5
2	d4	e6
3	c4	dxc4
4	e4	

Anand takes the game off the beaten track at a very early stage. 4 e3 would have led to normal lines of the Queen's Gambit Accepted.

4	...	b5
5	a4	c6
6	axb5	cxb5
7	b3	

Karpov was already spending a considerable amount of time, indicating his unfamiliarity with this unusual variation.

7	...	♗b7
8	bxc4	♗xe4
9	cxb5	♘f6
10	♗e2	

10 ♗d3 has been played more frequently.

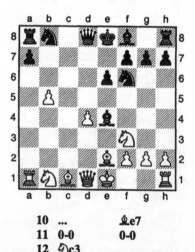

10	...	♗e7
11	0-0	0-0
12	♘c3	

From here the knight not only attacks the bishop, but also exerts some influence on the square in front of the isolated pawn – control of such a square is always important.

12 ...   ♗b7
13 ♘e5   a6

Karpov plays to liquidate the remaining pawn on the queenside. After 13...♗b4 14 ♗b2 ♗xc3 15 ♗xc3 a6 16 ♗f3! White retains an edge, for example 16...♘d5 17 ♗a5, followed by b6, and the advanced pawn is a potential danger.

14 ♗f3

Again White is fighting for control of d5.

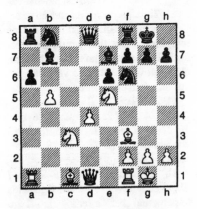

14 ...   ♘d5

After 14...♗xf3 15 ♕xf3 ♕xd4 16 ♕xa8 ♕xc3 17 ♗f4 White has a slight edge, although the extra exchange would prove hard to exploit in a position without queenside pawns. Karpov's move also leads to a slight plus for White.

15 ♘xd5   exd5

This change in the pawn structure rather favours White, since in the resulting symmetrical situation Black's b7-bishop is inactive and the white knight on e5 is an asset.

16 ♖b1

More dynamic than 16 ♕b3 axb5 17 ♖xa8 ♗xa8 18 ♕xb5, with just a minimal advantage for White.

16 ...   ♕b6

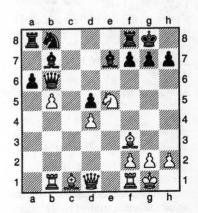

17 ♗e2!

This move shows flexibility of thought. Now that d5 is firmly blocked by a pawn, the bishop serves no real purpose on f3. The new target is Karpov's kingside, which is lacking defensive minor pieces. To this end the bishop is transferred to d3, at the same time lending support to the b5-pawn.

17 ...   axb5

Black continues his plan of gradual liquidation. If 17...a5, then 18 ♕a4 and White's passed b-pawn is more dangerous than Black's passed a-pawn since it is further advanced and supported by a rook.

18 ♖xb5   ♕c7
19 ♗f4   ♗d6
20 ♗d3   ♗a6

Karpov realizes that his kingside is in peril, and seeks to exchange White's dangerous light-squared bishop, even at the cost of giving up his central pawn.

After 20...♗c6 21 ♖b3, White would have a free hand with his attack.

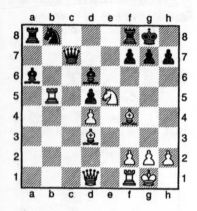

21 ♗xh7+!

A brave and absolutely correct decision. White could play 21 ♖xd5, with a clear extra pawn, but to win the resulting position would be far from easy. The relatively small number of remaining pawns increases the defender's drawing chances, and by exchanging on e5 Black might be able to reach an ending with 4 vs 3 on the same side, never easy to win even in favourable circumstances. Many players would have chosen this route because White has absolutely no risk of losing and can torture Black for a long time, but Anand is more interested in scoring the full point than achieving a nominal advantage.

The piece sacrifice offers excellent practical chances. Detailed analysis shows that White retains the advantage even against the best defence, and to find that optimum defence over the board proves too much even for such a noted defender as Karpov.

21	...	♔xh7
22	♕h5+	♔g8
23	♖b3	

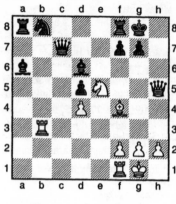

23 ... ♗xe5?

After this Black is lost. There were two alternatives that would have offered Black more defensive chances, although White retains a very dangerous attack in every line:

1) 23...♗c8? 24 ♖g3 and now:

1a) 24...♕e7 25 ♗h6 ♗xe5 26 dxe5 g6 27 e6 ♗xe6 (27...♕xe6 28 ♗xf8 wins material) 28 ♕e5 f6 29 ♖xg6+ wins for White.

1b) 24...♖a3 25 f3! (25 ♖xg7+? ♔xg7 26 ♗h6+ ♔f6 27 ♖e1 ♖g8 leads to perpetual check after 28 ♘g6 ♖xg6 29 ♕h4+ ♔f5 30 ♕h5+, or is unclear after 28 ♕h4+ ♔e6 29 ♘g4+ ♔d7 30 ♘f6+ ♔c6 31 ♖c1+ ♔b7 32 ♖xc7+ ♗xc7) 25...♕e7 26 ♖c1! ♕f6 27 ♗h6 ♗xe5 (if White is allowed to take on g7 then he should have the advantage) 28 dxe5 ♕b6+ 29 ♔h1 g6 30 ♗xf8 ♖c3 31 ♕h6 ♖xc1+ 32 ♕xc1 is winning for White.

2) 23...f6! 24 ♖h3 fxe5 (24...♗xe5? 25 dxe5 transposes to the game) 25 dxe5 ♕c4! (25...♖xf4? 26 e6 ♔f8 27

♕h8+ ♔e7 28 ♕xg7+ ♔xe6 29 ♖e1+ ♖e4 30 ♖h6+ forces mate) 26 ♖e1! (cutting off the enemy king's escape route) 26...♕xf4 27 ♕h7+ ♔f7 28 exd6 and now:

2a) 28...♖e8? 29 ♕h5+ g6 30 ♖e7+! ♖xe7 (30...♔f6 31 ♕f3! wins) 31 ♕h7+ ♔f6 (31...♔f8 32 dxe7+ ♔e8 33 ♕xg6+ ♔xe7 34 ♖h7+ forces mate) 32 ♕xe7+ ♔f5 33 ♕f8+ ♔e5 34 ♖e3+ leads to a decisive advantage for White.

2b) 28...♘c6 29 ♖f3 ♕xf3 30 gxf3 ♗c4 31 ♔h1 was Black's best chance, but White has the advantage because of his d-pawn and persisting attack.

24 ♖h3   f6
25 dxe5   ♕e7

25...♕c4 26 ♖e1 ♕xf4 27 ♕h7+ ♔f7 28 e6+ ♔e8 29 ♕g6+ is also hopeless for Black.

26 ♕h7+   ♔f7
27 ♖g3

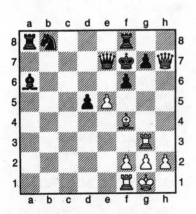

Although White does not have a large attacking force, he has a local superiority on the kingside since Black's queenside pieces are too far away to influence the struggle.

27 ...   ♔e8

Giving up the g-pawn is equivalent to resignation, but 27...♖g8 28 ♕g6+ ♔f8 29 exf6 is crushing.

28 ♖xg7

There are now several ways to win. One alternative is 28 exf6 gxf6 (or 28...♖xf6 29 ♖xg7 ♕e6 30 ♕h5+ ♖f7 31 ♖xf7 ♕xf7 32 ♖e1+) 29 ♖e3 ♕xe3 30 fxe3 ♗xf1 31 ♗d6 and White will have a decisive material advantage.

28 ...   ♕e6
29 exf6

With three pawns and an enormous attack for the piece, the end is not far off.

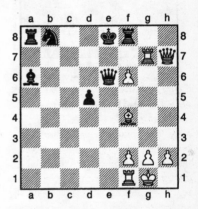

29 ...   ♘c6
30 ♖a1

The rook finally moves away from the attack of Black's bishop – Karpov never had time to take it.

30 ...   ♔d8
31 h4

White's position is so strong that he can afford the time to give his king a flight square.

31 ...   ♗b7

31...♘d4 loses to 32 ♗c7+ ♔c8 33 ♗a5.

32 ♖c1   ♗a6

33 ♖a1

Here, too, there are other routes to victory, e.g. 33 ♖xc6 ♕xc6 34 ♗c7+ ♔c8 35 ♕f5+ ♔b7 36 ♗a5+ ♔b8 37 ♕e5+ ♔c8 38 ♖c7+. However, there is nothing wrong with Anand's method.

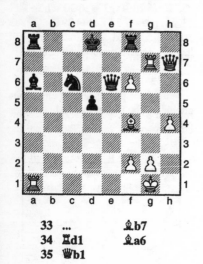

33	...	♗b7
34	♖d1	♗a6
35	♕b1	

A neat finish, switching the queen to the other side of the board, although 35 ♖e7 would have won at once.

35	...	♖xf6
36	♗g5	♔c8

1-0

Karpov lost on time while in the act of playing 36...♔c8. The reply 37 ♕b6 wins immediately.

Lessons from this game:

1) An unusual opening can be an effective one-off surprise weapon, but it is not a good idea to adopt such off-beat lines regularly.

2) In a direct attack on the king, what matters is not the overall material balance, but how many pieces each side has in the actual battle area.

3) Play the odds. Presenting your opponent with tough problems may give you better winning chances than a safe position with only a modest advantage.

Game 100
Vishy Anand – Joël Lautier
Biel 1997
Scandinavian Defence

The Players

Viswanathan ("Vishy") Anand (born 1969) was ranked number 3 in the world on the January 1998 rating list. He is the strongest-ever player from India and challenged unsuccessfully for the PCA World Championship in 1995. For more details see Game 88.

Joël Lautier (born 1973) is the first Frenchman ever to reach the Interzonal stage of the world championship. His first major success was winning the World Junior Championship in 1988; two years later he gained the grandmaster title and played in the Manila Interzonal. Since then he has made some progress, but without reaching the very top ranks of world chess. In 1997 he married the leading Moldovan woman player Almira Skripchenko. On the January 1998 rating list Lautier was ranked joint 38th.

The Game

A sharp opening line soon leads to a weird position in which White's king's rook has been developed via h3 to e3, while Black's light-squared bishop is trapped on g2. Anand is prepared to offer the exchange in order to round up this bishop, while Lautier hopes to sell it as dearly as possible. At the critical moment, Anand finds a stunning combination based on a queen sacrifice. Lautier's position cannot withstand this massive blow and promptly collapses.

1	e4	d5	
2	exd5	♕xd5	
3	♘c3	♕a5	

The Scandinavian is one of the success stories of the 1990s. At one time considered an eccentric and dubious response to 1 e4, it has gradually been accepted as a mainstream opening. Black's intention is to develop his c8-bishop to either f5 or g4, and then play ...e6. The result is a pawn-structure similar to the solid 4...♗f5 line of the Caro-Kann.

4	d4	♘f6	
5	♘f3	c6	

6	♗c4		

6 ♘e5 is another popular line.

6	...	♗f5	
7	♘e5		

The variations with 7 ♗d2 leave White with a slight edge, but Black's position is very solid. The text-move is a far more dynamic option.

7	...	e6	
8	g4	♗g6	
9	h4	♘bd7	

The most accurate; after 9...♗b4 10 ♗d2 ♘e4 11 f3! White gained some advantage in Campora – Curt Hansen, Palma de Mallorca 1989.

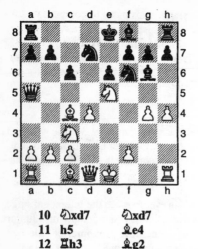

10	♘xd7　♘xd7
11	h5　♗e4
12	♖h3　♗g2

A key moment. The natural square for Black's bishop is d5, but this finesse intends to force the rook to g3 first, so that a later ...♗d6 will gain a tempo by attacking the rook. If White were indeed forced to play ♖g3, Black would benefit from this manoeuvre, but Anand demonstrates that he has a second option. Since Black appears unable to equalize in the game continuation, he should have abandoned his finesse and played 12...♗d5 at once, with an unclear position.

13 ♖e3!

Much better than 13 ♖g3. At first sight the rook is exposed to attack by ...♘b6-d5, but White is prepared to give up his rook in order to close the net around the bishop on g2. Of course, Black can remove his bishop from the trap by 13...♗d5, but this would be an admission of failure, as White would simply have gained the useful extra tempo ♖e3.

13 ...　♘b6

This is the critical continuation. After 13...b5 14 ♗d3 b4 15 ♘e4 Black

will have to play ...♗xe4 sooner or later, when White will be better due to his two bishops.

14 ♗d3!

14 ♗b3?! is inferior due to 14...c5!, when Black has good counterplay.

14 ...　♘d5

The obvious reply, attacking c3 and e3.

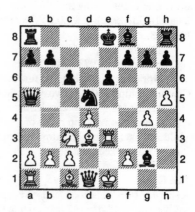

15 f3!

A remarkably calm move. White is willing to jettison considerable material in order to guarantee capture of the g2-bishop. In the resulting position Black will end up with a rook and some pawns against two bishops, which might favour him on a pure head-count, but other factors benefit White. The lack of open files means that there will be little scope for the black rooks to become active and in any case both rooks are still on their original squares, so any potential activity is quite far away. On the other hand, White's bishops will already be in play and, coupled with the advanced kingside pawns, they will give White excellent attacking chances should Black play ...0-0.

15 ... **♗b4**

After 15...♘xc3 16 bxc3 ♕xc3+ 17 ♗d2 ♕xd4 18 ♔f2 ♗xf3 19 ♔xf3 or 15...♘xe3 16 ♗xe3 ♕b6 17 ♔f2 ♗h3 18 ♖b1 a position of the type mentioned above is reached; White has the advantage in both cases.

16 ♔f2! **♗xc3**

The same comment also applies to the continuation 16...♘xc3 17 bxc3 ♗xc3 18 ♖b1 ♗xd4 19 ♔xg2 ♗xe3 20 ♗xe3.

17 bxc3 **♕xc3**

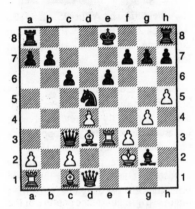

18 ♖b1 **♕xd4**

White wins after 18...♗xf3 19 ♕xf3 ♕xd4 20 ♖xb7 0-0 21 ♕e4, keeping the extra piece.

19 ♖xb7

Now Black cannot castle because of 20 ♗xh7+, so his king has to stay in the centre.

19 ... **♖d8**

The other critical lines are:

1) 19...♗h3 20 ♖xf7! c5 (threatening 21...♔xf7; if instead 20...♘xe3, then 21 ♗xe3 ♕d6 22 ♖f4 is very good for White) 21 ♖f5! ♘xe3 22 ♗xe3 ♕b2 23 ♖xc5 0-0 24 ♔g3! wins, because Black will probably not even get

a single extra pawn to compensate for the two bishops vs rook advantage.

2) 19...♘f4 20 ♔g3 ♕d6 21 ♗a3! ♘xh5+ (21...♕xa3 22 ♗e4! also wins) 22 ♔xg2 ♕g3+ 23 ♔f1 is winning for White.

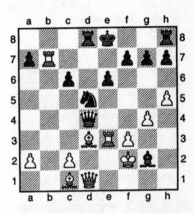

20 h6!

At first sight an odd move, because it is hard to see why the interpolation of h6 and ...gxh6 improves White's position. However, it is all based on a hidden tactical point. White would like to play the beautiful move 20 ♗g6, but after 20...♕xd1 21 ♖xe6+ ♔f8 22 ♗a3+ (or 22 ♖xf7+ ♔g8) 22...♘e7 23 ♗xe7+ ♔g8 the black king escapes and the attack fails.

The preliminary h6 is designed to induce the small change in the kingside pawn-structure which would make this combination work.

20 ... **gxh6?**

Lautier has missed the ♗g6 idea and allows White to demonstrate the main point of his play. The alternatives are:

1) 20...g6 (after this the combination also works) 21 ♗xg6! ♕xd1 22 ♖xe6+ ♔f8 23 ♖xf7+ ♔g8 24 ♖g7+

(utilizing the pawn on h6) 24...♔f8 25 ♗a3+ followed by mate.

2) 20...♘xe3 (the only move to avoid immediate defeat) 21 ♗xe3 ♕e5 22 hxg7 ♖g8 23 ♕c1! is very good for White. He threatens both 24 ♕a3 and 24 ♔xg2, and if 23...♕h2, then 24 ♗f4 ♕h3 25 ♕a3 wins.

21   ♗g6!!

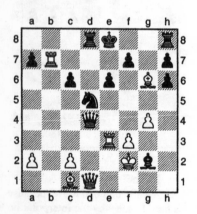

A really beautiful move, putting both queen and bishop *en prise*.

21   ...   ♘e7

There is no way out:

1) 21...♕xd1 22 ♖xe6+ ♔f8 23 ♗xh6+ ♔g8 24 ♗xf7#.

2) 21...♕xe3+ 22 ♗xe3 fxg6 23 ♗c5 wins.

3) 21...♕f6 22 ♗xf7+ ♕xf7 23 ♖xf7 ♘xe3 24 ♕xd8+! ♔xd8 25 ♗xe3 ♗h3 26 ♖xa7 ♖e8 27 ♖xh7 and Black loses several pawns, followed by his bishop!

22   ♕xd4   ♖xd4
23   ♖d3!

The clearest win. Black is doomed by his trapped bishop.

23   ...   ♖d8
24   ♖xd8+   ♔xd8
25   ♗d3!   1-0

A neat finish. After 25...♗h1 26 ♗b2 ♖e8 27 ♗f6 Black will soon be in zugzwang and have to surrender at least a piece.

Lessons from this game:

1) Be careful with clever little finesses, especially if they involve an unnatural move – after your opponent's reply they may not seem so clever.

2) A king trapped in the centre is exposed to attack – flouting this basic principle can cost the game, even for a grandmaster!

3) Weird positions often call for unusual moves.

Suat Atalik – Gyula Sax
Szeged 1997
Nimzo-Indian Defence

The Players

Suat Atalik (born 1964) was for many years Turkey's leading grandmaster, although he recently changed his national registration to that of Bosnia & Herzegovina. He has not broken through into the top ranks of world chess, but has achieved considerable success in team competitions. His direct style of play has produced a number of attractive games, but he is probably best known for the game below.

Gyula Sax (born 1951) is a Hungarian grandmaster who was very successful as a junior player and was European Junior Champion in 1971/2. He gained his grandmaster title in 1974 and won the Hungarian Championship for the first time in 1976. His career has spanned over 30 years of top-level chess, and while he has always been a dangerous opponent in individual games, he never acquired the consistency necessary to break into the world elite. His best period was 1988-91, during which he twice qualified for the Candidates' matches. In recent years his play has become more erratic, but he is still capable of playing excellent chess.

The Game

There has always been opening theory in chess, but in recent decades it has grown to such an extent that even rarely-played lines are often deeply analysed. The use of computers and the dissemination of information via the Internet have only served to fuel this growth. Some players have reacted by choosing quiet openings in which a detailed knowledge of theory is less important, while others have embraced the new paradigm and devoted more and more time to opening research. The stunning novelty which Atalik plays in this game shows how opening preparation can be a point-winner in tournament play. Sax enters a double-edged opening line which, at the time of this game, appeared playable for Black, only to be rocked back by a novelty. Atalik follows up with a blistering tactical display, and Sax's king is pounded to destruction along the long diagonal.

1	d4	♘f6
2	c4	e6
3	♘c3	♗b4
4	♕c2	

In recent decades this move has been one of White's most popular options against the Nimzo-Indian. At the cost of some time, White avoids the doubling of his c-pawns.

4	...	d5

Black tries to exploit White's slow play by opening up the centre. 4...c5 and 4...0-0 are Black's main alternatives.

5	a3	♗xc3+
6	♕xc3	♘e4
7	♕c2	♘c6

The start of a double-edged plan which results in Black gaining material but falling far behind in development. However, until this game Black's plan had not been refuted. 7...c5 8 dxc5 ♘c6 is a safer continuation.

8	e3	e5
9	cxd5	♕xd5
10	♗c4!	

Accepting the challenge. 10 ♘f3 is playable but less ambitious.

10	...	♕a5+
11	b4	♘xb4
12	♕xe4	

White allows Black a double check which leads to gain of material, but in return Black's pieces end up offside.

| 12 | ... | ♘c2++ |

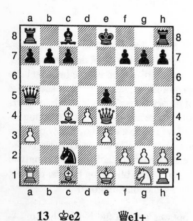

| 13 | ♔e2 | ♕e1+ |

This preliminary check is essential since it obstructs the development of White's kingside pieces. 13...♘xa1 14 ♘f3 is very good for White, despite the minus exchange, since he has a large lead in development and chances to trap the a1-knight.

| 14 | ♔f3 | ♘xa1 |

The position is tricky to assess. White's well-centralized pieces and attacking chances must be balanced against Black's material advantage and the fact that White's king may also become exposed. A recurring theme is the possible sacrifice of the h1-rook in order to bring the g1-knight into play with gain of time.

| 15 | ♗b2 | |

Development is all-important. The greedy 15 ♕xe5+ ♗e6 16 ♗xe6 would rebound after 16...0-0!.

| 15 | ... | 0-0 |

It is natural to speed the black king away from the centre, although White's pieces are also well placed for a kingside attack. 15...♗e6 has been played a few times, but after 16 d5 0-0-0 17 dxe6 fxe6 18 ♗xe5 White has the advantage.

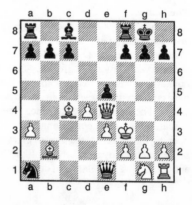

| 16 | ♔g3! | |

It is remarkable that White has time for this quiet move, which both safeguards his king and prepares an assault by ♘f3-g5. The immediate 16

♘h3 ♕xh1 17 ♘g5 fails to the simple 17...♕xh2.

16 ... **♔h8**

This move was regarded as best at the time the current game was played. The alternatives are:

1) 16...♗d7 17 ♘f3 ♕xh1 18 ♘g5 g6 19 ♕xe5 ♖ae8 20 ♕f6 ♖xe3+ 21 fxe3 ♕e1+ 22 ♔f3 ♕d1+ (Sadler – Tukmakov, Linares open 1995) and now 23 ♗e2 ♗g4+ 24 ♔f4! favours White.

2) 16...h6 is perhaps the last chance for Black in this variation, although nobody seems to have been motivated to try it!

17 dxe5!

This stunning novelty effectively killed the whole variation. Hitherto, White had continued 17 ♘f3 ♕xh1 18 ♘g5 f5 19 ♕xe5, but after 19...♗d7 20 ♘f7+ ♖xf7 21 ♗xf7 f4+ 22 exf4 ♕d1 (Hillarp Persson – Timman, Køge 1997) the position is totally unclear.

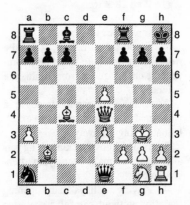

The text-move costs White a tempo, but it allows him to activate his dark-squared bishop. The main thrust of the attack will be along the long dark diagonal.

17 ... **♗e6**

Forced, as White was threatening an instant win by 18 ♗d3 g6 19 e6+ f6 20 e7.

18 ♘f3

The rook sacrifice is stronger now than a move earlier.

18 ... **♕xh1**
19 ♘g5 **g6**
20 ♘xf7+!!

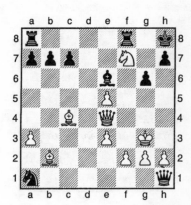

Already a rook and the exchange down, White throws in another piece in order to prise open the long diagonal. Without this follow-up, White's innovation at move 17 would have been pointless.

20 ... **♖xf7**
21 ♗xe6 **♖g7**

The first time Black had a genuine choice since the thunderbolt at move 17. The alternative was to aim for counterplay by 21...♖xf2!? 22 ♔xf2 ♖f8+ 23 ♔g3 ♕e1+ 24 ♔h3 ♔g7, but after the remarkable continuation 25 ♗d7! ♔h6 26 e6 ♖f5 27 ♗f6!! Black is lost; for example, 27...♖xf6 28 e7 or 27...♖h5+ 28 ♔g4 ♖f5 29 e7 ♕d1+ 30 ♔h4.

22 ♗f7!

The second surprising blow on the f7-square. White must move his bishop to prepare e6, and by moving to f7 White ensures that it will not be blocked when the e-pawn advances. Black is lost thanks to the extraordinary activity of White's bishops. 22 ♗g4?! is inferior since 22...♖f8! 23 e6 ♕f1 gives Black enough counterplay to hold the balance.

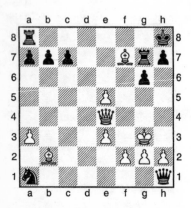

22 ...   ♖xf7?

Black can't stand the sight of the two deadly bishops and decides to eliminate one, but now White has a forced win. 22...♕d1, trying to bring the queen back into the game, offers slightly more of a fight, but after 23 e6 ♕d6+ (23...h5 loses to 24 e7 ♕d6+ 25 ♗e5) 24 ♗e5 ♕e7 25 ♗xa1 ♕g5+ (25...♖ag8 26 ♕f4 b5 27 ♗f6 ♕d6 28 ♕xd6 cxd6 29 e7 also wins for White) 26 ♕g4 ♕xg4+ (26...♕d8 27 ♕f4) 27 ♔xg4 h6 28 e7 White will emerge a piece up.

23 e6+   ♔g8

23...♖g7 24 e7 h5 25 ♕xg6 leads to mate.

24 ♕d4   ♔f8
25 exf7   ♔xf7

After 25...♔e7 26 ♗xa1 ♕c1 27 ♕g7 ♔e6 28 ♕g8! White will be a piece up.

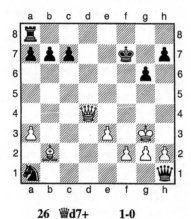

26 ♕d7+   1-0

White forces mate after 26...♔f8 27 ♕g7+ ♔e8 28 ♗f6.

Lessons from this game:

1) If you are attacking, it can be worth a considerable sacrifice to prevent the enemy queen from joining the defence.

2) A long diagonal aimed at a weakened kingside provides an excellent attacking highway.

3) Two bishops attacking along parallel diagonals make a terrifying offensive force.

4) Playing an ultra-sharp opening variation without careful preparation is very risky!

Boris Gelfand – Alexei Shirov
Rubinstein Memorial, Polanica Zdroj 1998
Grünfeld Defence, Modern Exchange Variation

The Players

Boris Gelfand (born 1968) has been one of the world's top grandmasters since 1990. See Game 88 for more details.

Alexei Shirov (born 1972) is arguably the most creative and aggressive of the current world elite. For more information see Game 89.

The Game

Play follows a complex theoretical opening line until Gelfand introduces a new idea, one that he thought up at the board. Shirov responds in aggressive manner, obliging Gelfand to demonstrate the full tactical basis for his idea. For several moves it seems that White's pieces will prove as loose as they appear, but with a couple of stunning blows Gelfand makes everything clear. Shirov has to give up his queen, whereupon Gelfand is able to combine ideas on both flanks to secure victory.

| 1 | d4 | ♘f6 |
| 2 | ♘f3 | |

This move-order allows Black to enter a Grünfeld without White being able to play the traditional form of the Exchange Variation that we saw in Game 53. However, theory had developed considerably in the intervening years. Starting in the late 1970s, the merits of putting the knight on f3 in the Exchange Variation had come to be appreciated, and the drawback of allowing ...♗g4 was considered less serious.

| 2 | ... | g6 |
| 3 | c4 | ♗g7 |

3...d5?! is a mistake, since after 4 cxd5 ♘xd5 5 e4 Black cannot exchange knights on c3, and must retreat his knight instead.

4 ♘c3

Now White intends to play e4, so Black must choose between a Grünfeld and a King's Indian.

| 4 | ... | d5 |

4...0-0 5 e4 d6 is a King's Indian.

5	cxd5	♘xd5
6	e4	♘xc3
7	bxc3	

We have now reached a position that can also arise via the move-order 1 d4 ♘f6 2 c4 g6 3 ♘c3 d5 4 cxd5 ♘xd5 5 e4 ♘xc3 6 bxc3 ♗g7 7 ♘f3. White does not fear the pin by ...♗g4 since he has various means of supporting his centre and/or counterattacking against the b7-pawn. One of White's main ideas in the ♘f3 Exchange Grünfeld is to play d5 after suitable preparation, establishing a big space advantage.

| 7 | ... | c5 |

It is considered best for Black to play this standard move immediately. Instead, 7...0-0 gives White more freedom, as Black can often put the tempo to better use in the fight against White's centre.

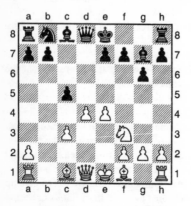

8 ℤb1

This is one of White's most popular lines. This odd-looking rook move was first popularized at the end of the 1970s by the Ukrainian player Viacheslav Eingorn, and quickly found a place in Garry Kasparov's repertoire. White puts pressure on b7, and also prepares to play d5 by taking the rook off the long diagonal. In several lines he is able to play this move as a pawn sacrifice.

8 ♗e3 is the main alternative. At the time this game was played, it was not regarded as a very threatening move, but Vladimir Kramnik later infused it with some subtle new ideas, most notably using it to score a critical victory over Garry Kasparov in their world championship match in 2000.

| 8 | ... | 0-0 |
| 9 | ♗e2 | cxd4 |

This exchange of pawns has served Black best, but he has several alternatives at this point. The lines following 9...♘c6 are highly instructive. White replies 10 d5, offering a pawn sacrifice that Black should probably decline:

1) 10...♗xc3+ 11 ♗d2 ♗xd2+ 12 ♕xd2 ♘a5 (12...♘d4 13 ♘xd4 cxd4 14 ♕xd4 simply leaves White better) 13 h4 gives White a dangerous attack for the pawn.

2) 10...♘e5 11 ♘xe5 ♗xe5 12 ♕d2 leads to very heavily analysed lines that are far from resolved, despite a great many games and a lot of analysis over a 20-year period. Black needs to play very resourcefully to avoid being overwhelmed by White's central majority.

| 10 | cxd4 | ♕a5+ |

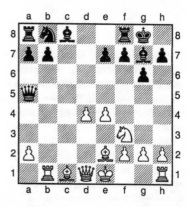

In the early days of the ℤb1 line, this generally led to an exchange of queens and a quiet endgame. After a while it became clear that Black could hold the endgame, so the spotlight was turned to the idea of sacrificing the a2-pawn and seeking compensation in a sharp middlegame.

11 ♗d2

11 ♕d2 ♕xd2+ 12 ♗xd2 is the quieter option; while not fully resolved, it seems that Black has a good enough share of the chances.

11 ...   ♕xa2

12 0-0

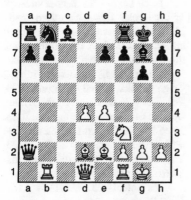

This is the key starting position for a massive body of opening theory. The initial impression is that White can't possibly have enough compensation for the pawn. Black has no weaknesses, no obvious problem pieces, his king is in no immediate danger, and he has two connected passed pawns on the queenside. White's development advantage is not large, and his bishops are not very actively placed. Part of the key to the position is the black queen. It is not in danger at present, but Black is naturally loath to retreat it voluntarily, as this would cost tempi that White could use to exert a strong grip on the position. Moreover, the queen would get in the way of the other pieces (on e6 it would obstruct the c8-bishop). However, if it stays on a2 for too long, White will start to generate threats against it. On the other hand,

the black queen has a definite nuisance value, and there are lines where Black holds the balance due to his queen hitting sensitive points in White's position. The other main key to the position is that Black's queenside development is not as easy as it looks. If the bishop moves, b7 is left loose, while c6 is not a stable square for the knight.

12 ...   ♗g4

Black decides not to be greedy, and seeks to disrupt White's centre while activating his pieces. This is the most popular line, and has been considered best since the late 1990s; alternatives include 12...♘d7, 12...♕e6, 12...a5 and 12...b6.

13 ♗g5

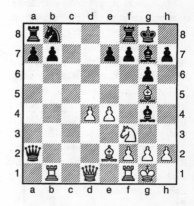

White defends his d4-pawn while putting his bishop on an active square. There is no immediate idea of taking on e7, but this is likely to become a real threat in due course.

13 ...   h6

Black forces the bishop to choose a diagonal.

14 ♗h4   a5

Black decides to seek counterplay by advancing his a-pawn. Obviously this strategy has its risks since White is given a freer hand in the centre and on the kingside. Black hopes that he will be able to deaden White's initiative, even at the cost of some material, as long as he can recoup the investment thanks to his a-pawn. 14...g5 15 &g3 ♘c6 is an alternative approach, focusing on the centre.

15   ♖xb7   g5
16   &g3   a4
17   h4

This move has since fallen out of favour due to the idea in the next note. Instead, 17 ♖c7 has similar ideas to Gelfand's 19th move, but Black has tended to survive after 17...♕b2.

17   ...   a3

17...♘c6 18 hxg5 hxg5 19 d5 &xf3 20 &xf3 ♘d4, as introduced by Ivan Sokolov, has proved very solid for Black. If White is not careful, the a-pawn could still prove very potent.

18   hxg5   hxg5

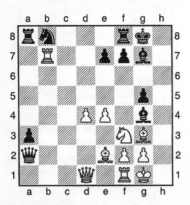

19   ♖c7!

This was a new move. According to Gelfand, it was an idea he had over the board, rather than one prepared at home. White prevents ...♘c6 and also

has ideas of ♖c2 and ♘xg5, or else &c4.

19   ...   ♘a6?

This turns out badly due to a brilliant sequence of tactics. Alternatives:

1) After 19...♘d7 Gelfand intended 20 e5! (directed against the g7-bishop and the d6-knight) 20...♕b2 (20...♖fc8 21 &c4 costs Black his queen since 21...♕b2?! allows 22 &xf7+ with a big attack) 21 ♖c2 ♕b3 (the queen stays with the a-pawn, which remains Black's principal counterchance) 22 ♘xg5 a2! (22...&xe2 23 ♕xe2 a2 24 ♖a1 ♕b1+ 25 ♖c1 is good for White; Gelfand gave the sample line 25...♖fb8 26 e6 ♕xc1+ 27 ♖xc1 ♖b1 28 exf7+ ♔f8 29 ♘e6+, winning) 23 ♖xa2! (23 ♖c1 ♕xd1 24 &xd1 &xd1 25 ♖cxd1 ♘b6 is not clear, since Black's a-pawn remains potent) 23...♕xd1 24 ♖xd1 ♖xa2 25 &xg4 with some advantage for White.

2) 19...♕b2 20 ♖c2!? ♕b6 (the alternative 20...♕b3 21 ♘xg5 a2 22 ♖xa2! ♕xd1 23 ♖xd1 ♖xa2 24 &xg4 looks good for White; note that he threatens ♘e6) 21 ♘xg5 was considered by Gelfand to favour White, based on ideas such as 21...♕xd4 (21...&xe2 22 ♕xe2 ♘d7 23 e5; 21...a2 22 ♖xa2 ♖xa2 23 &xg4) 22 ♕xd4 &xd4 23 &xg4 a2 24 ♖xa2 ♖xa2 25 ♘e6!.

20   ♖xe7   ♕b2
21   &c4

Taking aim against f7.

21   ...   ♕b4

This double attack appears to reveal a major flaw in White's idea. Instead:

1) 21...&f6 22 ♖xf7 ♖xf7 gives White a choice between 23 e5!? and 23 &xf7+ ♔xf7 24 ♘xg5+ &xg5 25 ♕xg4, winning in both cases.

2) 21...a2 loses to 22 ♖xf7 ♖xf7 23 ♗xf7+ ♔xf7 (23...♔h8 24 ♕a1) 24 ♘xg5+, when White's mating threats are more important than the a2-pawn.

22 ♗xf7+ ♔h8

Black relies on the fact that White's pieces on the 7th rank are somewhat loose. 22...♖xf7 23 ♖xf7 ♗xd4 24 ♖f5 ♗xf5 25 exf5 ♖d8 26 ♕e2 is hopeless for Black.

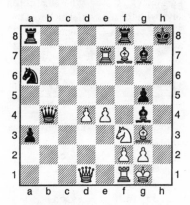

23 ♖d7!!

The logic is clear: if the bishop takes the rook, the f3-knight is free to take on g5, when White's mating threats will force major gains. Meanwhile, White threatens ♗d6, and it turns out that Black is unable to exploit White's loose pieces. 23 ♗e6!? ♗xf3 24 ♖xg7! ♗xd1 25 ♗e5! is also strong, but the move Gelfand chose is even stronger, and must have been somewhat easier to analyse over the board.

23 ... ♗xd7

Or:

1) 23...♕b5 allows 24 ♖d5, when White rescues his pieces and continues the attack.

2) 23...a2 24 ♗xa2 ♖xf3 (24...♗xd7 25 ♘xg5) 25 gxf3 ♗xd7 26 ♔g2 and

White's mating threats on the h-file are decisive.

3) 23...♗f6 is brilliantly defeated by 24 ♗e6! ♗xe6 25 ♘xg5.

24 ♘xg5 ♕b6

For a moment, it looks as if Black has found a defence.

25 ♗e6!

However, the bishop whose position appeared so precarious lands the lethal blow by blocking out Black's queen.

25 ... ♕xe6

There is nothing better than giving up the queen: 25...♗e8 26 ♕g4 ♗xd4 (or 26...♖f6 27 ♗e5!) 27 ♕h4+ ♔g7 28 ♕h7+ ♔f6 29 ♗h4 ♕c5 30 ♗d5 is terminal.

26 ♘xe6 ♗xe6

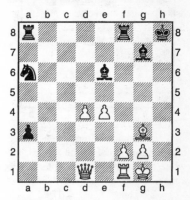

White has queen and three pawns vs rook, bishop and knight. If Black can coordinate his pieces and/or reinforce his a-pawn, he may yet be able to save the game. White must therefore continue vigorously.

27 ♗e5!?

27 ♗d6 is an alternative. Without going into enormous detail, Gelfand considered 27...♖fd8 28 ♗e5 ♗c4 29

♕h5+ ♔g8 30 ♕g6 ♖a7 31 ♖a1 a2 32 ♕c6 ♗f7 33 ♗xg7 ♔xg7 34 d5 ♘c7 to be the best defence, which he only gave as "much better for White".

27 ...   **♖f7**

27...♗c4 is best answered by the disruptive 28 ♕c1! (threatening ♕h6+, and so removing Black's more active bishop) 28...♗xe5 29 ♕xc4 ♗g7 30 ♖a1, when the a-pawn is more a target than a strength, while White's pawns are about to cause havoc.

28 ♕h5+   **♔g8**
29 ♕g6

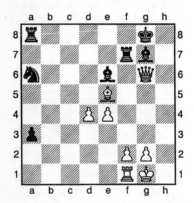

Black is denied time to consolidate his position; however he replies, the white queen will find fresh targets to attack.

29 ...   **♗d7**
30 ♗xg7

30 ♕g3 a2 31 ♖a1 is also strong.

30 ...   **♖xg7**
31 ♕d6   **♔h7**

31...♘c7 is a better try, but 32 ♕xc7 ♗h3 33 ♕c6 ♖a5 34 ♖c1! was analysed to a win by Gelfand. 34...♖xg2+ (34...♗xg2 35 ♕c8+ ♔h7 36 ♖c7; 34...a2 35 ♔h2 ♗xg2 36 d5! ♔h7 37

♕f6 ♖a8 38 d6) 35 ♔h1 a2 (35...♖g7 36 ♖c5) 36 ♕e8+ ♔h7 37 ♕e7+ ♔h6 38 ♖c6+ and the checks prove fatal.

32 ♕xa3

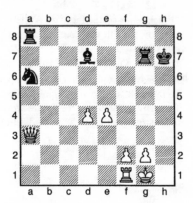

Now the four pawns simply prove too much.

32 ...   **♘c7**
33 ♕e3   **♘e6**
34 d5   **♘g5**
35 f4   **♘h3+**
36 ♔h1   **♖a2**
37 f5!

Avoiding 37 gxh3? ♖gg2!.

37 ...   **♘g5**
38 f6   **♖g6**
39 f7   **1-0**

Lessons from this game:

1) Compensation does not always take dramatic forms. Here a strong centre and a general awkwardness in Black's development provided full compensation for a pawn.

2) Sometimes excellent new opening ideas are found at the board.

3) An exposed king often allows all manner of tactical devices, dooming an otherwise healthy position.

Aleksandr Veingold – Daniel Fridman
Zonal tournament, Tallinn 1998
Queen's Gambit Declined, Semi-Slav Defence

The Players
Aleksandr Veingold (born 1953) is an international master from Estonia. Like many ex-Soviet players, he lacked opportunities to travel outside the USSR until the late 1980s. One of Veingold's most notable achievements was a victory over Kasparov in 1979 that the future world champion found sufficiently interesting and instructive that he annotated it in his games collections.

Daniel Fridman (born 1976) is a Latvian grandmaster who is in the world's top 150 players at the time of writing (January 2004).

The Game
In an ultra-sharp opening variation, Veingold introduces a sharp and complex new move. It may not be any better than the normal continuation, but it keeps the position extremely chaotic and gives his opponent some very difficult decisions. In such situations, errors are common, and Fridman allows Veingold to make an excellent queen sacrifice. His active pieces and a far-advanced pawn prove too much for Black, who is handicapped throughout the game by his exposed king.

1	d4	d5
2	♘f3	♘f6
3	c4	c6
4	♘c3	e6

This is a Semi-Slav, an opening we have already seen several times in this book.

5	♗g5	dxc4
6	e4	b5
7	e5	

Once more we have a Botvinnik System, an opening line that leads to extreme complications.

7	...	h6
8	♗h4	g5
9	♘xg5	hxg5
10	♗xg5	♘bd7
11	g3	

The alternative here is 11 exf6. It is possible for Black to direct the game along different lines according to which of these options White chooses, but very often he just ignores White's move-order. Thus 11...♗b7 12 g3 ♕b6 (for 12...c5 see Games 74 and 89) 13 ♗g2 transposes into the game.

11	...	♗b7
12	♗g2	♕b6
13	exf6	0-0-0
14	0-0	c5
15	d5	b4

Both players follow the main line.

16	♖b1	

This is a move we saw before in Game 98, while 16 ♘a4 was featured in Game 95.

16	...	♛a6
17	dxe6	♝xg2

Up until this point we have been following the same sequence as in Game 98. White now uncorked an extremely interesting new move.

18 ♖e1!?

Veingold keeps the maximum tension in the position and plays a very useful rook move. The pawn has considerable nuisance value on e6, and Black is kept guessing about its intentions. This move leads to great complications, and over the board it is no surprise that Fridman went astray. 18 e7 has been the normal move here. Recent practice has then seen 18...♝b7!? in addition to 18...♝xf1, which we saw Kramnik playing in Game 98.

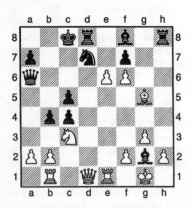

18 ... ♘e5?!

Fridman chooses a very natural and active move, but it allows a powerful queen sacrifice that puts Black in great difficulties. Alternatives:

1) 18...♛a8? loses immediately: 19 exd7+ ♖xd7 20 ♖e8+ ♔c7 21 ♝f4+ ♝d6 22 ♖xh8 ♝xf4 23 ♛g4.

2) After 18...♝c6?! 19 e7 bxc3 20 exd8♛+ (20 e8♛ and 20 bxc3 are also possible) 20...♔xd8 21 bxc3 it will be hard for Black to defend against White's plan of penetrating along the b-file, if not the central files.

3) 18...♛c6?! 19 exd7+ ♖xd7 20 ♛g4 and now:

3a) 20...bxc3? 21 ♖e8+ ♔c7 22 bxc3 leaves Black in desperate trouble: 22...♝h3 23 ♝f4+ ♝d6 24 ♝xd6+ ♖xd6 (24...♛xd6 loses to 25 ♛f3) 25 ♖e7+ ♖d7 26 ♛f4+ ♛d6 27 ♖xd7+ and Black loses his queen: 27...♔xd7 (27...♝xd7 is met the same way) 28 ♖b7+ ♔c6 29 ♛e4+ ♛d5 30 ♖c7+.

3b) 20...♝h3 21 ♖e8+ ♔b7 22 ♛e4 is at least somewhat better for White.

4) 18...bxc3 is one of the critical defences. 19 exd7+ ♖xd7 20 ♖e8+ ♔c7 and here:

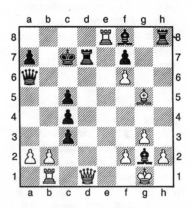

4a) 21 ♝f4+ leads to unclear play after both 21...♝d6 22 ♖xh8 ♝xf4 and 21...♔c6 22 ♛c2 ♝f3.

4b) 21 ♛e2 ♛xa2 (21...c2!? is another move Black could try) 22 ♝f4+ (22 ♔xg2 ♛xb1 23 ♝f4+ ♔b6 is also unclear) 22...♝d6 (22...♔b6 23 ♛c2 is good for White) 23 ♝xd6+ ♖xd6 24 ♖xh8 ♛xb1+ 25 ♔xg2 cxb2 and Black might well be hanging on; e.g.,

26 ♕e7+ ♔c6 27 ♖b8 ♔d5 28 ♖e8
♔c6 29 ♕xa7 ♕f5 30 ♕a8+ ♔c7 31
♕b8+ ♔c6 32 ♕xb2 ♕d5+ with perpetual check, since 33 f3? ♕d2+ 34
♕xd2 ♖xd2+ 35 ♔h3 c3 certainly isn't
a winning attempt for White.

5) 18...fxe6 19 ♔xg2 bxc3 (after
19...♕c6+ 20 ♘e4 ♘e5 21 ♕e2 ♘d3
White should probably choose 22 ♖h1,
defending against Black's ...♘xf2
idea) 20 bxc3 ♕c6+ 21 ♔g1 and then:

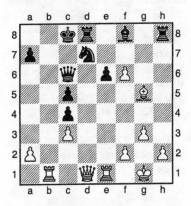

5a) 21...♘b6 22 ♕g4 was given by
Veingold as good for White.

5b) 21...♗d6 22 ♕g4 ♔c7 23 f7
♖df8 24 ♖xe6 ♘e5 25 ♖xe5 ♗xe5 26
♕xc4 ♗d6 27 ♖d1 is messy, but led to
a win for White in Pitkanen – Iaselli,
ICCF e-mail 2000.

5c) 21...♗h6 22 ♕g4 was considered unclear by Veingold. After the
continuation 22...♗xg5 (22...♖dg8?!
is met by 23 ♕xc4 followed by ♖xe6)
23 ♖xe6 ♕d5 White can try 24 ♕f5!?
(better than 24 ♕xc4?! ♘b6) 24...♕a8
(24...♘b6 25 ♖e5+ ♕d7 26 ♖xc5+;
not 24...♕xf5?? 25 ♖c6#) 25 ♖b5 with
a complete mess of a position.

19 ♕xd8+   ♔xd8
20 e7+   ♗xe7

20...♔e8 21 ♖xe5 ♗f3 might perhaps be a better try.

21 fxe7+   ♔e8

21...♔c7 22 ♖xe5 bxc3 23 ♗f4
leaves Black in serious difficulties.

22 ♖xe5   f6
23 ♖d1   fxe5

23...♗f7 24 ♖f5! bxc3 25 ♖xf6+
♕xf6 26 ♗xf6 ♔xf6 27 bxc3 and the
threat of ♖d8 means White reaches a
trivially won rook ending.

24 ♖d8+   ♔f7
25 ♖xh8   ♗c6

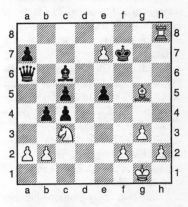

26 ♘e4

26 ♖f8+ is an alternative, and possibly clearer, way to win. 26...♔g7
(26...♔g6 27 ♖f6+ ♔xg5 28 ♘e4+!)
27 ♗f6+ ♔h7 (27...♔g6 28 ♗xe5 intending ♖f6+) 28 ♗xe5 intending
♖f7+ and ♖f6+.

26 ...   ♕xa2!?

26...♕a4 is best answered by 27
h4!, a multi-purpose move, defending
the bishop and giving the king a flight-
square on h2. Then:

1) 27...♗xe4 28 ♖f8+ ♔g7 29
♗f6+ ♔h6 30 ♖h8+ ♔g6 (30...♗h7
31 e8♕) 31 e8♕+ leads to an easily
won ending for White.

2) 27...♛d1+ 28 ♔h2 ♛e2 29 ♖h7+ ♔g6 30 ♖h6+ ♔f7 (30...♔f5 31 ♖xc6 ♔xe4 32 ♖f6 ♛h5 33 ♖f8) 31 ♖xc6 and Black has run out of tricks.

3) 27...c3 is most simply parried by 28 b3; for example, 28...♛xa2 29 ♖h7+ ♔g6 (29...♔e6 30 ♖h6+ ♔d5 {or 30...♔d7 31 ♖d6+} 31 ♖xc6) 30 ♖h6+ ♔f7 31 ♖xc6 ♛b1+ 32 ♔h2 (using the h2-square) 32...♛xe4 33 ♖c8 and White promotes and quickly mates.

27   ♖h7+   ♔g6

27...♔e6 28 ♖h6+ ♔d7 (28...♔f7 transposes to the game) 29 ♘xc5+ is hopeless for Black.

28   ♖h6+   ♔f7

Or:

1) 28...♔f5 29 f3! sets up a mating-net: 29...♛b1+ (29...♗xe4 30 ♗c1 ♗xf3 31 e8♛) 30 ♔f2 ♛xb2+ (or 30...♗xe4 31 ♗d2!) 31 ♗d2! ♛d4+ 32 ♗e3 ♛b2+ 33 ♘d2.

2) 28...♔g7 29 ♖xc6 ♛b1+ 30 ♗c1! leaves Black helpless, as his queen cannot reach the squares it needs.

29   ♖h7+

White could play 29 ♘d6+! immediately, but he decided to repeat the position, presumably in case any accidents happened on the way to the time-control. 29 ♖xc6?? ♛b1+ 30 ♗c1 ♛xe4 shows that White mustn't be careless.

29   ...   ♔g6
30   ♖h6+   ♔f7

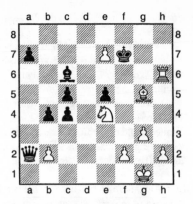

31   ♘d6+   ♔g8

After 31...♔g7 32 ♘f5+ ♔f7 33 ♖f6+ ♔g8 34 ♖xc6 ♛b1+ 35 ♗c1! Black is unable to stop the e-pawn: 35...♛xc1+ 36 ♔g2 ♔f7 37 ♖c8.

32   e8♛+!   ♗xe8
33   ♗f6

The threat of ♖h8# is unstoppable, and the white king can easily evade the checks.

33   ...   ♛b1+
34   ♔g2   ♗c6+
35   ♔h3   ♗d7+
36   ♔h4   1-0

Lessons from this game:

1) Keeping tension rather than releasing it is very often a good idea.

2) It is easy to go wrong when confronted with an unexpected move.

3) A queen on its own can sometimes prove surprisingly powerless.

Game 104

John Nunn – Igor-Alexandre Nataf
French Team Championship 1998/9
Sicilian Defence, Kalashnikov Variation

The Players

John Nunn (born 1955) is an English grandmaster who has had a successful playing career extending over more than a quarter of a century. For further details see Game 78.

Igor-Alexandre Nataf (born 1978) is a French grandmaster with a lively attacking style of play. For many decades French chess remained in the doldrums, but in the late 1980s and 1990s a new generation of young players emerged, starting with Lautier and followed later by Bacrot and Fressinet. These days France has a strong team, since their home-grown talent has been augmented by an influx of strong foreign players taking up residence there, such as Tkachev, Dorfman and Andrei Sokolov. Nataf has made rapid progress, with his rating increasing from the low 2300s in 1996 to the upper 2500s at the time of writing. He is currently ranked 9th in France.

The Game

In keeping with his style of play, Nataf's opening is based on piece activity at the cost of positional weaknesses. This is a risky strategy, because if the active pieces can be exchanged or nullified, then the positional weaknesses will be a long-term problem. Soon Black is forced to invest a pawn to keep his strategy going. However, curbing piece activity often demands accurate play, and in this game White made a crucial mistake on move 14. This gave Nataf the chance to launch an attack with a scintillating sacrifice on the traditional weak spot f2. This sacrifice is unusual because Black gives up a whole rook when three of his pieces are still on their original squares. However, analysis shows the sacrifice to be totally correct, although it only becomes clear that Black is winning after his brilliant 24th move.

1	e4	c5
2	♘f3	♘c6
3	d4	cxd4
4	♘xd4	e5

This move introduces the Kalashnikov Variation. The basic idea is similar to that of the Sveshnikov Variation (which starts with the moves 4...♘f6 5 ♘c3 e5), namely that Black gains time by chasing the white knight around.

The penalty is the weakening of the d5-square and the backwardness of Black's d-pawn.

5	♘b5	d6
6	c4	

This possibility is the main difference between the Kalashnikov and Sveshnikov variations. White consolidates his grip on d5 and prevents Black from expanding on the queenside by

...b5 as he does in the Sveshnikov. On the other hand, White weakens d4 and the additional pawn move means that he falls a little behind in development.

6 ...   ♗e7

More flexible than 6...♘f6. Black retains the option of exchanging his bad dark-squared bishop by ...♗g5 (perhaps supported by ...h6) or he may play for piece activity by ...f5. White is kept guessing.

7 ♘1c3

This move means that White's other knight will have to retreat to the offside square a3, but there is no perfect solution to the problem of how to deploy White's knights. If the one on b5 retreats to c3, then it prevents the most natural development of the b1-knight.

7 ...   a6

8 ♘a3

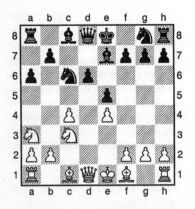

If White gets time, this knight might be activated by ♘c2 and possibly ♘e3.

8 ...   f5

Black's most dynamic continuation. He secures considerable piece activity at the cost of a further weakening of his pawn-structure.

9 ♗d3

White does not want to present Black with a development tempo by taking on f5, but this move allows Black to expand on the kingside. 9 exf5 ♗xf5, and then either 10 ♗d3 or 10 ♘c2, is a safer option.

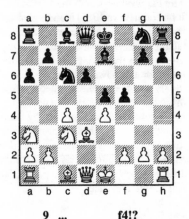

9 ...   f4!?

The f4-pawn obstructs White's development, and prevents White's intended manoeuvre ♘c2-e3.

10 g3

This is the critical continuation, trying to remove the annoying pawn by force.

10 ...   ♘f6

This pawn sacrifice is the only consistent follow-up to the previous move. After the limp 10...fxg3 11 hxg3 ♘f6 12 ♘c2 0-0 13 f3, followed by ♗e3, ♕d2 (or ♕e2) and 0-0-0, White has a clear advantage.

11 gxf4

White must accept or else he has simply wasted a tempo playing g3.

11 ...   exf4

12 ♗xf4   0-0

At first sight Black doesn't have very much for the pawn. Development is roughly equal, and although White's shattered kingside pawns make 0-0 uninviting, it doesn't seem particularly difficult for White to organize 0-0-0. However, several elements combine to make life awkward for White. The undefended f4-bishop represents a tactical weakness, and the f2-pawn is vulnerable. If we also take into account White's offside a3-knight and his slight weaknesses on the dark squares, we can see that Black has reasonable play for the pawn. However, objectively speaking White should probably be slightly better.

13 ♗g3

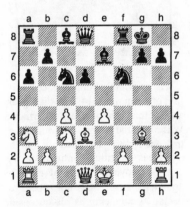

The most natural and best move. The bishop was vulnerable on f4 and would have to move sooner or later in any case, so moving it now preserves the greatest flexibility.

13 ... ♘g4

Black takes aim at the traditional weak spot of an uncastled king – the f2-square.

14 ♗e2?

White wants to drive Black's knight away, but the knight moves not backwards but forwards! The best move is

John Watson's suggestion 14 f4!, which may appear weakening but has two very positive points: it controls the important e5-square, and it prevents a sacrifice on f2. In this case White would have some advantage. The text-move is an error which has unexpectedly serious consequences.

14 ... ♘xf2!!

An absolutely stunning sacrifice. Black is willing to invest a whole rook in order to drive White's king out into the open. The remarkable feature of this sacrifice is that Black has no overall lead in development and indeed his queenside pieces are still largely sitting at home. Nevertheless, White's lack of dark-square control makes it very hard for him to fend off Black's threats.

15 ♕d5+

White cannot avoid this check, because 15 ♗xf2 ♖xf2! 16 ♔xf2 ♗h4+ 17 ♔g2 (17 ♔e3 ♕g5+ 18 ♔d3 ♘b4+ 19 ♔d4 ♕c5#) 17...♕g5+ 18 ♗g4 ♘e5 19 h3 h5 wins back a piece, while retaining a huge attack. With the queen on d5, Black no longer has a check on g5, so the sacrifice is less clear-cut.

15 ... ♔h8

16 ♗xf2?!

Objectively speaking, White should play 16 ♖f1, when 16...♘g4 is just slightly better for Black. However, in practice White is almost bound to accept Black's sacrifice, since at this stage it is far from clear that the outcome of the complications will be favourable for Black.

16 ... ♘b4?!

John Watson points out that the alternative move-order 16...♖xf2! 17 ♔xf2 ♘b4 would have been slightly more accurate, depriving White of the opportunity to bale out next move. In that case, 18 ♕f7 ♗h4+ 19 ♔f3 fails to the neat switchback 19...♘c6! 20 ♕f4 g5 21 ♕e3 ♗h3! with a decisive attack for Black, so White would have nothing better than 18 ♕h5, transposing to the game.

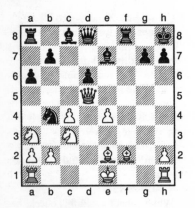

17 ♕h5?!

White is trying to retain control of g5 so as to prevent Black from giving a queen check on that square, but White's queen is soon driven away. The best chance was 17 ♕d4 ♖xf2! 18 ♖g1! (18 ♔xf2? ♗h4+ 19 ♔f3 ♗h3! 20 ♘d5 ♕g5 21 ♘f4 ♖f8! 22 ♕xd6 ♗g4+ 23 ♔e3 ♖xf4 24 ♕xf4 ♗f2+ 25 ♔xf2 ♕xf4+ wins for Black), although after 18...♖f7 Black retains a positional advantage thanks to his dark-square pressure.

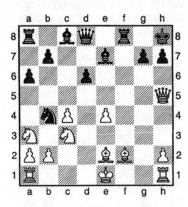

17 ... ♖xf2!

The inevitable consequence of the first offer on move 14. The disappearance of this bishop further undermines White's already poor dark-square control, and his king is forced out into the open.

18 ♔xf2 ♗h4+

Black's attack does not appear especially convincing as his queenside pieces have yet to join in, but in fact White is lost, although the attack demands high-quality play by Black. The key point is that White cannot prevent Black's queen from entering the attack with gain of tempo.

19 ♔g2

There is nothing better. 19 ♔g1 g6 20 ♕f3 ♕g5+ 21 ♔f1 transposes to the game, while 19 ♔e3 g6 20 ♕f3 ♕g5+ 21 ♕f4 ♕c5+ 22 ♔d2 ♗g5 picks up the queen.

19 ... g6

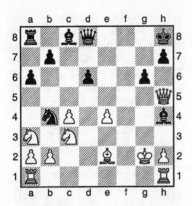

Now 20 ♕h6 loses to 20...♗g5, so White must surrender his control of g5.

20 ♕f3 ♕g5+

The entry of Black's queen into the attack is an important step on the road to victory.

21 ♔f1

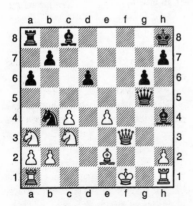

If White's pawn were on h3, then Black's attack would amount to nothing, but White never gets a spare tempo to defend himself.

21 ... ♗h3+!

Another sacrifice to keep White off-balance. It is worth investing a

further piece to activate the a8-rook with gain of tempo.

22 ♕xh3 ♖f8+
23 ♗f3

White cannot even escape by giving up his queen: after 23 ♕f3 ♖xf3+ 24 ♗xf3 ♕e3 25 ♔g2 ♕f2+ 26 ♔h3 ♕xf3+ 27 ♔xh4 h6 28 ♖hg1 g5+ 29 ♖xg5 hxg5+ 30 ♔xg5 ♕g2+, followed by ...♕xb2, Black is too far ahead on material.

23 ... ♕e3
24 ♕xh4

24 ♘d1 ♖xf3+ 25 ♕xf3 ♕xf3+ 26 ♔g1 ♘d3 leads to mate in a few moves.

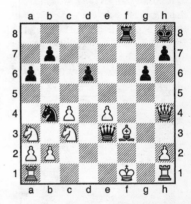

After the text-move Black's attack appears to have run out of steam, since 24...♕xf3+? 25 ♔g1 ♕e3+ 26 ♔g2 is only perpetual check, while the blunder 24...♖xf3+?? 25 ♔g2 would even lose for Black.

24 ... ♘d3!

Despite being a rook and two pieces down, Black has time for this lethal quiet move, bringing the last reserves into the attack. Black threatens mate in three by 25...♖xf3+ 26 ♔g2 ♘f4+ 27 ♕xf4 ♕f2#.

25 ♘d5

There is no escape for White. 25
♔g2 ♕xf3+ 26 ♔g1 ♘f4 mates in a
few moves.

25 ...   ♕xf3+

It doesn't make any difference to
the result of the game, but Black could
have forced mate in seven starting with
25...♖xf3+! 26 ♔g2 ♕e2+ 27 ♔g1 g5.

26 ♔g1   ♘f2

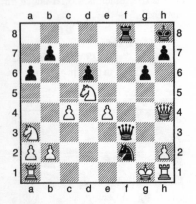

27 ♔f1

27 ♘f6 is the only way to play on,
but after 27...♘h3+ (the most accurate
move, since 27...♖xf6 28 ♕xf6+ ♕xf6
29 ♖f1 is less clear) 28 ♔xh3 ♕xh3 29
♖f1 ♕e3+ 30 ♔g2 ♕g5+ 31 ♔h3 ♖xf6
32 ♖xf6 ♕xf6 White loses in any case.

27 ...   ♕xh1+
28 ♔e2   ♕xa1

0-1

Lessons from this game:

1) Beginners are taught that when
White's king has not castled, f2 is a
vulnerable square. The same principle
applies even for grandmasters.

2) Once you have launched an all-
out attack, your commitment must be
total, no matter what the cost in material.

3) Total domination on squares on
one colour greatly increases the power
of an attack.

Garry Kasparov – Veselin Topalov
Wijk aan Zee 1999
Pirc Defence

The Players

Garry Kasparov (born 1963) is the greatest player of the modern era. Even after losing his world title in 2000, he remains by far the highest profile chess-player, and is still top of the rating list. See Game 71 for more details.

Veselin Topalov (born 1975) has occupied a high place on the world ranking list since the mid-1990s. For more information see Game 90.

The Game

You are about to witness one of the most extraordinary king-hunts in the history of chess. The opening and early middlegame are relatively quiet: Kasparov adopts an aggressive stance, but Topalov plays flexibly and obtains a fully acceptable position. Indeed, Kasparov is fighting not to be worse from move 14 to move 24, but as so often when a great champion's back is against the wall, he gives his opponent plenty of chances to go horribly wrong. In a moment of inspiration, an amazing idea pops into Kasparov's mind, and he embarks upon a sacrificial sequence. Topalov bravely decides to play down the main line when he had a perfectly safe alternative, but it turns out that Kasparov had been right: his pieces and pawns work in perfect harmony to hunt down the errant black king.

1 e4	d6

This move characterizes the Pirc Defence. 1...g6 is known as the Modern Defence, and has many ideas in common with the Pirc.

2 d4	♘f6
3 ♘c3	g6

As normal in the Pirc, Black adopts a set-up akin to the King's Indian Defence, but there is the major difference that White's c-pawn remains on c2, rather than advancing to c4. This gives White an extra tempo for development and makes his pawn-centre less of a target. However, it also means that there is less chance of White launching a queenside attack with a massive pawn advance. Therefore White tends to rely more on piece-play than in the King's Indian, and a kingside attack is a common plan for White, while it is often easier for Black to advance on the queenside.

4 ♗e3	

This flexible move is a very popular choice in modern practice. White keeps plenty of options open regarding the positioning of his king's knight and also with his f-pawn. It might advance to f4, to threaten a pawn-storm, or it could sit on f3, supporting the centre and covering the g4-square, or it could remain on f2.

4 ...	♗g7

This move looks completely natural, but it is quite a major decision. The drawback is that White can now play ♕d2 and ♗h6, and if Black meets this by playing ...♗xh6, then he will have lost a tempo compared to lines where he leaves his bishop on f8 and White replies in the same way. Of course, Black could not continue indefinitely without playing ...♗g7, but it is possible to delay this move while generating queenside play, in the hope that White will play something unduly committal or give up his ideas of a kingside attack.

4...♘g4 is possible, but is not considered a solution to Black's problems, since 5 ♗g5 relocates the bishop to another useful square, while Black's knight is unlikely to prosper on g4 for long.

4...c6 is the principal alternative, preparing ...b5. Then 5 ♕d2 ♘bd7 6 ♗d3 b5 7 ♘f3 e5 8 h3 ♗b7 is one possible line out of a great many, while 5 h3 is an interesting option, when f4 is often an idea for White.

5 ♕d2

Kasparov opts for the aggressive ♗h6 plan. However, note that he does not rush to play this move immediately; the possibility will not vanish, and he wants to make the exchange of bishops only in the most favourable situation. Simply exchanging off a fianchettoed bishop does not automatically lead to an attack – indeed, the further course of the game serves as an example of this fact.

5 ...   c6

Black sees no point in committing his king just yet, and opts for the ...c6 and ...b5 plan now that White has committed his queen to d2 and thus

has restricted his own choice of set-ups somewhat.

6 f3

White defends e4 to take the sting out of Black's ...b5-b4 advance, and also brings the g4 advance into the picture.

6 ...   b5

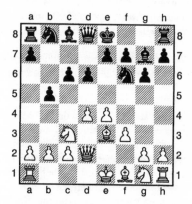

7 ♘ge2

Kasparov remains flexible. 7 0-0-0 gives Black a clear target, while 7 g4 (though highly dangerous) also defines White's plans rather more clearly than one might like. 7 ♗d3 is a natural-looking move, but the bishop lacks a clear role on this square.

7 ...   ♘bd7
8 ♗h6   ♗xh6
9 ♕xh6   ♗b7

Topalov simply develops his last minor piece and invites Kasparov to make the next committal decision. 9...♕a5?! is too blunt before White has castled; then 10 ♘c1 starts a convenient regrouping.

10 a3

Kasparov prevents ...b4 by simple means, and keeps the knight on e2 so that he can maintain the central tension

in the likely event of Black playing
...e5.

10 ...   e5

Black is not necessarily thinking of
exchanging on d4 any time soon, but
the idea will be there for some time to
come, and this move enables Black to
start bringing his king to a more secure
home on the queenside.

11 0-0-0   ♕e7
12 ♔b1   a6

Topalov secures his queenside structure. Although there is no immediate
threat to the b5-pawn, its only support
is from the c6-pawn, and at some point
it is bound to become an issue. For instance, 12...0-0-0 gives White the idea
of 13 d5. Kasparov gave 12...a5?! 13
♘c1 b4 14 dxe5! dxe5 15 ♘a4 bxa3
16 b3, which is very good for White,
as Black has achieved little apart from
damaging his own queenside.

13 ♘c1

Recycling the knight and freeing
the f1-bishop.

13 ...   0-0-0
14 ♘b3

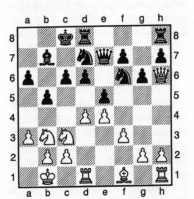

It is time to take stock. Clearly,
White's ideas of a kingside attack have

not come to fruition, and he could be
said to be a little behind in development. On the other hand, Black's king
is rather oddly situated on the queenside; while it is not in any imminent
danger, it isn't as secure as White's
king. White is now looking to get the
upper hand in a positional struggle: he
has plans with ♘a5 or maybe g3 and
♗h3. He will most likely bring his
queen back to e3 at some point. These
factors encouraged Topalov to put his
dynamic pluses to use...

14 ...   exd4!

Black opens the position and seeks
piece-play before White is fully coordinated.

15 ♖xd4

Kasparov does not want to give up
♘a5 ideas.

15 ...   c5
16 ♖d1   ♘b6!

Preparing ...d5, which would liquidate the backward pawn but more importantly activate his pieces. White
needs to find a creative response.

17 g3

White brings ♗h3+ ideas into the
picture, which enables the h1-rook to
be speedily developed. 17 ♘a5 is a
natural move to consider, but Black responds directly with 17...d5 (but not
17...♗a8?! 18 a4), because after 18
♘xb7 ♔xb7 19 exd5 ♘bxd5 Black's
strong centralized knight is no worse
than White's bishop, which is struggling to find a role due to the pawn-
structure.

17 ...   ♔b8

Topalov's sense of danger appears
to be intact at this stage of the game.
Instead, 17...d5?! 18 ♕f4 exposes
him to some unpleasant threats; e.g.,
18...d4 19 ♗h3+ ♘fd7 20 ♘d5 is an

excellent pawn sacrifice – and most likely a temporary one.

18 ♘a5   ♝a8

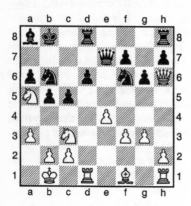

Black preserves the strong bishop. In order to put his knight to any use on a5, White will now need to drum up some attacking chances, but it is not immediately apparent how he might do so. It is a testament to Kasparov's imagination that seven moves from now, the game will have turned into perhaps the greatest king-hunt in the entire history of chess.

19 ♗h3   d5
20 ♕f4+   ♚a7
21 ♖he1   d4

21...dxe4? is wrong as after 22 fxe4 the position opens greatly to White's advantage.

22 ♘d5

22 ♘a2 is much too insipid.

22 ...   ♘bxd5
23 exd5   ♕d6
24 ♖xd4!?

This brave move is the start of a sensational sequence. At this point, Kasparov had not seen a win if Black took the rook, though he did have a safety-net in the form of perpetual

checks in some lines. Beliavsky and Mikhalchishin recommend 24 ♘c6+ ♝xc6 25 ♕xd6 ♖xd6 26 dxc6 ♚b6 27 ♖e7 ♚xc6 28 ♖de1 "when the threat of 29 ♖a7 ♚b6 30 ♖1e7 secures at least a draw".

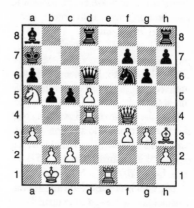

24 ...   cxd4?

Topalov decides to test Kasparov's idea, but this move was a fatal error. Or maybe his aesthetic sense got the better of him, and he was curious to see if Kasparov's idea really worked. Either way (win or lose), he could be certain that it would be a truly great game. Kasparov stated that while Topalov was pondering this decision, the game continuation up to move 37 flashed through his mind.

24...♚b6! would have saved Black, and meant that this game would have been quickly forgotten, perhaps to be dredged up when someone wrote an article about "brilliancies that only occurred in the notes". 25 ♘b3! (other moves are clearly bad) 25...♝xd5! (25...♘xd5? 26 ♕xf7; 25...cxd4? 26 ♕xd4+ ♚c7 27 ♕a7+ ♝b7 28 ♘c5 and 29 ♖e7+) 26 ♕xd6+ ♖xd6 27 ♖d2 ♖hd8 28 ♖ed1 was given as equal by Kasparov, but Beliavsky and Mikhalchishin prefer Black after 28...c4 (28...a5 is Christiansen's suggestion, when he considers Black to have a small edge) 29 ♘c1 (this move isn't forced) 29...♔c7. Perhaps Kasparov's "=" assessment essentially meant "I'm sure I wouldn't lose this".

25 ♖e7+!

The rook is immune, so Black's king must go for a walk. Not 25 ♕xd4+? ♕b6 26 ♖e7+ ♘d7, when White has nothing.

25 ...   ♔b6

25...♔b8 loses to 26 ♕xd4! ♘d7 27 ♗xd7! ♗xd5 28 c4!. 25...♕xe7? allows mate: 26 ♕xd4+ ♔b8 27 ♕b6+ ♗b7 28 ♘c6+ ♔a8 29 ♕a7#.

26 ♕xd4+   ♔xa5

26...♕c5 27 ♕xf6+ ♔d6 loses to the spectacular 28 ♗e6!! ♔xa5 (28...♖he8 29 b4!; 28...♗xd5 29 b4!) 29 b4+ ♔a4 30 ♕c3 ♗xd5 31 ♔b2 intending ♕b3+, mating.

27 b4+   ♔a4

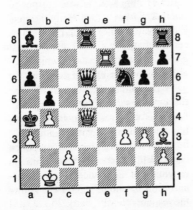

28 ♕c3

This leads to a grandiose finish, but 28 ♖a7! is slightly more accurate: 28...♗b7 (28...♘xd5 29 ♖xa6+! ♕xa6

30 ♕b2; 28...♗xd5 29 ♕c3) 29 ♖xb7 ♕xd5 (29...♘xd5 30 ♗d7! ♖xd7 31 ♕b2) 30 ♖b6! a5 (30...♖a8 31 ♕xf6) 31 ♖a6 ♖a8 32 ♕e3! ♖xa6 33 ♔b2 and Black has no defence.

28 ...   ♕xd5

28...♗xd5? 29 ♔b2 and ♕b3+ leads to mate.

29 ♖a7!

29 ♕c7? allows 29...♕d1+ with a draw. Nevertheless, this line is a good example of a safety-net that may have helped Kasparov to decide to sacrifice.

29 ...   ♗b7
30 ♖xb7!

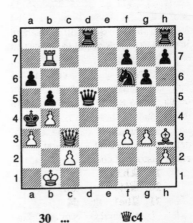

30 ...   ♕c4

Or:

1) 30...♖d6 loses to 31 ♖b6!, overloading the rook.

2) 30...♖he8 is a major alternative, when White must also find a highly creative solution: 31 ♖b6 ♖a8 32 ♗f1! (threatening ♖d6) and now:

2a) 32...♖ed8 (setting up a defence with ...♕d4 in answer to ♔b2) 33 ♖c6! ♘h5 (33...♘d7 34 ♖d6!) 34 ♖c5 ♖ac8 35 ♔b2! and White wins because the d8-rook is overloaded.

2b) 32...Ee1+! 33 ♕xe1 ♘d7 34 Eb7! and White wins; e.g., 34...♕xb7 (34...♘e5 35 ♕c3 ♖xf3 36 ♗d3 ♕d5 37 ♗e4) 35 ♕d1! ♔xa3 36 c3, mating.

3) 30...♘e4 31 fxe4 ♕c4 comes close to holding, but White wins by 32 Ea7! Ed1+ (32...Ea8 33 ♕e3) 33 ♔b2 ♕xc3+ 34 ♔xc3 Ed6 35 e5 Eb6 36 ♔b2; e.g., 36...Ee8 37 ♗g2 Ed8 38 ♗b7 ♖d7 39 ♗c6! Ed8 (39...Ed2 40 ♗e8; 39...Exa7 40 ♗d5 and 41 ♗b3#) 40 ♗d7 with c4 coming next.

31 ♕xf6   ♔xa3

31...Ed1+ leads to a less spectacular end, without changing the result: 32 ♔b2 Ea8 33 ♕b6 ♕d4+ 34 ♕xd4 Exd4 35 Exf7 a5 36 ♗e6 axb4 37 ♗b3+ ♔a5 38 axb4+ ♔b6 (38...Exb4 39 c3 traps the rook) 39 Exh7 and White will win this ending.

32 ♕xa6+   ♔xb4
33 c3+!   ♔xc3
34 ♕a1+   ♔d2

34...♔b4 loses to 35 ♕b2+ ♔a5 36 ♕a3+ ♕a4 37 Ea7+.

35 ♕b2+   ♔d1

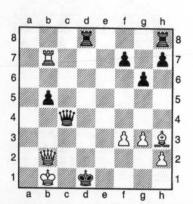

We have reached a famous position. Black's king has come all the way

down the board, and suddenly it seems that White's pieces are no longer coordinated. However, now comes a stunning 'one-two' that Kasparov had seen in his flash of inspiration many moves earlier...

36 ♗f1!

This overloads the black queen, but it appears that Black has a defence:

36 ...   Ed2

36...♕xf1 allows 37 ♕c2+ ♔e1 38 Ee7+ and mate next move.

Now, however, it even seems that White's king is in the greater danger, but it takes just one more move for everything to become clear.

37 Ed7!

The pin and diversion of the d2-rook cost Black his queen, and as the sting in the tail, Black's other rook gets picked off.

37 ...   Exd7
38 ♗xc4   bxc4
39 ♕xh8   Ed3
40 ♕a8   c3
41 ♕a4+   ♔e1
42 f4   f5
43 ♔c1   Ed2
44 ♕a7   1-0

Lessons from this game:

1) Delayed castling can greatly ease the defender's task when his opponent's set-up is geared towards attacking on one wing in particular.

2) Intuition is a powerful weapon in chess. While it shouldn't be dominant in your thought-process, an experienced chess-player should not ignore his instincts.

3) The difference between a king-hunt and a king-walk can depend on a few subtle nuances.

Game 106
Veselin Topalov – Vishy Anand
Linares 1999
Caro-Kann Defence, Advance Variation

The Players

Veselin Topalov (born 1975) has occupied a high place on the world ranking list since the mid-1990s. For more information see Game 90.

Viswanathan ("Vishy") Anand (born 1969) has been rated among the top three players in the world since the mid-1990s. In 2000 he won the FIDE World Championship. See Game 88 for more details.

The Game

Topalov plays the most aggressive line against Anand's solid Caro-Kann. Anand must give up a piece for three pawns, but does so in a new way. By advancing his kingside pawns, he makes it harder for White to smash open lines there. Topalov finds it necessary to sacrifice back the piece to gain some breathing room, whereupon Anand makes another piece sacrifice to generate attacking chances against the exposed white king, motivated by a general feeling that he "should" be better. The game remains finely balanced for several moves, but after a series of very difficult decisions, Topalov slips and allows Anand's small but well-coordinated army to smash through. The end result is a lost ending for White.

1 e4	**c6**	

This move introduces the Caro-Kann Defence, which is one of the openings referred to as the Semi-Open Games, by which Black responds asymmetrically to White's 1 e4. Of these openings, it is the third in popularity after the Sicilian and the French. In common with the French, Black prepares to challenge White in the centre by playing ...d5. It has the advantage over the French that the development of the c8-bishop is not obstructed, but in exchange there is the drawback that ...c6 is not a move that especially helps Black's development.

2 d4	**d5**	
3 e5		

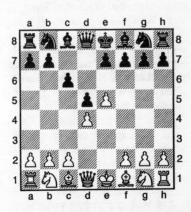

This is known for obvious reasons as the Advance Variation. It is a sharp and aggressive option for White. At first sight it appears strategically dubious for White to react in this way, since Black can develop his bishop to f5 and follow up with ...e6 and ...c5, establishing the type of position that he could only dream for in a French Defence. However, things are not so simple as that, since there are dynamic considerations that can enable White to generate a powerful initiative. Firstly, Black's bishop, if developed actively on f5, can also be used as a target: White can attack it with his pawns and knights, while if Black spends too much time securing a home on the kingside for this bishop (e.g. by playing ...h5), then White might simply swap it off by playing ♗d3 and put the time gained to good use to develop his initiative, notwithstanding the fact that he has exchanged a formally 'good' bishop for a formally 'bad' bishop. Secondly, Black will almost certainly need to play ...c5, both to generate counterplay and to free the c6-square for a knight. However, this clearly comes at the cost of a tempo. The third factor White can hope to exploit is that the bishop's absence from the queenside can leave the light squares highly sensitive, and this can lead to some violent tactics if Black allows the position to open up before he is sufficiently developed.

3 ♘c3 is the main line of the Caro-Kann. It generally leads to quieter play, where White has a slight space advantage. After 3...dxe4 4 ♘xe4 Black normally chooses between 4...♗f5 and 4...♘d7 intending ...♘gf6.

3 exd5 cxd5 4 c4 ♘f6 5 ♘c3 is another popular line, known as the Panov Attack. This leads to play similar to some lines of the Queen's Gambit; indeed, transpositions are possible.

3 ...   ♗f5

Black develops this bishop to its best square and challenges White to do his worst. 3...c5 has been played occasionally in high-level games, but has never achieved full respectability since Black often ends up having to play ...e6 before developing his queen's bishop.

4 ♘c3

White covers the e4-square in preparation for attacking the bishop with g4. He is burning his boats with this move, since Black's inevitable ...c5 advance will not be able to be met by c3, with the result that White's central pawn-chain will be broken. 4 g4?! ♗e4 5 f3 ♗g6 6 h4 h5 7 e6 ♕d6! is an instructive line, showing how a premature advance can rebound on White.

4 ...   e6
5 g4   ♗g6
6 ♘ge2

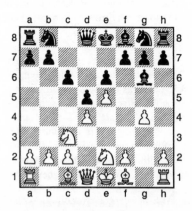

6 ...   ♘e7

6...c5 is also possible, and has been the subject of much analysis and practical testing. It would take us too far into the realms of opening theory to discuss in detail the arguments for 6...♘e7 vs

6...c5, but suffice it to say that Black has not given up on playing ...c5, but hopes that the benefits of delaying it a little while (less looseness, better support for the g6-bishop, and ...h5 ideas) will compensate for the fact that White has now been given more information about Black's kingside set-up. After 6...c5 White normally chooses between 7 ♗e3 and 7 h4.

7 ♘f4

7 f4 later acquired some popularity. One surprising idea is that 7...h5 is met by 8 f5 exf5 9 g5 shutting the g6-bishop out of play at the cost of a clear pawn. 7 ♗e3 and 7 h4 are both met by 7...h5.

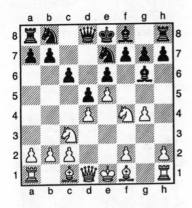

7 ... c5

Now that the knight has taken its eye off d4, Black plays this inevitable advance.

8 h4

With his centre crumbling, White pursues the bishop. 8 dxc5 is an alternative that was later played in several top-level games.

8 ... cxd4

This is the most consistent: Black destroys White's centre, even if this means having to give up the light-squared bishop for several pawns.

9 ♘b5

The threat of ♘d6+ disrupts Black's natural plan of ...♘bc6 and denies him time to rescue the g6-bishop.

9	...	♘ec6
10	h5	♗e4
11	f3	

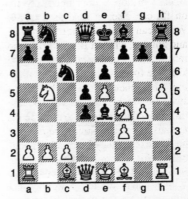

The bishop clearly has no escape, so Black must choose the best way to gain three healthy pawns in return. This had all been played in previous games, with Black continuing 11...♗xf3 12 ♕xf3 ♘xe5. Initially this was regarded as just unclear, but by the time of the current game, the verdict seemed to be swinging in White's favour due to his attacking chances after 13 ♕g3 ♘bc6 14 ♘d3. In some lines White played his pawns to h6 and g5 to open up attacking lines. Oddly enough, this fact provided part of Anand's inspiration for the new idea that he introduced with his next move. Anand wrote: "My trainer Ubilava and I wondered if Black could get these moves [...h6 and ...g5] in himself."

11 ... a6!

This also leads to positions with a piece vs three pawns, but with a rather different structure.

   12   ♘d6+   ♗xd6

   13   exd6

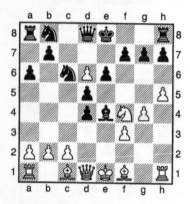

   13   ...   g5!

Again Anand attacks a white knight with a pawn, forcing it to choose a square before the central situation is resolved. This move also places a firm obstacle in the way of White's g-pawn. 13...e5?! 14 ♘g2 ♕d6 15 fxe4 dxe4 16 ♘e3 smoothly recycles the white knight, which now has some excellent squares at its disposal.

   14   ♘h3   h6

   15   fxe4   dxe4

   16   ♗g2   f5

Black has achieved an imposing pawn-front, and it is not easy to see a way for White to break it up, especially as his own king could easily become exposed.

   17   0-0   0-0!

This gives White some ideas based on a queen check on b3, but it turns out not to trouble Black unduly. Anand rejected 17...♖f8 because 18 gxf5 exf5 19 ♗xe4! fxe4 20 ♖xf8+ ♔xf8 21

♗xg5 hxg5 22 ♕g4 gives White good attacking chances.

   18   c3?

In keeping with his style and his sharp opening choice, Topalov plays aggressively, fighting for the initiative. However, the course of the game shows that Black now gets the upper hand. White should therefore seek safety, and the correct path is 18 gxf5 exf5 19 ♗xe4 fxe4 20 ♗xg5! ♖xf1+ 21 ♕xf1 hxg5 22 ♕f5 ♕d7 23 ♕g6+ ♕g7 24 ♕e8+ with perpetual check. There appear to be no significant improvements upon this line for either side.

   18   ...   ♕xd6

   19   gxf5   exf5

   20   ♕b3+

Anand points out that 20 ♗e3 ♘d7! 21 cxd4 ♘b6 followed by ...♘d5 is good for Black. He only has two pawns for the piece, but his knights are superb, while White's pieces are stymied by the pawn-structure.

   20   ...   ♔h8

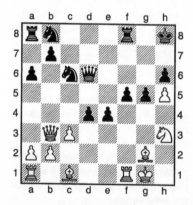

   21   ♗xe4!

Topalov gives up a piece to open some lines for his pieces before Black can consolidate. Instead, lines like 21 ♕xb7 ♘d7 22 ♕b3 ♘de5 and 21 cxd4 ♘xd4 22 ♕c3 ♘bc6 are simply miserable for him.

21	...	fxe4
22	♖xf8+	♕xf8
23	♕e6!	

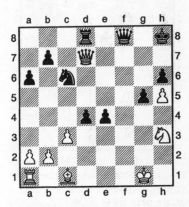

Threatening 24 ♗xg5 hxg5 25 ♖f1. Topalov is fighting back well, and Anand now needs to play with extreme vigour to stay on top.

23	...	♘d7!

Anand states that this was an intuitive sacrifice. He felt that he "should" be better, and so played a move that avoided drawish lines. This wasn't pure recklessness though; while he had certainly not calculated everything to a finish, in what appeared to him the critical line he had seen a way to bail out to a draw if nothing better became apparent as the critical position approached. This type of "safety-net" is an extremely useful thinking method, and one that computers can use too – they will often be programmed to rank a position where they can (but don't have to) force a draw as preferable to one where the only feasible outcome

is a draw. In the present case, Anand's intuition served him well, and there was indeed a better option.

Not 23...e3? 24 ♗xe3! followed by ♖f1.

24	♕xd7

24 ♗xg5? hxg5 25 ♕xd7 fails to 25...♖d8! 26 ♕e6 ♖e8 27 ♕g6 ♘e5.

24	...	♖d8

25	♕g4!

This is the best chance. 25 ♕xb7? is the move against which Anand had foreseen that he could take a draw if need be:

1) 25...♕f3(?) 26 ♘xg5 hxg5 27 ♕xc6 ♕g4+ is the draw.

2) 25...♕d6! is the best way to play for a win though: 26 ♔g2 ♕f6! 27 cxd4 ♕f3+! 28 ♔h2 ♘e5! 29 ♕c7 (29 dxe5 ♕e2+ leads to mate) 29...♘g4+ 30 ♔g1 ♕d1+ 31 ♔g2 ♖f8 and Black wins. It should be mentioned that this is a difficult sequence, despite its short length. Anand neither saw it at the board, nor when he wrote his initial set of notes, but only when he revised his notes with the help of a considerable amount of additional computer assistance. The difficulty stems from the

number of tempting alternatives that Black has on every move.

25   ...   e3

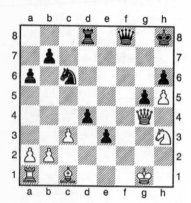

26   b3

Seeking to develop his queenside pieces – rather belatedly, but they both have prospects of coming into play with gain of tempo.

26 cxd4? ♖xd4 27 ♕e2 is another defensive idea. It seems crazy to help the black rook get into the attack, but White's queenside pieces can come quickly into play, and the black king is also more exposed now. However, Black can prevail as follows: 27...♕f5 (27...♖h4 28 ♗xe3! is less clear) 28 ♕xe3 (28 ♗xe3 loses to 28...♖g4+ 29 ♔h2 ♕e5+ 30 ♔h1 ♖g3! 31 ♕f1 ♕e6!! 32 ♘g1 ♖xe3) 28...♖g4+! 29 ♔h2 ♘e5 30 ♕b6! (30 ♘g1 ♖e4!) 30...♘f3+ 31 ♔h1 ♕d5! and Black wins since his king will run to the kingside to escape the checks from the white queen.

26   ...   ♘e5
27   ♕e4   ♕f6!
28   ♔g2?

This move appears to be White's fatal mistake. ...♘f3+ was not such a

devastating threat as it might appear. 28 ♗a3! gives him real chances of surviving, as the bishop covers some important squares while enabling the rook to fight for the f-file. 28...♘f3+ (28...dxc3 29 ♖f1 ♕e6 30 ♖f5 gives White just enough activity to survive; 28...d3 29 ♖f1 ♕e6 30 ♕xe3 ♕g4+ 31 ♔f2 ♕f5+ 32 ♔g1 ♕g4+ is perpetual check) 29 ♔g2! ♘d2 30 ♕g6 ♕xg6 31 hxg6 d3 (31...dxc3 32 ♗e7 ♖c8 33 ♗f6+ ♔g8 34 ♖c1 c2 35 ♗b2) 32 ♗c1 ♘xb3 33 axb3 d2 34 ♗xd2 ♖xd2+ "and Black is slightly better, although a draw is more likely than a win for Black" – Anand.

28   ...   e2!

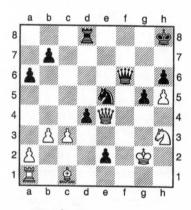

29   ♗xg5

Or:

1) 29 ♕xe2 loses to 29...d3! 30 ♕f2 ♕c6+ 31 ♔g3 ♕e6! 32 ♘g1 ♕g4+ 33 ♔h2 ♕xh5+ 34 ♔g2 ♘g4!.

2) 29 ♗d2 is a critical line, but Black is able to win with accurate play: 29...♖f8! 30 ♘g1 (30 cxd4 ♕f1+ 31 ♔h2 ♘f3+ 32 ♔g3 ♘xd2; 30 ♕xd4 ♖d8!) 30...d3! 31 ♖e1 (31 ♕d4 ♔h7!) 31...♕f2+ 32 ♔h1 ♕g3 33 ♕g2 ♕h4+ 34 ♕h2 ♕e4+ 35 ♕g2 ♘f3 36 ♘xf3

→xf3 37 ♞g1 ♕f5 and White is helpless.

29	...	hxg5
30	cxd4	♕c6
31	d5	

31 ♕xc6 ♞xc6 is hopeless for White, since he can't eliminate the e2-pawn without simplifying to a trivially lost ending.

| 31 | ... | ♕xd5 |

Trying to keep the queens on the board by 31...→xd5 32 →e1 gives Black less.

32	♕xd5	→xd5
33	→e1	→d2
34	♚f2!	→xa2

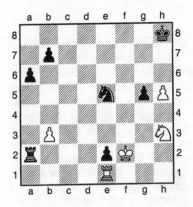

35   →xe2?!

Topalov finally removes the troublesome pawn, but he has missed a trick that makes Black's victory quite simple. Or maybe he played this move so as to set a little trap? 35 ♚e3! poses Black more problems, but 35...♞f7 36 →xe2 (or 36 ♞f2 ♚g7 37 →xe2 →xe2+ 38 ♚xe2 ♚h6) 36...→xe2+ 37 ♚xe2 ♚g7 38 ♚f3 ♚h6 39 ♚g4 a5 40 ♞f2 b5 41 ♞e4 a4 42 bxa4 bxa4 43 ♞c3 a3 is also a win for Black.

| 35 | ... | ♞d3+ |

36	♚e3	→xe2+
37	♚xe2	g4!

The trap is 37...♞f4+?? 38 ♞xf4 gxf4 39 ♚f3 with a drawn ending.

38	♞g5	♞c1+
39	♚e3	♞xb3
40	h6	a5
41	♚f4	♞d4!

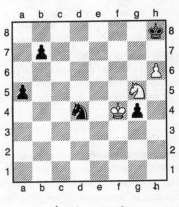

42	♚xg4	a4
43	♚h5	

Even in this hopeless ending, Topalov produces a mating threat.

| 43 | ... | ♞c6 |

43...a3?? loses to 44 ♚g6!. How painful that would have been!

0-1

Now Black will parry 44 ♚g6 with 44...♞e5+ 45 ♚f5 a3!.

Lessons from this game:

1) Advancing pawns in front of your king can make it safer, if this makes it harder for the opponent to open lines.

2) "Safety-nets" are an extremely useful concept when making difficult decisions at the chessboard.

3) When both kings are exposed, initiative matters more than material.

Game 107
Veselin Topalov – Vasily Ivanchuk
Linares 1999
English Opening

The Players

Veselin Topalov (born 1975) has been one of the world's leading players since he leaped up the rating list in 1993. At the time of writing (January 2004) he is ranked sixth in the world. For more information see Game 90.

Vasily Ivanchuk (born 1969) has been one of the world's top grandmasters for over 10 years and at the time of writing is ranked 13th in the world. Despite his enormous talent and his ability to play outstanding individual games, his nerves have prevented him from gaining a major title. For more information see Game 85.

The Game

Much opening theory is concerned with whether White can maintain the slight advantage of the first move, or whether Black can achieve equality. The idea of Black gaining the advantage is often hardly considered, but in practice White's one-tempo advantage can easily be surrendered by inaccurate play. In the following game Topalov makes a slip in the opening, allowing Black comfortable equality. However, White does not realize the danger he is in and continues to play as if he still had White's usual opening edge. Ivanchuk is quick to punish Topalov's failure to grasp the new situation and Black takes over the initiative with a series of powerful moves. Again and again White is on the verge of repairing the defects of his position, only to be kept off-balance by a new blow. Finally, a deadly piece sacrifice traps the white king in the centre and in the firing-line of Black's army. It is not often that a leading grandmaster loses with White in only 25 moves.

1	♘f3	c5
2	c4	♘c6
3	d4	cxd4
4	♘xd4	e6

Move-order finesses can be important in the Symmetrical English. This position is slightly unusual in that Black has played ...♘c6 rather than ...♘f6, a difference which introduces some novel factors.

5 g3?!

5 ♘c3 is more natural, and after 5...♘f6 a standard position arises. The text-move is too slow in this position as the added pressure on d4 afforded by ...♘c6 allows Black to play more actively than normal.

| 5 | ... | ♗b4+ |

5...♕b6 might be an even more effective way of exploiting White's inaccuracy.

6 ♘c3

6 ♗d2 ♕b6 7 ♘b3 is better, when White might still claim a very slight advantage.

6 ... ♕a5!

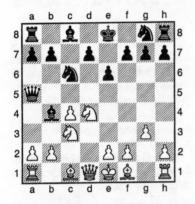

A very good move, pinpointing the fact that White is still two moves from castling.

7 ♘b5

In the corresponding position with ♗g2 and ...♘f6 included, White can offer a very strong pawn sacrifice by castling. Here this option isn't available, so White has to make a concession. If 7 ♘xc6, then Black has a comfortable position after either recapture. However, the move played, moving the knight a third time, is also not ideal.

7 ... d5

Black's active play in the centre gives him easy equality.

8 a3

If you are White, there is a tendency to assume that you must be better in the opening phase. Over the next couple of moves White plays as if he has the advantage, when in fact he does not. The result is that he takes unjustified risks for which he is severely

punished. After 8 ♗d2 a6! 9 cxd5 exd5 10 ♘a3 Black's position is also very comfortable, so White should have settled for the modest but safe 8 ♗f4 e5 9 ♗d2, with a roughly equal position.

8 ... ♗xc3+
9 bxc3?!

White hopes to use the active position of his knight on b5, but this is not a relevant factor. 9 ♘xc3 was better, with the idea of sacrificing the exchange after 9...d4 (9...dxc4 is safer) 10 b4 ♘xb4 11 axb4 ♕xa1 12 ♘b5. Then the position would be very unclear.

9 ... ♘f6

Having forced White into a variety of concessions (time-wasting knight moves and doubled c-pawns) Black rushes to complete his development.

10 ♗g2

Other moves also fail to equalize; e.g., 10 ♗f4 e5 11 ♗d2 0-0 or 10 ♘d6+ ♔e7 11 cxd5 exd5 12 ♗f4 ♕xc3+ 13 ♗d2 ♕c5 14 ♘xc8+ ♖hxc8.

10 ... 0-0

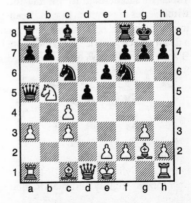

11 ♕b3

11 0-0 dxc4 and 11 cxd5 ♘xd5 12 ♕b3 a6 13 ♗xd5 exd5 14 ♘d6 d4 15

♘xc8 ♖axc8 are also favourable for Black.

11 ... dxc4

12 ♕xc4

A critical moment. White's king is still in the centre, but he is now threatening to castle. Black must use his lead in development to keep White off-balance.

12 ... e5

Freeing the c8-bishop. 12...♖d8 is also dangerous for White, although he might be able to hold on with 13 a4.

13 ♘d6?!

This move appears most natural, but now White's position is torn apart by a hurricane. 13 a4? ♗e6 14 ♕d3 ♖fd8 15 ♕c2 a6 and 13 0-0? ♗e6 14 ♕d3 ♖fd8 15 ♕b1 a6 are even worse options for White, since Black wins straight away. 13 ♕b3! is the best chance, although Black retains a clear advantage after 13...♗e6 14 ♕b2 ♖fd8 15 a4 a6.

13 ... ♗e6

14 ♕d3

Forced, as 14 ♘xb7 ♗xc4 15 ♘xa5 ♘xa5 16 ♗xa8 ♖xa8 is winning for Black.

Again we have a critical position in which indecisive play by Black would allow White to escape. The text-move offers a pawn in order to gain time to bring Black's rooks onto the central files.

15 ♘xe4

White must accept. The alternatives 15 ♕c2 ♘d4, 15 ♗xe4 ♘xe4 16 ♘xe4 ♖ad8, 15 ♕e3 ♘g4 16 ♕d2 ♖ad8 17 ♘xb7 ♕a4 18 ♘xd8 ♖xd8 and 15 ♕d2 ♖ad8 are all lost for White.

15 ... ♘xe4

16 ♗xe4 ♖ad8

17 ♕c2

17 ♕e3 ♖fe8 costs White material; for example, 18 f3 f5 19 ♗xc6 bxc6 followed by ...♗c4.

17 ... ♘d4

White is not given a moment's respite.

18 ♕b2

After 18 ♕b1 ♕xc3+ 19 ♔d2 (19 ♔f1 ♗h3+ 20 ♔g2 ♕c6 21 f3 ♘xe2 wins for Black) 19...♘c2+ White must give up the exchange since 20 ♗xc2 loses to 20...♕xd2+ 21 ♔f1 ♗h3+ 22 ♔g1 ♕xe2.

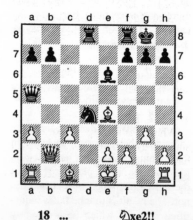

14 ... e4!

18 ... ♘xe2!!

This spectacular sacrifice pins the white king down in the centre of the board. 18...Ξfe8 would let White off the hook since 19 0-0! ♗h3 20 cxd4 ♗xf1 21 ♗d2 is roughly equal.

19 ♔xe2

White must accept as 19 ♕b4 loses to 19...♘xc3!.

19 ... Ξfe8

The best follow-up; Black brings his last piece into play and preserves all his options. White's king isn't going to run very far.

20 ♕b4

Black's attack breaks through no matter what White plays:

1) 20 ♗e3 ♗c4+ 21 ♔f3 Ξxe4 22 ♔xe4 (22 ♔g2 ♗d5 is also hopeless for White) 22...♕d5+ 23 ♔f4 h5! and Black mates in a few moves.

2) 20 Ξe1 ♕h5+! 21 ♔f1 ♗h3+ 22 ♔g1 ♕f3 mates.

3) 20 f3 f5! 21 ♗xb7 (after 21 ♕b4 ♕a6+ 22 ♔f2 fxe4 23 ♗e3 exf3 Black has a pawn more and a strong attack, while 21 ♗g5 fxe4 22 ♗xd8 exf3+ is crushing) 21...♕xc3!! (a beautiful finish) 22 ♕xc3 (22 ♔f1 ♗c4+ 23 ♔f2 ♕xb2+ 24 ♗xb2 Ξe2+ 25 ♔g1 Ξxb2 26 ♗c6 Ξd6 27 ♗a8 Ξb8 traps the bishop) 22...♗c4+ 23 ♔f2 Ξe2+ 24 ♔g1 Ξd1+ mates.

20 ... ♕h5+!

A neat queen switch. White cannot keep the black queen out forever.

21 f3 f5

22 g4

White tries to keep his extra piece, since if the bishop falls, White will have nothing to show for the terrible position of his king. 22 ♕c5 ♗d5! and 22 ♕xb7 fxe4 are also dead lost.

22 ... ♕h3!

Black continues accurately; for example, 22...fxg4?! 23 ♗e3 would allow White to fight on.

23 gxf5 ♗xf5!

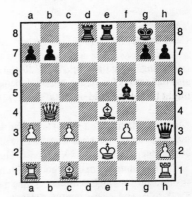

The last bastions protecting the white king are crumbling.

24 ♕c4+

24 ♔f2 ♗xe4 25 fxe4 Ξf8+ mates.

24 ... ♔h8

25 Ξe1 Ξxe4+

0-1

After 26 fxe4 ♗g4+ 27 ♔f2 ♕xh2+ it is mate next move.

Lessons from this game:

1) In the opening, pay attention to finesses in move-order; they can have more significance than is immediately apparent.

2) When you have gained the initiative, try to keep your opponent off-balance.

3) If the central files are open, it may be worth a considerable sacrifice to keep your opponent's king trapped in the centre.

Peter Svidler – Michael Adams
Neum 2000
Ruy Lopez (Spanish), Møller Variation

The Players

Peter Svidler (born 1976) is a grandmaster from St Petersburg. He showed enormous talent as a teenager, winning his first Russian Championship in 1994. He has been among the world's top 20 players since 1996, and a string of excellent results in 2003 (including his fourth Russian Championship title) boosted him to 4th place on the January 2004 list, behind only Kasparov, Kramnik and Anand.

Michael Adams (born 1971) is the British no. 1, and one of the world's leading grandmasters. He comes from Cornwall, in the extreme south-west of England. His temperament is ideally suited to chess; no matter what has happened in the game, he continues making good solid moves. Allied to his positional sense and the rarity with which he blunders, this makes Adams a formidable competitor. In 1993 he qualified for the Candidates stages of both the FIDE and PCA world championships, and has performed consistently well in FIDE's knockout-format world championship. He is currently world number 11, but it is rare for him to be outside the top ten.

The Game

Adams chooses a fashionable defence against the Lopez, in which Black relies on active piece-play. Svidler cunningly targets a weakness in Black's queenside, and there follows a tactical sequence in which the centre is blown open. White gets the better of the intricate complications that follow, and crowns off his achievement with a fine queen sacrifice after which his pieces prove much too active for Black to handle.

1	e4	e5
2	♘f3	♘c6
3	♗b5	a6
4	♗a4	♘f6
5	0-0	♗c5

This is known as the Møller Variation, and is a closely related idea to the Arkhangelsk Variation (5...b5 6 ♗b3 ♗b7), which we saw in Game 68. In putting his bishop on c5, it appears that Black is somehow aiming to prevent White from playing d4. However,

White can quite easily force through this advance, so we wonder what Black might be up to – if he has to respond by exchanging on d4 and retreating his bishop, surely he will get a miserable position? In fact, Black's set-up is heavily based on tactical ideas. The idea is that Black will not exchange on d4, but (having played ...b5 and ...d6) just drop his bishop back to b6 when White plays c3 and d4. Black will then seek to create quick pressure with his pieces against White's pawn-centre, forcing a concession of some sort. Pressure against d4, e4 and f2 are all common themes, and Black often makes a temporary pawn sacrifice in pursuing these goals. The move ...d5 is frequently seen too.

Black can implement this same idea by playing 5...b5 6 ♗b3 ♗c5, and this is also an important option. The main argument against that form of the line is that White can reply 7 a4, putting immediate pressure on Black's queen-side. This isn't necessarily a great problem for Black, but it is natural that the attempt to deny White this possibility should be explored, especially at times when Black appears to be struggling after 7 a4. In fact, the move-order chosen in the game also gives White some independent options, so the two forms of this defence have swung in and out of fashion, with its advocates switching from one line to the other and back again depending on the state of theory at the time. After 7 a4, one important line runs 7...♖b8 8 c3 (8 axb5 axb5 9 ♘xe5 ♘xe5 10 d4 is another idea for White) 8...d6 9 d4 ♗b6 10 ♘a3 0-0 11 axb5 axb5 12 ♘xb5 exd4 13 cxd4 ♗g4, which is only the starting point for a good deal of sophisticated opening theory; Black may well have enough play for the pawn.

6 c3

White has some alternatives here. 6 ♗xc6 dxc6 is a form of Exchange Variation where Black's bishop turns out to be quite well placed on c5, while the tactical trick 6 ♘xe5 ♘xe5 7 d4 leads to interesting open play, but Black has his full share of the chances. This trick is also available to White in the 5...b5

move-order, and is not considered a major problem for Black in that case either.

6 ... b5
7 ♗c2

White attempts to take advantage of Black's move-order by bringing his bishop directly to c2. Instead, 7 ♗b3 arrives at the same position as after 5...b5 6 ♗b3 ♗c5 7 c3. However, this is not an unequivocal gain for White, since although the bishop is useful on c2, and often ends up dropping back to that square in due course, it also serves a useful purpose on b3 too, where it eyes d5 and f7.

7 ... d6

7...d5 is a logical attempt to exploit the bishop's absence from the a2-g8 diagonal. However, it is by no means a simple solution to Black's problems; sharp and forcing play results after 8 d4 or the surprising 8 a4.

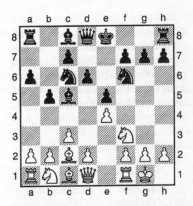

8 a4

8 d4 is another possibility, but after 8...♗b6 9 h3 (9 a4 is also important) 9...0-0 Black has a clearer target than in the game continuation.

8 ... ♗g4

This pin is one of Black's main ideas in this line.

9 d3

White cannot take any drastic action for now, and prepares to develop his queen's knight.

9	...	0-0
10	h3	♗h5
11	♘bd2	

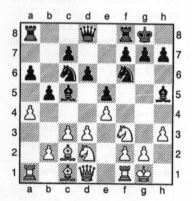

Now what should Black do? All his minor pieces are actively developed, and it is not fully clear where his major pieces belong. Also, White retains many options. While he is not immediately threatening to achieve the d4 advance, this idea is still hanging in the air, while he has several ways to play on either wing. Black must also look out for White playing g4 at a favourable moment.

11 ... b4

Adams removes White's possibilities of exchanging on b5, and hopes to generate some queenside play. The move's drawbacks are clear: White is granted the c4-square and Black's queenside structure is disrupted.

11...d5 looks very natural, but after 12 axb5 axb5 13 ♖xa8 ♕xa8 14 exd5

♘xd5 15 ♘e4 White's position is very harmonious, and he is probably a little better.

12 a5

White fixes the pawn on a6 and denies the a5- and b6-squares to Black's pieces.

| 12 | ... | ♖b8 |
| 13 | ♕e2!? | |

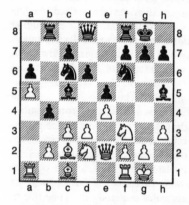

With this subtle move, a novelty that he had no doubt prepared beforehand, Svidler takes aim against the loose a6-pawn, an idea that takes on real form when you consider that White is thinking of playing d4. It is far from easy for Black to parry this in a simple way.

13 ... bxc3

13...♕c8 defends the a6-pawn, but after 14 ♖e1 White has a pleasant game, with the ♘f1-g3 regrouping on the agenda.

14 bxc3 d5

Adams hits back in the centre, and this leads to immense complications. This was a brave decision, given that Svidler was sure to have analysed this critical test of his novelty.

15 d4!

Backing out at this stage would make no sense.

15	...	exd4
16	**♛xa6**	

Taking stock, we see total chaos on the board. Black must decide whether to save his c6-knight, which would allow White to retain a pawn-centre of some sort, or to opt for exchanges, opening the centre completely.

16	...	dxc3

16...♛d6 is met by 17 e5 ♘xe5 18 ♛xd6 when, however Black responds, White will retain a grip on the centre and have a useful passed a-pawn.

17	**♛xc6**	cxd2
18	**♘xd2!**	

This is a somewhat surprising move, but otherwise White's kingside will become seriously weakened: 18 ♛xc5? dxc1♛ 19 ♖fxc1 ♗xf3 20 gxf3 ♘h5! is just bad for White, while 18 ♗xd2 dxe4! 19 ♛xc5 exf3 offers Black excellent counterplay.

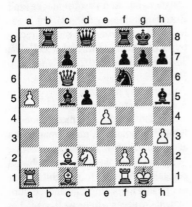

18	...	**♗d4**

The bishop doesn't have an ideal square. Its presence on d4 enables White to swing his queen's rook into action, but 18...♗a7 is well met by 19

e5!, when 19...♗d4 20 ♗a3! ♗xe5 21 ♗xf8 favours White.

19	**♖a4**	dxe4
20	**♘xe4**	**♘xe4!**
21	**♗xe4**	

White has ideas like 22 ♗xh7+ ♚xh7 23 ♛e4+, and simply 22 ♗f4, piling on the pressure. 21 ♛xe4 is another idea, aiming for simpler positions where the a-pawn will prove influential.

21	...	**♗e2**

Therefore Adams opts for a forcing line.

22	**♗xh7+**	**♚h8!**

22...♚xh7? 23 ♛e4+ is clearly not an option for Black.

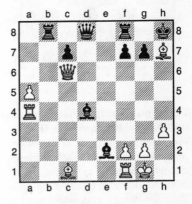

23	**♗c2**	

23 ♛e4? is very bad due to 23...♖e8! 24 ♖xd4 ♖xe4 25 ♖xd8+ ♖xd8 26 ♗xe4 ♗xf1 27 ♚xf1 ♖d1+, when Black is better.

23	...	**♖e8?**

Black's ideas involve counterplay against f2, but White has a good response. He should take the material, even though White has abundant compensation after 23...♗xf1 24 ♚xf1 g6 25 a6, as given by Svidler.

24 Ze1   Ze6

24...♕h4 is brilliantly parried by 25 ♗e3! ♖xe3 26 ♕xc7! ♖d8 (26...♖be8 is met by 27 ♖xd4 ♕xd4 28 fxe3 ♕xe3+ 29 ♔h2) 27 ♖xd4 ♖xd4 28 fxe3 ♕xe1+ 29 ♔h2, when Black is helpless despite his extra rook; e.g., 29...♖d3 30 ♗xd3 ♗xd3 31 ♕d8+ ♔h7 32 ♕xd3+.

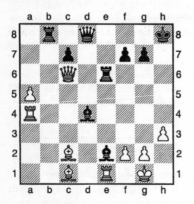

25 ♕xe6

This queen sacrifice is clearest, although 25 ♖xd4 ♕xd4 26 ♕xc7 is also good.

25 ...	fxe6
26 ♖xe2	**e5**
27 a6	**♕d7**
28 a7	**♖a8**
29 ♖xe5!	

This sacrifice releases the pent-up energy of the white pieces and turns the spotlight firmly onto Black's exposed king.

29 ...   g6

The critical line justifying White's previous move is 29...♗xe5 30 ♖h4+ ♔g8 31 ♗b3+ ♔f8 32 ♖h8+ ♔e7 33 ♖xa8 ♕c6 34 ♗g5+ ♗f6 35 ♗xf6+ gxf6 36 ♖g8 ♕c1+ 37 ♔h2 ♕f4+ 38 ♖g3 ♕e4 39 ♖e3.

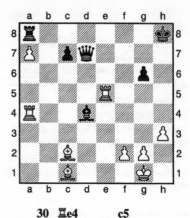

30 ♖e4	**c5**
31 ♖a6	

31 ♖h4+ is also very strong, but the text-move is more straightforward.

31 ...	**♖xa7**
32 ♖xg6	**♗g7**
33 ♗b2!	**♕b5**

33...♗xb2 34 ♖h4+ is terminal.

34 ♗c3

This was enough to cause Adams to resign, as he has no useful moves (and ♖b6 is one of many threats), but Svidler could have won even more directly by 34 ♖b6 ♕xb2 (34...♕xb6 35 ♖e8#) 35 ♖e8+ ♗f8 36 ♖xb2.

1-0

Lessons from this game:

1) Plans are often formed by identifying the opponent's main weaknesses and thinking of ways to target them.

2) In closed positions, one should constantly be alert to possibilities of the position opening up, and be sure that one's pieces will be well-placed in that event.

3) White's queen sacrifice gained time and enabled him to bring a rook and an unopposed bishop into the attack on the black king.

Game 109

Ivan Sokolov – Alexei Dreev

Dos Hermanas 2001
Queen's Gambit Declined, Semi-Slav Defence

The Players

Ivan Sokolov (born 1968) is originally from Bosnia & Herzegovina, but now resides in the Netherlands. He is an extremely creative and dynamic player, always willing to sacrifice material for the initiative. As a result, he creates many beautiful games, but also suffers the occasional disaster. He is currently (January 2004) world number 16.

Alexei Dreev (born 1969) is a grandmaster from Russia. He has a solid style of play, and the polished technical skills that one associates with pupils of the famous trainer Mark Dvoretsky. Dreev has represented Russia in several Olympiads and other team events. He is currently 20th in the world.

The Game

The opening is a true battle of the specialists; Dreev is one of the outstanding experts in the Moscow Variation, and Sokolov was one of the main pioneers of the aggressive gambit response to it. It appears as if Sokolov is smashing through Black's position in the centre, but Dreev turns out to have everything under control. A few quick stabs from his pawns reveal the true picture: the foundations of White's position are being dismantled, and this will deny his attacking pieces the back-up they require. In the end White's king is mated mid-board.

1	d4	d5
2	c4	c6
3	♘f3	♘f6
4	♘c3	e6

For the seventh time in this book, we have a Semi-Slav. It must be admitted that this is slightly out of proportion with the opening's relative popularity, but it does accurately reflect its importance in top-level games and the fact that it often leads to extremely interesting and complex battles.

| 5 | ♗g5 | h6 |

In Games 74, 89, 95, 98 and 103, we saw Black playing 5...dxc4, the Botvinnik System. The text-move, known

as the Moscow Variation, is an attempt to direct the game along quieter channels. Black's aim is to obtain the bishop-pair and a solid position, in return for which White has a space advantage and some pressure.

| 6 | ♗h4 |

6 ♗xf6 ♕xf6 was for many years the standard continuation here, and more or less the only line taken seriously. However, during the 1990s, the alternative, and far sharper, plan introduced by the text-move became popular. This was partly because Black's position was looking extremely solid in the lines following 6 ♗xf6, and

partly based on an increased willingness to play highly sharp, dynamic opening lines. The rise of computers has played a part in this change, since they enable players to try out speculative ideas in their home analysis, with the computer helping out with the analysis of highly tactical positions.

6 ...   dxc4

Otherwise Black would get a standard Queen's Gambit Declined position, where his early ...c6 and ...h6 would not be to his advantage. This is unlikely to satisfy many Semi-Slav players.

7 e4

Now White gets a big centre, and the sharp game that he was clearly seeking with his 5th and 6th moves.

7 ...   g5

This is the big difference from the Botvinnik System: Black can force the bishop back to g3. Instead, 7...b5 transposes to the Botvinnik System, which Black was clearly trying to avoid by playing 5...h6.

8 &g3   b5

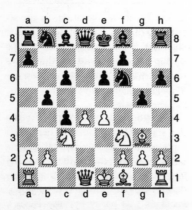

Now Black has an extra pawn, and there is no simple way for White to

regain it. Instead, he shall seek compensation in his development advantage, strong pawn-centre, and Black's vulnerable pawn-structure on both wings.

9 &e2

9 h4 had been successfully introduced by Sokolov, but by the time of this game looked unconvincing due to 9...g4 10 ♘e5 &b4. With the text-move, White is not abandoning the h4 idea, but wants to create more favourable circumstances for it.

9 ...   &b7

One of the greatest boosts for 6 &h4's popularity came when it was demonstrated that 9...b4 10 ♘a4 ♘xe4 11 &e5 ♘f6 (after 11...♖g8, both 12 ♛c2 and 12 &xc4 are considered promising for White) 12 ♘c5 leaves Black in considerable trouble, as he has no way to remove the e5-bishop and the paralysing grip it exerts.

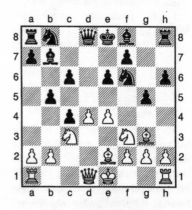

10 h4   b4!?

When he first faced this line, Dreev suffered a disaster: 10...g4 11 ♘e5 b4 12 ♘a4 ♘xe4 13 &xc4 ♘xg3 14 fxg3 ♘d7 15 ♘xf7! &xf7 16 ♛xg4 ♛e7 17 0-0+ &e8 18 &xe6 &c8 19 ♖ae1 gave

White a winning attack in Khalifman – Dreev, Elista 1998 (note that the black bishop's absence from c8 makes e6 more vulnerable here than in lines following 9 h4). Three years on, he was ready with a far more testing response.

11 ♘a4   ♘xe4
12 ♗e5

Clearly there are parallels with the line we saw following 9...b4. It is not immediately apparent whose extra move (h4 vs ...♗b7) will prove more useful. One significant point is that Black is one move closer to castling queenside.

12 ...   ♖g8

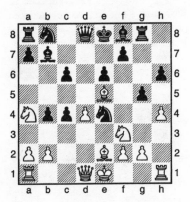

13 ♕c2

13 hxg5 hxg5 14 ♗xc4 ♘d7 15 ♕d3 g4 16 ♕xe4 gxf3 17 gxf3 (17 ♕xf3 ♘xe5 18 dxe5 ♕g5!) 17...♕a5 left Black somewhat better in the game Xu Jun – P.H. Nielsen, Istanbul Olympiad 2000.

13 ...   c5

This move is logical, as it puts the b7-bishop to work. However, it also exposes Black's king, and it seems all too easy for White to exploit this fact.

Dreev avoids 13...♘f6?! 14 ♘c5, when he risks the familiar paralysis; even though the f6-knight isn't pinned here, it still has problems, especially with the need to look out for ♕h7 ideas.

14 ♗xc4

It might be an improvement for White to exchange on g5 before playing this, but Black could also meet 14 hxg5 with 14...♕a5!?. 14 0-0-0 has been played in some later games, and leads to highly complicated play.

14 ...   g4

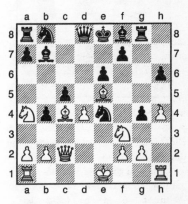

Black ploughs on with his counterplay. White's threats look very dangerous, but we may presume that Dreev was confident that he had enough activity and could disrupt White's potential reinforcements.

15 ♗b5+   ♘d7
16 dxc5?!

Sokolov opens the d-file, and it seems that d7 is bound to collapse, and Black's whole position with it. What does Black have against this? It seems that his pieces are poorly coordinated, and while he has two pawns that have advanced into White's half of the board, they do not appear likely to be part of any real counterattack. However, in view of the forcing sequence in the game, White needs to find an improvement here. 16 0-0-0 was Stohl's suggestion; after 16...gxf3 17 dxc5 fxg2 18 ♖hg1 ♗d5 19 c6 ♗d6 20 cxd7+ ♔e7 21 f3 White still has chances.

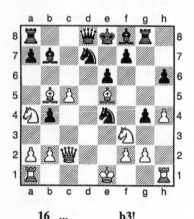

16 ...   **b3!**

This move is a vital link in the chain. It opens the a5-e1 diagonal with gain of time and disrupts White's coordination. 16...gxf3? 17 c6 is good for White.

17 ♕d3

17 ♕xb3 ♗d5 18 ♕d3 gxf3 19 c6 ♗b4+ is terrible for White (e.g., 20 ♘c3 ♘xe5 21 c7+ ♕d7 or 20 ♗c3 ♗xc3+ 21 ♘xc3 ♘xf2! – Stohl), while 17 axb3 ♕a5+ 18 ♘d2 ♘exc5 (or 18...♕xb5 19 ♘xe4 ♕b4+ 20 ♘ac3 ♗xc5) 19 ♘xc5 ♕xb5! 20 ♘xd7 ♕xd7, as given by Dreev, strongly favours Black, since White's king is still the one in more real danger.

17 ...   **gxf3**

17...♗xc5 risks letting White off the hook.

18 c6

18 ♖d1 ♗d5 blocks the d-file.

18 ...   **♗b4+**

Black activates his dark-squared bishop with gain of time and frees f8 for his king.

19 ♗c3

19 ♘c3 brings the knight back into play, but is very strongly answered by 19...♗xc6 20 ♗xc6 fxg2 21 ♖g1 ♘xf2!!, when Black is much better.

19 ...   **♗xc3+**
20 bxc3

Now both of Black's far-advanced pawns become major problems for White, but 20 ♘xc3 fxg2 21 ♖g1 ♘ec5 is quite safe for Black, and therefore gives him a large plus.

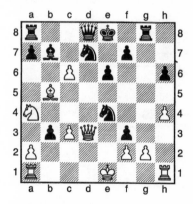

20 ...   **fxg2**
21 ♖g1   **b2!**

Overloading the a4-knight.

22 ♖d1

22 ♘xb2 ♘ec5 23 cxd7+ ♔e7 24 ♕d4 ♕c7 leaves White's position simply in ruins.

22 ...   **♕xh4!**
23 ♕xd7+   **♔f8**
24 ♕d4   **b1♕!**

Black's b-pawn has done its duty valiantly in this game, and now lays down its life to secure the d-file for Black's last undeveloped piece.

25 Rxb1 Rd8
26 cxb7

26 ♕e3 ♕h2 and 26 ♕b4+ Rd6 27 Rb2 ♕h1 are fatal for White.

26 ... Rxd4
27 b8♕+ Rd8
28 ♕xa7

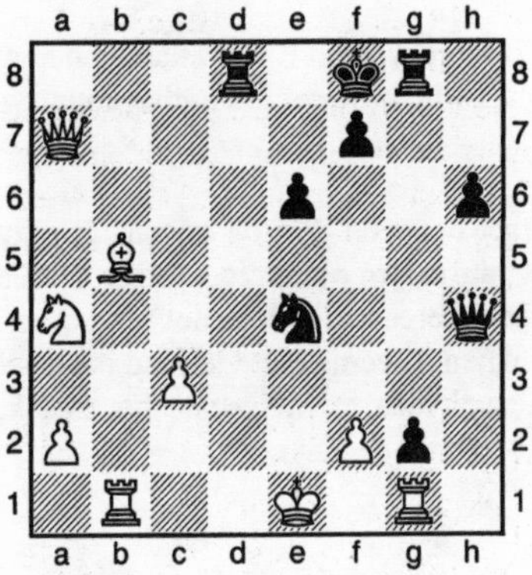

White has even acquired a material advantage, but Black has a mating attack.

28 ... ♕h2

29 ♔e2

29 f3 is the only other way to defend the rook, but it is also mate then: 29...♕g3+ 30 ♔e2 Rd2+, etc.

29 ... Rd2+
30 ♔e3 Rg3+!
31 ♔xe4

31 fxg3 ♕xg3+ 32 ♔xe4 f5# is a neat mate.

31 ... Rg4+
0-1

It is mate next move.

Lessons from this game:

1) In some positions the roles of attacker and defender are not very clearly defined; here Black had to go on the counterattack to keep his position afloat.

2) The fact that one player appears to be making all the running can be misleading; many of Black's pieces were forced to particular squares, but they proved very well placed nevertheless.

3) By knocking the support away from White's attack, Black robbed it of its strength.

Game 110

Boris Gelfand – Boris Kantsler

Israel 2001

King's Indian Defence, Classical Variation

The Players

Boris Gelfand (born 1968) has been one of the world's top grandmasters since 1990. See Game 88 for more details.

Boris Kantsler (born 1962) is a grandmaster originally from Kyrgyzstan who now lives in Israel – one of the many former Soviets who have settled in that country.

The Game

A standard King's Indian scenario arises: a race between White's queenside play and Black's kingside attack. Kantsler adopts a modern plan, recapturing with a knight on d6; while this makes a lot of subtle differences, it does not fundamentally change the nature of the position. Just when it seems that Gelfand is ahead in the race, Kantsler produces a most unusual idea to invigorate his attack. Gelfand falters, and Black's attack quickly becomes decisive.

1	d4	♘f6
2	c4	g6
3	♘c3	♗g7

Black chooses the King's Indian, in which Black allows White a big centre in the hope of chipping away at it, or else blocking the centre and playing on the wings. This brings about an interesting psychological situation, as the King's Indian is an opening that Gelfand has played as Black himself a great many times. It is never easy to face one's own favourite openings, despite the obvious advantage of being extremely familiar with the theory.

4	e4	d6
5	♘f3	0-0
6	♗e2	

White adopts the no-nonsense Classical set-up. He develops rapidly and avoids making any further pawn advances for the time being.

6	...	e5

Black makes his standard claim for a share of the centre. Several structures are now possible: Black exchanges on d4; White exchanges on e5; or White blocks the centre by playing d5. More often than not, it is the third of these possibilities that occurs, though White tends to delay the advance until Black forces it; generally White can expect some advantage if Black exchanges on d4.

7	0-0	♘c6

This is the standard move. Black more or less forces White to play d5. Black's knight will have to move again, but e7 is not a bad square at all, since from there it can be quickly transferred into a kingside attack.

8	d5	♘e7

Now White has a major decision. Almost all the logical moves (and quite a few bizarre-looking ones) have been tried in this position. White's problem is that whatever he does, he gives Black something on which to base his actions.

9 ♘e1

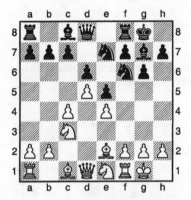

This is White's traditional main line. By retreating his knight, White discourages ...♘h5, makes it possible to support the e4-pawn by playing f3 if and when this becomes necessary, and also has in mind ♘d3, which supports the c5 advance, which is vital for White's queenside attack. However, the knight move does have its drawbacks: there are no longer any ideas of ♘g5 (which can be useful if Black plays for a quick ...f5), while the option of transferring the knight to c4 via d2 (where *en route* it also guards e4) is given up.

9 ... ♘e8

Although the position after White's 9th move has been subjected to intense scrutiny for more than half a century, this move only became topical in the 1990s. 9...♘d7 is the more standard move. In order to understand the subsequent play, it is important to note a

few important differences between the two moves. Firstly, on d7, the knight discourages White's thematic c5 advance; the fact that White has to spend extra time preparing this advance is the key reason for 9...♘d7's traditional main-line status. (Also, it supports the e5-square, meaning that ideas with f4 by White are not a great problem for Black; with the knight on e8, they are quite testing.) Black invariably plays ...f5. White will try to avoid replying with f3 (since this makes it easier to launch a standard attack with ...f4, ...g5, etc.), happy that if Black plays ...fxe4, a white minor piece will be well placed on the e4-square. Black will often need to play ...♘f6 if he wishes to force White to play f3. Clearly, the knight can equally well have manoeuvred via d7 or e8 from that viewpoint. In the subsequent play (once Black has played ...f4 and ...g5, and White has played c5 and exchanged pawns on d6), Black often finds it necessary to play ...♘e8 to cover the c7-square, where White often threatens to invade. We thus see a possible benefit of putting the knight on e8 immediately – if Black can somehow encourage White to play f3 by other means, then he might save two tempi by playing ...♘e8 directly, rather than ...♘d7-f6-e8. However, the "somehow" in that sentence is the key word – there are lines where Black has nothing better than playing ...♘f6 anyway. A further idea that can justify ...♘e8 is that he can reply to White's standard c5 and cxd6 idea by recapturing on d6 with the knight. This leads to a type of position that is far less well explored than that after ...cxd6. Clearly there are many subtle factors at work here, but White has not yet managed to demonstrate any persuasive argument for Black to abandon 9...♘e8.

10 ♗e3

Gelfand opts for a very direct approach, which is also a highly critical reply to 9...♘d7 (we saw it in Game 83). White puts his bishop on the most active diagonal available to it and prepares the c5 advance. The bishop's attack against a7 will quickly take on real form if White plays ♘b5. On the other hand, White will now have no choice but to meet ...f5 with f3. If he is to show up a defect of ...♘e8, it will be purely with his queenside attack.

10 ...   f5
11 f3   f4
12 ♗f2   h5

It looks a little odd to play this move before ...g5, but Black reasons that both moves will be necessary (with no knight on f6, the h-pawn's support is essential if Black is to play ...g4), and there is no harm in playing this move first. One possible argument against 12...g5 is that White could meet it with 13 g4, but there is little experience with White playing this move. Note that 12...♘f6? is simply a bad move. It leads to positions similar to those we saw in Game 83, but White's queenside attack will be a whole move faster because he can play c5 without supporting it with b4. This amounts to a virtually decisive advantage in this race-type situation. If Black is to make sense of his position, he will need to demonstrate the positive aspects of his knight being on e8.

13 c5   g5
14 a4

This move is useful in almost any scenario, so White plays it now, and

keeps Black guessing about how he will seek to smash open the queenside. In particular, White does not rush to play cxd6; although this is normally played, it is also possible for White to play c6 in some lines.

14 ...   ♘g6

14...♖f6, intending ...♖g6, is the main alternative. Black will then generally recapture with the knight on d6, since without his king's rook available to defend c7, Black will want to avoid ♘b5-c7 ideas.

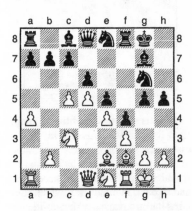

15 a5   ♖f7

15...♘f6?! is still poor, since White has made only useful moves on the queenside. 15...♗h6 is a move introduced by Kasparov, but after Korchnoi's idea 16 ♘b5! a6 17 ♘a3 ♔h8 18 ♘c4 Black is under pressure.

16 cxd6

16 c6!? is an alternative way to break open lines on the queenside.

16 ...   ♘xd6

16...cxd6?! is unwise here too, since White's time spent advancing his a-pawn is put to good effect by 17 ♘b5 a6 18 ♘c3 intending ♘a4-b6, eliminating Black's c8-bishop, whose vital role in Black's attack was shown in Game 83; we see a further example in our current game.

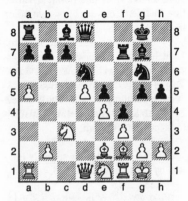

17 ♘d3

Kantsler intended to meet 17 ♘b5 with 17...♘xb5 18 ♗xb5 g4, exploiting the fact that the exchange on b5 has drawn White's bishop away from covering g4.

17 ... ♗f6

Freeing g7 for the rook, where it supports ...g4 and further g-file play. This aim could also be achieved by 17...♗h6. There are arguments for and against both moves; e.g. on h6 the bishop might get play on the h6-c1 diagonal and doesn't obstruct the queen; on f6 it covers the e5-pawn and can move to h4 in some lines.

18 ♘c5

This move highlights an obvious drawback of not recapturing with the pawn on d6. However, Black can cover e6 for now.

18 ... ♘f8

19 ♘b5

19 ♕b3 was played in Korchnoi – Relange, Cannes 1996 (where this position was reached via rather a different move-order). Black should probably reply 19...a6, preventing White from playing a6 himself.

19 ... ♖g7

20 a6

Both sides pursue their wing attacks.

20 ... bxa6

20...b6 is met by 21 ♘b7 (this isn't even a pawn sacrifice here) 21...♕e7 (21...♘xb7?! 22 axb7 ♗xb7 23 ♘xa7 leaves White's attack clearly the stronger) 22 ♖c1 ♘xb5 23 ♗xb5 g4 24 d6 cxd6 25 ♘xd6 ♗e6 26 ♘f5 ♗xf5 27 exf5, when White is unlikely to succumb to Black's kingside attack, though the situation is not wholly clear.

21 ♘xa6

21 ♘xd6 cxd6 22 ♘e6 ♘xe6 23 dxe6 ♗xe6 24 ♖xa6 ♗e7 leaves Black solid.

21 ... g4

Black rightly focuses on his attack. It is not enough for White's queenside play to pick off a pawn or two; he must also divert or remove some of Black's key attacking pieces, and Kantsler has foreseen a most imaginative way to prevent him from doing so.

22 ♘xa7 g3

23 ♗c5

23 hxg3 makes no sense, because ...♕h2+ is too easy for Black to arrange; White would prefer to conceal his king behind a black pawn on h2. 23...fxg3 24 ♗c5 ♗g5 25 ♘xc8 (25 ♘c6? allows Black to force mate by 25...♗e3+ 26 ♗xe3 ♕h4 27 ♖e1 ♕h2+ 28 ♔f1 ♕h1+ 29 ♗g1 ♗h3 30 gxh3 ♕xh3#) 25...♗f4 gives Black a strong attack.

After the text-move, it might seem that White is getting things under control. He is about to eliminate Black's important light-squared bishop, and it is no great problem if Black takes on h2. It isn't obvious how Black can quickly bring his queen into the attack either. Kantsler's next move shows great imagination, as it is by no means a standard idea in this type of position.

23   ...   ♗h3!!

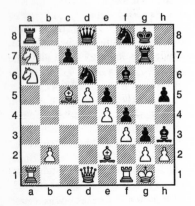

While it is quite normal for Black to play a ...♗xh3 sacrifice (taking a pawn), to sacrifice the bishop on the empty square is most unusual. Of course, a major part of the impetus here is to preserve the bishop from exchange, but the vital justification is that Black often has ...♗xg2 as his follow-up.

24 gxh3?

Gelfand challenges his opponent head-on to justify his sacrifice, but this turns out to be an unwise decision.

24 hxg3 is better. 24...♗xg2 (after 24...♖xg3 25 ♖f2 Black has no clear-cut follow-up, but it doesn't appear too bad for him either) and then:

1) 25 ♔xg2 ♖xg3+ 26 ♔f2 (26 ♔h1 ♖h3+ 27 ♔g2 ♖g3+ repeats) 26...♗h4 was given by Kantsler as "unclear", without any further analysis. 27 ♖g1

♕g5 28 ♔f1 ♘d7 29 ♗f2 ♖xg1+ 30 ♗xg1 ♖a7 31 ♗xa7 ♕g3 32 ♗b5 ♘xb5 33 ♗g1 ♕h3+ 34 ♔e2 ♕g2+ 35 ♔d3 ♕xb2 is one possible variation that certainly does not contradict that assessment.

2) 25 ♘c6 wasn't mentioned by Kantsler, but looks critical. The queen sacrifice 25...♗xf1 (25...♕d7 26 ♔xg2 ♖xg3+ 27 ♔f2 doesn't give Black enough for the piece) 26 ♘xd8 ♗xe2 27 ♕xe2 ♗xd8 may well be satisfactory for Black though.

24   ...   ♕d7

White's choice is now severely limited by the threat of ...♕xh3.

25 ♗d3

25 ♔g2? ♘g6 intending ...♘h4+ gives Black a winning attack, while 25 ♕c2 ♕xh3 26 ♗d3 ♘g6 27 ♕g2 transposes to the game continuation.

25   ...   ♕xh3
26 ♕e2   ♘g6

Black's main threat is the surprising ...♘h4-g2; watch out for this same idea over the next few moves.

27 ♕g2   ♕d7

Black of course avoids the exchange of queens and challenges White to find a way to meet the threat of ...♘h4.

28 ♘xc7

Gelfand tries to deflect the black queen and regain the initiative on the queenside. However, Kantsler simply ignores the knight. Instead, 28 ♖fc1 allows a brilliant win by 28...♘h4 29 ♕f1 ♘xf3+!! 30 ♕xf3 ♕h3.

28   ...   ♘h4

28...♕xc7? 29 ♘c6 gives White far too much play.

29 ♕e2   ♕h3!

Excellent. Black, already a piece down, shows no interest in the c7-knight, and instead leaves two of his pieces *en prise*. In return, he invigorates his already potent kingside attack. However, it is not yet obvious what his real threats are, since neither ...g2 nor ...gxh2++ is liable to lead to any clear result.

30 ♘e6

White strikes at the rook that is a major component in Black's attack, but it is too late to have any impact. Instead:

1) 30 ♗xd6? leads to immediate disaster: 30...♘g2! (30...♖xa7 is also strong: 31 ♖xa7 ♘xf3+ 32 ♖xf3 gxh2++ and mates) 31 hxg3 (31 ♕xg2 gxh2+ 32 ♔f2 ♖xg2+ 33 ♔e1 h1♕) 31...♖xg3 32 ♔f2 ♗h4 and White has no way out.

2) 30 ♘xa8 is also answered by 30...♘g2!! – indeed, this is Black's key idea in all variations. 31 ♖fc1 (31 hxg3 ♖xg3 32 ♔f2 ♗h4 is hopeless for White, despite his extra rook and bishop) 31...♕xh2+ 32 ♔f1 ♕h1+ 33 ♗g1 ♘h4 34 ♔e1 (34 ♖c2 g2+ 35 ♔f2 ♘hf5! is decisive) 34...♘xf3+ 35 ♔d1 ♕xg1+ 36 ♕f1 and now both 36...♕xf1+ 37 ♗xf1 g2 38 ♗xg2 ♖xg2 and 36...♕h2, intending ...g2, are easy wins for Black.

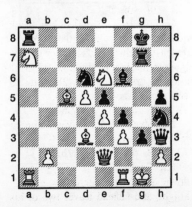

30 ... ♘g2!!

By now, this move will not come as any surprise to the reader. Black cuts the communication between the white queen and the h2-pawn, and if White takes the knight with his queen, then the pawn capture on h2 will be with check, meaning that the g7-rook being under attack will not matter.

31 ♖fc1

31 hxg3 ♖xg3 32 ♔f2 ♗h4 again cuts short the king's flight, so White provides his majesty with the f1-square.

31 ... ♕xh2+
32 ♔f1 ♕h1+
33 ♗g1 ♘h4!

Black threatens ...♘xf3, and there is very little White can do about it.

34 ♘xg7

34 ♖c2 parries the main threat but allows 34...♖gxa7 (34...♘xf3? 35 ♕g2 ♘h2+ 36 ♔e1) 35 ♖ac1 ♖a1, overloading the c2-rook; Black threatens 36...♖xc1+ 37 ♖xc1 ♘xf3 38 ♕g2 ♘h2+.

34 ... ♘xf3
0-1

White loses his queen, followed by further material: 35 ♕g2 (35 ♕c2 ♕xg1+ 36 ♔e2 ♕f2+ 37 ♔d1 ♕e1#) 35...♘h2+.

Lessons from this game:

1) A difference in the positioning of a single piece can have major implications for both sides' plans.

2) Even in very well-known types of positions, there is still scope for new and creative ideas.

3) When confronted by a surprising move, try to remain calm, and assess the position objectively. Of course, this is more easily said than done!

Vladimir Kramnik – Viswanathan Anand
Dortmund 2001
Queen's Gambit Accepted

The Players

Vladimir Kramnik (born 1975) defeated Garry Kasparov in a match for the BGN World Championship in 2000. At the time of writing (January 2004), he has not yet been required to defend his title. For further information, see Game 94.

Viswanathan ("Vishy") Anand (born 1969) has been rated among the top three players in the world since the mid-1990s. In 2000 he won the FIDE World Championship. See Game 88 for more details.

The Game

In an opening well-known to both players, Anand makes an unusual rook manoeuvre, in an attempt to improve the communication between his pieces. However, when his next move temporarily breaks this communication, Kramnik pounces with a thematic pawn sacrifice that is backed up by some surprising tactical ideas. In order to avoid an immediate catastrophe, Anand is forced to weaken his kingside. Kramnik plays vigorously to exploit this, and his attack continues even after the exchange of queens.

1	d4	d5
2	c4	dxc4

This is the standard Queen's Gambit Accepted (QGA). We saw a form of QGA arise via a different move-order in Game 99.

3 ♘f3

This is the traditional main line. In recent years it has reasserted itself as clearly the most popular line, after a period in the 1990s when 3 e4 was seen in a large proportion of top-level games (including Game 88 in this book).

3	...	♘f6
4	e3	

With this move, White simply aims to regain the pawn without making any concessions or overextending himself.

He will then try to put his central pawn-majority to good use.

4	...	e6

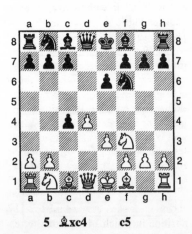

5	♗xc4	c5

This is Black's standard response. At some point an exchange is likely to take place on d4, but Black will not necessarily hurry to play ...cxd4, since this exchange frees White's c1-bishop to be developed actively.

    6 0-0   a6
    7 ♗b3

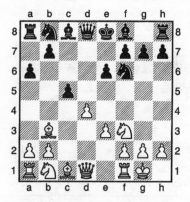

This appears to be rather a modest move, but it contains some cunning ideas, and has been used to good effect by both Kasparov and Kramnik in several top-level games.

    7 ...   cxd4

After 7...b5, which is a standard reply to moves such as 7 ♕e2, White would play 8 a4, when 8...b4 9 ♘bd2 gives him good prospects of keeping a significant edge. 7...♘c6 8 ♘c3 probably gives Black nothing better than exchanging on d4, transposing to the game. Instead, 8...♗e7 9 dxc5 tends to give White some advantage in a queenless middlegame, due to the tempo Black loses in playing ...♗e7xc5; 8...b5 gives White a choice between 9 d5!? exd5 10 a4 with interesting play, and 9 ♕e2 with a standard type of position in which Black would often prefer to have his knight on d7 instead of c6.

    8 exd4   ♘c6
    9 ♘c3

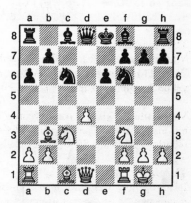

Compared to lines where White has played ♕e2, he has better chances of achieving the d5 advance here, with his queen still on d1.

    9 ...   ♗e7
    10 ♗g5   0-0
    11 ♕d2

White plays for a direct attack, transferring his queen to the kingside via f4. This also makes it difficult for Black to play ...h6, as this can often be powerfully met by a ♗xh6 sacrifice.

    11 ...   ♘a5
    12 ♗c2   b5
    13 ♕f4

13 ♖ad1 ♘c4 14 ♕f4 ♖a7 (not 14...♘xb2?? 15 ♗xf6 ♗xf6 16 ♕e4) transposes to note "2" to Black's 14th move.

    13 ...   ♖a7!?

This move looks a little odd, but certainly has its logic. There are many possible lines in which the e7-bishop can prove poorly defended, especially if White plays ♕h4 or makes the d5 pawn-break (often this is a powerful pawn sacrifice). The game Tkachev – Lesiège, FIDE Knockout, New Delhi 2000 featured instead 13...♗b7 14 ♖ad1 g6 15 ♗h6 ♘h5 16 ♕g4 f5 17 ♕h3 ♖c8 18 d5! with a big advantage for White.

14 ♖ad1

14 ♕h4 g6 15 ♖fe1 ♘h5!? and 14 ♘e5 ♘d5 15 ♕h4 g6 show some ideas behind Anand's rook move.

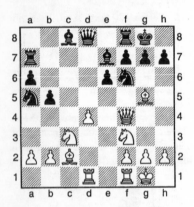

14 ...   ♗b7?!

However, this looks rather odd just after putting the rook on b7; Anand presumably felt that the blockage along his second rank would only be temporary and that the rook's potential would not be lessened. In this type of position, Black often has to perform a tricky balancing act to prevent White from making a successful d5 pawn-break, but often, as here, he just ends up inviting it. Alternatively:

1) 14...♖c7 can be met by 15 d5, but 15...exd5 (15...♘xd5? 16 ♗xe7 ♕xe7 17 ♖xd5) 16 ♗xf6 ♗xf6 17 ♖xd5 ♖d7 might not be too bad for Black.

2) 14...♘c4 occurred, by transposition, in a later game between the same players: 15 ♘e5 (15 ♕h4 g6 16 ♘e5 ♘d5 holds Black's defences together) 15...♖c7 (15...♘xb2!? 16 ♘c6 ♘xd1 17 ♘xd8 ♘xc3 is not too clear) 16 ♘xc4 bxc4 17 ♗xf6 ♗xf6 18 d5 e5 19 ♕f3 left White somewhat better in Kramnik – Anand, Advanced Chess match (game 3), Leon 2002.

15 d5!

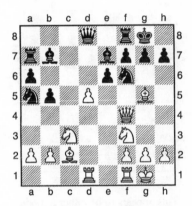

Kramnik plays with great vigour, detonating the centre before Black is fully organized.

15 ...   ♗xd5

Or:

1) 15...exd5? 16 ♕h4 causes an immediate collapse: 16...g6 is decisively met by 17 ♘e4! or the more standard 17 ♖fe1 threatening ♖xe7; 16...h6 17 ♗xh6 gxh6 18 ♕xh6 and Black is quickly routed.

2) 15...♘xd5?! is strongly met by 16 ♗xh7+! ♔xh7 17 ♕h4+ (normally with this set-up the point would be to win the e7-bishop; this doesn't apply here due to the a7-rook, but White has another idea) 17...♔g8 18 ♖xd5 ♗xd5 19 ♗xe7 ♕xe7 20 ♘g5 (the key point) 20...♕xg5 21 ♕xg5, when White has a big advantage.

16 ♘xd5   exd5

After 16...♘xd5 Kramnik demonstrated 17 ♖xd5! exd5 (17...♕xd5? 18 ♗xe7 ♖xe7 19 ♕h4) 18 ♗xh7+ ♔xh7 19 ♕h4+ ♔g8 20 ♗xe7 ♕xe7 21 ♘g5 (this idea again justifies White's play) 21...♕xg5 22 ♕xg5 ♖d7 23 h4 followed by h5 with a big plus.

17 ♕h4

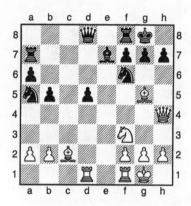

17 ...   h5

This odd-looking move is forced, as the alternatives lose in familiar ways: 17...g6? 18 ♖fe1 intending ♖xe7, and 17...h6? 18 ♗xh6! gxh6 19 ♕xh6 with a crushing attack.

After the ugly text-move, it is fairly clear that White should have some advantage, but he must play accurately and forcefully to make this advantage as large as possible.

18 ♖fe1

18 ♘d4 is also good, heading for the f5-square.

18 ...   ♘c6

18...♕c8 19 ♘d4 ♕g4 20 ♕xg4 hxg4 21 ♗d2! ♗d8 (21...b4 22 ♖xe7) 22 ♗b4 ♖e8 23 ♖xe8+ ♘xe8 24 ♗f5 leaves White well on top.

19 g4!

This weakens White's kingside, but Black is in no position to launch a counterattack. Meanwhile gxh5 and h6 is threatened, and the g4-pawn obviously cannot be captured. 19 ♗xf6 ♗xf6 20 ♕xh5 g6 gives White far less.

19 ...   ♕d6

Or:

1) 19...♖c7 20 gxh5 ♘h7?! loses to 21 ♗xh7+ ♔xh7 22 h6 g6 23 ♖xe7! ♘xe7 24 ♗f6.

2) 19...♖e8 20 ♗xf6 ♗xf6 21 ♕xh5 is now very good for White because 21...g6 is met by 22 ♗xg6.

20 gxh5   ♕b4

20...♘h7 21 ♗f4 ♕c5 (21...♕f6 22 ♕g3) 22 ♗xh7+ ♔xh7 23 ♕g4 keeps White on top.

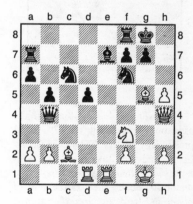

21 h6!

White's attack will remain potent even after the exchange of queens.

21 ...   ♕xh4

22 ♘xh4

Now hxg7 is a very serious threat.

22 ...   ♘e4

22...gxh6 23 ♗xh6 ♖c8 24 ♔h1 ♔h8 25 ♘f5 gives White a winning attack; e.g., 25...♘g4 26 ♗g7+ ♔g8 27

♖e2 ♗f6 28 ♖g1 ♗xg7 29 ♖xg4 f6 30 ♗b3 ♖d8 31 f4 (Kramnik).

	23	hxg7	♖c8
	24	♗xe7	♘xe7
	25	♗xe4	dxe4
	26	♖xe4	♔xg7

White is a pawn up with the more active pieces, but there are relatively few pawns remaining, so White must still play accurately.

27 ♖d6!

White targets the a6-pawn, and so threatens ♖xe7 in earnest. 27 ♖xe7 ♖xe7 28 ♘f5+ simplifies a little too much, and gives Black better drawing chances.

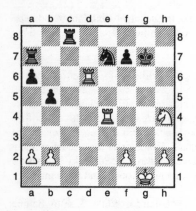

	27	...	♖c5
	28	♖g4+	♔h7
	29	♘f3	♘g6

29...♖c2 30 ♘g5+ ♔g7 31 ♘e6++ ♔f6 32 ♘d8+! ♔f5 33 ♖g7 leaves Black helpless.

| | 30 | ♘g5+ | ♔g7 |
| | 31 | ♘xf7 | |

The flashy 31 ♖xg6+? ♔xg6 32 ♘e4+ ♔h5 throws away White's advantage.

| | 31 | ... | ♖xf7 |
| | 32 | ♖dxg6+ | ♔h7 |

33 ♖6g5   ♖xg5

If Black avoids this exchange, White will play for mate.

| | 34 | ♖xg5 | ♖c7 |
| | 35 | a3! | |

35 ♖g3 ♖c2 36 ♖b3 is less incisive.

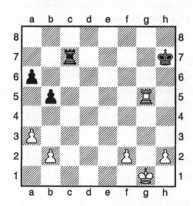

35 ...   b4

35...♖c2 36 b4 ♖a2 37 ♖g3 leaves White's rook better placed than in the previous note.

	36	axb4	♖c1+
	37	♔g2	♖b1
	38	♖a5	♖xb2
	39	♖a4	

Kramnik wisely avoids 39 ♖xa6?? ♖xb4 with a theoretically drawn ending (rook and f- and h-pawns vs rook).

1-0

Lessons from this game:

1) Be especially careful when playing unnatural-looking moves, even if they seem to be supported by analysis.

2) If there is a move you feel ought to be strategically desirable, search for a way to make it work.

3) An exchange of queens does not necessarily mean that an attack is at an end.

Emil Sutovsky – Ilia Smirin

Israeli Championship, Tel Aviv 2002

Sicilian Defence

The Players

Emil Sutovsky (born 1977) was born in Baku, Garry Kasparov's birthplace, but in 1991 he emigrated to Israel and has represented that country ever since. He learned to play chess at the age of four, and in 1996 he won the World Junior Championship. Since then he has won several grandmaster tournaments, but his greatest success was winning the European Championship in 2001. He is currently ranked 31st in the world, but this talented player could make further progress towards the top. Like some other famous chess-players, such as Smyslov and Taimanov, he is also musically talented.

Ilia Smirin (born 1968) is another former Soviet player who has emigrated to Israel. He is currently ranked 29th in the world. For more details, see Game 84.

The Game

The blocked pawn-structure in the centre gives White the freedom to launch an early flank attack against Black's king. An accurate response is required, but rather than trying to exchange off the attacking pieces, Black plays to win material. This gives White the chance to rip open Black's kingside with a sacrifice. Despite Black's exposed king, the outcome is far from a foregone conclusion since White has invested heavily in the attack. However, at the critical moment Black makes a serious error and the attack crashes through; Sutovsky finishes off with a queen sacrifice to chase the enemy king up the board and force mate.

1	e4	c5
2	♘c3	♘c6
3	♘f3	

This move-order is directed against the Sveshnikov (which normally arises after 2 ♘f3 ♘c6 3 d4 cxd4 4 ♘xd4 ♘f6 5 ♘c3 e5). If Black desperately wants to reach the Sveshnikov, then he can try 3...e6, so that after 4 d4 cxd4 5 ♘xd4 ♘f6 6 ♘db5 d6 7 ♗f4 e5 8 ♗g5 he reaches a standard Sveshnikov position. However, this move-order allows White to play the line 6 ♘xc6, which currently enjoys quite a good

reputation for White. 3...♘f6, hoping for 4 d4 cxd4 5 ♘xd4 e5, also has its defects, as after 4 ♗b5 Black is forced into a line of the Rossolimo Sicilian which he may not care to play. Hence Sveshnikov players often prefer 3...e5, which aims to 'punish' White for his anti-Sveshnikov move-order by ruling out the move d4 altogether. The defect is that Black's pawn-structure is inflexible and he weakens the d5-square.

3	...	e5
4	♗c4	d6
5	d3	♗e7

6 0-0   ♘f6
7 ♘g5

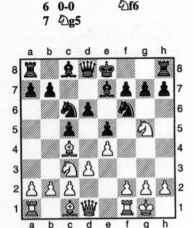

If Black is allowed to complete his development and start exchanging pieces, White will find it very hard to achieve more than a minimal advantage. The text-move aims to open up the position with f4, and thereby start a kingside attack. Although White has not yet completed his development, this early attack is justified by the fixed central pawn-structure, which makes it hard for Black to generate counterplay.

7 ...   0-0
8 f4   exf4
9 ♗xf4   h6?!

It looks natural to drive the knight back from the active g5-square, but in my view this move is inaccurate since it weakens Black's kingside. 9...♗g4 and 9...♘d4 are playable alternatives.

10 ♘f3   ♗e6
11 ♘d5

The seems to be the most dangerous continuation. After 11 ♕d2 d5 Black is able to free his position.

11 ...   ♗xd5
12 exd5

12 ♗xd5 ♘xd5 13 exd5 ♘e5 is only equal.

12 ...   ♘a5

It looks odd to play the knight offside but other moves are worse:

1) 12...♘e5 13 ♘xe5 dxe5 14 ♗xe5 ♘xd5 15 ♕h5 gives White two active bishops and attacking chances.

2) 12...♘b4 is the natural follow-up to Black's earlier play, but after 13 ♗d2 ♘bxd5 14 ♘h4, followed by ♘f5, White gets a dangerous attack in return for the sacrificed pawn.

13 ♘h4

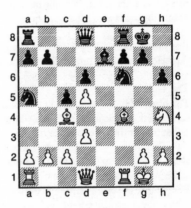

Here, too, the knight aims at the f5-square. Thanks to Black's earlier ...h6, he cannot play ...g6 to keep the knight out.

13 ...   b5?!

Black tries to solve his strategic problems by force, but violent actions often tend to rebound on the perpetrator. Other possibilities:

1) 13...♘xd5? 14 ♗xd5 ♗xh4 15 ♕h5 ♗f6 16 ♖ae1 gives White a very strong attack for the pawn.

2) 13...g5?! (a greedy move) 14 ♘f5 gxf4 15 ♘xh6+! ♔h7 (15...♔h8 16 ♖xf4 is also dangerous for Black)

16 ♘f5 ♖g8 17 ♖xf4 with a very strong attack for White. One possible continuation is 17...♖g6 18 ♕f3 ♘xc4 19 dxc4 ♗f8 20 ♖f1 (threatening 21 ♘h4) 20...♗g7 21 ♖e1! (threatening 22 ♖h4+ ♔g8 23 ♘e7+) 21...♗h6 22 ♕h3 ♕f8 23 ♖ef1 with a large advantage for White.

3) 13...♘xc4! 14 dxc4 ♘xd5 15 ♕xd5 ♗xh4 16 ♖ad1 b6 17 ♗xd6 ♗e7 looks like the best option for Black. White still has an edge but in Kramnik – Leko, Linares 2003, Black managed to steer the game to a draw.

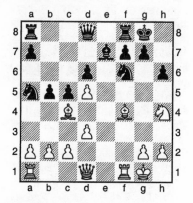

14 ♘f5!

Not 14 ♗xb5? ♘xd5 and Black manages to escape; e.g., 15 ♘f5 ♘xf4 16 ♖xf4 ♗g5 17 ♖f1 g6 and White's pieces are pushed back.

The text-move is the start of a remarkable sacrificial onslaught. In these days of powerful computers, it is normally possible to determine conclusively whether a particular sacrifice is sound. This case is an exception, since White's threats build up relatively slowly and push the compensation over the computer's horizon. My own view is that the sacrifice offers excellent

practical chances; White has a draw by perpetual check in hand, while Black must play with great accuracy simply to stay in the game.

14 ...   bxc4
15 ♗xh6!

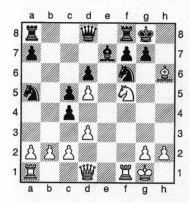

Both white bishops are sacrificed, the first passively and the second actively.

15 ...   gxh6

Black may as well accept the second offer, since 15...♘e8 16 ♕e1! gives White a blistering attack:

1) 16...♖h4 17 ♘xh4 gxh6 18 ♘g6 cxd3 (18...fxg6 loses to 19 ♕e6+ ♔g7 20 ♖xf8 ♔xf8 21 ♖f1+) 19 ♘e7+ ♔h8 20 ♕e3 ♕h7 21 ♕xd3+ ♔h8 22 ♘g6+ ♔g7 23 ♘xf8 ♔xf8 (23...♘f6 24 ♕c3) 24 ♖xf7+ ♔xf7 25 ♕h7+ with a decisive attack.

2) 16...♗f6 17 ♗d2 ♘b7 18 ♗c3 and now:

2a) 18...♗g5 19 h4 ♗f6 20 ♗xf6 ♘xf6 21 ♘e7+ ♔h7 22 ♖xf6 gxf6 23 ♕e4+ ♔h8 24 ♕e3 wins for White.

2b) 18...♖b8 19 ♕g3 ♗g5 (after 19...♗xc3 20 bxc3 g6 White wins by 21 ♖ae1 ♘f6 22 ♘e7+) 20 ♖ae1 cxd3 (20...g6 is met by 21 ♕h3) 21 h4 g6 22

hxg5 gxf5 23 ♕h3 is also winning for
White.

2c) 18...g6 19 ♗xf6 ♘xf6 20 ♘e7+
♔g7 21 ♘c6 ♕e8 22 ♕c3 ♕e3+ 23
♖f2 ♔h7 24 ♕xf6 with a large advantage for White.

16   ♘xh6+

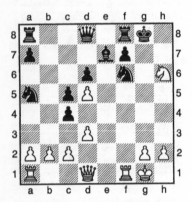

16 ...   ♔h7

A tough choice for Black, as it isn't
clear whether h8 or h7 is best for the
king. The alternative is 16...♔h8 17
♖xf6! ♗xf6 18 ♕h5, and now:

1) 18...♔g7? 19 ♘f5+ ♔g8 20 ♖f1
♖e8 (20...♕e8 21 ♕g4+ ♔h7 22 ♕h3+
♔g8 23 ♕g3+ ♔h7 24 ♖f4 and White
wins) 21 ♖f3! ♖e1+ (Black must free
e8 to avoid mate) 22 ♔f2 ♔f8 23
♔xe1 cxd3 24 cxd3 with a decisive attack for White.

2) 18...♗d4+ 19 ♔h1 and now:

2a) 19...♕c7 (Black aims to push
the f-pawn and thereby defend along
the second rank) 20 ♘f5+ (20 c3? is
too slow: 20...f5 21 ♘f7+ ♔g7 22
♘g5 ♔g8 23 cxd4 ♖f6 favours Black)
20...♔g8 21 ♕g5+ and now:

2a1) 21...♔h7 22 ♖f1! and, rather
surprisingly, Black is helpless despite
his large material advantage:

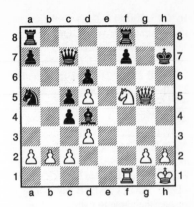

2a11) 22...f6 23 ♕h5+ ♔g8 24
♘h6+ ♔h8 (24...♔g7 25 ♖f3) 25 ♘f7+
♔g7 26 ♕h6+ ♔xf7 27 ♕h7+ ♔e8 28
♕xc7 and White wins.

2a12) 22...♖ae8 23 ♕h4+ ♔g8 24
♕g3+ ♔h7 25 ♖f4 leads to a forced
mate.

2a13) 22...♖fe8 23 c3! f6 24 ♕h4+
♔g8 25 ♘h6+ ♔h8 26 ♘f7+ ♔g7 27
♕h6+ ♔xf7 28 ♕h7+ ♔f8 29 ♕xc7
and White wins.

2a2) 21...♔h8 22 ♘e7 ♕xe7 23
♕xe7 cxd3 24 cxd3 with a large advantage for White.

2b) 19...♕e8 20 ♘f5+ ♔g8 21
♕g4+ ♔h7 22 ♕h4+ ♔g8 23 ♖e1 (23
♖f1!? is also interesting) 23...cxd3 24
cxd3 ♗xb2 (24...♕xe1+ 25 ♕xe1 ♘b7
26 ♕g3+ ♔h7 27 ♕h4+ ♔g6 28 ♕g4+
♔f6 29 h4 ♖g8 30 ♕f3 ♔g6 31 ♕f4
wins for White) 25 ♘e7+ ♕xe7 26
♕xe7 ♗e5 27 ♕c7 ♗c3 28 ♖f1 with
some advantage for White as the badly
placed knight and Black's exposed
king are more important than his slight
material plus.

17   ♘f5

17 ♖xf6? ♗xf6 18 ♕h5 no longer
works due to 18...♖h8 19 ♖f1 ♕e8
and Black wins.

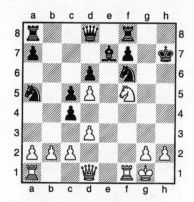

In the subsequent play, it is worth bearing in mind that if White regains one piece, then he may have excellent positional compensation for the remaining piece, based on his excellent f5-knight, Black's exposed king and the offside knight on a5.

17 ...   cxd3?

A very weak move, which allows the white queen to enter the attack with gain of tempo. The alternatives are:

1) 17...♖e8 18 ♖f3 ♗f8 (18...♔g8 loses to 19 ♕c1 ♘g4 20 ♖g3) 19 ♖h3+ ♔g8 (19...♔g6 20 ♕f3) 20 ♕f3 ♗g7 21 ♕g3 and White wins.

2) 17...♖g8 18 ♕e1 and now:

2a) 18...♗f8 19 ♕h4+ ♔g6 20 ♕g3+ ♔h7 21 ♕h3+ ♔g6 22 dxc4 (clearing d3 for the queen, and threatening 23 ♖f4) 22...♘h7 23 ♕d3 ♔h5 24 ♖ae1 with a winning attack.

2b) 18...♘xd5 19 ♕e4 ♖g6 (after 19...♗f6 20 ♕xd5 ♖f8 21 ♖f3 White is also much better) 20 ♕xd5 ♖e6 21 ♖ae1 with very strong pressure for White.

3) 17...♖h8 18 ♕e1 and then:

3a) 18...♘g8 19 ♕e2 ♔g6 (19...♕f8 20 ♕e4 ♗f6 21 ♖f3 is also bad for Black) 20 ♕e4 ♗f6 21 ♖f3 ♕e8 22 ♕g4+ ♗g5 23 h4 ♖h5 24 hxg5 ♖xg5 25 ♘h4+ ♔h6 26 ♕h3 gives White more than enough for the piece.

3b) 18...♘xd5 19 ♕e4 ♗f6 20 ♕xd5 ♔g8 21 ♖ae1 (threatening 22 ♘e7+) 21...♖h7 22 dxc4 ♗e5 23 g3 with very strong pressure in return for a small material investment.

4) 17...♔g8 is the best chance, but after 18 ♕e2 White gains the advantage in every line:

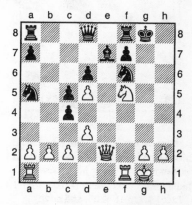

4a) 18...♘xd5 19 dxc4 ♘c6 20 cxd5 ♘e5 21 ♖ae1 ♗f6 (21...♗g5 is also met by 22 ♕h5) 22 ♕h5 (threatening 23 ♖xe5) 22...♘g6 23 ♖e6! with a winning attack.

4b) 18...♖e8 19 ♕e3 ♗f8 20 ♕g3+ (20 ♕g5+ ♔h8 21 ♘h6 ♕e7 22 ♖ae1 ♕xe1 23 ♘xf7+ ♔h7 24 ♕f5+ ♔g8 25 ♕g6+ ♗g7 26 ♘h6+ ♔h8 is only a draw) 20...♔h8 21 ♖f4 and now:

4b1) 21...♘h7 22 ♖g4 ♘f6 23 ♖h4+ ♘h7 24 ♕h3 ♕xh4 25 ♕xh4 is good for White since he retains his strong knight.

4b2) 21...♕c7 22 ♖h4+ ♘h7 23 ♖f1 f6 (23...cxd3 loses to 24 ♖xh7+ ♔xh7 25 ♖f4) 24 ♕g6 cxd3 25 cxd3

♖ab8 26 ♖g4 ♗g7 27 ♖f3 and White's attack is too strong.

4b3) 21...♖e5! 22 ♖h4+ ♘h7 23 ♕h3 ♕xh4 24 ♘xh4 and White is better, but Black still has some defensive chances.

18 ♕xd3

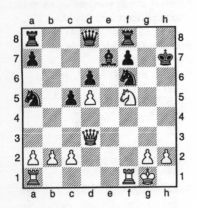

Now Black is lost, since he has to move his king and this gives White an extra tempo to bring his a1-rook into the attack.

18 ...   ♔h8
19 ♖ae1   ♕b6

After 19...♖e8 20 ♕c3 White wins at once.

20 ♕h3+

White could have won somewhat more quickly by 20 ♕g3.

20 ...   ♘h7
21 ♖xe7

Threatening to win by 22 ♕c3+ f6 23 ♕h3.

21 ...   c4+
22 ♔h1   ♕xb2

Preventing the check on c3, but White's attack is too strong.

23 ♖e4   ♖g8

Allowing a beautiful forced mate, but there was no defence in any case; for example, 23...♕f6 24 ♖h4 ♕g6 25 ♖g4 ♕f6 26 ♖g7 ♕xg7 27 ♘xg7 ♔xg7 28 ♕c3+ and White wins.

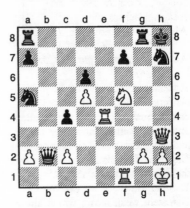

24 ♕xh7+!   1-0

Black resigned in anticipation of 24...♔xh7 25 ♖h4+ ♔g6 26 ♖h6+ ♔g5 27 h4+ ♔g4 28 ♘e3+ ♔g3 29 ♖f3#.

Lessons from this game:

1) An early attack may be justified if the centre is fixed and the opponent lacks obvious counterplay.

2) When faced with an attack, the priority is often to exchange off attacking pieces rather than to win material.

3) When you are defending, use every tempo to reinforce the defence; don't waste time on irrelevancies.

Index of Players

Numbers refer to pages.
A bold number indicates that the named player had White.

Index of Openings

Numbers refer to pages.

About the Authors

Graham Burgess is an experienced chess player and writer. He holds the FIDE Master title and in 1994 established a new world record for marathon blitz chess playing: an astonishing 510 games in three days. His *Mammoth Book of Chess* (also published by Robinson) won the prestigious British Chess Federation Book of the Year Award in 1997.

Dr John Nunn is a top-class grandmaster, who has won four individual gold medals in chess Olympiads in addition to three team silver medals. He finished sixth overall in the World Cup in 1988/9. He is one of the world's finest writers on chess, and is the only author to have won the British Chess Federation Book of the Year Award twice.

John Emms is also a grandmaster. He finished equal first in the super-strong 1997 British Championship, together with world championship semi-finalist Michael Adams. He plays and coaches professionally, and was chess columnist of the *Young Telegraph*.